D0883601

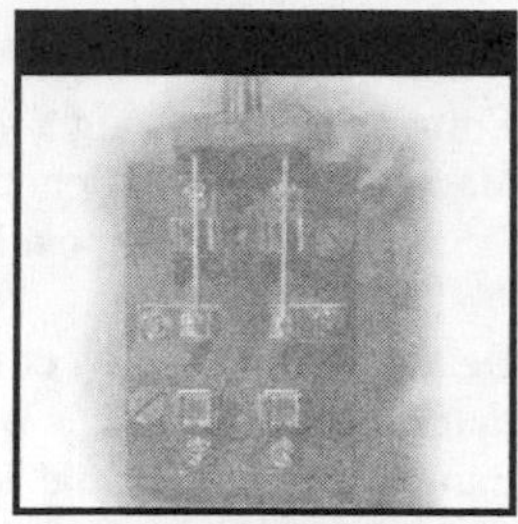

The Switch Book

The Complete Guide to LAN Switching Technology

Rich Seifert

Wiley Computer Publishing

John Wiley & Sons, Inc.

NEW YORK • CHICHESTER • WEINHEIM • BRISBANE • SINGAPORE • TORONTO

Publisher: Robert Ipsen
Editor: Carol A. Long
Managing Editor: Micheline Frederick
Text Design & Composition: North Market Street Graphics

This book is printed on acid-free paper. ♾

Published by John Wiley & Sons, Inc.

Published simultaneously in Canada.

Library of Congress Cataloging-in-Publication Data:

Seifert, Rich, 1952–
The switch book : the complete guide to LAN switching technology / Rich Seifert.
p. cm.
ISBN 0-471-34586-5 (cloth : alk. paper)
1. Local area networks (Computer networks) 2. Internetworking (Telecommunication) 3. Telecommunication—Switching systems. 4. Computer network architectures. I. Title.

TK5105.7.S455 2000
621.39'81—dc21 00-020735

Printed in the United States of America.

10 9 8 7

For Ellyn, in memory of Irv

Contents

Preface

The invasion of Local Area Networks (LANs) into the commercial, industrial, university, and even the home environment during the 1980s and 1990s has been nothing short of phenomenal. No longer do organizations consider *whether* they need a network, but only what type of network should be employed and what devices should be used to build the network infrastructure.

Most early LANs were designed around the use of a shared communications channel—for example, a coaxial cable bus. During the late 1980s and early 1990s, two phenomena occurred that would fundamentally change the way that end user LANs were designed:

- LAN topology migrated from the use of a shared medium to standardized structured wiring systems, implemented primarily using unshielded twisted pair (UTP) cable and central wiring hubs.
- End user computing equipment and application requirements advanced to the point where the capacity of a shared LAN could actually limit overall system performance.

These two factors (together with commensurate advances in silicon technology) fostered the development and deployment of LAN switches. While traditional, shared-bandwidth wiring hubs are still in use today, they are generally considered acceptable only at the edge of the network or when application demands do not seriously tax LAN performance. Switches have become almost ubiquitous for backbone interconnections. As switch prices decrease, they have become popular even for desktop use, as they can provide performance advantages and growth capability for only a very small premium over their non-switched counterparts.

Along with the power and performance advantages offered by switches comes an increase in features, options, and complexity. This book will guide both network users and product developers through the murky sea of issues surrounding the capabilities, use, and design of LAN switches and switched internetworks.

Who Should Read This Book

This book is aimed at the needs of:

Network users. This includes network planners, designers, installers, and administrators; MIS management; value-added resellers (VARs); and operations staff in any organization that selects, installs, or uses LAN switches and related network products. This book will help these people to understand and become more comfortable with switching technology and to make informed decisions regarding the selection, purchase, and deployment of LAN switches. In many cases today, these people depend primarily on equipment suppliers as their main source of information. Such information is always suspect, as suppliers have a strong motivation to sell their particular technology regardless of whether it is appropriate or not.

Network technologists. This includes engineers working in companies involved in the design and manufacture of computers, communications, and networking products; academics (both instructors and students); network product marketing and sales personnel; independent consultants; and anyone interested in understanding LAN switch operation beyond the level of detail typically available in product data sheets, trade journals, and general networking books.

The reader is assumed to be at least casually familiar with computer networks (in particular, Local Area Networks), network protocols, and common network application environments. No attempt is made to provide a complete, from-the-ground-up tutorial suitable for novices. Indeed, such a work would require an encyclopedia and would make it impossible to focus on the critical issues of LAN switching. Network technologists and users grounded in network fundamentals will learn everything they need to completely understand the workings of LAN switches; in the process they will gain enormous insight into the reasons why things are done the way they are, rather than just getting a presentation of cold facts.

Organization of the Book

The book is divided into two main sections.

Part I: Foundations of LAN Switches

The first part of the book teaches the essentials of LAN switches. It comprises six chapters:

Chapter 1, *Laying the Foundation*, provides a review of the core technologies underlying LAN switch design, including network architecture, addressing, LAN technology, and LAN standards. In addition, it introduces some key terms that are used throughout the book. While not intended as a primer for first-time networkers, this chapter sets the framework for the rest of the book and can serve as a refresher for readers who may not have looked at these subjects for a while. Some important insights are provided into the relationship between network architecture and implementation, along with a lot of the history behind the development of modern LAN technology and the relevant standards.

Chapter 2, *Transparent Bridges*, explains the details of how bridges operate to allow communication among stations on multiple LANs. In addition to explaining the functional behavior of bridges, the chapter explores bridge implementation and performance issues and provides a guide to the IEEE 802.1D bridge standard.

Chapter 3, *Bridging between Technologies*, looks at the problems that arise when bridges are used between dissimilar LANs and between LAN and Wide Area Network (WAN) technologies. The important issues of frame translation, encapsulation, checksum protection, bit-ordering, and so on, are all examined in detail, along with the solutions offered both by the standards and the commercial products. The chapter also explains the limitations inherent in such mixed technology bridged LANs.

Chapter 4, *Principles of LAN Switches*, bridges the gap (pun intentional) between the operation of bridges and modern switched LANs. The chapter shows how switches can be deployed in LAN environments, then goes on to look at (1) the evolution of switch design from its earliest days to modern, single-chip solutions, (2) commercial switch configurations, and (3) switch application environments from desktop to enterprise-wide use. Special treatment is given to Layer 3 switches and their implementation and application, as well as the issue of cut-through versus store-and-forward switch operation.

Chapter 5, *Loop Resolution*, explains how the Spanning Tree protocol provides for automatic detection and resolution of loops in bridged/switched

LANs. A detailed explanation of the operation of the protocol is provided, along with some important implementation issues and performance implications resulting from its use. The chapter also provides a guide to the relevant IEEE standard, along with a discussion of loop resolution across Wide Area Networks.

Chapter 6, *Source Routing*, explains the operation of this alternative method of LAN bridging that is available on Token Ring and FDDI networks. The concepts and operation of source routing are presented, followed by a detailed discussion of the source routing algorithms implemented in both end stations and bridges. The chapter provides an extensive discussion of the problems (and some solutions) associated with the use of source routing and transparent bridges in a mixed, heterogeneous LAN environment.

Part II: Advanced LAN Switch Concepts

The second part of the book builds on the fundamentals discussed earlier to explore many advanced features and capabilities being offered in modern switches.

Chapter 7, *Full Duplex Operation*, explains how dedicated media and dedicated switched bandwidth can be used to eliminate the access control algorithms common in shared LANs. Following an explanation of the operation of both full duplex Ethernet and Token Ring, the chapter goes on to consider the implications of full duplex operation both for end-user network design and for switch implementations, along with a discussion of the application environments that can best leverage full duplex technology.

Chapter 8, *LAN and Switch Flow Control*, looks at the problems of link congestion arising from the deployment of LAN switches. It first describes the various methods of backpressure that can be implemented in shared LANs, then explains the operation of the explicit flow control protocol used on full duplex Ethernets. Special consideration is given to some of the implementation details of this protocol, as well as to the IEEE 802.3x standard itself.

Chapter 9, *Link Aggregation*, explains how switches and end stations can use a group of independent LAN segments as if they were a single link (often called *trunking*). The chapter looks at the uses for aggregated links and some of the important effects on system and higher-layer protocol behavior arising from their use. A detailed discussion of the IEEE 802.3ad Link Aggregation standard is provided.

Chapter 10, *Multicast Pruning*, looks at the capability of switches to restrict the propagation of multicast traffic to exactly those links and stations that need to see it. It explains in detail how switches use the GARP Multicast Registration Protocol (GMRP) to distribute traffic along subsets of the spanning tree.

Chapter 11, *Virtual LANs: Applications and Concepts*, is the first chapter in a two-part miniseries. It introduces the ideas and principles underlying the design of Virtual LANs (VLANs) by first exploring the various uses for VLANs, then explaining the key concepts employed by devices that implement VLAN capability, including VLAN tagging, VLAN-awareness, and the application of VLAN association rules.

Chapter 12, *Virtual LANs: The IEEE Standard*, shows how the concepts presented in the previous chapter are applied in industry-standard VLANs. The chapter provides a guide to the IEEE 802.1Q standard, along with detailed explanations of VLAN tag and frame formats and the internal operation of standards-compliant switches. The design and use of the GARP VLAN Registration Protocol (GVRP) is explained, and there is also a discussion on the interrelationship between VLANs and the spanning tree.

Chapter 13, *Priority Operation*, explores the mechanisms employed by switches to provide preferred service to specific applications, users, and/or stations in the network. After a discussion of the native priority mechanisms available in some LAN technologies, the chapter explains how VLAN mechanisms can be used for explicit priority indication. Following this, a detailed examination of the internal operation of a priority-enabled switch is provided, including priority determination, class-of-service mapping, and output scheduling.

Chapter 14, *Switch Management*, considers the extra functionality required that both allows a switch to be configured and managed and also allows switches to monitor traffic in the catenet. The Simple Network Management Protocol (SNMP) is explained, along with the structure and content of the management database. Special consideration is given to network monitoring tools, including port and switch mirrors, and the implementation of Remote Monitor (RMON) capability within the switch. Alternatives to the use of SNMP are also presented.

Chapter 15, *Make the Switch!*, ties together all of the basic and advanced features discussed earlier and shows how these functions are combined and arranged in practical switch implementations. In addition to a walk-through of the block diagram of a hypothetical switch, an in-depth discussion of switching fabrics is provided, included shared memory, shared bus, and crosspoint matrix architectures.

References are sprinkled liberally throughout the book, both to indicate the sources of specific information or statements and to provide pointers to documents where the reader can research the area under discussion in ever greater detail. References are shown in the form:

[BOOG76]

where BOOG is the first letters of the name of the author (e.g., John Boogerhead) and 76 is the last two digits of the year Mr. Boogerhead's document was published. The full citation for all such references is provided in a separate section at the end of the book.

A glossary is also provided that gives definitions for all of the specialized terms and expressions used in the book as well as an expansion of all abbreviations and acronyms.

A Few Words from the Author

I would like to clarify two important points:

1. This book discusses the abstract engineering principles behind switch operation as well as the practical application of those principles in commercial products. Many of the examples and discussions of practical implementations are derived directly from real commercial products where the author was either involved in or personally responsible for the design. However, the book does not discuss the specific features, performance, or comparative value of products that may be available in the marketplace today; this work is not a selection or buyer's guide to LAN switches. The landscape of network products changes on an almost daily basis, and any attempt to present feature, performance, or price comparisons would be hopelessly obsolete in a very short time. Trade journals and trade shows are a good way to stay informed on the latest array of vendors, products, and features; this book should provide you with the tools to see through the marketing hype that often characterizes those information channels.

2. As discussed and reviewed in Chapter 1, LAN switches are most commonly deployed on some mix of Ethernet, Token Ring, and FDDI technologies. When it is necessary to distinguish among switch behaviors on these different LANs, I have provided separate, LAN-specific discussions and explanations. However, for many features and functions, the operation and behavior of a switch are independent of the underlying technology. In these cases, most explanations are provided in the context of Ethernet as the example LAN technology, since Ethernet comprises the vast majority of installed LANs; it is also the most common technology for which LAN switches are designed.

In some cases (e.g., full duplex flow control and link aggregation, as discussed in Chapters 8 and 9, respectively) certain switch features are applicable only to Ethernet LANs. Thus, some sections of the book may appear to be Ether-centric. However, I believe this to be appropriate considering the popularity of Ethernet relative to alternative LAN technologies.

The Laws of Networking

In my last book, *Gigabit Ethernet: Technology and Applications for High-Speed LANs* [SEIF98], I presented a few of "Seifert's Laws of Networking." These are a set of general principles that underlie good network design and/or implementation. I have been collecting and refining these principles over many years of teaching and working in the network industry. When the text discussed some specific situation that exemplified a basic design rule, I would often present the principle as one of these Laws of Networking. Feedback from that book indicated that many readers enjoyed these Laws and found that they could more easily appreciate the rationale behind certain design decisions when they understood the underlying principle.

As a result, I have expanded on the presentation of these Laws in this book. When an important discussion in the text is really a special case of a general network design axiom, I have attempted to present the principle succinctly as a Law of Networking. In some cases, the law is not mine; I have tried to give credit to others who have expounded the same principle in earlier works or public forums (including bars in hotels where network standards meeting are held). In addition, each Law is now packaged in a neat graphic at no extra cost to you—a significant improvement over the earlier book!

A Special Bonus for People Who Read Prefaces!

Following the introductory Chapter 1, Chapters 2 and 3 immediately delve into the technical details of transparent bridges as used between similar and dissimilar technologies. For over 140 pages, virtually no mention is made of a device called a switch. This may seem odd for a book that purports to be a treatise on LAN switches.

The answer to this puzzle is provided in Chapter 4, where we reveal (lo and behold!) that a LAN switch is, in fact, nothing more than a bridge. If you understand how a bridge works, you understand how a switch works, since they are simply different names for the same device. As explained in Chapter 4, *bridge* was the term popularized in the 1980s when the technology first emerged, and *switch* was the term popularized by network product marketers when they wanted to revive the technology in newer, speedier versions.

When reading Chapters 2 and 3, feel free to substitute the word *switch* anytime you see *bridge*. The text reads correctly either way. You will also save yourself from the tedium of the "homework assignment" that will be given in Chapter 4 for all readers who routinely skip over the preface in a book—they are told to go back and do what you will have already done.

My Thanks

It's a huge task to write a book of this depth and magnitude. Fortunately, I had the help of experts and colleagues who reviewed material, corrected my errors, and gave excellent advice on the content and organization of this work. Thanks to Scott Bradner, Norm Finn, Michael Gilbert, Kristin Hansen, Tony Jeffree, Mick Seaman, and Craig Wiesner for their time, reviews, and advice; to my students at the University of California at Berkeley who used the early manuscript chapters and pointed out where the book needed more clarity and detail; to Cisco Systems and Nortel Networks for permission to use the photographs in Chapter 4; to Addison-Wesley Longman for permission to use material from my earlier book, *Gigabit Ethernet*, as the basis of some of the text in this work; to Christina Berry, Micheline Frederick, and Kathryn Malm for their editorial assistance, and to Carol Long for managing the development process at John Wiley & Sons and picking up the tab at Salamander.

I also would like to thank all of my consulting clients, whose interesting projects give me the opportunity both to stay on top of current technology and to bring many of my ideas on switch architecture and design to commercial reality, along with my colleagues in the IEEE 802.1 and 802.3 Working Groups, who consistently develop the highest quality and most widely-adopted standards in the LAN industry.

Of course, any errors contained in this work are my responsibility alone.

Technology Updates

Network and switch technology changes quickly, especially in relation to the time required to write and publish a book such as this one. New products and features are constantly being introduced by equipment manufacturers. At the same time, the standards bodies (composed for the most part by those same equipment manufacturers) continually formalize and publish new technology standards relating to LANs and switching.

This book was written contemporaneously with a number of important standards developments, including the publication of the IEEE 802.3ad Link

Aggregation and IEEE 802.3ac VLAN Frame Extension standards (both of which I edited), and the IEEE 802.5r Dedicated/Full Duplex Token Ring standard. At the time of this writing, there are active projects considering modifications to the Spanning Tree protocol, LAN security and access control, enhanced VLAN characteristics, and 10 Gigabit Ethernet, among others. Outside of the standards community, amazing developments are occurring on a daily basis in switch chip development, network processors, and high-speed, hardware-based Layer 3 routing.

It is impossible to revise a printed book as fast as this industry moves. Therefore, to keep you informed with the most up-to-date information, including any corrections to this book, I will be maintaining a World Wide Web site for this purpose at:

www.wiley.com/compbooks/seifert

I will try to keep you pleasantly surprised with updates on technology and standards as they become available.

Contact the Author

I welcome your feedback, both on the usefulness (or not) of this book, as well as any additions or corrections that should be made in future editions. *Good* network-related stories, jokes, and puns are always welcome. Please feel free to contact me:

Rich Seifert
Networks & Communications Consulting
21885 Bear Creek Way
Los Gatos, CA 95033
(408) 395-5700
(408) 395-1966 (fax)
seifert@netcom.com

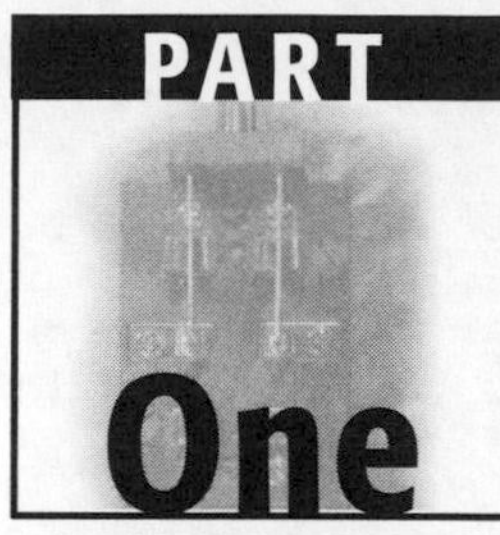

PART One

Foundations of LAN Switches

CHAPTER

1

Laying the Foundation

Before we delve into the details of Local Area Network (LAN) switch operation, we need to consider the foundation on which LAN switches are built. This chapter examines four important building blocks that will be indispensable to our understanding of LAN switches in later chapters:

- Network architecture
- Device addressing
- LAN technology
- LAN standards

Each is considered specifically in the context of Local Area Networks and its relevance to LAN switching.

In addition, this chapter introduces the terminology that will be used consistently throughout the book. Very often, speakers, writers, equipment vendors, and network operations personnel use different sets of terms to describe the elements and behavior of computer networks—is it an Ethernet *frame* or an Ethernet *packet* that is sent by a station?[1] While a name in itself is never inherently wrong—speakers and writers can define their own terminology any

[1] See Section 1.5.2 for the answer.

way they want—we need to agree on the meaning of a number of key words and phrases so that we can unambiguously describe and understand the behavior of network protocols and devices. I have tried throughout this book to use terminology in a way that both reflects common industry usage and is technically accurate. When there is a conflict between these points of view, I have opted for technical correctness. In any case, I have tried to be consistent and unambiguous.

It is not possible to provide a novice-level tutorial on every facet of networking that may be relevant to an understanding of LAN switches. This book is not intended to be an introduction to computer networks; it is a comprehensive treatise on the design, operation, and application of switch technology in LANs. Most of the discussions here and in later chapters presume that the reader has some experience with networks and LAN technology. While this first chapter does provide background information, it is not intended as a primer, but as a *reminder* of the technologies and concepts on which later chapters build.

1.1 Network Architecture

The art of networking comprises a wide range of operations and technologies. Casual end users may think that "the network" is the browser or e-mail screen interface; from their perspective this is all that they know (and probably all that they need to know) about networking. Programmers writing applications code that must communicate among multiple machines may need to know about the programming interfaces and network facilities provided by the local operating system, but are generally unconcerned about the actual mechanisms used to deliver messages. Designers of high-speed optical fiber links used to interconnect network routers and servers should not have to worry about the data structures in the e-mail messages that may traverse a link.

In addition, the applications, functions, and technologies of networking are constantly changing. Every year, we find ways to increase the data rate of the communications channels on which our networks operate. New applications are constantly being written that use existing network facilities to provide improved or even revolutionary new services for users. We need to make sure that advances in one area of network technology are not constrained by limitations in other areas. For example, we want to be able to install a higher-speed communications link without having to wait for a new application or protocol to be designed that can take advantage of that link. Similarly, we want to ensure that the new communications link does not cause previously working applications to fail because those applications depend on some idiosyncrasy endemic to the older technology.

The key to achieving these goals is to separate the totality of network functions into discrete partitions called *layers*. Layering allows the appropriate technology to be applied to each function and to be changed without unduly affecting other layers. The number of layers is rather arbitrary; the issue is separation of functions. Architectural layers are defined such that each layer provides a set of distinct, related functions. Ideally, these functions are grouped such that layers can be as independent of each other as possible; only a minimum of information should have to pass between layer entities.

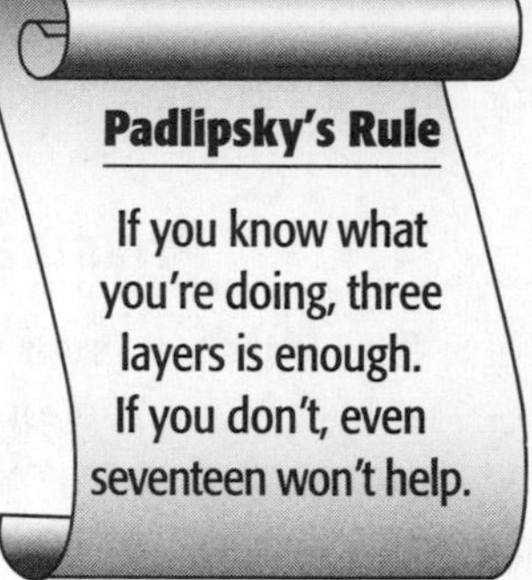

Padlipsky's Rule
If you know what you're doing, three layers is enough. If you don't, even seventeen won't help.

Figure 1.1 depicts the Open Systems Interconnect (OSI) model of network layering developed during the late

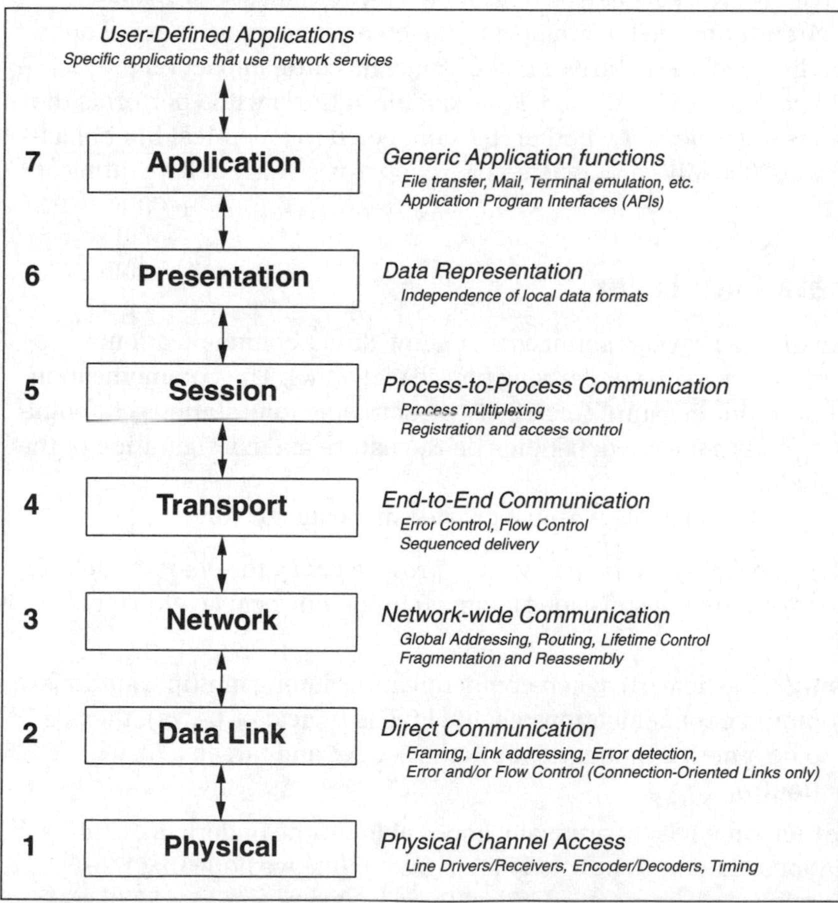

Figure 1.1 OSI reference model for network communications.

1970s and formally standardized in [ISO94]. It comprises seven layers of network system functions.

In the sections that follow, we will take a look at the functions provided by each of these layers, with particular concern for their relevance to LANs and LAN switches.

1.1.1 Physical Layer

The Physical layer comprises those elements involved with the actual transmission and reception of signals from the communications medium. The functions provided typically include line drivers and receivers, signal encoders and decoders, clock synchronization circuits, and so on. The exact nature of the device(s) implementing the Physical layer is a function of the design of the communications channel and the physical medium itself.

While a given networking device (e.g., a LAN switch) must obviously include the circuitry needed to connect to the communications channel on which it is to be used, the nature of that channel has little impact on the higher-level operation of the device. For example, a LAN switch performs the same functions regardless of whether it is connected to an optical fiber channel operating at 1000 Mb/s or a twisted pair copper wire channel operating at 10 Mb/s.

1.1.2 Data Link Layer

The Data Link layer provides services that allow direct communication between devices across the underlying physical channel. The communication can be point-to-point in nature (exactly two communicating stations) or point-to-multipoint (one-to-many), depending on the nature and configuration of the underlying channel.

In general, the Data Link layer must provide mechanisms for:

Framing The Data Link typically must provide a way to separate (delimit) discrete message transmissions (frames) in the Physical layer symbol stream.

Addressing Particularly when communicating among multiple stations on a common communications channel (as is typical of LANs), there needs to be a means to identify both the sender and target destination(s).

Error detection It is theoretically impossible for the underlying communications channel to be totally error free. While we hope that most transmissions will be received intact, there is always some residual rate of data errors, regardless of the technology employed within the Physical layer.[2] It is important that corrupted data not be delivered to higher-layer clients of the Data Link. At a minimum, the Data Link layer must detect virtually all errors. Depending on the design of the Data Link, it may either discard corrupted data (leaving error recovery to higher-layer entities) or take explicit action to correct or recover from the data corruption. These two modes of operation are explored in detail in Section 1.1.7.1.

In general, LAN technology exists primarily at the Data Link and Physical layers of the architecture. Likewise, the functions performed by a LAN switch occur mainly at the Data Link layer.[3] As a result, this book focuses heavily on Data Link operation and behavior. Throughout the book, we show how LAN switches significantly enhance the power and capabilities provided by the Data Link layer. As part of the design of these new features and the devices that implement them, we must often consider the impact of such Data Link modifications on the operation of higher-layer protocols.

Because it is so crucial to our understanding of LANs and LAN switching, Section 1.1.7 provides an in-depth look at Data Link layer operation.

1.1.3 Network Layer

While the Data Link is concerned with the direct exchange of frames among stations on a single communications channel, the Network layer is responsible for station-to-station data delivery across multiple Data Links. As such, this layer must often accommodate a wide variety of Data Link technologies (both local and wide area) and arbitrary topologies, including partially-complete meshes with multiple paths between endpoints. The Network layer is responsible for the routing of packets across the internetwork, usually through the action of intermediate relay stations known as *routers* (see Section 1.5.3).[4]

Examples of Network-layer protocols include the Internet Protocol (IP) used in the TCP/IP suite, the Internetwork Packet eXchange protocol (IPX) used in NetWare, and the Datagram Delivery Protocol (DDP) used in AppleTalk.

[2] Ultimately, quantum (thermal) noise will introduce random errors into any communications channel, regardless of the quality of the components used or the lack of external sources of interference.

[3] Chapter 4 discusses the operation of so-called *Layer 3 switches*, which implement Network layer functionality.

[4] Pronunciation guide:

rou-ter (rōō'tər) *noun*
A device that forwards traffic between networks.

rou-ter (rou'tər) *noun*
A machine tool that mills out the surface of metal or wood.

1.1.4 Transport Layer

In most network architectures, Transport is where the buck stops. While the underlying communications facilities may cause packets to be dropped, delivered out of sequence, or corrupted by errors, the Transport layer shields higher-layer applications from having to deal with these nasty details of network behavior. Transport provides its clients with a *perfect pipe:* an error-free, sequenced, guaranteed-delivery message service that allows process-to-process communications between stations across an internetwork, as long as there is a functioning communications path available.

To provide this end-to-end reliable delivery service, Transport often needs to include mechanisms for connection establishment, error recovery, traffic pacing (flow control), message sequencing, and segmentation/reassembly of large application data blocks. Examples of Transport protocols include the Transmission Control Protocol (TCP) of the TCP/IP suite, the Sequenced Packet eXchange (SPX) protocol of NetWare, and the AppleTalk Transaction Protocol (ATP).

1.1.5 The Layers Keep Lifting Me . . . Higher and Higher

The *Session layer* provides for the establishment of communications sessions between applications. It may deal with user authentication and access control (e.g., passwords), synchronization and checkpointing of data transfers, and so on.

The *Presentation layer* is responsible for the problems associated with communication between networked systems that use different methods of local data representation. When implemented, this layer allows data to be exchanged between machines that store information in different formats while maintaining consistent semantics (the meaning and interpretation of the data).

The *Application layer* provides generic application functions, such as electronic mail utilities, file transfer capability, and the like. It also provides the Application Program Interfaces (APIs) that allow user applications to communicate across the network. Note that, contrary to popular belief, the OSI Application layer does *not* include the user's networking applications; from an architectural perspective, end user applications reside above the OSI reference model altogether. The Application layer provides the facilities that allow user applications to easily use the network protocol stack, that is, generic application services and programming interfaces.

From the perspective of LAN switch operation, we rarely need to consider the operation of protocols above Transport. A well-designed and functioning Transport implementation effectively shields the higher-layers from all of the vagaries of networking.

1.1.6 Layering Makes a Good Servant but a Bad Master

Many people in the networking industry forget that the industry-standard layered architecture is not the OSI *reverence* model, to be worshipped, but a *reference* model, to be used as a basis for discussion. They believe that the standard model is like the Seven Commandments passed down from a network deity, and that any system that does not conform to the structure of the model is evil, or at least fundamentally flawed. This is complete and utter nonsense. The model is just that—a *model* for describing the operation of networks. It is not a standard to which networking protocols must adhere, or an engineering specification to which network components or devices must conform. The OSI reference model provides us with a common framework to discuss and describe the complete set of functions that may be performed in a practical network implementation. It should not, however, constrain any implementation from doing what is appropriate and right for its target application environment. Architectural purity may look nice on paper, but it doesn't make a system work properly.

Seifert's Law of Networking #6
Network architecture—where the rubber meets the sky!

In particular, our understanding of layered architecture should always be tempered by the following:

- *Not all layers are always required.* In many environments, the functions provided at some layers of the OSI model are simply not needed. For example, when transferring ASCII e-mail files between machines, there is no real need for a Presentation layer, since ASCII is universally understood. The layer can be eliminated completely with no loss of functionality. The standard TCP/IP protocol suite eliminates both the Session and Presentation layers, yet it works quite well.[5]
- *Any function not performed at one layer can be pushed up to a higher layer.* Just because a network system does not implement some OSI-prescribed function in an exposed module using the OSI name for that layer does not mean that the system must live without the use of that function. For example, if a protocol suite does not include a Presentation layer, this does not imply that all communicating systems must use the same method of local data representation.[6] Lacking a Presentation layer, the burden of data format conversion between dissimilar systems

[5] To be fair, TCP subsumes some of the OSI Session layer functions into the Transport layer.
[6] This is a good example, since the Presentation layer is rarely implemented as shown in the OSI reference model.

just becomes the responsibility of the application that is providing the data transfer. This is, in fact, common practice.

- *Don't confuse architecture with implementation.* Even if the architecture of a network device can be presented in a layered fashion according to the OSI model, this does not mean that the implementation of that device must necessarily be partitioned according to the architectural layering. Architecture defines the *functional* boundaries of a system. Implementation should follow *technology* boundaries. In many cases, it is perfectly acceptable for software modules to cross layer boundaries. A single segment of code may implement the functionality described by multiple layers; there may be no exposed interfaces between certain layer entities. The tradeoff here is modularity versus performance. In a system highly constrained by processing power and/or memory, it may even be necessary and appropriate to write an entire protocol stack in one software module.[7]

  This dichotomy between architecture and implementation is true for the hardware as well as the software components of a system. For example, many manufacturers produce integrated circuits designed to provide an interface to a local area network (LAN chip sets). Rarely does it make sense to build a "Data Link chip" and a "Physical layer chip." The partitioning of functions between devices in a chip set is determined by technology (analog versus digital process, clock domains, etc.), power consumption, and portability to multiple device applications rather than by any arbitrary layering prescribed by the OSI model.

- *An application can use the network at any layer, not just the Application layer.* Just because the OSI model defines one layer specifically for application interfaces does not mean that real applications must use that layer as their entry point to the network. An application can access network services at any layer in the hierarchy as long as it is willing to accept the level of service provided at that layer. For example, an application that only operates across a single link can interface directly to the Data Link layer; there is no need to incur the overhead of Network and higher-layer processing if those functions are not needed by that particular application.

  Similarly, there is no need for communications to pass through every layer between an entity and the underlying physical channel, even if they exist in the protocol suite in use. Layers can be skipped if the functional-

[7] A good example is the highly-unlayered implementation of DECnet for DOS-based systems. In an attempt to allow PCs to communicate with VAXen in the 1980s, Digital Equipment Corp. developed a DECnet protocol suite implementation that could run on an 8088-based computer with no more than 640 Kbytes of memory. In order to provide even marginally acceptable performance, the implementation had few exposed interlayer interfaces. This avoided a lot of the context switching required with strictly-layered implementations, at the expense of having a plate of difficult-to-maintain spaghetti code.

ity adds no benefit. Figure 1.2 depicts an example of a multi-protocol end station architecture incorporating TCP/IP, Local Area Transport (LAT), AppleTalk, and IPX. Note that not all seven layers are present in any of these protocol suites. In addition, many higher-layer protocols and applications skip layers where appropriate, and some modules encompass the functionality of multiple layers.

These important concepts are often lost between the study and the practice of networking. Layered architecture is how we describe the behavior of a system; implementation is how we actually build it. Neither one should control the other. In fact, no popular network system in use today exactly maps, module-for-module, to the OSI model. Any attempt to build such a system (or to describe a system as if it did map this way) is futile; this is not the purpose of the model.

1.1.7 Inside the Data Link Layer

Because this is a book about LAN switches, we need to examine the innards of the Data Link more than any other layer in the architecture. In this section, we look at the different modes of Data Link layer operation, the architectural subdivision of the Data Link layer, and the operation of the Logical Link Control protocol (LLC).

1.1.7.1 Modes of Operation

Data Links can operate in either of two basic modes: connectionless or connection-oriented.

1.1.7.1.1 Connectionless Operation

A connectionless link provides *best-effort service;* frames are sent among devices and should be properly received with high probability, but no guarantees are made and no mechanisms are invoked to recover from errors if they do occur. Error *detection* will prevent corrupted frames from being delivered to a higher-layer client (to the level of robustness provided by the error check algorithm). However, in the event of an error, it is not the connectionless Data Link's responsibility to invoke retransmissions or other recovery mechanisms; connectionless links do not provide error *control.*

Similarly, if a target destination is unable to receive a frame due to lack of resources (e.g., buffer memory), it is not a connectionless Data Link's responsibility to recover from this loss, or even to prevent transmission when such resources are not available; connectionless links do not normally provide flow control.

A connectionless link thus operates *open loop;* there is no feedback provided from the receiver to the sender. No acknowledgments are generated, no

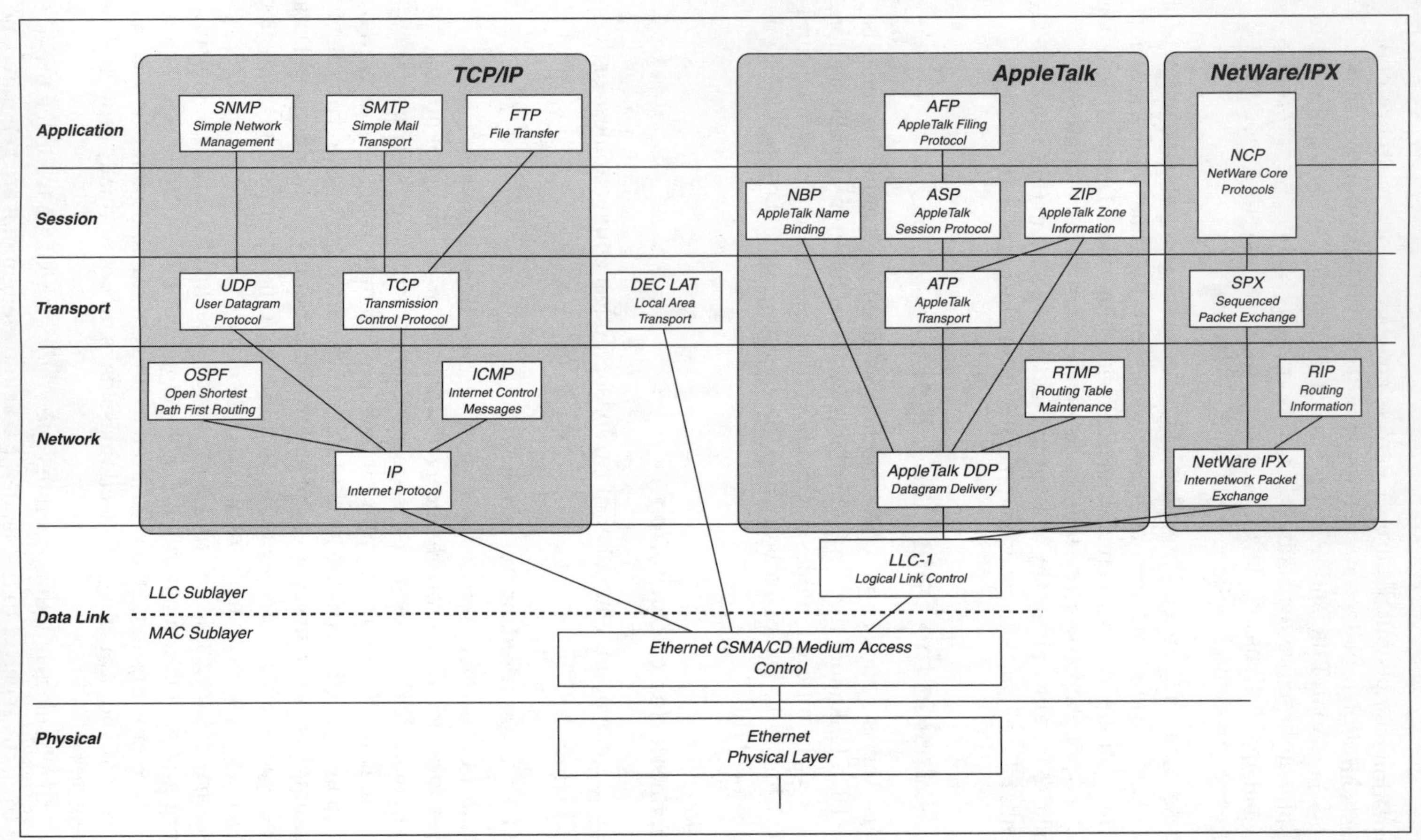

Figure 1.2 Multi-protocol layered architecture example.

information is provided about buffer availability, and no retransmission requests are produced in the event of frame loss. If connectionless operation is in use at the Data Link layer, and some higher-layer application requires a guarantee of successful data delivery, then reliable delivery mechanisms must be provided at a higher layer (typically Transport) or within the application itself.

1.1.7.1.2 Connection-Oriented Operation

A connection-oriented link usually provides for both error and flow control between the communicating partners. In general, this will require that the partners maintain a certain amount of state information about this ongoing stream of information being exchanged. In the event of an error, there must be some way to identify the particular frame(s) that were not received and to request their retransmission. Thus, sequence numbers are usually assigned to frames, and the communicating stations must keep track of which frames were received and which are either in process or require retransmission.

Prior to information exchange, partners in a connection-oriented link must generally invoke a call setup procedure, which establishes the link and initializes the sequence state information. Once set up, data can be exchanged, with error and/or flow control procedures operating to ensure orderly and error-free exchange during the course of the call. Once completed, the call can be torn down and the resources made available for other communications.

A connection-oriented link operates *closed loop;* once a connection is established, there is a continual exchange of data and feedback control information in both directions. Errors and frame loss can be corrected relatively quickly; the loop time constant need only accommodate the processing and propagation delays of the single link over which communication is occurring.

1.1.7.1.3 Connectionless versus Connection-Oriented Operation

A connectionless link provides no guarantees regarding frame delivery to the target destination(s). Frames will be delivered with high probability, but there are sure to be some frames that are not delivered due to errors in the physical channel or buffer unavailability at a receiver. A connection-oriented link provides some assurance of proper data delivery to its client (unless the physical channel is inoperative—there is nothing that a Data Link protocol can do to deliver data across a non-functioning channel!). As always, there is no free lunch; a price must be exacted for this assurance.[8]

[8] Actually, there are two kinds of free lunches—those you have already paid for and those you have not yet paid for. If you are using a connection-oriented link, you have already bought lunch. If you are considering using a connection-oriented link, remember that those luscious pictures of dishes on the menu have prices next to them.

- *Protocol complexity.* The link protocol must necessarily be more complex for a connection-oriented link than for a connectionless link. A connectionless protocol can consider each frame completely independent of any other. A connection-oriented protocol must generally provide mechanisms for frame sequencing, error recovery, and flow control. Typically, this involves a Positive Acknowledgment and Retransmission (PAR) protocol for error recovery and either a sliding window or buffer credit scheme for flow control. In addition, the connection-oriented protocol needs facilities for call setup and teardown, and possibly for restoration of a disrupted call.
- *Station complexity.* Stations participating in a connection-oriented link protocol must implement all of the functions demanded by that protocol (call setup/teardown, error control, flow control, etc.). For performance reasons, these functions are generally implemented in hardware within the link controller; the delay imposed by a software-based connection-oriented link protocol implementation is often unacceptable, particularly on high-speed links. This additional hardware adds to the cost of the link controller in every station using the protocol.
- *Connection-orientation.* The use of a connection-oriented link protocol presumes a connection orientation on the part of the higher-layer protocols and/or applications in the system. A connection-oriented link protocol may be appropriate if the communication indeed comprises a long-term stream of information exchanges. However, if the communicating applications exchange information only sporadically, the overhead of call setup and maintenance can be excessive. Examples of such sporadically-communicating applications include most Network-layer routing protocols (RIP, OSPF, etc.) and infrequent polling of devices for network management statistics (SNMP).

Connectionless links are uncomplicated; there is minimal overhead required in the frames exchanged, and the link hardware can be simpler and therefore lower in cost. Whether connectionless operation is acceptable depends primarily on the probability that frames will be delivered properly under normal operation. If the vast majority of frames are successfully delivered, connectionless operation is incredibly efficient. For the boundary case of a missing frame, higher-layer protocol mechanisms can still recover and maintain reliable delivery for the client application(s). Performance will suffer when errors occur, but if errors do not occur often, the effect is insignificant.

Connection-oriented links incur all of the overhead and complexity required for reliable delivery whether or not the underlying channel or the communicating devices ever need to invoke those mechanisms. If the communications channel is error prone, or if the communicating devices can be easily swamped by the speed of the channel (i.e., they have inadequate resources to prevent buffer overflow at the Data Link layer), then a connection-oriented link can provide efficient operation. Low-level hardware prevents such problems and limitations from propagating beyond the Data Link layer facilities; higher layer protocols and applications are unaware that errors are being corrected and buffer overflow is being prevented.

The communications channel in a LAN environment is generally of exceedingly high quality. Unlike long distance telephony circuits, microwave links, or satellite channels, LANs generally operate over carefully-designed media in a controlled environment. The error rates encountered in a typical LAN are on the order of 1×10^{-12} or better. For a workgroup-average frame length of 534 bytes [AMD96], this implies 1 lost frame due to bit errors for every 234 million frames sent. The complexity and overhead of a connection-oriented link are not easily justified for this level of errors. If the communications channel were an error prone Wide Area Network (WAN) link with an error rate of 1×10^{-6} (one bit in a million in error), there would instead be 1 lost frame for every 234 frames sent. This is a much more significant level of frame loss and could easily justify the complexity of a connection-oriented Data Link protocol.

Thus, LANs generally use connectionless Data Link protocols. The notable exception is the IBM LAN architecture and its use of Token Ring; this is discussed in detail in Chapter 3, *Bridging between Technologies*, and Chapter 6, *Source Routing*.

1.1.7.2 Data Link Sublayering

LANs are somewhat special in that they often comprise a shared channel among many stations (as opposed to a point-to-point link, as provided by a telephony T-carrier). That is, in addition to providing a connectionless or connection-oriented service to its client, a LAN generally requires some means to arbitrate among the stations for use of the shared, common channel.

Thus, we separate the Data Link layer into two distinct sublayers, as depicted in Figure 1.3:

- *Logical Link Control (LLC)*. This upper sublayer provides the Data Link service (connectionless or connection-oriented) to the higher layer client, independent of the nature of the underlying LAN. In this manner, higher layer clients are relieved from having to deal with the details of the particular LAN technology being employed. They can use the same service interface to the Data Link, whether it is operating over an Ethernet, Token Ring, FDDI, or other technology.[9]

[9] Note that a price is paid for this abstraction. With a uniform service interface, higher-layer clients can lose visibility into technology-specific features of the underlying LAN (e.g., the priority access mechanism provided by Token Ring).

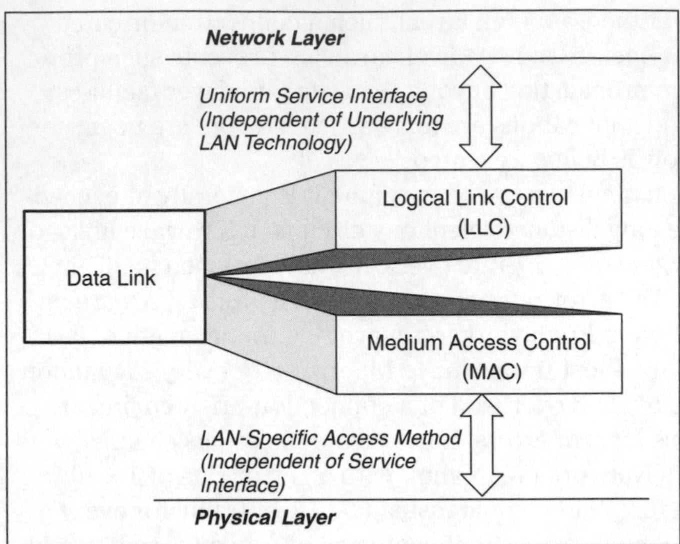

Figure 1.3 Data Link sublayering.

- *Medium Access Control (MAC).* This lower sublayer deals with the details of frame formats and channel arbitration associated with the particular LAN technology in use, independent of the class of service being provided to higher layer clients by LLC.

1.1.7.3 Logical Link Control

The Logical Link Control protocol was developed and standardized within the IEEE 802.2 Working Group (see Section 1.4.1) and provides for three types of service:

- *LLC Type 1: Connectionless Service.* This is a simple, best-effort delivery service. LLC-1 provides no call setup or maintenance procedures, no error recovery, and no flow control. The only protocol mechanism provided is for multiplexing of the Data Link to multiple higher-layer clients.
- *LLC Type 2: Connection-Oriented Service.* LLC-2 was derived directly from the High-Level Data Link Control protocol (HDLC) commonly used on wide area telecommunications links [ISO93, ANSI79]. It operates from the same set of principles; the main differences are a reduction in the number of connection modes available and the inclusion of both source and destination client identifiers. LLC-2 includes procedures for call establishment and teardown, error recovery using Positive Acknowledgment and Retransmission, and flow control using a fixed-length sliding window

of eight frames. Devices that implement LLC-2 must also implement LLC-1; connectionless operation is used to establish LLC-2 connections.

- *LLC Type 3: Acknowledged Connectionless Service.* LLC-3 is somewhat of a contrived, amalgamated service. It provides neither connections nor error or flow control, but does include support for immediate acknowledgment of frame delivery. A client using LLC-3 can immediately detect whether an individual frame was properly delivered and take necessary action (e.g., resubmitting the frame for transmission). In a true show of architectural impurity, LLC-3 was specifically designed to leverage a mechanism called *Request-with-Response* that is available in the IEEE 802.4 Token Bus LAN. Request-with-Response provides a low-level acknowledgment capability with very fast reaction time [IEEE90c]. As IEEE 802.4 Token Bus LANs never enjoyed widespread popularity, and applications that need an LLC-3 style of service never emerged, LLC-3 sees little (if any) commercial use.

Readers interested in the details of LLC protocol procedures should refer to [IEEE98b] for the complete set of specifications.

1.1.7.3.1 LLC Frame Format

Figure 1.4 depicts the format of an LLC frame for all three classes of service. The frame header comprises either 3 or 4 bytes; the longer version is used only for LLC-2 Information and Supervisory frames.

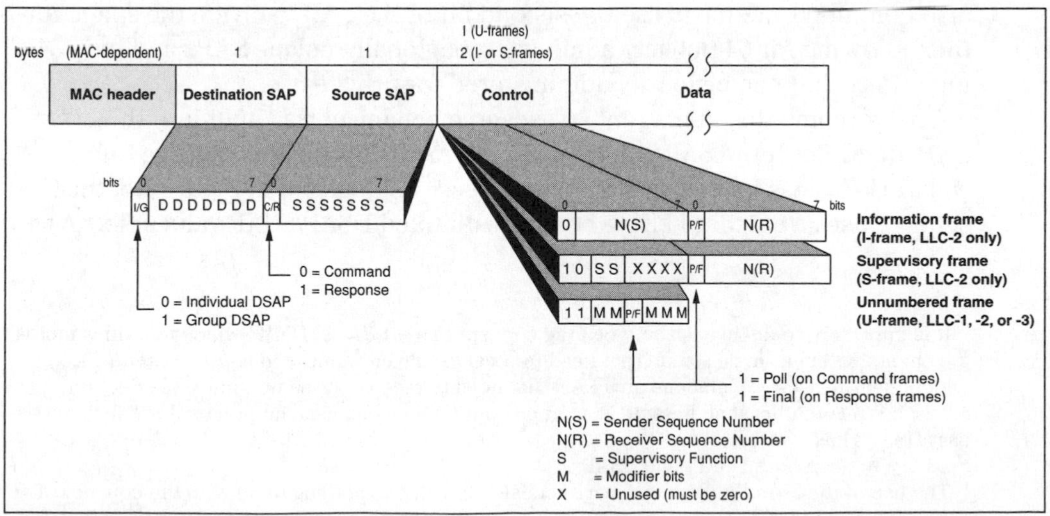

Figure 1.4 LLC frame format.

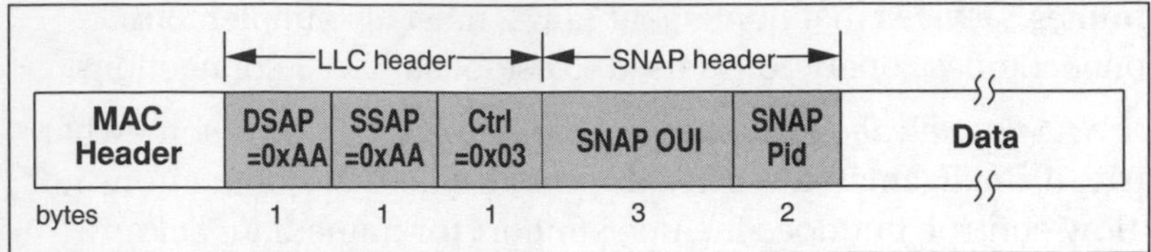

Figure 1.5 LLC-1/SNAP format.

LLC multiplexes among multiple higher-layer clients through the use of a Service Access Point (SAP) identifier. Both the client within the sender (Source SAP, or SSAP) and the target client within the receiver (Destination SAP, or DSAP) can be identified. SAP identifiers are 1 byte in length.

The first bit of the DSAP indicates whether the target is an individual client within the receiver or a set of multiple clients within the receiving station that need to see the received frame simultaneously.[10] This provision for SAP multicasting applies only to DSAPs; it is not even clear what would be meant by a multicast SSAP. The first bit of the SSAP is used to distinguish Command and Response frames.

1.1.7.3.2 SNAP Encapsulation

A problem arises with the use of LLC in its pure form. LLC SAPs (LSAPs[11]) are only 1 byte long; as a result, they can multiplex only among a maximum of 256 clients. However, as shown in Figure 1.4, the SAP space is further subdivided. Half of the space is reserved for group (i.e., multicast) SAPs, leaving only 128 multiplexing points for most purposes. Even within this restricted space, it is also common practice to use the second bit of the SAP to divide the space further, allowing for 64 publicly-administered, globally-unique SAPs and only 64 identifiers that can be locally administered for private use.

To overcome this limitation, an escape mechanism was built into the LLC SAP identifier. If the SAP is set equal to 0xAA, this indicates that the Sub-Network Access Protocol (SNAP) is in use.[12] As depicted in Figure 1.5, this scheme uses a standard LLC-1 header with fixed DSAP/SSAP values (0xAA)

[10] It is important to distinguish between the concept of a *multicast DSAP*, which identifies multiple clients within a single station that need to receive a given frame, and a *multicast address*, which identifies a set of stations on a LAN that need to receive the same frame (see Section 1.2.2.1). While multicast addressing is an important LAN mechanism, no practical use for multicast DSAPs has ever emerged.

[11] LSAPs include both DSAPs and SSAPs.

[12] The use of the term *Sub-Network* here is misleading. It has nothing to do with the concept of subnetworks in the TCP/IP protocol suite. It is used primarily to make the acronym SNAP sound, well, snappy. It's even more fun when we get to talk about SNAP SAPs.

and provides an expansion of the SAP space through a pair of fields following the LLC-1 U-frame header. An Organizationally-Unique Identifier (OUI, see Section 1.2.2.3) indicates the organization for which the Protocol Identifier (Pid) field is significant; the Pid is a higher-layer protocol identifier.

SNAP encapsulation allows any organization to have a set of 65,536 private higher-layer protocol identifiers, effectively eliminating the restriction of the 8-bit LSAP space.

1.2 Addressing

By definition, a network comprises multiple stations.[13] The purpose of the network is to allow information exchange among these multiple stations. An *address* is the means used to uniquely identify each station either as a sender or receiver of information (or both).

Every layer that supports data exchange among multiple stations must provide a means of unique identification, that is, some form of addressing.[14] Many Data Link technologies (e.g., LANs) allow multiple devices to share a single communications link; Data Link addresses allow unique identification of stations on that link. At the Network layer, we need to uniquely identify every station in a collection of multiple, interconnected links. Therefore, most network architectures provide for station addresses at both the Data Link and Network layers.

1.2.1 Local and Global Uniqueness

The only important characteristic of an address is its uniqueness; its purpose is to identify the particular sender and/or receiver of a given unit of information. Strictly speaking, an address need only be unique within the extent of the architectural layer at which it is operating. That is, a Data Link address need only be *locally-unique;* it must unambiguously identify each station on a particular link (e.g., a single LAN). It is not strictly necessary for a Data Link address to be able to distinguish stations on disjoint links, since such stations cannot directly communicate at the Data Link layer.

[13] A network consisting of one station is about as useful as a single walkie-talkie.

[14] Strictly speaking, station addresses are necessary only when communications can occur among some proper subset of the totality of stations present. For example, if every transmission is always intended for receipt by every station, then there is no need to identify the target receiver(s). However, this is a rather unique case, somewhat artificially contrived. In practice, we need to provide station addresses at every layer where there are multiple communicating stations.

At the Network layer, an address must uniquely identify each station in the entire internetwork. Network-layer addresses must therefore be globally-unique. Traditionally, globally-unique Network-layer addresses are constructed from locally-unique Data Link addresses in a hierarchical manner as depicted in Figure 1.6.

Note that each station's Data Link address (1, 2, 3, or 4) is locally-unique on its particular LAN. While there are multiple stations with the same Data Link address (1, 2, 3, or 4), no two stations have the same address on the same LAN. Thus, there is no ambiguity when Station 1 and Station 4 on Network 1 communicate at the Data Link layer; there is only one Station 1 and only one Station 4 on the instant link comprising Network 1.

Communication among stations on separate LANs can be accomplished at the Network layer through the use of the internetwork routers. Each station's

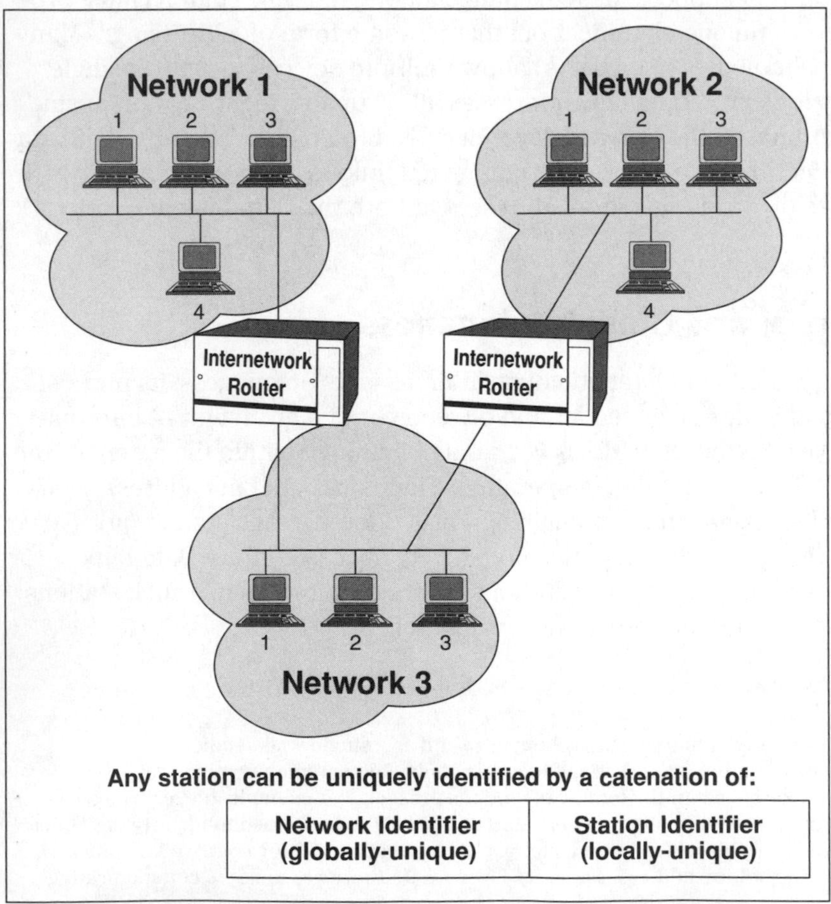

Figure 1.6 Hierarchical addresses.

Network-layer address can be formed by a catenation of its locally-unique Data Link address and a globally-unique Network identifier (Network 1, 2, or 3). Thus, [Network 1 | Station 1] can communicate with [Network 3 | Station 1]; though they have the same Data Link address, there is no ambiguity at the Network layer.

1.2.2 LAN Data Link Addresses

Until the 1980s, even large corporations rarely had more than a few hundred computers deployed throughout their entire organizations. Personal computers had not yet entered the workplace, and computing tended to be centralized under the control of a small cadre of knowledgeable technicians. In this environment, using manual means to administer individual device addresses was both reasonable and manageable. Network and computer configurations did not change frequently, and the task of maintaining address uniqueness was not particularly onerous. As such, most Data Link technologies at the time employed either 8- or 16-bit locally-unique addresses. Address assignment was accomplished either through software configuration or by setting switches or jumpers on the network interface hardware. As a side benefit, the relatively small address space saved transmission and processing overhead.

In 1979, the team that designed the commercial 10 Mb/s Ethernet (including this author) recognized that this situation was about to change dramatically. The advent of personal computing was at hand; while a human administrator might be able to manage the address assignments of dozens of computers, this method offered little hope of success if there were tens of thousands of addressable devices in the enterprise, especially when devices were being constantly added and moved throughout the company.

In response to this anticipated situation, the Ethernet designers consciously took a different approach to Data Link layer addressing. Rather than trying to save transmission overhead by conserving bits, we instead opted to create a huge address space capable of providing a globally-unique Data Link address to every device for all time. The Ethernet address space was designed to allow a unique address to be permanently assigned to every device that would ever attach to a LAN. Later, this same address scheme was endorsed and adopted by the IEEE 802 LAN Standards Committee in a slightly modified form.

Figure 1.7 depicts the format of the 48-bit addresses currently used in all industry-standard LANs. An address can identify either the sender (Source Address) or the target recipient (Destination Address) of a transmission. Since these addresses are used solely by the Medium Access Control sublayer within the Data Link, they are referred to as *MAC addresses*.

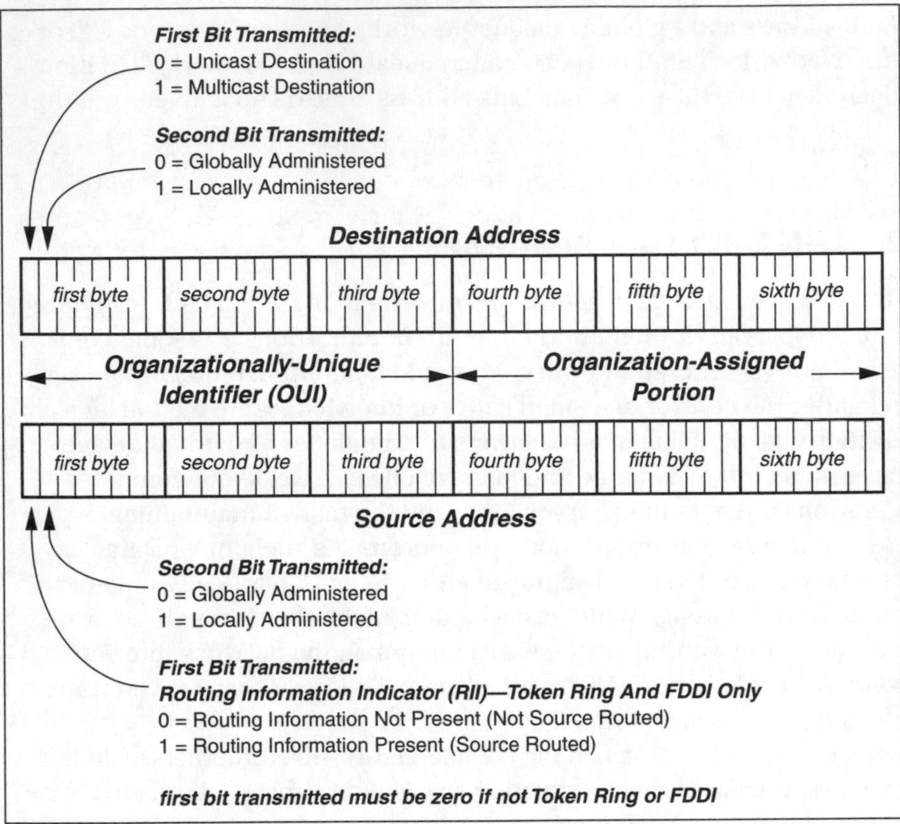

Figure 1.7 48-bit LAN address (MAC address) format.

1.2.2.1 Unicast and Multicast Addresses

The 48-bit address space is divided into two halves:

- A *unicast address* identifies a single device or network interface.[15] When frames are sent to an individual station on a LAN, the unicast identifier of the target is typically used as the destination address in all trans-

[15] There are actually two philosophies for interpreting unicast addresses. One philosophy follows the premise that a unicast address identifies a device (e.g., a workstation or server) as opposed to a network interface installed within the device. Under this philosophy, when a device has multiple interfaces, it uses the same address on all of them. This approach was used in the original Xerox Network System (XNS) and most Sun Microsystems' products. The other philosophy, that an address uniquely identifies the interface rather than the device, sees more widespread application today, and is the model assumed in this book (even though the author has an affection and longing for the "architectural purity" of the single-address-per-device model). Using the address-per-interface philosophy, a device with multiple interfaces will have multiple unicast addresses assigned to it. Both philosophies are valid in the sense that both can be made to work properly in a practical network. In neither case is there any ambiguity about the destination for a frame sent to a given unicast address.

mitted frames. The source address in transmitted frames (the identifier of the sender) is always unicast. Unicast addresses are sometimes called *individual addresses*, *physical addresses*, or *hardware addresses;* these terms are all synonymous.

- A *multicast address* identifies a group of logically-related devices. Most LAN technologies provide many-to-many connectivity among multiple stations on a shared communications channel; multicast addressing provides the means to send a frame to multiple destinations with a single transmission. (See Chapter 10, *Multicast Pruning*, for a complete discussion of how multicast addresses are used.) Multicast addresses are sometimes called *group addresses* or *logical addresses*.

The first bit of a destination address (called the Individual/Group or I/G bit in the IEEE standards) indicates whether the target recipient is an individual destination (I/G = 0 for unicast) or a group of destinations (I/G = 1 for multicast). Thus, there are 2^{47} possible unicast addresses and 2^{47} possible multicast addresses. Source addresses are always unicast; a transmission always emanates from a single device.

The multicast mechanism provided by this address structure is considerably more powerful than the simple broadcast mechanism provided in many link technologies. Broadcasting allows a station to send a frame to all stations on a LAN simultaneously. Multicasting allows a station to send a frame to an arbitrary subset of all stations on the LAN; this prevents needlessly bothering (and using the resources of) those stations that are not interested in, or unable to understand, the transmission. In fact, the broadcast address (all ones, in the IEEE standards) is just one of the 2^{47} multicast addresses available.

The first bit of a source address is always 0 on any LAN technology other than IEEE 802.5 Token Ring or FDDI. On those two technologies only, the first bit of the source address can be used as a Routing Information Indicator (RII), indicating the presence of source routing information. Source Routing and the use of the Routing Information Indicator are discussed in detail in Chapter 6.

1.2.2.2 Globally-Unique and Locally-Unique MAC Addresses

In the original Ethernet design, there was no concept of locally-unique MAC addresses. All addresses were intended to be globally-unique; no mechanism was provided for local control or address assignment. When the Ethernet address scheme was incorporated into the IEEE LAN standards, political considerations forced the adoption of a means to allow network administrators to manually assign addresses in a locally-unique manner. The second bit of an address (called the Global/Local or G/L bit in the standards[16]) indicates

[16] And sometimes the *IBM bit* by network architects.

whether the identifier is globally-unique (G/L = 0) or unique only to the LAN on which the station resides (G/L = 1). As discussed in Section 1.2.2.3, globally-unique addresses are assigned by equipment manufacturers at the time a device is produced. Locally unique addresses are manually assigned by a network administrator; it becomes the responsibility of that administrator to ensure that addresses on a given LAN are unique.

A Philosophical Aside

IS 48 BITS THE RIGHT NUMBER?

The 48-bit LAN address structure in common use today has served us well since its inception in 1980, but will it last forever? Will we need some new, wider address space soon, due to the proliferation of network devices?

Probably not. A 48-bit address provides 2^{48}, or about 281 million million, unique points in the address space. Even allowing for half of these to be used for multicast addresses, and further eliminating half of what is left for locally-unique assignments, there is still enough space for almost 12,000 network-addressable devices for every man, woman, and child on the planet. (Even *you* don't have that many computers on your desk!)

Looked at another way, if the industry produced 100 million LAN devices every day of the year (more than 500 times the current level of production), it would still take nearly 2,000 years to exhaust the address space.

Granted, the way that addresses are assigned tends to make sparse use of the available space, but there is no concern that we will run out of addresses anytime soon. More important, we will not run out of addresses in time for any of us who instituted this scheme to be blamed for it!

1.2.2.3 How LAN Addresses Are Assigned

As shown in Figure 1.7, the 48-bit address is divided into two parts. The first 24 bits of the address constitute an Organizationally-Unique Identifier (OUI). The OUI indicates the organization (typically a manufacturer) responsible for unique assignment of the remaining 24 bits of the address.[17] If a company builds devices that need globally-unique addresses assigned to them (e.g., network interfaces), the company must first obtain an OUI from the IEEE. This is a relatively straightforward procedure involving the filling out of a simple form and an exchange of currency.[18]

[17] In theory, any organization can obtain an OUI and assign globally-unique addresses for its own use; however, the vast majority of OUIs are obtained by network equipment manufacturers.

[18] Information on obtaining OUIs can be found at http://standards.ieee.org. In the period when the Ethernet standard existed prior to the completion of the IEEE LAN standards, OUIs were

The organization obtaining the OUI thus has 16,777,216 globally-unique unicast addresses (from the 24 bits in the organization-assigned portion of the address) available to assign to the devices it produces. Normally, each network-addressable device is configured with a Read-Only Memory (ROM) that contains the 48-bit address assigned by the manufacturer. (See Chapter 9, *Link Aggregation*, for a discussion on how device drivers can use and/or override this burned-in address.) It is the manufacturer's responsibility to ensure that it assigns the 24 bits under its control in a unique manner. It is the IEEE's responsibility to ensure that the same OUI is never assigned to two organizations. When a manufacturer uses up most of its 16 million-plus addresses, it can obtain another OUI.[19]

Note that an OUI assignment provides its owner with both 2^{24} unicast addresses *and* 2^{24} multicast addresses. By changing the first bit of the address from a 0 to a 1, the OUI holder gains a multicast space for its private use.

The second bit of an OUI is the Global/Local bit; if it is set to 1 (by a network administrator manually assigning addresses), this means that the entire scheme of OUIs and ROM-resident globally-unique addresses is being ignored and overridden for the device(s) being configured. A network administrator using this mechanism assumes total responsibility for ensuring that any such manually-configured station addresses are unique.

When assigning OUIs, the IEEE ensures that the G/L bit is always a 0; that is, the IEEE does not assign OUIs in the locally-administered address space. As stated earlier, the original Ethernet standard did not provide for locally-unique address assignment. Before the IEEE standards were produced, Xerox Corporation administered Ethernet OUI allocations. Xerox had no way of knowing that the address format would be modified in the future by the IEEE, and during that early period a number of OUI assignments were made that had their second bit set equal to 1.[20] These were globally-unique assignments that later appeared to be locally-unique due to the IEEE's modification of the 48-bit address semantics. Some of these devices still exist in the field; it is important

---

administered and assigned by Xerox Corporation; the $1000 fee was actually structured as a one-time, royalty-free license to build products that incorporated Xerox's patented Ethernet technology. Since that time, Xerox has waived its rights to those original patents; the IEEE now charges $1,500 for an OUI. This fee serves three purposes:

1. It pays for the paperwork and administration of OUIs.
2. It is low enough to be insignificant for any serious producer of network equipment.
3. It is high enough to discourage every graduate student taking a networking class from obtaining his or her own OUI (an important factor preventing the rapid depletion of OUIs!).

[19] Any organization that has shipped over 16 million network devices can afford another OUI.

[20] In particular, 3Com received an assignment of 02-60-8C-xx-yy-zz, and Digital Equipment Corp. received an assignment of AA-AA-03-xx-yy-zz.

that network administrators who manually assign locally-unique addresses not use this portion of the address space.

The IEEE maintains a list of current public OUI assignments on its Web site at http://standards.ieee.org. When obtaining an OUI, an organization may choose to keep its assignment private; private assignments are not published. There are no private assignments that encroach on the locally-administered address space.

1.2.2.4 Written Address Conventions

Strictly speaking, an address is a sequence of 48 bits. It is not a number; that is, it serves as a unique identifier but has no numerical significance. However, it is rather inconvenient (not to mention user-unfriendly) to have to write down a string of 48 ones and zeros every time we need to show an address; a 48-bit serial format is a rather unwieldy piece of baggage to lug around. Therefore, we use a shorthand convention when writing MAC addresses. It is important to remember that this is only a writing convention for the convenience of humans and network architects—regardless of how it looks on paper, the address is still the 48-bit string.

Addresses are normally written as a sequence of 12 hexadecimal digits separated by hyphens:[21]

aa-bb-cc-dd-ee-ff

Each pair of hexadecimal digits represents 1 byte of the 6-byte (48-bit) address. The bytes are written from left to right in the same order as transmitted; that is, the *aa* byte is transmitted first, the *bb* byte second, and the *ff* byte last. The *aa-bb-cc* portion is the OUI; the *dd-ee-ff* portion is normally assigned by the manufacturer.

The order of the bits transmitted within each byte varies with the LAN technology being employed (see Sections 1.3.1.4, 1.3.2.4, and 1.3.3.3). However, unless stated otherwise, addresses in this book are assumed to be in *canonical format;* that is, the bits within each byte are transmitted from the least significant to the most significant. This is the standard order on Ethernet LANs. Thus, the least significant bit of the first byte is the Individual/Group bit.[22] Chapter 3 contains an extensive discussion of the bit-ordering differences among LANs and their impact on LAN switch technology.

[21] Some manufacturers use colons instead of hyphens.

[22] This convention allows unicast addresses to be easily distinguished from multicast addresses. If the second hexadecimal digit in an address (i.e., aa-bb-cc-dd-ee-ff) is even (0, 2, 4, 6, 8, A, C, or E), the address is unicast. If the second digit is odd (1, 3, 5, 7, 9, B, D, or F), the address is multicast.

1.3 LAN Technology Review

In the context of this book, switches are used primarily to interconnect LANs.[23] Historically, dozens of different types and variations of LAN technology have been commercially produced; many have also been formalized and approved by official standards organizations or have become de-facto standards through market forces. However, only a small number of these LAN technologies have truly achieved widespread use.

In this section, we look at the three most popular LAN technologies in the order of their product volume and importance: Ethernet, Token Ring, and the Fiber Distributed Data Interface (FDDI). The vast majority of LAN switches are designed specifically for one or more of these three systems. At the end of the section we briefly consider some other, less-used LAN technologies.

1.3.1 Ethernet

Ethernet was originally conceived and implemented at Xerox Corporation in Palo Alto, California in 1973. The lab prototype, developed by Dr. Robert Metcalfe (generally regarded as the "father of Ethernet"), operated at 2.94 million bits per second. This *Experimental Ethernet* was used in some early Xerox products, including the Xerox Alto, the world's first networked personal workstation with a graphical user interface.

During 1979, Digital Equipment Corporation (DEC) and Intel joined forces with Xerox to standardize, commercialize, and promote the use of network products using Ethernet technology. This DEC–Intel–Xerox (DIX) cartel developed and published the standard for a 10 Mb/s version of Ethernet in September 1980 (Ethernet Version 1.0) [DIX80]. In 1982, a second revision of this standard was published (Version 2) [DIX82] that made some minor changes to the signaling and incorporated some network management features.

In parallel to the DIX work, the IEEE formed its now-famous Project 802 to provide a broader industry framework for the standardization of LAN technology. When it became clear that the IEEE 802 committee could not agree on a single standard for all Local Area Networks (the original mission), the committee subdivided into various Working Groups (WGs), each focusing on different LAN technologies. (See Section 1.4 for a complete discussion of the IEEE 802 history and organization.) In June of 1983, the IEEE 802.3 Working Group produced the first IEEE standard for LANs based on Ethernet technology. With a few minor differences, this was the same technology embodied in the DIX

[23] Interconnections among geographically-separated LANs using Wide Area Network (WAN) technologies are discussed in Chapter 3.

Ethernet specification. Indeed, much of the language of the two documents is identical. As the marketplace for Ethernet grew, this base standard was augmented with a set of repeater specifications and a variety of physical medium options: thinner coaxial cable for low-cost desktop attachments, unshielded twisted pair, optical fibers for interbuilding connections, and so on.

In 1991–1992, Grand Junction Networks developed a higher-speed version of Ethernet that had the same basic characteristics (frame format, software interface, access control dynamics) as Ethernet but operated at 100 Mb/s. This proved to be a huge success and once again fostered industry standards activity. The resulting Fast Ethernet standard [IEEE95b] spawned another wave of high-volume Ethernet products. In 1998, a version of Ethernet was standardized that operated at 1000 Mb/s (Gigabit Ethernet) [IEEE98e]. Work is continuing on even higher data rates and additional features for Ethernet-based systems.

There are literally hundreds of millions of Ethernet interfaces deployed throughout the world in personal computers, servers, internetworking devices, printers, test equipment, telephone switches, cable TV set-top boxes—the list is huge and increasing daily. In many products, there is no intent to connect the device to a traditional computer network; Ethernet is used simply as a low-cost, high-speed, general-purpose communications interface. Ethernet has become "the RS-232 of the 90s," very much as its designers intended [SEIF83].

1.3.1.1 Ethernet Medium Access Control (MAC)

The purpose of any MAC algorithm is to allow stations to decide when it is permissible for them to transmit on a shared physical channel. Ethernet uses a distributed algorithm known as Carrier Sense Multiple Access with Collision Detect (CSMA/CD). The IEEE 802.3 standard contains a precise, formalized specification of the CSMA/CD algorithm in Pascal code. Readers interested in the nitty-gritty details of CSMA/CD operation should refer to the standard itself [IEEE98a]. The description provided here is qualitative in nature, and does not take into account some of the low-level minutiae that must be considered in an actual implementation. A simplified flowchart of the CSMA/CD algorithm is provided in Figure 1.8.

1.3.1.1.1 Frame Transmission

When a station has a frame queued for transmission, it checks the physical channel to determine if it is currently in use by another station. This process is referred to as *sensing carrier.* If the channel is busy, the station *defers* to the ongoing traffic to avoid corrupting a transmission in progress.

Following the end of the transmission in progress (i.e., when carrier is no longer sensed), the station waits for a period of time known as an *interframe*

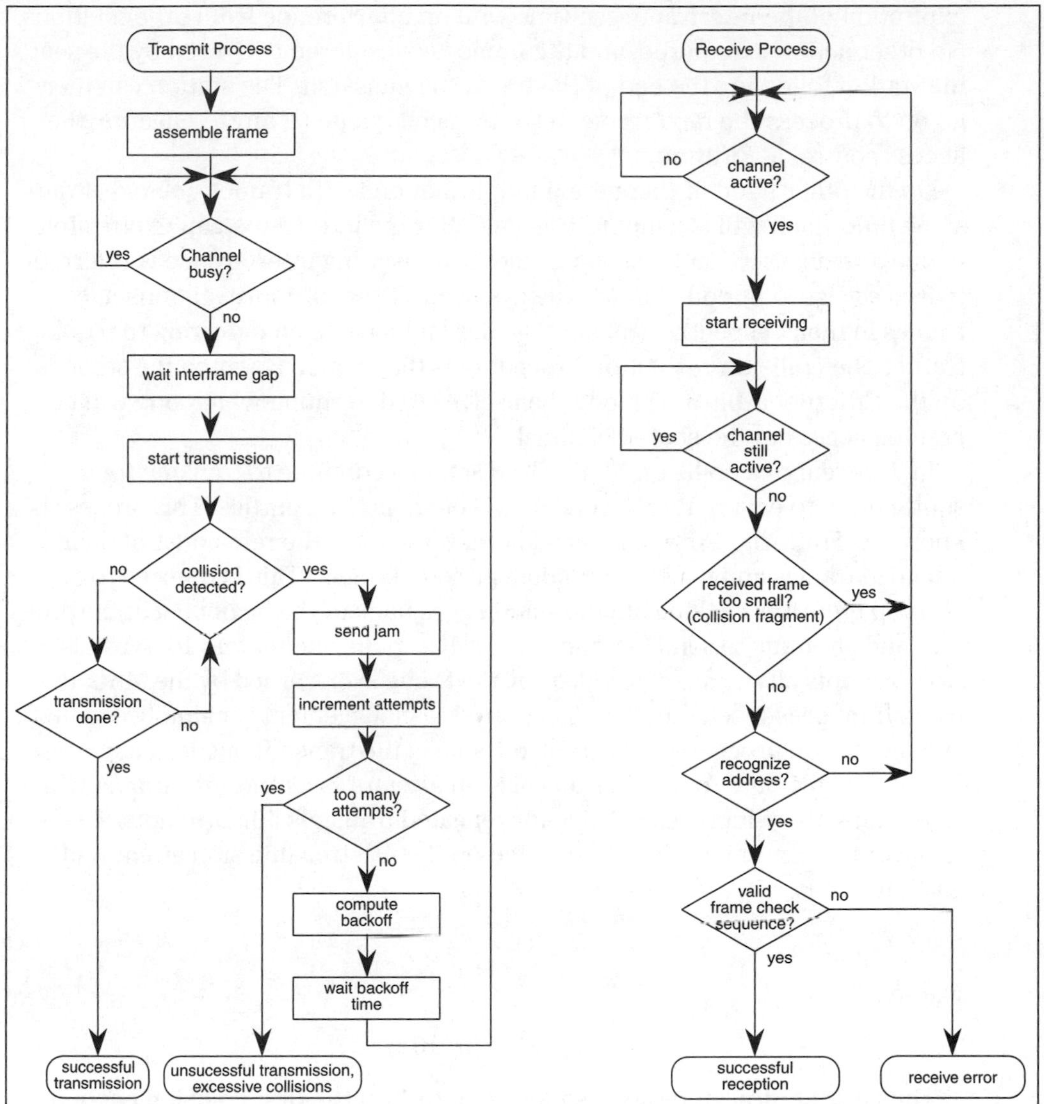

Figure 1.8 Ethernet MAC flow.

gap to allow the physical channel to stabilize and to additionally allow time for receivers to perform necessary housekeeping functions such as adjusting buffer pointers, updating management counters, interrupting a host processor, and so on. After the expiration of the interframe gap time, the station begins its transmission.

If this is the only station on the network with a frame queued for transmission at this time, the station should be able to send its frame following the expiration of the interframe gap time with no interference from other stations. No other action is required, and the frame is considered delivered by the sending station following the end of the frame transmission. The station can then go on to process the next frame in the transmit queue (if any), repeating the access control algorithm.

On the other hand, if there are multiple stations with frames queued at the same time, each will attempt to transmit after the interframe gap expires following the deassertion of carrier sense. The resulting interference is referred to as a *collision.* A collision will always occur if two or more stations have frames in their respective transmit queues and have been deferring to passing traffic. The collision resolution procedure is the means by which the stations on the Ethernet arbitrate among themselves to determine which one will be granted access to the shared channel.

In the event of a collision, all involved stations continue to transmit for a short period to ensure that the collision is obvious to all parties. This process is known as *jamming.* After jamming, the stations abort the remainder of their intended frames and wait for a random period of time.[24] This is referred to as *backing off.* After backing off, the station goes back to the beginning of the process and attempts to send the frame again. If a frame encounters 16 transmission attempts all resulting in collisions, the frame is discarded by the MAC, the backoff range is reset, the event is reported to management (or simply counted), and the station proceeds with the next frame in the transmit queue, if any.

The backoff time for any retransmission attempt is a random variable with an exponentially-increasing range for repeated transmission attempts. The range of the random variable r selected on the nth transmission attempt of a given frame is:

$$0 \leq r < 2^k$$

where

$$k = \text{MIN}\ (n,\ 10).$$

Thus, the station starts with a range of 0 to 1 on the first collision encountered by a given frame, and increases the range to 0 to 3, 0 to 7, 0 to 15, and so on, up to the maximum range of 0 to 1,023 with repeated collisions encountered by the same frame. The backoff time is measured in units of the worst-case round-trip propagation delay of the channel, known as the *slotTime.*[25]

[24] It is the aborting of the remainder of the frame upon detecting a collision that gives Ethernet its high performance relative to ALOHA-type protocols [KLEIN75]. The detection and resolution of collisions occur very quickly, and channel time is not wasted sending the rest of a frame that has already been corrupted.

[25] The slotTime is 512 bit times for all Ethernet data rates except 1000 Mb/s. This translates to a quantum of 51.2 μs at 10 Mb/s and 5.12 μs at 100 Mb/s. On Gigabit Ethernet, the slotTime is defined as 4,096 bit times, or 4.096 μs [SEIF98].

1.3.1.1.2 Frame Reception

On the receive side, a station monitors the channel for an indication that a frame is being received. When the channel becomes non-idle, the station begins receiving bits from the channel, looking for the Preamble and Start-of-Frame delimiter that indicate the beginning of the MAC frame (see Section 1.3.1.3). The station continues receiving until the end of the frame, as indicated by the underlying channel.

A receiving MAC discards any received frames that are less than one slotTime in length. This is because, by definition, these must be the result of a collision; valid frames will always be longer than the slotTime (i.e., the worst-case round-trip channel propagation delay). If the received frame meets the minimum length requirement, the Frame Check Sequence (FCS) is checked for validity and the frame discarded if the FCS does not match the proper value for the received frame. Assuming a valid FCS on a valid-length frame, the receiver will check the Destination Address to see if it matches either (1) the physical address of the receiving station (unicast) or (2) a multicast address that this station has been instructed to recognize. If either of these indicate that the frame is indeed destined for this station, the MAC passes the frame to its client (typically device driver software) and goes back to the beginning, looking for more frames to receive.

1.3.1.2 Ethernet Physical Layer Options and Nomenclature

When Ethernet first saw widespread commercial use, it supported only one data rate (10 Mb/s) and one physical medium (thick coaxial cable); the term *Ethernet* was therefore unambiguous in referring to this system. This clarity and simplicity was not to last, however. Ethernet was modified to operate over an increasing variety of physical media for reasons of cost, ease of installation and maintenance, use in electrically hostile environments, and so on. Later, the data rate changed, providing even more variations and physical media options. As such, there are a lot of very different communications systems available today, all called *Ethernet.*

In order to avoid having to say things like, "10 Mb/s Ethernet using two pairs of Category 3 unshielded twisted pair," or "Gigabit Ethernet on two optical fibers using long wavelength laser optics," the IEEE 802.3 committee developed a shorthand notation that allows us to refer to any particular standard implementation of Ethernet. A given flavor of Ethernet is referred to as:

n–signal–phy

where

n is the data rate in Mb/s (10, 100, 1000, etc.).

signal indicates either BASE, if the signaling used on the channel is baseband (i.e., the physical medium is dedicated to the Ethernet, with no other communications system sharing the medium) or BROAD, if the signaling is broadband (i.e., the physical medium can simultaneously support Ethernet and other, possibly non-Ethernet services).[26]

phy indicates the nature of the physical medium. In the first systems to which this notation was applied, *phy* indicated the maximum length of a cable segment in meters (rounded to the nearest 100 m). In later systems, this convention was dropped, and *phy* is simply a code for the particular media type.[27]

Table 1.1 provides a complete listing of the Ethernet reference designations that are currently defined.

1.3.1.3 Ethernet Frame Formats

Ethernet frames can take one of two forms, as depicted in Figure 1.9. The Preamble/SFD, address, and Frame Check Sequence fields are common to both Type Encapsulated and Length Encapsulated Ethernet frames.

Preamble/Start-of-Frame Delimiter All Ethernet frames begin with an 8 byte field comprising a Preamble and a Start-of-Frame Delimiter (SFD). The Preamble allows receivers to synchronize on the incoming frame and comprises 7 bytes, each containing the value 0x55; the SFD contains the value 0xD5. The effect is to send a serial stream of alternating ones and zeros (1 0 1 0 1 0 1 0 . . .) for 62 bits, followed by 2 ones, signifying the end of the delimiter sequence and the beginning of the Destination Address field.

Destination Address This field contains the 48-bit address of the target destination(s) of the frame. It may contain either a unicast or multicast address, as discussed in Section 1.2.2.1.

[26] The only Ethernet system using broadband signaling is 10BROAD36, which allows Ethernet to operate using three channels (in each direction) of a private CATV system. Other services (broadcast television, point-to-point modems, etc.) can use the other channels simultaneously. This system is not very popular, primarily due to its high cost.

[27] As part of this change in conventions, codes using the old style (length) convention do not use a hyphen between the signaling type and the physical medium designation (e.g., 10BASE5, 10BASE2); later designations always have a hyphen (e.g., 10BASE-T, 100BASE-FX) to show the change in meaning. In addition, the signaling designation is always capitalized. Now you can impress your coworkers and correct your boss when she writes *10BaseT* instead of the strictly-correct *10BASE-T*. Please be sure to update your resume before trying this.

Table 1.1 Ethernet Media Designations

1 MB/S SYSTEMS	
1BASE5	Unshielded twisted pair (UTP, 1 pair), 500 m maximum ("StarLAN")[28]
10 MB/S SYSTEMS	
10BASE5	Thick coaxial cable, 500 m maximum (Original Ethernet)
10BASE2	Thin coaxial cable, 185 m maximum ("Cheapernet")
10BROAD36	Broadband operation using 3 channels (each direction) of private CATV system, 3.6 km maximum diameter
10BASE-T	2 pairs of Category 3 (or better) UTP
10BASE-F	Generic designation for family of 10 Mb/s optical fiber systems
10BASE-FL	2 multimode optical fibers with asynchronous active hub, 2 km maximum
10BASE-FP	2 multimode optical fibers with passive hub, 1 km maximum
10BASE-FB	2 multimode optical fibers for synchronous active hubs, 2 km maximum
100 MB/S SYSTEMS	
100BASE-T	Generic designation for all 100 Mb/s systems[29]
100BASE-X	Generic designation for 100BASE-T systems using 4B/5B encoding
100BASE-TX	2 pairs Category 5 UTP or STP, 100 m maximum
100BASE-FX	2 multimode optical fibers, 2 km maximum
100BASE-T4	4 pairs Category 3 (or better) UTP, 100 m maximum
100BASE-T2	2 pairs Category 3 (or better) UTP, 100 m maximum[30]
1000 MB/S SYSTEMS	
1000BASE-X	Generic designation for 1000 Mb/s systems using 8B/10B encoding
1000BASE-CX	2 pairs 150 Ω shielded twisted pair, 25 m maximum
1000BASE-SX	2 multimode or single-mode optical fibers using shortwave laser optics
1000BASE-LX	2 multimode or single-mode optical fibers using longwave laser optics
1000BASE-T	4 pairs Category 5 UTP, 100 m maximum

[28] The 1BASE5 system was developed after the 10 Mb/s coaxial Ethernet but prior to 10BASE-T. It was never very successful commercially, and was rendered completely obsolete by 10BASE-T.

[29] Even though the 100 Mb/s family includes optical fiber, all are generically referred to as 100BASE-T.

[30] While there is an approved standard, no products using 100BASE-T2 signaling have ever been commercially produced.

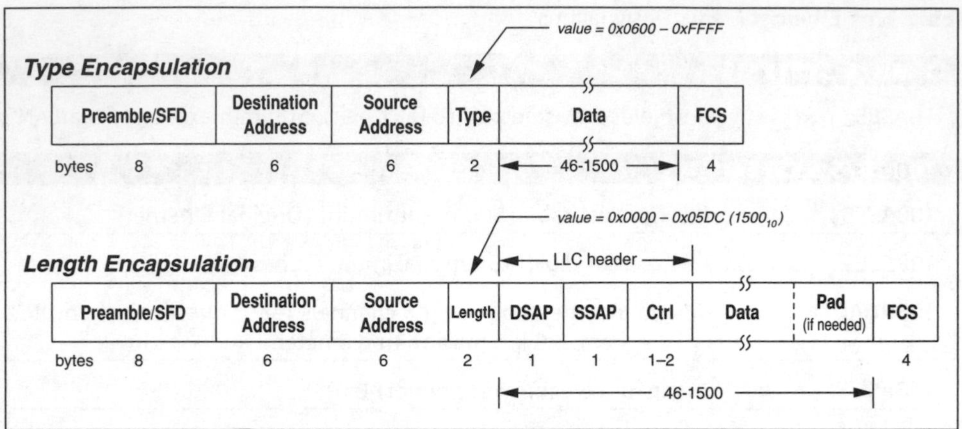

Figure 1.9 Ethernet frame formats.

Source Address This field contains the 48-bit unicast address of the station sending the frame.

Frame Check Sequence The FCS is a checksum computed on the contents of the frame from the Destination Address through the end of the data field, inclusive. The checksum algorithm is a 32-bit Cyclic Redundancy Check (CRC). The generator polynomial is:[31]

$$G(x) = x^{32} + x^{26} + x^{23} + x^{22} + x^{16} + x^{12} + x^{11} + x^{10} + x^{8} + x^{7} + x^{5} + x^{4} + x^{2} + x + 1$$

The FCS field is transmitted such that the first bit is the coefficient of the x^{31} term and the last bit is the coefficient of the x^0 term. Thus the bits of the CRC are transmitted: $x^{31}, x^{30}, \ldots, x^1, x^0$.

1.3.1.3.1 Type Encapsulation

In the DIX Ethernet specifications (both Version 1 and Version 2), Type Encapsulation was the only frame format specified. For this reason, it is often called *Ethernet Version 2* encapsulation, reflecting the more widely distributed version of that standard.

Type field When Type Encapsulation is used, a *Type field* identifies the nature of the client protocol running above the Ethernet. Using Type fields, an Ethernet can upward multiplex among various higher-layer protocols (IP, IPX, AppleTalk, etc.). Ethernet controllers do not typically

[31] A complete discussion of CRCs is beyond the scope of this book. The reader is referred to [PETER72] for a general discussion, and to [HAMM75] for the detailed behavior of the particular algorithm used in Ethernet.

interpret this field, but use it to determine the destination process within the attached computer. Originally, Type field assignments were made by Xerox Corporation; however, in 1997 this responsibility was transferred to the IEEE.[32] Type fields are 16-bit values in the range of 0x0600 to 0xFFFF.

Data field The Data field encapsulates the higher-layer protocol information being transferred across the Ethernet. Ethernet frames must be of a certain minimum length due to the restrictions of the CSMA/CD algorithm.[33] When using Type Encapsulation, it is the responsibility of the higher layer protocol client to ensure that there are always at least 46 bytes in the Data field. If fewer actual data bytes are required, the higher layer protocol must implement some (unspecified) padding mechanism. The upper bound of the data field length is arbitrary and has been set at 1,500 bytes.[34]

1.3.1.3.2 Length Encapsulation

Originally, the IEEE 802.3 standard supported only Length Encapsulated frames and did not permit the use of Type Encapsulation. Despite this lack of official sanction, Type Encapsulation was (and is) widely used; it has always been the more popular frame format on Ethernet. In 1997, the standard was supplemented to include support for Type fields, and both encapsulations are now part of the IEEE standard.

When using Length Encapsulation, the 2 bytes following the Source Address are used as an indicator of the length of the valid data in the Data field rather than as an upward multiplexing mechanism.

Length and Pad fields The 16-bit Length field is used to indicate the number of valid bytes composing the Data field in the range of 0 to 1,500 bytes (0x0000 to 0x05DC). Note that this value may be less than the 46 byte minimum required for proper operation of the Ethernet MAC. When using Length Encapsulation, it is assumed that the Ethernet MAC will provide any needed pad (in the Pad field shown in Figure 1.9); the Length field contains the length of the unpadded data.

[32] See http://standards.ieee.org for information about obtaining a Type field and the current list of assignments.

[33] A minimum frame length is necessary to ensure that collisions are always detected on a maximum-length Ethernet.

[34] There are many pros and cons of allowing longer Ethernet frames, including the effect on access latency and frame error rates. However, the real reason for the specified maximum was the cost of memory in 1979 (when the 10 Mb/s Ethernet was being designed) and the buffering requirements of low-cost LAN controllers. For a more detailed discussion, see [SEIF91]. Chapter 12, *Virtual LANs: The IEEE Standard,* discusses the need to increase the overall length of the Ethernet frame slightly to support Virtual LAN tags.

With the Type field eliminated, there is now no way for the Ethernet MAC to indicate the higher-layer protocol client (upward multiplexing point) within the sending or receiving station. Frames using a Length field are therefore assumed to encapsulate Logical Link Control (LLC) data, as discussed in Section 1.1.7.3. The first bytes of the Data field therefore contain the LLC header information shown in Figure 1.9. LLC (rather than a Type field) provides the mechanism for multiplexing among multiple clients of the Ethernet.

1.3.1.3.3 Length versus Type Encapsulation

While these two approaches appear to be in conflict with each other (they use the same field in the frame for different purposes), in practice they can easily coexist. The 2-byte Type/Length field can carry a numerical value between 0 and $2^{16} - 1$ (65,535). The maximum allowable value for Length Encapsulated frames is 1,500, as this is the longest valid length of the Data field. Thus, the values between 1,501 and 65,535 can be used as Type field identifiers without interfering with the use of the same field as a Length indication. We have simply made sure that all of the Type field value assignments were made from this noninterfering space. In practice, all values of this field between 1,536 and 65,535 inclusive (0x0600 through 0xFFFF) are reserved for Type field assignment; all values from 0 to 1,500 are reserved for Length field assignment.[35]

In this manner, clients using Length Encapsulation and LLC can communicate among themselves, and clients using Type Encapsulation can communicate among themselves, on the same LAN. Of course, the two types of clients cannot intercommunicate, unless a device driver or higher layer protocol understands both formats. Most higher layer protocols, including TCP/IP, IPX (NetWare), DECnet Phase 4, and LAT (DEC's Local Area Transport), use Type Encapsulation. Length Encapsulation is most commonly used with AppleTalk, NetBIOS, and some IPX (NetWare) implementations. Chapter 3 contains a complete discussion of the issues related to the use of different encapsulation formats by different protocol clients.

Note that when Type Encapsulation is used, the Logical Link Control (LLC) protocol is not used, and need not even be present. If a device supports some clients that use Type Encapsulation and others that use Length Encapsulation, the MAC can upward multiplex to both sets of clients simultaneously, as depicted in Figure 1.2 on page 12.

1.3.1.3.4 SNAP Encapsulation

Any frame encapsulating LLC data can use the LLC SNAP SAP[36] as discussed in Section 1.1.7.3.2 to expand the upward-multiplexing capability of LLC. Figure 1.10 depicts a Length Encapsulated Ethernet frame containing LLC/SNAP encapsulated data.

[35] The range of 1,501 to 1,535 was intentionally left undefined.
[36] See, I told you it was fun to say this!

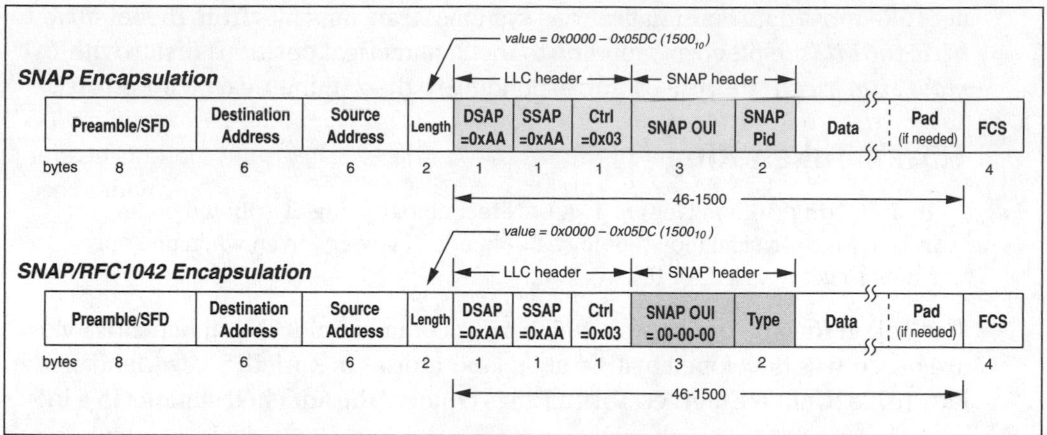

Figure 1.10 SNAP and RFC1042 encapsulation on Ethernet.

In its generic form, the SNAP OUI indicates the globally-unique identifier of the organization for which the SNAP Protocol Identifier (Pid) field is significant. For example, Apple Computer has an assigned OUI of 08-00-07, and most AppleTalk protocols are encapsulated using LLC/SNAP with this value of SNAP OUI. A SNAP OUI of all zeros (00-00-00) has a special meaning; it signifies that the SNAP Pid field has the same semantics as an Ethernet Type field. That is, the SNAP Pid field is interpreted as a globally-unique Type field, with the same value assignments as are used for native Type Encapsulated frames, rather than being reserved for private use. This allows a client protocol to use Length Encapsulation, LLC, and SNAP along with the set of standard Type field assignments.

Using this approach, SNAP encapsulation can provide the equivalent of Type field encoding on LANs that do not provide native support for it (e.g., Token Ring, discussed in Section 1.3.2). If the SNAP OUI is not equal to 00-00-00, then there is no assurance that the SNAP Pid field has the same semantics as an Ethernet Type field; the organization controlling the non-zero OUI can define the Pid field in any manner it chooses.

The original purpose for this special case of SNAP encapsulation was to allow the TCP/IP protocol suite to use Type field encoding consistently across all LAN types regardless of their ability to natively support Type Encapsulation. The procedure is specified in [RFC1042] and is referred to as RFC1042 Encapsulation. Figure 1.10 depicts an Ethernet frame using RFC1042 Encapsulation.[37]

1.3.1.4 Bit-Ordering

When transmitting an Ethernet frame onto the LAN medium, bytes are transmitted in the order shown in Figure 1.9 from left to right. Within each byte, Ether-

[37] Often, the term *SNAP Encapsulation* is used when what is really meant is RFC1042 Encapsulation (i.e., SNAP Encapsulation with an OUI of all zeros). The RFC1042 form is more common than SNAP used with a non-zero SNAP OUI.

net (like most data communications systems) transmits bits from the *least significant bit* (the bit corresponding to the 2^0 numerical position) first, to the *most significant bit* (the bit corresponding to the 2^7 numerical position) last.

1.3.2 Token Ring

To·ken Ring (tō′kən rĭng) *n.* **1.** A LAN technology using distributed polling arbitration on a physical loop topology. **2.** A piece of jewelry given when one only wants to get married for the weekend.

The Token Ring technology on which most commercial LAN implementations are based was developed by IBM at its laboratories in Zurich, Switzerland, in the late 1970s. Unlike Ethernet, Token Rings connect the attached stations in a loop

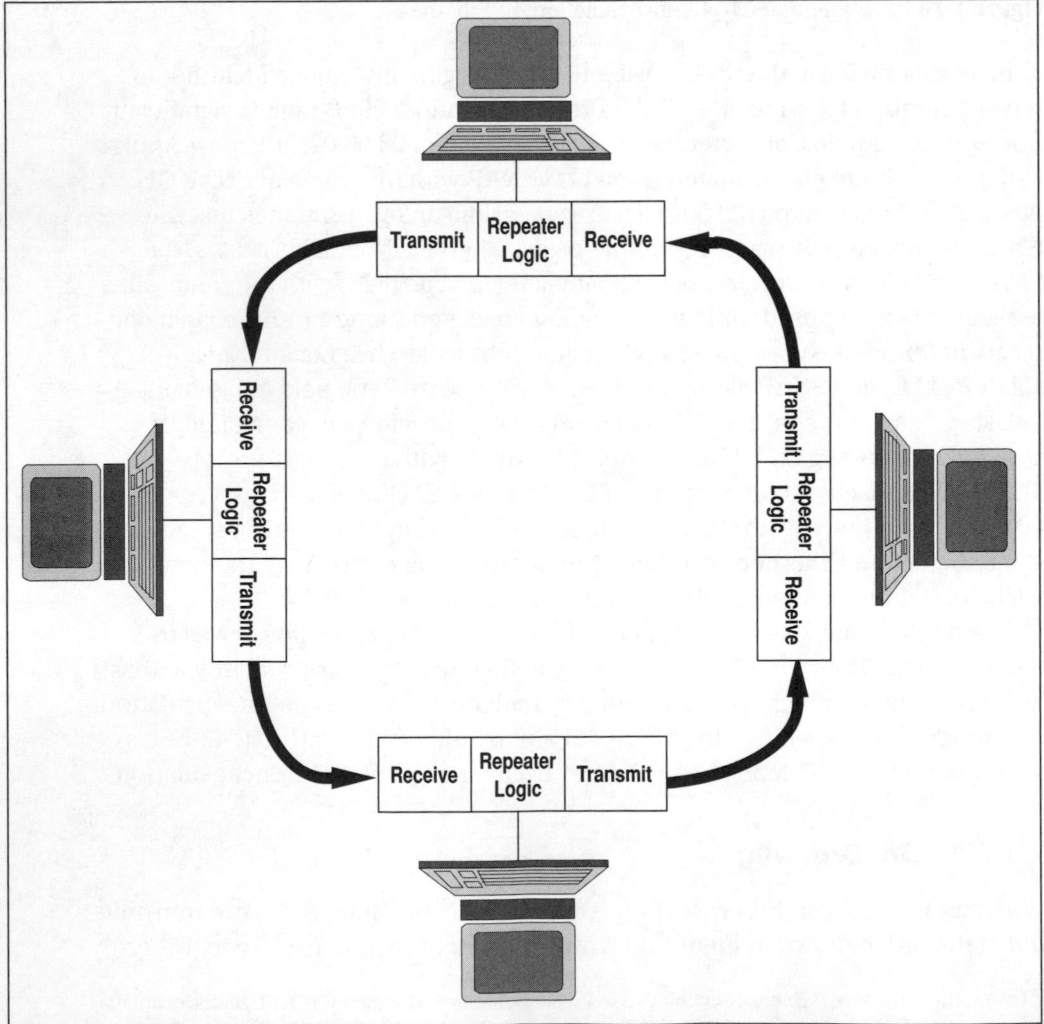

Figure 1.11 Token Ring configuration.

configuration, as depicted in Figure 1.11. Each station can transmit information directly only to its downstream neighbor, and can receive directly only from its upstream neighbor. Many-to-many communication is effected by having each station repeat the signals from its upstream neighbor to the downstream one.

When a station transmits on its own behalf, it inserts its data into the circulating stream. All other (non-transmitting) stations repeat the data until it returns to the originating station, which is responsible for removing it from the ring.

Similar to what occurred with Ethernet, IBM both wrote its own specification formalizing Token Ring operation and also brought its technology to the IEEE 802 LAN Standards Committee during the early 1980s. IBM's Token Ring architecture became the basis of the IEEE 802.5 standard, first published in 1985.

The original Token Ring standard specified operation at either 4 or 16 Mb/s. Initially, most commercial products operated at the lower data rate. During the late 1980s and early 1990s, 16 Mb/s Token Ring products became more widely available; by the late 1990s, virtually all Token Ring installations operated at the 16 Mb/s data rate. In 1998, the IEEE 802.5 Working Group approved a standard for Token Ring operation at 100 Mb/s; however, this has not seen significant commercial deployment.

1.3.2.1 Token Ring Medium Access Control

Proper operation of a Token Ring requires that only one station be using it to transmit its own data at any given time. That is, only one station ever has permission to transmit; this "permission slip" is called a token.[38]

The token circulates from station-to-station around the ring. Each station repeats the token, effectively passing it to its downstream neighbor. When a station wishes to transmit data, it waits for the token to arrive and then changes a single bit (from a 0 to a 1) in the token frame. This single bit change (the Token bit in the Access Control field, see Figure 1.12) converts the token to a data frame; the station then proceeds with the transmission of its data, which circulates throughout the ring.

All stations on the ring inspect the contents of the data frame as they repeat it to their respective neighbors. If the destination address within the frame indicates that they are intended recipients, the station(s) copy the frame into a local buffer and pass it to the higher-layer client (typically LLC) for further processing. In any event, the device continues to repeat the frame around the ring in case there are other potential receiving stations (e.g., a multicast destination), and to allow the frame to return to the original sender.

When the original sender sees its own frame returning after its arduous journey, it removes the frame from the ring and transmits a new token to its

[38] I have discovered that many students find it easier to understand Token Ring operation if, when reading material on the subject, they substitute the phrase *permission to transmit* for *token* in their heads.

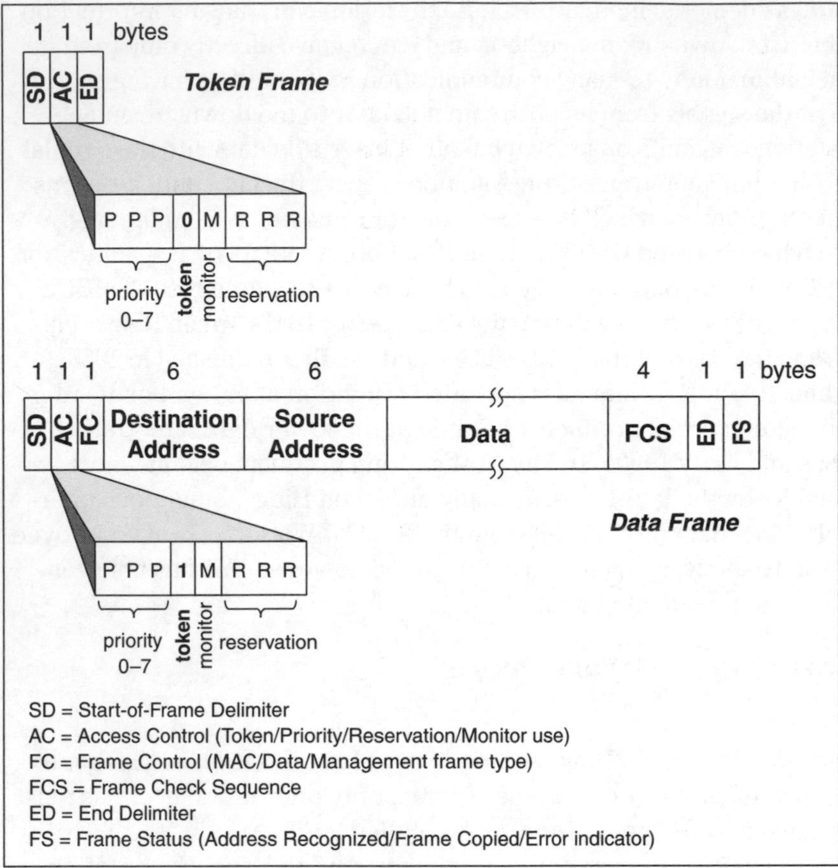

Figure 1.12 Token Ring frame format.

downstream neighbor (by flipping the Token bit back to a 0 value), effectively passing the baton to the next potential sender.[39]

1.3.2.2 Token Ring Physical Layer Options

The original Token Ring standard specified operation using a specialized shielded twisted pair cable developed as part of IBM's overall building wiring architecture [IBM82]. Virtually all early Token Ring customers used these cables, although they were extremely expensive, physically heavy, and diffi-

[39] What is presented here is a highly simplified explanation of Token Ring operation. There are many special features (token reservation, early release, priority, etc.) and boundary conditions (ring initialization, lost token recovery, etc.) that can only be understood from a detailed examination of the Token Ring access protocol specifications. Interested readers should refer to [CARL98] or the standard itself [IEEE98h]. Fortunately, a detailed understanding of the Token Ring MAC is not necessary for the purpose of understanding LAN switching in this book.

cult to terminate. The emergence of structured wiring systems using unshielded twisted pair (UTP) cable in the 1990s created a market demand for Token Ring products that could operate over this easier-to-use, lower cost wire. While the official standard for Token Ring operation over UTP cable was not formally published until 1998 [IEEE98h], many suppliers offered commercial products supporting Token Ring operation over UTP cable both at 4 and 16 Mb/s for a decade before the standard was approved.

In 1998, an amendment to IEEE 802.5 was approved that specified the operation of 16 Mb/s Token Ring over multimode optical fiber [IEEE98f]. Again, the date indicated only that the formal standard was catching up with common commercial practice many years after the fact.

The standard for Token Ring operation at 100 Mb/s uses the identical twisted pair physical layer specifications used for 100 Mb/s Ethernet (100BASE-TX).[40] That is, the same wiring system and physical layer signaling components can be used for either Ethernet or Token Ring operation at 100 Mb/s.

1.3.2.3 Token Ring Frame Formats

The Token Ring frame format is depicted in Figure 1.12.

Start-of-Frame Delimiter (SD) This field contains a unique pattern (as defined by the underlying physical signaling method) that allows a receiver to distinguish the start of a data frame from the idle signals used between frames.

Access Control (AC) This field comprises four subfields used to communicate information to the Token Ring access control process:

- The *priority bits* (P) indicate the priority level of the token or data frame. (See Chapter 13 for a discussion of priority operation and the use of the priority bits.)
- The *token bit* (T) is used to differentiate a token frame (T = 0) from a data frame (T = 1).
- The *monitor bit* (M) is used by a special *active monitor station* to detect various error conditions (circulating high priority token, frame initiator no longer present to remove its frame from the ring, etc.).
- The *reservation bits* (R) are used to request future use of a token at a specified priority level.

Frame Control (FC) The Frame Control field is used to differentiate user data frames from network management data frames.

[40] Actually, Ethernet "borrowed" (a nicer word than *ripped off*) these same Physical layer specifications from FDDI-over-copper [ANSI95] for use in 100 Mb/s Fast Ethernet. High Speed (100 Mb/s) Token Ring simply followed the long-standing tradition of using an existing, proven technology for a purpose other than that for which it was originally designed.

Destination Address This field contains the 48-bit address of the target destination(s) of the frame. It may contain either a unicast or multicast address, as discussed in Section 1.2.2.1.

Source Address This field contains the 48-bit unicast address of the station sending the frame. (Chapter 6 discusses the use of the first bit of the Source Address as a Routing Information Indicator for Source Routing.)

Data Field The Data field encapsulates the higher-layer protocol information being transferred across the LAN. Unlike Ethernet frames, Token Ring frames have no minimum length; there can be 0 bytes present in the Data field. The maximum length of the Data field is 4,528 bytes when operating at 4 Mb/s, and 18,173 bytes when operating at 16 or 100 Mb/s.

Frame Check Sequence The FCS is a checksum computed on the contents of the frame from the FC field through the end of the data field inclusive. The checksum algorithm is identical to that used in Ethernet (see Section 1.3.1.3).

End Delimiter (ED) This field contains a unique pattern (as defined by the underlying physical signaling method) that allows a receiver to unambiguously determine the end of the frame.

Frame Status (FS) This field contains status bits that allow a sending station to determine whether any intended recipients on the ring recognized the destination address, copied the frame into a local buffer, and/or detected an error during reception.

1.3.2.4 Bit-Ordering on Token Ring LANs

When a Token Ring frame is transmitted onto the LAN medium, bytes are transmitted in the order shown in Figure 1.12 from left-to-right. Within each byte, Token Ring transmits bits from the *most significant bit* (the bit corresponding to the 2^7 numerical position) first, to the *least significant bit* (the bit corresponding to the 2^0 numerical position) last. This is the opposite convention from that used in Ethernet.

Chapter 3 contains a complete discussion of the problems encountered due to this difference in bit-ordering as well as with the use of the Frame Status field when bridging between Ethernet and Token Ring LANs.

1.3.3 Fiber Distributed Data Interface

The Fiber Distributed Data Interface (FDDI) was the first standard local and metropolitan area network technology capable of operating at 100 Mb/s; until 1993, it was the only practical network alternative operating at a data rate in excess of 16 Mb/s. Developed under the auspices of the American National

Standards Institute (ANSI) during the mid-1980s, it had support from dozens of network equipment manufacturers. FDDI is now an ISO International Standard [ISO89a, ISO89b, ISO90]. While FDDI is not strictly part of the IEEE 802 family of standards, it is fully compatible with them. Architecturally, FDDI operates like an IEEE 802-style MAC, and it uses the same 48-bit address structure. Like its Token Ring cousin, FDDI requires LLC (with or without SNAP encapsulation) to upward multiplex among multiple client protocols and applications.

Originally, FDDI was intended for a wide variety of applications:

- *Front-end networks.* A high-speed replacement for desktop LANs (i.e., an Ethernet upgrade)
- *Back-end networks.* A processor-to-processor communications system for server interconnections, multiprocessing systems, and so on
- *Backbone networks.* A means of interconnecting other networks

In practice, FDDI flourished only in the backbone application environment. This is primarily due to its initial use of fiber media exclusively (effectively eliminating widespread deployment in the high-volume desktop market) and its high cost.

1.3.3.1 FDDI Operation

FDDI was designed around the use of a shared fiber medium configured in a dual ring topology, with media arbitration accomplished through token passing (similar to the IEEE 802.5 Token Ring MAC). This is depicted in Figure 1.13.

FDDI supports a maximum of 500 stations in the ring. All stations operate at a single, common data rate of 100 Mb/s. A token circulates around the ring; when a station wishes to transmit data, it waits for the token to arrive and then substitutes its data frame(s) for the token. Following successful transmission of the data frame(s) in its transmit queue, the station releases a new token, allowing the next station in the ring to similarly send data.[41]

1.3.3.2 FDDI Physical Signaling

Obviously from its name, FDDI was originally designed for fiber media (otherwise, we would just have called it DDI!). At the time it was being developed

[41] Like the previous discussion of Token Ring operation, this is a highly simplified description of the FDDI access method. In addition to some of the same boundary conditions and features of the IEEE 802.5 Token Ring, FDDI also provides mechanisms for use of the redundant second ring, restricted token behavior, synchronous bandwidth reservation, and so on. These details are not presented here as they are not necessary for an understanding of the use of FDDI in a switched LAN environment. Readers interested in the details of the FDDI MAC should refer to [SHAH93] or the official standard [ISO89a].

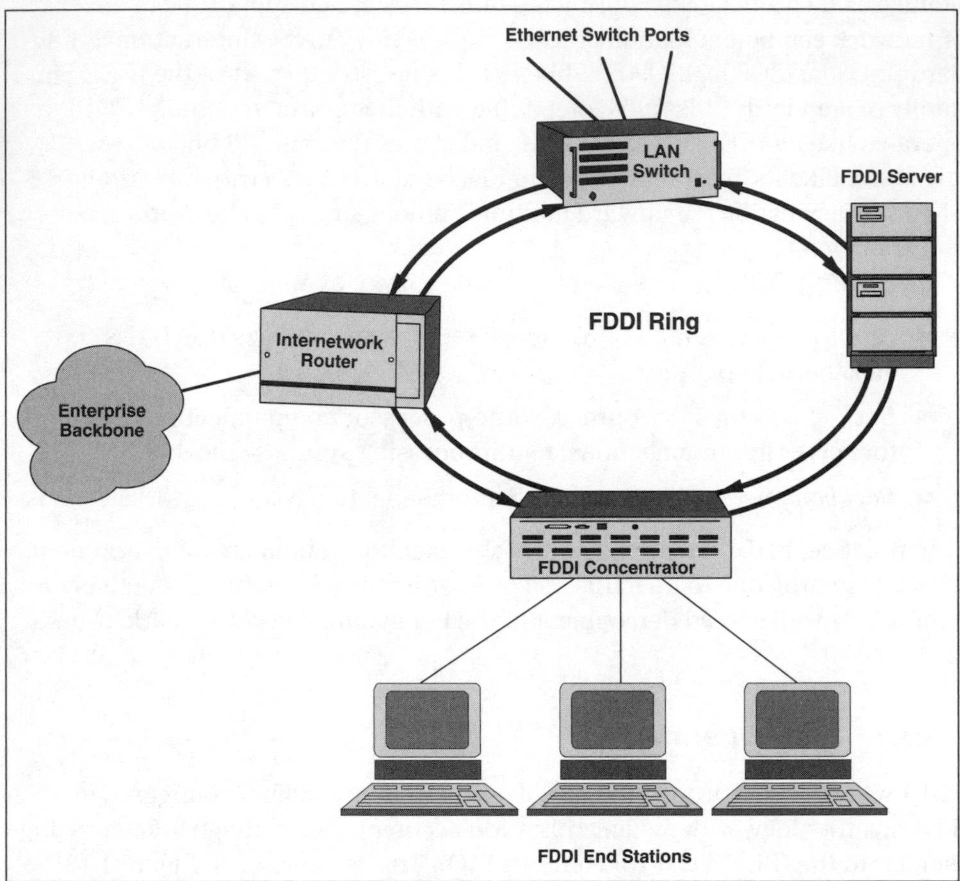

Figure 1.13 FDDI ring.

(around 1985), operation at 100 Mb/s over copper media was considered impractical. (At that time, even 10 Mb/s operation over twisted pair was inconceivable, much less 100 Mb/s operation!) In addition, backbone applications normally require relatively long-distance links (on the order of kilometers), which is impractical even today using low cost copper media. Thus, the original FDDI standard specified the use of multimode optical fiber exclusively. The standard provided for distances of up to 2 km between stations on the ring.

In order to reduce the signaling rate on the fiber, a block data-encoding scheme was employed. FDDI systems encode four bits of data into five code bits (4B/5B encoding). This results in a channel signaling rate of 125 Mbaud (100 Mb/s × ⁵⁄₄). The 4B/5B encoding system was later adopted for use in 100 Mb/s Ethernet systems.

In an effort to expand the marketplace for FDDI, a system for operating FDDI over twisted pair copper media was developed during the early 1990s. The key technical challenge was to develop a means of signaling at 125 Mbaud

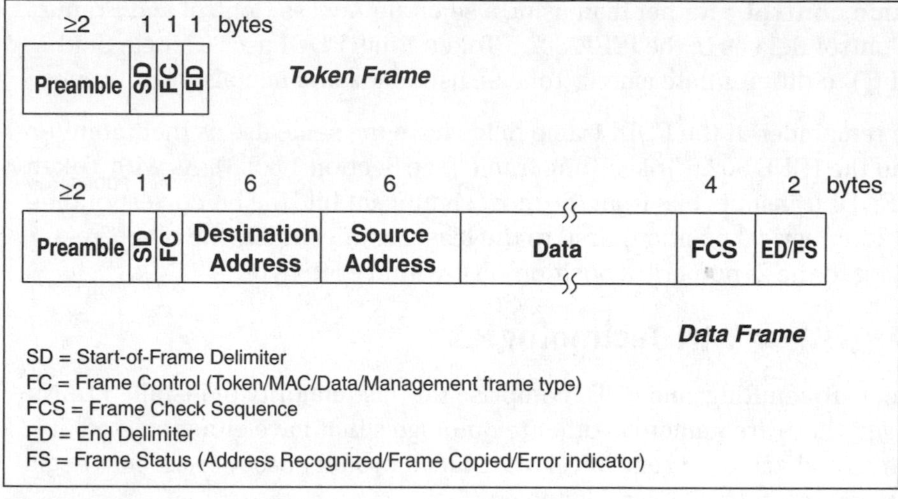

Figure 1.14 FDDI frame format.

in such a way that the signal was still decodable after passing through 100 m of UTP cable while not violating electromagnetic interference (EMI) regulations. The result was a line encoding system called Multi-Level Threshold (MLT-3), which used ternary (three level) rather than binary signaling to reduce the high-frequency spectrum of the transmissions.[42] The use of FDDI protocols over copper media is known as either Copper Distributed Data Interface (CDDI), a trade name of Cisco Systems, or Twisted Pair-Physical Medium-Dependent signaling (TP-PMD) in ISO terminology. The MLT-3 line encoding scheme is the same as that used in 100 Mb/s Ethernet and Token Ring.

FDDI is supported in standards-compliant devices over multimode optical fiber (2 km maximum), and both Category 5 UTP and STP (100 m maximum). Proprietary systems are also available that use singlemode fiber over longer distances.

1.3.3.3 FDDI Frame Format

FDDI, being a variant of Token Ring, uses a frame format similar to that of IEEE 802.5, as depicted in Figure 1.14.

Preamble Similar to Ethernet, the FDDI Preamble allows receivers to synchronize on the incoming frame.

[42] While officially MLT stands for Multi-Level Threshold, in reality it is the initials of the founders of the company that developed the technology (Crescendo Communications, later acquired by Cisco Systems): **M**ario Mazzola, **L**uca Cafiero, and **T**azio De Nicolo.

Frame control Rather than using a separate Access Control and Frame Control field as in the IEEE 802.5 Token Ring, FDDI uses a single field (FC) to differentiate among Tokens, user data, and management frames.

The remainder of the FDDI frame fields have the same use as their counterparts in the IEEE 802.5 Token Ring frame (see Section 1.3.2.3). As with Token Ring, FDDI transmits bits from the most significant bit (the bit corresponding to the 2^7 numerical position) first, to the least significant bit (the bit corresponding to the 2^0 numerical position) last within each byte.

1.3.4 Other LAN Technologies

Ethernet, Token Ring, and FDDI comprise the vast majority of installed LANs. However, there are numerous other technologies that have either existed at one time (and achieved some level of installed product base) or are just beginning to emerge in the LAN marketplace.

From a LAN switching perspective, most of these other technologies can be treated as variants of one of the more popular LANs. Differences in frame formats, shared medium access methods, or protocol semantics may affect the low-level implementation details of the devices employing a given technology, but do not change the fundamental behavior or operational algorithms in a switch from those used with the more popular technologies. In many cases, generic Data Link protocols such as LLC shield higher-layer clients from the details of the underlying LAN.

Some of the LAN technologies that have ended up in a ditch along the shoulder of the Information Superhighway include:

- Token Bus, as specified in IEEE 802.4 and used in Manufacturing Automation Protocol (MAP) systems
- Distributed Queue/Dual Bus (DQDB) systems, as specified in IEEE 802.6 and used in Switched Multimegabit Data Service (SMDS) offerings
- isoEthernet, specified in IEEE 802.9a
- 100VG-AnyLAN, specified in IEEE 802.12

Virtually none of these systems ever achieved any significant degree of market penetration or installed base of product, nor are manufacturers actively developing new products using these technologies.

One alternative LAN technology that did achieve considerable success was the Attached Resource Computer network (ARCnet), developed by Datapoint Corporation during the mid-1970s. Designed to operate over coaxial cable using a branching tree topology and a Token Passing Bus access method, ARCnet was arguably the most widely-installed LAN technology in the early 1980s. Until Ethernet components achieved commodity status, ARCnet's low cost made it attractive for small personal computer networks. Furthermore, its relatively low data rate of 2.5 Mb/s was not a limiting factor in that early, low performance networking environment.[43]

The biggest problem with ARCnet (from a LAN switching perspective) is that it uses locally administered, manually-configured, 8-bit addresses. When installing an ARCnet interface into a computer, the installer must select and configure the device's address, often by setting switches or jumpers on the interface card itself.

As discussed in Chapter 2, the fact that ARCnet does not use globally-administered addresses makes it unsuitable for use with LAN bridges operating at the Data Link layer. While it is possible to build an internetwork of multiple LANs comprising a combination of ARCnet and other technologies, Network-layer routers (not LAN bridges or switches) must be used for the interconnection. ARCnet LANs cannot even be bridged to themselves, much less to Ethernets, Token Rings, or other standard LANs.

Fortunately for the deployment of LAN switches, ARCnet is rarely used today in commercial networks. It is occasionally encountered in embedded process control systems used for factory automation.

1.4 IEEE LAN Standards

The Institute of Electrical and Electronics Engineers (IEEE) supports the development of industry standards in a wide range of technologies, from power generation to electronic instrumentation to programming languages. In February 1980, a meeting was held at the Jack Tar Hotel in San Francisco, California, to discuss the development of an industry standard for Local Area Networks.[44] That meeting (and many others subsequent to it) spawned the creation of IEEE Project 802, one of the largest and longest-running activities within the IEEE standards organization.

The original intent of Project 802 was to develop a single standard for local area computer networks. Recognizing that a number of different skill sets were involved in this endeavor, the group originally split into three subcommittees:

1. A *Higher-Layer Interface* (*HILI*) group would be responsible for the development of service and programming interfaces for higher layer protocol clients. In addition, this group would deal with all of the issues that

[43] A 20 Mb/s version (dubbed ARCnet Plus) was developed in the late 1980s, but never successfully commercialized.

[44] I was at that meeting. The Jack Tar Hotel no longer exists (the Cathedral Hill Hotel is now located at the same site), but the IEEE 802 LAN/MAN Standards Committee does. Interestingly, although much of the constituency of the IEEE 802 committee comes from Northern California (Silicon Valley), that first meeting was the only time that a full IEEE 802 (plenary) session was held anywhere in the San Francisco Bay Area. It's much more fun to travel to Maui, Montreal, New Orleans, and the like than to stay at home and work.

are generally addressed with software technology, such as network management.

2. A *Medium Access Control* (*MAC*) group would be responsible for the development of the MAC algorithm to be used on the LAN.
3. A *Physical Layer* (*PHY*) group would be responsible for the actual wiring, encoding, and signaling used on the medium.

Over the next few years, it became clear that the MAC and PHY groups would never achieve consensus on a single technology or medium to be *the* standard for all users. There was one large faction of Ethernet supporters promoting CSMA/CD on baseband coaxial cable, a second faction arguing for the use of a Token Passing Bus on broadband coaxial cable, and a third group endorsing Token Ring on shielded twisted pair cable.

Since no agreement would be forthcoming, the committee decided to pursue all three approaches. Each faction formed a separate Working Group and developed a set of specifications around its favorite technology. The HILI group split in two as well, one subcommittee dealing with architecture, interworking, and management issues, and the other with the definition of the generic Logical Link Control protocol. Thus, there were five Working Groups:

IEEE 802.1: Overview, Architecture, Interworking, and Management

IEEE 802.2: Logical Link Control

IEEE 802.3: CSMA/CD MAC and PHY

IEEE 802.4: Token Bus MAC and PHY

IEEE 802.5: Token Ring MAC and PHY

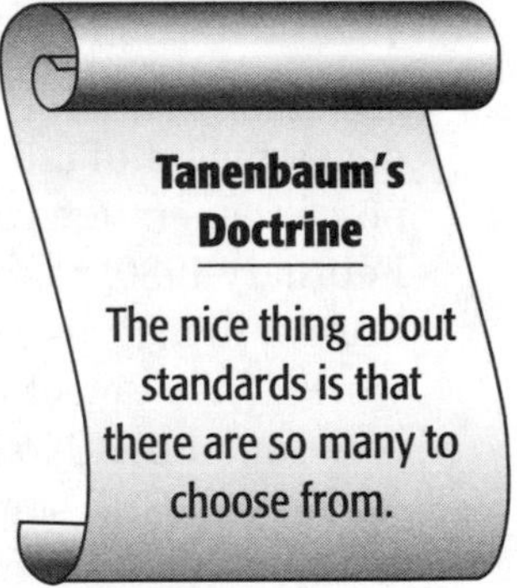

Tanenbaum's Doctrine
The nice thing about standards is that there are so many to choose from.

Over the years, additional Working Groups were formed, and a large number of standards were produced. IEEE Project 802 is internationally recognized as the official body responsible for the development of local and metropolitan area network standards. Many of the standards developed are adopted and endorsed by national standards bodies, for example, the American National Standards Institute (ANSI) in the United States, as well as the International Organization for Standardization (ISO). While IEEE 802 is ostensibly a U.S. organization, its membership is global, with significant representation from individuals and organizations in Europe, Asia, and Israel.

1.4.1 IEEE 802 Organization

Figure 1.15 depicts the current IEEE 802 organization, composed of 13 Working Groups (WGs) and two Technical Action Groups (TAGs). The groups in boldface are currently active and hold regular meetings to work on outstand-

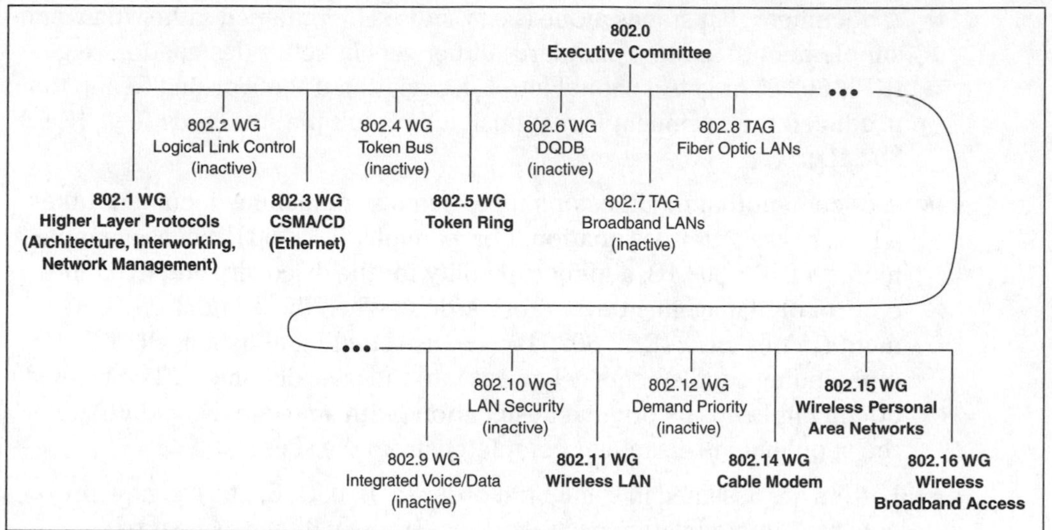

Figure 1.15 IEEE 802 organization.

ing projects and issues.[45] The others are in *hibernation*, meaning that there is no ongoing activity, no projects are outstanding, and no meetings are held; former members of those groups can be contacted if questions arise about the interpretation of a standard developed when the group was active.

Information on current IEEE 802 Working Group activities and meetings, and on obtaining the standards themselves, can be found at http://standards.ieee.org.

As we wish to focus on those areas pertinent to LAN switching, Sections 1.4.3, 1.4.4, and 1.4.5 look more closely at the activities of the IEEE 802.1 WG and the IEEE 802.3 and 802.5 WGs (Ethernet and Token Ring), respectively.

1.4.2 IEEE 802 Naming Conventions, or "Mind Your p's and Q's"

You may notice (both in this book and in industry literature) that IEEE documents are sometimes called "IEEE so-and-so," and at other times "P802-dot-whatever." Also, some documents use lower-case letters and some upper-case. While some of the variation is due to sloppiness and inconsistency in publication practices,[46] there is actually a method to the madness—a code system by which we assign designations to Task Forces and the documents that they produce. IEEE 802 uses the following conventions:

[45] As I write this, I am preparing to leave for the November 1999 meeting in Kauai, Hawaii, as editor of the IEEE 802.3ad Link Aggregation standard. Hey, *somebody* has to do it!

[46] A problem never encountered at John Wiley & Sons.

- A document that stands alone (i.e., that is self-contained rather than a supplement to another standard) either gets no letter designation (e.g., IEEE 802.3) or gets a capital letter designation if the Working Group that produced the document is responsible for multiple standards (e.g., IEEE 802.1D).
- A document that modifies or supplements a standalone document takes a lower-case letter designation. For example, IEEE 802.1k was a supplement to IEEE 802.1B, adding capability for the discovery and dynamic control of management event forwarding. When the foundation document (in this case, IEEE 802.1B) is revised and republished, all of the outstanding supplements get swept into the base document. The base document keeps its original designation (with a new revision date), and the supplements disappear completely from the scene.
- Letters are assigned in sequential order (a, B, c, D, E, etc.) as new projects are initiated within each Working Group, without respect to whether they are capitalized or not. There is no relationship between the letter designation assigned to a supplement and the letter of the foundation document that it modifies. The letter designation uniquely identifies both the document and the Working Group Task Force that develops it.
- Approved standards have an IEEE name (e.g., IEEE 802.1Q). Unapproved drafts leading up to an approved standard are designated P802 (dot whatever), signifying that they are the work of an ongoing project (hence the P). The P802 name is usually followed by the draft number. Thus, P802.1p/D9 was the ninth (and final) draft of a supplement to IEEE 802.1D. It turned out that the schedule for publication of IEEE 802.1p (the approved standard resulting from P802.1p) coincided with the time for the revision and republication of its foundation document, IEEE 802.1D. Thus, it was expedient to sweep the supplement into the base document immediately rather than waiting as much as a few years for the next revision cycle. So IEEE 802.1p (an important standard on multicast pruning and priority bridge operation) was never published on its own.

Is it all clear now?

1.4.3 IEEE 802.1

IEEE 802.1 is the Working Group responsible for all of those aspects of LAN technology that cross MAC sublayer and Physical layer technology boundaries. As such, it has become a catch-all group for a variety of issues and standards development activities, including network management, addressing, and the IEEE 802 architecture itself.

At the time of this writing, there are seven extant IEEE 802.1 standards:

IEEE 802: Overview and Architecture [IEEE00][47] This is the foundation document for the entire series of IEEE 802 standards. It contains key concepts applicable across all LANs, including the structure of 48-bit addresses and Organizationally-Unique Identifiers and the architectural reference model for the other IEEE 802 standards.

IEEE 802.1B: Management [IEEE95c] This standard provides a protocol and mechanisms for remote management of IEEE 802 LANs. As the de facto standard for LAN Management is the Simple Network Management Protocol (SNMP) [RFC1157, ROSE96], IEEE 802.1B is largely ignored. There are few, if any, commercial implementations.

IEEE 802.1D: MAC Bridges [IEEE98a] This is the most widely-known and implemented IEEE 802.1 standard; it forms the basis for all LAN bridges and switches. The operation of bridges built to this standard is discussed extensively in Chapters 2 to 6 of this book. The 1998 edition includes facilities for multicast pruning and priority operation, as discussed in Chapter 10, *Multicast Pruning*, and Chapter 13, *Priority Operation.* Prior to this revision, these functions were described in the supplement to IEEE 802.1D, designated P802.1p.

IEEE 802.1E: System Load Protocol [IEEE94] This largely unknown but very useful and interesting standard defines a protocol for the reliable downloading of bulk data simultaneously to multiple devices using the multicast addressing capability of IEEE 802 LANs. The protocol avoids the need to individually download multiple devices with the same information (e.g., operational code), yet provides for guaranteed delivery to all destinations, invoking retransmission only when needed by one of the multiple target devices.

IEEE 802.1F: Common Definitions for Management [IEEE93b] This standard provides a set of generic definitions for management information common across the range of other IEEE 802 standards. It is modeled toward use with the ISO Common Management Information Protocol (CMIP) [ISO89c]. Since most systems today ignore CMIP and instead provide management based on SNMP, this standard sees little application.

IEEE 802.1G: Remote MAC Bridging [IEEE98c] This standard defines an architecture and set of requirements for bridges that interconnect geographically dispersed sites using Wide Area Network (WAN) technology. As discussed in Chapter 3, the standard provides little practical informa-

[47] Note that the name of this standard is IEEE 802, not 802-dot-anything. While not strictly an IEEE 802.1 document, it was developed under the auspices of the IEEE 802.1 WG, and by the same people who developed other IEEE 802.1 standards.

tion and is generally ignored by both product developers and network administrators.

IEEE 802.1H: Bridging of Ethernet [IEEE95a] This important document is officially a Technical Recommendation, as opposed to a standard.[48] It describes the method used by bridges to convert between Type Encapsulated frames (as used on Ethernet) and both SNAP and RFC1042 encapsulation (as used on LANs that do not support native Type Encapsulation). The procedures specified in this standard are discussed extensively in Chapter 3.

IEEE 802.1Q: Virtual Bridged LANs [IEEE98d] This standard defines the requirements for bridges operating in a Virtual LAN (VLAN) environment. VLAN operation is discussed in Chapter 11, *Virtual LANs: Applications and Concepts*, and Chapter 12.

From a LAN switch perspective, the important IEEE 802.1 documents are IEEE 802, IEEE 802.1D, IEEE 802.1H, and IEEE 802.1Q.

1.4.4 IEEE 802.3

IEEE 802.3 is the standard for MAC and Physical Layer operation of CSMA/CD LANs. Unlike IEEE 802.1, only one self-contained document is controlled by the IEEE 802.3 Working Group—the IEEE 802.3 standard. Over the years, there have been numerous supplements and revisions; at the time of this writing, the letter designations for IEEE 802.3 projects have reached P802.3af, having used all 26 letters and wrapped around to 2-letter designations.

The 1998 version of IEEE 802.3 is over 1,200 pages long; it is affectionately referred to as the *Doorstop Edition* in deference to one of the alternative uses for such a massive work. It includes all of the supplements through IEEE 802.3z (Gigabit Ethernet).

Some of the key supplements to IEEE 802.3 include:

IEEE 802.3a (Thin wire coaxial cable, 10BASE2), 1988

IEEE 802.3c (Repeater specifications), 1985

IEEE 802.3d (Fiber optic inter-repeater link, FOIRL), 1987

IEEE 802.3i (UTP cable, 10BASE-T), 1990

IEEE 802.3j (Fiber optic LAN, 10BASE-F), 1993

IEEE 802.3u (Fast Ethernet, 100BASE-T), 1995

IEEE 802.3x (Full duplex operation and flow control), 1997

[48] Technical Recommendations carry less weight than official standards. Indeed, the IEEE 802.1H recommendation comprises only 29 pages and weighs about 70 grams, as compared to the IEEE 802.1G standard, a weighty tome at over half a kilo!

IEEE 802.3z (Gigabit Ethernet over optical fiber), 1998

IEEE 802.3ab (Gigabit Ethernet over UTP cable, 1000BASE-T), 1999

IEEE 802.3ac (Frame Extensions for VLAN-tagging), 1998

Throughout this book, the terms *Ethernet* and *IEEE 802.3* are used interchangeably.

1.4.5 IEEE 802.5

IEEE 802.5 is the standard for MAC and Physical Layer operation of Token Ring LANs. As with IEEE 802.3, this Working Group controls only one base document—the IEEE 802.5 standard. That standard has been supplemented to include:

IEEE 802.5c (Dual ring redundant configuration), 1991

IEEE 802.5j (Optical fiber media), 1997

IEEE 802.5r (Dedicated Token Ring/Full duplex operation), 1997

IEEE 802.5t (100 Mb/s High Speed Token Ring), 1998

1.4.6 Other Standards Organizations

IEEE Project 802 is not the only organization in the world concerned with the development and dissemination of network standards. In particular, the formal charter of IEEE 802 restricts its activities to technologies operating at the Data Link and Physical layers exclusively. While these comprise a large part of what most people consider a LAN, any practical networking system will also require services above these lower layers. Thus, some aspects of networking are outside the scope of IEEE 802 standardization.

The IEEE is a professional society existing for the benefit of its members and the engineering community. It derives whatever authority it has from the assent of the industry. It is not a government agency, nor does it have any power or ability to enforce compliance with its standards other than the willingness of the industry to accept those standards as meaningful.

Many national and international standards bodies look to IEEE 802 for guidance in setting their official standardization policies. As such, many of the important IEEE 802 standards have also been approved as standards by the American National Standards Institute (ANSI). ANSI is the U.S. representative to the International Organization for Standardization; ISO has adopted many of the IEEE 802 standards and published them under the ISO name. Thus, IEEE 802.3 is also available as ISO 8802-3, IEEE 802.1D is available as ISO 15802-3, etc. Typically, ISO adoption and publication of IEEE 802 standards lags approximately one year behind their approval by IEEE.

Some of the important standards organizations working on technologies related to LANs and LAN switching include:

- *American National Standards Institute.* ANSI is responsible for much of the work on higher-layer protocols in the ISO protocol suite, including the ISO Connectionless Network Protocol (CLNP), ISO Transport Protocol, and so on. ANSI was also responsible for the development of FDDI.
- *Internet Engineering Task Force.* The IETF is responsible for all of the higher-layer protocols in the TCP/IP family.
- *International Organization for Standardization.* While ISO does not generally develop standards itself, it does adopt and endorse standards developed by other organizations, including IEEE and ANSI. Many national governments and legal agencies adopt ISO standards either intact or as the foundation for their own national standards; in some cases, these agencies may forbid the sale of products in their countries that do not conform to the relevant ISO standard.
- *Electronic Industries Association/Telecommunications Industries Association.* The EIA/TIA vendor consortium has been responsible for the development of the standards for the structured building wiring on which most modern LANs operate. They also developed many other standard communications technologies, including RS-232, RS-422, and so on.
- *International Telecommunications Union.* The ITU-T (formerly known as the International Consultative Committee on Telephony and Telegraphy, or CCITT) is the agency of the United Nations responsible for many of the standards for long-distance telecommunications and interfaces to public data network equipment (e.g., modems).

1.5 Terminology

Q: Does a station send *frames* or *packets* onto a network?
Q: Is a device that interconnects Ethernets to an FDDI backbone called a *bridge* or a *router?*
Q: Should you care?
A: Yes, yes, and yes.

Writers (especially in the lay or trade press) often get "free and loose" with terminology. *Packets* and *frames* are treated interchangeably; *routers* are called *bridges*, or *bridges* are called *gateways*. In many cases, it really doesn't matter whether the wording reflects strict technical correctness. Such details are usually not vital for a broad, high-level understanding of system behavior. We, however, have no such luxury here. This book examines the behavior of stations and internetworking devices at a highly detailed level. As such, we often need to be precise in our terminology, so that it is clear exactly what is being discussed or manipulated.

Network terminology tends to follow the layered architectural model. We use different terms to describe the devices, objects, and processes that implement the functions of each layer. This actually makes life somewhat easier; we can generally tell which architectural layer is being discussed just from the terms being used.

1.5.1 Applications, Clients, and Service Providers

As depicted in Figure 1.16, each layer in a suite of protocols can be seen to use the services of a lower-layer *service provider* and to provide services to a higher-layer *client*. Information is passed across the service interfaces between the layers, but a given layer simply does its defined job—processing transmission requests from higher-layer clients and passing them down to the next lower layer, or processing received information from a lower layer service provider and delivering the contained payload up the stack. If we look at a protocol suite from a standpoint of architectural purity, each layer is unaware of the nature of the layers both above and below it. A Network layer entity (e.g., an IP implementation) is unaware whether its client is TCP, UDP, OSPF, or some other entity. Similarly, the IP entity performs the same functions whether it is operating over an Ethernet or WAN link.

In particular, there is no way for a given layer entity to know the architectural layer at which its client resides. As discussed in Section 1.1.6, an end user application may invoke network services at any layer of the architecture. The entity providing services at some middle layer has no idea whether its client is a protocol at the next higher layer or an end user application. From the perspective of any given layer, every entity using its services is a *client application*. In this book, we use the term *application* in this very broad sense, meaning any client using the services of the layer entity under discussion. Thus, from the perspective of IP, a Transport protocol (e.g., TCP), a Network Management agent (e.g., SNMP/UDP), and a routing protocol (e.g., OSPF) are all client applications. The terms *higher layer protocols* and *client applications* are synonymous.

1.5.2 Encapsulation

As data is passed from a user application down the protocol stack for ultimate transmission onto a network, each layer generally adds some control information to the transmission, so that its peer entity at the receiver can properly interpret it and take appropriate action upon its receipt. This process is known as

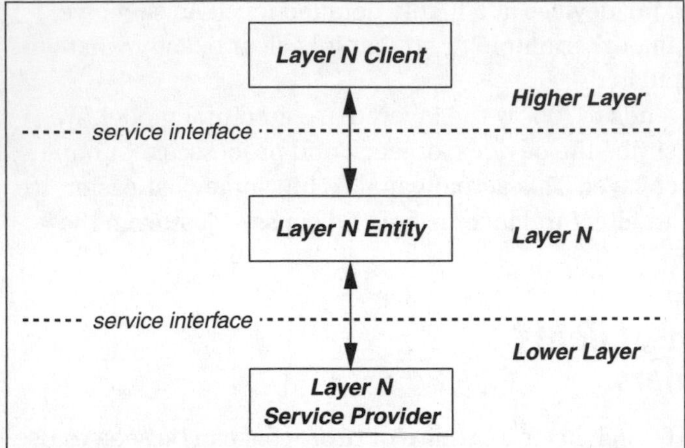

Figure 1.16 Clients and service providers.

encapsulation. Each layer entity takes the information provided by its higher-layer client (called a *Service Data Unit,* or SDU), adds layer-specific control information (typically in the form of a *protocol header* and/or *trailer*), and passes this combined *Protocol Data Unit* (PDU) to its lower layer service provider. Similarly, as the information is processed in the receiving device, each layer parses, interprets, and acts upon its layer-specific control information, strips away the header and trailer, and passes the decapsulated information up to its higher-layer client. As depicted in Figure 1.17, a Transport layer PDU thus becomes the Network layer SDU; the Network layer adds a protocol header to its SDU to create a Network layer PDU, which becomes the SDU of the Data Link layer, and so on.

The unit of data at each protocol layer (the Protocol Data Unit) has a distinct name:

- A Transport PDU is called a *segment,* or in some protocol suites, a *message.*
- A Network PDU is called a *packet.* In the IP protocol suite, the term *datagram* is often used to denote a connectionless IP packet.
- A Data Link PDU is called a *frame.*
- A Physical layer PDU is called a *symbol stream,* or more commonly, a *stream.*

Thus, we can speak of TCP segments, IP packets, and Ethernet frames. Strictly speaking, there is no such thing as an Ethernet packet, since an Ethernet entity (operating at the Data Link layer) deals only with its own encapsulation (a frame). An Ethernet frame encapsulates an IP packet, which encapsulates a TCP segment, as depicted in Figure 1.18. Throughout this book, these terms will take their strict interpretation as stated here.

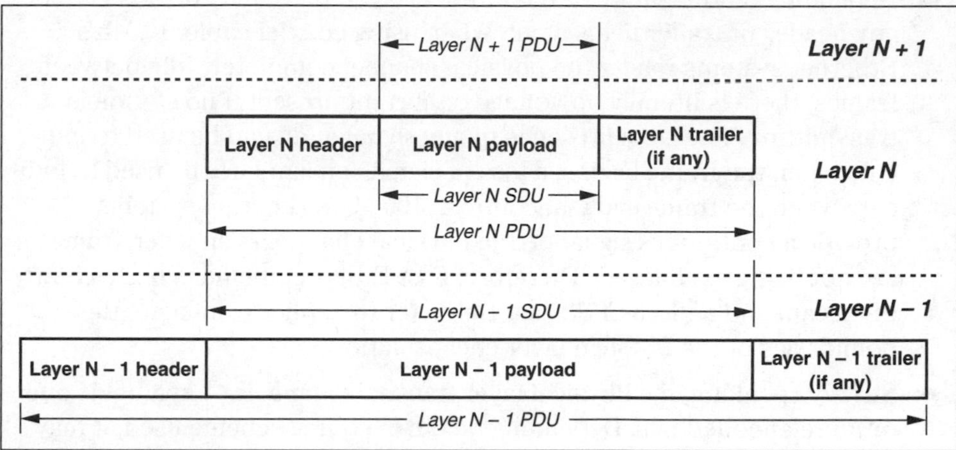

Figure 1.17 Service and Protocol Data Units.

A few points should be noted:

- If a frame is the encapsulation at the Data Link layer, then it should seem curious that the Ethernet Start-of-Frame Delimiter occurs *within* the Ethernet header; if it truly delimited the start of the frame, it should come at the end of the Physical layer encapsulation (see Section 1.3.1.3.) This is an artifact of the evolution of Ethernet from its DEC–Intel–Xerox roots to the IEEE 802.3 standard. In the original specification, the Ethernet Preamble was considered part of the Physical layer header; in the later IEEE 802.3 standard, the Preamble was defined to be part of the Data Link encapsulation. Thus, in the earlier standard, the Start-of-Frame Delimiter did actually mark the start of the Data Link frame.

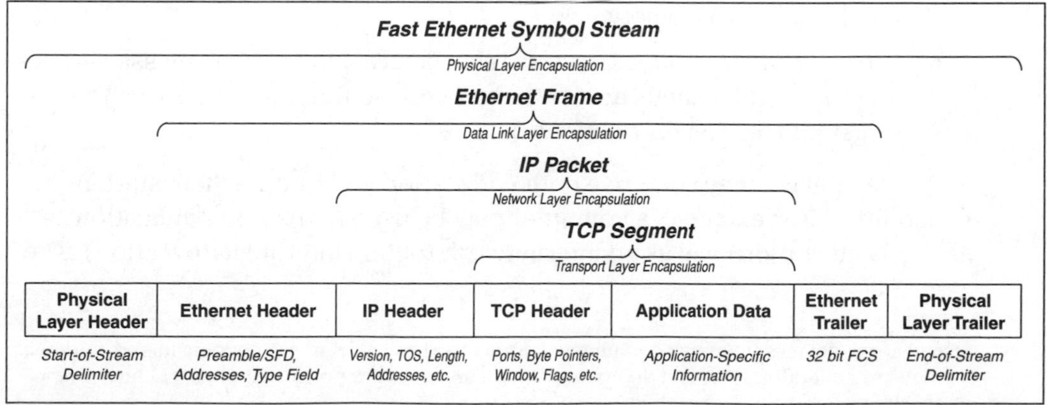

Figure 1.18 Example of layer encapsulation.

- Depending on the nature of the Physical layer, there may be no need for any header or trailer fields at all. When using coaxial cable, 10 Mb/s Ethernet systems render the physical channel completely idle between frames; there is literally no voltage or current present if no station is transmitting. Thus, the presence of any signal at all can be used to indicate when the frame begins; a loss of signal can similarly be used to indicate when the frame ends. In contrast, 100 Mb/s Ethernet systems provide a continuous signal on the physical channel even when frames are not being exchanged. Therefore, Fast Ethernet includes both a Start-of-Stream and an End-of-Stream Delimiter to explicitly indicate the boundaries of the Physical layer encapsulation.
- Strictly speaking, the Physical layer transmits *symbols.* A symbol is one or more encoded bits. Depending on the encoding scheme used, it may not even be possible to transmit a single bit on the physical channel. For example, Fast Ethernet uses an encoding system whereby 4 bits of data are encoded into a 5-bit symbol (so-called 4B/5B encoding). Data is always transferred in 4-bit nibbles; it is not possible to send a single bit on a Fast Ethernet. On a 10 Mb/s Ethernet, the Manchester encoding scheme used does permit individual encoded bits to be transmitted. Regardless of the encoding used, we often speak of the physical channel encapsulation as a *bit stream,* even though it is symbols (encoded bits) that are actually exchanged.

1.5.3 Stations and Interconnections

Any device that implements network services at the Data Link layer or above is called a *station.*[49] There are two types of stations:

- *End stations.* Support one or more user network applications. End stations are the source and ultimate destination (sink) of all user data communicated across a network.
- *Intermediate stations.* Serve as relay devices, forwarding messages generated by end stations across the network so that they can reach their target end station destination(s).

A given device may comprise both end station and intermediate station capabilities. For example, a computer may be used both as an application server (end station) and as an internetwork router (intermediate station). The

[49] In general, devices operating completely within the Physical layer are not considered stations, as they are not addressable and do not implement any network protocols. Thus, cabling components and repeaters do not qualify as stations.

term *workstation* generally denotes a device that provides end station functionality exclusively.

Intermediate stations are classified by the layer in the architecture at which they provide their relay function:

Data Link Layer An intermediate station relaying frames among various Data Links is called a *bridge.* A collection of LANs bridged together is called a *catenet* (catenated network) or a *bridged LAN.*

Network Layer An intermediate station relaying packets among networks is called an *internetwork router,* or simply a *router.* A collection of networks interconnected by routers is called an *internetwork,* or simply an *internet.* The Network-layer protocol used on an internetwork is called an *internetwork protocol,* or simply an *internet protocol.*

Note that *internet* and *internet protocol* are intentionally spelled here with lower-case letters. Any set of networks interconnected by routers is an internet, regardless of the internet protocol in use. Thus, one can build AppleTalk/DDP internets, NetWare/IPX internets, IP internets, and so on. One well-known IP internet is *the Internet* (capitalization intentional). The internet protocol used on the Internet is the Internet Protocol (IP).[50] This distinction between an internet and the Internet is maintained consistently throughout this book.

A *gateway* strictly refers to a device that provides interconnection between dissimilar protocol architectures. It is typically application-specific; for example, an e-mail gateway may be able to translate messages between the Simple Mail Transfer Protocol (SMTP) operating over a TCP/IP stack and the IBM-proprietary PROFS system operating in an IBM SNA protocol environment, thus allowing mail interaction between users on a private SNA system and the Internet.

Historically, IP routers were often called gateways (IP gateways). While current literature and most modern products now use the (more correct) term *router,* many IP standards documents and protocols (and some old-time IP fogies) still carry this terminology baggage, for example, the Border Gateway Protocol (BGP).

In practice, *gateway* has become a marketing term for any device that connects anything to anything else. Since it evokes a much more pleasant visual image than either *bridge* or *router,*[51] it has been used to sell everything from true Application-layer translators to RS-232 adapter connectors. Fortunately, we do not need this term for anything in this book.

[50] This has to be one of the oddest sentences ever written in a networking text, but it does make complete sense.

[51] It always reminds me of the Gateway Arch, and a wonderful time I had in St. Louis, Missouri, in 1983.

Table 1.2 Network Terminology Summary

	UNIT OF DATA	INTERCONNECTION DEVICE	MAXIMUM EXTENT (LAN CONTEXT)
APPLICATION		Gateway	
PRESENTATION			
SESSION			
TRANSPORT	Segment or Message		
NETWORK	Packet	Router	internetwork or internet
DATA LINK	Frame	Bridge	Catenet or Bridged LAN
PHYSICAL	Symbol or Bit Stream	Repeater	Local Area Network

1.5.4 Terminology Summary

Table 1.2 shows the seven layer OSI reference model along with the terms used for encapsulation and interconnection at each layer. Where no standard term exists, the table is empty. Fortunately, we will not need terms for these entries. (In fact, if there were a general need for these missing table entries, standard terms would have been developed long ago.)

CHAPTER

2

Transparent Bridges

OK, the history lesson and abstract architectural introductions are over. It's time to look at how things actually work. In this chapter, we delve into the gory depths of transparent bridges. The concepts and practices presented here provide the foundation for all of the advanced switch design and esoteric features discussed in later chapters. The treatment here is in five parts:

1. Principles of operation (what a bridge does)
2. Architecture (how a bridge appears to the stations and applications)
3. Implementation (critical design issues)
4. Performance
5. IEEE 802.1D (the official standard for transparent bridges)

2.1 Principles of Operation

This first section describes the fundamental transparent bridge algorithms. The presentation here is primarily from a behavioral perspective, that is, how the bridge behaves in response to received frames.

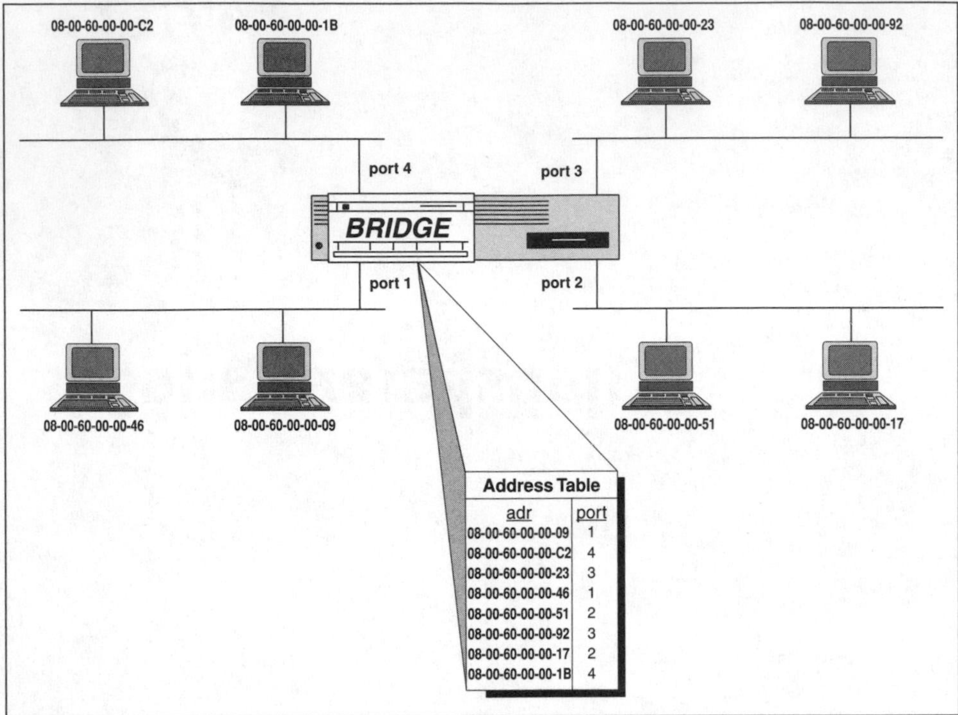

Figure 2.1 Bridged LANs[1].

Figure 2.1 depicts a simple bridged LAN configuration. Note that:

- There are multiple, distinct LAN segments interconnected by the bridge. (The figure shows four such segments, but there is no architectural limit on the number of LANs that may be interconnected by a single bridge.)
- Each station has a globally-unique 48-bit unicast address. This is critical; proper bridge operation depends on the use of globally-unique addresses at the link layer.
- The bridge has a *port,* or interface, on each of the LANs to which it connects.
- There is a table within the bridge that maps station addresses to bridge ports; that is, the bridge knows through which port each station can be reached.

[1] In this figure, and in many others in this book, LANs are depicted as shared-media buses. There is no intent to imply that this logical topology necessarily reflects the physical topology in use. Most modern LANs use dedicated media connections, a star-wired topology, and a central hub. The depiction of LANs as shared-media buses is intended to differentiate them from switched LANs that require dedicated media, as discussed in later chapters. In every case where a LAN is depicted using shared-media, a star-wired configuration with a repeater hub can also be used.

- The bridge operates in *promiscuous mode;* that is, it receives (or at least attempts to receive) every frame on every port, regardless of the destination address (target) of the frame. A typical end station will only attempt to receive those frames whose destination address matches that of the station; in contrast, a bridge receives all frames regardless of the intended destination.

2.1.1 Unicast Operation

When a frame is received on any port, the bridge extracts the destination address from the frame, looks it up in the table, and determines the port to which that address maps. If the port on which the frame is received is the same port where the target destination resides, the bridge can simply discard the frame, since it can be assumed that the target will have received the frame through the normal LAN delivery mechanisms. In the first case shown in Figure 2.2, the bridge receives a frame on port 1 being sent from station 08-00-60-00-00-46 to 08-00-60-00-00-09; the bridge will discard this frame, since the address table indicates that station 08-00-60-00-00-09 is on port 1 and the frame was received on port 1. This is called *filtering* the frame. The bridge filters all frames whose destination resides on the same port as that on which the frame arrived. It is important that the bridge not retransmit the frame onto port 1 (the port of arrival). This would cause a duplication of the frame that

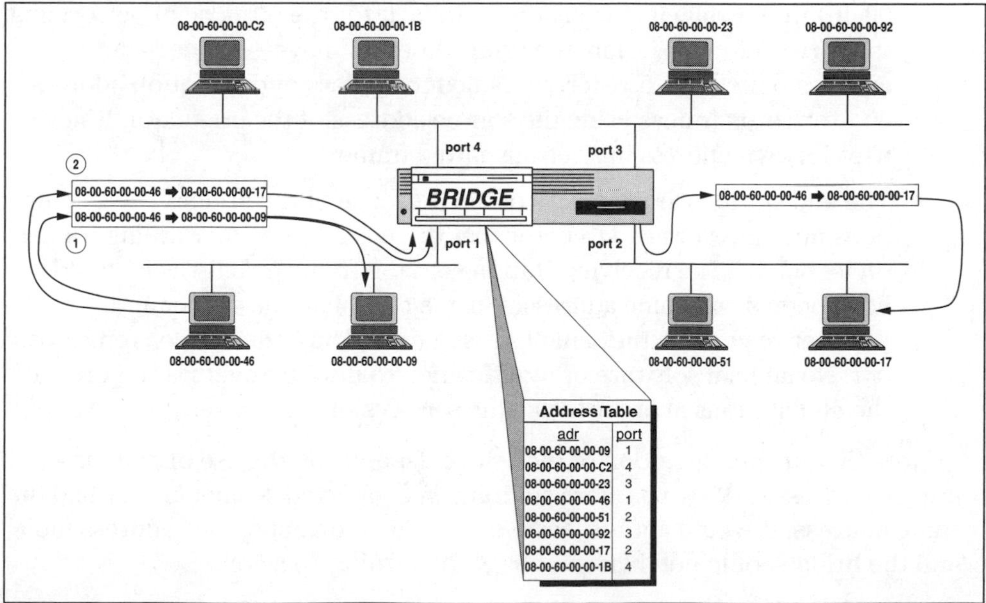

Figure 2.2 Unicast operation.

could cause problems in the end station(s), not to mention doubling the traffic on every port.[2] This is discussed further in Section 2.2.1.1.

If station 08-00-60-00-00-46 now sends a frame to station 08-00-60-00-00-17, the bridge will receive this frame on port 1 (being in promiscuous mode, it is receiving all frames) and look up station 08-00-60-00-00-17 in the address table. The table indicates that the target destination is reachable through port 2. In order for the target to properly receive the frame, the bridge must now *forward* the frame onto port 2. Note that in the process of forwarding the frame:

- The bridge cannot simply forward the frame without regard to other stations on that LAN. It must behave according to the normal Medium Access Control (MAC) rules for that port. This means that the bridge must defer, detect collisions, back off, and so on, on an Ethernet port, just like any other Ethernet device. On a token-passing LAN, the bridge must wait until it has obtained the token before forwarding frames.
- There can be significant delay in forwarding frames on output ports. This is known as the *bridge transit delay.* If a target output port is not immediately available or is congested, frames will queue up inside the bridge, waiting for available times to be transmitted. In the worst-case, a bridge's output queue may fill, causing the bridge to discard frames rather than forward them, due to lack of bridge resources (buffers) in which to store frames.
- When the bridge forwards the frame, it uses for the source address the address of the original sender of the frame (in this example, 08-00-60-00-00-46) rather than its own address. In fact, for the purpose of performing the forwarding operation, the bridge does not have—or need—an address of its own. It receives frames regardless of destination address, and forwards frames using the source address of the originator. It never uses its own address in a retransmitted frame.
- The end stations are unaware of the presence of the bridge. The sender does not know or need to know that there is a bridge forwarding frames on its behalf. The receiving station sees the frame exactly as it would have been seen (same addresses, same data) had the sender and receiver resided on the same LAN segment. Thus, the bridge is *transparent.* No special software or modification to device drivers is required in the end stations in order to use the services of the bridge.

Note that proper operation of the bridge depends on the use of globally-unique addresses. If two or more stations on connected segments ever had the same address, it would not be possible to build an unambiguous address table, and the bridge could not make a correct forwarding decision.

[2] It could be worse. Consider the case of multiple bridges with ports on the same LAN!

2.1.2 Unknown and Multicast Destinations

What if station 08-00-60-00-00-46 sends a frame to station 08-00-60-00-00-2C in Figure 2.2? The bridge will receive the frame on port 1 and perform the requisite lookup in the address table. However, the destination is not in the table. The bridge does not know the relative location of the target destination. What should the bridge do?

There are two possible choices: (1) Discard the frame; (2) Queue the frame for transmission on all ports except the port on which it arrived. Forwarding a frame onto all ports except the port of arrival is known as *flooding*.

There are three possibilities for the whereabouts of our unknown target destination, as depicted in Figure 2.3:

1. The station could be present on port 1, unbeknownst to the bridge.
2. The station could be nonexistent (or equivalently, turned off), unbeknownst to the bridge.
3. The station could be present on a port other than port 1, unbeknownst to the bridge.

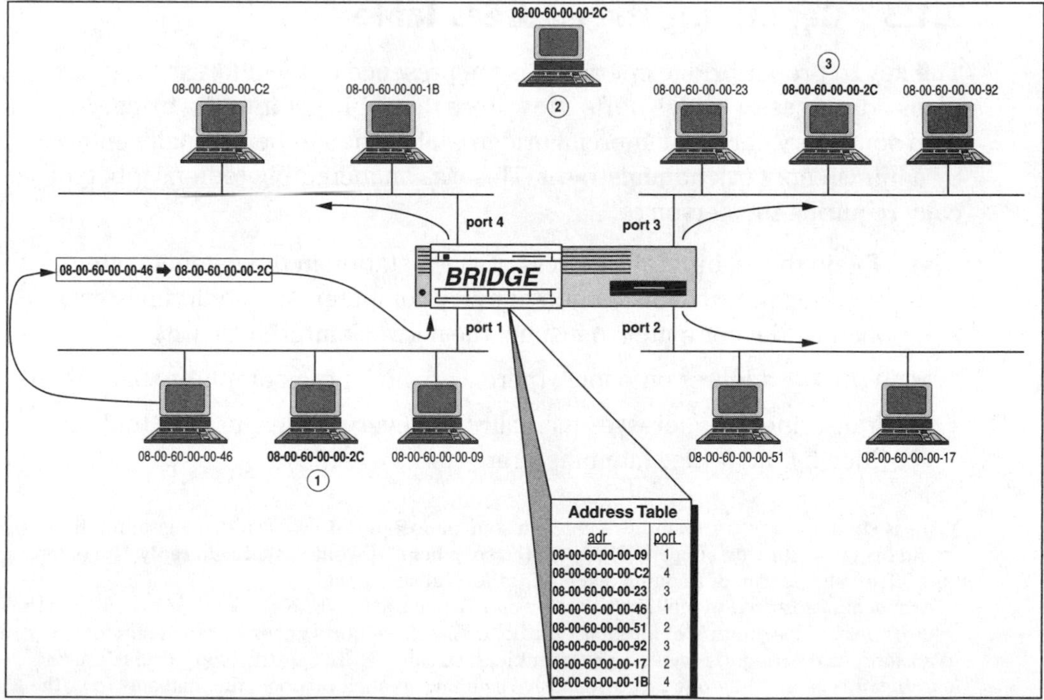

Figure 2.3 An unknown destination.

If we assume that the attached LANs have excess capacity (i.e., they are overprovisioned) and that traffic sent to unknown destinations constitutes a relatively small fraction of the total traffic seen by the bridge in the steady-state, then flooding does not constitute a significant burden for the catenet. The issue then is not one of whether capacity is being wasted (it is, but who cares?), but whether flooding will actually allow communications to proceed. In case 1, flooding does not help the source and destination to communicate, since the destination will see the frame directly on its own LAN without any action by the bridge. In case 2, flooding also does not help, since the bridge cannot do anything to provide communications with a nonexistent device. However, in the third case, flooding does help, as it allows communication with the target regardless of the port on which it resides.

Thus, flooding will permit communication with destinations unknown to the bridge in the event that the destination is present on some bridge port other than the port of arrival. Other than generating some excess traffic, it does no real harm.[3]

Similarly, if a station sends a frame to a multicast address, a bridge will forward that frame onto all ports except the one on which it arrived, as the bridge cannot tell which stations are listening to a given multicast address and so must not restrict distribution of such frames to particular target output ports.[4]

2.1.3 Generating the Address Table

The key to proper bridge operation is the presence of the address table that maps addresses to bridge ports. How does this table get into the bridge?

In some very early commercial bridges, tables had to be manually entered by a human network administrator. This was an incredibly tedious job, typically requiring the person to:

- Obtain the 48-bit MAC address of every station in the catenet (often requiring physical inspection of every computer, and sometimes even opening the computer to inspect the network interface card)
- Write the address on paper (there were no laptop computers back then)
- Transcribe the addresses manually into every bridge, using a tool provided by the bridge manufacturer

[3] This is similar to my grandmother's chicken soup philosophy. If I was sick, my grandmother would bring me chicken soup. "Bubbe, will the soup help?" I would ask. She'd reply, "It couldn't hurt!" The same is true of flooding, except for the Yiddish accent.

[4] The mechanisms used in multicast pruning and Virtual LANs (VLANs) specifically deal with the issue of proper distribution of multicast traffic to only those ports necessary to ensure delivery to all stations desiring to receive a given multicast stream [IEEE98a, IEEE98d]. Unlike unicast learning, this cannot be done through passive listening; explicit protocol mechanisms (e.g., the Generic Attribute Registration Protocol, GARP, and its companion, the GARP Multicast Registration Protocol, GMRP) are needed to register multicast addresses with particular bridge ports. This is discussed in Chapter 10.

In an organization with hundreds or thousands of end stations and multiple bridges, the probability of correctly recording and transcribing every address was approximately the same as that of winning the lottery![5] If any errors were made, and the address tables were incorrect or inconsistent, there could be serious communications problems that were difficult to troubleshoot. Perhaps more important, any time a station was moved, it was necessary to manually update the bridge tables to reflect the change. This is clearly an unwieldy situation in any sizable organization.

Fortunately, manual address table administration can be avoided. The address table can be built automagically by considering the Source Address in received frames. Bridges perform a table lookup on the Destination Address in order to determine on which port(s) to forward a given frame. The bridge can also perform a table lookup for an entry corresponding to the Source Address, indicating the station that sent the frame. If an entry is not found (i.e., the bridge has not heard from this station previously), the bridge creates a table entry for this newly-learned address, with the port mapping indicating the port on which the frame arrived. If an entry is already in the table, the port mapping is updated to reflect the port on which the latest frame arrived. This allows the bridge to properly map stations that have moved from one LAN segment to another. Over time, as stations send frames, the bridge will learn the address-to-port mapping for all active stations.

2.1.4 Address Table Aging

If all we ever did was add learned addresses to the table and never removed them, we would have two problems on our hands:

1. For many lookup algorithms, the larger the table, the more time the lookup will require (see Section 2.3.2). The performance of a bridge is (to a certain extent) a function of the bridge's ability to perform table lookups and make forwarding decisions quickly. If we never removed stale entries, the table could get quite large. We might be forcing the lookup algorithm to deal with an unnecessarily big table, thereby artificially reducing the performance of the bridge. Thus, it makes sense to restrict entries in the table to only those stations that are known to be currently active.
2. If a station moves from one port to another, the table will incorrectly indicate the old port until the station sends traffic that would cause the bridge to learn its new location. Depending on the nature of the higher-layer protocols and applications running on that station, this may take a long time (or forever, with a poorly designed protocol). Consider a device that responds only to specific requests from other stations, and

[5] Interestingly, the probability of winning the lottery is approximately the same whether or not you buy a ticket.

never initiates communications of its own accord. If this station moves (making the address table incorrect), requests may not be forwarded properly to the station in question. The bridge can re-learn the proper port only if the station sends traffic, yet the protocol is designed not to send traffic until specifically requested. But until the station does send traffic, it will not hear the requests! This is a deadlock situation.

A simple solution to both problems is to age entries out of the address table when a station has not been heard from for some period of time. Thus, when we perform the table lookup for the Source Address, we not only make a new entry (or update the port mapping for an existing entry), we flag the entry as being still active. On a regular basis, we check the table for *stale entries*—entries that have not been flagged as active for some period of time—and remove them from the table. Once a station entry is aged out, further communications directed to that station will be flooded as the station address is now unknown. This will allow communications to be re-established with the station regardless of its new attachment port. As discussed in Section 2.5.1.1, the standard default value for the aging time is 5 minutes. Methods for implementing the aging algorithm are discussed in Section 2.3.4.

Seifert's Law of Networking #9
If you never say anything, no one will know that you're there.

Note that the definition of activity for aging purposes is based on the address appearing as a Source Address, not as a destination. We learn (and age) table entries based on senders, not receivers, of data. The fact that someone may be trying to send traffic to a station must not prolong the life of that station's entry in the address table. Consider what would happen in the case of our poorly-designed protocol from case 2 in the preceding list; continued requests from other stations would prevent the target from being aged out of the table, prolonging the deadlock situation.

2.1.5 Process Model of Table Operation

We can think of the dynamic operations on the Bridge Address Table as being performed by three independent processes, as depicted in Figure 2.4:

1. A *lookup process* compares the Destination Address in incoming frames to the entries in the table to determine whether to discard the frame, forward it to a specific port, or flood it to all ports.
2. A *learning process* compares the Source Address in incoming frames to the entries in the table and updates the port mapping and activity indicators or creates new entries as needed.
3. An *aging process* removes stale entries from the table on a regular basis.

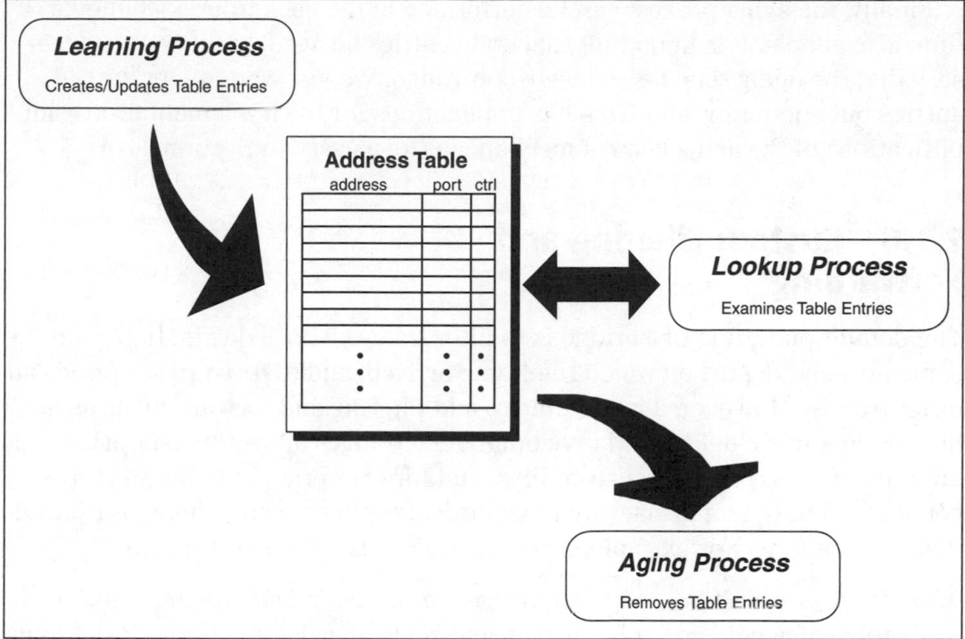

Figure 2.4 Processes operating on address table.

As discussed in Section 2.3.1, this is also the order of priority for these operations. Destination lookup must be performed in real-time, on a frame-by-frame basis. Any delay in performing lookups will reduce the performance of the bridge for user data traffic, both limiting throughput and increasing bridge latency.

Address learning is important, but is not in the critical path of frame forwarding. In fact, if the bridge cannot perform address learning on every frame under worst-case traffic conditions, it may have little effect on overall performance. New stations sending traffic may not be learned immediately, but this will not impede communications; traffic sent to these stations will be flooded rather than directed to a specific port. As long as the unknown station continues to send traffic, its address will be learned in due course, when the traffic peak subsides and the bridge has time to perform the learning process.[6]

[6] Some early commercial bridge designs anticipated that they would not be able to perform the learning algorithm on all frames at full traffic load. They intentionally learned only every *n*th address seen (e.g., learn on every third frame) to reduce the burden. As long as traffic patterns were somewhat irregular, the bridge would ultimately learn all of the addresses. Of course, woe be it if the traffic patterns were such that a given source appeared exactly every *n*th frame and was consistently overlooked by the learning algorithm. This is similar to how a strobe light can make motion appear stationary if the motion occurs at the same frequency as the strobe.

Finally, the aging process can be performed in the background whenever time is available. It is important that stale entries be aged, but it is not necessary that the aging time be precisely controlled. We just want to get the old entries out sooner or later. This has implications for the implementation (simplification) of the aging control mechanisms, discussed in Section 2.3.4.

2.1.6 Custom Filtering and Forwarding

The default operation of a bridge is to filter frames whose destination is on the same port as the port on which the frame arrived, and to forward (or flood) all other frames. However, it is possible to add filtering and forwarding criteria beyond just these defaults. Many commercial bridges allow the network administrator to program custom filter and forward criteria; these allow the bridge to behave in a manner that may provide some added benefits for particular applications. For example, a network administrator may wish to:

- *Prevent specific users from accessing certain resources.* A primitive form of access control may be achieved by disallowing frame forwarding onto certain output ports based on the Source Address in received frames.
- *Prevent sensitive traffic from being allowed to propagate beyond a set of controlled LANs.* Some degree of privacy can be achieved by filtering traffic based on Source and/or Destination Address, protocol types, and so on.
- *Limit the amount of multicast traffic that is flooded onto certain LANs.* A rate-limiting mechanism can be applied to the flooding algorithm to prevent excess multicast traffic under heavy load conditions.

The possibilities are virtually endless. Most bridges that support such custom filters provide tools for specifying the filter criteria (e.g., addresses and/or protocol types) and the action(s) to be taken when frames arrive that meet the criteria (filter, forward to a specific set of ports, report to a network administrator, etc.). In many cases, bridge performance may be adversely affected by the use of custom filters. Each set of filter criteria must be applied to every frame; this is usually a processor-intensive activity that can significantly degrade performance, depending on the implementation.

Seifert's Law of Networking #23
The only real security is physical security.

A note is in order about the use of custom bridge filters for providing network "security." While primitive access and privacy controls can be implemented in this manner, these mechanisms are notoriously easy to defeat by a determined intruder. In fact, no amount of electronic security (passwords, encryption, etc.) will prevent 100 percent of attacks. Ultimately, all data security reduces to *physical* security.[7] Electronic security mechanisms simply make the job of the intruder more difficult, and will prevent intrusions only from those attackers who are unwilling to expend the effort necessary to break the level of protection you have provided.

2.1.7 Multiple Bridge Topologies

The previous discussions all assumed that we were dealing with a group of LANs interconnected by a single bridge. (Well, you have to start *somewhere!*) Of course, the environment may require that multiple bridges be used for interconnection. It turns out that this does not change the operation of the bridge or the end stations at all. Bridges are not only transparent to end stations, they are transparent to each other. Consider the situation depicted in Figure 2.5.

From the perspective of bridge X, stations A, B, and C reside on port 2, and every other station in the catenet is on port 1, including all of the stations in building 1. Since all of the bridges forward traffic transparently without modifying Source or Destination Addresses, bridge X will see all traffic that is not originating from port 2 as originating from port 1, regardless of the actual location of the originating station and the number of bridges that the traffic has to traverse to reach bridge X. Similarly, none of the other bridges will be able to determine whether a Source Address seen on an input port reflects a station that is actually resident on that port or one that is some number of bridge hops away. The actual location is irrelevant; the bridge table reflects the fact that a given address is reachable through a given port, not that it is actually resident on the LAN attached to that port.

Note that, in reality, there are no end stations at all that actually reside on the LAN connected to port 1 of bridge X (the building 2 backbone). Address table entries in bridge X that map to port 1 can be created from only that traffic that other bridges have forwarded onto this network, either because of entries in their own address tables or due to flooding of unknown destinations. Thus, bridge X may not have address table entries for every station in the catenet, even in the steady-state. Traffic from stations that only need to communicate locally within building 1 never needs to be forwarded into building 2; those stations will never appear in bridge X's address table. As a result, while the address tables in all of the bridges should be consistent (i.e., not in contradiction with each other), they may not be identical due to locality of traffic patterns.

[7] If I really want your data badly enough, I don't have to become an electronic spy. I simply point a gun to your head and say, "Give me your data." Most users comply with this request.

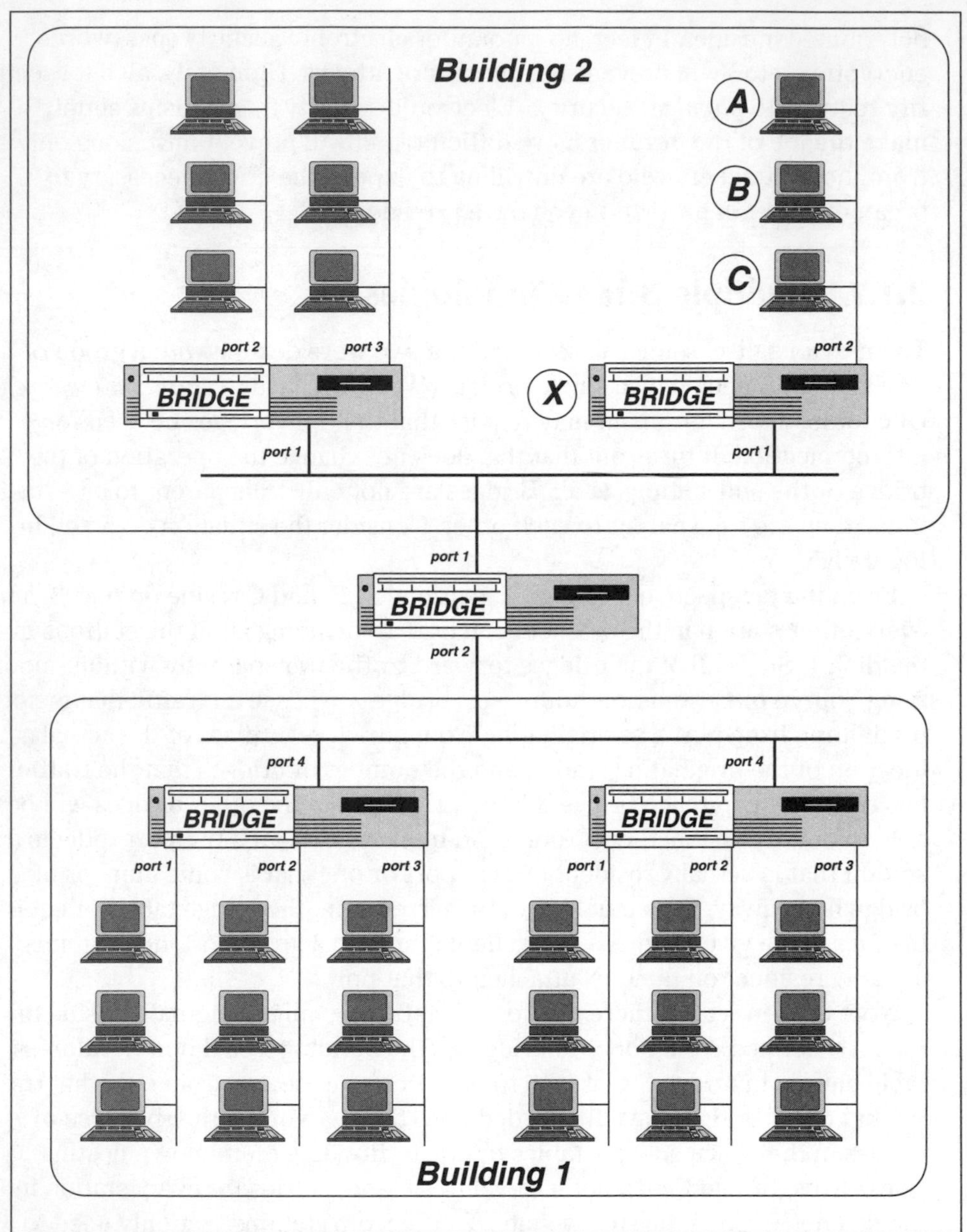

Figure 2.5 Multiple bridges.

There is no theoretical limit on the number of bridges that may be interconnected in tandem. Practical limits arise from the need to limit flooding of multicast traffic and from the requirements of higher-layer protocols and applications. This is discussed in greater detail in Section 2.5.1.2.

2.2 Transparent Bridge Architecture

In this section we look at how transparent bridges map into and provide the services for communication in the context of the OSI seven layer reference model [ISO94]. In addition, we consider how the insertion of transparent bridges between end stations affects the architectural invariants of the Data Link as seen by higher-layer protocols and applications within those stations. If abstract architecture bores you, you may safely skip this entire section with no loss of continuity.[8]

Transparent bridges, dealing exclusively with globally-unique MAC addresses, provide internetworking services at the Data Link layer of the OSI model.[9] This is depicted in Figure 2.6. For simplicity, the figure shows only a two port bridge, although the architecture is the same regardless of the number of ports present.

Each port on the bridge comprises a MAC and Physical layer entity, which communicate with their peer entities in the end stations on the attached LANs. On any given port, all of the devices [both the end station(s) and the bridge port itself] must use the same MAC method (e.g., Ethernet) and the same Physical layer data rate (e.g., 10 Mb/s or 100 Mb/s). Different ports of the bridge may use different data rates and/or different MAC technologies. Chapter 3, *Bridging between Technologies*, discusses the implications of bridging between dissimilar MAC technologies.

The bridge contains a *relay entity*, which implements the bridging function as described in Section 2.1. This relay entity takes frames received from the various MACs, makes the determination of what to do with them (i.e., discard, forward to a specific port, or flood), and submits them as necessary for transmission on other ports. The Bridge Address Table is contained within the relay entity. The relay entity (and the relay function itself) is completely transparent to the end stations; they are totally unaware of the presence of the bridge at the Data Link layer. Another way to say this is that the bridge does not terminate the link. Data Link communication (e.g., LLC) occurs between the end stations directly, rather than from end station to bridge and bridge to end station.[10]

[8] I only wish that I could do the same.

[9] OK, to be absolutely precise, the service is provided at the MAC sublayer of the Data Link layer.

[10] This is different from Network layer routing, where communication occurs explicitly between end stations and routers. Routers are not transparent at the Data link, and do terminate the link from an end station.

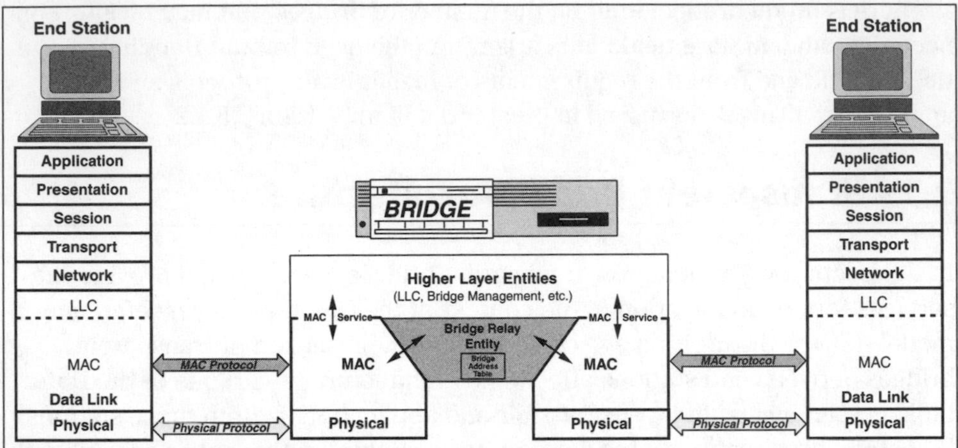

Figure 2.6 Bridge architecture.

From the perspective of the client of the Data Link, the bridge is invisible. This is true regardless of whether the client is using connectionless (e.g., LLC-1) or connection-oriented (e.g., LLC-2) link services.

Let's try to separate the concept of an "architectural bridge" (the bridge relay) from that of a device called, and sold as, a bridge (a "real bridge"). The bridge relay neither sources nor sinks any frames on its own behalf. That is, all frames originate in a sending end station and terminate in a receiving end station. The bridge relay (together with its associated network interfaces) constitutes an *intermediate station* providing the internetworking function at the Data Link layer.

A real bridge may of course include many capabilities besides just those required to implement the bridge relay. Typical features include network management, the Spanning Tree Protocol (discussed in Chapter 5, *Loop Resolution*), Network layer routing, and possibly some network server functions. The operation of a bridge relay is the same regardless of the real bridge within which it is packaged. The additional functions provided in the real bridge exist above the MAC layer, and are typically not transparent to other end stations. That is, a real bridge appears as an end station in its role of implementing those capabilities not associated with the bridge relay. In this manner, a real bridge may source and sink data frames (e.g., network management messages) on its own behalf.

2.2.1 Maintaining the Link Invariants

A bridge tries to make a catenet appear to the end stations as if it is a single LAN. That is, from the perspective of the higher-layer protocols and applications, the station is connected to *a* LAN, and not an interconnected set of LANs. As such, the protocols and applications may be reasonably assumed to expect single-LAN-like behavior from the catenet.

A LAN Data Link exhibits a number of important characteristics, as shown in Table 2.1.

Table 2.1 LAN Data Link Invariants

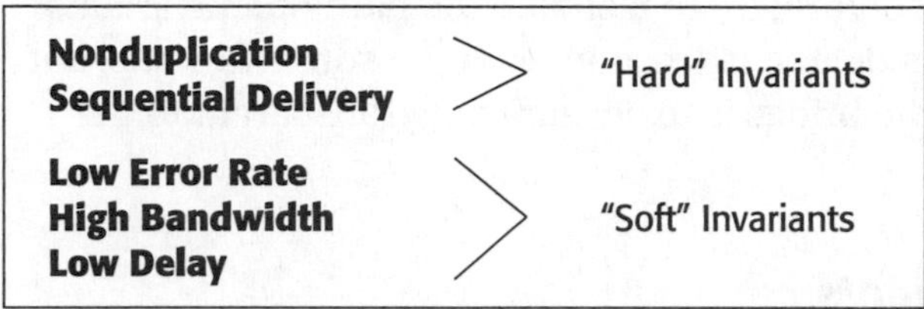

These characteristics are referred to as *invariants* of the LAN. The "hard" invariants are absolute strictures. Individual LANs always exhibit these behaviors. The "soft" invariants reflect services generally provided by a LAN, but there is a little more flexibility here. Yes, the error rate should be low, but it is not expected to be zero, and it can vary somewhat over time. Similarly, LANs provide low delay, but often the upper bound (and the tolerance of higher-layer protocols) is much greater than the typical delays encountered in practice.

Notice that there are no protocol mechanisms required to establish these invariants. For example, Ethernet controllers do not look for duplicate frames and delete extra copies, nor does Ethernet incorporate sequence numbers into the frames and require receivers to check for proper ordering. It is simply a natural consequence of the LAN itself that gives rise to these invariant behaviors.

A protocol designed to operate directly above a LAN-based Data Link (e.g., a Network-layer protocol or an application using the LAN Data Link without any intervening protocols) can simply assume the invariant behaviors of the LAN. If the protocol knows that it is operating over a LAN, then it never needs to consider the possibility that frames may be received out-of-order or that multiple copies of the same frame may be received. Assuming the invariant behavior greatly simplifies the design, and can improve the performance of the client protocol or application. Since frames will never be received out-of-order, there is no need to deal with or even consider that possibility; the client protocol does not need to implement any mechanisms for frame re-ordering (or eliminating duplicate frames), since these events never occur.[11]

[11] Note that while these are invariants of a LAN Data Link, they may not be invariants of some Network-layer protocols. That is, the simplifying assumption is only valid when dealing directly with the LAN; if the protocol or application is communicating through a Network-layer protocol that does not guarantee message ordering or non-duplication (e.g., IP), then the application must deal with that possibility and incur whatever complexity is needed.

Bridges complicate the issue. They make multiple LANs appear as one. They have internal memory, and, unless we take specific action to prevent it, there is a possibility that frames could be replicated or delivered out-of-order. Such a bridge would be violating a hard link invariant; an application or protocol running on a bridged catenet rather than a single LAN could be dealt a situation that it never expected. As a result, the application may display unpredictable behavior (read: it may crash).

Simply put, it is incumbent on bridges to maintain the hard link invariants absolutely.[12] There is a certain degree of freedom with the soft invariants, but they need to be respected if the bridge is to appear truly transparent to the end station applications.

2.2.1.1 The Hard Invariants Are Hard Indeed

Strictly speaking, a bridge must not re-order the sequence of frames between any Source-Destination Address pair *at a given priority level;* that is, higher-priority frames may be sent ahead of lower-priority frames regardless of their order of generation. Some LAN technologies (e.g., Token Ring and Token Bus) can encode priority directly into the frame; Ethernet has no native priority mechanism. Therefore, in the absence of external priority mechanisms (e.g., priority tags and VLAN tags, as discussed in Chapter 11, *Virtual LANs: Applications and Concepts*, and Chapter 12, *Virtual LANs: The IEEE Standard*), priority is not an issue for Ethernets. All frames are at the same priority level, and ordering must be maintained on the entire sequence of frames between any Source-Destination Address pair.

Note that the invariant behavior is a constraint on the traffic flow between a Source and Destination Address pair, regardless of the "packaging" of the devices using those addresses. A given physical device may be listening to (or transmitting from) more than one address. Consider the situation depicted in Figure 2.7. Here we have two devices, with two application communication sequences occurring between them. One of the applications is sending unicast frames and the other is sending multicast frames. This can occur in many common situations, such as a pair of routers that are exchanging both file transfer data (FTP unicast) and routing protocol information (RIP broadcasts).

The FTP traffic carries a unicast Destination Address, and the routing protocol traffic carries a multicast Destination Address. Thus, the Source-Destination Address pairs are different between the two sequences; there is no requirement on the bridge to maintain the relative order between the

[12] Or to a degree of probability such that violations are so infrequent that we are willing to accept the consequences.

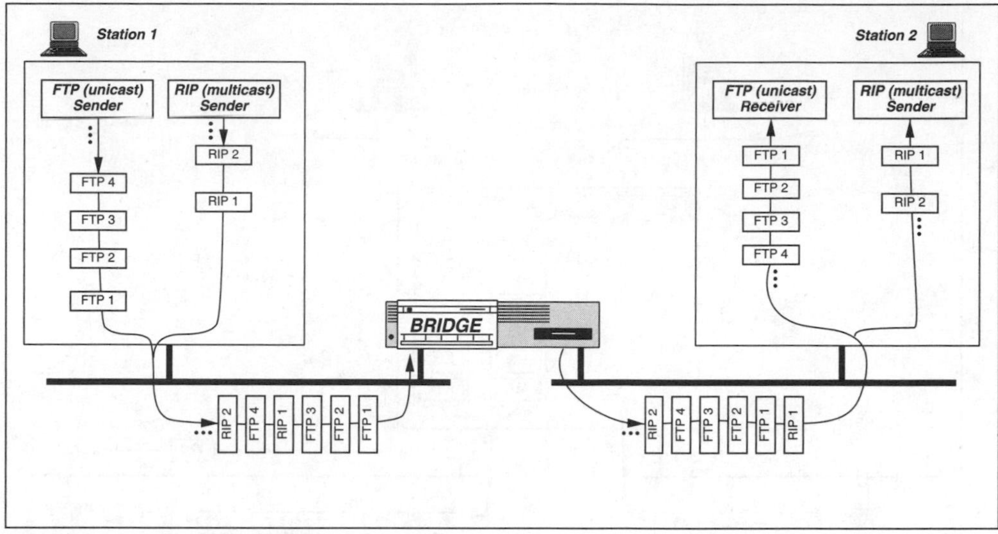

Figure 2.7 Unicast and multicast traffic sequences.

sequences. The unicast traffic must be delivered in order, as must the multicast traffic, but there is no strict ordering requirement on the total traffic stream between the stations. This can greatly simplify the design of the bridge, depending on the data flow architecture (see Chapter 15, *Make the Switch!*). In particular, it is permissible to use separate queues for multicast and unicast traffic without concern for the rates at which the queues are filled or emptied.[13] As shown in the figure, the bridge has reordered the RIP traffic relative to the FTP traffic, but there is no impact on the operation of these applications in the stations.

There is one classic difficulty (read: "gotcha!") that merits discussion here. The normal observable behavior of a bridge with respect to frames sent to unknown unicast destinations is the same as that for multicast destinations—in both cases the bridge will flood the frame. It therefore seems like a reasonable design approach to use the same data path within the bridge to handle both multicasts and unknown unicasts. If separate queues are being used for multicast traffic and unicast traffic, then unknown unicasts will appear in the multicast queue. Now consider the situation depicted in Figure 2.8.

[13] The formal specification of the ordering invariant is contained in the MAC Service Specification [ISO95]. The current document specifies the ordering constraints just described. However, an earlier version of this specification [ISO91] specified that ordering needed to be maintained between *stations* rather than just Source-Destination Address pairs. Some commercial bridges (including several designed by me) incorporated considerable complexity to meet this particular requirement in order to claim strict compliance with the standard. Most bridge designers ignored the issue (or didn't realize it existed). In practice, it does not matter whether the stricter ordering invariant is maintained. The standard was changed to reflect this fact, in part due to my own desire to eliminate the cost of the added complexity.

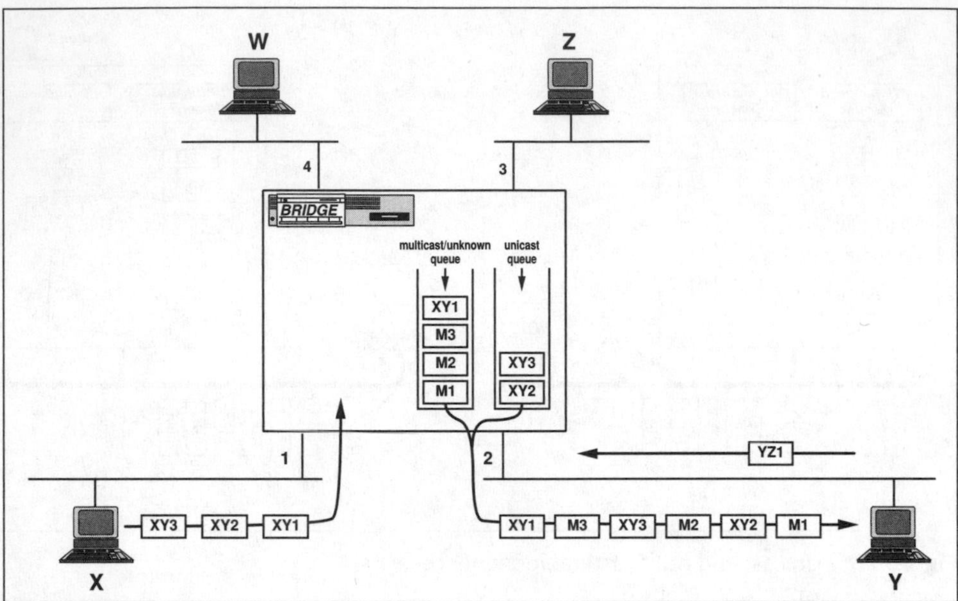

Figure 2.8 Inadvertent ordering change.

The bridge receives a frame (XY1) for destination Y from source X; station Y is currently unknown. As such, the bridge treats it as a multicast and prepares to flood the frame using the same internal mechanisms as are used for multicast traffic. This results in the frame appearing in the multicast queues of all output ports, including the one on which Y actually resides. In the figure, there is a certain amount of multicast traffic (M1, M2, M3) already in the queue awaiting transmission, so the frame destined for Y must wait.

While waiting in the queue, we now receive a frame (YZ1) sent by Y on port 2. In addition to filtering or forwarding the frame sent by Y, we now learn Y's address in the address table and map it to port 2. X continues to send unicast frames (XY2, XY3) to Y, perhaps as part of a large file transfer. However, Y is no longer an unknown address, having been learned from YZ1. Frames XY2 and XY3 are handled as normal unicasts, rather than as multicasts. In the figure, the unicast queue for port 2 is empty. Unless we take some extraordinary precaution, XY2 and XY3 will be transmitted out port 2 before XY1, which is still waiting in the multicast queue! By treating unknown unicasts as multicasts, we risk violating the ordering invariant.

There is no easy solution to this problem. A number of approaches have been taken in commercial products:

- Use a single queue for both unicast and multicast traffic (which has its own set of difficulties).
- Use a time-synchronization mechanism between the two queues.

- Discard the later unicast traffic until the earlier frames have been sent from the multicast queue.
- Ignore the problem and hope nothing breaks.

The exact method used depends on the particular architecture and implementation of the bridge.

Maintaining the non-duplication invariant is much easier. By the very nature of the filtering algorithm, a bridge will never forward a frame onto the port from which it arrived. As long as there are no paths in the catenet that create a topology loop, frame replication will not occur. Chapter 5 is devoted to the subject of loop resolution.

2.2.1.2 Soft Invariants

A bridge tries to make a catenet appear to higher-layer protocols as if it is a single LAN. While it is possible to maintain the hard invariants of a LAN across a bridged catenet (in fact, we go to great pains to make this happen), it is not possible to provide bridge services without degrading the soft invariant behaviors to some extent. Fortunately, we have some flexibility here. As long as the catenet exhibits behavior acceptable to the higher-layer protocols and applications, it is permissible to degrade the service relative to that provided by a single LAN. Put another way, bridges benefit from the fact that higher-layer protocols are designed to tolerate worse performance from LANs than what the LANs actually provide.

2.2.1.2.1 Error Rate

An individual LAN exhibits some inherent error rate; that is, some fraction of the frames sent on that LAN will be corrupted due to errors induced in the physical channel. A catenet will always have a higher error rate than any individual LAN in the set, since a frame traversing multiple LANs has multiple opportunities for induced errors. The more LANs that must be traversed, the more errors that may be induced. Since no popular LAN technology uses forward error correction techniques, any error induced by the physical channel should result in a frame discard.[14] A single bit error introduced on any link in the catenet will cause that frame to be discarded by the next receiver (either a bridge or the final destination).

[14] All common LANs use some form of check sequence (e.g., a Cyclic Redundancy Check) that is able to detect (but not correct) virtually all channel-induced errors. (There will always be some residual, undetected frame errors, even with a strong check sequence.) Forward error correction algorithms are able to detect *and* correct certain classes of errors transparent to their clients. The tradeoff is increased complexity of the algorithm and reduced channel capacity due to the need to send information in a redundant manner. Since LAN error rates are typically quite low, the use of forward error correction is generally unjustified.

What makes the combined errors acceptable is that LANs typically exhibit extremely low error rates to begin with. Consider a 10BASE-T Ethernet LAN in a benign office environment. The worst-case specified bit-error rate (BER) for this LAN is 1×10^{-8} [IEEE98e, Clause 14]. A more typical value is on the order of 1×10^{-12}. An application streaming continuous data at the full channel data rate using maximum-length frames (the worst case) can expect a frame loss rate (FLR) of:

$$\text{FLR} = 1 - (1 - \text{BER})^L = 1.2 \times 10^{-8}$$

where L is the length of a maximum-length Ethernet frame (12,176 bits). For a catenet requiring the frame to traverse n such LANs, the combined FLR reduces to:

$$\text{Combined FLR} = 1 - (1 - \text{FLR})^n = 8.4 \times 10^{-8}$$

for a catenet comprising seven bridge hops ($n = 7$, the maximum per IEEE 802.1D, see Section 2.5.1.2). This frame loss rate (less than 1 in 10 million) does not significantly degrade the performance of most higher-layer protocols and applications. Even if the LANs exhibited the worst-case BER rather than the typical values, the combined FLR would be still be less than 0.01 percent (1 in 10 thousand), which would not generally cause a significant problem.

A second issue is the introduction of errors by the bridge itself. In the process of receiving, storing, and queuing frames for transmission, a bridge may introduce errors into the data. These errors may be caused by memory faults, internal bus errors, or possibly software problems within the bridge. With proper design, these errors should occur extremely infrequently—much lower than the physical channel error rate. Even so, it would be nice if these errors were at least detectable so that we could discard such frames rather than pass them along with undetected errors.

Consider the situation depicted in Figure 2.9. The originating station X generates a frame of data with a valid Frame Check Sequence (FCS). If an error is induced on the link between X and the bridge, the bridge will detect this error by checking the FCS and discarding the frame. (There is no reason to process and forward a frame that is known to contain an error.) Similarly, if an error is induced on the link between the bridge and station Y, station Y will determine this by checking the FCS on the retransmitted frame (FCS′) and discarding the frame in error. However, if the bridge introduces an error, it is possible for that error to go undetected. The following sequence could occur:

- The network interface for port 1 receives the frame, checks the FCS, and declares it valid.
- The address table lookup algorithm determines that the frame is destined for station Y on port 2.

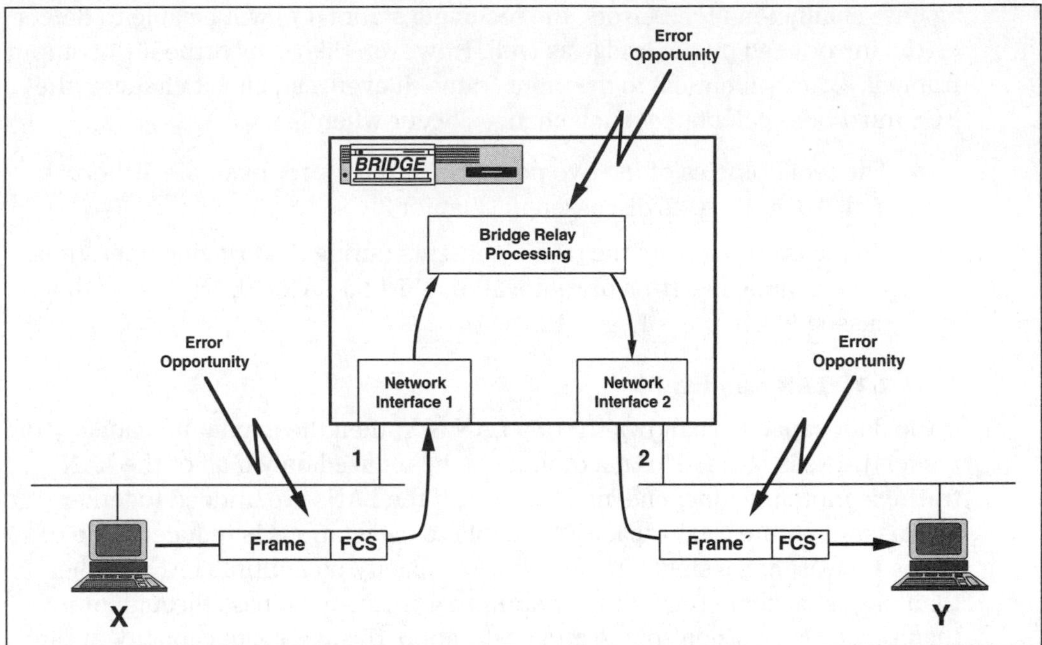

Figure 2.9 Error detection.

- The bridge copies the frame to a buffer for port 2 and introduces an error during the copy operation.
- The network interface for port 2 generates a new, correct FCS′ for the incorrect data in its output buffer and transmits the frame to station Y.
- Station Y receives the frame, checks the FCS′, and declares it valid, even though the data contains an error.

The bridge has thus introduced an error that is undetectable, at least at the Data Link layer. Such errors are detectable if higher-layer protocols perform some additional, end-to-end error checking, but this is often not done due to performance or protocol limitations.

Seifert's Law of
Networking #3
Thou shalt not
present bad data
as good.

However, we have a way to prevent this occurrence, at least much of the time. If the output port uses the exact same frame format as the input port (e.g., both ports are Ethernets), then the forwarded frame will be identical, bit-for-bit, to the received frame. There is no need for the network interface on the output port to recalculate the FCS. It can (and should) use the FCS that was received and declared valid at the input port, rather than generating a new FCS′. If this is done, not only will the FCS protect against channel-induced errors, the receiving station (Y) will be able to detect errors introduced by the bridge as well. However, this is only true if the output frame is exactly identical to the input frame. If even a single bit changes, the FCS must be recalculated. Such changes occur when:

- The technologies of the two ports are different, for example, Ethernet and Token Ring, as discussed in Chapter 3.
- Changes are made to the frame contents during the bridging operation, for example, insertion or removal of a Virtual LAN (VLAN) tag, as discussed in Chapters 11 and 12.

2.2.1.2.2 LAN Bandwidth

If the data capacity (bandwidth) of a LAN is X, then the maximum capacity of n such LANs is $n \times X$. This maximum can be realized only if all of the LAN traffic is mutually independent. However, if the LANs are bridged together into a catenet, the total capacity available to end stations is reduced. Due to frame forwarding, a single frame will use capacity on multiple LANs, rather than on just a single LAN. To the extent that traffic must pass through more than one LAN between source and destination, the aggregate capacity of the catenet is reduced.[15]

Thus, bridges impact the soft invariant that LANs provide high bandwidth to end station applications; bridged traffic may experience lower throughput than traffic that remains local to the LAN. However, LAN bandwidth is generally well overprovisioned; the typical utilization of a LAN is much less than its maximum capacity over any reasonable averaging period. Thus, while the theoretically-available bandwidth is decreased by the use of bridges, it is still within limits acceptable to higher-layer protocols in a properly configured catenet.

2.2.1.2.3 Delay and Latency

Similarly, higher-layer protocols expect LANs to provide low-delay data delivery service.[16] Bridges increase delay (latency) in three ways:

1. By forwarding frames across multiple LANs between source and destination, the frames experience the sum total of the access delays of all intervening LANs.
2. Due to traffic patterns, short-term congestion, and/or speed differences between ports, a bridge introduces queuing delay.
3. Due to its internal operation (e.g., address table lookup and frame forwarding), a bridge introduces processing delay.

[15] If all traffic is local (i.e., the destinations are always on the same LAN as the source), then the total capacity is not reduced. However, there is also no need for bridges in this situation!
[16] This is known as de-lay of de-LAN.

The delay issue is managed in a manner similar to the bandwidth issue from the perspective of maintaining the soft invariant. While delays are definitely increased, the delay tolerance of the Data Link client is generally much greater than that introduced by the catenet as a whole. The unavoidable increase in delay is offset by the advantages and convenience of using bridges.

As discussed in Section 2.5.1.2, the IEEE 802.1D standard provides an upper bound on the delay introduced both by any given bridge and by the catenet as a whole. A detailed technical treatment of latency is deferred to the discussion of switches and switch architecture in Chapter 4, *Principles of LAN Switches*, and Chapter 15, *Make the Switch!*

2.3 Implementing the Bridge Address Table

Much of the performance of a bridge is dependent on the design of the address table and the table search algorithm. In this section, we look at some of the practical design issues facing bridge architects. Readers with no interest in product implementation can safely skip this entire section with no loss of continuity (even though this is really interesting stuff!).

2.3.1 Table Operations

There are three operations that need to be performed on the Bridge Address Table: Destination Address lookup, Source Address learning, and entry aging. As discussed in Section 2.1.5, this is also the order of importance of the operations. The architecture and organization of the address table are intimately coupled to the search algorithm being used; they are designed as one. Considering the priority of operations, the table design should be optimized for fast, real-time lookup, at the expense of slower and/or more complex update and aging algorithms if need be.

As a counterexample of this approach, consider a design employing a linear search table (i.e., a non-ordered, simple linear list of address and port mappings). With this design, it is very easy to add new entries; new entries may be simply added to the end of the list in a single operation. However, the lookup algorithm requires (in the worst case) inspecting every entry in the table, a tedious and time-consuming operation. Thus a linear organization is an example of poor Bridge Address Table design, since it optimizes the less-critical update operation rather than the more important lookup task. In the next section we look at some more popular (and much more efficient) methods of organizing the table.

2.3.2 Search Algorithms

A truly exhaustive discussion of table search algorithms is beyond the scope of this book. The reader is referred to [KNUT98] or [WEIS98] for a more comprehensive treatment. Here we will look at three popular table designs that have been used in many commercial bridges.

2.3.2.1 *Hash Tables*

"In the old days," bridge tables and the table algorithms were implemented primarily in software. A general-purpose computer implemented the algorithms, and the Bridge Address Table resided in the computer's main memory. The design problem became that of finding the memory location with the port mapping for a given 48-bit address.

The simplest idea would be to use the 48-bit address itself as a memory pointer. This would allow software to determine the port mapping in a single operation. Unfortunately, the address space is huge. Recognizing that a traditional bridge only needs to look up unicast addresses, there are still 2^{47} possible entries. Even if the port mapping and age indicators only required a single byte of storage, this would imply over 140,000 gigabytes of memory for the table![17] Clearly, this is impractical. What is needed is a way to map the 48-bit address into a smaller pointer space. A hash function provides this capability.

Hashing means applying a function that takes the 48-bit address and produces a shorter field that can be used as a pointer to a subset of the table structure in memory. The function must:

- Produce a consistent value for the same address (be repeatable)
- Produce a relatively uniform distribution of output values (memory pointers) for any arbitrary set of input values (addresses)

That is, the function should not cause an uneven spreading of addresses to output values. Each output value should have (approximately) the same number of addresses mapped to it, and the distribution should appear to be random relative to the input values. This latter requirement is especially important when hashing MAC addresses, since it is possible that many addresses on a catenet will be numerically close to each other. If most network equipment is purchased from the same (or a small number of) manufacturer(s), the addresses may all contain the same first 24 bits (the OUI), and perhaps a narrow range of values for the remaining 24 bits (depending on manufacturing practices).

[17] This is the memory of over 2 million computers with 64 Mbyte each.

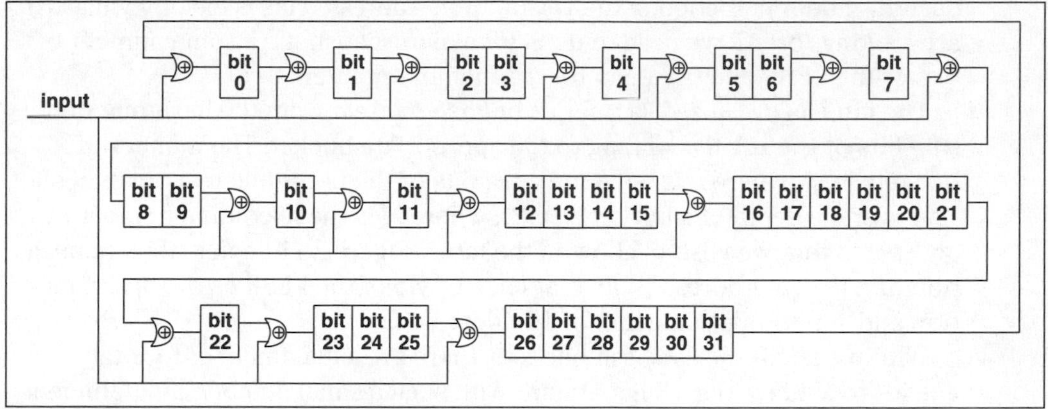

Figure 2.10 Linear feedback FCS checker.

The standard literature describes lots of useful (and easy to compute) hash functions, including exclusive-ORs and other simple arithmetical operations. When computing a hash function in software, simplicity of computation translates directly into lookup performance. However, we have a unique situation with bridges, as they need to compute a hash function on incoming data. Network interfaces have a natural, built-in hash function—the FCS checker.

A network interface computes the frame check sequence on incoming data in order to determine its validity. Typically, the FCS is checked in hardware, and is computed continuously on a bit-by-bit or word-parallel basis.[18] When the frame is complete, the FCS computation register is checked for a specific value that indicates that all of the received data (including the received FCS that was generated by the sender) is valid. Figure 2.10 depicts one common implementation of a checker for the CRC-32 algorithm used in most LANs, using a Linear Feedback Shift Register (LFSR).

The CRC-32 algorithm is a wonderful "number stirrer." The value in the shift register at any given time is a deterministic function of the input bits, yet the pattern appears random due to the complex feedback paths. It is a perfect hash function generator.[19]

In Ethernet, the first bits of a frame comprise the destination address. That is, the contents of the LFSR after the first 48 bits have been received are a

[18] Bit serial FCS computation was invariably used with 10 Mb/s Ethernet. With extremely high-speed LANs, such as Gigabit Ethernet, it becomes impractical to compute the FCS serially; more complex (but faster) multi-bit parallel checking methods are usually used. However, there is no change from the bridge's perspective. The intermediate values of the FCS are still available in real-time.

[19] I personally evaluated the uniformity of the hash distribution from CRC-32 in the early 1980s. It exhibits near-perfect behavior, regardless of which bits of the CRC are used for the hash! Unfortunately, the documentation of this research has been lost to the ages, but the proof is in the pudding, or rather the bridges that use this approach.

pseudo-random function of the Destination Address. This is exactly what we are looking for! All we need to do is to take a "snapshot" of some number of bits of the LFSR and use them for the memory pointer.

The table is organized as a series of *hash buckets*, with the hash function (the bits of the LFSR) pointing to the appropriate bucket. The number of buckets is 2^n, where n is the number of bits of the LFSR taken in our snapshot. The average depth of a bucket is $M/2^n$, where M is the maximum number of addresses that we wish to allow in the table. Figure 2.11 depicts the organization of a Bridge Address Table that uses 1 byte of the LFSR as the hash function and supports a maximum of 1K addresses.

Within each of the 256 hash buckets, there are a maximum of four table entries to achieve our 1K maximum. With such a small number, an inefficient (but simple) linear search within the bucket is adequate. Increasing the width of the hash (the number of buckets) can increase the maximum table size supportable, at the expense of additional memory. Hash tables such as this were very common in early bridges. They made for simple software implementation, but suffered from a few problems:

- While the hash computation on the destination address is performed naturally by the hardware, the Source Address computation, which is needed to update the table, is not so simple. Since the Source Address

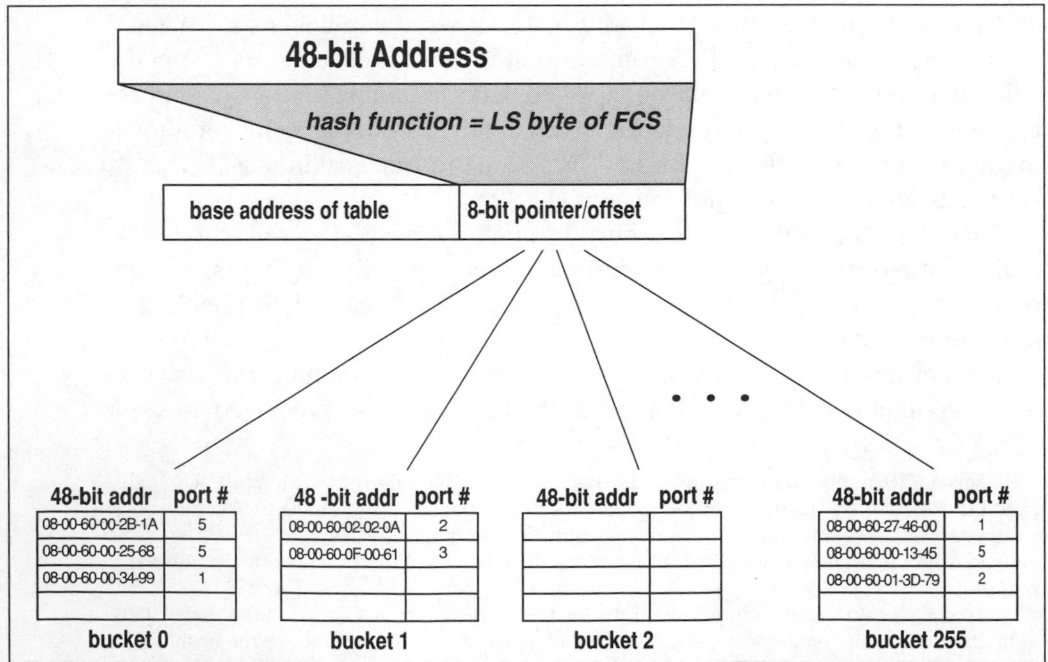

Figure 2.11 Hashed Bridge Address Table.

follows the Destination Address in the frame, the same LFSR cannot be used for the computation. Either the hash function on the Source Address must be computed in software (very difficult for a CRC-32 function) or a second LFSR is needed.[20]

- Depending on the values of the addresses in the catenet, there is some possibility that the hash buckets will not fill uniformly. The table can only be filled to its maximum if the addresses hash evenly across all buckets. In the example in Figure 2.11, it is possible that five addresses out of hundreds in the catenet might hash to the same bucket, yet each bucket can only hold four entries. The table thus appears to be filled after only four addresses have been learned; the bridge is unable to learn the fifth address. Various methods have been employed to get around this problem, including providing special overflow buckets for this case and even changing the hash function when this occurs (e.g., by changing the bits of the LFSR that are selected). The tradeoff is added complexity versus the ability to support more addresses under worst-case conditions.

2.3.2.2 Binary Search

If the address table is sorted in numerical order, it becomes possible to perform a binary search for addresses, as depicted in Figure 2.12.

The search begins in the middle of the table, at the "numerical center." The address being searched is compared to the table entry at the middle. If the address is a match, we're done. If not (you never get *that* lucky!), you note whether the address at the center of the table is numerically greater or less than the one you are searching for. This allows you to restrict the remainder of the search to the half of the table that may contain the entry. Then the process is repeated; the search goes to the middle of the identified half of the table, and so on. Each operation reduces the unsearched entries by one-half, until either the entry is found or it is determined that the entry is not there.

A binary search table has a number of advantages:

+ The maximum number of operations required to perform a complete search is ($\log_2 N + 1$), where N is the number of entries in the table. This is reasonably efficient; a search of a 4K entry table requires only 13 operations, and each doubling of the table size adds only a single extra search operation.

+ There is no problem with inefficient filling of the table, as with hash algorithms. The entire available table can always be used, regardless of the numerical values of the addresses.

[20] Most early bridges used the software approach. This is a good example of how the bridge table design can be optimized for lookup ease at the expense of difficult update capability.

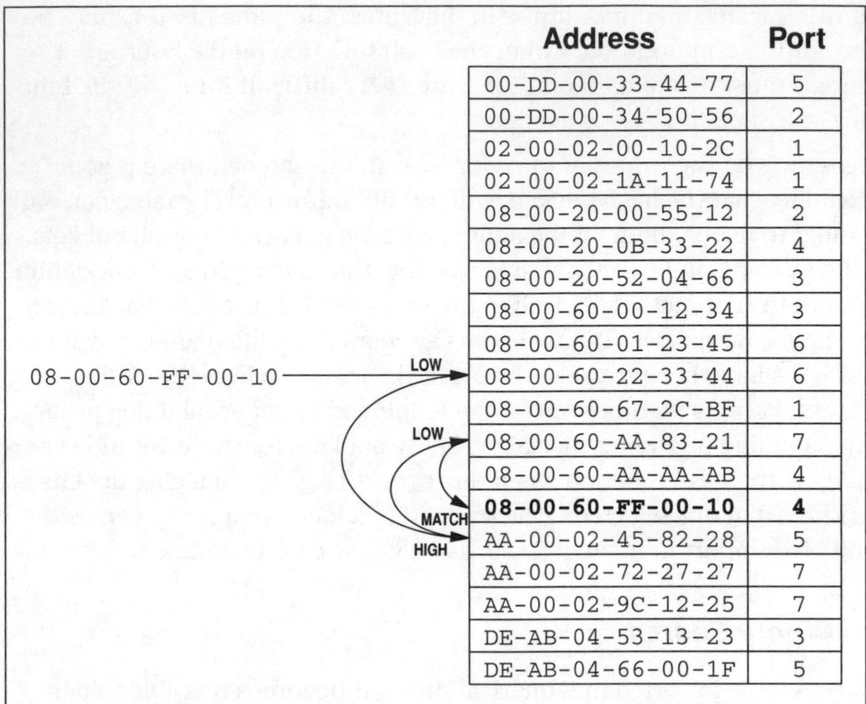

Address
Port
00-DD-00-33-44-77 5
00-DD-00-34-50-56 2
02-00-02-00-10-2C 1
02-00-02-1A-11-74 1
08-00-20-00-55-12 2
08-00-20-0B-33-22 4
08-00-20-52-04-66 3
08-00-60-00-12-34 3
08-00-60-01-23-45 6
08-00-60-FF-00-10
LOW
08-00-60-22-33-44 6
08-00-60-67-2C-BF 1
LOW
08-00-60-AA-83-21 7
08-00-60-AA-AA-AB 4
MATCH
08-00-60-FF-00-10 4
HIGH
AA-00-02-45-82-28 5
AA-00-02-72-27-27 7
AA-00-02-9C-12-25 7
DE-AB-04-53-13-23 3
DE-AB-04-66-00-1F 5

Figure 2.12 Binary search table.

+ The algorithm is highly conducive to hardware implementation. The recursive procedure can be coded into a simple, finite-state machine with relatively little logic and embedded into application-specific silicon (ASIC). This is a very popular approach in modern bridges.[21]

The main disadvantage is that, depending on the data structure used for the table, updates may be difficult to perform. To add or remove an address from the table requires re-sorting the entire table into numerical order (or re-linking pointers to achieve the same effect). The number of operations required for a traditional re-sort is proportional to the number of entries in the table (rather than the logarithm of the number of entries, as for lookup). In general, the table cannot be used for lookups while it is being re-sorted during updates, as the entries are being changed or moved. Considerable complexity is required

[21] Some implementations have incorporated simultaneous parallel comparisons of multiple search recursions. For example, by checking the middle entry of the table and the middle entries of each of the two halves in parallel, the algorithm can divide the table in fourths (rather than in half) in a single operation. Recursing this way, the total number of operations is halved, improving performance accordingly, for a simple second implementation of the comparison hardware logic.

to allow table coherency for lookup during a re-sorting sequence. The most common solutions to this problem are:

- *Defer updates to periods of low activity, and disable lookups while re-sorting the table.* This can cause erratic performance problems, since traffic activity cannot be predicted in advance, and the table generally must be completely updated and re-sorted before resuming lookup operations. In some cases, updates may be deferred for a long period of time, forcing traffic to be unnecessarily flooded or preventing timely table aging.
- *Keep two copies of the table.* One copy is used for lookups; the other is used for updates and is re-sorted in the background. When an update cycle is complete, the "tables are turned"; the now-updated table is used for lookups, and the original lookup table is brought up-to-date. This effectively solves the problem at the expense of doubling the memory required for the table (or equivalently, halving the number of entries that can be supported).

2.3.2.3 Content-Addressable Memories (CAM)

If I ask you to think about pizza, most of you will conjure up thoughts of melted cheese, your favorite toppings, and perhaps some event you associate with pizza.[22] You are able to retrieve these related thoughts without knowing *where* in your memory they were stored. The keyword *pizza* allows you to access this associated data without having to know its location in memory.

In traditional computer memories (e.g., RAM and ROM), you need to know the address where information is stored in order to retrieve it. In a *content-addressable memory* (CAM), you use the storage contents as a key for retrieving data associated with those contents. Thus, rather than specifying a location in memory, the logic presents a data value (and sometimes a bit mask over it) and the CAM returns either the associated data or an indication that the requested data value is not present in the CAM. When storing information in the CAM, the logic presents the key and the associated data, and the CAM stores it in any available location. (Since we don't access the memory by specifying the address, the actual location where a given data element is stored is irrelevant.) As such, a CAM functions as a virtually-instantaneous hardware search-and-update function element. For a bridge application, a common CAM organization uses a 48-bit key (the address) and a 16-bit associated data field that contains the port mapping, aging, and control information, as depicted in Figure 2.13.

[22] I immediately think of beer and a little place that used to be on 12th Street near Washington Square.

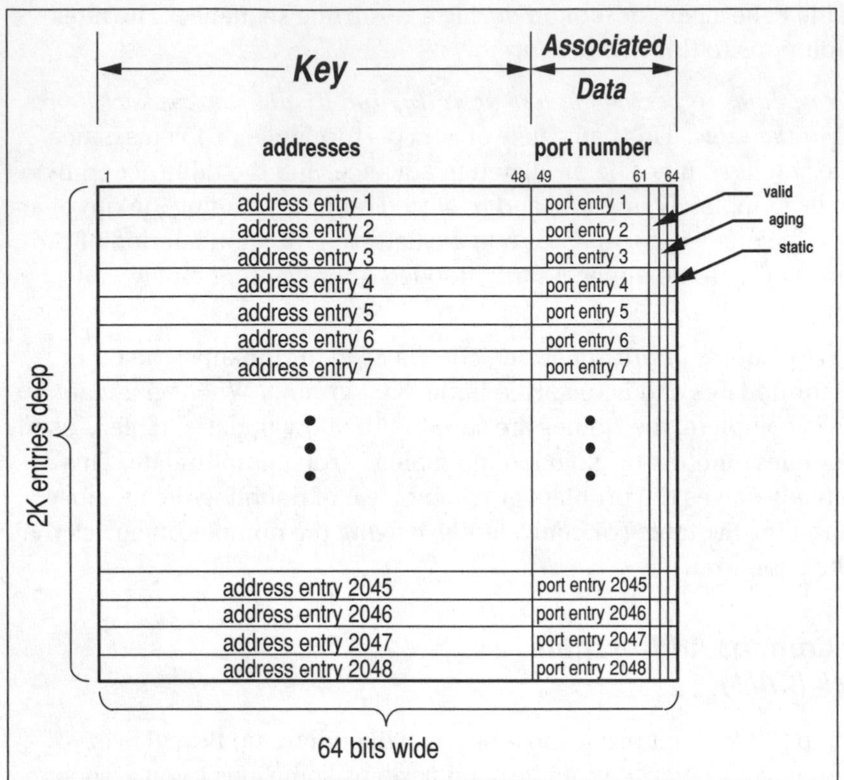

Figure 2.13 Content-Addressable Memory organization.

CAMs are specialized hardware devices whose usefulness for implementing a Bridge Address Table is obvious.[23] A number of manufacturers make devices specifically for this application. They are available in a wide variety of sizes and organizations, and are commonly used in commercial bridges.

There are only two real problems with CAMs:

1. *CAMs are expensive.* A CAM may cost 4–5 times as much as a conventional RAM of the same size. Unless the added performance is absolutely necessary, a solution using conventional memory and a search algorithm will usually be less expensive.

2. *CAMs have limited storage capacity.* Because of their silicon-intensive design, CAMs tend to have much less memory capacity than RAMs of the same size.

[23] CAMs have many other uses, such as for a System Page Table to perform virtual-to-physical memory mapping or as database accelerators.

In the early days of bridges, one very popular CAM could hold 1K addresses (64 bits wide × 1K deep), performed a lookup or update in 80 ns or less, and cost about $25 in quantity. At the time of this writing, CAMs are available both as packaged parts and as semiconductor cores that can hold 32K addresses (64 bits wide × 32K deep), perform a lookup in under 20 ns, and cost less than $20. Still, this is more expensive than a traditional memory, and is justified only for high-performance bridges.

2.3.3 How Deep Is Your Table?

A common question asked is, "How big should the address table be?" Ideally, the table should be deep enough to hold an entry for every active station in the catenet. How many entries this constitutes depends on the nature of the catenet. A bridge designed for small office or workgroup interconnection may only need to support a few hundred entries. A bridge being used as a collapsed backbone for a large campus may need to support tens of thousands of entries. Chapter 4 discusses application environments and table size requirements.

If the table can hold more entries than there are stations in the catenet, there is clearly no problem (other than that you may have bought more bridge than you needed). But what happens if the table is too small to hold all of the active stations in the catenet? Does the network experience catastrophic failures? Will applications in the end stations crash? Is it the end of life as we know it? Actually, very few problems occur under this scenario. If the table is too small to hold all of the active entries, then the addresses of some stations cannot be learned. Traffic sent to these stations is not discarded, but flooded, since an unlearned address is (by definition) an unknown address. All stations will still be able to communicate successfully, even those whose addresses are not in the table. The bridge will simply flood (wasting bandwidth) rather than send traffic out the specific port where an unlearned destination resides. The bridge trades off bandwidth utilization for communications continuity.

The next obvious question is, "If the table is full, what should I do with new potential entries?" There are three possibilities:

1. Learn the new address and discard an entry already in the table.
2. Decrease the aging time to prune the table more rapidly.
3. Don't change anything, and ignore the new addresses until normal aging makes entry space available.

All three solutions have their proponents. The problem with the first approach is the difficulty in determining which existing entry should be discarded. Conceivably, you might want to discard the entry that has not had traffic sent to it for the longest time, using a least-recently-used (LRU) algorithm. But this would require:

- *A timestamp with a finer granularity than that used for the aging timer.* In order to discard an entry sooner than the aging algorithm would, you need a time measurement shorter than the aging time.
- *A timestamp based on the use of the address as a destination, rather than a source.* Remember that aging is based on how recently the entry was seen as a sender of traffic, not as a receiver. If you wanted to prune the address table earlier than dictated by normal aging, you would want to eliminate those addresses that don't need to be looked up. This reflects its use as a destination, not a source.

The added complexity is not easily justified.

The second approach assumes that the catenet can tolerate shorter aging. The aging time should reflect the slowest rate of transmission by an active station. That is, bridges assume that if a station has not been heard from in an aging time, then the station is really inactive or has moved. If the aging timer can be reduced when the table is filled, why not reduce it all the time and improve convergence time for moved stations? In general, it is safer to have a longer-than-needed aging time than one that is too short. If the aging time is set too short, the table can "thrash." Stations that are really active (but with a transmission frequency lower than the aging period) will be aged out prematurely and must be constantly relearned. As the table design is generally optimized for lookup (and not learning, which occurs less frequently), this thrashing can be expensive in terms of bridge resources.

The third approach is both the easiest and most appropriate. If the overload condition is transient, the aging process will soon make room for the new entries. If the overload condition is sustained, this indicates a configuration problem, which should be solved by a reconfiguration rather than an algorithm modification. (You bought the wrong bridge, buddy!)

2.3.4 Aging Entries from the Table

Finally we can relax a little. Table lookup and update may be relatively difficult, but aging is easy. We need to age out stale entries to allow station mobility and keep the table as short as possible, but:

- The aging process is a non-critical, low priority task. It can be done in the background, on a "when you get around to it" basis, without any significant performance or operational penalty.
- The time scale for aging is very long relative to other table operations. Lookups must be performed in microseconds (or less), but aging occurs on the order of minutes.

- The accuracy of the aging time is non-critical. While the standard default aging time is 5 minutes, for most purposes it matters little whether stale entries are aged out in 3 minutes, 8 minutes, or anything in between.

Given these conditions, we can implement table aging in a very efficient manner. There is no need to record or maintain accurate timestamps for table entries. Figure 2.14 depicts one mechanism that is commonly used.

Only two bits are required to record and maintain aging information. The *valid* (V) bit indicates that a table entry is valid; the *hit* (H) bit indicates that this entry has been "hit," that is, seen as a source address, during the most recent aging process cycle.

When a new entry is recorded, the learning process sets both the V and H bits to indicate a valid, active entry. When an existing entry is being updated (i.e., when the address has been seen as a source and already has a table entry), the learning process sets the H bit if it has been cleared, to indicate that the entry is still active and is not ready to be aged out.

In the background, the aging process is operating to clear the bits. Once per specified cycle time (typically on the order of minutes), the aging process checks each entry's H bit. If it is currently set, the aging process clears the H bit for that entry. If it is currently clear, the aging process clears the V bit for that entry. In this way, any address that has not been heard from in two aging process cycles will be cleared from the table (V bit clear). Stations that are regularly heard from will have their H bits alternately cleared by the aging process and reset by the learning process, with the V bit staying set.

This provides the needed aging function with little table or process overhead. The resolution of the aging time is quite coarse, but still acceptable; using this method, the actual aging time for a given entry can vary over a 2:1 range.

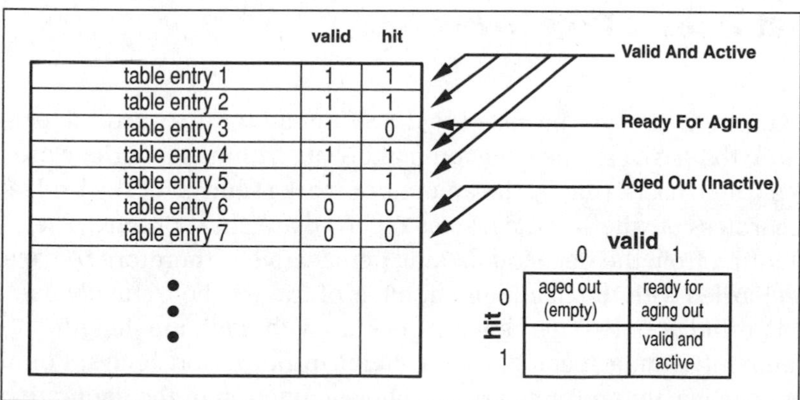

Figure 2.14 Table aging mechanism.

Other than its accuracy and resolution, another issue is the aging time itself. Long aging times allow stations that communicate very infrequently to remain active in the address table. This avoids constantly re-learning their addresses and flooding traffic in the interim. On the other hand, very long aging times can prevent communications with stations that have moved yet not transmitted. Since stations rarely move, and move times are typically on the order of minutes or more, most aging times are in this range. The actual value is rarely critical. In Chapter 5, we discuss the need to accelerate table aging when the topology of the catenet changes.

Finally, some address table assignments may be *static;* they are never removed from the table or allowed to have their port mapping updated. This may be done to implement custom filters, as discussed in Section 2.1.6, or to support specific higher-layer protocols with reserved address assignments (see Section 2.5.3). Therefore, a practical address table needs a mechanism for specifying that aging should not be performed on specific entries. A single control bit is adequate for this purpose, as shown in Figure 2.13.

2.4 Bridge Performance

A bridge performs two performance-intensive operations:

1. It implements the decision-making algorithms—table lookup, filter/forward decision, and table maintenance.
2. It moves data among its ports (data flow).

A deficiency in either element can reduce the bridge's performance below the theoretical best-case.

2.4.1 What Does It Take to Be the Best?

The most that a bridge can ever be asked to do is filter and/or forward 100 percent of the traffic that arrives. The decision-making algorithms of a bridge are performed on a frame basis; that is, the amount of work required of the bridge is the same regardless of whether the frames received are short or long. The worst-case situation from the decision-making perspective is therefore to have every port bombarded with the maximum number of frames theoretically possible in a given period of time. This generally occurs with minimum-length frames, minimum interframe spacing, and negligible propagation delays. For a given LAN port, the maximum frame arrival rate is a function of the data rate and the LAN technology employed. Table 2.2 lists the maximum frame arrival rates for some popular LAN technologies.

Table 2.2 Maximum Frame Arrival Rates

TECHNOLOGY	DATA RATE (Mb/S)	MAXIMUM RATE (SECONDS/FRAME)	MAXIMUM RATE (FRAMES/SECOND)
Ethernet	10	67.2 µs	14,881.0
	100	6.72 µs	148,809.5
	1000	672.0 ns	1,488,095.2
Token Ring	4	50.0 µs	20,000.0
	16	14.5 µs	68,965.5
	100	2.88 µs	347,222.2
FDDI	100	2.0 µs	500,000.0

Note: Figures for Token Ring and FDDI assume LLC-1, zero length data, and full duplex operation.

From the data flow perspective, the worst case is to have the longest-possible frames. That is, if all of the LAN bandwidth is consumed by frame data that must be forwarded among the ports of the bridge, this constitutes the highest stress condition for the bridge's data flow mechanisms. While there is always some small overhead due to the LAN technology itself (e.g., interframe gaps, tokens, frame delimiters, and the like), it is generally assumed that, in order to avoid a performance bottleneck, the capacity of the data flow architecture must equal or exceed the sum of the raw data capacities of all of its ports.[24] For example, a bridge with 24 ports of 100 Mb/s Ethernet should be prepared to deal with

$$24 \times 100 \text{ Mb/s} = 2.4 \text{ Gb/s}$$

of data flowing through it.[25]

Thus, there are two separate criteria for determining whether a bridge may ever become a performance bottleneck: (1) its ability to make a filter/forward decision under conditions of maximum-rate frame arrivals on all ports simultaneously and (2) its ability to move the totality of the ports' data-carrying capacity arbitrarily among all ports. A bridge capable of performing both of these tasks is said to operate at *wire speed,* or to be *non-blocking.*

Some manufacturers use the term *wire speed* to refer to only the first criterion (table lookup performance); some others use *non-blocking operation* to mean only that their product passes the second test (data flow). Depending on the design, either table lookup or data flow capacity may in fact be the limit-

[24] The difference between the raw channel capacity and the effective maximum capacity after accounting for Physical layer overhead is rarely more than a few percent, and can be ignored.

[25] This assumes full duplex operation, as discussed in Chapter 7, *Full Duplex Operation.*

ing factor for bridge performance. With few ports (or mostly low-speed ports), table lookup is generally the more difficult test. With large numbers of high-speed ports, data flow capacity is more often the limiting factor. In this book, the terms are used interchangeably and mean that both tests are met.

The design of data flow mechanisms for non-blocking operation is discussed in Chapter 15.

2.4.2 If You're Not the Best, How Good Are You?

"In the old days," wire-speed bridges were rare indeed. The few available wire-speed bridges in the late 1980s commanded a price premium of 100 percent or more over their lower-performing counterparts. In practice, wire-speed operation provides no real benefit in most networks. No practical applications spew out long streams of minimum-length frames, and few networks see anywhere near 100 percent utilization for long periods of time on large numbers of bridge ports. So, why bother with trying to achieve wire speed at all?

There are a few reasons:

- With modern, hardware-based designs, it is possible to achieve wire-speed operation with little cost impact. This is especially true with lower-speed ports (e.g., 10 Mb/s Ethernet).
- If a product can truly operate at wire-speed, then there is never a question about its performance. Such a device will never be the bottleneck for network operation, and no competitor's product will be able to properly claim higher performance.

Wire-speed operation thus becomes a competitive issue in the "battle of the data sheets." Once some manufacturer can provide a wire-speed bridge at a reasonable price (for a given technology and number of ports), then any other manufacturer not meeting this standard must either provide a significant price advantage or spend a lot of time explaining to its customers why wire-speed operation makes little difference in practical networks. To make things worse, some of the test procedures and benchmarks used by interoperability test labs and trade magazine "product shootouts" stress wire-speed operation both for lookup and data flow [RFC2544]. A product that is deficient in this benchmark will have a market perception problem, even if it doesn't have a problem serving the needs of practical networks.

If a product does not meet wire-speed criteria, there are a few factors that can be used to consider its relative performance:

Filter performance This refers to the ability of the bridge to perform the lookup algorithm. The best possible filter performance is the maximum frame rate on all ports simultaneously. Short of this, a bridge may achieve some number of frames-per-second that is less than the theoretical maximum.

For a less-than-wire-speed bridge, it is useful to be able to determine whether the available filter performance can be arbitrarily distributed among its ports or whether there is a per-port limitation as well. For example, consider a bridge with eight ports of 100 Mb/s Ethernet and a maximum filter rate of 600,000 frames per second. (Wire-speed performance for this bridge would be ~1.2 million frames per second.) Can the bridge support four of its ports at wire-speed when the other four are idle, or is the maximum filter rate one-half of wire-speed on a port basis? The lower performance may be on a port-by-port basis (the worse of the two situations) or only in the aggregate.

Data flow capacity Similarly, a bridge may not be able to handle sustained, maximum data flow from all ports simultaneously. There will be some maximum data capacity for the bridge that is less than wire-speed. As in the case of filter performance, this limitation may be on a port-by-port basis or only for the aggregate.

The discussion of a third performance metric—bridge latency—is deferred to Chapter 4, *Principles of LAN Switches*, since it is closely associated with the issue of cut-through switch architectures.

2.5 The IEEE 802.1D Standard

IEEE 802.1D is the international standard for MAC bridges [IEEE90a, IEEE93a, IEEE98a]. The explanations of bridge operation presented in this chapter are consistent with the formal description in that standard. In order to be unambiguous and rigorously precise, standards are written in a style and language that is not conducive to a tutorial. The purpose is to document the requirements for proper operation and interoperability, not to educate the reader. That task is left to books like this one.

In addition to the formal description of transparent bridge operation, the standard provides:

- An architectural framework for the operation of bridges, including formal specifications for interlayer services
- A formal description of the Bridge Address Table,[26] frame filtering, and forwarding, including support for static and dynamic entries, forwarding rules, and custom filter definitions

[26] The standard calls this the *Filtering Database;* however, I find the term *address table* much more intuitive and useful.

- A set of operating parameters for interoperation of bridged catenets
- A convention for address assignment to bridges and bridge ports
- A reserved block of MAC addresses for which standard-compliant bridges must exhibit specific behavior
- A formal specification of a loop resolution algorithm and protocol
- A specification of a minimum set of management objects, to allow interoperable management of a multi-vendor catenet

The first two items are artifacts of the standard itself; that is, they are necessary for an IEEE standard but not for understanding the real-world operation of a bridge. The operating parameters, address assignment, and reserved address block are discussed in the following text. The loop resolution algorithm is explained in Chapter 5; bridge management is covered in Chapter 14, *Switch Management*.

2.5.1 Operating Parameters and Requirements

The standard specifies certain key operating parameters of the bridge algorithms, as well as some specific behaviors expected of conformant bridges.

2.5.1.1 Aging Time

The *aging time* parameter controls the pruning of old entries from the Bridge Address Table. The standard allows a range of aging times from 10 seconds to 1 million seconds (11.6 days), with a recommended default of 300 seconds (5 minutes). Most commercial bridges use this default value or a value close to it.

2.5.1.2 Bridge Transit Delay

The client (a higher-layer protocol or application) of a LAN Data Link in an end station can generally expect low delay, at least relative to a complex internetwork that includes slow WAN links. While this is not a hard invariant like sequential delivery and non-duplication, it is nevertheless a reasonable expectation. Some LAN-centric protocols (e.g., NetBIOS/NetBEUI and LAT) make assumptions about the delay of the underlying communications system and do not perform properly when the delays are large. As such, these protocols are suitable only for use on low-delay LANs or catenets that exhibit similar characteristics. While the protocols can tolerate some increase in delay over that provided by a single LAN, the delay cannot be made arbitrarily high without some serious consequences (such as protocol failure or lost connections).

Most Network-layer protocols include a means for explicit control of delivery delay across the internetwork. IP includes a *Time To Live* field that routers use to estimate the amount of time that a packet has been delayed in transit (normally by counting routing hops); if the delivery delay exceeds the upper bound placed on it by the sending station, then the packet is discarded.[27] This protocol mechanism prevents excessively-late delivery at the Network layer. The communicating application may have to deal with a discarded packet (as must any application running on a connectionless network), but it doesn't have to concern itself with overly-delayed messages due to the explicit lifetime control provided by the Network-layer protocol.

Unfortunately, there is no explicit lifetime control provided for LAN Data Links. In the original design of most LANs, bridged catenets were not considered, and there is no need for explicit delay control in a single-LAN environment. The delay imposed by typical LANs is low enough to be ignored by any practical higher-layer protocol.

This changed with the introduction of bridged catenets. In a large catenet, it is possible that a frame may encounter considerable delay as it is forwarded across multiple bridges with processing and queuing delays in each bridge. The bridges are designed to provide transparent connectivity across multiple LANs, but the increased delay may not be acceptable to some higher-layer protocols. In order to keep the delay within some reasonable upper bound, the standard imposes two restrictions:

1. *An upper bound on the delay that may be introduced by a single bridge.* This is known as the Maximum Bridge Transit Delay. The recommended value is 1 second; the maximum permitted value is 4 seconds. A bridge is required to discard any frames that have been received that cannot be forwarded within the Maximum Bridge Transit Delay.[28]

[27] AppleTalk DDP and the DECnet Routing Protocol each provide an equivalent mechanism using a Hop Count field.

[28] The implication of this requirement is that a bridge must either be designed so that it is inherently incapable of imposing a transit delay in excess of the Maximum Bridge Transit Delay, or every frame must be timestamped upon arrival and the timestamp checked prior to transmission on any output port. While the accuracy of the timestamp is not especially critical, some form of timestamping and time-checking may be needed for standards compliance, depending on the bridge design. Many commercial bridges neither implement timestamping nor provide any inherent limit on transit delay and are therefore not strictly standards-compliant.

One possible way to avoid timestamping is for a bridge to have such a limited buffer memory that it is not possible for a frame to remain within the bridge for more than a Maximum Bridge Transit Delay. That is, if the bridge does not have 1 second's-worth of buffer, then it will naturally discard any frames that would have been held longer than that time. This argument is valid as long as there is no access-control delay on the output ports (e.g., the output ports operate in full duplex mode). If there can be an arbitrary delay in obtaining access to an output port, then a frame may be delayed more than a Maximum Bridge Transit Delay even if the bridge has limited buffer capacity. This is more of an issue with slow-speed links than with high-speed LANs; a 1-second buffer on a Gigabit Ethernet requires over 100 Mbytes of memory!

2. *An upper bound on the number of bridge hops across a catenet.* The standard recommends a maximum diameter of seven bridges. In practice, few network planners use bridges to this extent; most modern networks use bridges for high-speed local connections and internetwork routers for site interconnectivity (see Chapter 4).

By combining these two restrictions, we get an implicit upper bound on the delay of a catenet equal to the maximum number of bridge hops multiplied by the maximum transit delay of each bridge. In theory, this can be as high as 28 seconds; in practice, it rarely exceeds a few seconds. The actual delay experienced by a given frame will usually be much lower than this; the specification is for the worst case. This is adequately low for proper operation of most delay-sensitive client protocols.

2.5.1.3 Additional Operating Requirements

The standard makes some additional statements about the behavior of conformant bridges:

FCS checking Bridges are required to check the Frame Check Sequence (FCS) in all incoming frames. If a frame is received with an FCS error, it is discarded by the bridge. It makes no sense for a bridge to forward a frame that contains an error, since end stations would have to discard the frame anyway. Furthermore, since FCS error only indicates that an error is present (and not where in the frame the error is), the bridge cannot then depend on the integrity of the address fields in the received frame. With the address fields in question, the lookup, filter, and forwarding algorithms are moot—we have no idea whether the addresses we are using to make the bridging decisions are valid.

Note that the requirement to check the FCS makes any device that begins frame transmission on an output port before the frame is fully received at the input (a so-called *cut-through bridge*, discussed in Chapter 4) non-compliant with the standard. While the bridge may begin to process the frame before it is fully received (e.g., starting the address lookup engine), it cannot actually transmit the frame on any output port until it has validated the FCS.

Similarly, it is important that a bridge not learn addresses from frames that contain FCS errors, since those addresses are suspect. A bridge may begin the learning process, but it must be prepared to abort the procedure (and if necessary, "back out" any such incorrectly learned or updated table entry) upon detecting an FCS error in the frame.[29]

Same Source and Destination Address The original standard [IEEE93a] considered the special case of a frame that contains the same Source and Destination Address. Some higher-layer protocols use frames of this sort either for loopback testing or to determine if there are multiple stations with the same address [IEEE98b]. (If you send a frame to yourself and someone else responds, that's a pretty good hint that there is more than one station with the same address!)

If the Bridge Address Table indicates that the address in question is on the same port as that on which the frame arrived, there is no difficulty—the bridge will simply filter the frame. But what if the address table indicates a different port for that address? Should the bridge forward the frame to the indicated port and then learn the new port mapping, or should it learn the new mapping first and not forward the frame? Similarly, if the address is currently unknown, should the bridge flood the frame and then learn the address, or learn the address first and not flood? The standards say nothing about the internal implementation of a bridge; a given design can forward and then learn, or learn and then forward, or do both simultaneously. These are all valid implementations.

The original standard neatly skirted this issue. To quote:

> A MAC Bridge that claims conformance to this standard . . . shall either (a) Filter frames with equal source and destination addresses, or (b) Not filter frames with equal source and destination addresses . . . [IEEE93]

That helped a lot. Implementations could do whichever they wanted. The later version of the standard [IEEE98] doesn't mention this case at all.

2.5.2 Bridge Address Assignment

Strictly speaking, a bridge does not need an address in order to perform the bridge relay function. It receives all frames regardless of destination, and forwards them using the Source Address of the originating end station. At no time does the bridge use any address of its own for filtering or forwarding of frames. However, the standard actually requires a bridge to have a unique address for every port of the bridge, as well as an address used to denote the bridge as a whole.

[29] Depending on the particular implementation, this may be quite a difficult task. Some commercial bridges incorrectly learn and update their address tables from frames with FCS errors. Fortunately, FCS errors should not occur frequently, and the probability that an incorrectly-learned address-port mapping conflicts with a valid entry is quite low.

There are two reasons for requiring an address for each port:

1. Some LAN technologies invoke special MAC frames that communicate between MACs in order to maintain and/or control LAN operation. Token Ring, Token Bus, and FDDI LANs all exchange MAC frames in order to initialize, recover from errors, and maintain logical ring operation. For proper operation of such LANs it is a requirement for each port to have a unique address. Since a bridge may have multiple ports on the same LAN (discussed in Chapter 5), these addresses must be unique across all of the bridge ports as well.
2. Higher-layer protocols operating within a "real bridge" (see Section 2.2) often need to send frames that can be uniquely identified as being sourced from a specific port (e.g., address resolution protocols and/or network management).

That said, there are many commercial bridges that provide only a single address for the entire bridge. Unlike the token-passing technologies, Ethernet does not require the use of MAC frames for LAN maintenance, and thus does not impose the need for unique port addresses. An address can be assigned to the bridge as a whole and used for all higher-layer protocols (including the Spanning Tree Protocol, discussed in Chapter 5.) In most environments, this works, in that the system can function in a practical network without protocol or application failure. However, it makes troubleshooting especially difficult; a network protocol analyzer or frame capture device may be able to determine which bridge sent a given frame, but it cannot determine the port from which the frame was sent. In a problem-solving situation, especially one involving loops in a catenet, it is extremely useful to be able to determine the port that sent a given frame. The use of a single address for multiple bridge ports may also cause other bridges in the catenet to see that address on multiple input ports (e.g., as a result of management traffic emanating from the bridge in question) and therefore modify their address tables accordingly. Using the same MAC address on multiple bridge ports effectively violates the assumption that interfaces have globally-unique addresses; the consequences are the same as if multiple devices had the same MAC address. Under some circumstances, this situation could cause the management entity in the bridge to become unreachable from some locations in the catenet. The practice of assigning a single address to a bridge may save the manufacturer some design complexity and cost, but it ultimately makes life more difficult for end users and network administrators.

In addition to the port addresses, a bridge is assigned an address for the bridge as a whole. This is used as part of the Bridge Identifier in the Spanning Tree Protocol (see Chapter 5) as well as any other higher-layer protocols operating within a real bridge. There is no need for the bridge address to be unique

Table 2.3 Reserved Multicast Addresses

ADDRESS	USAGE
01-80-C2-00-00-00	Spanning Tree Protocol (See Chapter 5)
01-80-C2-00-00-01	IEEE 802.3 Full Duplex PAUSE (See Chapter 8)
01-80-C2-00-00-02	Slow Protocols (e.g., Link Aggregation Control and Marker Protocols; see Chapter 9)
01-80-C2-00-00-03	Reserved for future use
. . .	. . .
01-80-C2-00-00-0F	Reserved for future use

from all port addresses; the recommended convention is to use the address of the lowest-numbered port for the bridge address.

2.5.3 Reserved Addresses

Normally, a bridge floods frames sent to any multicast address, as discussed in Section 2.1.2. However, the standard reserves a specific group of multicast addresses that are never forwarded by a bridge, much less flooded to all ports. These multicast addresses are used by specific protocols and applications that require their transmissions to be limited in scope to a single link. Table 2.3 lists these 16 reserved addresses and their usage.

Regardless of whether a particular bridge implements any of the protocols that use these addresses, the bridge must not forward or flood frames sent to any reserved address. Frames sent to any of these addresses will either be received and interpreted by the bridge itself (for those protocols it supports) or discarded.

CHAPTER

3

Bridging between Technologies

Up to now, we have made the tacit assumption in our discussion of bridges that all of the bridge ports employed the same technology. Whether interconnecting multiple Ethernets, Token Rings, or FDDI LANs, bridges operate seamlessly and transparently, shuttling frames among ports according to the rules described in Chapter 2. End stations can communicate as if they were on the same LAN, regardless of their relative location. Everything is right with the world.

If we now allow a bridge to connect LANs employing dissimilar technologies, things get uglier than a pick-up date at closing time. The purpose of the bridge is still to allow end stations to communicate transparently. However, the technologies employed on the bridge's ports may provide different:

- Access control methods
- Frame formats
- Frame semantics (the meaning of the fields in the frame)
- Allowable data length
- Bit-ordering, and so on

How can we even consider using a device as simple as a bridge to interconnect such fundamentally incompatible technologies? The answer can be found in the way that the bridge itself operates. While the LAN interfaces on a bridge must of course support the technology of the attached LAN (that is, a bridge needs a 10 Mb/s Ethernet interface on a 10 Mb/s Ethernet port, a 16 Mb/s Token Ring interface on a 16 Mb/s Token Ring port, etc.), the bridge algorithms themselves don't care about the nature of the underlying technology. Bridges filter, forward, and learn solely on the basis of received destination and source addresses. As long as the interconnected technologies support globally-unique addressing from a common address space, they can be interconnected with a transparent bridge, at least in theory.

All of the IEEE 802 LAN technologies as well as FDDI support the use of globally-unique, 48-bit addresses drawn from the same address space. The frame formats of all of these LANs each include both a Source and Destination Address. Thus, it should be possible to use a transparent bridge to interconnect devices attached to all of these dissimilar LANs.

In this chapter, we discover that while such seamless interconnection is possible in theory, in practice a series of problems must be overcome in order to make the system work properly from the end station and application perspective. These problems can be solved (more or less), but they impose added complexity, loss of technology-specific features, and/or restrictions on the configurations permitted. Hang on, it's going to be a bumpy ride.

As long as we are looking at interconnections between dissimilar LANs, we might as well investigate interconnections between LAN and Wide Area Network (WAN) technologies (remote bridges). Surprisingly, this is easier and more straightforward than the LAN interconnection issue.

3.1 Bridging the LAN Gap

While all of the standard LAN technologies may share the same addressing mechanisms, no one would argue that they are all the same. Each uses a different method for managing access to the LAN, each has a different frame format, and each provides a different set of features and services. In this section we look at how it is possible to transparently bridge among these LANs.

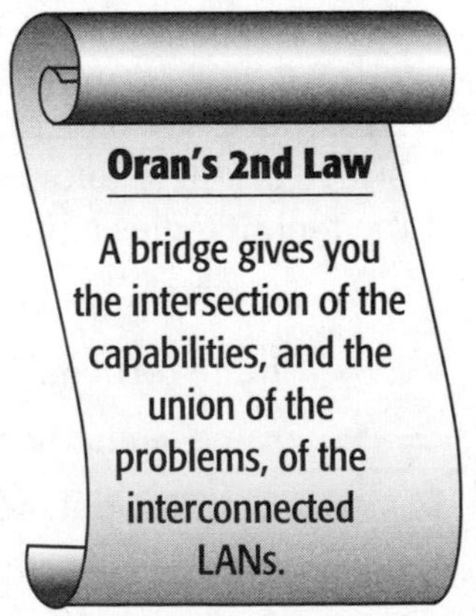

Oran's 2nd Law
A bridge gives you the intersection of the capabilities, and the union of the problems, of the interconnected LANs.

The discussion uses examples of bridges among Ethernet (IEEE 802.3), Token Ring (IEEE 802.5), and FDDI (ISO 9314) LANs, primarily because these constitute the vast bulk of the installed base today. No other LAN technology supported by transparent bridging has any significant market share.[1] In addition, our focus is on the use of

[1] At the time of this writing, FDDI still has an installed base, but is not commonly used for new network installations. As such, the impact of FDDI will only decrease over time, and any FDDI bridging issues will become of historical, rather than practical, interest.

transparent bridges, as discussed in Chapter 2. No consideration is given (in this chapter) to Source Routing as used in Token Ring and FDDI or to interconnections between Source Routed and Transparently Bridged catenets.

3.1.1 LAN Operational Mechanisms

Figure 3.1 depicts a bridge with connections to a variety of different LANs. Other than the fact that the bridge may be forwarding frames among the attached LANs, the operation of each individual LAN is independent of all others. In fact, the stations (including the LAN interfaces within the bridge itself) are unaware that there are even any other LANs in the catenet at all; the catenet operates transparently.

Thus, the operational mechanisms of each LAN remain unchanged in a bridged environment. In particular:

- Access control for each LAN is unchanged, and is independent of any other LAN in the catenet. Each Ethernet interface executes its CSMA/CD algorithm, and each Token Ring and FDDI interface performs its token passing and handling procedures independently.

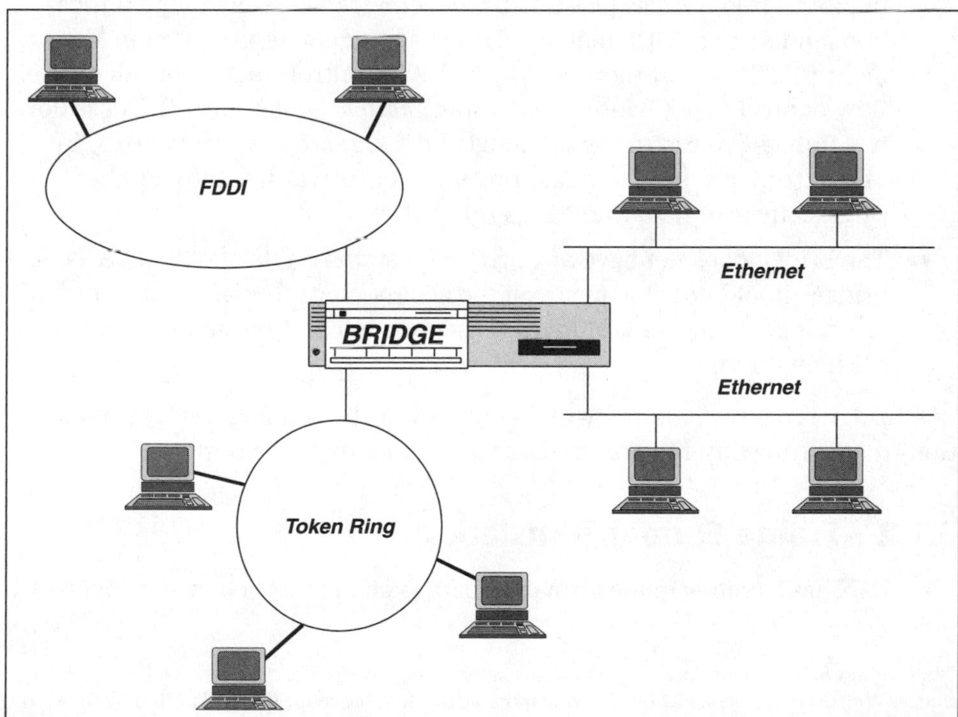

Figure 3.1 Bridging between dissimilar LANs.

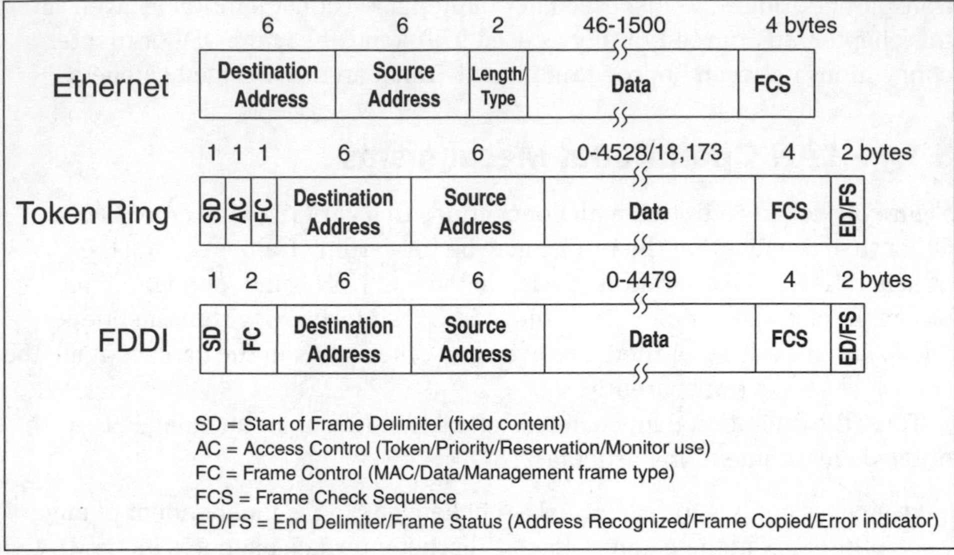

Figure 3.2 Data frame formats.

- Most LANs use some special control frames to manage the operation of the LAN. Token Rings use Tokens, Beacon frames, Neighbor Notification, and so on; FDDI includes Station Management/Connection Management (SMT/CMT); Ethernet can use MAC Control frames for full duplex flow control (see Chapter 8, *LAN and Switch Flow Control*). These control frames are restricted to a single LAN and are never forwarded by a bridge (e.g., a token from one ring is never forwarded onto another ring). Only user data frames are bridged.
- The bridge does not have any privileged status on its attached LANs. A bridge should not violate any of the access control rules just because it is a bridge. It appears to the LAN as any other station, sending and receiving frames.[2]

A bridge is simply a device with many LAN ports, running a relay "application" that is transparently forwarding frames among those ports.

3.1.2 Frame Format Translation

Each LAN has a unique frame format for data exchange, as depicted in Figure 3.2.

[2] In Chapter 8, we discuss some vendors' attempts to improve performance by violating LAN access control rules, typically by allowing more aggressive behavior than permitted by the standard algorithms.

The bridge always transmits frames using the format appropriate for each LAN. Thus, when a bridge receives a frame on one LAN that must be forwarded onto a LAN that uses a different frame format, the bridge must perform a translation between the frame formats of the two LANs. For this reason, a transparent bridge that interconnects dissimilar LANs is often called a *translational bridge.*

There are two parts to the translation:

1. The bridge must map between the MAC-specific fields of the various frames, for instance, Source and Destination Addresses, access control and frame control, protocol type, and so on.
2. The bridge must map between the different methods used to encapsulate user data among the various LANs, in particular between Ethernet Type field encoding and the Logical Link Control/Sub-Network Access Control Protocol (LLC/SNAP) encoding as used on Token Ring and FDDI.

3.1.2.1 MAC-Specific Fields

As depicted in Figure 3.2, the frame formats used on each LAN contain some variable-content fields in common, plus some fields unique to each technology, as shown in Table 3.1.

Clearly, some technologies have fields that don't exist in others. Even when two technologies have a field with a common name (e.g., Frame Control), the semantics of the bits within the field are different between the technologies. When bridging between dissimilar LANs, depending on the direction of frame

Table 3.1 Data Frame Contents

ETHERNET	TOKEN RING	FDDI
	Access Control	
	Frame Control	Frame Control
Destination Address	Destination Address	Destination Address
Source Address	Source Address	Source Address
Length/Type		
Data	Data	Data
FCS	FCS	FCS
	End Delimiter/Frame Status	End Delimiter/Frame Status

forwarding, either some information must be discarded or some new field contents must be generated to form the outgoing frame. Specifically:

- When forwarding to a Token Ring, an Access Control field must be formed. Access Control has four subfields: a token bit, a priority field, a priority reservation field, and a monitor bit (see Figure 1.12). In a forwarded frame:
  - The token and monitor bits will always be set to 0; a data frame is never a token and the monitor bit is always initially set to 0.
  - The current token priority is a function of administrative policy and the operation of the Token Ring MAC, and is typically generated automatically by the LAN controller circuitry.
  - Some value for priority reservation must be created. This will generally be a static configuration parameter; that is, some value of priority is chosen for bridge operation (by an administrator or the designer of the bridge), and it remains constant.
- When forwarding to a Token Ring or FDDI, a Frame Control field must be formed. Since the only frames forwarded are user data frames, this field will always indicate that the frame is user data (rather than a MAC or Management frame). User priority information must also be provided. If the received frame carries user priority information, then this can be used to create the user priority value in this field; otherwise, some static, administratively-configured parameter is used for the priority.[3]
- When forwarding to a Token Ring or FDDI, an End Delimiter/Frame Status field must be formed. This field contains bits to indicate whether a received frame passed the address check successfully, was copied into a local buffer, and/or contained a detected error. On transmit, each of these indicators is set to 0—that is, they are set to 1 only as part of the ring operation by receiving stations. The interesting issue of what a bridge should do with the Address Recognized and Frame Copied bits upon receiving a frame from a Token Ring or FDDI is discussed in Section 3.1.3.5.1.

Note that when forwarding a frame onto an Ethernet, any FDDI or Token Ring–specific fields are simply discarded.

[3] Ethernet has no native mechanism for signaling user priority. Thus, when bridging from an Ethernet to a Token Ring or FDDI, some priority value must be made up (configured by an administrator). If VLAN or Priority tags are being used on Ethernet (see Chapter 12), then the priority value contained within the tag can be used to form the native priority value in the Frame Control field.

3.1.2.2 User Data Encapsulation

That takes care of the technology-specific details of the MAC frame formats. However, there are a number of different ways in which user data can be encapsulated into the payload of the frame:

- Ethernet supports *native Type field encoding.* In this method, the Length/Type field in the Ethernet frame contains a Type value indicating the higher-layer protocol that is being encapsulated. The data portion of the frame simply carries the payload for this higher-layer protocol with no additional overhead. Type field encoding is the most common encapsulation used on Ethernet.
- Any LAN can use *pure LLC encoding.* In this method, the LLC header contains a Destination and Source Service Access Point (DSAP/SSAP) field that identifies the higher layer protocol.[4] A control field carries a value indicating the type of frame. LLC-1 uses "Unnumbered Information" (connectionless, best effort service) only. LLC-2 can provide reliable, connection-oriented services[5] [IEEE98b].
- Any LAN can use Sub-Network Access Protocol (SNAP) encapsulation. This method uses a standard LLC-1 header with fixed DSAP/SSAP values (0xAA) and provides an expansion of the SAP space with a pair of fields following the LLC-1 header. An Organizationally-Unique Identifier (OUI) indicates the organization for which the Protocol Identifier (Pid) field is significant; the Pid is a higher-layer protocol identifier. An OUI of all zeros (0x000000) signifies that the Pid field has the same semantics as an Ethernet Type field; that is, SNAP encapsulation can be used to provide Type field encoding on a LAN that does not support it natively. (See Chapter 1, *Laying the Foundation,* [IEEE90b], and [RFC1042].)

Figure 3.3 depicts the three encapsulations described. While the figure shows these encapsulations in the context of an Ethernet frame, both LLC and SNAP encapsulation can be used on any other LAN technology. (Type encapsulation can only be used on Ethernet.) Table 3.2 shows which encapsulations are used by many popular protocols both on Ethernet and non-Ethernet (Token Ring and FDDI) LANs.

[4] Okay, to be strictly correct architecturally, the LLC SAP is not a protocol identifier in the same way that an Ethernet Type field is. Unlike a Type field, a SAP is intended to identify a client process to the LLC sublayer, but not the nature of that client; this results in the need for separate Destination and Source SAP fields. However, this "architecturally-correct" usage of LLC SAPs has not been widely adopted; most LLC implementations use SAPs as protocol identifiers.

[5] Since a bridge does not interpret the LLC information, it treats LLC-1 and LLC-2 exactly the same. LLC-3 (acknowledged connectionless service) is virtually unheard-of in practical LANs.

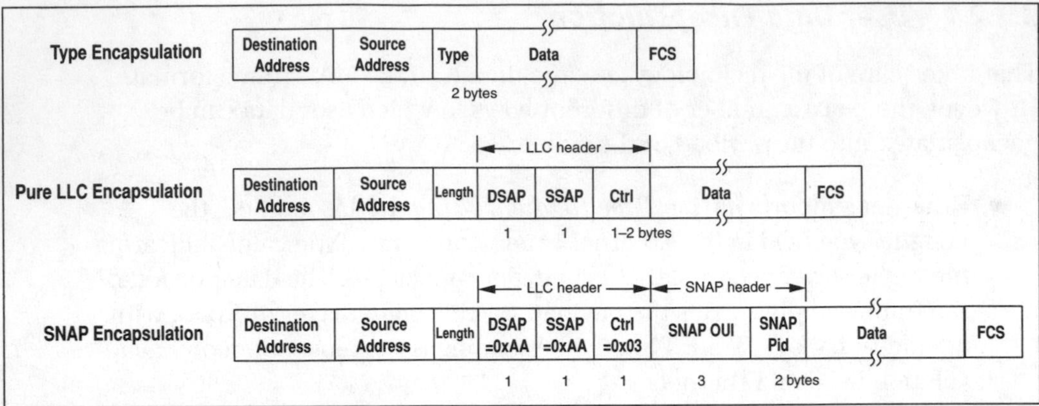

Figure 3.3 Data encapsulation formats.

It is not especially difficult to transform from one encapsulation to another. Figure 3.4 depicts the transformation between native Type field encoding and SNAP encoding, using an Ethernet-to-FDDI LAN translation as an example.

A bridge need only deal with data encapsulation transformations between Ethernet and non-Ethernet LANs, and then only between Type field encapsulation and SNAP encapsulation. This is because:

- Ethernet is the only LAN that supports native Type field encapsulation. Token Ring and FDDI (and every other LAN) support both pure LLC and SNAP encapsulation, so there is never a need to convert between formats.
- It is not possible to convert between Type field and pure LLC encapsulation, since the semantics of the DSAP/SSAP fields are different from those of the Type field used in Ethernet.[6]

Note that the transformation increases the size of the data payload by 8 bytes (for the LLC and SNAP headers). Fortunately, the transformation from Type to SNAP encapsulation is only performed from an Ethernet to a Token Ring or FDDI LAN; since both Token Ring and FDDI support larger frames than Ethernet, there is no architectural problem.

Dang! I almost forgot one nasty little "gotcha." Consider the case depicted in Figure 3.5. When forwarding frames from the Ethernet to the FDDI, a bridge's task is straightforward: If the frame is Type encapsulated, convert it

[6] In theory, you could build a table that mapped the Type field semantics to the appropriate LLC SAP for those protocols supported, but this is never done in practice. The selection of appropriate encapsulation by the end stations on the attached LANs eliminates any need to do this.

Table 3.2 Encapsulations and Encoding for Standard Protocols

PROTOCOL	ENCAPSULATION/ENCODING(S) ON ETHERNET LANS	ENCAPSULATION/ENCODING(S) ON NON-ETHERNET LANS
IP (datagrams)	Type = 0x0800	SNAP: OUI = 0x000000, Pid = 0x0800
IP (address resolution)	Type = 0x0806	SNAP: OUI = 0x000000, Pid = 0x0806
AppleTalk (datagrams)	SNAP: OUI = 0x080007, Pid = 0x809B	
AppleTalk (address resolution)	SNAP: OUI = 0x000000, Pid = 0x80F3	
Novell IPX (see note)	Type = 0x8137	
	Pure LLC-1: DSAP = SSAP = 0xE0	Pure LLC-1: DSAP = SSAP = 0xE0
	SNAP: OUI = 0x000000, Pid = 0x8137	SNAP: OUI = 0x000000, Pid = 0x8137
DECnet Phase IV	Type = 0x6003	SNAP: OUI = 0x000000, Pid = 0x6003
NetBIOS/NetBEUI	Pure LLC-2: DSAP = SSAP = 0xF0	
ISO 8473 CLNP	Pure LLC-1: DSAP = SSAP = 0xFE	
Spanning Tree	Pure LLC-1: DSAP = SSAP = 0x42	

IPX supports any of the encapsulations shown; the specific one used is controlled by a parameter in a configuration file read upon protocol initialization. IPX also supports a format on Ethernet LANs known as *Raw 802.3,* which uses a Length field with no LLC or SNAP identifiers. The use of this format is discouraged, as it makes protocol identification difficult. See Chapter 11 and the Appendix for more information on identification of protocol types in different encapsulations.

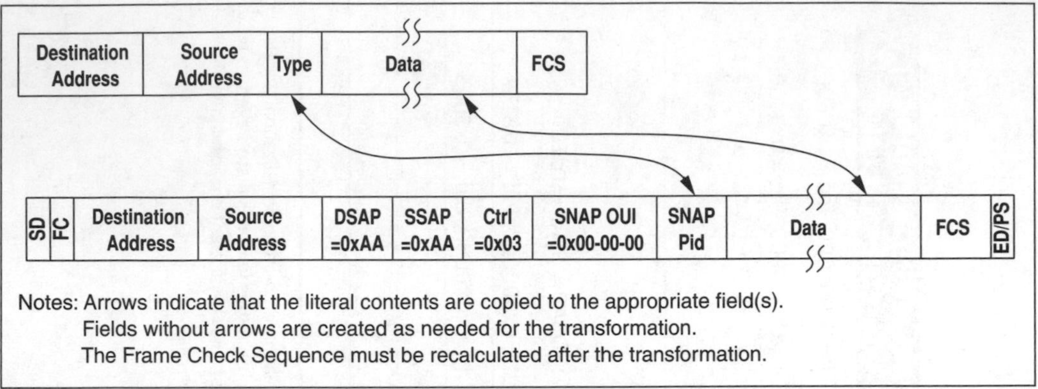

Figure 3.4 Transforming one encapsulation into another.

to SNAP encapsulation on the FDDI; if the frame is in pure LLC or SNAP encapsulation, pass it through with no transformation.

However, when a bridge is forwarding frames from the FDDI to the Ethernet, there are three cases to consider:

1. If the frame is pure LLC encapsulated, pass it through with no transformation.

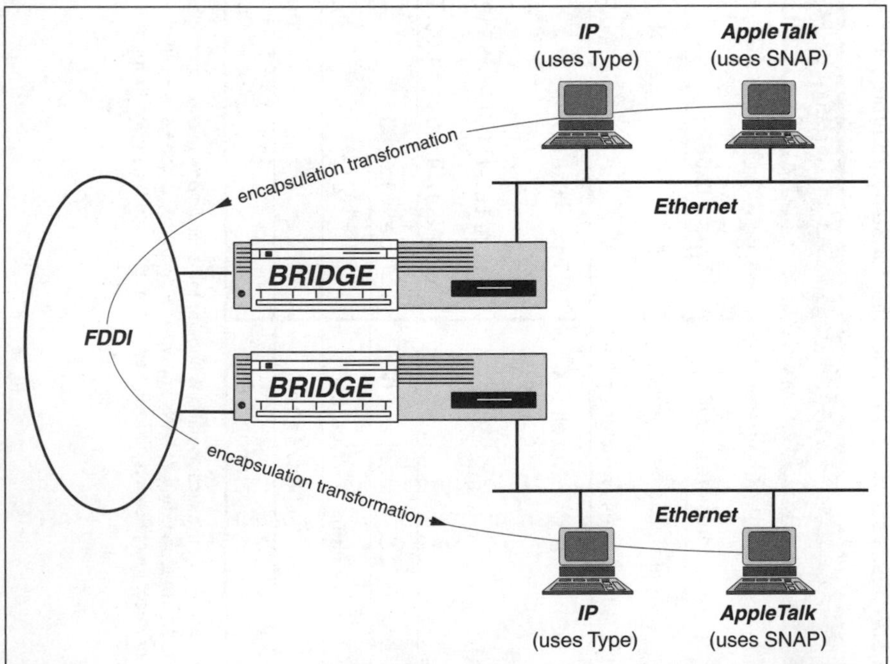

Figure 3.5 Two-way transformations.

2. If the frame is SNAP encapsulated with an OUI other than all zeros, pass it through with no transformation. A non-zero OUI means that the semantics of the Pid field that follows may not be the same as for Ethernet Types, so no transformation is possible.
3. If the frame is SNAP encapsulated with an OUI of all zeros, there are two choices. The bridge can pass the frame unchanged (Ethernet also supports SNAP encapsulation) or it can transform it to Type encapsulation. What to do, what to do?

If we were to pass the frame through in SNAP format, we would have to require every station on an Ethernet to understand two encapsulations (Type and SNAP) for every higher-layer protocol that uses Ethernet Type fields (most protocols, per Table 3.2). Frames received from stations on the local LAN would arrive Type encapsulated, while frames received from stations on other LANs through a bridge would arrive SNAP encapsulated. This is an unreasonable burden to place on the end stations. Therefore, it seems appropriate to transform all SNAP encapsulated frames with an OUI of all zeros to Type encapsulation when forwarding onto an Ethernet.

However, look at the entry for AppleTalk address resolution (AppleTalk ARP) in Table 3.2. As you can see, the end stations use SNAP encapsulation, with an OUI of all zeros, *even on an Ethernet.* An AppleTalk station never uses Type encapsulation, and does not understand this format. If we transform all SNAP encapsulated frames with an OUI of all zeros into Type encapsulation, AppleTalk address resolution packets will not be understood by the AppleTalk stations on the Ethernet and AppleTalk won't work across the bridge.

Unfortunately, this problem was discovered not in someone's notebook, but in the field. No one really thought about this until people started deploying Ethernet-to-FDDI bridges and tried to run AppleTalk over them. Of course, it didn't work. The problem arises from an error on the part of Apple's protocol architects. They should either have required AppleTalk devices to understand both encapsulations on an Ethernet or used a non-zero value for the OUI when transmitting AppleTalk ARP packets in SNAP format.[7]

While this is an AppleTalk-specific problem, there were (and are) millions of devices in use running this protocol suite.[8] As such, the IEEE 802.1 committee formulated an industry standard Recommended Practice that "solves" the problem.[9] [IEEE95] Simply put, a bridge needs to look at the Pid field before

[7] There were a number of heated exchanges on this topic with Apple's representative to IEEE 802.1, cooled down only by lots of beer, at the meetings where this problem was being addressed.

[8] Including the machine I am using to write this book!

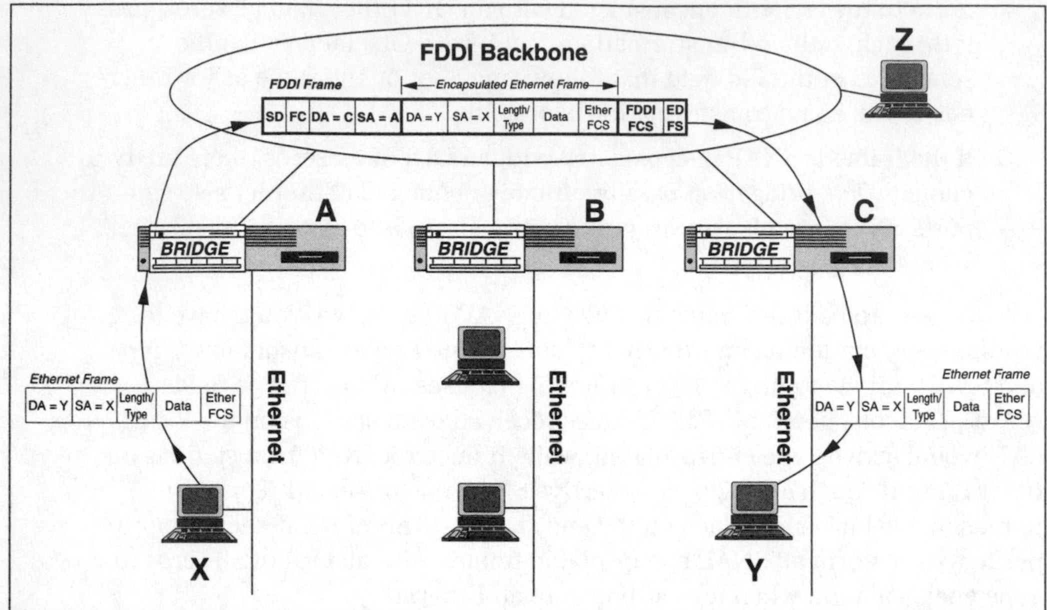

Figure 3.6 Encapsulating bridges.

deciding whether to transform a frame into Type encapsulation. If the protocol is anything except AppleTalk ARP, it makes the transformation. For AppleTalk ARP, the SNAP encapsulated frame is passed through unchanged. It's ugly, but it works.

3.1.2.3 Translating versus Encapsulating Bridges

There is an alternative to the problems of translation between the formats imposed by dissimilar LANs. Rather than converting the MAC-specific fields of the frame and the user data encapsulation, you can simply encapsulate the entire received frame (lock, stock, and MAC headers) into the data field of the transmitted frame, as depicted in Figure 3.6.

In the figure, stations on the Ethernets (e.g., station X) transmit normal Ethernet frames (transparently) to their intended destination(s). These frames are taken by a bridge and "wrapped up" in a FDDI frame.[10] The Source and Destination Addresses used in the FDDI frame are associated with the bridges

[9] IEEE Recommended Practices are technical proposals that deal with interoperability issues but do not carry the weight of a formal Standard. Implementors may choose to adopt a Recommended Practice or not and still claim conformance to the standard.
[10] Both FDDI and Token Ring support a larger data field than Ethernet, making this possible.

themselves (A and B, in the example); they are not the original Source and Destination Addresses from the Ethernet frame. The frame is forwarded across the FDDI to the appropriate bridge, where the FDDI headers and trailers are stripped off, and the original Ethernet frame is delivered to the intended recipient. Bridges that operate in this manner are referred to as *encapsulating bridges*, as opposed to the translational bridges discussed earlier.[11] There are a number of pros and cons to using the encapsulation approach:

+ Encapsulation avoids any need to transform the user data encapsulation as described earlier. The original frame structure is carried end-to-end.
+ The original FCS can be carried end-to-end, providing protection against errors introduced within the bridges. (See Section 3.1.3.2 for a complete discussion of this issue.)
+ The bridges do not need to operate in promiscuous mode on the encapsulating port (backbone). Since encapsulating bridges forward frames to the specific bridge with a connection to the intended destination, the bridges need only receive the frames that actually require forwarding, rather than all frames.[12]

On the other hand:[13]

- Encapsulating bridges cannot provide connectivity to end stations on the encapsulating port (backbone) unless those stations subsume the functionality of an encapsulating bridge and understand the original frame format. In order to extract the original frame, station Z in Figure 3.6 must understand Ethernet frame format in addition to the encapsulation being used. In practice, this requirement restricts the use of encapsulating bridges to "pure" backbones (i.e., those with no attached end stations).
- There needs to be some auxiliary protocol (similar to the routing protocols used by Network layer routers) for the bridges to exchange their address table information. Since encapsulated frames are forwarded to a specific bridge on the backbone, the bridges must somehow map the

[11] Another name for this is *tunneling*, as opposed to bridging.

[12] This was the original rationale for encapsulating bridges. In the early days of FDDI, achieving wire-speed performance on a 100 Mb/s LAN was difficult and expensive. Encapsulating bridges allowed users to install FDDI backbones without spending a fortune on the bridges.

[13] A prospective consulting client once told me, "Rich, I'm looking for a one-armed consultant." I inquired about this rather strange request (thinking perhaps that he had had an experience similar to Dr. Richard Kimball in *The Fugitive*). He replied, "No, I'm just looking for a straight answer, but every consultant that comes in here starts off, "Well, on the one hand, you could do it *this* way . . ."

original frame's Destination Address to the address of the bridge responsible for it. Since there is no industry-standard for this exchange of Bridge Address Tables, encapsulating bridges are proprietary and must usually all be purchased from the same vendor.

– The backbone technology must support a data field length longer than that of the LAN being encapsulated.

Encapsulating bridges were popular in the early 1990s, primarily because of the challenges of providing high-performance during the nascent era of FDDI. Today's LAN bridges hardly ever employ encapsulation in this manner.

3.1.3 Issues in Bridging Dissimilar LANs

If you thought things got ugly with AppleTalk ARP and SNAP encapsulation, that's just one tiny problem related to using bridges between dissimilar LANs. In the sections that follow, we consider a number of other, more generic problems faced by the network architect.

3.1.3.1 Maximum Transmission Unit (MTU)

While most LANs support variable-length frames, each technology imposes some maximum length of data that may be exchanged in a single frame. This upper bound of a frame's data payload is called the *Maximum Transmission Unit* (MTU), and is depicted in Figure 3.7.

In general, larger MTUs:

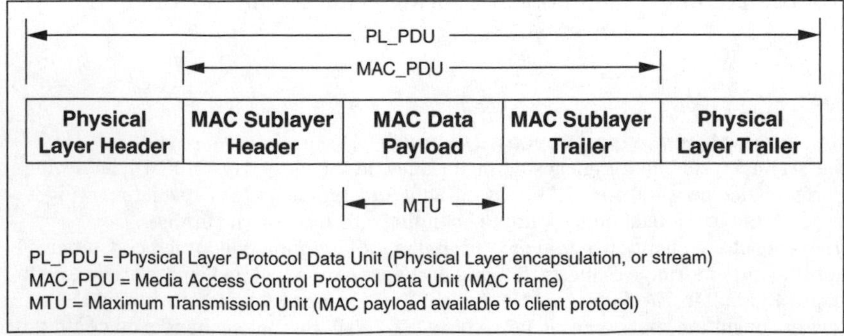

Figure 3.7 Maximum Transmission Unit.

+ *Increase the channel efficiency.* Physical and Data Link layer overhead is on a per-frame basis. If the MTU is larger, more data can be exchanged with the same overhead, providing greater efficiency.[14]
+ *Reduce processing overhead.* Every device sending and receiving frames has some per-frame processing overhead for buffer management, interrupt service, and so on. Larger MTUs allow a given volume of data to be exchanged using fewer frames, reducing the processing overhead.

On the downside, larger MTUs:

– *Increase delay.* If a station is allowed to transmit very long frames on a shared communications channel, other stations must wait this longer time before sending their frames.

– *Increase the probability of collisions in Ethernet.* A collision is guaranteed among all frames that have been queued for transmission in multiple stations while waiting for a frame-in-progress to complete. If frames can be very long, this allows more time for stations to queue frames that are guaranteed to collide, which in turn increases the probability that frames will be queued in multiple stations.

– *Increase the probability of frame loss.* Since a single-bit error will (in general) cause a frame to be discarded, the more bits in the frame, the higher the probability that one of them will be in error.[15]

– *Increase the minimum memory requirement.* Any network device must have some minimum number of frame buffers for reasonable transmit and receive performance. The amount of memory required is therefore a function of the MTU.

In the end, designers of popular LAN technologies have chosen different MTUs for a combination of the reasons just discussed.[16] Table 3.3 lists the MTU and maximum frame lengths for all of the IEEE 802 and FDDI LAN technologies.

[14] In practice, the increase in *efficiency* from larger MTUs is not especially significant. The maximum channel efficiency for Ethernet is:

$$\frac{\text{MTU}}{\text{MTU} + \text{MAC\_Overhead} + \text{Physical\_Overhead}} = \frac{1{,}500 \text{ bytes}}{1{,}500 + 26 + 12 \text{ bytes}} = 97.5\%$$

If the MTU was increased to as much as 9,000 bytes, the efficiency would increase to only

$$\frac{9{,}000 \text{ bytes}}{9{,}000 + 26 + 12 \text{ bytes}} = 99.6\%$$

The difference for a 6:1 MTU change is only a 2.1% efficiency increase.

[15] Consider the limiting case: For a frame with an infinite MTU, there is a 100 percent probability of a bit error for any non-zero bit error rate.

[16] A complete discussion of the rationale behind the Ethernet MTU is given in [SEIF98] and [SEIF91].

Table 3.3 Maximum Transmission Units and Frame Lengths

TECHNOLOGY	MTU[1] (MAXIMUM DATA PAYLOAD)	MAXIMUM FRAME LENGTH[2] (INCLUDING DATA LINK OVERHEAD)
IEEE 802.3/Ethernet	1,500 bytes	1,522 bytes
IEEE 802.4/Token Bus	8,174 bytes	8,193 bytes
IEEE 802.5/Token Ring[3]		
4 Mb/s	4,528 bytes	4,550 bytes
16 Mb/s	18,173 bytes	18,200 bytes
100 Mb/s	18,173 bytes	18,200 bytes
IEEE 802.6/DQDB[4]	9,191 bytes	9,240 bytes
IEEE 802.9a/isoEthernet	1,500 bytes	1,518 bytes
IEEE 802.11/Wireless	2,304 bytes	2,346 bytes
IEEE 802.12/Demand Priority		
Ethernet Mode	1,500 bytes	1,518 bytes
Token Ring Mode	4,502 bytes	4,528 bytes
ISO 9314/FDDI	4,479 bytes	4,500 bytes

[1] This is the maximum payload available to a client above the MAC; LLC/SNAP overhead (if used) must be deducted from the value shown.
[2] Not including Preamble, where used.
[3] Assumes no Source Routing information is present.
[4] IEEE 802.6 segments the values shown for transmission using ATM-like cells, transparent to the Data Link Client.

3.1.3.1.1 Dealing with the MTU Problem within the MAC Layer

A problem occurs when we use a bridge to interconnect two LANs with different MTUs, as depicted in Figure 3.8. As shown, station X (on the FDDI) can send frames with 4,479 bytes of client payload. If such a frame is sent to station Y (on the Ethernet), the bridge is expected to transparently forward the frame to the destination. However, the frame is too large to be legally transmitted on an Ethernet, which only supports a 1,500 byte MTU.

A "pure" bridge (as discussed in Chapter 2, *Transparent Bridges*), has only two options for dealing with a received frame. It can filter (discard) the frame, or it can forward it. In this case, the bridge would like to forward the frame (as station Y is present on the Ethernet), but it must instead discard the frame, as forwarding would violate the Ethernet rules. Even if the bridge chose to

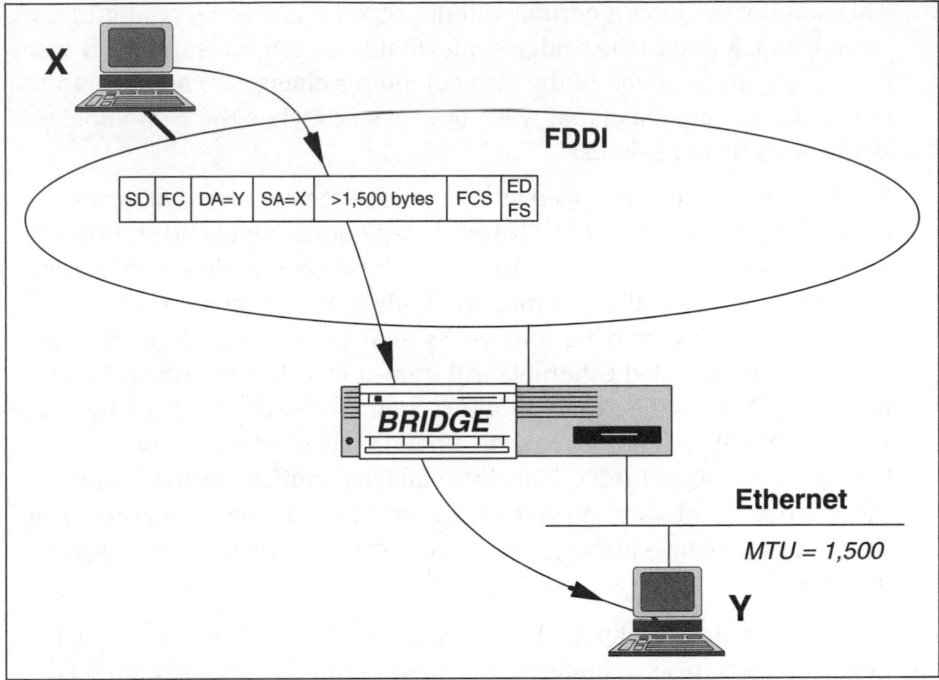

Figure 3.8 Bridging dissimilar MTUs.

break the rules and send the too-long frame on the Ethernet, station Y was not designed to receive such long frames, and would most likely discard this frame anyway. We are stuck! Transparent communications are not possible in this scenario.

This is where Oran's Second Law comes to bite us. The "intersection of the capabilities," that is, the lowest common denominator of MTU between the two LANs, is the smaller Ethernet limitation. Even though an FDDI can carry larger frames, a catenet mixing FDDI and Ethernet can (practically) only support the Ethernet MTU. The greater capability of FDDI is not available if the bridge is to function correctly.

Since we know that FDDI-to-Ethernet bridges do exist (if you didn't, you do now), how do we circumvent this problem? There are two methods for dealing with this particular issue within the Data Link layer (methods for handling this problem above the Data Link are discussed later):

1. A straightforward approach is to configure the device drivers of the devices on the FDDI to use smaller frames carrying a maximum of 1,500 bytes of client payload. This reduces the efficiency of the FDDI, but allows the bridge to function normally. Communication is possible among all stations, regardless of the type of LAN on which they reside.

This solution requires a certain amount of tedious manual configuration. In addition, it makes the bridge somewhat less than transparent (translucent?); the introduction of the bridge requires changes to be made to the end stations, something that was not necessary when the technologies being bridged were similar.

2. FDDI is most commonly used as a backbone technology; that is, it is used to interconnect other LANs, and may not have any end stations directly connected to it. If it is used as a backbone (as depicted in Figure 3.9), then there is really no problem. While FDDI can support long frames, frames can only be sourced by end stations, and all of these are on the interconnected Ethernets. All frames will start out on an Ethernet, and will meet the Ethernet MTU requirement. The fact that they traverse an FDDI en route to their destination has no effect on the transparency of the bridge. This is, in fact, a common configuration. If there are any end stations on the backbone (e.g., common servers or network management stations), these can be manually configured as just described.

You may be wondering why the bridge can't simply take the larger FDDI frame, break it up into some number of Ethernet frames (three maximum), and forward these onto the destination port? Actually, the bridge *can* fragment the frame as described. The problem is that there is no mechanism within the

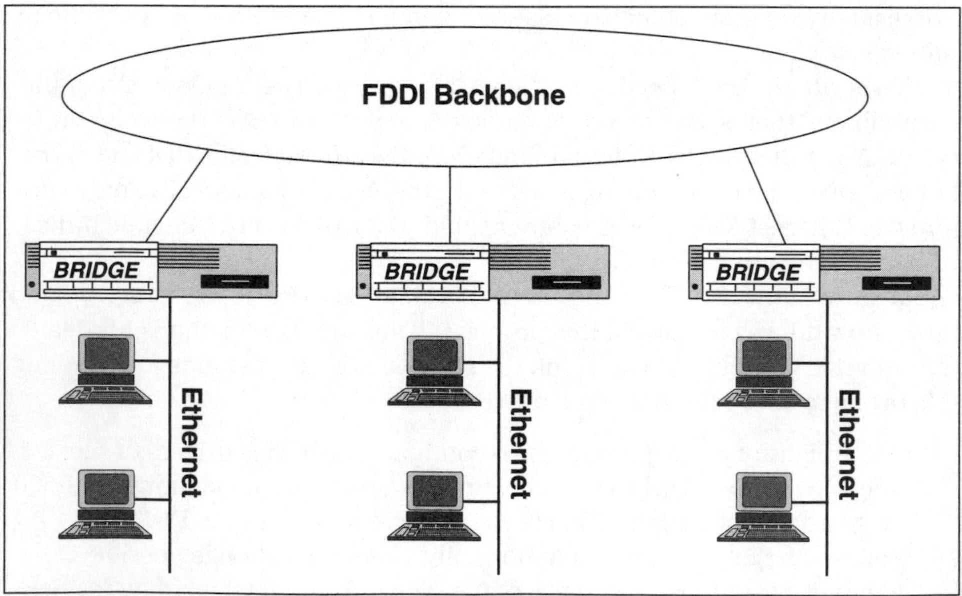

Figure 3.9 FDDI backbone.

Ethernet (or any other popular LAN Data Link) for reassembling the fragments back into the original frame at the receiving station. Look at the frame format for Ethernet (Figure 3.2). There are no fields to identify a frame as being part of a larger construct, to indicate the first, intermediate, and/or last frames in a sequence, and so on. LANs do not generally include mechanisms for fragmentation and reassembly, and this is why the bridge (which operates within the Data Link) cannot invoke such facilities. A Data Link client in the FDDI station cannot submit a single frame for transmission on the LAN, have three frames delivered to its peer client in the Ethernet station, and expect the system to work properly. It would require a redesign of the Ethernet protocol to allow for such reassembly.

Humpty-Dumpty's Law
Never take something apart if you don't know how to put it back together again.

3.1.3.1.2 Dealing with the MTU Problem at the Network Layer

If we allow ourselves to invoke Network Layer mechanisms, we find some additional tools at our disposal for dealing with the MTU problem. Of course, this won't be "pure" bridging (which is by definition a Data Link layer mechanism), but if it solves the problem and makes the customer happy, so be it.

Transparent IP Fragmentation The Internet Protocol (IP) [RFC791] does provide a means for fragmentation and reassembly of IP datagrams. Traditionally, such fragmentation/reassembly would be performed by a router (rather than a bridge) that interconnects LANs with dissimilar MTUs. However, we can have our bridge perform just the fragmentation function without implementing a full-blown router. The bridge in Figure 3.8 can have the capability to fragment IP datagrams, and could actually emit three Ethernet frames for a received maximum-length FDDI frame carrying an IP datagram. Unlike a router, the bridge in this case would not:

Seifert's Law of Networking #11
Architectural purity goes out the window when purchase orders come in the door.

- *Be visible to the end stations.* The end stations would still send their frames directly to each other. The two interconnected LANs would appear as a single IP network, and would not require the services of a router to move datagrams between them.
- *Make forwarding decisions based on IP addresses.* The bridge still makes the filter/forward decision based on the MAC addresses in the Data Link frames and not on Network Layer addresses in the IP datagram.

- *Participate in the IP Routing Protocol.* The bridge remains transparent to both end stations and other routers.

Reassembly of the fragments occurs in the end station, at the Network Layer. Unlike the LAN Data Link, IP does have means for reassembling fragments into a single message for delivery to its client. Other than the performance impact of fragmentation and reassembly (which can be significant), there is no connectivity problem.

This mechanism works only for IP datagrams. No other popular Network-layer protocol has any mechanism for fragmentation and reassembly of messages.[17]

MTU Discovery Another approach is to have the end stations, prior to initiating communications, "discover" the maximum length frame that can be carried between them. Again, such a mechanism must typically be invoked at the Network layer (or higher).[18]

In IP, a station can send Echo Request/Reply packets (commonly referred to as *pinging* the other station [RFC792]; see Chapter 14, *Switch Management*), using various packet lengths, to determine the maximum length that can be successfully exchanged across the link. Typically, the station would first attempt to communicate using the MTU of its local link, and reduce that value if it received no response from its intended partner.[19]

Unlike the approach of statically reducing the MTU in the device driver, this approach allows the stations to use the maximum frame lengths permitted for communication both with stations on their own LAN (e.g., the FDDI) and with stations on a transparently bridged LAN with lower MTU. The downside is that the end station needs to know that there is a bridge in the catenet (otherwise, why even bother to invoke this mechanism) and to maintain some state information about which stations are on which side of the bridge. In most cases this is a heavy price to pay for the small performance improvement achieved.

Use of small datagrams Most other protocols "solve" the MTU problem by limiting the size of the datagram used at the Network layer. DECnet Phase IV generally limits transmissions to the Ethernet MTU of 1,500

[17] The ISO Connectionless Network Protocol (CLNP) [ISO87] has a mechanism similar to IP for segmentation and reassembly, but this protocol has never achieved widespread use.

[18] Source Routing, used in Token Ring and FDDI, does have a mechanism for coarse MTU Discovery; however, it is restricted to use within a Source Routed domain. By definition, this is not transparent bridging and cannot be used with stations on an Ethernet. LLC Test frames could also be used to provide MTU Discovery, but many systems do not implement LLC (e.g., most Ethernet-based systems) or do not implement the Test function even if LLC is implemented.

[19] This is a variation of the MTU Discovery mechanism described in [RFC1191]. Traditional MTU Discovery relies on intermediate routers issuing "Datagram Too Big" responses. The MTU Discovery discussed in this text does not require any intermediate router responses.

bytes [DEC82]. Since this is the smallest MTU of the popular LANs, it avoids most MTU problems. Similarly, AppleTalk limits transmissions to 600 bytes or fewer.[20] Before implementing MTU Discovery (as just discussed), NetWare solved the MTU problem by limiting transmissions to 512 bytes when a frame had to leave the local LAN (i.e., when sending frames to a router). This approach avoids the problems of fragmentation and MTU incompatibility, at the expense of the inefficiency of using small frames.

3.1.3.2 Frame Check Protection

A second problem involves the ability of the Frame Check Sequence (FCS) to protect against errors introduced by the bridge itself. As discussed in Chapter 2, the FCS protects the frame against errors introduced anywhere from the point at which the FCS is calculated to the point at which it is checked. As long as a bridge does not change the contents of a forwarded frame (not even a single bit!), the FCS will protect the frame from errors introduced by the bridge itself. Such protection occurs naturally when bridging between similar technologies, even at different data rates. Since an Ethernet (or Token Ring) frame is identical regardless of data rate, a bridge interconnecting only Ethernets (or Token Rings) will not compromise the error-detecting ability of the FCS.

However, a bridge interconnecting dissimilar technologies *must* make changes to forwarded frames. The basic frame format is different among Ethernets, Token Rings, FDDIs, and so on, and the bridge must emit validly-formed frames for the particular technology used on a given port. Thus, there will assuredly be changes made to frames between reception and forwarding among the bridge ports. The FCS will protect against errors introduced on the various links, but cannot protect against errors introduced by the bridge itself.

Fortunately, this is not a significant issue for practical products. There are three likely sources of errors attributable to a bridge:

1. *Memory errors.* It is possible for a memory chip to have an internal fault on a bit, or to be struck by an alpha particle or cosmic ray, resulting in an unintentional change in a bit's value.[21] In the old days, semiconductor memories were unreliable, and large memory arrays used for critical applications required more expensive error-correcting (ECC) memories. Today's memories are much more reliable, and error-correcting memories are rarely used in commercial products. If memory reliability is an issue, simple parity-checking memory can be used.[22]

[20] This lower-than-Ethernet MTU provides backward compatibility with the LocalTalk LAN technology used in early Macintosh computers.

[21] Seriously, background particle emissions are a measurable source of memory errors!

[22] The original VAX super-minicomputer used ECC memory on arrays of 1 Mbyte or more.

2. *Internal bus errors.* The data paths within the bridge may incur errors due to noise or component failure, resulting in data changes during transfer between the subassemblies of the bridge. Again, this is a low-probability event, and can be protected using simple parity-checking on the internal data paths.
3. *Design flaws.* A design flaw (e.g., software bug) in a bridge may cause data corruption under some set of conditions.

None of these error sources create large numbers of undetected errors. If there were some serious fault or design flaw causing lots of data errors, it will probably become obvious from application misbehavior, regardless of the inability of the FCS to detect the error at the Data Link layer![23] The issue is really the occasional rare error event that goes undetected and for which there is no end-to-end error checking provided. Such insidious problems can greatly increase the aspirin consumption of network administrators and can be virtually impossible to troubleshoot.

Short of employing some end-to-end error checking (e.g., TCP checksums), there is no absolute solution to this problem. Bridge designers can reduce the probability of the bridge introducing undetected errors into the data stream by using good design practices and instituting memory/bus parity checking where appropriate.

If a designer is really paranoid (or the application environment demands superior error protection), some sophisticated methods may be used to extend the FCS coverage over most of the internal data paths and memory of the bridge.

Seifert's Law of Networking #8

Just because you're paranoid doesn't mean that they're not out to get you!

In the simpler approach (which is the one most commonly used in commercial products), the received FCS is checked (to determine whether the received frame contains an error) and then discarded. The frame contents are forwarded to the appropriate output port, where frame translation takes place. A new FCS is calculated at the output, based solely on the frame contents and the new frame headers. Any errors introduced between the time the incoming FCS is discarded and the time the new FCS is calculated at the output are undetectable at the Data Link layer.

In a second approach, the original received FCS is checked as before, but is also carried to the output along with the forwarded frame contents. Rather than the FCS being computed for the outgoing frame as a function of the frame contents and newly-generated headers, the outgoing FCS is computed

[23] Of course, if the error were to move the decimal point to the right in everyone's paychecks, who would complain?

as a function of the received FCS and the changes (additions, deletions, and/or modifications) made to the frame contents and headers. That is, the bridge computes the effect of the frame changes on the FCS and applies those changes to the FCS that was received. This approach is more complex, but provides superior error-detection; it is described more fully in [IEEE98a, Annex G]. Using this method, a bridge can protect against memory, bus, and design errors in the data paths from input to output port. What is still left unprotected is the circuitry used to compute the new FCS and (depending on the particular implementation) some of the circuitry used to communicate the changes made to the frame. This method is considerably less error prone than the first (simpler) method, where the entire frame contents and all of the memory and data paths within the bridge are exposed to undetected errors. The probability of undetected errors can thus be reduced to a negligible level.

3.1.3.3 Bit-Ordering

Most LAN technologies use some form of encoded serial transmission to exchange bits across the communications medium. That is, a sequence of bytes (or wider fields) meaningful to some higher-layer protocol or application is squeezed into a serial bit stream, transmitted across a medium, and reorganized into bytes at the receiving end for delivery to the peer entity. Two questions arise in the design of this process:

1. In what order should we send the bytes of the frame?
2. In what order should we send the bits within each byte?

The first question is rarely controversial at the Data Link layer; we send the first byte first, the second byte second, and so on. That is, the LAN interface takes a byte stream and transmits it on a first-come, first-served basis.[24]

The second question has two opposing camps: Those who send bits serially from the least-significant bit (LSB) to the most-significant bit (MSB) within a byte, and those who send bits serially from MSB to LSB. The former are known as *Little Endians*, the latter as *Big Endians*.[25] Figure 3.10 depicts these byte- and bit-ordering methods.

[24] The issue of byte-significance in numerical fields comprising more than 1 byte is of interest only to the higher-layer protocol, and can use whatever convention it chooses. Different clients of the Data Link can use different conventions (e.g., least-significant byte first or most-significant byte first) without conflict.

[25] The terms *Little Endian* and *Big Endian* for bit ordering were coined by Danny Cohen in his landmark paper, "On Holy Wars and a Plea for Peace," [COHE80] originally published in April 1980 and then in the *Communications of the Association for Computing Machinery.* It is widely available on the World Wide Web. The terms come from the eighteenth-century novel *Gulliver's Travels* by Jonathan Swift.

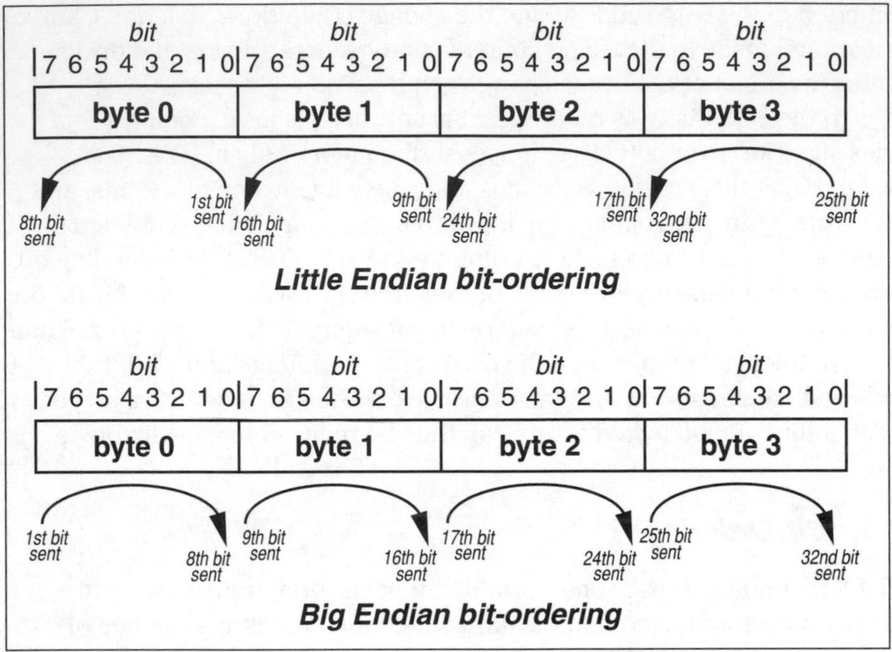

Figure 3.10 Bit-ordering.

Neither method is right or wrong. It is simply a convention; as long as everyone does it the same way, there should not be any argument over the interpretation of the bits within the bytes. The problem is that not everyone does it the same way! The vast majority of communications systems (including RS-232, Ethernet, and most other LANs) send bits in Little Endian order. Because of the extremely common use of Little Endian bit order, it is also referred to as *canonical format.* The notable exceptions are Token Ring and FDDI, which use Big Endian bit order for the data payload of the frame.[26] However, the MAC Destination and Source Address fields in a frame are not numerical fields, and so there is really no concept of least-significant bit or most-significant bit. An address is simply a string of 48 bits. When transmitted serially, the first bit must always be the unicast/multicast bit, the second bit the local/global bit, and so on, regardless of the endian-ness used for user data in the frame payload. A device may choose to store MAC addresses in internal memory in any fashion it chooses, as long as the bits are transmitted in the correct order on the underlying communications channel. To make the transmission of addresses and data payload fields consistent in Token Ring systems, most implementations store the address in bit-reversed order relative to an Ethernet.

[26] Maybe it's no coincidence that both of these are high speed token-passing systems; perhaps the bits got turned the other way from all that whirling around the rings. Maybe not.

SORTING OUT THE BIG ENDIAN VERSUS LITTLE ENDIAN ADDRESS CONFUSION

The subject of MAC addresses and endian-ness has been a source of confusion to many newcomers to networking. Let's take a concrete example and look at how it is handled in both an Ethernet and Token Ring station. Consider the 48-bit address AC-DE-48-03-67-80 (written in canonical format).

Regardless of the way the value may be stored in a station's memory, the bits will always be transmitted serially as:

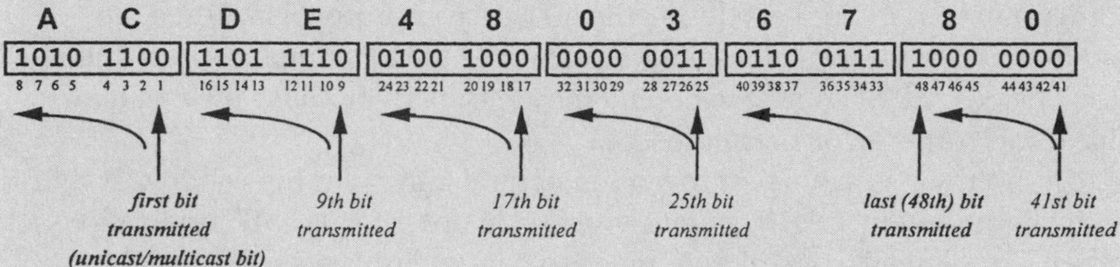

Ethernet devices transmit data in Little Endian bit order, so the address can most easily be stored in memory exactly as shown in the preceding schematic, with the least-significant bit being the rightmost bit in each byte.

Since Token Ring devices transmit data in Big Endian bit order, the same address can most easily be stored in memory as shown in the following schematic, with the least-significant bit being the leftmost bit in each byte:

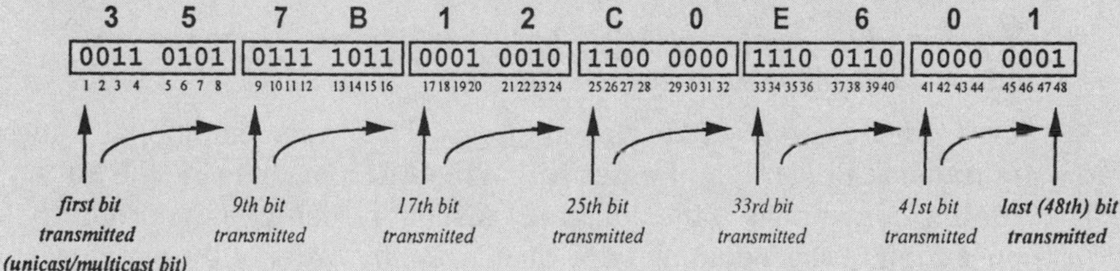

Note that the 48-bit sequence is exactly the same in both cases. An address is an address is an address. However, the apparent "numerical value" (i.e., how the address would look as a number if the bits had numerical significance) changes depending on how the field is stored in memory.

The address AC-DE-48-03-67-80 stored in Little Endian format is the exact same address as 35-7B-12-C0-E6-01 stored in Big Endian format. They are not different addresses, just different storage representations of the same address.

Network administrators of Ethernet networks most commonly write addresses assuming Little Endian (canonical) storage format. Network administrators of Token Ring networks normally write addresses assuming Big Endian storage format. You should always be aware of which format is being used.[27]

[27] In this book, addresses are always written in canonical format unless otherwise noted.

A problem arises when higher-layer protocols also need to exchange MAC address information embedded into the fields of the higher-layer message, unbeknownst to the underlying LAN. This is exemplified by the address resolution protocols used by IP (ARP) [RFC826, COME95] and AppleTalk (AARP) [APPL90]. A complete discussion of ARP and AppleTalk ARP is beyond the scope of this book; for the purposes of this discussion, the critical issue is that these protocols require a MAC address carried in the data payload portion of a frame to be exchanged between two devices that interpret bits in the opposite order. If the bridge simply "does its thing" (i.e., sends the frame in the bit order appropriate for each LAN), the higher-layer protocols will see the address in a bit-reversed fashion. This will result in communications failure; the devices will be unable to communicate properly because they will not have each other's correct addresses.

The solution is again to throw architectural purity out the window. It is critically important that ARP operate properly in order for TCP/IP applications to work, so we need to tweak the bridge to deal with this special case. Rather than simply forwarding the frames transparently, a transparent bridge that interconnects Ethernets with Token Rings and that needs to support TCP/IP applications (basically, any bridge with both an Ethernet and Token Ring interface), must:

- *Look specifically for ARP packets being transferred.* ARP packets are identified by the protocol type field on Ethernet or the SNAP protocol identifier on Token Ring.
- *Understand the syntax of ARP.* The bridge "knows" where the MAC address fields are within the ARP packet.
- *Correct the bit order in the address fields.* The bridge intentionally does not transmit the MAC addresses within the ARP packet using the bit-ordering convention of the outgoing LAN, but rather uses the ordering convention of the incoming LAN. That is, the bit order of these fields is maintained across LAN types. Note that this only affects the addresses that are encapsulated in the ARP packet; the rest of the fields are sent in the correct order for the outgoing LAN, as depicted in Figure 3.11.

Ethernet preceded Token Ring in the marketplace;[28] ARP was specifically designed to deal with the address mapping problem between 32-bit IP addresses and 48-bit Ethernet addresses. Bit-ordering only became a problem when Token Ring technology emerged a few years later and users tried to bridge between their Ethernets and Token Rings. FDDI technology (which is also Big Endian in nature) was developed in the late 1980s, after the ARP/bit-order problem was discovered with Token Ring. In an effort to avoid prolifer-

[28] Commercial 10 Mb/s Ethernet products were available as early as 1981. Commercial 4 Mb/s Token Ring products became available in 1985.

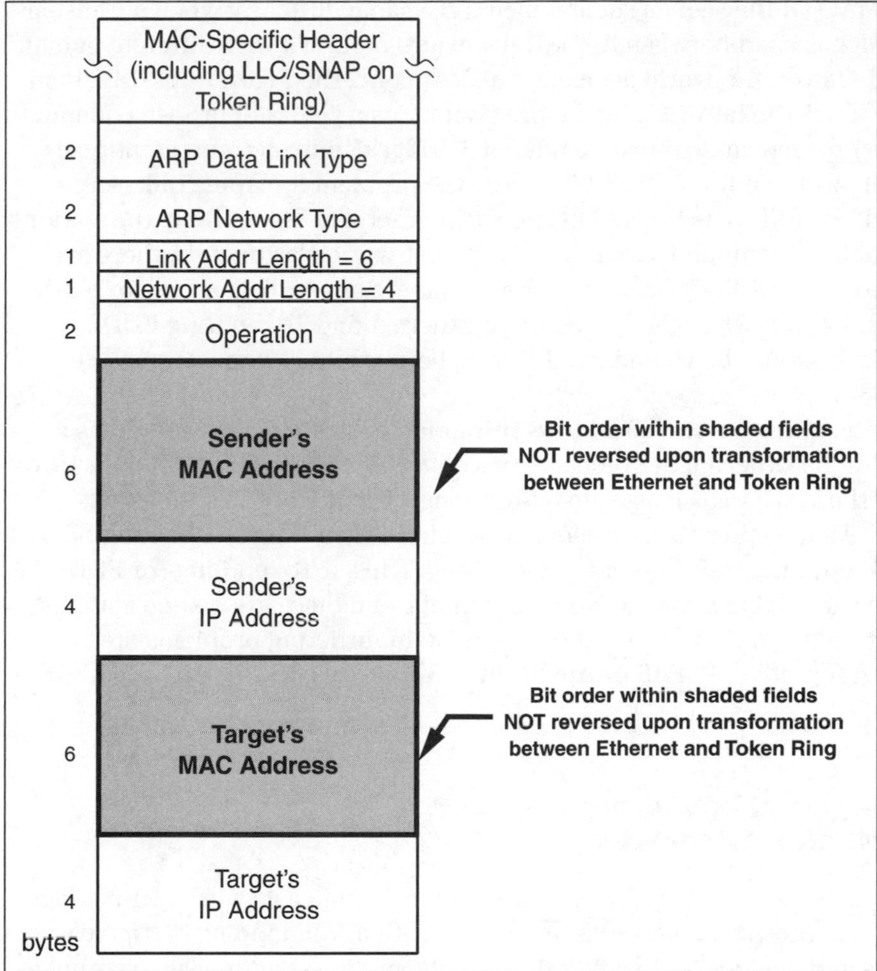

Figure 3.11 ARP transformation.

ating the (admittedly ugly) solution implemented for Token Ring–to–Ethernet bridging just described, the designers of TCP/IP chose to implement ARP on FDDI in a manner that preserves MAC address bit-order relative to Ethernet. That is, when ARP is used on a FDDI LAN, the MAC addresses in the ARP packet are inserted as if they were to be transmitted in Little Endian bit order, regardless of the fact that the underlying LAN is Big Endian [RFC1390]. Because of this, a bridge interconnecting FDDI and Ethernet does not need to treat ARP packets differently from any other; the algorithm described above for Token Ring bridging is unnecessary.

In the AppleTalk protocol suite, AppleTalk ARP provides the same function as does ARP for TCP/IP; it maps 24-bit AppleTalk Network layer addresses to

48-bit MAC addresses. As such, it incurs the same difficulty when a transparent bridge is used between AppleTalk devices on LANs with different endianness. However, the world is, in general, less concerned with AppleTalk than with TCP/IP; the latter is much more popular as a general-purpose communications protocol suite. Most commercial bridges address (pun intentional) the ARP problem for TCP/IP, but ignore the problem for AppleTalk. As a result, if AppleTalk is bridged between Ethernet and Token Ring, the stations are unable to communicate. It simply doesn't work. Fortunately, there are very few AppleTalk devices with direct connections to Token Ring or FDDI LANs; however, when there is a mix of Ethernet and Token Ring/FDDI, AppleTalk should be routed, not bridged, between the two networks[29] [SEIF93].

An interesting twist: The address resolution problem occurs if there is a change in bit-ordering between stations on transparently bridged LANs. However, if there are *two* changes in bit-ordering, then the problem doesn't occur![30] That is, there is a problem in bridging Token Ring to Ethernet, but not from Token Ring-to-Ethernet-to-Token Ring. Thus, if Token Ring (or FDDI) is being used as a backbone between Ethernets, and there are no end stations directly connected to the backbone, then no bit-ordering problems are incurred for either TCP/IP or AppleTalk. Two wrongs do sometimes make a right![31]

3.1.3.4 Functional Groups versus True Multicast Addressing

As discussed in Chapter 1, LAN addresses can be unicast (with a 1:1 mapping between address and device) or multicast (with a 1:*n* mapping between address and devices). When first devised, the multicast addressing was not a widely understood mechanism. Most network architects understood how unicast addresses would be used, and broadcast (a multicast signifying the set of all stations on the LAN) was available in many technologies, but a generalized multicast address representing an arbitrary set of devices was not a commonly available construct.[32]

[29] Note that, unlike TCP/IP, AppleTalk incurs the bit ordering problem when either Token Ring or FDDI is bridged to Ethernet.
[30] To be precise, there is no problem for any even number of changes in bit-ordering.
[31] Even if two wrongs don't make a right, three lefts always do.
[32] In fact, many network architects, including the designers of many of the support protocols for TCP/IP, ignored generalized multicast and relied on the old-fashioned broadcast address for protocols such as ARP and RIP. This is much less efficient for end stations, as all devices needed to receive and interpret these packets, only to throw them away if they did not support the protocol in question.

Two schools of thought emerged for the use of multicast addressing:

- In the Ethernet world, multicast addressing was treated as a logical address space perfectly parallel to the unicast space. That is, a 48-bit address provided for 2^{47} unicast addresses (when the first bit was 0) and 2^{47} multicast addresses (when the first bit was 1). Any of these 2^{47} multicast addresses could be used for any purpose whatsoever. This is referred to as *true multicast addressing*, and was the original intent of the address design [DALA81].
- In the Token Ring world, true multicast addressing was possible, but generally avoided. Instead, Token Ring networks used a concept called Functional Group addressing, where each bit of the multicast address represented a specific function and a device could subscribe to that function by recognizing frames that had that particular bit set in the Destination Address field. A multicast group could be assigned to any bit in the address field and used for any purpose. In theory, functional group addressing allows a total of only 47 possible multicast addresses, one for each available bit. In practice (due to the encoding), only 31 such Functional Group addresses are available, as depicted in Figure 3.12.

A Functional Group address is encoded as a locally-administered (manually configured) multicast, with the most-significant bit of the third byte equal to 0, as shown in Figure 3.12. Functional Group addressing is used exclusively on Token Ring networks; it is not supported on Ethernet. Thus, the semantics of a multicast address change when bridging between a Token Ring and an Ethernet. For example, the multicast address used to indicate "All AppleTalk Stations" is different on an Ethernet (0x09-00-07-FF-FF-FF, in Little Endian format) than on a Token Ring (0xC0-00-40-00-00-00, in Big Endian format). Similarly, AppleTalk can support up to 253 network "zones" on an Ethernet

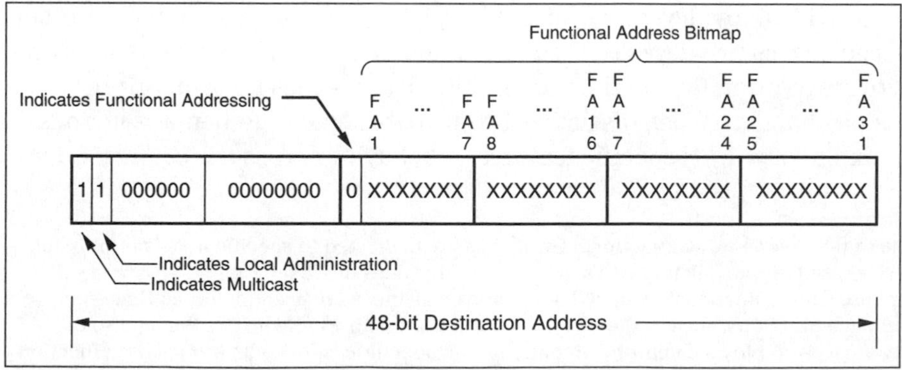

Figure 3.12 Functional group addressing.

(using 253 different multicast addresses), but only 19 zones on a Token Ring, due to the limited addressing provided by Functional Groups.[33]

A bridge that interconnects Ethernet(s) and Token Ring(s) must translate between the multicast address formats used on the two different LANs. Functional Group addresses are (for the most part) manually-administered; therefore, the mapping between all multicast addresses used in the catenet must be manually configured in each of the bridges interconnecting Token Ring LANs to other types. This is a tedious process at best.[34]

Why use functional addresses at all? When a meaning is assigned to each bit of the address (as opposed to all 48 bits taken together), the address decode function is easier to implement in hardware. A device that wants to receive frames for a set of multicast groups needs only to apply a bit mask to the destination address in received frames. The station looks at those functional group bits corresponding to the multicast groups of interest, and receives the frame if any of those bits is equal to 1. This requires much less hardware than is needed to decode a set of true multicast addresses; only a single 48-bit comparator is required to support functional group addresses, as opposed to a 48-bit comparator for each address when using true multicast.[35] Thus, functional group addressing allows for simpler hardware at the expense of limiting the number of available multicast groups and requiring manual administration of multicast addresses. While this tradeoff may have seemed appropriate in the mid-1980s, when hardware was much more expensive, most architects today would opt for the larger address space and ease of application use afforded by true multicast. The additional hardware complexity is insignificant with modern silicon technology.

3.1.3.5 LAN-Specific Features

Some LAN technologies exhibit (or at least claim to exhibit) unique features and behaviors specific to those technologies. For example, Token Ring networks provide a low-level mechanism for priority access; a station can obtain preferred access privileges (i.e., get the token more often) by manipulating the priority reservation field in the frame. Ethernet provides no such priority-access mechanism. When dissimilar LANs are bridged together, it is not possible to extend any LAN-specific features or behavior across the catenet. Such

[33] Some of the remaining 30 Functional Group bits are dedicated to specific non-AppleTalk functions, restricting AppleTalk usage to a maximum of 19 zones on Token Ring.
[34] There are a few Functional Groups that are universal; these are used for Token Ring–specific maintenance functions, such as the Active Monitor, Configuration Report Server, and so on.
[35] Many devices employ a compromise solution for true multicast decode, using a hash function with imperfect multicast filtering. The hardware complexity is comparable to that required for Functional Group address decode, but the results must still be examined by software, resulting in some performance degradation.

Table 3.4 A and C Bit Semantics

A	C	INTERPRETATION
0	0	No intended receiver recognized the frame as being destined for itself.
1	0	An intended receiver recognized the frame as being destined for itself, but did not have a buffer available to store it.
1	1	An intended receiver recognized the frame as being destined for itself and copied it into a buffer.
0	1	Error (this encoding is not used).

features can only be provided on the local LAN. Unfortunately, the bridge is transparent; a station on a LAN may *think* that it can depend on some particular feature of the technology to which it is directly connected and not realize that these features are lost when the frames cross the bridge. Remember, you only get the intersection of the features (the lowest common denominator).

3.1.3.5.1 Address Recognized (A) and Frame Copied (C) Bits

Token Ring and FDDI LANs provide a low-level acknowledgment mechanism. Unlike the case with Ethernet, on a ring network a transmitting station receives its own transmissions once they have circulated around the LAN. The Token Ring and FDDI MACs provide a pair of bits that allow the other stations on the ring to furnish some feedback regarding frame reception back to the sender of the frame.[36] The indications provided are embodied by the Address Recognized (A) and Frame Copied (C) bits in the End Delimiter (Token Ring) or Frame Status fields (FDDI).

These bits are always transmitted as 0 by the sending station. If any station on the ring recognizes its address in the Destination Address field of the frame, it sets the A bit to 1 as the frame passes by. If the station is also able to copy the frame into a local buffer, it sets the C bit as well.[37] Thus, when the frame arrives back at the sender, the status of the frame can be inferred from the A and C bits as shown in Table 3.4.

The A and C bits thus provide a low-level acknowledgment mechanism on a Token Ring or FDDI LAN. In the old days, device drivers for Token Ring networks would check these bits and initiate retransmission (often many times, if

[36] These bits are sent multiple times in Token Ring, for increased reliability, as they are not protected by the FCS.

[37] Note that in the case of a multicast destination, these bits can only indicate that at least one receiver properly recognized its address and/or copied the frame. There is no assurance that all members of the multicast group properly received the frame. Thus, the indicators are really only useful for unicast transmissions. Reliable multicast delivery is a much more complex problem.

necessary) if the A and C bits were not both set (indicating successful reception by the target). On the surface, this would seem to be a reasonable strategy.

Unfortunately, bridges complicate matters. (What else is new?) Consider the situation depicted in Figure 3.13. When station X sends its frame, what should the bridge do with the A and C bits? There are really three possible strategies:

1. *Leave the A and C bits alone (i.e., don't set them) on any frame.* Since the bridge is not the intended destination for the frame (the bridge is receiving it solely to consider forwarding it to another port), this is the strictly proper action, based on the stated semantics of the A and C bits. Unfortunately, if the device driver in station X is using a policy of continued retransmission until the A and C bits are set (or until some timer expires), this will cause a flood of retransmissions for every frame.
2. *Set the A and C bits for every frame that passes by.* This is simple for the bridge to do, and ensures that the sending station will not retransmit any frames. However, it gives a false sense of security; Station X is convinced that every frame is being properly received (regardless of

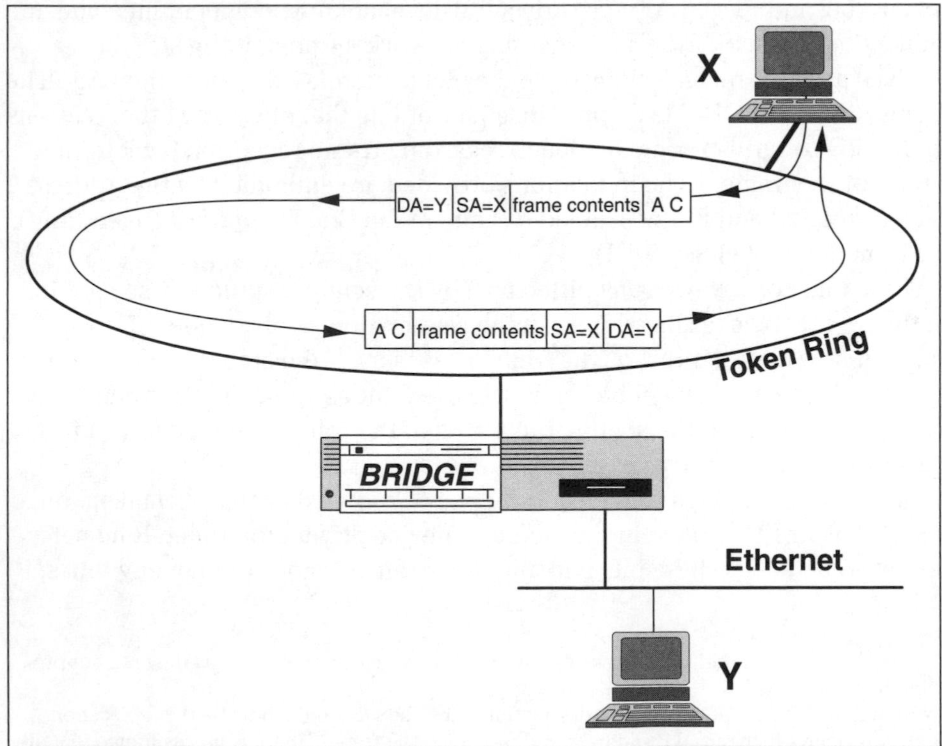

Figure 3.13 Dealing with the A and C bits.

whether the destination is on the local ring or not). This policy effectively nullifies any legitimate use of the A and C bits as intended.

3. *Set the A and/or C bits only for frames that the bridge must forward to another port.* This would seem a prudent middle ground; the bridge would set the bits as a proxy for the intended receiver on another port. There are a few problems with this approach, however:
   - Station X will think that station Y has properly received and buffered the frame, while it is only the bridge that has done so. Station Y may not even exist!
   - The bridge will have to set the bits for all unknown unicast destinations, again providing a misleading indication to station X about the status of the frame.
   - Most important, the bridge must complete its table lookup and make the forwarding determination before the frame has passed by. The A and C bits are contained in the End Delimiter/Frame Status field at the tail of the frame. For a passing frame with a very short data field, this is an extreme time constraint on bridge performance.

It is this last issue that makes the third policy unworkable. The bottom line is that the A and C bit mechanism doesn't work in a bridged catenet. Worse, since stations on a LAN cannot know (without manual configuration) whether they are on a stand-alone LAN or are part of a larger catenet (the bridges are, after all, transparent), the A and C bit acknowledgment mechanism really cannot be used at all.[38] Most modern device drivers and network protocol suites completely ignore these bits, but there was a painful transition period between the old days and modern times.

The standard [IEEE98a] neatly ducks the issue of what a bridge should do:

> The Address Recognized (A) bits . . . may be set to 1 . . . otherwise the A bits shall not be set. . . . If the A bits are set to 1, the Frame Copied (C) bits may be set to 1 to reflect the availability of receive buffering; otherwise the C bits shall not be set.

In essence, a bridge can do whatever it wants with the A and C bits and be compliant, other than setting C without setting A.

3.1.3.5.2 Bounded Latency

One of the popular beliefs about Token Ring and FDDI LANs is that they provide a degree of bounded latency. If each station has some maximum length of

[38] Some early Network Operating System implementations relied heavily on the A and C bit mechanism on Token Ring LANs, initiating repeated retransmissions when not properly set by a receiving station. This caused total failure of end user networks when transparent bridges were introduced.

time that it is allowed to transmit, then for a given number of stations on the LAN, each station can expect to get the token (permission to transmit) within a bounded time roughly equal to the maximum transmission time multiplied by the number of stations.[39]

Putting aside the question of whether the bounded latency assumption is valid,[40] any such latency bound is lost when frames cross a transparent bridge in the catenet. The station on the ring LAN may still get to transmit its frames within the specified bound, but there may be considerable delay before the intended recipient receives the frames. From an application perspective, it is irrelevant that a frame was sent if it is languishing in a bridge's buffer memory. The reason why a network application designer uses a LAN with bounded latency is because the demands of the application are such that there is a need to exchange information in a timely fashion (i.e., not longer than the upper bound provided by the network). Bridges remove this upper bound (or at least increase it by orders of magnitude); an application depending on real-time exchanges (on the order of the latency bound) will be disappointed with the service provided through a bridged catenet.

3.1.4 Thoughts on Bridging Dissimilar LANs

If all of these discussions make it sound like bridging dissimilar LANs is a Bad Thing™, then I have made myself clear. Such bridges "work," but only in very specialized environments and with all of the constraints discussed earlier. In general, a bridged catenet comprising heterogeneous LAN technologies requires careful planning and management by a network administrator. A good rule of thumb is:

Never, never bridge dissimilar LANs unless you really, really, have to.[41]

In general, it is usually more appropriate to use a Network layer router to interconnect dissimilar LANs. Routers may be more expensive and/or complex, but the problems of dissimilar LAN interconnection are handled more easily at the Network layer, where the end station can be better insulated from the vagaries of the interconnection technologies. An even better approach is to use one LAN technology consistently across the organization, simplifying the operation of both bridges and routers wherever they are used.

[39] This is true only for stations operating at the highest access priority. Lower priority stations can be delayed beyond this bound by sustained high priority accesses from other stations. It is partly for this reason that virtually all traffic on Token Ring LANs is sent at the highest user priority available. Of course, if everyone is at the highest priority, priority becomes meaningless.

[40] Such discussions generally get much too loud and require too much beer to be included here.

[41] See [HEIM83] for a discussion of this concept applied to a somewhat different decision!

3.2 Bridging between Local and Wide Area Networks

In the first section, we considered the local interconnection of LANs using dissimilar technologies. In this next section, we look at interconnecting remote LANs through an intervening Wide Area Network (WAN). While admittedly not a trivial task, bridging between LAN and WAN technologies is in many ways easier than bridging between dissimilar LANs. The problems and issues have more to do with the impact on application performance and vendor interoperability than with any particular implementation difficulty. In addition, WAN links are commonly used to interconnect bridges solely to other bridges; we generally do not need to consider direct end station attachments to a WAN link.

3.2.1 Applications of Remote Bridges

Up to now, all of the LANs in our catenets were assumed to be in the same place geographically; the bridged LAN environment spanned a building or a small campus. However, it is also possible to use transparent bridges to interconnect LANs in geographically-separate locations, using intermediate WAN communications links between bridges, as depicted in Figure 3.14.[42]

There are many environments where such interconnections may be appropriate:

- An organization has multiple campuses with many users at each site, all requiring intercommunications for various applications.
- The enterprise has a central campus and some number of remote branch offices, each requiring connectivity back to the central organization.
- The organization needs to support individuals working from remote sites, for example telecommuters or traveling employees.[43]

Each application scenario places different demands upon the communication links used for the remote interconnection.

[42] Remote interconnection can often be accomplished using either Data Link layer bridges or Network layer routers. The discussion in this chapter on the differences between LAN and WAN technology, and the decisions related to technology selection, are applicable both to the use of bridges or routers. The question of bridging versus routing is discussed in Chapter 4, *Principles of LAN Switches*.

[43] This application can often be treated as if it were a very small branch office; it is sometimes referred to as a "branch of one."

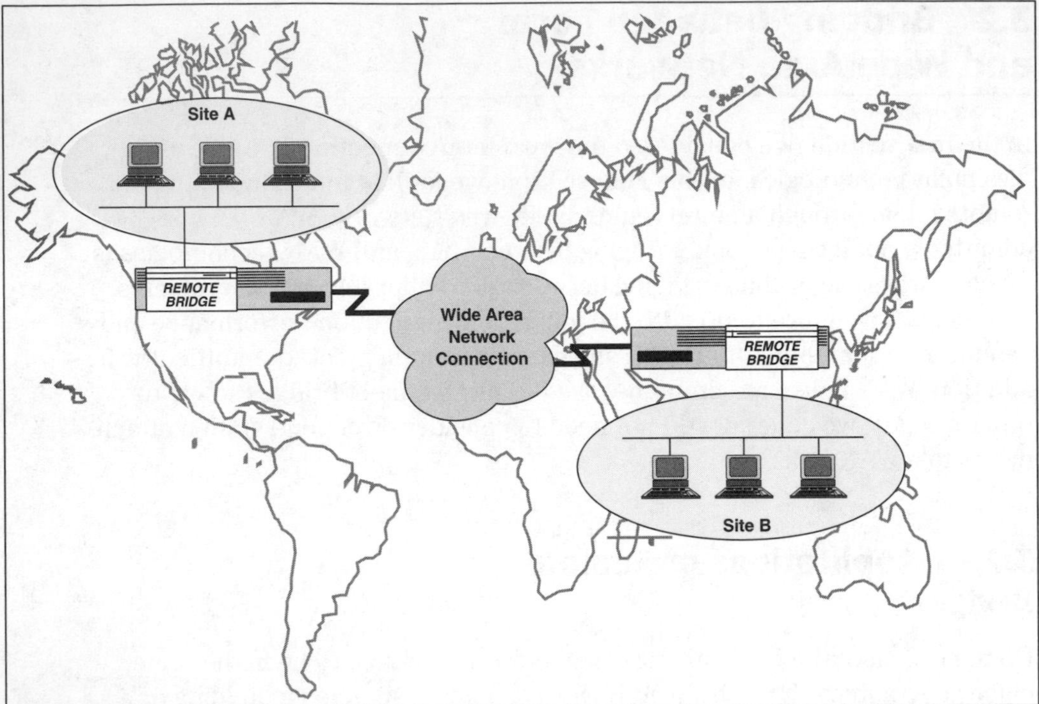

Figure 3.14 WAN interconnection using remote bridges.

3.2.2 Technologies for Remote Bridges

There are some key differences between the technologies used in LANs and WANs. Both the technology differences and the differing application requirements will affect any decision to use (or not to use) some particular technology. Some important factors affecting the technology decision include:

- *Data rate.* In general, WAN links offer significantly lower data rates than the LANs they interconnect. While LANs may operate at 10, 100, or 1000 Mb/s or more, the typical remote bridge link operates at a raw data rate on the order of 1 to 2 Mb/s (T1/E1/Frame Relay); many operate at submegabit data rates. While higher rate links are available, their cost tends to be prohibitive for all but the most demanding applications.
- *Error rate.* The error rates experienced on a WAN link are typically orders-of-magnitude worse than those of LANs (see Section 3.2.4.1). This can have an impact on the behavior of higher-layer protocols and applications that may be assuming the low frame loss rates associated with LAN links.

- *Cost.* On a LAN, bandwidth is essentially free. Once the LAN is installed, there is no recurring cost to use the available capacity (other than for personnel and equipment to maintain the network, which is needed independent of whether the technology is LAN or WAN). WAN links (other than privately-owned lines and/or satellites, which are relatively uncommon) generally must be leased from a service provider. That provider has invested capital in the installation of the lines and supporting equipment, and levies a charge appropriate to recover those costs plus maintenance expenses and profit. Thus, while in a LAN bandwidth is free, WAN bandwidth costs money. Typically, the cost is a function of both the data rate and the distance being spanned.

Table 3.5 provides a comparison of many of the popular WAN technologies as related to their use for remote bridge applications.

3.2.3 Encapsulation

While it is possible to translate between native frame formats when bridging between dissimilar LANs, this is not true when bridging to conventional WANs. This is because the WAN technologies used for remote bridge interconnection do not directly support 48-bit globally-unique addressing. That is, there is no way to transform a LAN frame into a WAN frame without losing some of the information necessary to deliver it to its intended recipient. As a result, we invariably encapsulate (as opposed to translate) LAN frames into a format suitable for transmission across the WAN.[44]

In the old days, the most popular format for data transmission across the synchronous serial technologies commonly used for WANs was borrowed from the High-Level Data Link Control (HDLC) protocol [ISO93, ANSI79]. HDLC normally provides mechanisms for:

- Delimiting the frame within the synchronous bit stream (framing)
- Addressing stations on the link
- Connection-oriented link control, flow control, and error control

Remote bridges are usually deployed on statically-configured point-to-point links, and the LAN technologies being bridged already have their own address information. Thus, it was generally unnecessary to use the HDLC address and/or link control fields. In addition, the complexity and delay imposed by

[44] One exception is Switched Multi-Megabit Data Service (SMDS), which actually does support 48 bit IEEE-style addresses. SMDS thus appears like a very long-distance LAN, making it possible to build a true translational bridge between a LAN and an SMDS WAN. The problem is that SMDS is virtually non-existent in practice.

Table 3.5 Comparison of WAN Technologies for Remote Bridges

TECHNOLOGY	TYPICAL USE	DATA RATE	COST	COMMENTS
Point-to-point privately-owned lines	Within a single organization, across a large campus or metropolitan area. Copper connections provide lower data rate; fiber can be used to 2.5 Gb/s or more. Some municipalities may have "dark fiber" available for more extensive connections.	1.5, 45, 100, 155, 622 Mb/s; 1, 2.5 Gb/s.	Installation only. No recurring costs.	Requires ownership of right-of-way privileges for installation.
Point-to-point leased lines	Site interconnection for short-to-moderate distances and limited number of sites.	56 kb/s–1.5, 2, 34, 45, 155 Mb/s common. 622 Mb/s and 2.4 Gb/s becoming available.	Based on data rate and distance.	Longer distances typically use frame relay service rather than dedicated links.
Frame Relay Service	For cost-effective long distance interconnection, especially when many sites are involved.	1.5 Mb/s (and lower), 45 Mb/s.	Based on raw data rate (burst rate), Committed Information Rate (CIR), and number of virtual circuits provided.	Requires leased line from user's site to service provider's Point of Presence (POP).
Asynchronous Transfer Mode (ATM) Service	Very high speed site interconnection.	1.5, 155, 622 Mb/s.	Highly variable; depends on individual carrier's pricing structure.	Appears as a virtual point-to-point link to the user. Limited availability.

ISDN	Site interconnection, branch office interconnection, and telecommuting applications where data rate is not critical.	64 or 128 kb/s.	Based on data rate and connect time.	Not popular for bridges today, due to difficulties of setting up and tearing down connections and mapping addresses to phone numbers. More commonly used for branch office routing.
Satellite	Very high speed connections over very long (global) distances.	1.5–10+ Mb/s.	Highly variable; depends on nature of specific service being provided.	May use a shared channel or dedicated channel (or transponder), depending on need.
Microwave/Infrared	Point-to-point interconnection over short-to-moderate distances (metropolitan area).	1–10+ Mb/s.	Installation only. No recurring costs.	Useful for crossing public right-of-way. Characteristics may vary with atmospheric conditions.

HDLC Flow and Error Control was inappropriate for a remote bridge application. All that was really needed was the HDLC framing mechanism.[45]

Figure 3.15 depicts a common method of LAN frame encapsulation using HDLC-like framing as implemented by early remote bridges. The FLAG fields denoted the start and/or end of the frame; within the encapsulated frame, *bit stuffing* was used to ensure that the FLAG character never appeared as part of the data payload. While never a formal standard, this encapsulation was quite popular, primarily due to its simplicity.

As internetworking products matured during the 1990s, the Point-to-Point Protocol (PPP) [RFC1661] was developed to meet the need for a more general encapsulation mechanism. PPP provides:

- Support for a single device encapsulating multiple protocols across a WAN link
- Vendor interoperability across a WAN link
- Error detection

PPP does not explicitly provide any mechanism for frame delimiting on a synchronous link. Thus, PPP frames are typically encapsulated within an HDLC frame to obtain the benefit of HDLC frame delimiters and bit stuffing. Figure 3.15 depicts the typical PPP encapsulation used on synchronous serial links.

While PPP was actually designed to support interoperable multiprotocol routing across a WAN, it has become the most popular method for encapsulating native LAN frames between remote bridges. In fact, it is fairly common for a single device to be routing some protocols and bridging others across the same WAN link, using PPP encapsulation for all transmissions.

3.2.4 Issues in Remote Bridges

While remote bridges "work," in the sense that they can provide the ability to transparently interconnect geographically dispersed users, they do have an effect on application behavior and performance. As discussed in Chapter 2, even a LAN-to-LAN bridge impacts the soft invariants of the Data Link; the use of intermediate WAN links can stretch these soft invariant behaviors even further, sometimes beyond the limit of usefulness. While higher-layer protocols are usually designed to tolerate worse performance from LANs than what the LANs actually provide, the use of remote bridges can make it more difficult to meet even the minimal performance demands of some higher layer entities.

[45] While most bridges employed just the framing aspects of HDLC, many modern bridges can be configured to use the full HDLC protocol, including support for link flow and error control.

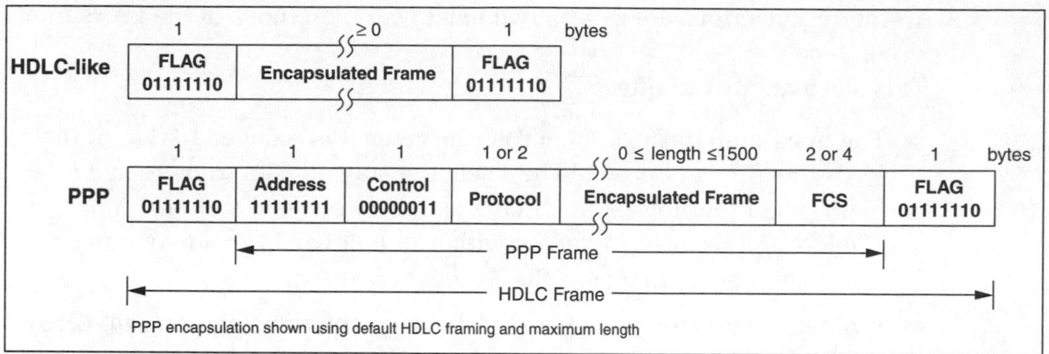

Figure 3.15 WAN encapsulations.

3.2.4.1 *Error Rate*

LANs provide very low error rates, typically on the order of 1×10^{-12} or better (see Chapter 2). Such low rates are possible because of the high quality cables, short cable lengths, and the relatively benign environment common to LANs. WAN links traverse much longer distances, must endure environmental stresses due to their exposure to the outside world, and often must pass through many devices (e.g., telephone switching equipments) between their end points. All of these factors account for a greater residual error rate in the underlying channel.

The most commonly used technologies (e.g., T-carrier links as used for Frame Relay service) provide error rates orders of magnitude worse than those of the typical LAN. However, there is little that can be done, other than to grin and bear it. While it is possible to use an error detection/retransmission scheme on the WAN link (e.g., HDLC error control), such protocols generally incur unacceptable delay when an error does occur. It's like squeezing a sausage; you can pull it in one place, but it pops out somewhere else.

On channels with extremely poor error performance (e.g., satellites), a forward error-correction scheme is often used. This allows error correction to occur transparently to the service using the channel, with little delay, at the expense of reducing the channel capacity.

3.2.4.2 *LAN Bandwidth and Delay*

Network designers are always balancing a three-way tradeoff among capacity, distance, and cost. It is always possible to get higher capacity at lower cost within a LAN than across a WAN, because the distances are so much shorter. To achieve the longer distances of a WAN, the user is forced either to accept a lower data rate or to pay more money. As a result, the link data rates used for

WAN interconnections are generally much lower than those of the LANs they interconnect.

This has a number of effects:

- The maximum throughput across the catenet is reduced to that of the WAN link. It is not possible to achieve sustained data transfer at a rate higher than the slowest link in the path between end stations. A pair of 100 Mb/s LANs interconnected with a T1 link will have a maximum throughput equal to that of the T1 link (1.5 Mb/s).
- Frame delivery delay is increased, because the transmission rate across the WAN link is less than that of the LANs; that is, it simply takes more time to transmit a frame on a slow link than on a fast one. A maximum-length Ethernet frame requires 120 μs for transmission on a 100 Mb/s Ethernet; on a T1 link the same frame takes 7.9 ms—an increase by a factor of 66.
- Since the WAN link is likely to be a bottleneck for traffic flow, delay is further increased due to queuing within the remote bridge. During periods of congestion, frames will spend longer periods of time in the remote bridge waiting for transmission onto the WAN link. This can impose delays on the order of tens-to-hundreds of milliseconds, depending on the level of congestion and the data rate of the WAN link.

Thus, the introduction of WAN technologies can both decrease the bandwidth as well as increase the delay across the catenet. At a minimum, this will reduce application performance. Whether it will cause application failure depends on the application itself.

Some higher-layer protocols were designed specifically to operate over local networks and are inherently delay-sensitive. Two examples are NetBIOS/NetBEUI and DEC LAT. Both protocols can provide efficient service when used on high-speed, low delay channels. In order to react quickly to problems, both protocols use fairly short timers for their internal error and flow control mechanisms. When a WAN link is introduced into a transparently bridged catenet, the added delay can (in some cases) cause total failure of these protocols. Worse, if the delays are highly variable (e.g., as a result of transient congestion), the behavior of applications using these protocols may be intermittently unacceptable and difficult to diagnose.

Various fixes have been attempted, including "spoofing" the protocols by having the bridge respond to the stations as a proxy for the real protocol partner across the WAN. However, like putting a Band-Aid on a broken leg, these fixes simply mask the fundamental underlying problem; we are trying to run an application in an environment different from that for which it was designed. The results are rarely satisfying. In the end, we must trade off performance and cost against the benefits of transparent remote bridging.

3.2.5 IEEE 802.1G—Not!

In 1989, the IEEE 802.1 Working Group started a Task Force to address issues related to remote bridging. Ideally, this group should have produced a standard to allow vendor-interoperable bridging across WAN links, addressing all of the encapsulation, performance, and behavioral issues just discussed. Unfortunately, this group chose to ignore all of the issues considered important by users, and instead produced a standard (IEEE 802.1G) [IEEE98c] that has little if any value [SEIF90]. What IEEE 802.1G provides is:

- An architectural framework for describing Remote Bridged LANs
- Interoperability with existing, IEEE 802.1D LAN bridges
- An optional extension to the Spanning Tree Protocol (See Chapter 5, *Loop Resolution*) for use on WAN links

None of the fundamental problems of remote bridges are solved by the standard. It doesn't even provide a standardized means of encapsulating LAN frames for transmission on WAN links.[46] As a result, few people outside of the standards committee have ever heard of this standard.

[46] At the time the IEEE 802.1G Task Force was working on the standard, PPP had not yet become widely used, and interoperable encapsulation of frames between remote bridges was a real problem that should have been addressed by the committee. By the time the standard was published in 1998, PPP had become the de facto standard for WAN encapsulation (neither aided nor supported by 802.1G), rendering this issue moot.

CHAPTER 4

Principles of LAN Switches

Those of you who read the preface before starting in on the rest of the book have been primed for what happens now. (After this, I bet you'll read the preface of the next book you buy.) Here we are, in Chapter 4 of a book about LAN switches, and all we've talked about so far are bridges. When do we get to the switching stuff?

Well, we already did, but you didn't realize it. Those of you who read the preface and followed its instructions are excused from the homework assignment.

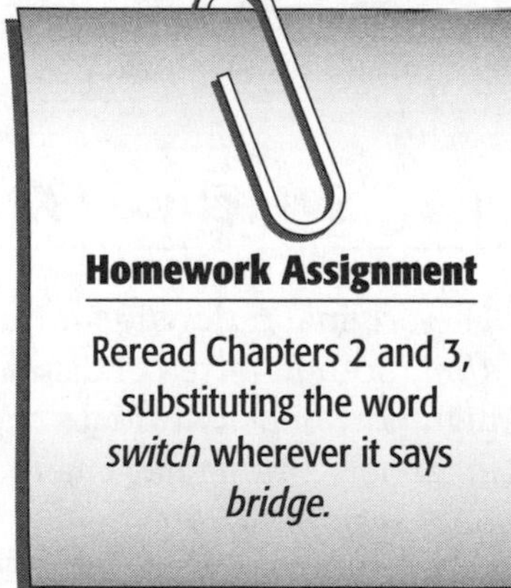

Homework Assignment
Reread Chapters 2 and 3, substituting the word *switch* wherever it says *bridge.*

4.1 A Switch Is a Bridge Is a Switch

LAN bridges have been commercially available since 1984.[1] For most of their early life, bridges were used to segment LANs, extend their distance, and increase the number of devices allowed beyond the limitations of a shared-bandwidth segment.

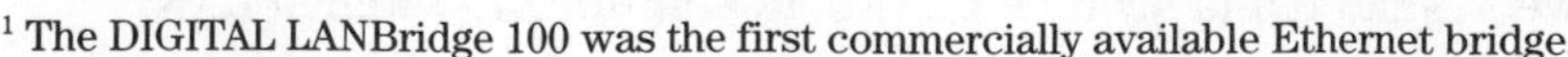
[1] The DIGITAL LANBridge 100 was the first commercially available Ethernet bridge.

Early LAN bridges rarely had more than two ports. Performance of these bridges was limited by the (now viewed as) primitive hardware and software capabilities available at the time. Many bridges sold in the old days could not support even two ports at wire-speed. Those that did support wire-speed operation commanded a premium price. Increasing the number of ports on these bridges did not make much sense, as the performance was usually limited not by the LAN attachments but by the internal bridging capacity. It simply was impractical to build high port-density bridges until the semiconductor technology advanced to bring the price point down to commercial reality.

During the 1990s, this is exactly what happened. Application-Specific Integrated Circuit (ASIC), processor, and memory technology advanced to the point where it was feasible to build LAN bridges with large numbers of ports capable of forwarding frames at wire-speed on all ports. Bridges built this way were marketed as *switches*. It is important to note that the distinction between a bridge and a switch is a marketing distinction, not a technical one. The functions performed by a switch are identical to those performed by a bridge; a switch *is* a bridge. Marketers chose to call their products switches primarily to differentiate them from the (more primitive) bridges of old.

In this book, the terms *bridge* and *switch* are used interchangeably. More consideration is paid to the application environment than the functional behavior of the device. That is, when talking about high port-density bridges used in modern applications, we generally call them switches, and refer to the environment as a *switched LAN*. Similarly, we use the term *switching hub* to refer to a geographically central device that performs the bridging function among its ports. This is in contrast to the traditional shared LAN, and is discussed in the following text. This usage of the terminology is consistent with common industry practice.

4.2 Switched LAN Concepts

The original rationale for the development of LAN bridges was LAN *extension*, both in terms of distance and numbers of stations. With the advent of high-port-density bridges capable of wire-speed operation, a new paradigm for local networking has emerged: the switched LAN, whose primary rationale is LAN *segmentation*.

A switched LAN is an alternative to a traditional shared-bandwidth LAN. In terms of product deployment in a structured wiring environment, the only apparent difference is that the hub is a switching hub (bridge) rather than a shared hub (repeater). The behavior of the network changes considerably, however, between shared and switched LANs. In addition, a switched LAN offers the possibility of configurations that were not available to the shared LAN user. As usual, all of this comes at a price.

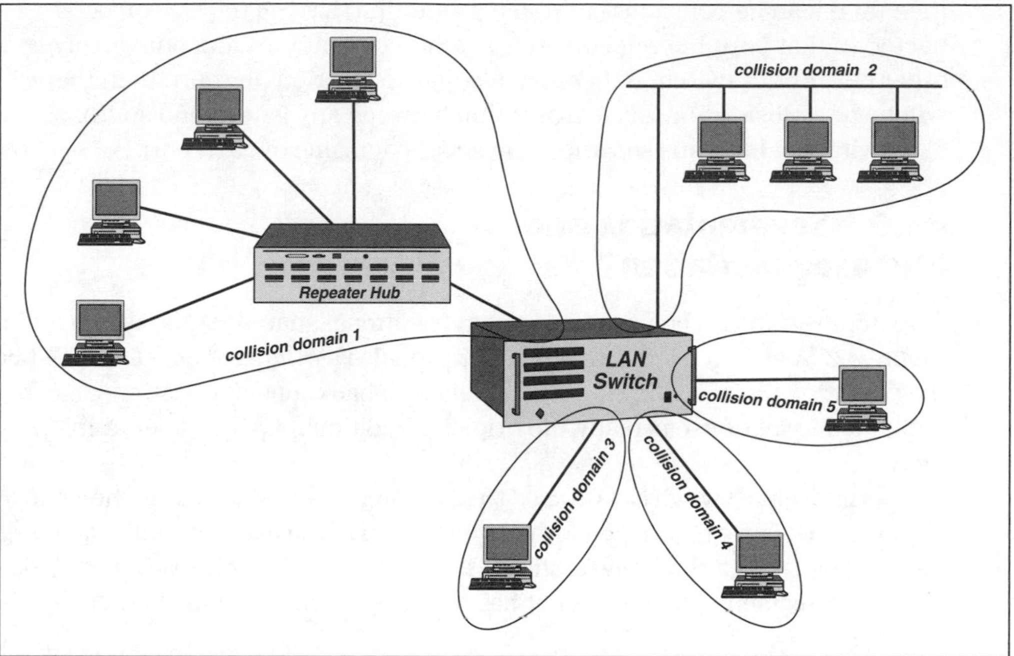

Figure 4.1 Collision domains.

4.2.1 Separate Access Domains

In a shared Ethernet LAN, the CSMA/CD MAC algorithm is used to arbitrate for use of the shared channel. If two or more stations have frames queued for transmission at the same time, there will be a collision among them. The set of stations contending for access to a shared Ethernet LAN is known as a *collision domain*. Similarly, the set of stations contending for the use of a token on a token-passing LAN can be referred to as a *token domain*. Both are examples of *access domains*—the set of stations sharing a given LAN and arbitrating among themselves using whatever access control mechanism is appropriate for that LAN.

As shown in Figure 4.1, stations in the same collision domain can experience access contention, with the resulting collision and backoff. Stations in separate collision domains do not contend for access to a common channel, and so do not experience collisions among themselves.[2]

In a switched LAN, each switch port is the terminus for the access domain associated with that port. If there is a shared LAN attached to a given port,

[2] While the figure and the ensuing discussion use the context of collision domains on Ethernet, an exactly analogous situation exists for token-passing (or any other shared) LANs. Stations in the same token domain must arbitrate among themselves for LAN usage using the token-passing access control mechanism. Stations in separate token domains (i.e., connected to different Token Ring switch ports) do not have to arbitrate for use of a shared channel.

then there can be collisions (or token arbitration) among the stations connected to that port, but not between a station on that port and one on any other port of the switch. If there is only one end station per port, then there will be no collisions or token arbitration between any pair of end stations.

A switching hub thus separates the access domains of each port.

4.2.2 Segmentation and Microsegmentation

A switching hub can be used to segment traditional shared LANs, as shown in Figure 4.2. A switch used in this manner provides a *collapsed backbone.*[3] While the performance of switches used in collapsed backbone applications may be high, the model of use is really the original, traditional LAN segmentation model.

Alternatively, a switch can be used to interconnect end stations, as shown in Figure 4.3. Here we have taken LAN segmentation to the extreme, with each "segment" comprising a single end station. This is referred to as *microsegmentation.*

A microsegmented environment has a number of interesting characteristics:

- There is no access contention (e.g., collisions) between end stations. Each end station is in its own access domain. It is still possible to have collisions between an Ethernet end station and the MAC in the switch port.[4]
- It may be possible to eliminate access control (e.g., collisions) altogether through the use of full duplex operation (see Chapter 7, *Full Duplex Operation*).
- Each end station has *dedicated bandwidth;* that is, a LAN segment is available for the exclusive use of each individual station.

[3] A backbone is a network whose primary purpose is the interconnection of other networks, as opposed to interconnecting end stations. A backbone may be either distributed or collapsed. In a distributed backbone, the backbone network is brought to the internetworking devices. Geographically dispersed internetworking devices are connected to the backbone, typically at wiring closets, to provide common interconnectivity. FDDI is an example of a technology once popularly used for distributed LAN backbones. In a collapsed backbone, the backbone consists of a high-performance internetworking device, such as a switch. The disjoint networks must be "brought to" the backbone, often through point-to-point links.

[4] There is a common misconception that, if there is only one station connected to a port of a switch, that there will be no collisions on that link. If the port is operating in half duplex mode (i.e., using normal CSMA/CD) this is simply not true. If the station has a frame queued for transmission to the switch at the same time that the switch has a frame queued for transmission to the station (a common event), then there will be a collision between the station and the switch itself. This is perfectly normal, and will resolve itself using the CSMA/CD algorithm. It is important to recognize that there really are two stations on each "LAN"; the station attached to the switch port, and the switch itself. The confusion arises because, in a microsegmented environment, it may be possible to configure the devices to use full duplex mode, which does eliminate all collisions. This is discussed extensively in Chapter 7. Microsegmentation alone does not eliminate collisions; full duplex operation (which requires microsegmentation as a prerequisite) does.

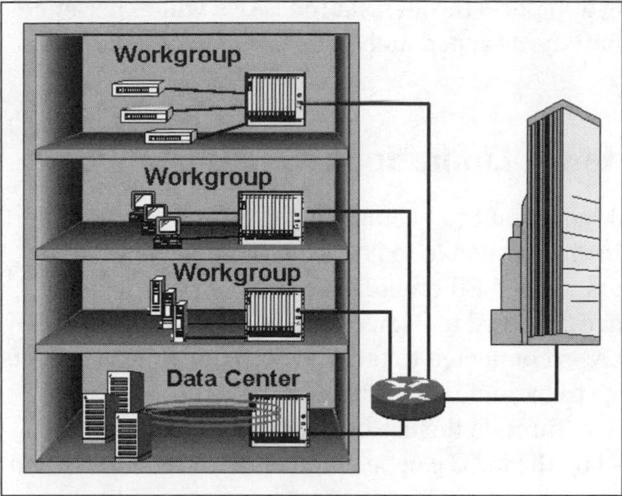

Figure 4.2 Collapsed backbone.

- The data rate of each station can be independent of any other. There can be devices connected to the same switch operating at 10 Mb/s, 100 Mb/s, 1000 Mb/s, and so on. This is not possible when using a shared LAN hub.

Of course, there can be a combination of shared LANs and single-station (microsegmented) attachments on a given switching hub, as shown in Figure

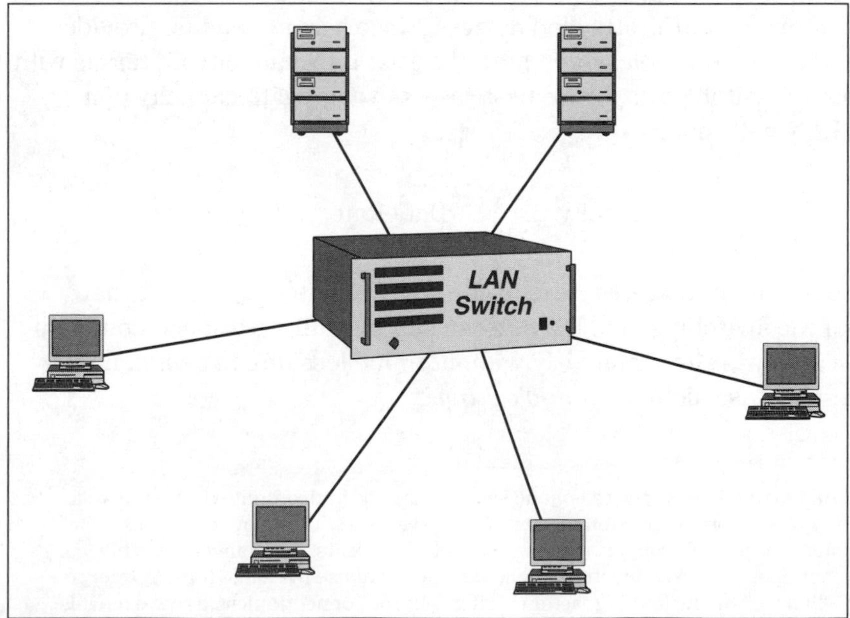

Figure 4.3 Microsegmentation.

4.1. Stations connected to switch ports through shared LANs will experience shared-LAN behavior, and stations attached individually will have microsegmented capabilities.

4.2.3 Extended Distance Limitations

Switches allow us to extend the distance coverage of a LAN. Each switch port is a distinct LAN, so each port has available to it the full distance extent provided by the technology. Thus, shared Ethernet LANs attached to a switch port operating at 10 Mb/s have the full 2 to 3 km distance limit available, regardless of the length of LANs connected to other switch ports. This reflects the traditional use of a bridge to extend LAN distances.

We will see in Chapter 7 that, through the use of full duplex operation, any distance constraints imposed by the MAC can be eliminated entirely on switch ports with microsegmented connections. This is an important capability provided by the use of switching that is simply not available with shared hubs. It is especially important for technologies such as Fast Ethernet and Gigabit Ethernet, where the distance constraints imposed by CSMA/CD effectively eliminate any possibility of using half duplex links for campus backbone applications.

4.2.4 Increased Aggregate Capacity

A switch provides greater data-carrying capacity than a shared LAN. In a shared LAN, the LAN capacity (be it 10 Mb/s, 16 Mb/s, 100 Mb/s, or 1000 Mb/s) is shared among all of the attached devices. Since a switched hub provides dedicated capacity on each switch port, the total LAN capacity increases with the number of switch ports. In the best-case, the aggregate capacity of a switched LAN will equal:

$$\text{capacity}_{\text{agg}} = \sum_{\text{port}=1}^{n} \text{Data Rate}_{\text{port}}$$

In practice, the total aggregate capacity will be limited by the internal capacity of the switching hub. If a hub can support full wire-speed communications on all ports simultaneously without frame loss due to switch limitations, the switch is said to be *non-blocking.*[5]

[5] This is a term borrowed from the telephone switch industry. In that context, it refers to a switch's ability to support connection requests (calls) without withholding resources—that is, having sufficient capacity to support calls from all attached users simultaneously. While a LAN switch does not operate in a connection-oriented manner, we use the same term to refer to a switch that will never be the limiting factor (bottleneck) for connectionless frame exchange. Output congestion may still limit aggregate throughput below that of the switch's internal capacity. See Chapter 15, *Make the Switch!*, for further discussion of switch architecture and non-blocking operation.

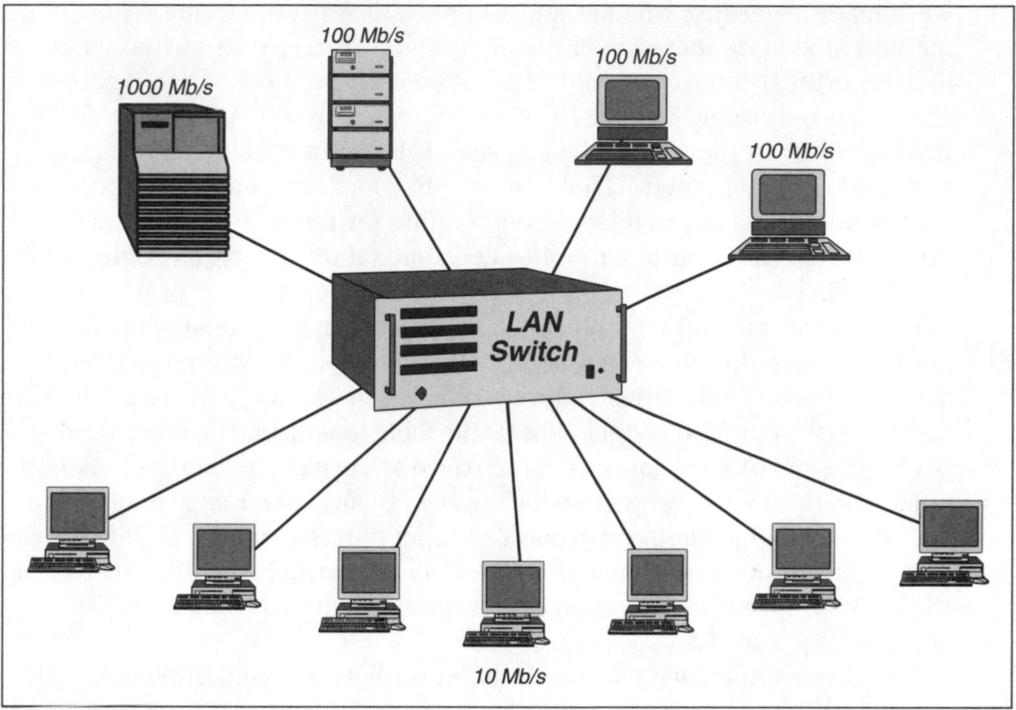

Figure 4.4 Mixing data rates on a single switch.

4.2.5 Data Rate Flexibility

All devices connected to a given shared LAN must operate at the same data rate. Independent LANs can operate at different data rates. Since each port of a switch connects to an independent LAN, each port can operate at a different data rate. This allows complete flexibility in deploying end stations at different data rates, especially in a microsegmented environment. When a switching hub is used, each attached station can be provided with a LAN interface (NIC) at the data rate appropriate for the applications being supported on that station, as depicted in Figure 4.4.

High performance workstations, servers, and routers can be provided with 100 Mb/s or 1000 Mb/s connections, while most end stations are provided with 10 Mb/s or 100 Mb/s connections. This provides higher performance where needed without burdening all users with the higher costs associated with a faster LAN.

4.3 Cut-Through versus Store-and-Forward Operation

In all the previous descriptions of bridge and switch operation, we implied that each frame was received (stored) completely before any decisions were made regarding whether and where to forward the frame. This method of switch operation is called *store-and-forward.* A switch makes its time-critical filter/forward decision based on the Destination Address in each received frame. The Destination Address is usually one of the first fields present in the frame. (In Ethernet, it is *the* first field following the Start-of-Frame Delimiter.) Thus, the switch can start the table lookup and forwarding-decision process without waiting for the rest of the frame to arrive; it has all the information it needs once the Destination Address has been received.

It takes some time for a frame to be fully received; a maximum-length Ethernet frame has a duration of about 1.2 ms (at 10 Mb/s). However, the Destination Address has fully arrived after a maximum of 11.2 μs (including Preamble and Start-of-Frame Delimiter). What if the table lookup can be completed before the end of the frame has even arrived at the input? Once the lookup is complete, the switch knows to which port(s) (if any) the frame should be forwarded; assuming that the appropriate output port is available, the switch can begin transmitting the frame before the frame has even been fully received at the input. This method of switch operation is called *cut-through,* and is depicted in Figure 4.5.

The most conspicuous, observable difference between a cut-through and a traditional store-and-forward switch is that the *latency* of the switch, measured from first-bit-in to first-bit-out, will be less for a frame forwarded in cut-through mode. This fact was not lost on the people who marketed the first cut-through switches;

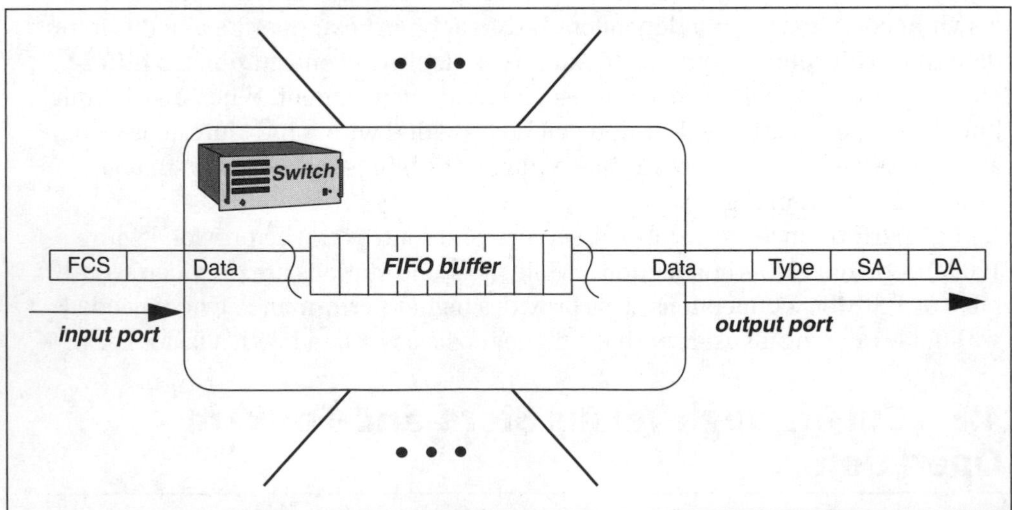

Figure 4.5 Cut-through switch operation.

it became the primary selling point for such designs.[6] For a maximum-length frame, a store-and-forward 10 Mb/s switch has a minimum latency of 1.2 ms (the frame duration). Allowing for lookup time, practical cut-through switches (from the same early 1990s era) had latencies on the order of 50 µs or less. This is a factor of more than 20:1; the implication was that a cut-through switch provided a 20:1 performance improvement over a store-and-forward switch.

There are a number of fallacies with this conclusion:

- *Absolute latency is not a significant issue for most higher-layer protocols and applications (at least not latency on the order of a few milliseconds).* When performing file transfers using TCP, a station does not need to wait for an immediate acknowledgment after sending one packet before sending additional packets. TCP provides a transmission window that creates a pipeline between sender and receiver. There can be many outstanding, unacknowledged packets in the pipe without impacting throughput.[7] As long as the TCP window is larger than the total round-trip delay of the network, file transfers can be accomplished at the maximum throughput offered by the channel. Each packet will be delayed by the store-and-forward switch, but the delay is not cumulative; any additional latency (on the order of a millisecond) accrues on a per-file-transfer basis, not a per-packet basis. A 10 Mbyte file transfer consumes about 7,200 maximum-length Ethernet frames; however, the total latency difference between using a cut-through versus a store-and-forward switch is only about 1 ms, not 7,200 times this value. The first packet arrives a millisecond later, but so does the last packet. The time difference is insignificant relative to the file transfer time (about 1.1 seconds with high-performing systems on a 10 Mb/s Ethernet). Confusing latency with throughput is like confusing the length of a hose with its thickness. They are not related.
- *For those protocols that are sensitive to latency, the switch is only a small part of the problem.* The Internetwork Packet eXchange (IPX) protocol suite provides an example of a Transport protocol where throughput *is* related to latency. This is because, in its original mode of operation, IPX does not provide a transmission window of more than one packet.[8] That is,

[6] The first commercial cut-through Ethernet switches were marketed by Kalpana Corporation, which was later acquired by Cisco Systems. *Kalpana* means *imagination* in Hindi; more important, it was the name of the wife of the company's founder (Vinod Bhardwaj). Moral: If you are going to form a high-technology start-up company where you will have to spend more time in the office than at home, at least name the company after your wife.

[7] Typical default TCP window sizes range from 8 to 32 Kbytes, which is the equivalent of 6 to 22 unacknowledged, maximum-length Ethernet frames. This corresponds to a network round-trip delay on the order of 7 to 26 ms at 10 Mb/s.

[8] In later incarnations, IPX included a burst-mode, where there can be multiple, outstanding unacknowledged packets. In this mode, it behaves more like TCP, although burst-mode IPX is still a stop-and-wait protocol, albeit for a burst of packets rather than for individual ones. The impact of network and switch latency is reduced, but it is still cumulative over the bursts.

a sender using IPX will wait for an acknowledgment for each packet before sending additional packets. With this type of stop-and-wait protocol design, the absolute round-trip network latency is a critical factor for throughput.

However, the switch latency is only a part of the total round-trip latency. Other elements in the path between sending a packet and receiving an acknowledgment include:

1. Protocol and device driver processing in the sending station.
2. Queuing delays in the sending station. (This is especially significant if there are other protocols and applications running on the same machine. IPX packets may have to wait in a queue behind multiple packets from other sources within the machine.)
3. Routing delays (including both processing and queuing) in intermediate routers and/or switches in the network.
4. Queuing delays in the receiving station. (Again, this can be significant if there are other applications using the network on the receiving station. In the case of a server, this is highly likely.)
5. Protocol processing, acknowledgment generation, and device driver processing in the receiving/acknowledging station.
6. Items 2, 3, and 4 applied to acknowledgments in the return path.
7. Acknowledgment processing in the original sending station.

Of all these latency components, switch latency comprises only a small portion of item 3. Reducing the latency of a switch will not significantly improve the throughput achieved by the end systems. A much greater performance improvement can be achieved by using a protocol that provides a transmission window larger than a single packet; that is, protocols such as traditional IPX are not optimized for performance—designing a switch to provide a minuscule performance improvement for an inherently low-performance protocol is not a particularly effective method of operation.[9]

- *Any latency benefit accrues only when the output port is available.* Cut-through operation is only possible if the intended output port is

[9] While IPX may not provide extremely high performance, its advantage lies in that it imposes very little memory and processing burden on the end stations. A sender needs only a single transmit buffer (which is used to retransmit a packet in the event of an error), and a receiver needs only a single receive buffer per connection; there will never be more than one outstanding unacknowledged packet in any given data stream. In addition, the receiver never needs to resequence a stream of packets, since they are always received in the order sent. For a memory-and-processor-constrained system, these can be significant benefits. IPX was originally designed to operate on low-end 8088-class PCs with very limited memory; the protocol design reflects this application environment.

available at the time the frame is received. If not, then the switch must buffer the incoming frame and transmit it at a time when the port is available. That is, cut-through is not an *alternative* to store-and-forward operation, it is *in addition* to it. The switch must still be capable of store-and-forward operation when the output port is in use.

We receive the latency benefit of cut-through operation only if output ports are available when needed, that is, when traffic through the switch is light. If the switch is heavily loaded with traffic, ports are likely to be in use, with a queue of frames waiting for transmission. Put another way, we get the latency benefit of cut-through operation only when we don't need it—when traffic is light. If traffic is really light, why do we even need a switch? A shared-LAN hub offers even lower latency, since it does not incur any delay for address table lookup.

- *Cut-through operation is generally not possible for multicast or unknown destination addresses.* Unless all ports are simultaneously available when the frame arrives, it will not be possible to cut-through a frame that must be forwarded through multiple output ports. Again, the switch must store-and-forward such frames.

When cut-through switches first arrived on the scene, many opponents of this approach (read: competitors selling store-and-forward switches against the aggressive marketing of cut-through switches based on latency) raised the issue of what happens when a frame arrives with an error due to corruption within the physical channel. The error will result in an invalid FCS; a store-and-forward switch will check the FCS and discard the frame in error. However, since the FCS is the last field received, a cut-through switch has already forwarded almost the entire frame by the time it recognizes the error. It cannot put the cat back in the bag. This would seem to be a serious problem; cut-through switches propagate frames with errors.

In defense of cut-through switching, this is not nearly the problem its opponents made it out to be. While it is true that a cut-through switch can propagate frames containing errors, in any practical network the number of such frames is vanishingly small. A 100 Mb/s Ethernet, experiencing 30 percent utilization over a 10 hour period with an average frame length of 250 bytes in an environment generating a BER of 1×10^{-12}, will see one FCS error on average (out of a total of 500 million frames exchanged during that time). This is simply not a big deal.

Of greater significance is the fact that, on an Ethernet, it is necessary to wait until at least 64 bytes have arrived before you can be sure that the frame being received is not a fragment resulting from a collision. This is a much more common event than an FCS error. Fortunately, it is a simple matter to delay any cut-through switching until the end of the first 64 bytes; in many cases this time is needed for the table lookup anyway.

Finally, it should be noted that cut-through switching only works if both the input and output ports are operating at the same data rate. It is not effective to cut-through between ports of dissimilar speed. In the case of forwarding frames from a slow-speed to a high-speed port, the switch must make sure that it doesn't run out of bits to send at the output. For a 10:1 ratio of port speeds (e.g., 10 Mb/s to 100 Mb/s), this implies buffering at least 90 percent of the incoming frame before starting to transmit at the output. Compared with buffering 100 percent of the frame, any latency benefit is minimal. In the case of switching from a high-speed port to a low-speed port, there is no issue of running out of bits to send, but the fact that bits cannot be forwarded at the same rate as they are received will force the switch to buffer the difference; again, this requires buffering at least 90 percent of the frame, with no real benefit accrued.

The Cut-Through versus Store-and-Forward Debate (A Red Herring)

Let's cut through all the nonsense and hype—the bottom line is that there is really no significant benefit (or detriment) to cut-through switching over the store-and-forward approach. Virtually all of the controversy was artificially created by the people marketing cut-through switches, as a way to differentiate their products. The one supposed benefit—reduced latency—does not provide any real performance improvement from the user perspective. However, this has not stopped hundreds of people from measuring switch latency to exacting standards.

Most manufacturers of switches now provide multiple, selectable modes of operation: store-and-forward, pure cut-through, and fragment-free cut-through (64 byte minimum buffer to prevent collision fragment forwarding). Some even provide a means to operate the switch in cut-through mode unless the error rate exceeds some threshold; the switch then changes to store-and-forward mode to prevent error propagation. Cut-through mode has become a data sheet "checklist" item, with no practical significance.[10]

4.4 Layer 3 Switches

Up to now, all of our discussion has concentrated on switching (bridging) at the Data Link layer (Layer 2) of the OSI model. Remember that the term *switch*

[10] Another reason that the controversy is now moot is that two of the early proponents of both cut-through switching (Kalpana) and store-and-forward switching (Grand Junction Networks) were both acquired by Cisco Systems! There was no longer any desire to fight between themselves for market share.

was simply market-speak for a high-performance implementation of a bridge. When bridge technology was first developed, it was impractical to build wire-speed bridges with large numbers of high-speed ports. With improved silicon technology, we were able to move many functions previously implemented in software into the hardware, thus increasing performance and enabling manufacturers to build reasonably-priced wire-speed switches.

A similar phenomenon occurred in the evolution of Network layer routers. Routers provide functionality beyond that offered by Data Link layer bridges; as a result, they naturally entail greater complexity. Like early bridges, routers were traditionally implemented in software, often running on a special-purpose communications processing platform. For a given level of performance, a software-based router has traditionally cost more than either a hardware- or software-based bridge. (Looked at the other way, for a given cost, a software-based router would typically have a lower level of performance than a bridge.)

Continual advances in silicon technology have made it possible to implement even this more complex Network layer functionality in hardware. By using integrated circuits with ample, low-cost logic, we can build Network layer routing engines at costs comparable to those of Layer 2 bridges. While a router still implements more functions than a bridge, the cost difference implied by this increased complexity shrinks as a function of the availability of inexpensive logic in silicon.[11]

Seifert's Law of Networking #20
When gates are plentiful, complexity is cheap.

4.4.1 A Router by Any Other Name Would Still Forward Packets

Marketing provides its practitioners with tools that are not often available to those who only practice engineering.[12] If you want to make a product that behaves like a bridge, but doesn't carry the emotional baggage of 1980s-era

[11] There were two fairly well-known early attempts to build hardware-based routers. During the late 1980s and early 1990s, a company called Protocol Engines unsuccessfully attempted to build a hardware-based Transport and Network Layer protocol chipset [CHES91]. The attempt failed primarily because the approach involved developing a new protocol suite (the eXpress Transport Protocol, XTP) that was simpler than TCP/IP and more amenable to silicon implementation with available technology. The scheme required that applications use this new protocol in lieu of TCP/IP to achieve the higher performance level. This approach met with significant resistance from the industry, especially as IP became the dominant Network layer protocol. Secondarily, even with the reduced protocol requirements or XTP, its complexity was at the limit of (some say beyond) the capability of then-available silicon technology. Cisco Systems successfully deployed a Silicon Switching Engine (SSE) in its router product line for many years. While this doesn't implement the entire IP protocol as a state machine, it performs certain time-critical tasks (e.g., routing table and ARP cache lookups) as hardware subroutines, significantly accelerating IP routing performance.

[12] Being one who practices both marketing and engineering, I need a larger tool belt than most.

bridges, just give it a new name—call it a switch. As a result of successful marketing (not to mention successful and useful products), the term *switch* served to differentiate next-generation implementations from their bridge roots, and became synonymous with high-speed, hardware-based internetworking. Through market positioning, switches became desirable while bridges were perceived as unattractive, even though the two technologies were functionally identical. Perhaps more important was the change in the relationship between bridges and routers; switches came to be viewed as a high-performance, low-cost means of internetworking, while routers were considered slow and expensive.

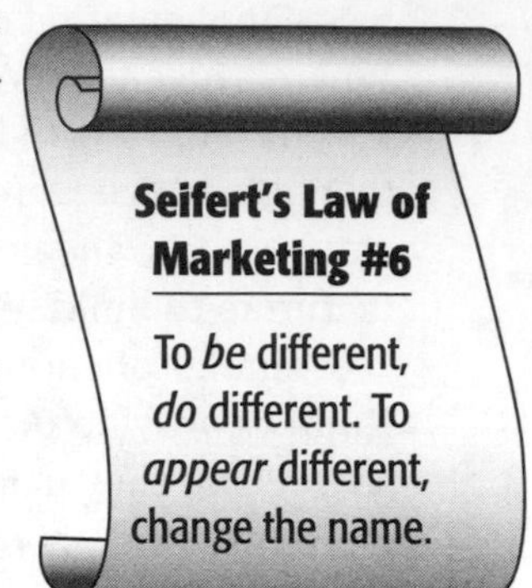

Seifert's Law of Marketing #6
To *be* different, *do* different. To *appear* different, change the name.

If we now implement Network layer routing functionality with high-performance hardware such that we can build wire-speed routers with large numbers of ports at a reasonable cost, marketing once again needs to differentiate this class of product from the customer image of routers as being slow, lumbering apes. The marketing solution was to leverage the good image of switching that was created for bridges operating at the Data Link layer. A *Layer 3 switch* carries the image of switching as high-performance, cost-effective, hardware-based internetworking, together with the feature set associated with Network-layer protocols.

In the same way that a Layer 2 switch is another name for a bridge, a Layer 3 switch is another name for a router. "Switching" does not represent any fundamentally new internetworking technology; we are still dealing with bridges and routers. It is just that the implementations are now such that those performance-intensive functions that were previously performed in software can be moved into hardware, with a resulting improvement in performance, reliability, and cost. The choice of using a bridge or a router for a given internetworking application should be based on the requirements of that application (as discussed in Section 4.7), not on whether the device is called a switch or not.

Table 4.1 presents a timeline of internetworking product development from a product marketing perspective.

4.4.2 Layer 3 Switch Operation

While a Layer 3 switch *is* indeed a router, a thorough treatment of routing and Network layer operation is beyond the scope of this book. Fortunately, many other books provide good foundation information on these subjects, including [COME95], [COME98], and [STEV94].[13] It is assumed in the discussions that follow that the reader is familiar with the operation of Network-layer proto-

[13] The interested reader should also consult the relevant RFCs. IPX routing is discussed in the Novell NetWare product documentation, and in [MALA90].

Table 4.1 Internetworking Product Timeline

THE BRIDGE ERA	
mid-1980s	Commercial bridges first become available. Most products are software-based. Two-port devices are the most common. Wire-speed operation is rare and commands a significant price premium. Bridges are used for interconnection of shared LANs.
THE ROUTER VERSUS BRIDGE ERA	
late 1980s–early 1990s	The market for commercial routers grows rapidly with the expansion of the Internet. Performance is less than that of bridges, so routers are sold on their extensive, software-based features (security, firewalls, reduction of multicast proliferation, multiple protocols, etc.). Market perception is that routers may be somewhat slower than bridges, but provide much more functionality. The common wisdom is, "Route when you can, bridge when you must."
THE SWITCH VERSUS ROUTER ERA	
early–mid 1990s	Hardware-based LAN bridges become available. Wire-speed performance is possible on large numbers of ports at competitive prices. To differentiate these bridges from their earlier, low-performance counterparts, they are marketed as *switches.* Market perception is that these inexpensive switches significantly outperform slow, software-based routers that command much higher prices. Switches can be used for individual station attachments rather than interconnection of shared LANs. Routers are seen as necessary evils for administrative isolation and Internet connection. The common wisdom becomes, "Switch when you can, route when you must."
THE "SWITCH EVERYTHING" ERA	
late 1990s–	Hardware-based routing becomes practical. Wire-speed routing is achievable in virtually all of the environments previously served by switches operating at the Data Link layer. To differentiate these routers from their earlier, low-performance counterparts, they are marketed as *Layer 3 switches.* Market perception is that all traffic can now be switched; whether Layer 2 or Layer 3 switching is used is determined by the nature of the attached devices and administrative needs.

cols (in particular, IP) and routing in general. The discussion here focuses on those performance-intensive operations that move into hardware in a Layer 3 switch implementation.

Until fairly recently, a variety of Network-layer protocols were still in widespread use, so that a commercially-viable router would need to implement multiple protocols in order to support the installed base. IP, IPX, DECnet Phase IV, AppleTalk, and the OSI CLNP (as well as some other, more obscure protocols) were often needed to support many customers' internetwork environments.

The number of protocols that are important in new routing products today is much fewer than in the old days. While there is still an installed base of DECnet, AppleTalk, and even some XNS-based systems, the growth of the Internet has made IP the most important Network-layer protocol by far, and many of the protocols that used to be popular have fallen by the wayside. Most corporations, universities, and other institutions are building (or migrating) their enterprise networks to IP-only operation. In addition, most legacy protocols can be encapsulated into IP, making an IP-only routing solution acceptable for many high-speed backbone networks. Thus, a Layer 3 switch may only need to implement hardware-based routing for IP. Other protocols (if needed) can be implemented in software; they are generally required more for connectivity to a shrinking installed base than for performance reasons.[14]

In addition, IP has matured as a protocol. The operation and behavior of the IP routing core is well-defined, and is unlikely to change significantly. Indeed, it would be quite difficult to gain widespread acceptance for any change that caused an incompatibility with the tens-of-millions of installed IP devices.[15] This is an important factor for Layer 3 switching. A traditional software-based router is more amenable to changes and updates without incurring field hardware replacement. With the stability of IP, the risk of hardware implementation is greatly reduced.

4.4.2.1 Separating Fast Path Functionality

A router with even a few ports operating at very high data rates must be prepared to handle millions of packets per second. Enterprise routers supporting moderate-to-large numbers of ports operating at gigabit data rates and higher need to process tens-to-hundreds of millions of packets per second in real-time. However, most Network-layer protocols provide many features and functions that either are rarely used (e.g., routing options) or that can be performed in the background of high-speed data forwarding (routing protocol operation, performance monitoring, etc.). A complete IP routing implementation (including all of the neces-

Seifert's Law of Networking #12
Optimize for the typical case, not the boundary case.

[14] After IP, IPX and AppleTalk are the most widely deployed protocols in enterprise internetworks. Some commercial Layer 3 switches do support IPX routing in hardware in addition to IP.
[15] While there is considerable activity in the area of new routing protocols, multicast operation, resource reservation (RSVP), and so on, the *core* functionality of an IP router is quite stable. The operations required to perform packet parsing, routing table lookup, lifetime control, fragmentation, and so on, are unlikely to change and can be committed to silicon with little risk.

sary functionality and support protocols) is impractical in hardware today; fortunately, it is also unnecessary. A router does not need to be able to perform wire-speed routing when infrequently-used options are present in the packet. Since these boundary cases generally comprise only a small fraction of the total traffic, they can be handled as exception conditions. Similarly, there is no need to provide (and pay for) high performance for housekeeping and support functions such as ICMP, SNMP, and so on. The switch architecture can be optimized for those functions that must be performed in real-time, on a packet-by-packet basis, for the majority of packets, known as the *fast path* of the flow.[16] A Layer 3 switch only needs to implement this fast path in hardware. For background tasks, or exception conditions that must only be dealt with on an occasional basis, it is both easier and less expensive to use a traditional software implementation.[17]

4.4.2.2 The IP Fast Path

What are those functions of the protocol that are in the fast path? This varies somewhat from protocol-to-protocol, but for the purpose of this discussion we will consider the case of IP unicast traffic, because:

- IP is the most widely used protocol suite in enterprise networks today.
- IP comprises a superset of the functionality of popular connectionless network protocols; that is, most other protocols incorporate a subset of the capabilities of IP. The IP fast path is therefore the most complex that needs to be investigated.
- IP multicast traffic currently comprises a small fraction of the total traffic on most IP internetworks, and therefore does not currently justify fast path handling.[18]

[16] The term *fast path* comes from the way protocol processing software is typically designed. The code thread that is traversed most often is scrutinized and optimized most by the programmer, as it has the greatest effect on system performance. Packets that do not deviate from the typical (i.e., they generate no exception conditions) receive the highest performance because they require fewer instructions to process (this code path is executed faster).

[17] This approach does have one nasty pitfall; there is a class of security attack that can be mounted by sending high volumes of traffic that the attacker knows will traverse the slow path, with the intent to overload the processor executing the exception condition software. Under such overload, it is possible that the router may fail altogether or be unable to perform some other important function, allowing an intruder to bypass security control mechanisms and/or avoid detection.

[18] This assumption may change if either voice/video conferencing or streaming multicast video over IP begins to see widespread use. Depending on the switch architecture and the organization of the routing tables, it is actually possible to implement multicast handling in the fast path with little impact on cost or complexity; some Layer 3 switches today already provide this capability. The discussion in the text is confined to the unicast case for simplicity and to avoid restricting the discussion to specific table organizations (e.g., compressed binary trees).

The format of an IP datagram is depicted in Figure 4.6. The Options field(s) is present only if the Header Length field indicates that the header is longer than five 32-bit words (20 bytes). This fact will be useful for separating those packets that contain IP routing options, which do not normally need to be handled in the fast path.

IP addresses are 32-bit, fixed-length fields that comprise two portions:

- A *network identifier*, which indicates the network on which the addressed station resides.
- A *station identifier*, denoting the individual station within the network to which the address refers. IP station identifiers are locally-unique, being meaningful only in the context of the network identified in the network portion of the address.

An example of this separation is shown in Figure 4.7.

Each IP address has associated with it a *subnet mask* of the same length as the address (32 bits). The bits of the address that comprise the network portion are identified by setting the corresponding bits of the subnet mask to 1; the station portion of the IP address is identified by those bits of the subnet mask that are set to 0.

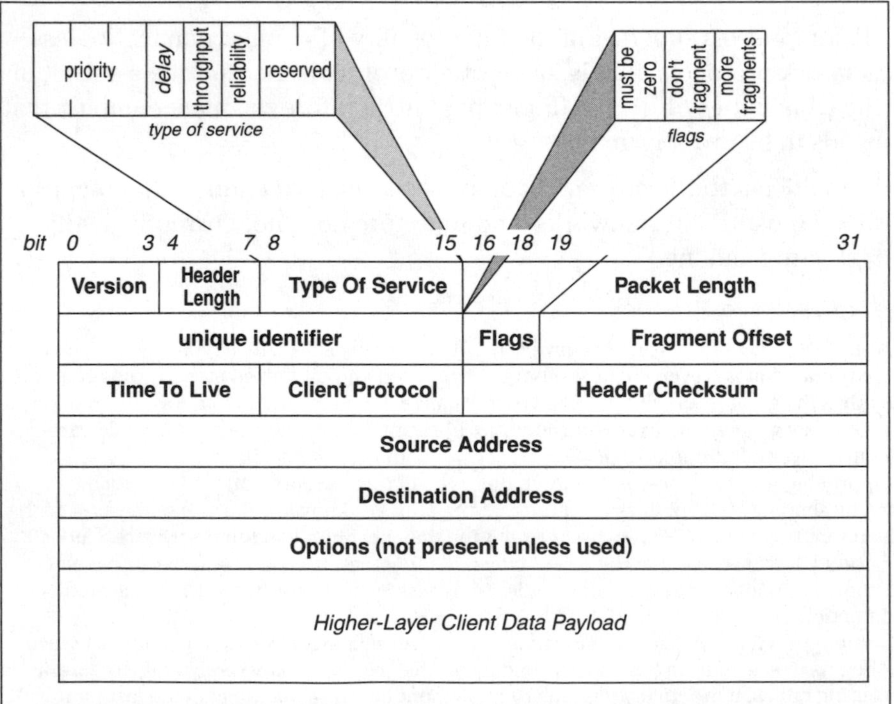

Figure 4.6 IP datagram format.

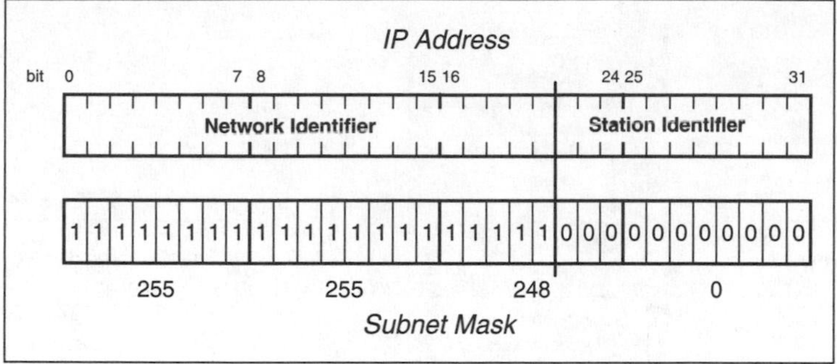

Figure 4.7 IP address format.

While not strictly required by IP, the network and station portions of the address generally comprise contiguous strings of bits, with the network portion being the first bits and the station portion the remaining bits. Using this convention, it is unnecessary to actually store subnet masks as 32-bit strings of ones and zeros; all of the relevant information can be provided by a 5-bit value indicating the number of leading bits that comprise the network portion of the address. This condensation can be used to advantage in high-speed routing table lookup operations. Aside from the dependence of some lookup algorithms on this common subnet convention, the use of discontiguous subnet masks can create huge difficulties in administering and managing an enterprise network. In particular, it becomes difficult even to determine which stations belong to the same network from a casual inspection of their addresses. As a result, any deviation from the convention of using contiguous subnet masks is highly discouraged in practice.

Seifert's Law of Networking #29
Anyone caught assigning discontiguous subnet masks will be summarily executed.

As depicted in Figure 4.8, the fast path for unicast IP routing entails:

Packet parsing and validation The router needs to separate the various fields in the received packet to determine the type of handling required and to check that the received packet is properly formed for the protocol before proceeding with protocol processing. In the case of IP, this means:

- Checking the protocol version number.
- Checking the header length field. The value must indicate a minimum of five 32-bit words (20 bytes) for a valid IP header; a higher value indicates that IP options are present in the packet.
- Calculating the header checksum.

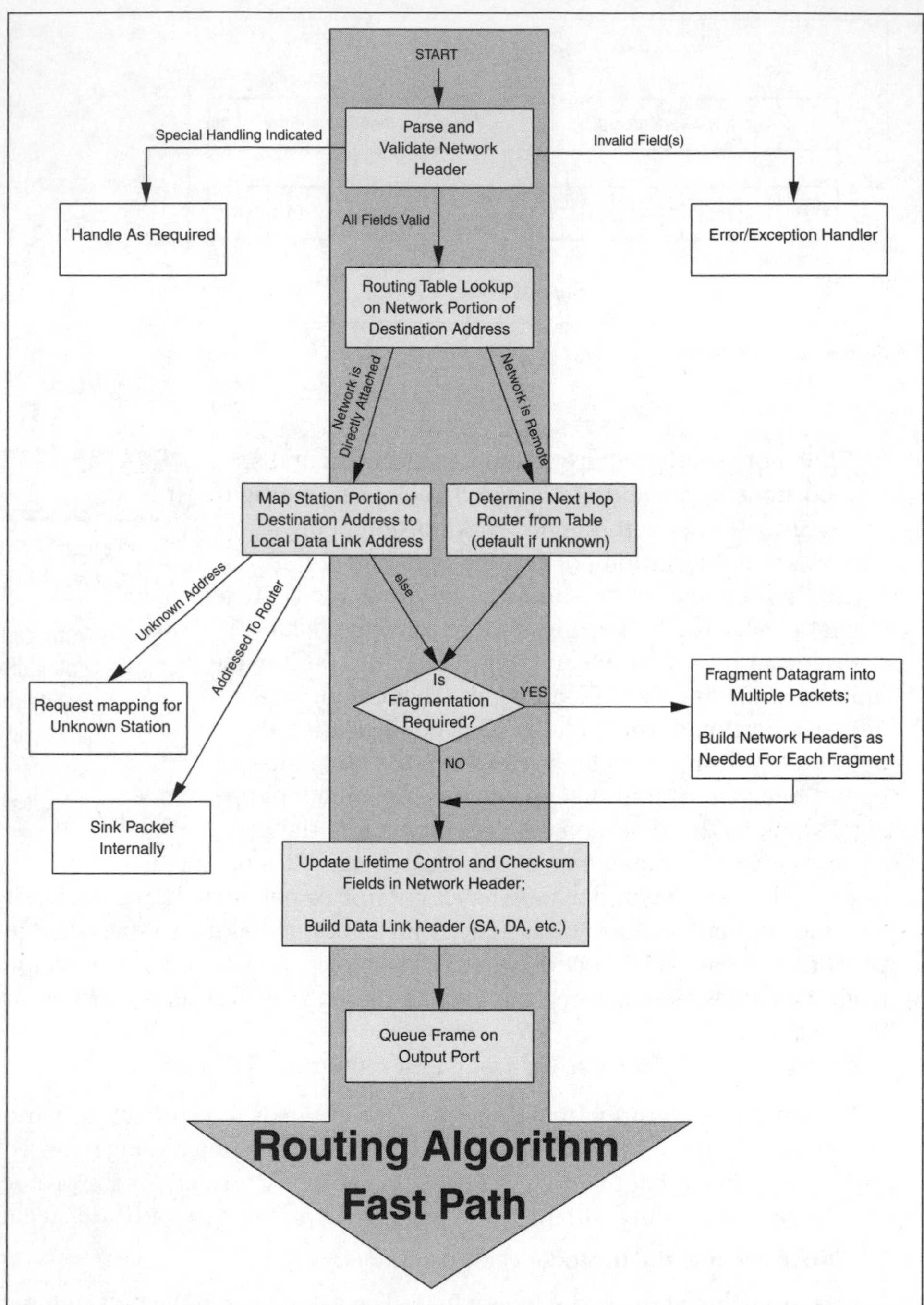

START
Parse and Validate Network Header
Special Handling Indicated
Invalid Field(s)
Handle As Required
Error/Exception Handler
All Fields Valid
Routing Table Lookup on Network Portion of Destination Address
Network is Directly Attached
Network is Remote
Map Station Portion of Destination Address to Local Data Link Address
Determine Next Hop Router from Table (default if unknown)
Unknown Address
Addressed To Router
else
Is Fragmentation Required?
YES
NO
Fragment Datagram into Multiple Packets;
Build Network Headers as Needed For Each Fragment
Request mapping for Unknown Station
Sink Packet Internally
Update Lifetime Control and Checksum Fields in Network Header;
Build Data Link header (SA, DA, etc.)
Queue Frame on Output Port
Routing Algorithm Fast Path

Figure 4.8 IP fast path.

- Validating the Source Address (e.g., rejecting multicast sources).

  Packets with errors can be passed to an error handler that operates outside the fast path. Similarly, packets requiring special handling (e.g., incorporating IP routing options such as source routing or route recording) can also be handled as exception cases outside of the fast path.[19]

Routing table lookup The router performs a table lookup to determine the output port onto which to direct the packet, and the next hop along this route, based upon the network portion of the Destination Address in the received packet. The result of this lookup will be that either:

- *The destination network is reachable only by forwarding the packet to another router (remote network).* This may occur due to a match of the destination network against a known table entry, or to the selection of a default route in the event of an unknown destination network. In either case, the lookup will return the address of the next-hop router, and the port through which that router can be reached.[20]
- *The destination network is known to be directly-attached to the router.* The lookup will return the port through which this directly-attached network is reachable, including the possibility of using an internal port (or pseudo-port) for sinking packets addressed to the router itself. For directly-attached networks, an additional step must be taken to map the station portion of the destination address to the data link address for the output port (address resolution using the ARP cache, discussed later).

It should be noted that table lookup in an IP router may be considerably more complex than for a bridge. At the Data Link layer, addresses are 48-bit, fixed-length fields. In addition, the address space is flat; there is no hierarchy or relevant subdivision of the address into distinct parts. Thus, address lookup in a bridge entails searching for an exact match on a fixed length field. This relatively straightforward operation lends itself well to the algorithms and technologies discussed in Chapter 2, *Transparent Bridges* (hash tables, CAMs, etc.).

IP addresses comprise two parts: the network identifier and the station identifier. The routing lookup operation in an IP router is used to deter-

[19] With increased silicon integration, it may be possible to handle these exception cases in fast path hardware as well. However, few IP packets today require option processing; IP options are used primarily for test, diagnostic, and control purposes, and comprise a tiny fraction of the total traffic on most internetworks.

[20] One special case must also be considered, where the destination network is unknown yet there is no default route configured. In this case, the packet will be discarded, and (optionally) an ICMP *Destination Unreachable* message will be sent to the originator.

mine the output port and next-hop data associated just with the network identifier portion of the address. The station identifier portion is examined only in the event that the network lookup indicates that the destination is locally-attached. In all but the simplest IP configurations, the dividing line between the network identifier and the station identifier will not be in a fixed position throughout the internetwork. Routing table entries can exist for network identifiers of various lengths, from 0 (usually signifying a default route) to 32 bits (for host-specific routes). A given destination address may yield a valid match simultaneously against multiple entries in the routing table, depending on the number of bits being considered. According to IP routing procedures, the lookup result returned should be the one corresponding to the entry that matches the maximum number of bits in the network identifier. Thus, unlike a bridge, where the lookup is for an exact match against a fixed-length field, IP routing lookups imply a search for the longest match against a variable-length field.

Appropriate algorithms for such a search are necessarily more complex than those suitable only for bridging. Many routers use a compressed binary tree (e.g., a radix or PATRICIA tree) data structure, which lends itself well to variable-length searches. In addition, a binary tree may allow the routing table to be integrated with the ARP cache, as discussed later. It may even be possible to incorporate Layer 2 bridge tables within the same data structure; a binary tree permits a combined Layer 2/Layer 3 switch to use one common data structure and lookup engine for both functions. While a pure Layer 2 device would generally not need the added complexity required to support variable length lookups, it costs little or nothing to use the more-powerful mechanism for the simpler bridge table lookups, if it is available.

Many hardware-based Layer 3 switches implement the lookup engine as a finite-state machine, with the data structure stored in RAM. Some semiconductor manufacturers produce merchant silicon products specifically designed for routing table lookup in IP routers, either as state machines or as content-addressable memories (CAM).

Mapping the destination to a local Data Link address (ARP mapping) The structure of Network layer addresses in IP does not provide a simple mapping to Data Link addresses for the common case of a Data Link that uses 48-bit addresses (i.e., for an IEEE 802-type LAN). That is, it is not possible to determine the 48-bit Data Link address for a given station solely from the station portion of the IP address. Thus, for packets destined for stations on locally-attached networks (i.e., the case where the router in question comprises the last Network layer hop in the route), we must perform a second lookup operation to find the destination address to use in the Data Link header of the frame encapsulating the forwarded packet. Depending on the organization of the lookup tables, this could be a secondary operation (i.e., independent routing table and ARP cache) or simply a continuation of the lookup operation that determined that the destination network was locally attached.

The result of this final lookup will fall into one of three classes:

1. *The packet is destined for the router itself.* That is, the IP Destination Address (network and station portion combined) corresponds to one of the IP addresses of the router. In this case, the packet must be passed to the appropriate higher-layer entity within the router and not forwarded to any external port.
2. *The ARP mapping for the indicated station is unknown.* In this case, the router must initiate a discovery procedure (ARP request) to determine the mapping. As this may take some time, the router may drop the packet that resulted in the initiation of the discovery procedure. Thus, ARP request generation can be outside the fast path of the routing code. Under steady-state conditions, the router will have a valid mapping available for all currently-communicating stations; the discovery procedure will only need to be invoked upon initiation of a new communication session with a station previously-unheard-from.
3. *The packet is destined for a known station on the directly-attached network.* In this, the most common case, the router successfully determines the mapping from the ARP cache and continues with the routing process.

Fragmentation Each available output port has associated with it a *Maximum Transmission Unit* (MTU). The MTU indicates the largest frame data payload that can be carried on the interface; it is generally a function of the particular networking technology in use (Ethernet, Token Ring, PPP, etc.). If the packet being forwarded is larger than the available payload space as indicated by the MTU, the packet must be fragmented into smaller pieces for transmission on this particular network.

Remember that a bridge is unable to fragment frames when forwarding between LANs of dissimilar MTUs, since connectionless Data Links generally have no mechanism for fragment reassembly in the receiver (see Chapter 3, *Bridging between Technologies*). At the Network layer, IP is capable of overcoming this limitation; packets can be subdivided into smaller pieces if needed to traverse a link with a smaller MTU. However, fragmentation is a mixed blessing. While it does provide the means to communicate across dissimilar link technologies, the processing burden to accomplish the fragmentation is significant.

In the case of a non-fragmented packet, the router's job (between packet reception and packet transmission on the output port) comprises simple manipulation of the fields in the IP header. Fragmentation implies additional tasks; in particular, the router must generate multiple packets for transmission as a result of a single received packet. Multiple IP headers must be generated (one for each fragment), necessitating memory allocation for the new headers and the linking of these headers to the appropriate subset of the original data payload.

As a rule, it is best to avoid fragmentation if possible. It is considerably more efficient (from the router's perspective) for the originating station to send packets that will not require fragmentation anywhere along the path to the target destination than to send large packets and demand that intermediate routers perform fragmentation. If necessary, stations and routers can determine the maximum MTU available along a path through the use of *MTU Discovery* [RFC1191]. The ultimate destination station is going to be receiving smaller packets one way or the other; any benefit gained through the use of larger packets is ultimately lost.

There is little a router can do when faced with a requirement to fragment, other than biting the bullet and doing the job. However, the burden of fragmentation does not need to be placed in the fast path of the code. Fragmentation is generally considered an exception condition; the function must be available if needed, but performance will suffer when it is invoked.

Fortunately, fragmentation is never needed in many high-performance routing environments. Consider the case of a campus

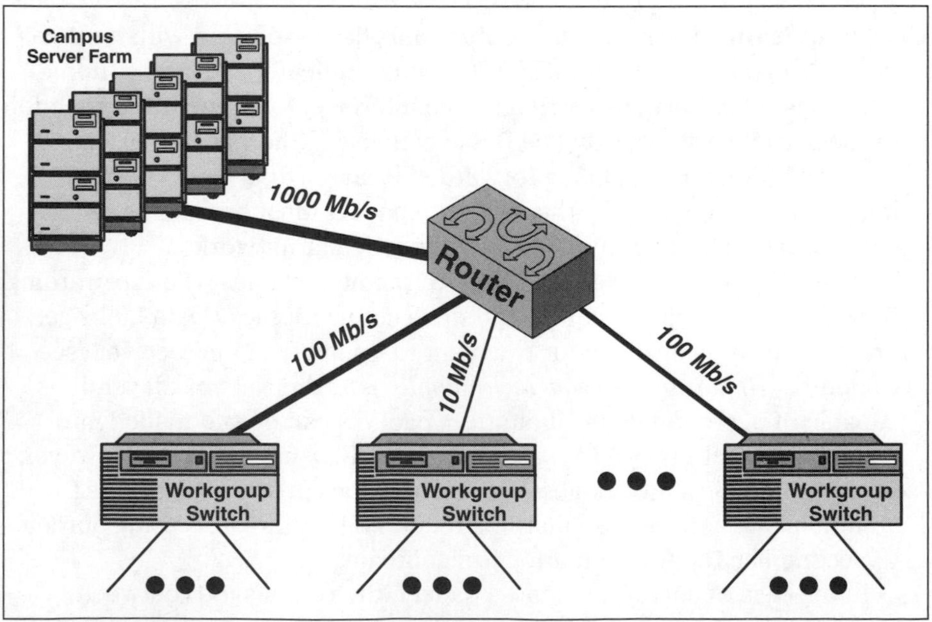

Figure 4.9 Campus Ethernet router configuration.

router providing interconnection among Ethernet LANs operating at 10, 100 and 1000 Mb/s, as depicted in Figure 4.9. Since the MTU of Ethernet is the same regardless of data rate, this router will never need to fragment; there is no possibility that a valid received frame will contain more data than can be encapsulated into the available MTU of any output port.[21] In fact, if a product supports only Ethernet ports (a common configuration), the router does not need to implement the IP fragmentation function at all, much less in the fast path. If a packet is received that is too large to be forwarded, it represents an error condition—some device on the input port has clearly violated the Ethernet MTU rules. Rather than performing fragmentation, the router can simply discard the packet.

Thus, fragmentation will be an issue only when the router supports links using dissimilar technologies, where the MTU of the output port can be smaller than some received packets. This can occur for a router that supports a mix of Ethernet, Token Ring, FDDI, and/or certain WAN technologies, but not in a homogeneous environment. As Ethernet (with its common 1,500 byte MTU) is pervasive in the desktop as well as most building and campus backbone environments, Layer 3 switches designed specifically for these applications can be simplified through the elimination of fragmentation.

Update lifetime control and checksum The router adjusts the Time to Live (TTL) field in the packet, which is used to prevent packets from circulating endlessly throughout the internetwork. Packets being routed to output ports have their TTL value decremented, then checked again to see if the packets have any life before actual forwarding occurs. Packets whose lifetimes are exceeded are discarded by the router (and may cause an error message to be generated to the original sender).

Finally, the header checksum must be recalculated, due to the change in the TTL field. Fortunately, the checksum algorithm employed (16-bit, ones-complement addition of the header fields) is both commutative and associative, allowing simple differential recomputation.[22]

That's it. The vast majority of packets flowing through an IP router need only have these operations performed on them. While this is not trivial, it is

[21] This result is one of the reasons why the MTU of Ethernet was not changed during the development of both Fast and Gigabit Ethernet. While greater efficiencies might be obtained in some situations through the use of longer Ethernet frames, the advantages of seamless, fragmentation-free internetworking were considered much more important. A similar argument holds against the use of so-called *jumbo frames*, where an attempt is made to improve server performance by using frames larger than allowed by the Ethernet standard.

[22] If the only change to the IP header is a decrement of the TTL field, the new checksum can be generated by taking the received checksum value and performing a subtract-with-borrow of the same value decremented from the TTL field. This operation is simple to implement in hardware.

possible to implement the entire fast path in hardware, providing performance suitable for large numbers of high-speed ports.

4.4.2.3 Off the Fast Path

There are many functions that must be implemented in a router other than those in the fast path. Some are performed on a packet-by-packet basis (i.e., optional or exception conditions) and some as background tasks. All of these can be generally implemented in software, as they are not time critical. For IP these functions include those shown in Table 4.2.

4.4.2.4 IPX Routing Issues

The fast path for IPX requires even less work than for IP:

- Since IPX uses a 32-bit, fixed-length network identifier, no subnet mask needs to be applied to extract the network portion from the address field.
- IPX addresses use a 48-bit field for the station portion of the Network layer address. The value used is the same as the 48-bit, globally-unique Data Link address of the interface to the underlying LAN. This allows a direct 1:1 mapping of the station portion of the Network address to the Data Link address, eliminating the ARP cache lookup and the concept of an ARP protocol altogether.
- IPX does not incorporate the concept of generalized network layer multicast, reducing the number and complexity of the possible routing decisions.
- IPX Lifetime Control is implemented as an increment of 1 to a Hop Count field, rather than as a potentially variable decrement as in IP.
- IPX implementations almost invariably disable checksumming; thus no update to the checksum field is usually required.

Table 4.2 Router Functions off the Fast Path

PACKET-BY-PACKET OPERATION	BACKGROUND TASKS
Fragmentation and reassembly	Routing protocols (RIP, OSPF, BGP etc.)
Source Routing option	Network management (SNMP)
Route Recording option	Configuration (BOOTP, DHCP, etc.)
Timestamp option	
ICMP message generation	

Therefore, hardware capable of performing IP fast path routing can be adapted to perform IPX routing as well. IPX routing functionality is a proper subset of IP routing. The only significant difference is in the syntax of the network address. There is little extra cost associated with supporting both protocols in the same product (if it is designed with this in mind from the outset).

4.4.3 Layer 4 Switching

A number of manufacturers actively market products that they call *Layer 4 switches*. Layer 4, the Transport layer of the OSI model, normally provides end station–to–end station services across an underlying internetwork. For example, the Transmission Control Protocol (TCP) is a popular Layer 4 protocol that provides reliable error- and flow-controlled connection-oriented data transport across a connectionless internetwork. As depicted in Figure 4.10, TCP (like all Layer 4 protocols) operates directly between the end stations; the bridges and/or routers in the path between the stations are not involved in TCP processes. In fact, they are generally blissfully unaware of the nature or presence of any protocols above the layer in which they operate (Data Link and/or Network, respectively). Any transport-related protocol information is simply part of the data payload being forwarded by the internetworking devices.

Strictly speaking, there is no such thing as a Layer 4 switch—at least not in the same sense that we have used the word *switch* up to now. Transport infor-

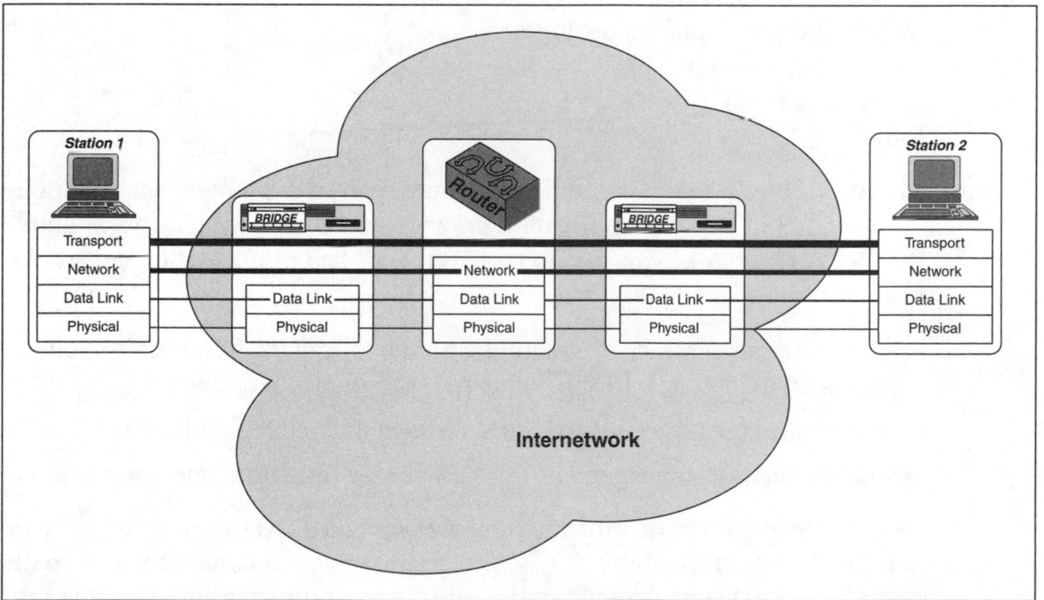

Figure 4.10 Transparent pass-through of Transport protocol information.

mation does not convey station identification; there is no way to determine to which station a given message is being sent by examining only the information available at Layer 4. Thus, it is not possible to direct packets to their appropriate destinations based solely on this information.

However, recall from Chapter 2 that a bridge (operating at the Data Link layer) can implement custom filters based on higher-layer information. For example, a bridge may separate and prioritize traffic as a function of Network-layer protocol type. While the bridging function itself is still based on Layer 2 information [i.e., the output port(s) is determined by the Destination Address in the received frame], certain aspects of bridging *policy* may be tempered by higher-layer information, including traffic priority, maintenance of sequential delivery invariants, and so on. The device is still a Layer 2 internetworking device (a bridge), but it can use higher-layer information to influence its operation.

Similarly, a Network layer router can implement routing policies based on higher-layer information. For example, a network administrator may want to prioritize certain classes of application traffic relative to others. Under congestion conditions, delay-sensitive applications may need to have their traffic moved to the head of the queue in order to provide good user performance. Applications can often be identified by their Transport layer process identifier (TCP port number). Thus, the router can inspect this higher layer information and use it to adjust its routing behavior. For example, one set of application priorities might be:

Network management (SNMP)	highest
Interactive voice/video	.
Interactive terminal (Telnet/rlogin)	.
World Wide Web (HTTP)	.
E-mail (SMTP/POP)	.
Bulk file transfer (FTP)	lowest

Alternatively, a network administrator may wish to implement security policies based on higher-layer application information. By applying custom filters at the Network layer based (in part) on Transport layer information, an administrator could (for example):

- Allow Telnet sessions originating within the organization but prohibit users from logging into the company's servers from outside
- Prohibit external access to Web servers dedicated to intranet use
- Allow Network Management (SNMP) access only from specific stations

By considering only the information available at the Network layer, we can generally identify traffic flow only to the granularity of a communicating pair of end stations. Through consideration of transport information, we can narrow the granularity to an individual process within a specific station and apply policies based on this finer-grained information. A stream of packets between a set of communicating processes is sometimes referred to as an *application flow*.

Most highly-featured routers have always provided this capability. However, such features, being both potentially complex and highly individualized, were always implemented in software, and invariably outside the fast path of the routing code. Thus, a network administrator who chose to implement such policy-based routing using higher-layer application information did so at the expense of significantly reduced performance. Such features would generally preclude the use of available hardware acceleration, and could reduce performance by orders-of-magnitude. As a result, they were used sparingly.

If advanced silicon technology now allows the implementation of complex routing policies based on application flow information, we can (once again) differentiate this capability from earlier, software-based implementations by calling it a switch. *Layer 4 switch* is a marketing name for a router that can implement application-based policy decisions without significantly affecting performance. Note that, despite the name, it is not really a Layer 4 device; there is no implementation of a Transport protocol as part of the switching function.[23] A Layer 2 switch implements Layer 2 functions; a Layer 3 switch implements Layer 3 functions. A Layer 4 switch does not implement Layer 4 functionality; it is still a Layer 3 device.

Marketing legerdemain notwithstanding, Layer 4 switching is not a trivial task. Depending on the device's position in the internetworking hierarchy, the number of possible application flows that must be parsed, distinguished, and have policy rules applied to them can be huge. A classic Network layer router in the backbone of a large Internet Service Provider (ISP) may need to know about tens-of-thousands of possible routes. The number of routes is a function of the number of reachable networks in the Internet. However, the number of possible application flows is a function of the number of station pairs that may be communicating, and the number of possible applications initiating data flow within each of those stations. The number of possible active flows can be on the order of millions to tens-of-millions. Worse, this number will only grow with the expansion of stations and differentiated applications running on them. A high-performance Layer 4 switch must be able to deal with a much larger number of cases than a router that does not need to consider such higher-layer flow information.

By now it should be clear that the term *switch* has simply come to mean a "high-speed *anything*"; typically, it implies a high-performance, hardware-based implementation of some function that was previously implemented in software. A Layer 2 switch is a bridge; a Layer 3 switch is a router, a Layer 4

[23] A Transport protocol may be present in a practical product for management purposes (e.g., SNMP over UDP, or Telnet over TCP); however, this is unrelated to its implementation of high-performance switching.

switch is a router with process-based flow policy, and so on. I fully expect some company to implement a complete, high-layer application in hardware and start calling it a Layer 7 switch. Just remember, you heard it here first.

For the remainder of this book, the term *switch* will be used to refer to a Layer 2 device (bridge) unless otherwise noted.

4.5 Four Generations of Switch Integration

As switches have moved from (what we would now consider) primitive bridges to more modern implementations, there have been continual changes and improvements in the level of integration. Higher levels of integration provide lower cost, higher reliability, smaller size, and lower power. In many cases, it is simply not possible to achieve the desired performance level *without* high integration; the merging of logical functions into a single IC permits the switch forwarding function and the data flow itself to operate much faster.

Switch designs have progressed through four stages of development:[24]

Zero integration (1984–1988) Some early bridges were built using general-purpose computers with standard network interfaces (NICs). A small computer with two (rarely more) NICs could be programmed through software to behave as a bridge. Frames were received by the NICs, stored in main memory, processed by the bridge software, and queued for transmission (if necessary) on the appropriate output port.[25]

Embedded system (board-level) integration (1986–1991) Once the market for bridges was established in the mid-1980s, many companies began to manufacture and sell bridge products. With growing demand and lots of competition, cost quickly became a factor. It was no longer practical to sell a zero-integration bridge into this market, since the cost of the general-purpose computer (and all of its normal supporting hardware) was an unnecessary burden in the bridge application. Special-purpose

[24] The levels of integration discussed here are applicable both to switches and routers (Layer 3 switches). Routers require a higher level of functionality; hence, the level of integration being achieved typically lags that of switches by at least one generation. Other than this developmental skew, the integration of routing functions into silicon is proceeding in a manner parallel to that of the Layer 2 switches described here.

[25] In some cases, such devices were built solely as *proof of concept vehicles* (i.e., prototypes) for a later, more highly integrated product. In other cases, zero-integration bridges were actually sold as is. In particular, most early Token Ring bridges were built this way. To this day, freeware/shareware software is available that allows a user to build a simple bridge using a personal computer and two or more standard NICs. While the performance achieved is far below that available from more highly-integrated switches, the cost is virtually zero (especially if you have spare computers and NIC hardware). If what is needed is connectivity, rather than performance, such an implementation may be perfectly adequate.

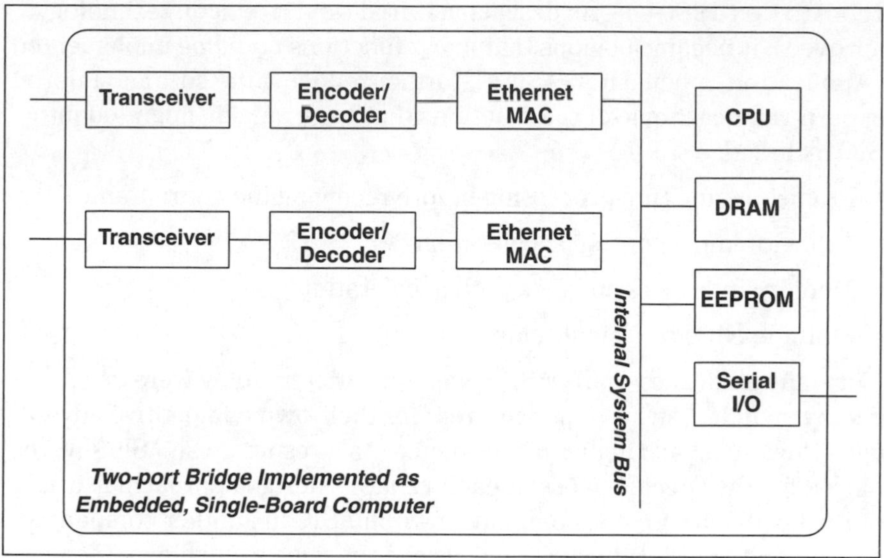

Figure 4.11 Board-level bridge block diagram.

embedded systems were developed that allowed a bridge to be built for much lower cost; a typical configuration is depicted in Figure 4.11.

Note that the architecture was essentially the same as that of a zero-integration bridge. It was simply optimized for single-purpose (bridge) use. A board-level bridge typically used a standard microprocessor, RAM, and network controller ICs.[26] What was eliminated was the chassis of the computer, the backplane, and all unnecessary peripheral interfaces (e.g., monitor and keyboard).

Bridge software was either pre-configured in ROM[27] or downloaded from a boot server over the network. Either approach eliminated the need for a storage device on the bridge (e.g., floppy disk), which would have been expensive and unreliable. In the latter case, a minimal boot ROM was needed to run diagnostics and to access the server for the operational code load.[28] There were literally dozens of manufacturers of such bridges during the late 1980s.

[26] Commonly used microprocessors for this application included the Intel 80186 and the Motorola 68000 families.

[27] In most cases, Electrically-Erasable, Programmable ROM (EEPROM) was used to allow software upgrades to installed devices. EEPROM download was generally accomplished through a local serial port.

[28] The widespread use of server-downloadable bridges was a key factor driving the development of the IEEE 802.1E standard (System Load Protocol) [IEEE94]. This standard provides a method for reliable multicast download, allowing large numbers of bridges (or other devices) to be simultaneously loaded with their operational code (as opposed to the tedious, one-at-a-time method) at initialization or as a result of power restoration.

Switch ASICs (1989–) As designs matured (and as silicon technology improved), it became obvious that many functions could be implemented in Application-Specific ICs (ASICs), further reducing the cost and improving performance. Some of the functions that were quickly migrated into ASIC included:

- Frame parsing (pre-processing before receiving the entire frame)
- Table lookup algorithm acceleration
- Memory interfaces and data path acceleration
- Multiple NICs on a single chip

Virtually all of these early ASICs were proprietary; they were developed by switch systems manufacturers for their own competitive advantage—lower cost and higher performance. As a result, these ASICs were tailored for the specific needs of each vendor's design approach. It was not reasonable to use one company's switch ASIC in another company's product, and few (if any) such devices ever became available on the merchant semiconductor market.

The evolution of switch ASICs led to the more complete integration of switch chipsets and to the merchant switch-on-a-chip solutions currently available.

Switch-on-a-chip (1997–) With the constant need to increase performance and reduce cost, even higher levels of integration have been achieved in switch design. During the late 1990s, *switch chipsets* became available on the merchant semiconductor market from a number of suppliers. These chipsets allowed a system designer to build a high-performance, high-port-density switch with minimal effort. Figure 4.12 depicts the architecture of a switch using one such chipset.

While many different architectures (and products) were available, this particular design integrated:

- Four NICs, address table CAM and lookup, RAM controller, and PCI control logic into a single IC
- Crossbar matrix data path and all control logic into a second IC

This allowed a manufacturer to build up to a 48-port 10/100 Mb/s Ethernet switch using very few components.

Of course, integration never stops. Later designs (using denser silicon technology) provided the first switch-on-a-chip implementations, depicted in Figure 4.13.

In this design, not only are the NICs (now eight of them) integrated with the data flow engine, but even the physical line interfaces are integrated into the same device. The only major external components needed are for the physical media connection and memory.

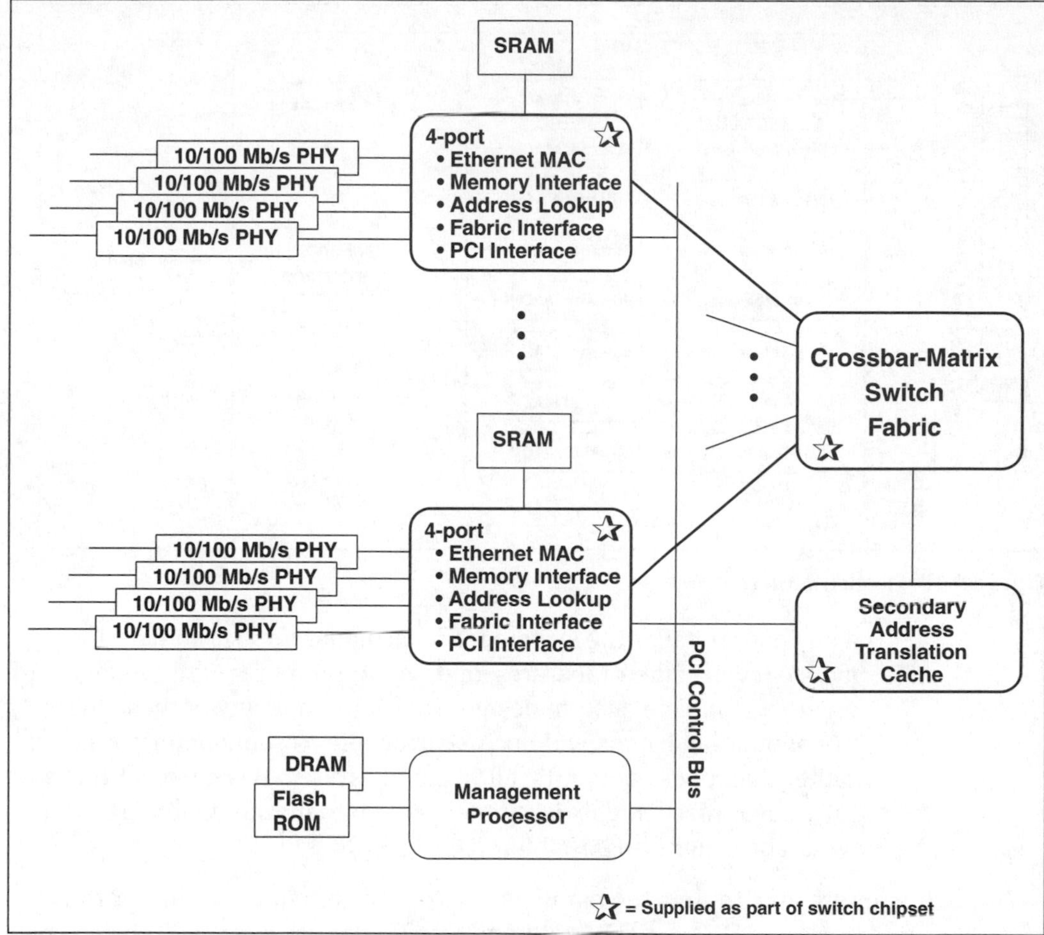

Figure 4.12 Switch implementation using commercial chipset.

It is expected that future designs will take one of two paths:

- For high-volume, well-defined applications (e.g., desktop switches), functions will be integrated even further. Single chip solutions are expected that incorporate not only the NIC, physical interface, and data flow engines, but the RAM and management CPU as well. Such devices will drive these application spaces to become pure commodity markets, similar to the shared-LAN hub market of the mid-1990s.
- For applications where flexibility is more important than cost (e.g., backbone switches), a more modular integration approach will evolve. Standard building blocks will be available (e.g., multiport NICs at various speeds, crossbar matrix blocks, and so on) that allow

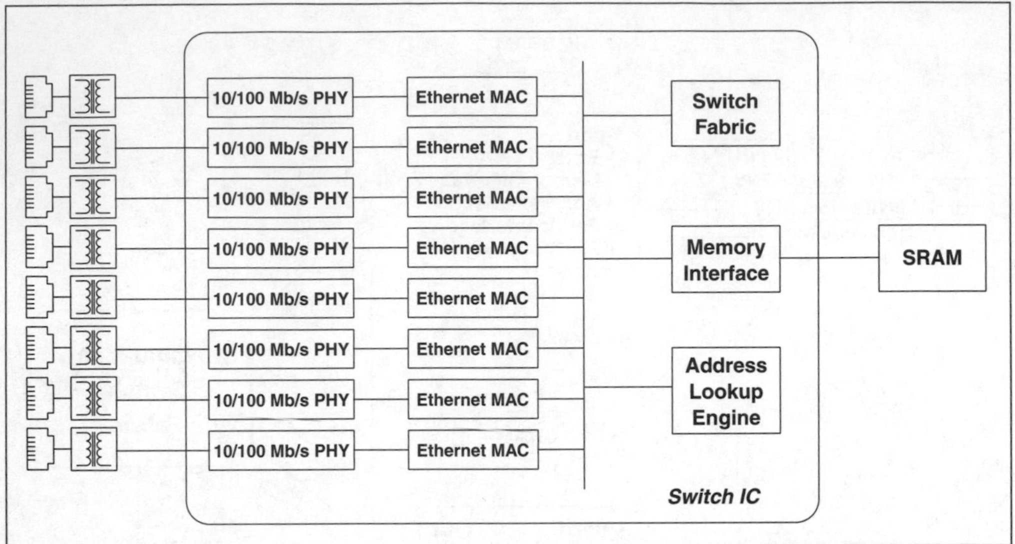

Figure 4.13 Switch-on-a-chip.

a designer to tailor the system for a particular application, performance level, cadre of features, and number of ports without having to create a complete custom design from scratch. Many of these functional building blocks will become available as semiconductor cores rather than packaged parts, allowing the system designer to bring a fully-customized, highly integrated switch to market much faster than would be otherwise possible.

It is interesting to note the parallels between switch integration and the earlier integration of NICs and shared-LAN hubs. In the old days, NIC design was an art. Few people had the skills to design a network interface and, as a result, there were few NIC manufacturers. As NIC designs were integrated, first in simple gate-array ASICs and then later as full-custom chips, the task of NIC design became much simpler. Rather than requiring any knowledge about networking, it became more of a cookbook exercise; you simply selected the appropriate chips and made sure that the rest of your circuitry interfaced properly with it. As a result, NICs became commodity items; prices for a 10 Mb/s NIC dropped from a range of $1,500 to $3,500 in 1982 to less than $10 in 1998.[29]

Similarly, shared-LAN hubs constituted a design challenge when they first

[29] Believe it or not, the DEC DEUNA 10 Mb/s Ethernet interface sold for a list price of $3,500 in 1982 (including the H4000 transceiver). There was virtually no network silicon integration employed; the design used Schottky TTL and 10K ECL logic. The NIC covered two large circuit boards with over 200 devices on each board, and consumed 5 VDC power at up to 12 Amps!

came on the market in the late 1980s. However, once they were fully integrated, low-cost commodity hubs could be had for under $4 per port. Switches (at least for the desktop and workgroup markets) are rapidly approaching this level of integration and commodity pricing.

4.6 Switch Configurations

Most commercial switches are packaged and sold in one of three classes of configurations:

- Bounded systems
- Stackable switches
- Chassis switches

The tradeoff among these is cost versus flexibility. Bounded systems offer the lowest cost and flexibility, while chassis switches offer the widest configuration flexibility at a commensurably higher price. Stackable switches offer a compromise solution.

4.6.1 Bounded Systems

A *bounded system* provides a fixed, predetermined configuration. A given product will have a specified number of ports, port technologies, and data rates. There are generally no options to select, and no means of system expansion beyond the prescribed configuration. Figure 4.14 depicts a typical bounded switch.

The primary advantage of a bounded configuration is that if the configuration provided matches the needs of the application environment, then it will be the lowest cost solution available for the user. The user does not pay for

Figure 4.14 Bounded system. (Courtesy of Cisco Systems)

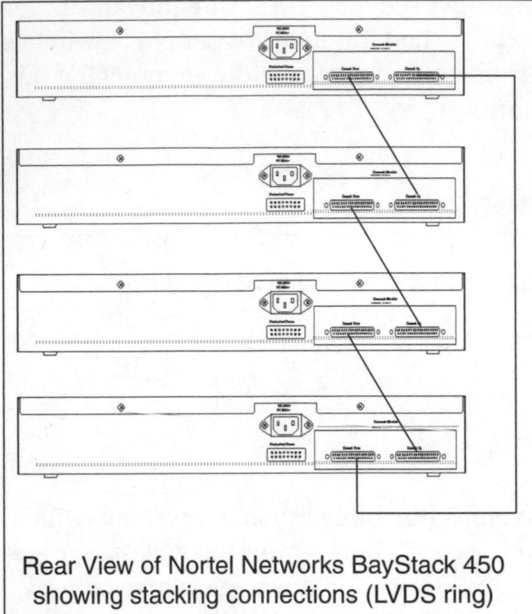

Rear View of Nortel Networks BayStack 450
showing stacking connections (LVDS ring)

Figure 4.15 Stackable switch. (Courtesy of Nortel Networks)

expansion capabilities or options that are not needed in the target network. The obvious disadvantage is that, if the user's needs change such that the bounded system is no longer appropriate, the user must generally purchase a replacement switch, since an upgrade or reconfiguration is not possible.

Due to their nature, bounded systems are most often manufactured and used for those application environments that are mature (i.e., well-known and understood) and high in volume. In these environments, competitive pressures usually force manufacturers to offer the lowest-cost solutions. Some common configurations include:

- Eight or 12-ports of 10 Mb/s Ethernet plus 1 or 2 ports of 10/100 Mb/s Ethernet (uplink); appropriate for a low-end desktop switch
- Sixteen or 24-ports of 10/100 Mb/s Ethernet; appropriate for a higher performance desktop switch or server cluster application
- Sixteen or 24-ports of 10/100 Mb/s Ethernet plus 1 or 2 ports of 1000 Mb/s Ethernet (uplink); appropriate for a workgroup switch[30]

[30] In this one particular case, it is common to provide at least one of the 1000 Mb/s ports as a plug-in option. Since 1000 Mb/s connections are considerably more expensive, it is not necessary to include the port hardware unless and until it is needed.

4.6.2 Stackable Switches

A *stackable switch* provides a means whereby a user can grow a system without having to discard hardware at each upgrade. Stackable configurations allow multiple physically separate switches to be clustered such that they function (and appear to management) as a single device. A stackable switch configuration is depicted in Figure 4.15.

The advantage of a stackable switch is ease of migration. A network planner can purchase a switch supporting the number of ports appropriate for a given environment. If the number of devices or users grows beyond the capabilities of the original switch, the switch can be expanded through stacking. A typical stackable switch may provide 24-ports per switch and be stackable up to 200 ports or more. This provides more than adequate growth, especially for desktop switching applications.

4.6.2.1 Stacking the Deck

The technology used to interconnect the switches in a stack is usually intrinsic to the particular product. In general, it is not possible to stack switches from different manufacturers in a single configuration. Technologies used for stacking include:

Uplink ports Some products use one of the switch's uplinks for the stacking connection. For example, a stackable 10/100 Mb/s switch may use a 1000 Mb/s uplink to interconnect switches in the stack.

Proprietary links A proprietary technology may be used to interconnect the switches. This may be a high-speed parallel channel, a high-speed serial bus, or a serial ring.[31]

Bus extension A stackable switch may simply use its internal system bus (e.g., PCI) for the stack interconnection, extending its distance by using high-current line drivers. In this manner, the internal bus becomes a backplane among the switches in the stack.

[31] It is becoming common to use Low Voltage Differential Signaling (LVDS) for switch stack interconnection. This low-cost technology offers the ability to operate at very high data rates (1 to 2 Gb/s or more) over short lengths of cable. Since switch stacks generally reside within the same equipment rack, the cabling limitations are usually acceptable. A ring topology is commonly used as a shared-media channel among the switches, since LVDS is more suited for point-to-point link connections [BAXT95, WIRB98].

4.6.2.2 A Block in the Ointment

Depending on the technology used for the stack interconnection, it is possible that a switch that would be non-blocking if used in a standalone configuration may no longer be non-blocking in a stacked configuration. If the stack technology is incapable of handling the sum of all traffic from all ports across the stack under worst-case traffic patterns, then it may become a performance limitation for the combined system. Such a stack limitation is quite common in commercial products; few stack interconnection technologies are able to support the aggregate sum of all traffic from all ports, especially when a stack provides for 100 Mb/s port densities of 50 to 100 or more.

Whether this manifests itself as a problem in the user environment depends on the traffic levels and patterns. If the traffic load exceeds the stack capability for only a short period (transient overload), buffer memory in the individual switches may be sufficient to ride through the event. If a problem is being caused by a specific, recurring traffic flow (e.g., a server-to-server path that is often used for bulk data transfer), a performance improvement may be achieved by ensuring that both endpoints of the flow connect to ports on the same physical switch; this relieves the stack interconnection from carrying the heavy load and frees it up for other user traffic.

4.6.2.3 United, We Are One

Properly designed, a stackable switch configuration appears as if it were a single switch, regardless of the number of physical devices in the stack. As a result, the entire stack can be managed as if it were a single device. All of the switches in the stack can be more easily and consistently configured; the alternative—individually configuring each set of switch parameters (e.g., custom filters)—is both tedious and error prone. From the perspective of a standard network management station using the Simple Network Management Protocol (SNMP), the switch has a single address and a single, integrated Management Information Base (MIB). This greatly simplifies troubleshooting and performance monitoring.

It may appear that a second advantage accrues to a stack appearing as a single switch—that it counts as only one hop in the catenet. As discussed in Chapter 2, we generally limit the extent of a catenet in order to maintain the delay invariant of the Data Link. However, this benefit of stackable switches is ephemeral; while the stack configuration may make it appear that data is only crossing a single switch, in reality data must pass through multiple devices, each with its own processing and queuing delays. Simply calling the stack a single switch doesn't reduce the delay, which was the reason we imposed the hop limit in the first place. This is one case where marketing cannot change reality.

A PENNY SAVED IS OFTEN LOST IN THE CAR SEAT

The main selling point of stackable switches is that they future-proof a network design. If your organization grows beyond the limits of an individual device, the device can be expanded through stacking to preserve your investment. This gives network planners an easy escape path; in particular, it allows them to avoid having to make an accurate estimate of the number of users that will need network access. The designer's job thus entails lower risk, since the product capabilities can be adjusted over time.

However, this escape path comes at a price. For any given configuration, a stackable switch will cost more than a bounded system with the same number of ports. In many cases, the expansion capability is never needed or used; a large percentage of stackable switches are sold that never have more than one device in the stack. Often, if the organization grows such that more ports are needed, many other factors are changing as well (e.g., an upgrade from 10 Mb/s to 100 Mb/s NICs); the stacking capability is wasted, as totally new hubs are needed anyway.

In some cases, the price of stackability exceeds the cost of discarding an old, bounded switch and buying a new one. It may be cheaper to discard (or redeploy somewhere else in the network) a 12-port desktop switch and buy a new 24-port device than to purchase a stackable switch in the first place. This is especially true when we consider the rapid decline in switch prices over time; the 24-port switch purchased a year or two later may cost less than the original 12-port device due to competition and advances in integration. The political reality is that it's hard to convince most managers that throwing out a piece of equipment is the most cost-effective solution, even if it's true. To be blunt, stackable switches are a way for network planners to avoid the *appearance* of making a mistake, even if it costs more in the end. This fact is not lost on the professionals marketing stackable switches; network designer job-preservation is an effective sales tool.

4.6.3 Chassis Switches

A *chassis switch* provides the ultimate in flexibility. The switch is designed to accept a variety of plug-in modules in its slots; the exact configuration (e.g., ports, data rates, features) is a function of the plug-in modules deployed. The user purchases a base chassis, which usually includes a power supply, backplane, and possibly a management processor and other necessary features, and selects modules based on the application environment. Modules can be easily changed, often without powering down the chassis or disrupting the network; this is called *hot-swap* operation.

The chassis provides some fixed number of module slots; common configurations may provide as few as 2 or as many as 10 or more slots. The options often correspond to the height specifications of popular 19″ rack-mount equipment. Figure 4.16 depicts a typical chassis switch.

The base chassis generally will have some maximum performance limitation. This is usually a result of the method used to interconnect the modules in the chassis (e.g., the backplane). Regardless of the modules selected, it is not possible to obtain performance in excess of that supported by the base chassis. A manufacturer may have a variety of base chassis available at different performance levels.

Modules are selected based on the technology requirements of the application. Popular modules include:

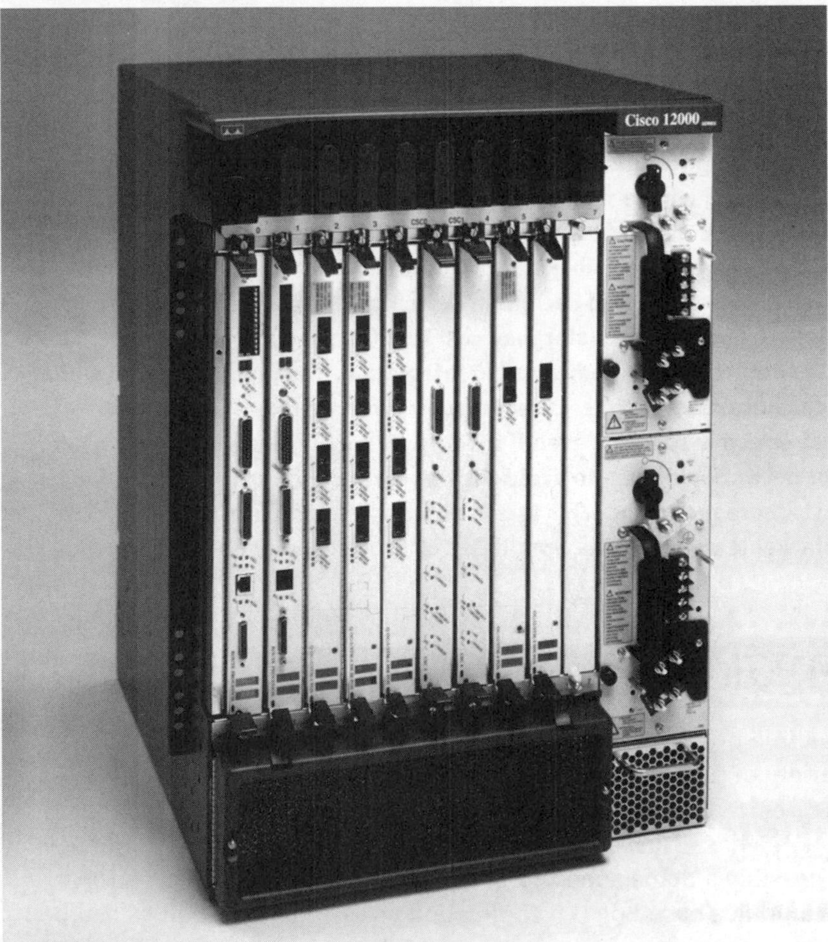

Figure 4.16 Chassis switch. (Courtesy of Cisco Systems)

- Multi-port 10 Mb/s and 10/100 Mb/s Ethernet interfaces
- Multi-port 16 Mb/s Token Ring interfaces
- Multi-port high-speed serial interfaces for WAN connections
- SONET interfaces supporting packet-over-SONET communications

Chassis switches provide the highest performance and maximum flexibility; of course, they usually command the highest price. Given the combination of performance, price, configuration flexibility, and hot-swap capability, chassis switches are most commonly deployed in backbone environments, either at the campus or enterprise level of the hierarchy.

4.7 Switch Application Environments

Large-scale LAN interconnection is generally implemented in a hierarchical manner, as depicted in Figure 4.17.

There are a number of reasons why such hierarchical structures are often employed:

- The burden imposed on the internetworking device(s) is only that of the level at which it is deployed; for example, desktop switches need only accommodate the needs of the desktop environment. If a *flat* intercon-

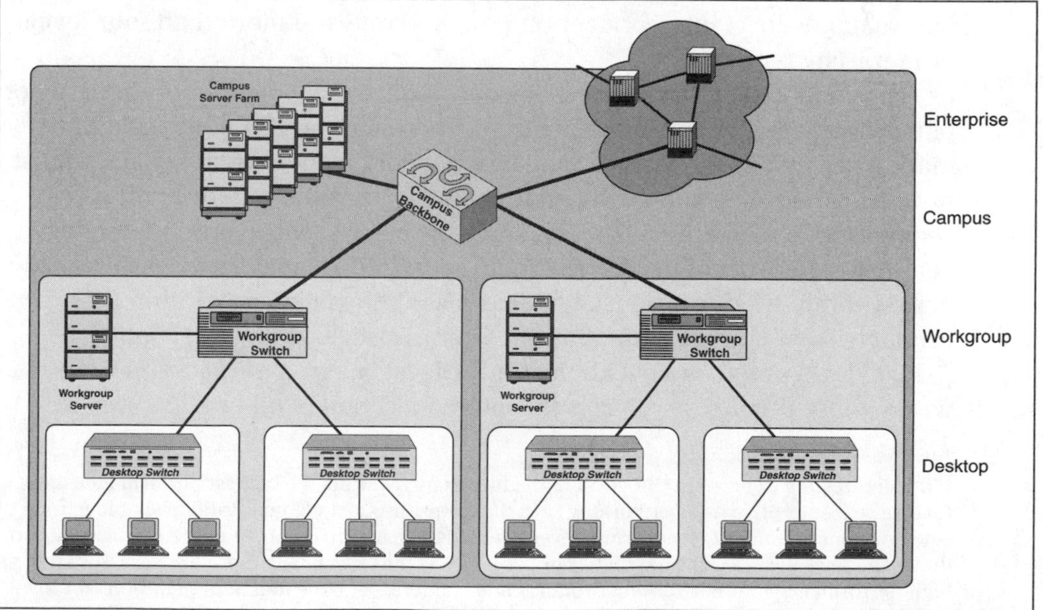

Figure 4.17 LAN interconnection hierarchy.

nection strategy were used (i.e., a single backbone interconnecting all users with no hierarchy), then every interconnection device would need to deal with the issues and complexities of enterprise-wide internetworking, resulting in the use of many more expensive devices.

- The burden imposed on the network administrator is similarly restricted to the level at which the given person operates. Local (departmental) administrators need deal only with the problems associated with the department or workgroup, and not the enterprise as a whole. Similarly, an enterprise administrator does not have to deal directly with the problems of individual users.
- Problems are more naturally isolated; network disruptions typically affect only the users or interconnection at the level of the fault. For most failure modes, the number of users affected by a network disruption is minimized. A failure of the enterprise backbone only disrupts intercampus communications, and allows most workgroup computing to continue unimpeded. A failure of a desktop switch would only affect the users directly connected.

In a given organization, not all levels of the hierarchy are necessarily required. A small company may only operate within a single building and not require campus or enterprise internetworking capability. A geographically separate workgroup in a large company may connect from its workgroup directly to the enterprise backbone without imposing a campus level in the hierarchy, even though other sites within the organization may indeed have campus-level interconnection points. Rarely are more than four levels of hierarchy required.

The terminology used here has become industry standard, both for network planners and equipment manufacturers. These four levels define most of the market segments for switches (and internetworking devices in general). Most products are specifically designed to meet the needs of one (or at most two) segments of this hierarchy. In fact, some companies' entire product strategy centers on a subset of the hierarchy. It is possible to build a successful business without offering products at all levels (although interoperation with products from other manufacturers becomes critical).[32]

Each level provides a backbone for the level below. A *backbone* is a network whose primary purpose is the interconnection of other networks. In

[32] It is interesting to note that the level in the hierarchy requiring the highest performance and feature set (enterprise internetworking) has the lowest product volume (total available market). An enormous amount of engineering development is required to compete in the market that produces the fewest sales (albeit at higher prices). This is the reason why there are very few truly high-performance internetworking products and vendors, yet large numbers of options for low-end desktop products, where the required performance and features are less demanding and the potential volumes are orders-of-magnitude greater.

practice, end users are connected only at the desktop level, never to a backbone. The only devices generally attached directly to a backbone are:

- Interconnection devices (repeaters/bridges/switches/routers)
- Servers (for the given hierarchical level)
- Network management stations (for the network administrator)

Keeping end user attachments off the backbone avoids the possibility of user application problems (e.g., software faults, misconfiguration, desktop hardware failures, and so on) affecting multiple users through disruption of a backbone. Imagine an application or device driver gone berserk (or worse, a malicious user!) generating extremely heavy traffic loads, errors, misdirected traffic, and the like on a campus backbone; such behavior could potentially disrupt thousands of users. In general, it is good practice to limit backbone connections to the devices just listed.

4.7.1 Desktop Level

This is the lowest level in the backbone hierarchy. At this level end-user devices (the "leaves" of the tree) are attached. Depending on the performance level required (and cost constraints), each switch port may support only a single user (microsegmentation), or small shared-LAN hubs (typically 4 to 12-ports) may be used to allow multiple end users to share a single port.

4.7.2 Workgroup Level

Sometimes referred to as the *departmental network*, this level is used to provide intercommunication among desktop switches (if any). A workgroup backbone will generally be constrained within a single building (typically a single floor). In addition to the desktop switch connections, this level provides attachments for departmental servers (that is, servers owned by and dedicated to the department, providing common application services, printer sharing, etc.) and possibly a department network administrator. A workgroup switch is generally located in a wiring closet within the building in which the department is housed. In many cases it may be in the same rack of equipment as the desktop switches to which it is connected; there is usually no need for long-distance links.

In the event that desktop switches are not deployed (i.e., end users are all on shared LANs) or the department is relatively small, the desktop level can be eliminated, and the workgroup level becomes the bottom of the switch hierarchy. This was the typical case in the past, before desktop switching became economically feasible.

4.7.3 Campus Level

The *campus backbone* provides interconnection among workgroups within a single location. Despite the name, in some cases the campus may be within a single building containing multiple departments. In the more general case, it connects departments across multiple buildings within a single organization (e.g., a corporation or university). The interbuilding links are assumed to be owned and/or controlled by the organization, so that common-carrier WAN technologies (with their lower data rates and monthly charges) are not required at the campus level.

4.7.4 Enterprise Level

At the enterprise level, we are interconnecting geographically separated sites, possibly world-wide. Rarely are the links under the ownership or control of the enterprise being interconnected; in general, we must deal with WAN common carriers (long distance telecommunications service providers).

Many of the issues that arise in private enterprise internetworking also apply to Internet backbone design. Indeed, some organizations have begun using the public Internet as their enterprise backbone (occasionally through the use of a Virtual Private Network construct). Thus, much of the information presented here relating to enterprise-level internetwork requirement also applies to the requirements for devices being used within the Internet itself. There are some key differences, however:

- A private enterprise network will likely have many fewer networks within its scope than the Internet; as such, the size of routing tables in these devices will be lower than in a router being deployed by an Internet Service Provider (ISP).
- By definition, the Internet is an IP-only backbone. Private enterprise backbones may also support other protocols (e.g., IPX).
- Private enterprise networks may choose to bridge rather than route some traffic (especially non-routable protocols such as LAT and NetBIOS); bridging is not supported across the Internet backbone.

4.7.5 The Needs Change with the Level

The functional requirements of an internetworking device depend on the application environment targeted by its designer. It is unlikely that any single product could be used at all layers; such a product would either cost too much for desktop use or be too limited in capability for a campus or enterprise backbone. The following sections identify some of the important product characteristics that vary depending on the application level. If you are a user, you can use the information presented here to compare the general set of requirements to your particular needs. If you are a manufacturer, you can use the same information to identify the product requirements in the various market segments.

Of course, the information provided here should be considered as general guidelines only; your particular needs (or product requirements) will vary according to the precise application scenario. In addition, application and product requirements will change over time as new technologies evolve.

Table 4.3 provides a complete summary, in matrix form, of the functional requirements relative to the hierarchical interconnection levels. The discussion in the following sections should help the reader to understand the relevance and interpretation of the data in the table.

4.7.5.1 Numbers of Ports

A port is an interface to a LAN or WAN link. In most devices, there are two types of ports to consider:

- *Attachment ports* are used to connect to devices at the hierarchical level at which the device is being used; for example, the attachment ports on a desktop switch are those ports connecting to desktop devices.
- *Uplink ports* are used either to connect to the next tier in the hierarchy or to connect to a high-performance device (e.g., a server) at the current level. Though this is not always the case, uplink ports usually operate at a higher data rate than attachment ports. This is appropriate when aggregating attachment traffic to a higher-level backbone, or for server connections.[33]

Depending on the level in the hierarchy, there are differing needs for both attachment and uplink ports. At the desktop and workgroup levels, devices with anywhere from 4 to 24 attachment ports are practical. Greater port densities are appropriate at the campus and enterprise levels, where there is a need for higher link concentrations.

The number of uplink/server ports required is generally an order of magnitude less than the number of attachment ports. This is due to the typical ratios of clients to servers, as well as to the data rates associated with each hierarchical level (e.g., 10/100/1000 Mb/s).

[33] The use of link aggregation to create a high-performance uplink from multiple lower-speed ports is discussed in Chapter 9, *Link Aggregation*.

Table 4.3 LAN Interconnection Product Characteristics/Application Environment Matrix

	DESKTOP	WORKGROUP	CAMPUS	ENTERPRISE/ISP
Number of Ports				
Attachments	4–24	8–24	8–48+	16–48
Uplinks	1–2	2–4	2–8	Not applicable
Switching versus Routing	Switching only	Primarily switching, some routing for intergroup communications	Primarily routing, some switching for non-routable protocols	Predominantly routing, some switching for non-routable protocols (enterprise) Routing only (ISP)
Higher Layer Protocol Support	Not applicable	IP, IPX, AppleTalk, possibly DECnet Phase IV	IP, IPX, AppleTalk	IP, IPX, AppleTalk (enterprise) IP only (ISP)
Number of Switch Table Entries	32–256 MAC addresses	256–2K MAC addresses	2K–64K MAC addresses	8K–64K MAC addresses (enterprise) N/A (ISP)
Number of Routing Table Entries	Not applicable	16–64 routes 256–2K ARP cache entries	64–1K routes 32–256 ARP cache entries	256–2K routes (enterprise) 10K–100K+ routes (ISP) 16–128 ARP cache entries
Link Technologies				
Attachments	Ethernet	Ethernet, some legacy Token Ring	Ethernet, some legacy FDDI	FT1/T1/T3 (with/without Frame Relay), ISDN PRI, SONET OC-3/12/48/192 (with/without ATM), WDM
Uplinks	Ethernet	Ethernet	WAN technology	Not applicable

Port Data Rates				
Attachments	10 Mb/s, 100 Mb/s	Primarily 100 Mb/s, some legacy 10 Mb/s and 16 Mb/s	100 Mb/s, 1000 Mb/s	≤1.5–45–155 Mb/s, migrating to 622 Mb/s–2.4 Gb/s+
Uplinks	100 Mb/s	100 Mb/s, 1000 Mb/s	56 kb/s–1.5 Mb/s–45 Mb/s, migrating to 155–622–2500 Mb/s+	Not applicable
Aggregate Capacity	<1000 Mb/s	500 Mb/s–4 Gb/s	2–40 Gb/s	20–100+ Gb/s
Virtual LAN Support (see Chapters 11 and 12)	None, Port, or MAC address–based	Port, MAC address, protocol and/or subnet-based	Port, MAC address, protocol and/or subnet-based	Port, MAC address, protocol and/or subnet-based (if switching is deployed)
Media Support				
Attachments	UTP	UTP	Fiber	WAN media
Uplinks	UTP	UTP, Fiber	WAN media	Not applicable
Installed Location	Wiring closet or ad hoc	Wiring closet, server room	Campus central wiring hub or data center	Corporate Data Center, Telco Central Office, ISP Point-of-Presence (POP)
Cost	Critical (cost-driven market)	Moderately important	Not as important as features, performance, and support	Not as important as features, performance, and support
Available Market Size	Tens of millions of ports; millions of devices	Millions of ports; tens–hundreds of thousands of devices	Tens of thousands of devices	Thousands–tens of thousands of devices
Customer	Departmental Network Planner/Administrator	Departmental Network Planner/Administrator	Facilities Network Planner, Corporate MIS Planner	Corporate MIS Planner (Enterprise) Internet Service Provider (ISP)

4.7.5.2 Layer 2 versus Layer 3 Switching (Bridging versus Routing)

In the old days, there were religious wars fought over the issue of bridging (switching) versus routing [SEIF89, SEIF90, PERL92]. Whole corporations came into existence (some subsequently dying) on one side or the other of this battlefield. Bridges provided high performance (for a given cost), plug-and-play installation, protocol independence, and automatic configuration. Routers provided additional functionality (e.g., IP fragmentation), full mesh topologies with multiple paths, better administrator control, and limited multicast propagation.

Today, few network designers use either technology to the exclusion of the other. Each has its place in the LAN interconnection hierarchy. This is due to a number of factors:

- With constantly improving technology, the cost performance tradeoff does not favor bridges as strongly as it used to. When wire-speed bridges were considered leading-edge technology (late 1980s), wire-speed routers were virtually unheard of or available only at a severe price penalty. Today, as a result of semiconductor integration, it is possible to build both wire-speed, high port-density bridges (switches) and routers at reasonable cost.
- Enterprise networks have grown enormously in recent years, such that simplistic approaches (i.e., "bridge everything" or "route everything") no longer make sense. The range of application environments is wide enough to require a broad variety of products and technologies.
- The growth of IP networks, and the Internet in particular, has made routing a necessity. At a minimum, routing is required at the point where the enterprise network connects to the Internet.
- Security concerns have increased the need for firewalls, which are most easily implemented at a router.

Both technologies are appropriate and necessary; the issue is where to deploy them to achieve the best combination of features, functions, and cost.

It is rarely useful to route within a single logical workgroup. At this level, a flat network makes sense. If internetworking technology is deployed here, it will be in the form of a LAN switch. Thus, practical desktop interconnection devices can be implemented as pure switches, with no routing capability.[34]

[34] In addition, if a router were used for desktop interconnection, then each user workstation would need to have an IP subnet assigned to it exclusively. (By definition, routers interconnect networks, even if the network has only a single user.) This could easily wreak havoc with a company's subnet allocation strategy and internal architecture.

At the workgroup backbone, there will be a need both for switching (for communications between users and a workgroup server) and routing (for intergroup communications). The bulk of the traffic is likely to be between clients and the local servers, although this is changing as organizations move toward Web-style intranetworks with centralized server farms. Since workgroup LANs often incorporate a high mix of equipment types (e.g., PCs running NetWare, Macintosh, UNIX workstations, and so on), a router at this level may have to deal with a wide variety of higher-layer protocols. IP is clearly necessary, but there is still a large installed base of IPX, AppleTalk, and even some DECnet Phase IV-based applications.

At the campus level, there is likely to be a high mix of switched and routed traffic, although it should be possible to restrict the number of routed protocols to one or two. IP (for Internet and enterprise intranet use) and IPX (to support the large NetWare installed base) are the most likely candidates for campus-wide internetworking. Other protocols can either be constrained to the workgroup or tunneled through those protocols that are natively supported (e.g., AURP tunneling of AppleTalk through IP) [RFC1504].

Enterprise backbone design (especially for Internet Service Providers) leans heavily toward a pure IP-routed environment.

4.7.5.3 Table Sizes

In general, organizations do not build huge, flat, switched networks.[35] Beyond some number of users, it becomes desirable to provide the administrative separation, security/firewall capabilities, and multicast traffic isolation provided by routers. While there are internetworks (e.g., the Internet) that support literally millions of computers using routers, rarely does a single switched LAN comprise more than a few thousand active stations. A station capability of 64K addresses is considered adequate for even the largest switched catenet.

Routing protocols usually embody the concept of a *default route*—a path that is chosen when none of the explicitly-known paths to given destinations apply. This allows a router to operate in an environment with large numbers of networks (potentially tens-of-thousands) without having to know about every network explicitly. Thus, the number of route entries can be a function only of the number of networks at or below the current hierarchical level. Similarly, a switch can use an uplink as a *default port*, reducing its lookup table requirement from encompassing every MAC address in the entire switched infrastruc-

[35] A Layer 2 switched LAN is referred to as *flat* because there is no hierarchy to the address space. Network layer protocols (as used in a routed internetwork) always provide some structure to their address space, for example using network identifiers for making routing decisions independent of the individual station identifiers.

ture to those at or below the current level by using a modified frame forwarding policy:

- It directs traffic among its non-uplink ports in the normal fashion, forwarding traffic to a given port when the destination address lookup indicates that the target receiver is reachable through that port.
- In the event of a lookup failure (e.g., a destination is unknown to the switch), rather than flooding the frame onto all ports, the switch can choose to forward the frame onto the uplink port on the assumption that the intended receiver is connected to some switch reachable through the next tier of the hierarchy.[36]

Using this modified policy, the address capability of the switches at lower levels of the hierarchy can be greatly reduced. They only need to support the maximum number of stations that are connected to their local ports, and do not need to keep track of all stations in the catenet (as is normally required of a switch). Thus, a practical desktop switch need only support a few dozen stations, and a workgroup switch only hundreds, rather than tens of thousands as might be present in the entire catenet. This can reduce the cost and complexity of these products considerably.

In IP networks, there is also the consideration of ARP caches. Since there can be no implicit mapping of IP addresses to MAC addresses (due to IP's limited address space), there must be an explicit (table-driven) mapping provided. The ARP cache provides the mapping of IP-to-MAC addresses. In general, there must be an entry in the ARP cache for each station with which a router directly communicates. This is different from the number of network identifiers (routes) that the router may know about.

Depending on the level in the hierarchy, the size of the required ARP cache will vary, most often in an inverse relationship to the number of routing table entries. At the workgroup level, a router may not need to know about very many networks, but it will likely have to know about a large number of directly attached devices (i.e., every IP end station in the department). At the other extreme, an Internet backbone router may need to know about a lot of networks, but has very few directly connected devices (i.e., the adjacent routers, with few if any end stations).[37]

[36] Some accommodation must be made for learning new and/or changed addresses on local ports; in practice, the policy becomes somewhat more complex than described here. The switch needs to (at least initially and/or occasionally) flood unknown traffic to all ports to discover new or moved stations.

[37] This inverse relationship between the number of routes and the number of ARP cache entries can be used to advantage. If a single, common data structure is used for the lookup of both routes and ARP mappings (as discussed in Section 4.4.2.2), a single memory allocation may be appropriate in a wide variety of application environments. At the workgroup level, most of the table entries will consist of ARP mappings; in the enterprise backbone, most entries will be network routes. A compressed binary tree data structure supports this duality well.

4.7.5.4 Link Technologies

The technologies deployed can also vary with the position in the hierarchy. At the desktop, there is a huge installed base of Ethernet that must be accommodated. Thus, Ethernet-only desktop switches are a reasonable solution for many users. Ethernet appears to be firmly ensconced at the desktop and workgroup levels, and is not likely to change in the near future. Campus backbones today include a wider mix of technologies, including Token Ring, FDDI, and some ATM, although Fast and Gigabit Ethernet are the de-facto standards at this level.

At the enterprise level, a router needs to support a wide variety of technologies, from T-carrier and SONET (the predominant approaches today) to Wavelength-Division Multiplexed (WDM) links in the future.

4.7.5.5 Port Data Rates and Aggregate Capacity

Clearly, the data rate of the ports on a switch should correspond to the data rate of the devices connecting to those ports. There is no need to provide greater interconnection capability than can be used by the attached devices. The issue thus becomes, "What are the current (and anticipated future) data rates that are to be found at the various hierarchical levels?"

Desktop attachments today commonly operate at either 10 or 100 Mb/s (with over 100 million installed interfaces). The higher speed is quickly becoming dominant for new installations, if only because the cost of the increased data rate is minimal. Workgroup server ports today use 100 Mb/s Ethernet extensively, and are rapidly migrating to 1000 Mb/s connections. Campus backbone connections often comprise a mix of 100 Mb/s and 1000 Mb/s connections, as they may need to serve thousands of users. Enterprise WAN connections vary from fractional T1 to SONET links operating at 2.4 Gb/s (OC-48) or higher.

In addition to the data rate of the links, there is the issue of the aggregate capacity of the switch itself. If the switch is touted as being non-blocking, its aggregate capacity should be greater than or equal to the sum of the capacities of the individual ports.

It is possible (especially with modular switches supporting very high port data rates, see Section 4.6.3) that a device may be non-blocking for certain configurations, but not for all possible valid configurations. This does not necessarily constitute a problem per se; depending on the traffic patterns and offered load distribution, the internal capacity limitation may never manifest itself as a degradation in application performance. Any such problems can be similarly avoided by avoiding those configurations that exceed the aggregate capacity of the device.[38]

It is also possible (depending on the architecture and the hardware/software trade offs made by the designer) that an internetworking device may operate in a non-blocking manner for certain classes of traffic (e.g., Layer 2 switching and IP routing) but not for others (e.g., IPX and AppleTalk routing). Whether this is appropriate depends on the traffic levels and protocols in use in the target environment.

4.7.5.6 Media Support

As we move from the desktop to the campus, the media of choice changes due to distance requirements, cost, and the need for easy reconfiguration. Unshielded twisted pair (UTP) cable is by far the most popular medium for desktop connections; therefore a desktop interconnection device should be designed with this medium in mind.

A workgroup interconnection device, being similarly restricted in scope to a single floor or building, may also use UTP as its primary attachment medium. Uplink ports from a workgroup device may need to support optical fiber for connection to a campus backbone. At the campus backbone level, fiber is the medium of choice, due to the need to support longer distances and to provide electrical isolation for interbuilding connections.

[38] For example, just because a device has 12 slots and the manufacturer offers an OC-48 interface does not mean that 12 OC-48 ports constitutes a reasonable or non-blocking configuration.

CHAPTER

5

Loop Resolution

In a networking context, bridges may indeed be the greatest invention since sliced bread.[1] However, they are not without their limitations. All of the discussions in earlier chapters made the assumption that the underlying topology could support bridge operation. In this chapter, we consider the topological restrictions imposed by the use of bridges and the means by which we can implement and enforce these restrictions.

5.1 Diary of a Loopy LAN

Consider the situation depicted in Figure 5.1. In this scenario, we have two LANs interconnected by two bridges that are effectively in parallel. Let's make a few assumptions:

- Both bridges are "plain vanilla" (i.e., they don't have any special features or characteristics designed to accommodate this specific situation).
- The address tables within both bridges, at least initially, properly reflect the relative locations of the stations shown. (We will see in a moment that this condition is difficult, if not impossible, to achieve.)

[1] I have always wondered what the greatest invention was *before* sliced bread.

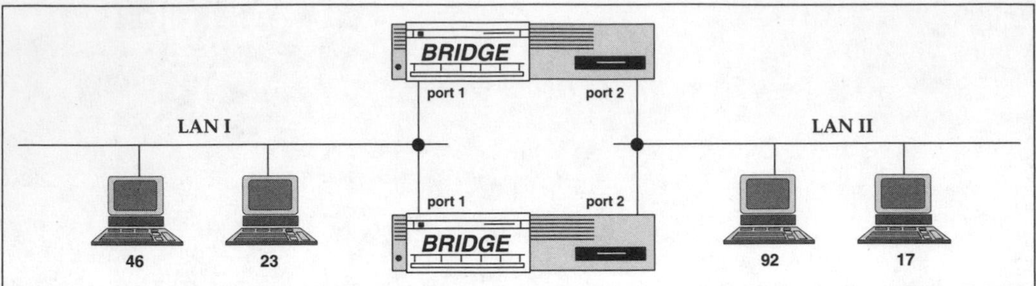

Figure 5.1 Two LANs, two bridges, one problem.

- Both bridges operate according to the principles discussed in Chapter 2, *Transparent Bridges*, with respect to frame filtering, forwarding, and address learning.

Given these assumptions, what will be the resulting behavior?

If station 46 sends a frame to station 17, each bridge will receive the frame on (its respective) port 1. Each bridge will perform a Destination Address lookup and determine that the frame should be queued for transmission on port 2. Ultimately (when each bridge's queue empties sufficiently) the frame will be transmitted on port 2 and received by station 17. Thus, station 17 will receive two copies of every unicast frame destined for it that originates on LAN I. In fact, *every* station on LAN II will receive two copies of every appropriately-addressed unicast frame originating on LAN I. This violates the non-duplication invariant of LANs—a LAN should never deliver multiple frames to a given destination for a single frame transmission. This can result in undesirable behavior in the end stations (read: higher-layer protocol or application crash).

But it gets worse. What happens if station 46 sends a frame to a multicast destination? As in the unicast case, bridges A and B will both forward the frame onto port 2, but bridge A will receive bridge B's forwarded transmission on its port 2 (and similarly, bridge B will receive bridge A's forwarded transmission). Each bridge will execute the relay algorithm for a frame with a multicast destination, which is to forward it onto all ports except the port of arrival. Thus bridge A will forward the multicast frame forwarded by bridge B back onto port 1, and bridge B will forward the multicast frame forwarded by bridge A onto its port 1 as well. The multicast frame just keeps going around in a loop, getting repeated with each revolution. Additional multicasts add to this fray and never disappear from the catenet. This will continue until either the LAN's or the bridges' resources become saturated from the circulating multicasts (which can happen quickly), at which point little real communication can occur.

We're not done yet. Consider what happens when bridge A forwards the unicast frame from station 46 to station 17 in the first example. When the frame is ultimately transmitted on LAN II, bridge B will receive it on its port 2. While it will not forward the unicast frame back onto port I (the address table shows that the destination is indeed present on port 2), it *will* see station 46 as a Source Address on port 2. Bridge B has no choice but to believe that station 46 has moved, and update the address table accordingly as part of the learning process. When station 46 sends another frame, bridge B will hear it on port 1 (station 46 hasn't really moved) and again update the address table back to the way it was in the first place. In fact, as stations continue to send frames (and as the bridges forward them), the address tables will never converge to reflect the proper topology. At any given time, the address tables may or may not contain the correct information; they will be hopelessly thrashing.[2] Since normal bridge operation depends on a stable and proper address table configuration, we surely cannot expect such a situation to achieve useful results. This is a fine mess we've gotten ourselves into this time, Ollie!

5.1.1 Getting Yourself in the Loop

How could we do this? What misguided logic drove us to configure our network this way? There are actually a few reasons why you might get a topology loop as described:

- *Two bridges are better than one?* In the old days, many (if not most) bridges could not operate at wire speed. A poorly performing bridge could be a traffic bottleneck for the catenet. Some (under-informed) network designers actually believed that they could get increased performance by using two (low performance) bridges in a parallel configuration. While it is possible to achieve such a performance improvement with Network layer routers (depending on the routing protocol employed), we can see that such an approach is misguided for bridged catenets.
- *But I didn't know!* In a complex network, it is often difficult to keep close tabs on the actual configuration at any point in time. Network documentation may be incomplete or inaccurate (it is often compiled by those fallible humans), or the configuration may have changed since the documentation was last updated. In many environments, stations, links, and internetwork equipment configurations change so often that it is virtually impossible to be sure that the documentation in hand exactly reflects the network configuration at a given time. Given this uncertainty, it is always possible that a network administrator may inadver-

[2] Another way to look at this is that, from the perspective of bridge B, bridge A either makes station 46 appear to be simultaneously resident on both LANs I and II, or makes it appear that there are two stations 46. This violates either the laws of physics or the bridges' assumption of globally unique addressing. Take your pick.

tently create a loop topology by inserting or enabling a bridge into an active catenet. As we have seen, the results can be catastrophic for the users.

- *Redundancy—you can say that again!*[3] There may be some portions of the catenet that need high availability. A network planner may be willing to pay the price of deploying multiple devices simply to ensure that at least one device will be operational at any given time. Similarly, it may be necessary to take an operating device out of service. To prevent network disruption between the time when a device is removed and the time its replacement is installed, it would help if we could install the replacement first and then remove the original bridge. Unfortunately, unless we change the behavior of bridges, such an action would cause worse problems than just removing the first bridge.

5.1.2 Getting out of the Loop

Obviously, loops are to be avoided in bridged catenets. Even the most simple loop in the active topology as shown in Figure 5.1 results in:

Patient: "Doctor, it hurts when I do that."

Doctor: "Don't do that."

- Unicast frame duplication
- Multicast frame multiplication
- Address table nonconvergence

The inability to tolerate active loops is a fundamental restriction on the topology of bridged catenets. Such loops must be eliminated to ensure proper operation. There are two ways to achieve this end: manual or automatic configuration.

- *Manual topology configuration.* Here's a simple method to avoid loops: Just don't do it! If the catenet is not configured into a loop, there is no problem. Unfortunately, as just discussed, it is not always possible or even desirable to manually configure a loop-free topology. Manual configuration is acceptable for small catenets where network availability is not a major concern, but is not a solution for the general application of bridges.

- *To fix your loops, find a pro to call!* Give a network architect a problem, and the solution is usually to invent a protocol. The problem of loops in a catenet is no exception.

[3] OK: "Redundancy."

5.2 The Spanning Tree Protocol

Since the problem of loop elimination in bridged catenets is universal, it was deemed appropriate to design a vendor-independent protocol to solve the problem, even if loops were created among bridges made by different manufacturers. That is, while any vendor might be able to implement a loop-elimination mechanism for use in all of its own products, there would be no guarantee that the customer's network would consist of that one vendor's products exclusively. (Although the vendor in question might surely want it to be that way!) The original standard for LAN bridges (IEEE 802.1D) [IEEE90a] included such a universal loop resolution protocol.

5.2.1 History of the Spanning Tree Protocol

LAN bridges were first conceived and developed during the mid-1980s, primarily at Digital Equipment Corp. (DEC). It was recognized even then that depending on human beings to properly configure a loop-free topology was problematic at best, and that an automatic topology configuration mechanism was needed.

As a result, DEC developed a protocol that operated among the bridges in the catenet to automatically detect and resolve loops and to configure the catenet in the best possible arrangement, where "best possible" was defined by the parameters of the protocol. Early DEC-manufactured bridges, including the popular DEC LANBridge 100, implemented this protocol.

Seifert's Law of Networking #7
Human beings make misteaks.

Industry interest in bridge technology grew rapidly during the 1980s, with many manufacturers trying to get a piece of the rapidly-growing market for such products. During 1985, in an effort to "make the world safe for bridges," discussions began within the IEEE 802.1 Interworking Task Force (IEEE 802.1D) toward developing an industry standard for transparent bridge operation that would provide users a measure of assurance that they could buy products that would interoperate properly from multiple vendors. The Task Force created a standard that included a Spanning Tree Protocol (STP), based on the original DEC protocol, that provided loop resolution for the catenet.[4]

Unfortunately, the STP defined in the IEEE standard is similar to, but not precisely the same as, the original DEC STP. While the two protocols are

[4] The IEEE 802.1D standard has been revised and reaffirmed a number of times since, with no significant changes to the Spanning Tree Protocol [IEEE93a, IEEE98a].

based on the same operating principles, they differ slightly in their details, both in the algorithm used within the bridges and the format of the messages exchanged on the links. As such, the two protocols do not interoperate. To assure resolution to a loop-free configuration, it is necessary that all of the bridges use the same protocol, either the DEC version or the IEEE version.

In theory, it is possible that disparate sections of a catenet could each use a different STP and still operate properly. As long as any potential loops included only bridges using a single protocol, the catenet would properly resolve to a loop-free topology. However, the probability that such a configuration would arise by itself is quite low. A network administrator would have to take great care to ensure that there were no loops that ever included bridges using different STPs. In addition, there would be no protection against the accidental insertion of a bridge between the disparate sections causing a loop that would not be eliminated by either protocol, resulting in severe network disruption. During the transition period when both protocols were in common use, such situations occasionally arose.

There was a transition period during the late 1980s and early 1990s in which user networks often comprised products that implemented the DEC protocol, the IEEE 802.1D protocol, or both. Many vendors supported both protocols, with the actual protocol in use controlled by a user-configurable software switch. Virtually all products in use from the mid-1990s onward use the IEEE 802.1D STP exclusively. If users have a choice of protocols (as a configurable parameter), they should invariably select the IEEE STP for maximum interoperability, unless they absolutely must support some piece of ancient DEC-compatible equipment in their network.[5] The descriptions and discussion of the STP that follow in this and other chapters relate exclusively to the IEEE 802.1D version of the protocol.

5.2.2 Spanning Tree Protocol Operation

Okay, everyone knows that the Spanning Tree Protocol eliminates active loops in a bridged catenet. (If you didn't know this before, now you do.) The formal specification of the protocol is contained in the IEEE 802.1D standard [IEEE90a]. However, like most standards, IEEE 802.1D is more suitable as a cure for insomnia than as a practical guide to network operations.[6] The following sections provide an explanation of the principles, operation, and behavior of the STP at a level of detail not found elsewhere. If your interest stops at knowing what the protocol does (without caring *how* it does it), you can safely skip the rest of this section and go directly to Section 5.3. (Do not pass Go, do not collect $200.) If you are an implementor responsible for

[5] Users in this category know who they are!

[6] It can also be an effective contraceptive, if read at the appropriate time.

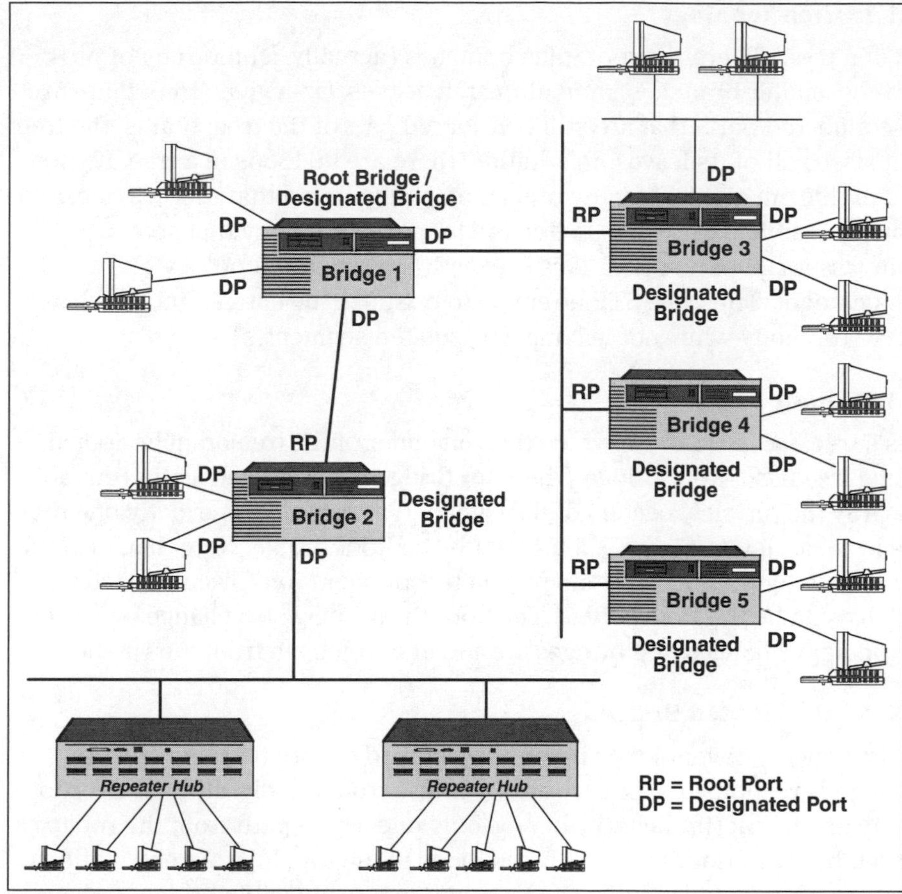

Figure 5.2 Spanning tree concepts.

designing a product that must conform to the official standard, or a network administrator trying to troubleshoot spanning tree–related problems in a bridged catenet, the explanations given here will help you greatly, but you should still refer to the IEEE standard for the official conformance and interoperability requirements of the protocol.[7]

5.2.2.1 Spanning Tree Protocol Concepts

Before we can delve into a discussion of how the spanning tree itself is calculated and maintained, we first need to understand some basic concepts employed by the protocol. Figure 5.2 depicts a representative set of LANs interconnected by bridges in a spanning tree, and is useful for understanding these concepts.

[7] The standard includes a reference C language definition of the protocol.

5.2.2.1.1 Tree Topology

Think of a tree.[8] There is a root, plus branches (actually, a hierarchy of progressively smaller branches), and ultimately leaves. On a given tree, there are no disconnected parts that are still considered part of the tree; that is, the tree encompasses all of its leaves. In addition, there are no loops in a tree. If you trace a path from any leaf to any other leaf, you will find that there is one, and only one, possible path.[9] Thus, a tree is a loop-free topology that spans (encompasses) all of its parts. This is exactly the desired topology for our bridged catenet. Thus, the STP attempts to organize the catenet into such a loop-free topology while not leaving any isolated segment(s).

5.2.2.1.2 Root Bridge

Just as a tree has a root from which the remainder of the tree branches out, a spanning tree has a Root Bridge. The Root Bridge is the logical center (but not necessarily the physical center) of the catenet. There is always exactly one root bridge in a catenet. In Figure 5.2, bridge 1 is the Root Bridge. Note that, depending on the configuration of certain parameters of operation (discussed later), any bridge can be the Root Bridge. The Root Bridge may also change over time if the topology changes or if bridges are added or removed from the catenet.

5.2.2.1.3 Designated Bridges

A simple way to prevent loops in the catenet is to ensure that one and only one bridge is responsible for forwarding traffic from the direction of the root onto any given link (branch). If there is only one active path from the root to a link, then by definition there will be no loops in the topology. As end stations (leaves) are connected to links (LANs), this "one responsible bridge" policy will ensure that there is only one path between any pair of end stations. The bridge responsible for forwarding traffic in the direction from the root to a given link is known as the Designated Bridge for that link.

Each link will have exactly one Designated Bridge. The Designated Bridge for a given link is directly connected to that link. The Root Bridge is always the Designated Bridge for all links to which it is directly connected. Non-Root Bridges (such as bridges 2 and 3 in Figure 5.2) may be the Designated Bridges

[8] It may help to look at one outside your window, unless you are in a major city or highly-developed area. In that case, you will have to wait until the standards committee develops a "Spanning Ugly Building" protocol to replace the Spanning Tree Protocol.

[9] Okay, okay, there is also a very strange sort of tree, called a Banyan, that actually does appear to contain loops. Banyan tree branches can send down new vertical growths, which root themselves into the ground to start a new trunk, which then forms more branches, continuing the process. The tree can spread over a very wide area. If you look at the tree, it appears as if there were lots of separate trees whose branches have grown together. It is very unnerving (like watching an episode of *The Twilight Zone*) to see a branch leave one tree trunk and appear to end in the trunk of another, different tree, rather than tapering into smaller branches and leaves. There is a very large, famous Banyan tree that occupies more than 3 acres of land in a park in Lahaina, on the island of Maui in the Hawaiian Islands. Go there and check it out. Send me a postcard.

for no links, one link, or more than one link in the catenet. It is possible that every bridge in the catenet may be a Designated Bridge for some link.

5.2.2.1.4 Designated Ports and Root Ports

For a given Designated Bridge, there are three types of ports:

- A *Designated Port* is a port in the active topology used to forward traffic away from the root onto the link(s) for which this bridge is the Designated Bridge. That is, a Designated Bridge attaches to the link(s) for which it is designated through a Designated Port. For example, in Figure 5.2, bridge 5 has two Designated Ports (attaching to microsegmented individual station links). A Designated Bridge will have as many Designated Ports as it has links for which it is the Designated Bridge.
- A *Root Port* is the port in the active topology that provides connectivity from the Designated Bridge toward the root. With one exception, a given Designated Bridge will have exactly one Root Port, since (as we all remember) there is exactly one Root. The exception is the Root Bridge itself. While the Root Bridge is indeed a Designated Bridge, it has no Root Port.

  Designated Bridges will forward traffic from the Root Port to one or more of its Designated Ports, as determined by the normal forwarding rules of the bridge. Similarly, a Designated Bridge will also forward traffic from its Designated Port(s) to its Root Port, as determined by those same forwarding rules.
- All other ports of a Designated Bridge will be inactive (disabled or blocking) in the steady-state. That is, a bridge only forwards traffic to and from its Root and Designated Ports. All other ports are not part of the active topology of the catenet. The bridge may still listen for, and possibly transmit, STP messages on these links in order to properly maintain the active topology, as discussed later in this chapter.

5.2.2.1.5 Bridge Identifiers and Port Identifiers

In order for bridges to properly configure, calculate, and maintain the spanning tree, there needs to be a way to uniquely identify each bridge in the catenet and each port within a bridge. A Bridge Identifier is a 64-bit (8 byte) field unique to each bridge in the catenet.[10] Depicted in Figure 5.3, the Bridge Identifier is a concatenation of a globally-unique 48-bit field and a 16-bit "priority" value.

Now, where are we going to get a 48-bit globally-unique field to use for the Bridge Identifier? Hmmm . . . let's use a MAC address! Since a bridge is used to interconnect LANs, and LANs (at least those compatible with IEEE 802 addressing conventions) generally use 48-bit globally-unique MAC addresses, the bridge should have a MAC address associated with each LAN to which it connects. We

[10] Properly implemented, the Bridge Identifier is actually unique to each bridge in the universe!

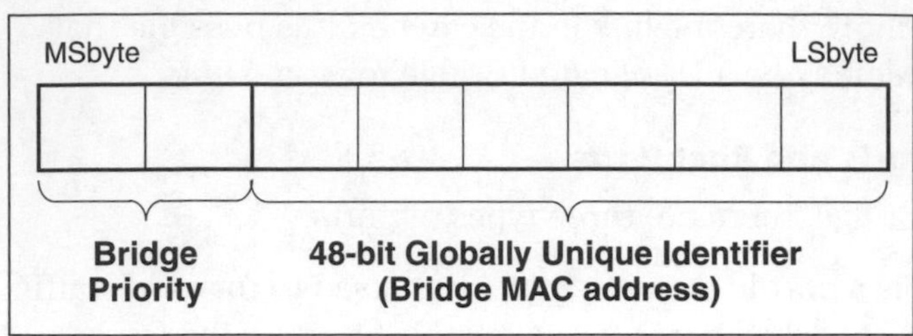

Figure 5.3 Bridge Identifier.

can simply use one of those addresses as the 48-bit portion of the Bridge Identifier. Since all we care about is uniqueness, it doesn't really matter which of the bridge's port MAC addresses we use, although popular convention uses the address of the lowest-numbered port, referred to as the Bridge MAC address.

MAC addresses (as discussed in Chapter 1, *Laying the Foundation*) consist of a globally-assigned Organizationally-Unique Identifier (OUI) and a manufacturer-assigned field. OUIs are not assigned in any particular order; a given manufacturer may have a numerically high or low value regardless of when the OUI assignment was made. This is usually of no concern, since MAC addresses normally do not have any numerical significance; that is, they are identifiers and not numbers. It is unimportant from the perspective of LAN operation whether one MAC address is numerically greater or less than any other; the value does not impart any advantage one way or the other. However, for the purposes of calculating the spanning tree (as discussed later in this chapter), this is no longer the case. The determination of Root and Designated Bridges is dependent in part on the numerical value of the Bridge Identifier. Because of this dependency, and the fact that we would like the resultant topology to be both deterministic and independent of the manufacturer of the bridge or interface, we append a "priority" field to the MAC address to create the Bridge Identifier.

The priority field allows a network administrator to control the topology independently from that which would result if she depended solely on the numerical nature of the 48-bit MAC address(es). Thus, a manufacturer whose OUI provided a numerical advantage over another's would not automatically cause that company's bridges to become the Root or Designated Bridges. The network administrator can configure priority values such that the spanning tree will resolve to any desired topology, with specific administrator-selected bridges becoming the Root, Designated Bridges, and so on. This is discussed in more detail in Section 5.6. The priority field of the Bridge Identifier can be in the range of 0 to 65,535 (0xFFFF); the default value is the center of the range (32,768, or 0x8000).

Each port on a bridge is assigned a Port Identifier, as depicted in Figure 5.4. Similar to the Bridge Identifier, a Port Identifier concatenates a unique 8-bit port number with a configurable priority field.

Port numbers are locally-unique (to the bridge), and simply denote the number of the physical attachment on the bridge. They are numbered from 1 to *N*,

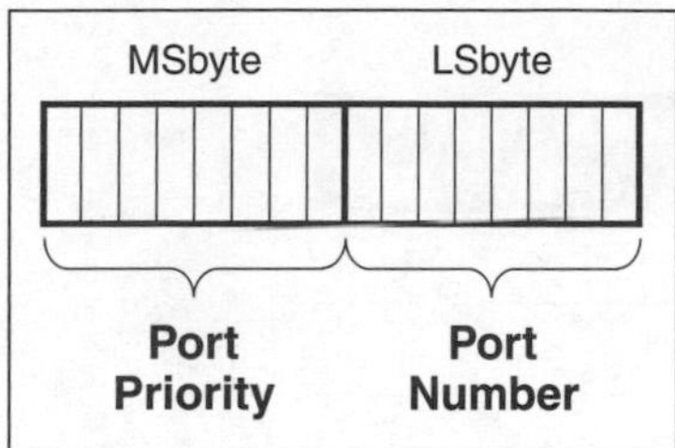

Figure 5.4 Port Identifier.

where N is the number of ports on the device. The priority field in the Port Identifier is used in a manner identical to the priority field in the Bridge Identifier. Network administrators can configure this value so that the topology is independent of the numbering of the ports within a bridge. The priority field of the Port Identifier can be in the range of 0 to 255 (0xFF); the default value is the center of the range (128, or 0x80).

5.2.2.1.6 Links and Link Costs

Each port on a bridge connects to a link. That link may be a high-speed LAN or, alternatively, some wide area communications technology. The STP attempts to configure the catenet such that every leaf (end station) is reachable from the root through the path with the lowest cost. By default, the cost of a given link was originally specified [IEEE90a] to be inversely proportional to the data rate of the link:

$$\text{Link Cost} = \frac{1000}{\text{Data Rate}_{\text{Mb/s}}}$$

Thus, a 10 Mb/s Ethernet "costs" 100, a 16 Mb/s Token Ring costs 62, etc.[11] This default cost equation served the needs of bridged catenets for many years, when LAN data rates were on the order of tens to hundreds of megabits per second. However, since the cost metric is an integer, this default sets an upper bound of 1 Gb/s on the data rate of a link. There were extensive discussions about this problem within the IEEE 802.1 committee, as this limit was reached with the emergence of Gigabit Ethernet and threatens to be exceeded with the use of technologies such as frames-over-SONET at OC-48 rates and above. As such, the 1998 revision of IEEE 802.1 [IEEE98a] offers a somewhat modified link cost algorithm, with a range of values for any given data rate and a recommended value that has a non-linear relationship between link cost and data rate for very high-speed LANs, as shown in Table 5.1.

These recommendations allow backward compatibility with the original default equation (the recommended ranges for all links slower than 1 Gb/s

[11] It is possible for a network administrator to change a link cost from the default to any arbitrary value in order to make the catenet configure as desired, although this is rarely (if ever) done.

Table 5.1 Link Cost Recommendations

DATA RATE	RECOMMENDED LINK COST RANGE	RECOMMENDED LINK COST VALUE
4 Mb/s	100–1000	250
10 Mb/s	50–600	100
16 Mb/s	40–400	62
100 Mb/s	10–60	19
1 Gb/s	3–10	4
10 Gb/s	1–5	2

ONE-BYTE PORT NUMBERS AND DENSE SWITCHES

The STP was developed during the 1980s. At that time, bridges were used primarily to interconnect shared LANs, typically with tens or hundreds of devices on them. Given this usage and the fact that bridges were relatively expensive, practical bridges had few ports. Two-port bridges were extremely common, and bridges with more than eight ports were virtually unheard of. In this context, an 8 bit port number was considered more than adequate.

The decision to use 8 bit port numbers failed to anticipate the emergence of switched LANs and microsegmentation. When inexpensive bridges are used to connect to individual end stations rather than shared LANs, we get the distinct possibility that a manufacturer may wish to build a bridge with more than 255 ports. The current design of the STP does not easily support such a configuration. (It is possible to overcome the limitation by making a single bridge appear as multiple bridges, each with 255 ports or fewer.)

This issue has been discussed extensively within the standards committee. The consensus is that a change should be made to allow some number of bits of the Port priority field to be used instead for the Port Number, thus increasing the maximum number of ports identifiable on a single bridge. Activity is currently under way in IEEE 802.1 to implement this change in a manner backward-compatible with the existing usage of these fields. In the meantime, some manufacturers that build switches with extremely high port densities have implemented their own proprietary workarounds to the port number limitation.

In practice, the problem emerges only if a large number of ports attach to the same LAN; this is not likely to be the case for a switch used in a desktop, microsegmented environment.

encompass the value from the original equation), yet provide some flexibility and extension for links of 1 Gb/s and higher, at least for a few years.

5.2.2.1.7 Path Cost

As stated earlier, the STP attempts to configure the catenet such that every station is reachable from the root through the path with the lowest cost. The cost of a path is the sum of the costs of the links attached to the root ports in that path, as calculated earlier.

5.2.2.2 Calculating and Maintaining the Spanning Tree

The spanning tree topology for a given set of links and bridges is determined by the Bridge Identifiers, the link costs, and (if necessary) the Port Identifiers associated with the bridges in the catenet. Logically, we need to perform three operations:

1. Determine (elect) a Root Bridge.
2. Determine (elect) the Designated Bridges and Designated Ports for each link.
3. Maintain the topology over time.

In practice, all of these are done in parallel, through the spanning tree algorithm operating identically and independently in each bridge.

5.2.2.2.1 Elect a Root

Since there can be only one Root Bridge, and any bridge is theoretically capable of becoming the root, we hold an election to determine which bridge it will be. The election algorithm is simple: The bridge with the numerically-lowest Bridge Identifier becomes the Root Bridge at any given time. A change in the catenet involving the lowest-numbered bridge (either adding a new bridge with a lower-numbered Bridge Identifier or removing the current Root Bridge) will cause the spanning tree to reconfigure such that Root Bridge always has the lowest-numbered Bridge Identifier.

Network administrators can control which bridge will be the default root, and the order in which other bridges will assume root responsibility, by manipulating the priority field in the Bridge Identifiers. Since the priority field constitutes the most-significant bits of the Bridge Identifier, it always overrides any effect of the remaining 48 bits.

5.2.2.2.2 Elect the Designated Bridges and Designated Ports

Once there is a Root Bridge, we need to identify, for each and every link in the catenet, a single bridge responsible for forwarding traffic from the root to that link. This is the Designated Bridge for the link in question. By definition, the Root Bridge is the Designated Bridge for each link to which it attaches. The Designated Bridge for each other link will be the bridge that offers the lowest-cost path back to the root. Remember that the path cost is simply the sum of the link costs over the path, with the link costs determined by the data rate of each link. Thus, the spanning tree will form such that the highest-capacity links are always used, rather than diverting traffic needlessly through slower links.

It is possible that two bridges can offer the same path cost back to the root. In Figure 5.5, both bridges 14 and 7 offer a path cost back to the root of 100 for link B and are thus equally qualified to serve as Designated Bridge for link B. In the event of such a tie, the bridge with the lowest-numbered Bridge Identifier will become the Designated Bridge.

Similarly, it is possible that a Designated Bridge can have two ports on the same link. (See bridge 7 in Figure 5.5.) Only one of the ports can be the Designated Port for the link; this honor goes to the port with the lowest-numbered Port Identifier. Again, network administrators can decide in advance exactly which ports will become designated through manipulation of the priority field in the Port Identifiers. The spanning tree is completely defined by the set of Designated Bridges (including the Root Bridge) and Designated Ports.

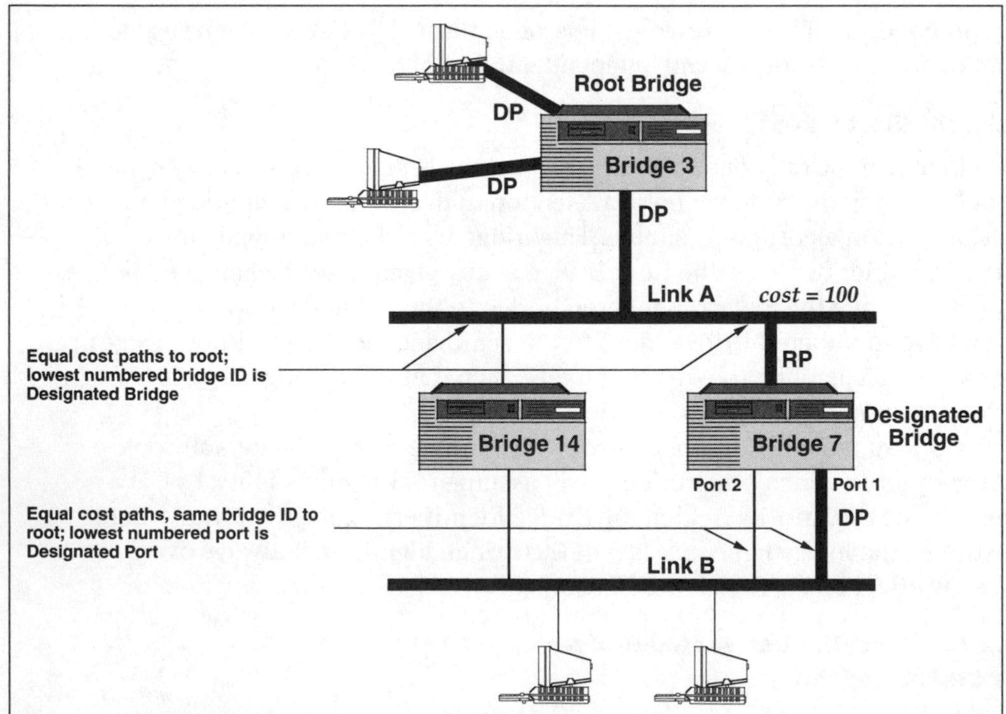

Figure 5.5 Breaking a tie.

5.2.2.2.3 Gardening in the LAN Arboretum (Spanning Tree Maintenance)

Now that we have our beautiful, healthy spanning tree,[12] we need to maintain a constant watch over it to ensure that changes don't cause loops to form or portions of the catenet to become separated from the tree. The events that might instigate a change in the topology are the removal, addition, failure, or recovery of a bridge or link, or the reconfiguration of any of the spanning tree election parameters through network management. Note that the initialization or "cold start" of a catenet is simply a special case of spanning tree maintenance. There may be a lot of bridges and/or links being added at once; the operation of the protocol accommodates this without invoking any special start-up mechanisms.[13]

The STP operates on the principle that all Designated Bridges (including the root) advertise their current understanding of the spanning tree and their internal state by emitting, on a regular basis through their Designated Ports, Configuration Messages (encoded as Bridge Protocol Data Units, or BPDUs; see Section 5.2.2.3). All bridges listen to these Configuration Messages and compare the advertised information to their own internal information. When a bridge's internal information (e.g., Bridge Identifier or path cost) indicates that it has a better claim to become the Root Bridge, Designated Bridge, and so on, than that being advertised, it takes action to change the topology appropriately.

When the spanning tree has converged to the proper topology, the regular emission of Configuration Messages maintains that topology, keeping inactive bridges and ports from becoming active and creating undesirable loops. In the event of a link or bridge failure, the lack of regular Configuration Messages from the now-failed link or bridge (i.e., a timeout) may cause previously inactive bridges and ports to become active in order to maintain maximum connectivity. The spanning tree topology will then reconverge to the best topology now available.

In normal (steady-state) operation, the protocol operates as follows:

1. Once every Hello time (typically 2 seconds, discussed further in Section 5.2.2.6), the Root Bridge transmits a Configuration Message encoded as a BPDU. This message indicates that the sender is the Root Bridge (the Root Identifier will be the same as the Bridge Identifier in the BPDU) and that the path cost is zero (since it is being sent by the root).

2. All bridges sharing links with the Root Bridge (e.g., bridges 2 and 3 in Figure 5.2) receive the message and pass it to the STP entity within the

[12] I promise to refrain from using any fertilizer analogies!

[13] The STP does assume that the topology is quasi-static, that is, it does not change faster than the ability of the algorithm to converge on the new topology. The STP will not provide a stable, usable configuration if bridges and links are being constantly added and/or removed. It is presumed that such changes occur infrequently relative to the timers employed by the protocol.

bridge. BPDUs are never forwarded through a bridge as are data frames from end stations.

3. Designated Bridges (or bridges preparing to become designated) use the information received from the Root Bridge to create a new Configuration Message, updating the values of the Bridge Identifier, path cost, Port Identifier, and other fields appropriately, and transmit this message out each of its Designated Ports.
4. Similarly, bridges sharing links with each of these Designated Bridges receive this second-tier message; as a result, the Designated Bridges for the next tier in the tree will transmit new, modified messages through their own Designated Ports. This process continues until there are no more Designated Bridges (i.e., the tree has reached the leaves).

Every bridge receiving Configuration Messages compares the information received with its own internal state and knowledge. Specifically, a bridge compares:

- The Root Identifier in received messages to its own Bridge Identifier. If a bridge's own identifier is numerically lower than the currently-advertised Root Identifier, then this bridge should attempt to become the root. It would do so by initiating a topology change and then sending Configuration Messages with its own Bridge Identifier as the Root Identifier.
- The path cost in received messages to the path cost available to this bridge through any other ports. That is, if a bridge believes that it can offer a lower-cost path to a given link than the cost currently being advertised by a Designated Bridge, then it will initiate a topology change and attempt to become the Designated Bridge for that link. In the case of equal path costs, a bridge will compare the advertised Bridge Identifier to its own to see if it should attempt to become the Designated Bridge due to having a lower Bridge Identifier. In the case of both equal path costs and equal Bridge Identifiers, the bridge will compare the advertised Port Identifier with the Port Identifier of the port on which the message was received to see if it should change Designated Ports within the bridge.

In this manner, the operation of the STP state machine for each bridge port always determines whether the current spanning tree configuration is correct, and takes corrective (topology change) action when it is not.

5.2.2.3 Bridge Protocol Data Units

Bridge Protocol Data Units (BPDUs) are the messages used by bridges implementing the STP to learn about the existence of other bridges and to obtain the information needed to calculate and maintain the spanning tree.[14]

[14] The pronunciation of BPDU as "bip-a-doo" has never really caught on. I don't know why.

5.2.2.3.1 BPDU Format

Figure 5.6 depicts the BPDU message format. As can be seen, the message includes all of the information necessary for a bridge port to convey its current state to other bridge ports on the link and to compute a new state based upon similar information received from other bridge ports. All of the relevant protocol timer parameters (discussed further in Section 5.2.2.6) are also included so that STP operation can be consistent across all bridges in the catenet.

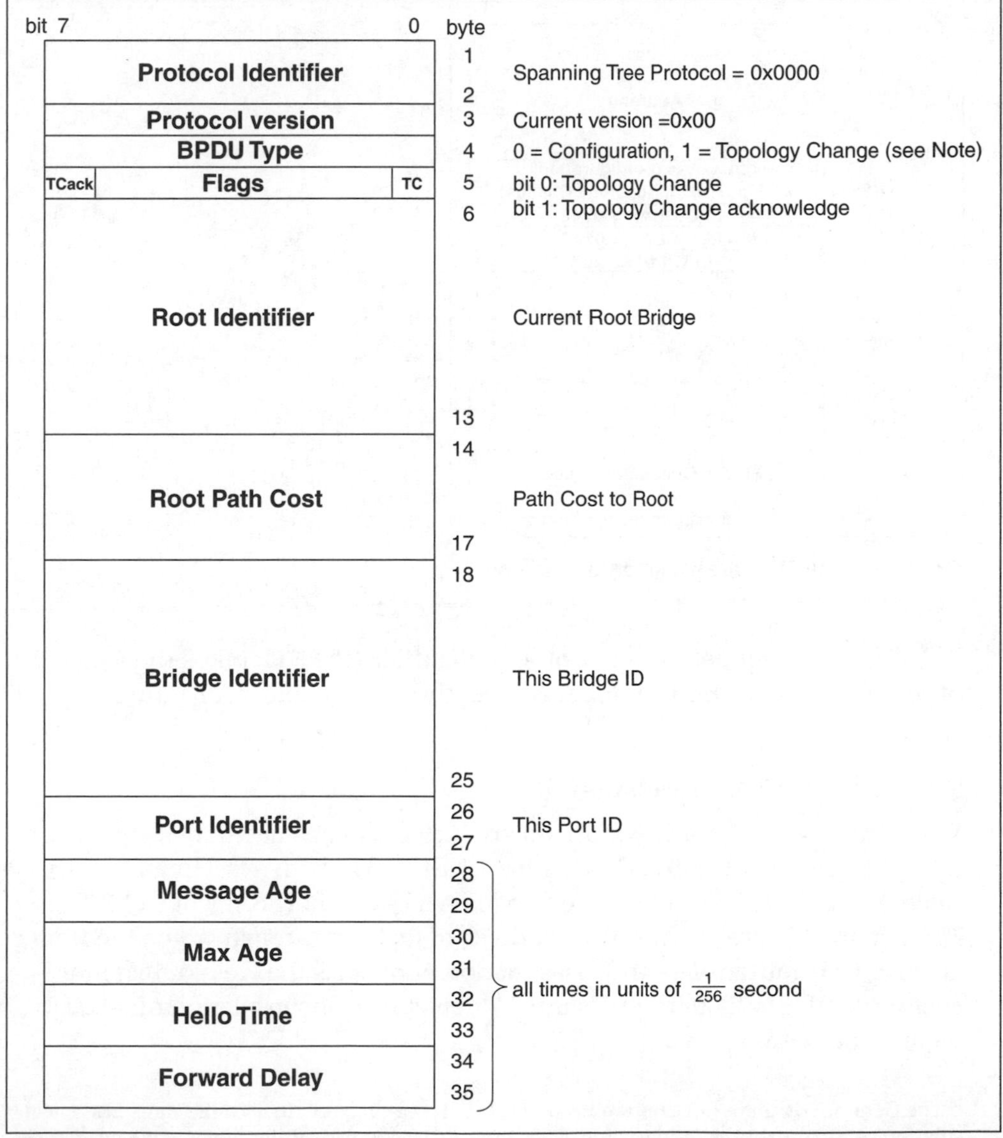

Figure 5.6 BPDU format. (Note: For a Topology Change BPDU, all fields after the BPDU Type are not present.)

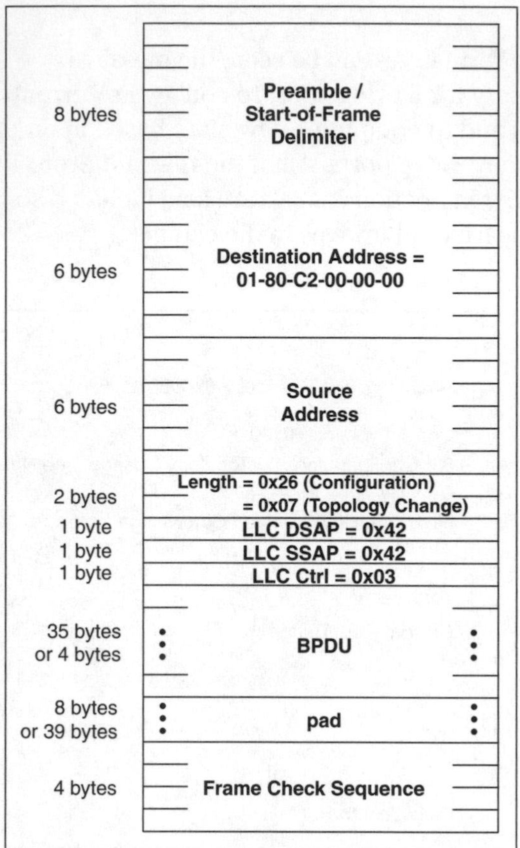

Figure 5.7 BPDU encapsulation on Ethernet.

The BPDU includes both a protocol identifier (the STP takes the value of 0x0000) and a version number (currently 0x00) to allow for future extensions.[15]

5.2.2.3.2 BPDU Encapsulation

When transmitted on a LAN, BPDUs are further encapsulated in MAC frames using Logical Link Control (LLC) Type 1 [IEEE98b], with a Destination Service Access Point (DSAP) and Source Service Access Point (SSAP) of 0x42. The MAC Source Address is the MAC address of the port through which the frame is being transmitted. The MAC Destination Address is the well-known multicast value 01-80-C2-00-00-00. Figure 5.7 depicts the encapsulation of a BPDU on an Ethernet LAN.

[15] The Generic Attribute Registration Protocol (GARP, see Chapter 10) uses the same LLC encapsulation as BPDUs, but takes the value 0x0001 for the protocol identifier to distinguish BPDUs from GARP messages.

AND THE ANSWER IS . . . FORTY-TWO!

The choice of 0x42 as the LLC SAP value for BPDUs has an interesting history. First, the chair and editor of the IEEE 802.1D Task Force (Mick Seaman) was British, and 42 is "The Answer to the Ultimate Question of Life, the Universe, and Everything" in *The Hitchhiker's Guide to the Galaxy* [ADAM79], a popular British book, radio, and television series at the time of the development of the original standard.

Even in the United States, the series was so popular that the original Digital Equipment Corp. bridge architecture specification was titled *eXtended LAN Interface Interconnect,* or XLII, the Roman representation of 42.

Finally, 0x42 is a palindrome; it has the same binary pattern regardless of whether one transmits the most-significant bit first or the least-significant bit first—0100 0010. This eliminates any confusion regarding bit ordering of the field when transmitted on Little Endian (e.g., Ethernet) versus Big Endian (e.g., Token Ring) networks, although this side benefit was not recognized until after the value was assigned.

The use of a well-known multicast address as the destination for all spanning tree BPDUs is important. This allows bridges to send BPDUs to all other bridges without having to know the unicast address(es) of the bridge ports that will receive the BPDU, or whether there are any bridges on the link to hear the message at all. Note that this address is within the range of addresses reserved by IEEE 802.1D for link-constrained protocols. As discussed in Chapter 2, frames with Destination Addresses in the range of 01-80-C2-00-00-00 through 01-80-C2-00-00-0F are never forwarded by an IEEE 802.1D-conformant bridge. This prevents the unwanted propagation of BPDUs beyond the link on which they are significant. In Section 5.7, we discuss the implications of bridges that do not implement the STP and that may forward BPDUs as if they were normal multicast frames.

5.2.2.4 Port States

Each port on a bridge can be in one of five states, as controlled by a relatively simple finite-state machine depicted in Figure 5.8. Table 5.2 summarizes the behavior of a port for each of the five possible states.

5.2.2.4.1 Disabled

A *disabled* port is just what it sounds like. When disabled, a port will neither receive nor transmit data frames or STP messages (BPDUs). Typically, a port is in this state because it is broken, its associated link has failed, or it has been intentionally disabled by a network administrator.

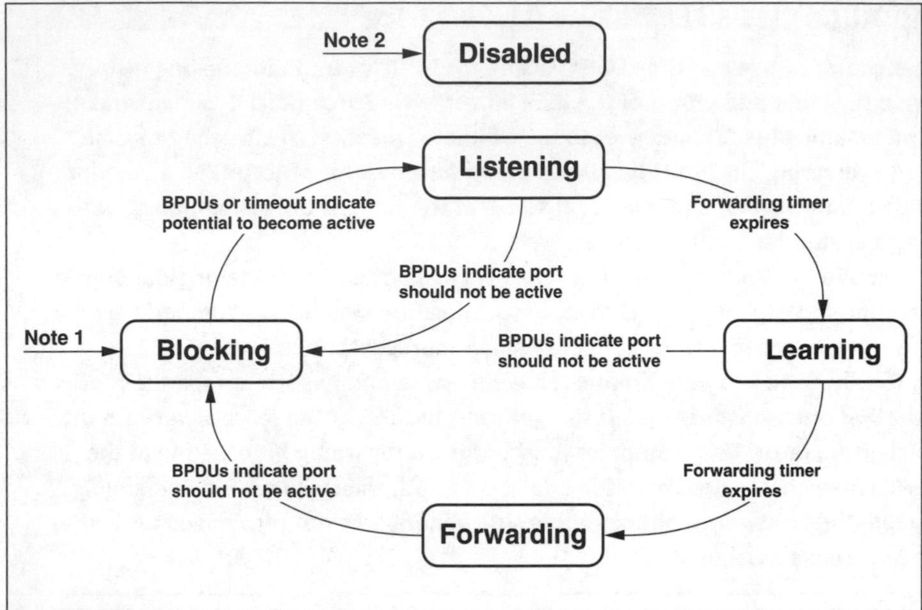

Figure 5.8 Port states. (Note 1: Unconditional transition into blocking state occurs upon initialization or management control. Note 2: Unconditional transition into disabled state occurs upon failure or management control.)

5.2.2.4.2 Blocking

A port that is enabled, but that is neither a Designated Port nor a Root Port, will be in the *blocking* state. This is the "standby" mode; such a port is not currently needed for the spanning tree. A blocking port will not receive or forward data frames, nor will it transmit BPDUs, but instead it will listen for others' BPDUs (and will time out if there are no BPDUs heard) to determine if and when the port should consider becoming active in the spanning tree. The blocking state is typically entered upon initialization (power up) of a port. Upon learning (through

Table 5.2 Port State Behavior

	RECEIVE BPDUS	TRANSMIT BPDUS	LEARN ADDRESSES	FORWARD DATA FRAMES
Disabled	—	—	—	—
Blocking	✓	—	—	—
Listening	✓	✓	—	—
Learning	✓	✓	✓	—
Forwarding	✓	✓	✓	✓

BPDUs or timeout) that it might need to become active, the port will move toward the forwarding state in three steps: listening, learning, then forwarding.

5.2.2.4.3 Listening

In this state, the port is still not forwarding data traffic, but is listening to (and possibly sending) BPDUs in order to compute the spanning tree. Depending on the content of its own and others' BPDUs, the port may decide that it is or is not best-qualified to become designated for this link, and proceed to the learning or back to the blocking state accordingly. This is the essence of the election algorithm. The port is comparing its own information (path cost, Bridge Identifier, Port Identifier) with information received from other candidates and deciding which is best suited for inclusion in the spanning tree.

5.2.2.4.4 Learning

In this state, the port is preparing to forward data traffic. Since the port's address table may be empty (for example, upon initialization), it is generally not a good idea to begin forwarding traffic yet, since a bridge with an empty address table will, by default, flood all received frames onto all other ports. This can cause significant congestion until the bridge learns the relative locations of attached stations and begins filtering traffic appropriately. As such, a port waits for a period of time to build its address table somewhat before actually forwarding data traffic. This time is known as the *forwarding delay.*

5.2.2.4.5 Forwarding

Once the bridge has spent some time learning addresses, it is allowed to forward data frames. This is the steady state for a bridge port that is part of the active spanning tree.

5.2.2.5 Topology Changes

Once an optimum spanning tree is determined and set in place, there is rarely any need to change the topology. Topology changes need to occur only if:

- A Designated Bridge (including the Root Bridge) fails, is powered off, or is disabled by management
- A Designated or Root Port within a Designated Bridge fails, is removed, or is disabled by management
- An active link within the spanning tree fails or is disconnected
- Management adjusts bridge priorities, port priorities, or link costs such that the optimum spanning tree has changed
- A new link is added to an existing topology that provides lower path cost to some segment of the catenet than the existing spanning tree

- A new bridge or port is added to an existing catenet that similarly provides lower path cost to some segment of the catenet

Such events occur rarely on an operational network. In the case of management-induced changes, they can occur at controlled times if desired. Thus, while the STP accommodates topology changes, they are considered unusual or boundary events; the protocol favors simplicity over efficient and rapid convergence to new topologies.

It would be nice if information could be detected and disseminated instantaneously. In a distributed network, unfortunately, this would require violating the laws of physics; it takes time for information to propagate (that darn Einstein guy again!). Because of this delay, changes in the topology of the catenet can occur without all bridges being immediately aware of them. To provide a smoother transition between topologies during a change, a mechanism is employed that:

- Provides for explicit topology change detection and notification
- Provides for acknowledgment of the topology change to all concerned bridges
- Uses timers to:
    1. Prevent rapid transition between the blocking and forwarding states, thus preventing the formation of transient loops during topology changes.
    2. Allow all bridges to participate in the election of new Designated Bridges and Ports, rather than just the one(s) that actually detected the topology change. This ensures that the optimum topology is selected, and avoids invoking topology change mechanisms recursively.

Before transitioning into the forwarding state on any port as a result of a topology change, a bridge waits for the new topology information to propagate throughout the catenet and for a time sufficient to ensure that any frames forwarded using the old topology have either reached their destination or been discarded.

5.2.2.5.1 Detecting When the Topology Must Change

Not every event will cause a topology change. Even the powering up of a new bridge, or the addition of a new link, may not invoke a topology change unless the new configuration causes the spanning tree to change. Bridges always listen to the Configuration Messages on their links before attempting to initiate a topology change; if the received information is superior to the bridge's internal information (i.e., the currently-active bridges and ports have a better right to be part of the spanning tree than the bridge in question), then the bridge will not initiate a topology change.

Topology changes will occur only when a bridge, port, link, or management event occurs such that the optimum set of Designated Bridges and Ports (as determined by the STP) is different from the currently active set. This occurs only after the exchange of Configuration Messages on the affected link(s); that is, the election procedure determines what the new topology should be and then the change is initiated.

5.2.2.5.2 Notifying the Authorities

When a bridge that is not the Root Bridge changes the active topology of the catenet, it transmits a Topology Change Message through its Root Port. This is repeated until the bridge receives an acknowledgment from the Designated Bridge for that link (through the TCack bit in the Flags field; see Figure 5.6). That Designated Bridge similarly transmits a Topology Change Message notification through its Root Port to the next Designated Bridge, until the message ultimately reaches the Root Bridge.

When the Root Bridge is informed of the change, it sets the Topology Change flag (TC) in all Configuration Messages transmitted for some time, so that all bridges become aware of the topology change. During the time that this flag is set, bridges use a shortened period for aging entries in their address tables, as described in Section 5.2.2.6.

5.2.2.6 *Protocol Timers*

The STP incorporates a number of timers that control the behavior of the bridges and the convergence of the spanning tree topology within the catenet. All of these timers are normally configurable through management, but most network administrators leave them at their default values, which ensures appropriate behavior under most conditions.

5.2.2.6.1 Table Aging

Bridges learn the relative locations of end stations by inspecting the Source Addresses in received frames. The bridge, on a frame-by-frame basis, updates its address table with the current port-to-address mapping for each end station heard. When making forwarding decisions (based on the Destination Address in received frames), the bridge invokes a table lookup to determine the appropriate output port(s) for each frame. It behooves the bridge to keep the address table as short as possible to minimize this lookup operation (which must be performed in real-time). Thus, if a station has not been heard from in some period of time, its entry should be removed from the table to improve bridge performance and to make room for new entries that may need to be made.

There is a trade-off that has to be made in the selection of the table aging parameter. If the timer is set to a large value, then stations that transmit only infrequently will remain in the table. Frames sent to these stations will be properly filtered and sent only on the appropriate port for each station. On the other hand, with a long aging time, stations that have become inactive will not be removed, and the bridge will be forced to perform a lookup in a table that is unnecessarily deep.

If the timer is set to a very short value, then the table will be purged quickly. This can make the lookup more efficient, but stations that transmit infrequently (relative to the aging timer) will have to be constantly re-learned, with traffic flooding onto all ports until the learning is complete. Thus, the tradeoff is between lookup efficiency and LAN utilization.

The standard specifies that the aging time can be set to any value in the range of 10 seconds to 11.6 days, but the default (and most common) value is 5 minutes.

5.2.2.6.2 Fast Aging on Topology Changes

Funny things can happen when the spanning tree topology changes. Even though no stations have physically moved, it can appear to the bridges that huge numbers of stations have been lifted from one link and plunked down onto another. Consider the situation in Figure 5.9. If link A fails, the topology will change as indicated in the figure. From the perspective of bridge 2, all of the stations directly connected to bridge 1 will appear to have moved from port 1 to port 2, even though they haven't gone anywhere.

Once this occurs, the address table in bridge 2 (and possibly many other bridges) will be incorrect for all of those stations either until they all send traffic that is seen by bridge 2 or until the aging timer expires. This can cause a disruption in service, dropped connections, and so forth, depending on the behavior of the application(s) running on those stations. Rather than risk disrupting service for 5 minutes (or worse, 11.6 days!), bridges switch to a short aging time during a spanning tree topology change. Rather than using the normal value for the aging timer, bridges use the value of the Forward Delay[16] (nominally 15 seconds) to age out unheard-from entries in the address table.

5.2.2.6.3 Hello Timer

The Hello time is the time between Configuration Messages emitted by the Root Bridge (and, by extension, by all Designated Bridges). Fast Hello times will result in faster detection of topology changes at the expense of increased STP traffic and bridge STP processing. The Hello time is always in the range of 1 to 10 seconds, and is nominally 2 seconds. The value is included in Con-

[16] This is the same parameter that determines the length of time spent transitioning from the listening to the learning to the forwarding states of a port.

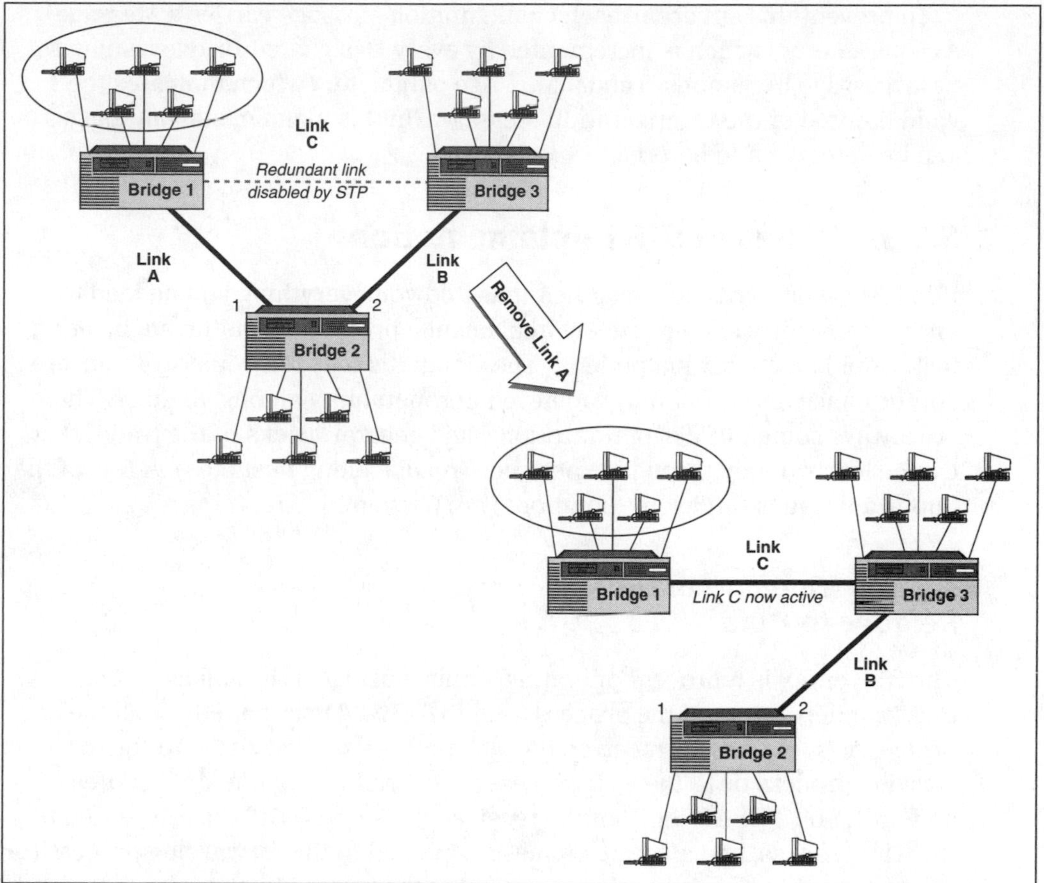

Figure 5.9 Stations appear to move.

figuration Messages so that all bridges know how often to expect these messages and to set their timeout values accordingly.

5.2.2.6.4 Message Aging

Every Hello time, the Root Bridge initiates a Configuration Message that is then processed by all receiving bridges. Designated Bridges then generate new, updated Configuration Messages, with the process repeating until the information propagates out to the leaves of the tree. If there are many bridges and tiers in the hierarchy, it may take quite some time for a Configuration Message to propagate in this way. If a Topology Change occurs during this time, the information in the Configuration Message may become stale and represent a topology and state that no longer exist. If a bridge processed and reacted to such a stale message, it might inadvertently countermand the topology change in progress. It is possible that the spanning tree might never converge to the correct topology.

To prevent this situation, each Configuration Message carries a Message Age parameter (which is incremented by every Designated Bridge issuing a new message in response) and a Max Age parameter (which indicates the valid lifetime of the Configuration Message). In this manner, stale messages can be detected and ignored.

5.2.3 Issues in STP Implementation

If industry standards and specifications told you everything you needed to know to properly and effectively implement a protocol, then the engineering task would be greatly simplified.[17] The standards only tell you how to ensure conformance and (hopefully) achieve interoperability among vendors. There are always some pitfalls, optimizations, and general "tricks of the trade" that can be learned only through experience (read: making mistakes). A few of the important issues (and some solutions) are presented here.

5.2.3.1 Queuing of BPDUs Relative to Data

The STP entity is a process operating within a bridge. It is, at least architecturally, independent of the process used to forward user data through the bridge. As such, frames received on each port are passed either to the forwarding process or to the STP process as determined by the MAC address and/or the LLC DSAP/SSAP of the received frame. STP BPDUs are passed to the STP process, and all other frames are passed to the forwarding process (or discarded subject to frame filters applied at the input). As a result of received BPDUs and protocol timers, the STP process creates BPDUs for transmission on its Designated Ports. The times at which these BPDUs are queued for transmission on an output port are independent of any traffic being queued by the normal forwarding process used for user data frames.

Problems can arise if a single queue is used for transmission of both forwarded data frames and STP BPDUs. If the queue is deep (e.g., because there is currently heavy traffic load destined for this port), the BPDU may be delayed significantly while waiting in the queue. Depending on the interrelationships among various STP and bridge parameters (in particular the Hello time and the Bridge Max Transit Delay), it is possible that Configuration Messages may be delayed for such a long period of time that a topology change is invoked by other bridges that time out due to an excessively delayed BPDU. This could be exacerbated even further by the use of flow control, as discussed in Chapter 8, *LAN and Switch Flow Control.* While preventing frame loss in the receiver, link flow control imposes additional transparent delays on the transmission of frames in the queue.

[17] And there would be no need for consultants! Fortunately this is not the case.

Similarly, a Topology Change Message could be delayed, causing the STP to take longer than necessary to converge to the new topology—or worse to create a transient loop in the catenet.

The easiest solution to this problem is to use a separate queue for transmission of BPDUs. Since there can be only one outstanding BPDU transmission for any given port, this second "queue" is really just a single buffer, requiring 35 bytes plus any MAC encapsulation.[18] Additionally, the BPDU should be given priority over forwarded data traffic. Such priority will not affect data throughput significantly, since it is only one short frame. This policy eliminates any concern over BPDU queuing delay.

5.2.3.2 Save a Receive Buffer for Me!

An analogous problem occurs on the receive side of the equation. BPDUs must not only be transmitted promptly, they must be properly received. While the protocol is tolerant of occasional frame loss,[19] care should be taken to prevent such frame loss when possible. From the perspective of the STP entity within the bridge, there is no difference between a frame being lost due to an error on the link (an infrequent event) and a frame being lost due to buffer unavailability in the receiver.

If there is heavy traffic load, it is possible that the bridge will become starved for receive buffers, as there is only finite memory in the bridge. The bridge will discard data frames in excess of its buffering capacity, requiring end stations to recover through appropriate higher-layer protocol mechanisms (e.g., Transport-layer retransmission). However, while it may be acceptable to discard data frames under such conditions, it is generally unacceptable to discard STP BPDUs. The loss of successive BPDUs under periods of heavy traffic can cause topology change and reconfiguration. When the load then subsides, the topology will have to go through another change to go back to the original configuration. Remember, the original topology was "the best" in terms of the STP; when the BPDUs can get through (later, when the traffic subsides), the original configuration is still the best and demands another topology change. Such a situation can cause thrashing of the topology and repeated network disruption during the topology change periods.

Again, the solution is to reserve a receive buffer specifically for the STP messages. This avoids unnecessary reconfiguration when data frame buffers are exhausted. This is a general rule for any critical protocol; it is prudent to reserve resources for those applications that can either cause severe problems when starved or that provide a last-chance hope of recovery from catastrophic failure. This is particularly effective when the reserved resources are minimal

[18] A BPDU fits within a minimum-length Ethernet frame of 64 bytes.

[19] It must be, as LANs provide only connectionless (best effort) frame delivery, and the STP does not incorporate any mechanisms for reliable, guaranteed service.

(e.g., a single, small buffer). The STP is just one example; Flow Control (described in Chapter 8, *LAN and Switch Flow Control*), Link Aggregation Control (discussed in Chapter 9, *Link Aggregation*), and certain network management protocols may also be good candidates for this policy.[20]

5.2.3.3 Spanning Tree Protocol Performance

Seifert's Law of Networking #62
Save your last buffer for something important.

One nice feature of the STP is that it demands relatively little processing on the part of the bridge. Under steady-state conditions, there will be only one BPDU received or transmitted on any port every 2 seconds. On high-speed LANs where the frame rates can be on the order of hundreds of thousands of frames per second, the STP does not constitute significant load for the network or make significant demands on the processor.

In general, the same processor that is used for general housekeeping functions within the bridge (e.g., initialization, network management, and so on) will be used to implement the STP. In the case of some low-end bridge products, the processor can be quite primitive and still provide acceptable performance.[21]

In early bridges, the bridge functions themselves (i.e., address table lookup and frame forwarding) were performed in software on a traditional processor. Similar to the use of a common buffer pool for both data and BPDUs, it is possible that heavy data traffic load could interfere with STP responsiveness in such implementations. Thus, if the processor is being shared between the STP and other functions, it is important that the STP take appropriate priority.

While today most bridges do not implement real-time data forwarding functions in software, the processor may still be shared among multiple processes. It is important that the STP be assured of processor availability, even under heavy traffic load conditions.

5.3 Loops in a Remotely Bridged (WAN) Catenet

In the preceding discussions, all of the links were presumed to be high-speed LANs. However, bridges are often used to interconnect geographically-separated locations using intermediate Wide Area Network (WAN) links, as discussed in Chapter 3, *Bridging between Technologies*. While the STP will

[20] Perhaps the most important protocol would be one that provides for a remote reset (reboot) of a device in the event all else fails. If there is no buffer to receive this message, the system will be hopelessly deadlocked.

[21] I once implemented the STP, along with a variety of other housekeeping functions, on an 8 MHz, 8-bit 8051 CPU embedded in a larger ASIC.

properly resolve loops in such a configuration (and is sometimes even used for this purpose), there are some important issues that arise from the differences between LAN and WAN technologies. In Chapter 3, we discussed the issues relating to data flow on wide area bridged catenets; in this section we examine issues relating to the use of the STP on such links.

5.3.1 There's More than a One-Letter Difference

There are two significant differences that affect the behavior and operation of bridged catenets using the STP:

- *Link speeds are lower.* In general, the data rates of WAN links are much lower than those of local networks. While LANs usually operate in the range of 10 to 1000 Mb/s or more, WAN bridge interconnections today typically operate in the range of 56 kb/s to 155 Mb/s. The most popular site interconnection links operate at rates of 56/64 kb/s to 2 Mb/s. STP link costs will be higher on WAN links than on LANs. The range of values for the link cost (1 to 65, 535) can accommodate links as slow as 15 kb/s using the default recommendation for cost calculation.
- *Links cost money every month.* Unlike LANs, WAN links usually incur a recurring monthly cost. LANs are owned and operated by the user organization, whereas WAN links usually must be leased from a common carrier. Therefore, there is a monetary cost associated with the use of WAN links, and that cost generally increases with both distance and data rate. For a given distance between sites, or between a site and a carrier's Point of Presence (you usually don't have much flexibility in relocating your business locations to accommodate the needs of the STP!), users will want to use the slowest link that provides acceptable performance. This only exacerbates the problems.

5.3.2 Spanning Tree on a WAN

Regardless of the mix of LAN and/or WAN links in the catenet, we still need to ensure that there is exactly one active path between any pair of end stations in order to maintain proper data link operation. In a pure LAN environment, the STP provides a simple, effective means of loop resolution. The protocol is optimized primarily for LAN operation; in doing so, the STP makes a few (sometimes unstated) assumptions about the underlying technology:

- *Link capacity is highly overprovisioned.* It is assumed that the links have lots of excess capacity. This is generally true for low-cost, high-speed LANs. Because of this overprovisioning, we generally don't worry that some traffic will have to pass through a disinterested link, that is, a link that contains neither the sender nor the receiver of the information, but that is part of the spanning tree.

- *Link delay is generally insignificant.* On a catenet of high-speed LANs, whether a frame passes through one, two, or more links does not significantly affect end-to-end throughput or the behavior of higher-layer protocols or applications.
- *STP overhead is insignificant relative to user data traffic.* STP configuration messages do not consume any appreciable fraction of the link capacity.
- *Bandwidth is cheaper than complexity.* If user performance is affected by the behavior of a spanning tree, it is usually easier and less expensive to simply upgrade the capacity of those links that are causing the problem, rather than invoking some complex mechanisms to use bandwidth more efficiently.

All of these assumptions may be invalidated when the catenet is extended across a WAN. As a result, the STP may produce undesirable behavior in a WAN environment. Let's look at some of the problems that may result.

5.3.2.1 Link Utilization

With relatively slow WAN links, average utilization will be higher than on the attached LANs (over any averaging period). Worse, since the STP may force traffic to pass through disinterested links, the total load presented to a WAN link may increase when a spanning tree topology is used. This will cause utilization to increase even more. While increased utilization is not a problem in and of itself (most people like the idea of getting a lot of use from their WAN links), a link that is heavily used will impose delay in the catenet.

5.3.2.2 Delay

WAN links are worse than LAN links in both transmission and queuing delay (discussed in Chapter 3). Not only is the transmission delay much greater due to the lower data rate and longer extent, but the queuing delay will generally be greater due to the higher utilization of the link. When it rains, it pours.

To add insult to injury, any overhead imposed by the STP itself constitutes a greater percentage of the available capacity for a WAN link and adds to the utilization and delay.

5.3.2.3 Using a Single Path for All Traffic

By definition, the STP defines a single path (the tree) over which all traffic flows through the catenet. The STP specifically blocks any ports that would cause multiple, parallel paths the be active. Thus, it is not possible to load share traffic across multiple, parallel paths. This is usually acceptable in a

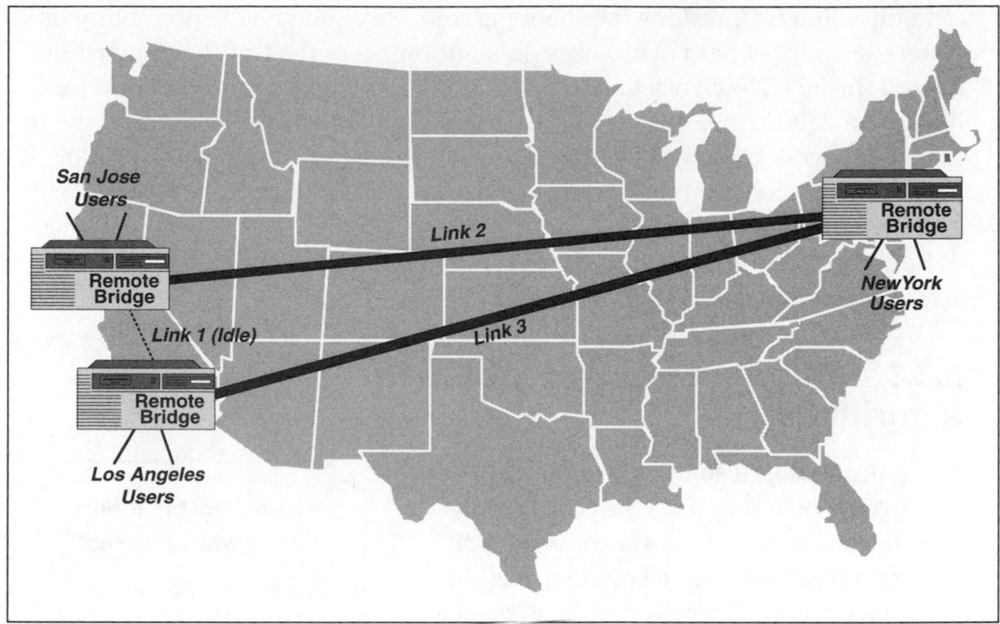

Figure 5.10 A WAN loop.

LAN environment, where LAN capacity far exceeds application requirements. LANs are generally highly overprovisioned; it is usually easier to increase the data rate of the LAN than to add complexity to allow load sharing across multiple links.[22] However, in a WAN context, link capacity may be *the* bottleneck for throughput. If two or more links could be used in parallel, then additional performance could be gained that might be worth the added cost. Unfortunately, the STP precludes such topologies.

Consider the situation depicted in Figure 5.10. Because of the STP, one of the WAN links in the figure must be devoid of user traffic. Which one it will be is a function of the Bridge Identifiers and the link costs, but one of the links must be idled to create the spanning tree. In the figure, the link from San Jose to Los Angeles is shown idled.

In this scenario, all traffic from San Jose destined for stations in Los Angeles must travel across the country twice, across links 2 and 3, to New York and back. There is no avoiding this situation if the STP is in effect. Traffic is unnecessarily forwarded across two links when there is only one link physically separating any site, and worse, both links are slow WAN links with long delay. Ideally, we would want the traffic from San Jose to Los Angeles to flow across link 1, San Jose to New York to flow across link 2, and New York to Los Angeles to flow on link 3, but the STP does not permit such behavior.

[22] Link Aggregation (as discussed in Chapter 9) does provide such load sharing, but does so transparently so that the STP sees the aggregation as a single link. In addition, Link Aggregation is restricted to a very limited set of topologies.

In directing traffic along the spanning tree, we eliminate the possibility of using the shortest path in all cases. In addition, all of the traffic that must be passed through New York to reach Los Angeles increases the utilization (and hence the delay) on both sets of links unnecessarily. Moreover, we are paying for Link 1 every month, yet getting no real benefit from it, other than having it available for backup in the event of a link or bridge failure. This is not a very effective use of either bandwidth or money.

Because of these problems, the STP is generally unacceptable for use on any but the simplest WAN topologies.[23]

5.3.3 Proprietary Loop Resolution Algorithms

When the standard solution to a problem creates even worse problems, you can be sure that ingenious engineers will come up with better alternatives. A number of such alternatives have emerged for the problems associated with the use of the STP on WANs. Clearly, what is desired is a mechanism to allow:

> **Patient: "Doctor, it hurts when I do that."**
>
> **Doctor: "Don't do that."**
>
> ***Still Wise Advice***

- All links to be used to their maximum extent whenever possible
- Traffic always to be directed across the lowest-delay path
- Parallel data paths to be used for load-sharing, if available
- The data link invariants (non-duplication and sequential delivery between endpoints) to be maintained
- Automatic configuration and reconfiguration to be performed in the event of topology changes

A number of algorithms and protocols have been developed that meet all of these goals [PERL92]. Essentially, all of these solutions provide for a single active path between any pair of end stations, yet allow all links to be used. Various methods of distributing traffic across multiple parallel paths have been implemented; most determine the path to be used as a function of the source and/or destination address of the frames being forwarded.[24]

[23] For example, if the topology is loop-free by its own virtue, then the STP simply confirms that topology.

[24] If the path chosen is an unambiguous function of both the Source Address (SA) and the Destination Address (DA), then all traffic for any SA/DA pair will always flow across a single link, which maintains the link invariants. The challenge becomes twofold: selecting a function that distributes traffic efficiently for an arbitrary set of SA/DA pairs (i.e., traffic patterns) and automatically detecting the presence of multiple available paths that can be chosen at any given point in time. This is exactly the same as the problems of frame distribution and link configuration for aggregated links, as discussed in Chapter 9.

The only problem is that all of these mechanisms are proprietary; various manufacturers have each developed their own methods for WAN load sharing. There is no vendor-interoperable standard for optimized loop resolution in a catenet comprising WAN links. The only agreed-upon standard is the STP, which is obviously less-than-optimum in most cases. As a result, users must generally purchase all of their WAN bridging equipment from the same vendor (or from some set of vendors that support the same proprietary algorithm).[25] In practice, this is often a good policy from the perspective of product support; it can be difficult to maintain a complex WAN catenet with products from multiple vendors, each with different management capabilities and tools. Thus, many users opt for a single vendor for support reasons rather than from any limitation of load sharing algorithms.

5.3.4 Routing versus Bridging on the WAN

The difficulties discussed in the previous sections all arise from our attempt to view a collection of LAN and WAN links as a single Data Link entity. Bridges allow end stations to treat a catenet as if it were a single LAN. However, if we drop this fiction, we can employ other, well-established means for efficient use of WANs for data communications. If we choose to perform our internetworking at a higher layer in the protocol architecture, solutions already exist for these problems.

A general-purpose enterprise-wide or worldwide internetworking technology must deal with using WAN technology in a performance- and cost-efficient manner. As a result, most Network-layer protocols support the use of multiple paths in an internetwork between end stations. Widely-used protocol suites such as IP and IPX provide for load sharing, automatic topology change detection, and so on. The routing protocols employed (e.g., OSPF [RFC2328] and NLSP [WYCK95]) do not attempt to form a spanning tree topology. The trade-off is that these protocols are considerably more complex than the STP. The STP is a very simple protocol that works well in a LAN catenet. For a general wide area internetwork, more complex Network-layer mechanisms usually provide superior performance. Thus, routers are more commonly used for wide area interconnection than are bridges.

[25] In theory, if there is more than one disjoint set of WAN links in the catenet, it should be possible to use equipment from different manufacturers in each disjoint set of WAN links. (These are referred to as *clusters* in the IEEE 802.1G Remote Bridge standard) [IEEE98c]. However, at least one vendor's proprietary algorithm required that one of its bridges be configured as the root of the spanning tree. If this is true for more than one manufacturer, then those choices become mutually incompatible. (They can't both be the root!)

5.4 An Example of Loop Resolution

Rather than deal with all of the concepts in abstract and algorithmic terms, let's take a look at an example of a catenet with loops and see how the STP works to resolve the loops and achieve a tree topology.

> **WARNING!**
>
> **You are watching a trained network professional. The stunts being performed entail a high degree of risk, require years of practice, and should not be attempted by amateurs or young children. Don't try this at home.**

Before you go off and build a replica of the depicted catenet for use in your organization, be aware that the example is primarily designed to demonstrate STP behavior; as such, it includes a number of interesting boundary conditions and link configurations that rarely occur in most environments. That is, the example is not necessarily practical or useful for any normal purposes. Given that caveat, consider the configuration shown in Figure 5.11.

For simplicity, we assume that all of the Bridge and Port Priorities are left at their default values (or set to a common value, which amounts to the same thing). Each bridge is shown with a (simplified) numerical Bridge Identifier, each port with a Port Identifier, and each link with an associated cost.

Following the algorithm described in Section 5.2.2.2, we can calculate the spanning tree as follows:

1. The Root Bridge will be bridge 109, since it has the numerically-lowest Bridge Identifier in the catenet. This bridge will be the Designated Bridge for every link to which it connects, including a 100 Mb/s FDDI on port 1 (link A, cost = 19) and a T1 WAN link on port 2 (link C, cost = 651).
2. There are two potential Designated Bridges for link B, a 10 Mb/s Ethernet (cost = 100). Both bridge 175 and bridge 447 offer a path cost of 19 back to the root, so we have to go to the next determinant to resolve the tie. For equal cost paths, we next consider the Bridge Identifiers. Since bridge 175 is numerically lower than bridge 447, it becomes the Designated Bridge for link B on its port 1. Both bridges 175 and 447 are Designated Bridges for their respective port 3, there being no other possible choice.
3. Next, let's consider link E, a 10 Mb/s shared Ethernet. There are two possible Designated Bridges. Bridge 492 is only one hop away from the root, but it incurs a path cost of 651 (through T1 WAN link C). Bridge 562 may be farther from the root in terms of number of hops, but the path cost is

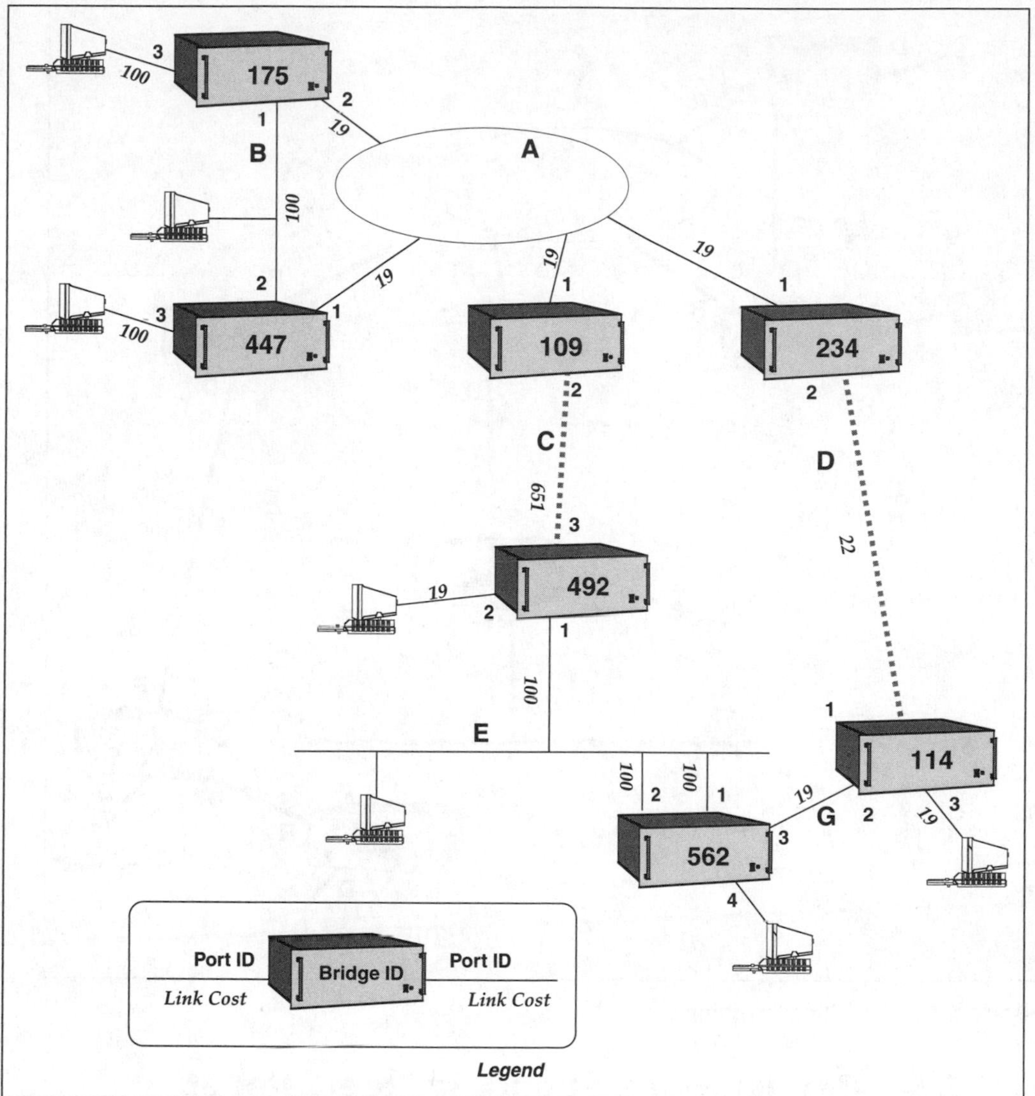

Figure 5.11 Example configuration.

only 60, being the sum of link G, a 100 Mb/s Ethernet (cost = 19), link D, a T3 WAN link (cost = 22), and link A, the 100 Mb/s FDDI (cost = 19). Thus bridge 562 is the Designated Bridge for link E. Since it has two ports on this link, the Designated Port will be the one with the numerically-lower Port Identifier (port 1).

Figure 5.12 depicts the resulting spanning tree. Note that every bridge is a Designated Bridge (for some link). All active bridge ports have been labeled either R for Root Port or D for Designated Port.

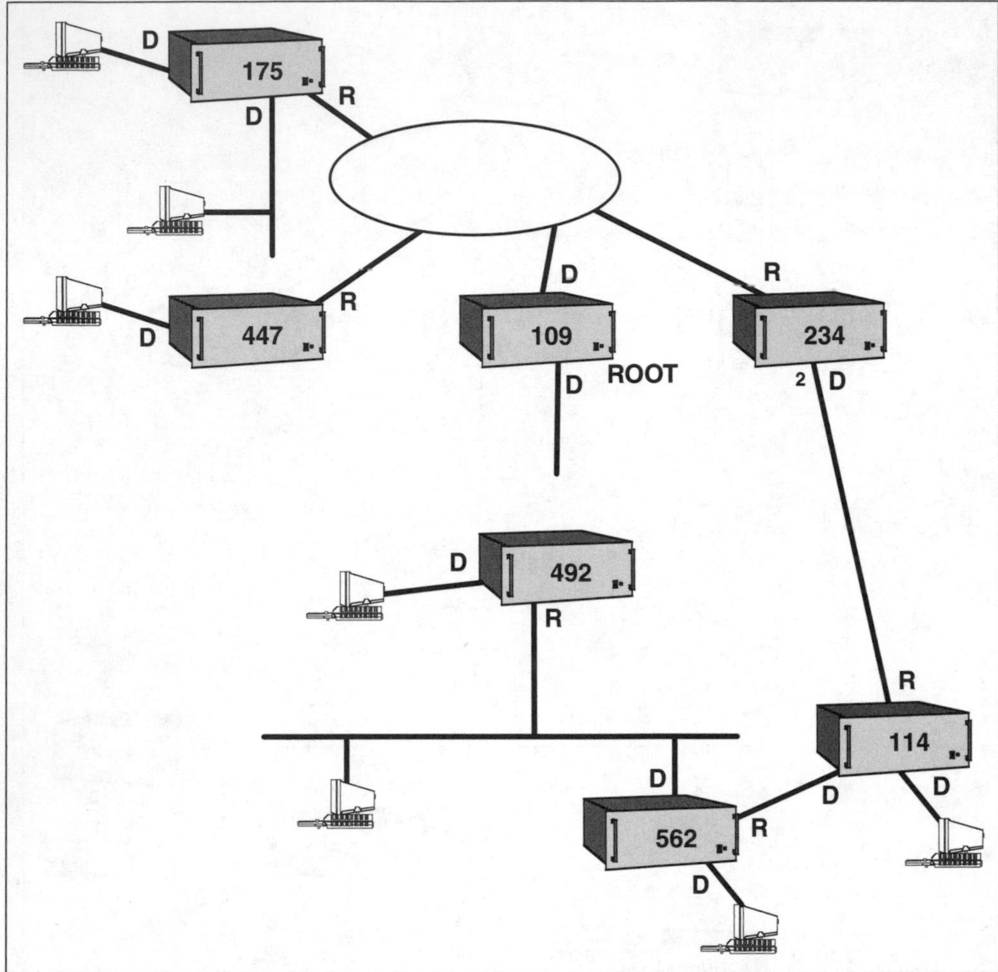

Figure 5.12 Resulting spanning tree.

5.5 Behavior of a Spanning Tree Catenet

There are many approaches that could be used to maintain proper end station behavior in a bridged catenet. The decision to use a spanning tree arises mostly from the simplicity of the algorithm, which allows low cost bridges to be easily built. When the catenet consists of high-speed LANs in a local environment, this seems a reasonable decision. In different environments, other factors must be considered. For example, the STP prohibits load-sharing across multiple paths to the same destination. This may be acceptable in a bridged catenet, but is generally intolerable in a complex WAN (such as the Internet), where link bandwidth is expensive and needs to be used to its maximum capabilities.

In this section we look at the behaviors exhibited by catenets using a spanning tree topology.

5.5.1 Maintaining the Link Invariants

A single, standalone (unbridged) LAN exhibits the following invariant behaviors:

- *Sequential delivery.* It is not possible for frames to be sent by a source on the LAN and received by a destination in a different order from that in which they were sent. It is possible that some frames might not be delivered, but there is no way for the sequence of frames to be changed.
- *Non-duplication.* Similarly, there is no means for a station to send a single frame and have another station receive multiple copies of that frame.

These are so-called *hard invariants* discussed in Chapter 2. There are no provisions made in the protocols (e.g., sequence numbers) to ensure these behaviors; they occur naturally. An application or higher-layer protocol that interfaces directly to the Data Link can simply assume such behavior on the part of the LAN. There is no need for such a higher-layer entity to make accommodation for duplicate or out-of-order frames; when operating on a LAN, such events simply cannot occur.[26]

Transparent bridges make a catenet appear as if it were a single LAN to the end stations. Therefore, these bridges must ensure that the invariant behaviors of a single LAN are maintained across the catenet. That is, bridges must guarantee that there is no duplication of frames or change in frame ordering. A spanning tree topology ensures this behavior. By providing only a single path between any pair of stations, ordering and non-duplication can be maintained.

5.5.2 Data Flow on the Spanning Tree

The spanning tree defines the path along which all data in the catenet flows. Regardless of the presence of other physical paths, all traffic will travel along the spanning tree. This implies that all links, bridges, and ports that are not part of the spanning tree are completely void of data traffic.[27] The links are available for *hot standby* in the event of a link or bridge failure (or reconfiguration of the catenet); they do not add to the data-carrying capacity of the network. In a local environment where link capacity does not incur a recurring cost, this is generally acceptable, but it is usually inappropriate in a WAN context, as discussed in Section 5.3.

[26] Note that higher-layer protocols or applications may not make such guarantees to *their* clients. For example, IP does not guarantee sequential delivery to TCP and, as such, TCP must incorporate mechanisms to deal with the possibility of receiving out-of-order IP datagrams.

[27] There may be BPDUs flowing into these idled bridges and ports to maintain the topology, but no data traffic is carried between end stations.

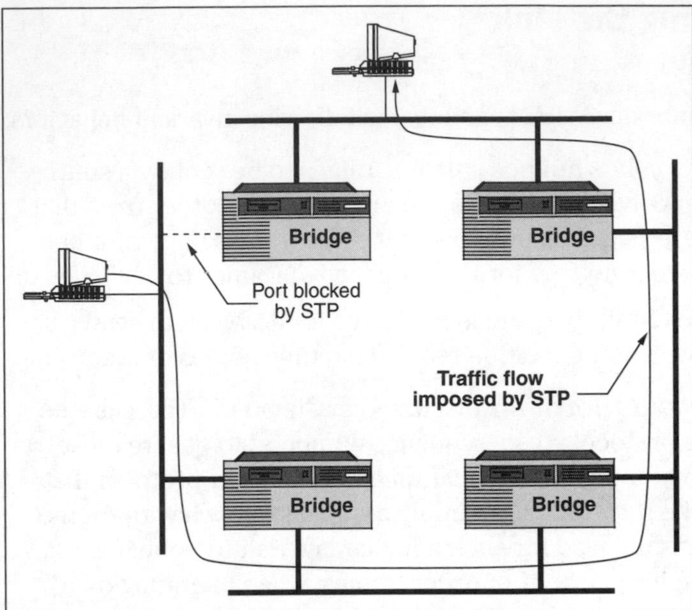

Figure 5.13 Traffic flow on the spanning tree.

For some configurations of links, the use of a spanning tree will actually provide a non-optimum path for some set of end stations. Consider the catenet depicted in Figure 5.13. For the catenet to resolve to a spanning tree, one of the bridge ports must be in the blocking state, as determined by the Bridge Identifiers, link costs, and Port Identifiers. Regardless of which port becomes blocking, there will always be a *long path* between some set of LANs at the edges of the resulting spanning tree. While these LANs actually have a single-hop physical path available, the use of a spanning tree forces all of their traffic to travel across multiple LANs and bridges.

Thus, while the spanning tree optimizes the topology according to its own metrics, there may be particular paths that are worse than they would be if some other topology were used. Depending on the traffic patterns in the catenet, the performance may actually be degraded. Administrators need to be aware of this characteristic; adjustments can be made to the spanning tree parameters (e.g., Bridge Priorities) to minimize this effect.

5.5.3 Traffic Congregation at the Root

The STP will force traffic to cross LANs and bridges as needed to reach its intended destination(s). Because the root is at the logical center of the catenet (the catenet is built up from the root, through the lowest-cost paths), traffic tends to be heaviest near the root.[28] If we understand this behavior, we can take steps to design the catenet for best performance. In particular, the Root Bridge should be a high-performance device (i.e., it should not become a bottleneck for traffic), and it should attach to highest-speed LANs, preferably in the backbone of the catenet. This is discussed further in Section 5.6.1.

5.5.4 Topology Changes and Disruption

In the steady-state, a bridged catenet provides full connectivity among all stations. In the event of a bridge change (addition or removal/failure) or a link change, the STP will attempt to reconfigure the catenet to the new "best" topology according to its algorithm and the assigned metrics.

A basic principle guiding the design of the STP is that such changes happen infrequently. STP timers (in particular the Forward Delay, Maximum Message Age, and Hello time) are all on the order of seconds. While the protocol is stable (i.e., it will converge to the proper topology) as long as changes do not occur frequently relative to these timers, a spanning tree topology change is considered a major event in the life of the catenet. Depending on the nature of the change and the extent (number and nature of links) of the catenet, it may require tens of seconds or even minutes for the topology to converge and the catenet to resume normal operation. During this reconfiguration time, ports may be blocked, frames may be discarded, and communication between some stations may be impossible. Thus, while the STP does perform its intended function, it is wise to avoid invoking topology change mechanisms unnecessarily.

It may be possible to reduce the convergence time of the STP by manipulating the protocol timers; however, there is a tradeoff involved. (So, what's new?) Reducing the Hello time will increase STP traffic on all links; reducing the Maximum Message Age may reduce the maximum extent of the catenet.

At the time of this writing, the IEEE 802.1 committee is considering some modifications to the spanning tree algorithm that will improve convergence time in the event of topology changes in a manner backward-compatible with existing implementations. Stay tuned for further developments.

5.6 Configuring the Spanning Tree

Well-designed systems allow "power users" to custom-tailor a configuration to their specific needs, but provide defaults that are appropriate for the vast major-

[28] Of course, this is somewhat dependent on the unique traffic patterns in the catenet. The assumption here is that traffic is relatively uniformly distributed among all stations. In this case, LANs and bridges at or near the root will tend to carry more traffic than those near the periphery of the catenet.

ity of situations.[29] If left to its default behavior, the STP it will automatically select a root, Designated Bridges, and Designated Ports according to the algorithm described in Section 5.2.2.2. For many users, this is perfectly adequate; the catenet will properly resolve loops and provide full connectivity along the best available paths. However, the STP also incorporates a great deal of flexibility for the network administrator who, for example:

- Has a complex configuration of bridges, with many potential Designated Bridges for a given link
- Wants to carefully control the configuration and topology change behavior in anticipation of specific events (bridge failures, link failures, and so on)
- Knows that the default behavior will result in an undesirable configuration (e.g., a known numerically-low Bridge Identifier is present on a bridge connected to a low-speed link at the edge of the catenet)
- Needs to configure a specific bridge as root, possibly as a requirement for a proprietary WAN load-sharing algorithm
- Wants to tune the performance and convergence of the protocol for specific needs

> **Seifert's Law of Networking #26**
>
> Defaults are guardian angels for the clueless.

The STP allows the network administrator to adjust the STP parameters to achieve almost any desired behavior. In the following sections, we discuss some of the important parameters and the reason why they might need to be changed from their default values.

5.6.1 "We'll All Be Planning That Root . . ."[30]

The Root Bridge is an important element of any spanning tree. The root is at the logical center of the catenet. Assuming that traffic is (relatively) uniformly distributed among the stations and LANs present, traffic will tend to be heavier through the root (and on the links to which the root connects) than through other Designated Bridges and their links.

The root will always be the bridge with the numerically-lowest Bridge Identifier. Using the default values of the STP, the root will be determined by the OUIs and manufacturing practices of the various bridge vendors whose products are deployed in the catenet. This may or may not result in an appropriate configuration, depending on the specific link arrangement and a certain

[29] The VMS Operating System comes to mind as one of the great examples of this principle.

[30] With apologies to Brian Wilson and the Beach Boys.

amount of chance. It is quite easy to specify any desired bridge to be the root—simply assign that bridge a numerically-lower value for the Bridge Priority than any other bridge in the catenet. Since the Bridge Priority constitutes the most-significant bits of the Bridge Identifier, it effectively overrides any OUI or address assignment artifacts.

Similarly, by assigning Bridge Priorities appropriately to all bridges, a network administrator can choose the exact order of ascension to the root position in the tree. In the event of failure of the desired primary root, the root responsibilities will shift to the next lowest assigned (or defaulted) Bridge Priority value in the catenet. The procedure is fully deterministic and controllable.

In general, it is good practice to:

- Select a root bridge that can handle a high level of traffic. Since traffic congregates near the root, an underperforming bridge used as a root can affect performance for many users.
- Make sure that the root attaches to the highest speed links in the catenet. This is often a backbone network in a building or campus.
- Select a root that is topologically central. Again, this will often be a bridge that attaches to a building or campus backbone network.

5.6.2 Assigning Link Costs

By default, the link cost is proportional to the reciprocal of the link data rate, as discussed in Section 5.2.2.1. For almost all links, this default leads to the best overall performance. Occasionally it may be desirable to deviate from this norm. In particular, it may be appropriate to manually set link costs for WAN links in the spanning tree so that traffic is directed in a manner appropriate for a given, known traffic pattern. For example, in Figure 5.10, if it is known in advance that the heaviest traffic will be between stations located in San Jose and Los Angeles, the spanning tree can be forced to include the direct link through adjustment of the link costs of the WAN links, rather than allowing the default behavior to force intrastate traffic to cross the country twice.

Similarly, if it is known that a given WAN link is prone to failure, then it may be appropriate to increase its link cost above the default value so that the link is kept out of the spanning tree unless absolutely needed. This avoids unnecessary topology changes (and their associated traffic disruption) when the expected link failures occur.

5.6.3 Setting Protocol Timers

The default values for the controllable STP timers are shown in Table 5.3.

In almost all cases, there will never be a need to adjust any of these timers, and it is generally not recommended practice. It is possible to reduce conver-

Table 5.3 STP Timers

PARAMETER	DEFAULT VALUE	ALLOWABLE RANGE
Hello time	2 s	1–10 s
Max Age	20 s	6–40 s
Forward Delay	15 s	4–30 s

gence time for the STP by reducing both the Hello time and the Forward Delay; however, this incurs a tradeoff against the maximum extent of the catenet. That is, if the protocol is tuned to respond more quickly, it cannot support environments where there is a large delay across the catenet.

In particular, for stability and proper convergence of the STP, it is important that:

- Max Age always be less than twice the Forward Delay
- Max Age always be greater than twice the Hello time

5.6.4 Managing the Extent of the Catenet

If bridges are so wonderful, why don't we make the entire universe one giant bridged catenet and be done with it? While the plug-and-play benefits of bridges provide a welcome relief from the tedious configuration demanded by internetwork routers, it is generally impractical to deploy huge catenets.

Even ignoring the administrative issues regarding Network layer addressing, security, and traffic isolation, extremely large catenets impose their own set of problems even within the link layer in which they operate. If a very large number of links and bridges are present between a pair of end stations, the (supposedly transparent) delays imposed may cause significant problems for some higher-layer protocols and applications. Time sensitive protocols such as NetBIOS, NetBEUI, and DEC's Local Area Transport (LAT) and Local Area VAXcluster (LAVc) protocols will simply not behave properly in catenets with excessive delay. This is the reason for the seemingly arbitrary limit of seven bridge hops across a catenet. Combined with an imposed upper bound on the transit time of a frame through a bridge, this puts an upper limit on the lifetime of a frame in the catenet.

Also, remember that topology changes are assumed to be infrequent, and can result in global disruption of the catenet for periods of minutes while a spanning tree computation takes place. By keeping a catenet relatively small, such disruptions can be localized. Thus, there is a tradeoff between the ease of use of bridges and the effects of topology changes on end users.

5.7 Up a Tree without a Protocol?

What if (heaven forbid!) someone built a bridge that did not include support for the STP or any other loop resolution algorithm? Would the Catenet Police arrest the person and confiscate the equipment? Would the person be banned for life from IEEE meetings?[31] More important, would it affect users?

5.7.1 Why Would Anyone Do This?

What would be the benefit to building a bridge or switch with no support for the STP? There are three reasons:

- Cost
- Cost
- Cost

In addition, it may be possible to save money by not including STP support. At the low end of the marketplace, every penny spent on the product weighs against the product competitively. The idea behind eliminating STP support is to avoid having to put any kind of control processor within the device. If a switch is built that does not require a processor for the data forwarding or lookup functions (e.g., it uses a finite-state machine implemented completely in hardware), then adding a processor simply to execute the STP constitutes an incremental expense.

Such a device would clearly be a "no-frills" switch. In addition to not supporting the STP, it could not support any standard network management protocols (e.g., SNMP), Link Aggregation Control, and so on. Because of this, such devices are sometimes referred to as *unmanaged switches*.

For better or for worse, there is a marketplace for such products, and they do exist. They fall into two classes:

1. *Connectivity devices.* These are simple bridges, generally with few ports (2 to 4, typically) that are used to provide connections between local networks. They are deployed almost like hubs; their purpose is to provide basic connectivity rather than performance or manageability. They are tactical products rather than constituting an internetworking strategy. Such devices are very low in cost, and are often sold through catalogs, retail channels, or resellers. Few major internetworking vendors provide such products, since they cannot be managed using standard tools.
2. *Edge devices.* These may be high-performance switches with large numbers of ports, but they are specifically designed and sold for use at the edge of a network (e.g., desktop switches). Since such devices are

[31] If so, I will build a bridge like this immediately!

expected to connect only to leaves of the tree, there should never be a loop in the catenet that includes such an edge device. Thus, their participation (or not) in the STP is irrelevant.

5.7.2 Interoperability

Though such a device may not participate in the STP, it must not prevent other bridges in the catenet from doing so. In order to achieve this end, a bridge that does not implement the STP should not sink STP BPDUs. That is, the bridge should forward BPDUs like normal multicast frames, even though their Destination Address is in the reserved range that the IEEE 802.1 standard stipulates must not be forwarded. If you are going to violate the standard, you need to violate it all the way!

If a bridge neither forwarded nor processed STP BPDUs, then any loop that included the suspect device could not be resolved by other bridges that did implement the STP. As long as there is at least one bridge in a loop that implements the STP, the loop will be properly resolved if all other (non-conformant) bridges forward the BPDUs.

This is more important for a connectivity device than for an edge device. Connectivity devices may be deployed anywhere within the catenet. Edge devices, if deployed the way they are intended, will not be part of a loop, so their behavior with respect to STP BPDUs is less important.

A loop that consists exclusively of bridges that do not implement the STP cannot be resolved, and will generally result in massive communications failure.

5.7.3 What to Do, What to Do?

The safest approach is to make sure that all of the bridges in the catenet implement the STP, regardless of their intended usage. While a switch may be intended for edge deployment, it is just too easy to inadvertently move it to a place in the catenet where the lack of a loop resolution protocol is harmful. Sometimes the move is "just temporary, until we replace it," but then becomes permanent through time and apathy. Only when a major network disruption occurs does anyone even look for problems of this nature, and they are hard to find. The personnel at the time of the disruption may be different from those who made the change, and they may not even be aware that all of the switches in the catenet don't implement the STP.

While you might save some money by buying a low-cost bridge, the cost (in network downtime) in the event of a loop usually exceeds any such savings. Remember that a bridge without the STP is also a bridge without any network management capability; such devices are generally unacceptable in all but the simplest catenets. At a minimum, any use of non-STP-conformant bridges should be restricted to the edge of the catenet.

CHAPTER

6

Source Routing

Until now, the only bridges we have considered have been those that operate using the transparent algorithms discussed in Chapter 2, *Transparent Bridges*. Transparent bridges can be used on all types of LANs, including Ethernets, Token Rings, FDDIs, and others. In this chapter we look at a completely different beast, called a *source routing bridge*, that is used exclusively on Token Rings and some FDDI networks.

While both types of devices may be called *bridges*, it is important to recognize that there is almost nothing in common between transparent and source routing bridge operation. The two technologies were developed independently by different groups of people from different companies, were conceived from a completely different set of underlying assumptions, operate on completely different principles, and provide a completely different style of internetwork behavior. The world of bridged LANs is really divided in two: Token Rings that use source routing, and everything else. Source routing is not, and has never been, supported on Ethernet LANs. In Section 6.6, we discuss methods for communicating between these parallel universes; except as noted in that section, the discussions of source routing in this chapter do not apply to Ethernet at all.

Following a brief overview of source routing operation, we will look at:

- The history of source routing
- The concepts underlying its design

- The details of source routing operation in end stations and bridges
- Issues related to the interconnection of source routed and transparently bridged catenets

6.1 Overview of Source Routing Operation

Consider the source routed catenet depicted in Figure 6.1, and the communications among stations X, Y, and Z.

Stations X and Y are on the same ring (ring 1); as a result, they can communicate directly without the use of source routing or any other type of bridge. Frames sent from station X to station Y carry a Destination Address of Y, a Source Address of X, and the data payload associated with the frame. Since the frame does not need to pass through any bridges, no source routing information is required.

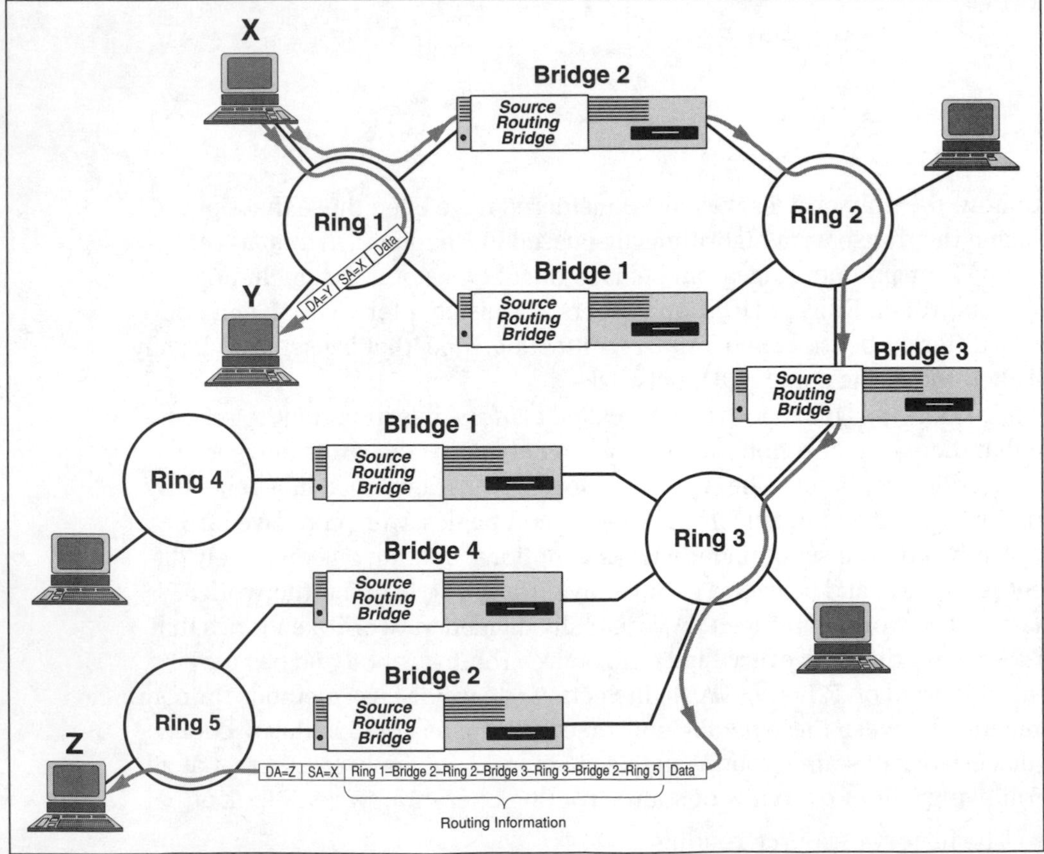

Figure 6.1 Source routing.

Stations X and Z can only communicate through a series of intervening rings and bridges. Four different paths are available between these two stations:

1. Ring 1–bridge 1–ring 2–bridge 3–ring 3–bridge 4–ring 5.
2. Ring 1–bridge 1–ring 2–bridge 3–ring 3–bridge 2–ring 5.
3. Ring 1–bridge 2–ring 2–bridge 3–ring 3–bridge 4–ring 5.
4. Ring 1–bridge 2–ring 2–bridge 3–ring 3–bridge 2–ring 5.

Prior to communicating with station Z, station X (not the bridges) must learn the routes that are available using a *Route Discovery* process. Station X then selects one of the routes (in the example shown, station X has chosen the fourth route from the preceding list) and inserts the explicit list of intervening rings and bridges in all frames sent to station Z. That is, the frame itself is modified to include routing information that describes the path taken by the frame through the catenet. The source routing bridges look at the encapsulated routing information and use it to forward frames along the indicated path.

Thus, the sending station (the source) determines the route taken by its frames; hence the name *source routing*. The destination station can use the same route the reverse direction, avoiding the need for Route Discovery by both endpoints of a communication session. In Section 6.5, the operation of end stations and bridges in a source routed catenet is explained in detail.

6.2 Eine Kleine Sourceroutinggeschichte

Source Routing was developed by IBM as part of its overall design of the Token Ring LAN architecture[1] [IBM87]. For the first 10 years of its life (1985–1995) virtually all Token Ring installations used source routing bridges exclusively. Transparent bridges were rarely used on Token Ring networks; few vendors even provided such products. Because of the differences in behavior between source routed and transparently bridged catenets, users that needed to support both Token Ring and Ethernet LANs within their orga-

[1] While most network equipment manufacturers offered Token Ring products, IBM was the only computer systems manufacturer that endorsed Token Ring (and source routing) as its LAN strategy. In contrast, numerous computer systems manufacturers endorsed Ethernet and transparent bridging, including Digital Equipment Corp., Sun Microsystems, Hewlett-Packard, Apple Computer, and many others. Thus, Token Ring LANs and source routing bridges were deployed primarily within IBM's customer base, particularly those customers who used IBM mainframes and mid-range computers.

For many years, Token Ring was the only LAN technology supported on these systems, virtually creating its own market from IBM's dominance of this segment of the industry. In later years, IBM began to support Ethernet on almost all of its computer systems, driven by its customers' migration from "True Blue" to mixed-vendor, heterogeneous computing environments. Since the early 1990s, IBM has shipped more Ethernet attachments each year than Token Ring.

nizations had to carefully partition network resources such that any traffic traversing between the two worlds passed through devices specifically designed to deal with the complexities of source routing-to-transparent bridge interconnection (see Section 6.6).

In the old days, Token Ring catenets consisted primarily of 4 Mb/s desktop rings interconnected by 16 Mb/s backbones. In this environment, source routing posed no great obstacle, since it was equally supported at both data rates. Customers could deploy source routing bridges throughout their Token Ring-based catenets and be assured that no serious interoperability problems would result.

By the early 1990s, FDDI emerged as a popular high-speed backbone technology. With its 100 Mb/s data rate, it provided the highest-capacity LAN technology of its day. FDDI was widely used to interconnect Ethernet desktop LANs; in fact, its use in this regard emerged as the primary application of FDDI. Since FDDI uses the same 48-bit globally-administered address space as IEEE 802 LANs, it was relatively easy to incorporate support for FDDI into the transparent bridge standard; the FDDI supplement to that standard was included in the 1993 edition of IEEE 802.1D [IEEE93a].

By the 1990s, 16 Mb/s Token Rings were quickly obsoleting their 4 Mb/s counterparts, even for desktop attachments. As FDDI was the only LAN technology supporting a data rate in excess of 16 Mb/s at the time, it made sense to use it for a backbone among the increasing number of 16 Mb/s Token Rings. FDDI is a natural technology to use for Token Ring interconnection. It uses the same address format, supports the same Frame Status indicators, and perhaps most important, uses the same bit-ordering (Big Endian) as Token Ring. As such, IBM and its adherents incorporated support for source routing into their FDDI products, so that the installed base of Token Ring users could use this higher-speed backbone technology. While source routing is supported on FDDI, this capability is needed only when the FDDI is being used to interconnect Token Ring LANs. In the vast majority of installations where FDDI is used to interconnect Ethernets, there is no need for products to support source route bridging.

Source routing (in its pure, native form) is an IBM-proprietary technology, described in the IBM Token Ring Architecture Reference [IBM87]. When used to the exclusion of transparent bridges, it has never been part of any approved national or international standard. In 1993, IEEE 802.1 incorporated an Annex to the IEEE 802.1D Bridge standard that provided support for source routing, but only in a device that supports both source routing and transparent bridging—the so-called SRT bridge, discussed in Section 6.6.3.

As Token Ring has evolved, many long-time Token Ring users have deployed Token Ring switches to increase aggregate network capacity. In much the same way that Ethernet switches allow microsegmentation and interconnection of 10, 100, and 1000 Mb/s Ethernets, Token Ring switches support links comprising 4, 16, and 100 Mb/s rings. Many of these Token Ring switches operate as transparent bridges and forgo source routing altogether. In this case, the only difference between a Token Ring switch and an Ethernet switch is the nature of the interface; the behavior of the switch is the same as discussed in Chapter 4.

6.3 Source Routing Concepts

I know it's difficult, but try to temporarily put aside everything you learned in the previous chapters. None of the concepts of transparent bridges apply to a source routed environment. Table 6.1 provides a summary of the differences between transparent and source routing bridges.

6.3.1 Nontransparency, or "Peek-a-Boo—I See You!"

Transparent bridges are, well . . . transparent. End stations communicating across a transparently-bridged catenet are completely unaware both of the path that their frames take through the catenet and of the presence of the bridges themselves. Conversely, the bridges are aware of the communicating end stations. Transparent bridges maintain address tables indicating those stations that are currently active and their relative locations (i.e., through which bridge port they are reachable). Forwarding decisions are made based on the information in the address table and the Destination Addresses in received frames.

The exact opposite relationships hold in a source routed environment. Source routing bridges are completely unaware of end stations in the catenet. They don't maintain tables of station addresses or any other state information regarding end station communications. Source routing bridges don't even examine the Destination Address field in received frames when making frame forwarding decisions. End station behavior in a source routed environment is also the antithesis of transparent operation. End stations in a source routed catenet are aware of both the paths their frames take through the catenet and of the source routing bridges along those paths. The source routing device driver within each station makes the decision as to the exact sequence of rings and bridges through which each frame it transmits will propagate.[2]

6.3.2 Who's the Boss?

We see that the role of the station and the bridge are reversed between source routing and transparent bridging. In transparent bridging, bridges make all of

[2] Source routing is the same as transparent bridging, if you stand on your head in front of a mirror.

Table 6.1 Summary of Differences between Transparent and Source Route Bridging

CHARACTERISTIC	TRANSPARENT BRIDGING	SOURCE ROUTE BRIDGING
Transparency	Bridges and multiple LANs are transparent to end stations. All end stations appear to each other to be on the same LAN. No end station difference between bridged and non-bridged traffic.	Bridges and multiple rings are exposed to end stations. End stations know which other stations are on the same versus different rings. End stations send frames differently to local versus bridged stations.
Topology knowledge	Address table and port mappings are learned and maintained by bridges.	Routes are learned and maintained by end stations.
Frame format	Unchanged by bridging.	Route information is inserted in frames.
Frame forwarding	Bridges make all forwarding decisions. No end station involvement	End stations make all forwarding decisions. Bridges follow end station instructions..
Bridge mode	Promiscuous; bridges intercept all traffic on all ports.	Bridges only intercept frames carrying source routing information.
Data Link operation	Connectionless or connection-oriented.	Connection-oriented.
Link utilization	All traffic follows the single spanning tree. Links not in the spanning tree are idle.	All links can be used for data traffic. Multicast and some route discovery traffic follows the spanning tree.
Ring/Bridge numbering	Not required.	Manually configured.
MTU discovery	Not supported.	End stations learn MTU of available path(s).

the frame forwarding decisions; end stations have neither responsibility for nor control of frame propagation through the catenet.

When source routing is used, the end stations have complete responsibility for directing traffic through the catenet. Stations decide if, when, and how to route frames across the various rings and bridges present. Source routing bridges simply follow the forwarding instructions (routing information) inserted into the frames by the end stations. They neither maintain address tables nor perform any frame-by-frame table lookup operations.

The rationale for this approach came from the belief that continuous promiscuous mode operation (as required for transparent bridging) constituted a prohibitive performance burden on a bridge and was therefore impractical for use in a commercial product. Source routing bridges examine and act only on those frames that must be forwarded across multiple rings. If most traffic is between desktop clients and a local server on the same ring, the performance burden on the bridge is greatly reduced. Historically, traffic patterns followed the 80/20 rule; 80 percent of network traffic was local and only 20 percent was targeted at a remote destination. Under this assumption, source routing indeed reduces the performance burden and lowers the cost of the bridge. With the modern trend toward enterprise intranetworks with centralized server farms, the 80/20 rule gets turned inside-out; most traffic traverses multiple LANs between client and server, and bridges need to forward the majority of frames present on a given LAN.

BRIDGE OPTIMIZATION VERSUS SYSTEM OPTIMIZATION

Source routing can reduce the performance burden on bridges, and hence their cost. However, as with most engineering decisions, there is a price to pay. In this case, the price is an increase in the performance burden placed on *every end station in the catenet.* By moving the route decision-making process from the bridge to the end station, we have increased the processing required of those end stations.

Total system complexity and cost is a function of the sum of the complexity of all of the devices in the system. Since there are generally many more end stations than bridges, the decision to place the routing burden on the end stations appears to be a sub-optimization; it reduces the cost of the bridges, but increases the overall cost of the system. More total CPU cycles will be needed to implement the frame forwarding process in every station than for a system that centralizes that task in a transparent bridge.

Of course, if you are in the business of selling CPU cycles, the end station approach makes good sense. Source routing increases the need for higher-performance processors on every desktop. Given that IBM was the industry-leading manufacturer of personal computers in the mid-1980s and, at the time,

had insignificant market share in internetworking products (transparent bridges and routers), it is not surprising that the company followed the Source Routing path.[3]

6.3.3 Connection-Orientation

When using source routing, end stations set up a path through the intervening rings and bridges at the time they open a communication session with a partner station (e.g., a server). This path is used for the duration of the session. In contrast, transparent bridges make their forwarding decision on a frame-by-frame basis; there is no concept of a communication session, and no forwarding history is maintained between frames.

Thus, source routing presumes that the communicating stations are using connection-oriented virtual circuits within the Data Link; the source routing path is typically selected at the same time the circuit is established. Since end stations using virtual circuits must already maintain state information for those circuits (e.g., flow and error control), the additional source routing state is relatively insignificant.[4]

This assumption of connection-orientation at the Data Link layer was endemic to IBM's model of network communications at the time source routing was developed. While the use of distinct Transport and Network-layer protocols (such as TCP and IP) is often taken for granted today, IBM's early LAN communications model did not provide these capabilities at the same architectural layers. As depicted in Figure 6.2, the original architecture that IBM-based systems used for LAN communications had high-level applications communicating directly with the Data Link. It was assumed in this model that the Data Link would provide:

- The error and flow control functions normally provided by the Transport layer
- The internetwork routing function normally provided by the Network layer in other data communications architectures

This model eliminated the Transport and Network layers altogether, and folded those functions into the Data Link. As such, the Data Link became more complex, comprising all of the connection-oriented features normally associated with higher-layer communications. This dichotomy permeates not

[3] The same underlying philosophy may be behind Intel's and Microsoft's activities with respect to desktop video delivery, LAN conferencing applications, multimedia games, and so on. These applications all require more memory and more CPU cycles at the desktop, implying a regular need for new hardware purchases and software upgrades.

[4] While the state information needed to perform source routing (i.e., the path being used) may be minimal, the complexity required to determine and establish the path is not.

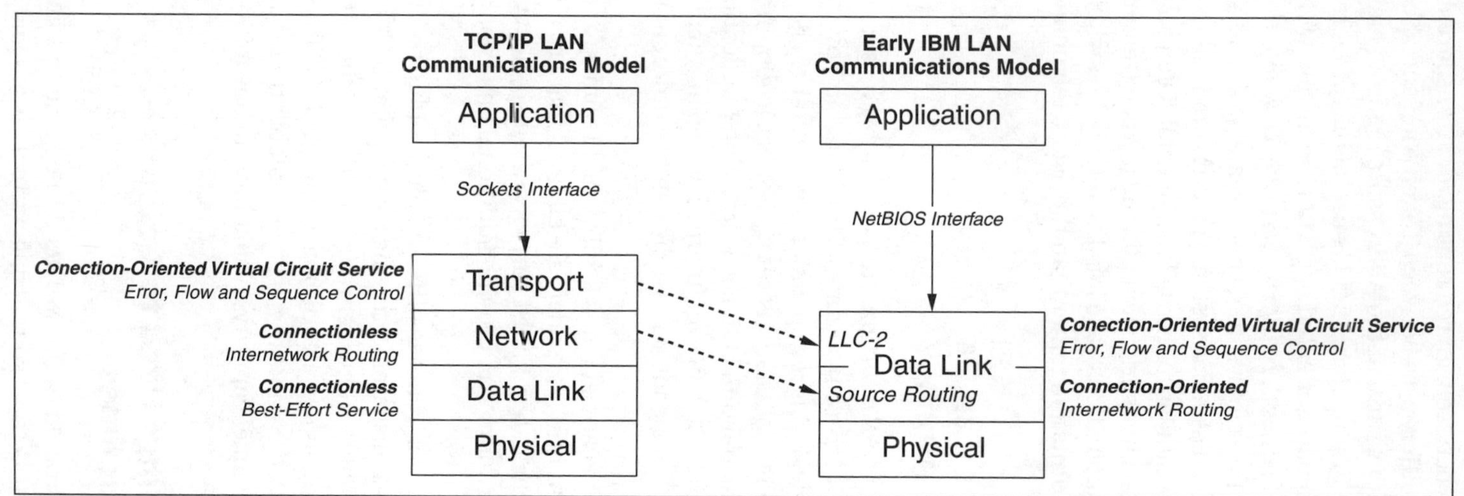

Figure 6.2 TCP/IP versus early IBM LAN communications architecture.

only most of the differences between source routing and transparent bridging, but also some fundamental differences between Token Ring and Ethernet LANs. For example, Token Ring's use of the Address Recognized and Frame Copied (A and C) bits in the Frame Status field is useful only if there is some form of acknowledged connection-oriented operation occurring within the Data Link. As discussed in Chapter 3, *Bridging between Technologies*, these functions are useless in a connectionless LAN and create problems when transparent bridging between dissimilar systems is attempted.

Source routing behavior is similar to the method of establishing a path through a telecommunications network when making a voice (telephone) call, except that in the telecommunications case it is the telephone switches that maintain the call routing information rather than the users' telephones.

6.3.4 Be All that You Can Be (Without Joining the Army)

As discussed in Chapter 5, *Loop Resolution*, transparent bridges maintain the non-duplication and frame ordering invariants of the Data Link by ensuring that all traffic follows a single, loop-free spanning tree path through the catenet. In a source routed catenet, stations set up a specific loop-free path through the catenet for each communication session. Non-duplication and frame ordering is thus maintained; however, there is no requirement that all sessions use the same path. Independent sessions can use different paths, as long as each is loop-free.

As a result, a source routed catenet can use all available links for active communications; transparent bridges render idle all links that are not part of the single spanning tree. If the catenet must carry a sustained, heavy traffic load, this feature of source routing can provide additional link capacity that would otherwise go unused.

Again, this dichotomy derives from the differing philosophies of LAN usage; proponents of Ethernet and transparent bridging assume that LAN capacity is relatively inexpensive and that it is cheaper to overprovision the network than to burden end stations with complex algorithms. Proponents of Token Ring and source routing believe that complexity is an acceptable tradeoff in exchange for maximizing channel capacity, availability, and usability.

6.3.5 Even Token Rings Need to Get Out of the Loop Sometimes

For some classes of source routed traffic, we need to be able to send frames between stations without (or before) setting up a virtual circuit and establishing a path through the catenet. Two important cases include:

Multicast exchanges It is usually not feasible to set up a virtual circuit with a single source and multiple endpoints, as would be implied by a multicast connection. Multicast traffic is generally connectionless in nature.

Route Discovery We may need to send frames without duplication for the purpose of establishing the source route for a given virtual circuit.

For these purposes, we create a loop-free subset of the topology that includes all rings in the catenet—a spanning tree. The important differences between the spanning tree used in transparently-bridged catenets and that used in source routed catenets are:

- In a transparently-bridged catenet, the spanning tree path is used for all traffic; in a source routed catenet, only a small portion of the total traffic is typically sent along the spanning tree (primarily multicasts and route discovery messages).
- Often, the spanning tree in a source routed catenet is manually configured. Rather than using the automatic Spanning Tree Protocol, a human network administrator decides which rings, bridges, and bridge ports will be part of the spanning tree, and configures these parameters with a proprietary software tool.

  If the spanning tree is manually configured, there is generally no mechanism for automatic reconfiguration of the tree in the event of the failure of a ring, bridge, or bridge port. Single failures can cause the catenet to fracture into disjoint logical partitions until the network administrator reconfigures the spanning tree parameters.

6.3.6 Ring and Bridge Numbering

In a source routed catenet, every frame that passes through multiple rings carries an explicit list of those rings and bridges through which the frame must pass to reach the intended destination ring(s) from the source station. Thus, each ring and each bridge must be uniquely identifiable, so that the path description is unambiguous.

When the source routing algorithms were being designed, it would have been a straightforward matter to provide 48-bit, globally-unique identifiers for rings and bridges. Each ring could be identified by the address of one of the stations present on that ring,[5] and (in a manner similar to transparent bridges participating in the Spanning Tree Protocol) each bridge could use the address of one of its interfaces as a unique identifier. However, this was not done.

[5] Since Token Ring network operation requires that exactly one station become an Active Monitor on each ring, it would have been a logical choice to use the address of the Active Monitor as the ring identifier.

Instead, each ring within a source routed catenet is assigned a unique 12 bit ring number, allowing for a maximum of 4,096 rings in a single catenet. (Don't worry; no source routed catenet has ever approached this limit, or likely ever will.) Bridges are assigned a 4-bit bridge number between 1 and 15 (bridge number 0 is reserved).[6,7] While this may appear to limit the number of bridges in the catenet to 15, this is not the case. Bridge numbers do not need to be unique even within a given catenet; they must only be unique on the rings to which a given set of bridges connect, as depicted in Figure 6.3. That is, there can be a maximum of 15 bridges connected to any ring, which is more than most users will ever want.

As a result of the small, locally administered ring and bridge number space, these values must be manually assigned. Each source routing bridge must be manually configured with its own bridge number as well as the ring number associated with each of its ports. Improper or inconsistent configuration can result in various types of communications failures.

6.3.7 Route Discovery

Source routing requires that an end station know about and use specific path(s) through the catenet to reach each other station with which it communicates. In a generalized catenet with an arbitrary topology (e.g., the topology shown in Figure 6.1), there may be multiple paths present between a given pair of stations. In addition, the number and nature of the available paths may change over time as the configuration of the catenet changes due to the addition, removal, or failure of rings and bridges. Thus, it is necessary for each station to learn what route(s) are available just prior to initiating a communication session with another station, using the Route Discovery process described in detail in Section 6.5.1.

[6] Part of the reason for not using 48-bit ring and bridge identifiers was to save space in the frame; a route descriptor using 48-bit ring and bridge identifiers would require 12 bytes ([48 + 48] bits = 96 bits = 12 bytes) rather than 2 bytes ([12 + 4] bits) for each hop. A second reason is that IBM never really subscribed to the concept of globally unique addressing, opting instead to use locally administered addresses in most Token Ring systems. Since IBM customers already needed to manually administer all of the station addresses, the job of administering ring and bridge numbers was considered a small incremental burden.

[7] Strictly speaking, these should be called ring and bridge *identifiers* rather than *numbers*, since the values assigned have no numerical significance. That is, they are compared for an exact match, but not to determine whether they are numerically greater or less than some value, and arithmetic operations are never performed on them. The IEEE standard calls them LAN Identifiers and Bridge Numbers, respectively. Nonetheless, common usage is to call them ring and bridge numbers, and this book follows that convention.

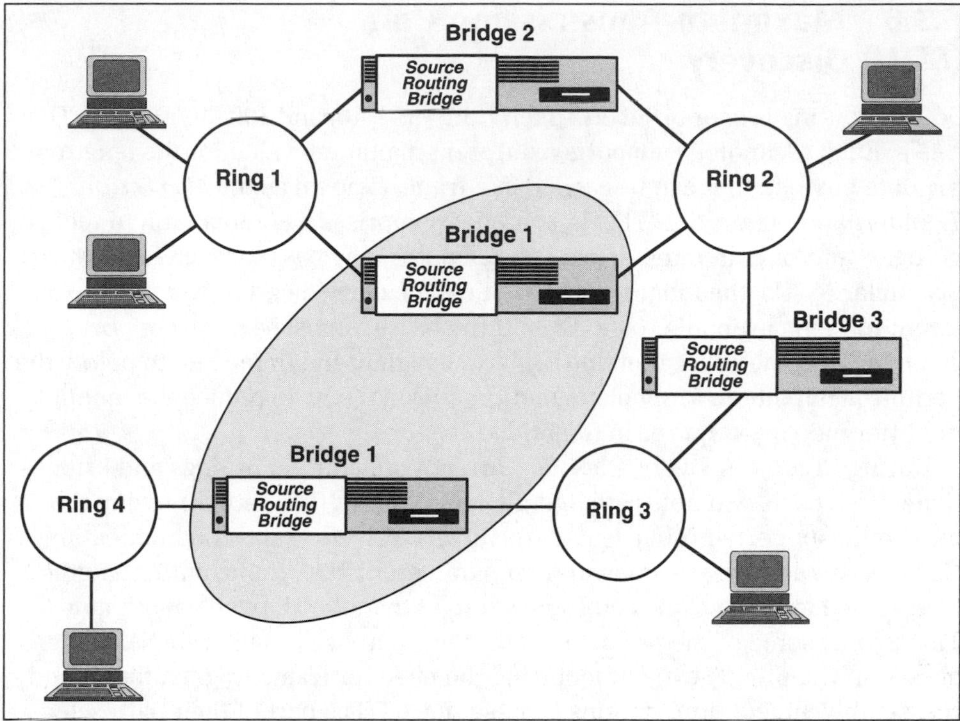

Figure 6.3 Same bridge number on different rings.

Route Discovery is normally invoked prior to each new communication session. The initiating station learns all of the available source routed paths between itself and the target destination, and chooses one using a set of station-specific selection criteria. Normally, the target destination station uses the same route (in reverse) for frames it sends back to the station that initiated the session. The selected route is cached (stored) within the device driver software and used for the duration of the communication session.

During Route Discovery, a station may learn that its target destination is on the same ring as itself (i.e., one of the paths it learns has no bridges in it). In this case, the stations will communicate directly, without the use of source routing.

In general, the route is flushed from the cache at the termination of the communication session; no history is kept between sessions. Each new communication session reinvokes the Route Discovery process; this allows the system to adapt to topology and configuration changes between sessions.

6.3.8 Maximum Transmission Unit (MTU) Discovery

Source routing is supported on Token Ring (at 4, 16, and 100 Mb/s), and FDDI LANs. Each technology supports a different maximum value for the length of the data payload that can be carried in a frame (known as the *Maximum Transmission Unit*, or MTU). If a catenet comprises a combination of technologies and/or data rates, source routed paths may pass through LANs with dissimilar MTUs; the longest frame that can be carried end-to-end may be different for each available route. Even if the LANs themselves can support a given MTU, some source routing bridges may limit the frame length below the permitted maximum for implementation reasons (e.g., to reduce the amount of buffer memory required in the bridge).

During Route Discovery, stations learn not only the set of rings and bridges that define each available path, but also the MTU of that path. Knowing the maximum supported frame length, the device drivers in the communicating stations can adjust their transmission parameters (e.g., frame buffer lengths) to ensure that they never send frames longer than the allowable maximum. This avoids some of the problems of bridging across dissimilar LANs (as discussed in Chapter 3) without incurring the need for frame fragmentation and reassembly. In addition, stations can use the MTU as part of their path selection criteria; a station can choose to use only those paths that can carry some minimum frame length; or may opt for a path that comprises more bridge hops but supports larger frames (e.g., for a bulk file transfer application that wants to maximize throughput at the expense of latency).

6.4 Source Routed Frames

Stations that implement source routing insert routing information into all frames that must traverse multiple rings. Thus, the frame format differs between bridged and non-bridged traffic.

6.4.1 Differentiating Source Routed and Non-Source Routed Frames

Source routing operation was fully defined after the development of the underlying Token Ring and FDDI technologies over which it operates. Thus, there was originally no accommodation made within the respective frame formats to allow a bridge to easily distinguish between source routed and non-source routed frames. Such differentiation is clearly needed—a key factor in the design of source routing is that bridges need only consider those frames that contain routing information; we do not want source routing bridges to have to operate in promiscuous mode.

In looking for a place to squeeze additional information into the frame, we can observe that, while a frame may be sent *to* either a unicast or a multicast destination, frames are always sent *from* an individual station. The first bit of the Destination Address indicates the unicast or multicast nature of the recipient(s). When used in its originally-intended manner, the first bit of a Source Address should always be 0, indicating an individual sending station. Source routing uses this "wasted" bit to indicate the presence of source routing information, as shown in Figure 6.4. If the first bit is 0, the frame does not contain source routing information; if the first bit is 1, routing information is assumed to be present immediately following the Source Address field. The first bit of the Source Address is therefore renamed the *Routing Information Indicator* (RII) on Token Ring and FDDI LANs.

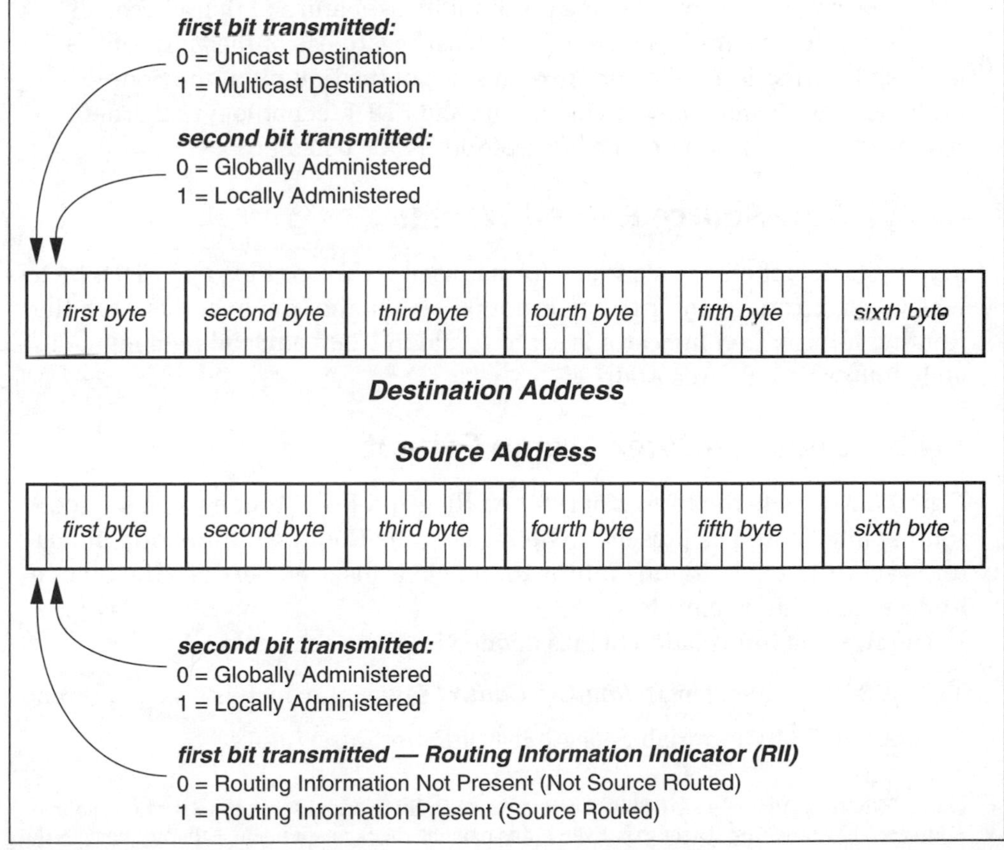

Figure 6.4 Routing Information Indicator in Source Address.

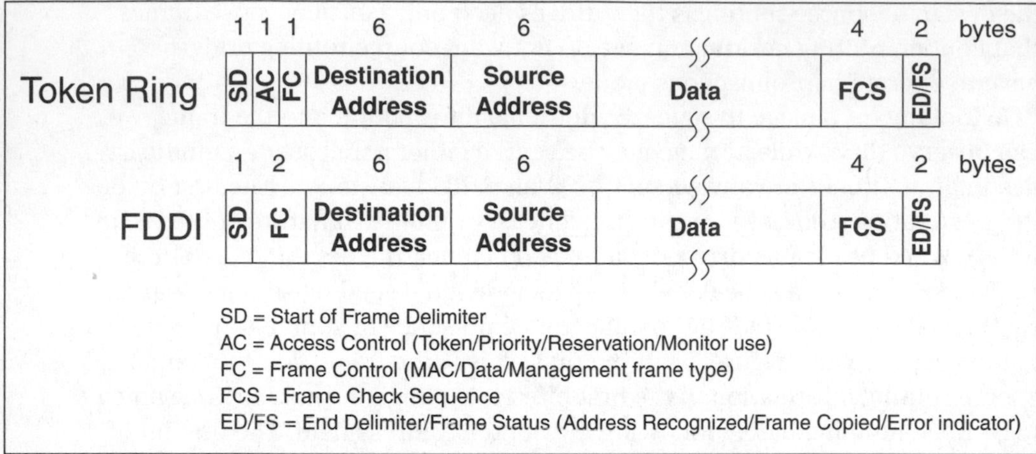

Figure 6.5 Token Ring/FDDI frame formats (no source routing information).

Note that setting the first bit of the address to 1 in a Source Address does not imply anything about the unicast or multicast nature of the source; all Source Addresses are assumed to be unicast regardless of the value of the Routing Information Indicator. Also, this use of the first bit of the Source Address is applicable only to Token Ring and FDDI technology; Ethernet requires that the first bit of the Source Address be 0 in all cases.[8]

6.4.2 Non-Source Routed Frames

Figure 6.5 depicts the basic frame format used on Token Ring and FDDI LANs when source routing information is not present in the frame. In this case, the Routing Information Indicator is set to 0, and the data payload field immediately follows the Source Address.

6.4.3 Source Routed Frame Format

Figure 6.6 depicts the format of a Token Ring and FDDI frame when source routing information is present. In both cases, the Routing Information Indicator is set to 1, and a Routing Information field is inserted between the Source Address and the data payload.

The Routing Information field is divided into two segments:

1. A 2-byte, fixed-length *Routing Control* segment, which is always present.
2. A 0 to 28 byte, variable-length list of *Route Descriptors*.

[8] Some Ethernet devices specifically check for this condition and discard frames whose Source Addresses have the first bit set to 0. Even if this explicit check is not made, Ethernet devices do not understand or act on natively-encapsulated source routing information. Source routing can only be accomplished on an Ethernet (if desired) by encapsulating the routing information using the Virtual LAN mechanisms discussed in Chapter 12, *Virtual LANs: the IEEE Standard.*

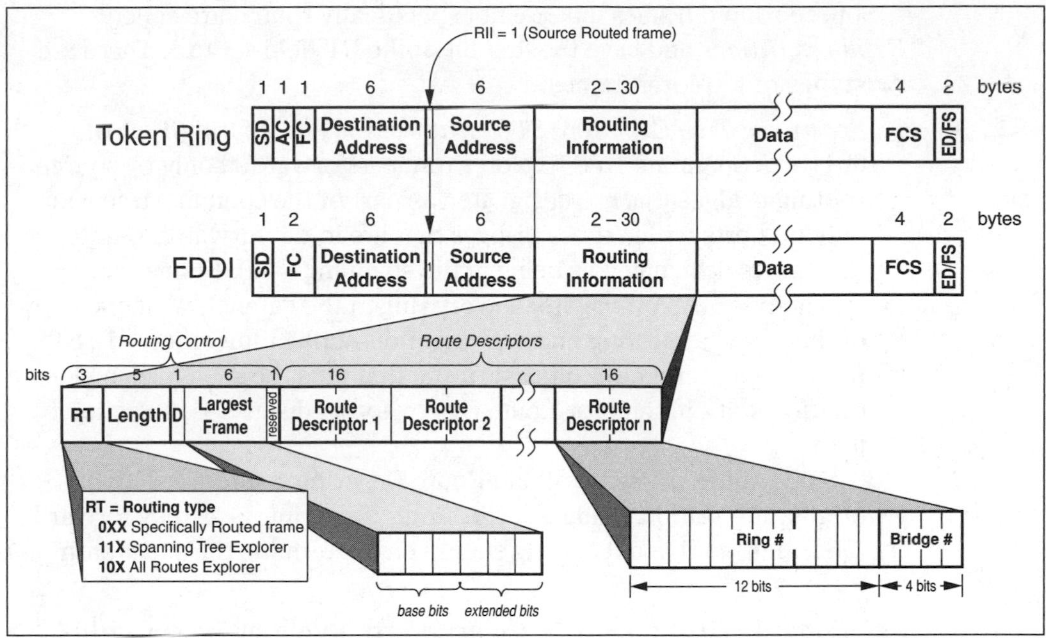

Figure 6.6 Source routed frame formats.

Each of these segments and their encapsulated fields are described in the following text. As per the normal convention in Token Ring and FDDI, bits are transmitted within each byte from the most-significant bit to the least-significant bit; in all figures, the left-most bit shown is the most significant within each byte.

6.4.3.1 Routing Control Fields

Routing Control comprises five fields, as follows:

Routing Type (RT) This field indicates the type of source routed frame being sent. Three types of source routed frames can be indicated:

1. *Specifically Routed Frames (SRFs)*. Carry a Routing Type of 0b0XX. (The first bit is set to 0, and the other 2 bits, indicated by XX in Figure 6.6, are ignored.[9]) A Specifically Routed Frame carries an explicit list of Route Descriptors, and is forwarded by source routing bridges along this single route through the catenet. This routing type is used for the bulk of traffic sent between stations on different rings (file transfers, client-server transactions, etc.).

[9] The XX bits are used for a path trace function in IBM-proprietary systems; they are ignored in systems that conform to the IEEE 802 standards.

Source routed frames that are not specifically routed are called *Explorer frames* and have the first bit of the RT field set to 1. There are two types of Explorer frames:

2. *Spanning Tree Explorer (STE) frames.* Carry a Routing Type of 0b11X. A Spanning Tree Explorer frame is forwarded only by source routing bridges that are designated as part of the spanning tree, and only on ports within those bridges that are in the forwarding state (i.e., ports designated as being in the spanning tree). Frames sent in this manner will propagate to every ring in the catenet, with one copy of the frame appearing on each ring (non-duplication enforced). STE frames are useful for multicast traffic that must be seen by many destination stations, and for Route Discovery, as discussed in Section 6.5.1.

   STE frames are sent with no Route Descriptors provided by the originating station. Bridges insert Route Descriptors as they forward the frame, so that a receiving station can determine the exact path taken.

3. *All Routes Explorer (ARE) frames.* Carry a Routing Type of 0b10X. An ARE frame is forwarded by all source routing bridges along every possible path between the source and destination. Thus, the destination may receive multiple copies of the same frame, one for every route available between the sender and itself. ARE frames are used for Route Discovery, as discussed in Section 6.5.1.[10,11]

   Similar to Spanning Tree Explorers, ARE frames are sent with no Route Descriptors by the originating station. Bridges insert Route Descriptors as they forward the frame, so that the receiving station can determine the path taken.

Traffic that remains local to the ring (i.e., non-source routed traffic) is not indicated by the Routing Type field. Local traffic is indicated by setting the RII to 0 and eliminating the Routing Information field altogether. Frames sent in this manner will never be forwarded off a ring by a source routing bridge.

Length (LTH) Since Routing Information can comprise a variable number of Route Descriptors, a Length field is used to indicate the total num-

[10] Note that bridges do not enforce a non-duplication invariant for ARE frames. Indeed, ARE frames are specifically sent so that a replica is created for each possible path through the catenet.

[11] IBM documentation calls a Specifically Routed Frame a *Source Routed Frame* (SRF), a Spanning Tree Explorer a *Single Route Broadcast* (SRB), and an All Routes Explorer an *All Routes Broadcast* (ARB). This book uses the IEEE standard terminology throughout.

ber of bytes present (including both the Routing Control and Route Descriptor segments). The Routing Control segment is always present and comprises 16 bits; therefore the minimum value of the Length field is 2 bytes. An arbitrary maximum is set at 30 bytes, which places the upper bound on the extent of a source routed catenet at 14 Route Descriptors.[12] Since Route Descriptors are 2 bytes each, the Length field should always be an even number.

Direction (D) The Direction bit indicates whether the Route Descriptors should be read from left-to-right (D = 0) or from right-to-left (D = 1) within the Routing Information field. This allows communicating stations to keep most of the Routing Information field identical during frame exchanges. Rather than requiring software to build the list of Route Descriptors in reverse order, a single list of descriptors can be used in both directions by simply inverting the Direction bit.

The D bit is meaningful only in Specifically Routed Frames; it must be zero in all Explorer Frames (STE and ARE).

Largest Frame (LF) Source Routing supports the capability for a pair of communicating stations to determine the largest data payload field (MTU) that can be supported by the complete set of rings and bridges between them. This allows the stations to optimize bulk data transfers by using the largest frames possible without incurring fragmentation by higher layer protocols. (See Section 6.3.8.)

If the LF field was encoded as the number of bytes that could be carried, 16 bits would be needed to represent all of the possible values needed. In order to save bits in the frame header, the range of possible LF values was encoded into a maximum of 6 bits. Thus, complexity and granularity were sacrificed for a savings of 10 bits.[13]

Before the incorporation of the source routing option into the IEEE 802.1D standard (i.e., when it was defined solely in the IBM documentation), the LF field used only 3 bits and provided eight levels of MTU granularity. During the standardization effort, the LF field was expanded to the 6 bits shown in Figure 6.6. As such, provisions were made to support both earlier devices that considered only 3 bits of LF information (called *base bits*) and those that considered all 6 bits (*extended bits*).

Table 6.2 shows the encoding of the LF field. Devices that consider

[12] While the architecture and industry standard may allow a frame to traverse up to 14 rings, the IBM specification and most commercial product implementations restrict the extent to eight Route Descriptors (seven bridge hops, LTH = 18).

[13] I personally believe that this was a mistake (although a relatively minor one). Given that LANs are designed to have lots of excess capacity, an increase in source routing overhead of 2 bytes does not seem unreasonable, especially in light of the encoding complexity that resulted from this decision.

Table 6.2 LF Encoding of MTU

Base Bit Encoding	Extension Bit Encoding							
	000	001	010	011	100	101	110	111
000	516	635	754	873	993	1,112	1,231	1,350
001	1,470	1,542	1,615	1,688	1,761	1,833	1,906	1,979
010	2,052	2,345	2,638	2,932	3,225	3,518	3,812	4,105
011	4,399	4,865	5,331	5,798	6,264	6,730	7,197	7,663
100	8,130	8,539	8,949	9,358	9,768	10,178	10,587	10,997
101	11,407	12,169	12,992	13,785	14,578	15,370	16,163	16,956
110	17,749	20,730	23,711	26,963	29,674	32,655	35,637	38,618
111	>17,749[1] 41,600[2]	44,591	47,583	50,575	53,567	56,559	59,551	>59,551

[1] This value is used by devices supporting only the base bits.
[2] This value is used by devices supporting both the base and extension bits.

only the base bits use the values in the (shaded) column associated with an extension of 0b000, regardless of the actual value of the extended bits.

The LF field is meaningful only in Explorer frames (both STE and ARE). Stations initially set the value to the largest payload length that they want to use. When forwarding Explorer frames, source routing bridges either leave this value intact (if they support the indicated LF length) or reduce it as a function of the LF capabilities of the bridge or the ports through which it is receiving or forwarding the frame. The LF field is ignored in Specifically Routed Frames; it is used only during route discovery to determine the maximum length of any Specifically Routed Frames to be sent later.

Reserved One bit is reserved for future (unspecified) use. Source routing bridges ignore the value, but propagate it as received in any forwarded frames.

6.4.3.2 Route Descriptors

The Route Descriptor segment comprises a sequence of Ring Numbers and Bridge Numbers specifying a path between a pair of communicating stations. Each Route Descriptor is a 2 byte, fixed-length field comprising a 12-bit Ring Number and a 4-bit Bridge Number.

IT'S NOT QUITE AS WEIRD AS IT LOOKS

While the LF field encoding may seem like a tabular representation of the output from a random number generator, there is some method to the madness. The values chosen for the base bit encoding were derived from some practical implementation environments:

- **516 bytes is the payload resulting from the use of minimum MTU packets in the ISO CLNP [ISO87] after allowing for LLC and Routing Information overhead.**
- **1,470 bytes is the payload resulting from a 1,500 byte Ethernet frame after subtracting 30 bytes for the maximum Routing Information field. While Ethernet systems do not support native source routing, the encoding allows for this possibility.**
- **2,052 bytes represents an 80 × 24 character screen display, with an allowance for control overhead (commonly used in IBM SNA applications).**
- **4,399 bytes represents the payload available on FDDI and 4 Mb/s Token Ring systems using default configuration parameters, after subtracting the Routing Information overhead.**
- **8,130 byte payloads could be carried on IEEE 802.4 Token Bus systems if they supported source routing (which they don't).**
- **11,407 byte payloads can be carried on 4 Mb/s Token Ring systems if a reduction in the error robustness can be tolerated (i.e., a reduction of the Hamming distance from 4 to 3).**
- **17,749 bytes represents the payload available on 16 and 100 Mb/s Token Ring systems after subtracting the Routing Information overhead.**

The remaining entries in the table are linear interpolations between these listed values.

The number of Route Descriptors present can be determined from the Length field as:

$$N_{RD} = \frac{\text{Length} - 2}{2}$$

and can vary from 0 (for an Explorer frame on the ring where it was initially generated) to 14 (for a Length field equal to the maximum value of 30).

Note that while it is possible to have no Route Descriptors present, the presence of only a single Route Descriptor (Length = 4) constitutes an error. Since frames always terminate on a ring (rather than in a bridge), a source routed path will always comprise at least two Route Descriptors, indicating a ring-bridge-ring sequence. The Bridge Number in the last Route Descriptor is always set to 0.

6.5 Source Routing Operation

There are two aspects to source routing operation:

1. The Route Discovery process by which stations learn and select among the available paths for frames to traverse the catenet.
2. The steady-state operation of the system for frames that follow the selected path.

In the sections that follow, we look at the details of the operation of both end stations and bridges with respect to both aspects of source routing operation.

6.5.1 Route Discovery

Before any pair of stations can communicate using Specifically Routed Frames across a catenet, they must first perform a Route Discovery procedure in which the stations learn which (if any) paths are available, and select one of those paths to use for frame exchanges during the instant session. Prior to the discovery of such a route, stations can still communicate across multiple rings by using Spanning Tree Explorer frames, although this obviates any benefits of source routing.

While it is theoretically possible to modify the source route dynamically over the duration of a session, in practice the Route Discovery process is invoked once and the selected route is used for the duration of the session, be it minutes or days. Source routes are generally not cached (remembered) between sessions; opening a new session with the same device invokes the Route Discovery process anew.

6.5.1.1 Route Discovery Algorithms

Before attempting to discover a route through the catenet, a station can try to communicate with its target destination without the use of source routing. If the target is present on the same ring as the session initiator, it will respond directly. If not, the initiating station must try to find a route to the target through the bridges in the catenet. Many different Route Discovery algorithms are possible. The two most common Route Discovery algorithms that have been used in commercial products are:

- *All Routes Explorer request, Specifically Routed response.* As shown in

Figure 6.7, the station wishing to initiate communications sends an All Routes Explorer frame to the target destination. Through the operation of the bridges, one copy of the original ARE frame will arrive on the destination ring for each possible path through the source routed catenet.

The target destination receives the All Routes Explorer frame(s); each one displays the path taken by that particular frame through the catenet in its Route Descriptor list. The destination chooses one of the available routes (see Section 6.5.1.3 for a discussion of route selection) and sends a single Specifically Routed Frame back to the initiator along the selected path. Once this frame is received by the initiator, both parties know the path selected and can communicate using Specifically Routed Frames until the end of the session.

Note that, using this algorithm, route selection is at the discretion of the destination station, not the initiator of the exchange. Only the destination sees all of the available routes, being the target of an All Routes Explorer frame. Also, a greater processing burden is placed on the target destination than on the initiator, since the target destination must receive all of the resulting Explorer frames.

In a variation of this algorithm, the target destination sends a Specifically Routed Frame back to the initiator for each ARE frame received. This action shifts the burden (or honor, depending on your point of view) of route selection back to the session initiator.

- *Spanning Tree request, All Routes response.* As shown in Figure 6.8, the station wishing to initiate communications sends a Spanning Tree Explorer frame to the intended destination. Bridges will forward this

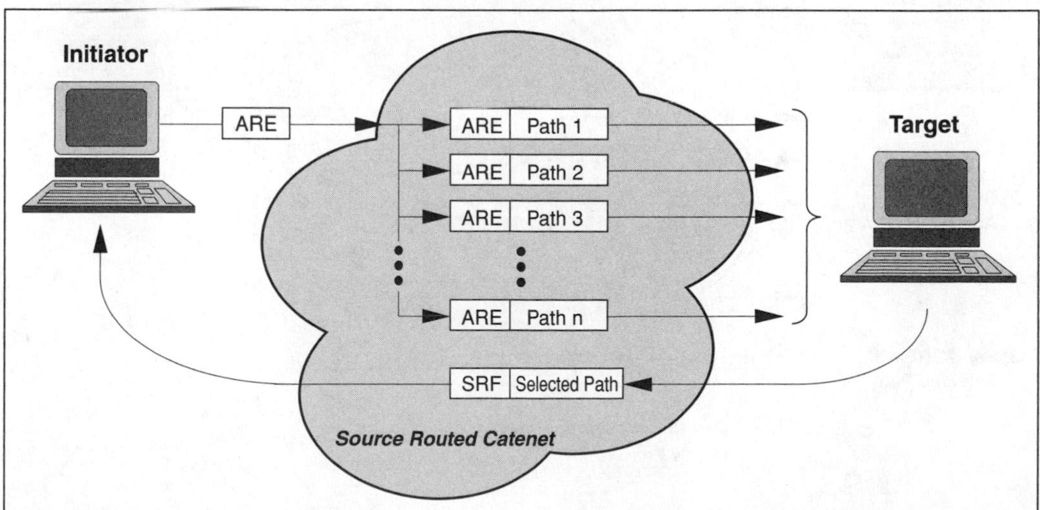

Figure 6.7 Route Discovery using ARE request, SRF response.

frame along the spanning tree, such that one copy of the frame will appear on every ring in the catenet and at the target destination.

The target receives the Spanning Tree Explorer frame and responds with an All Routes Explorer to the initiating station. The ARE frame(s) propagates back, with the bridges generating a copy of the frame for every possible path between the target and the initiator. The initiating station then selects a route from those shown to be available, indicates that route to the target with a Specifically Routed Frame, and uses it for communications for the duration of this session.

Using this method, route selection is at the discretion of the initiating station rather than the target. Similarly, the greater processing burden is placed on the initiator. In many application environments, communication sessions take place between a client and a server station, with a single server supporting many clients. Using this second method, Route Discovery processing is spread more evenly; the clients (who generally initiate sessions) accept both the Explorer frame processing burden and the responsibility for route selection for their own sessions, rather than requiring the server to do the combined work for all clients. For this reason, this algorithm is the most widely used, and is specified in the IEEE standard. Unless otherwise noted, it will be assumed in the discussions that follow that this method of Route Discovery is being used.

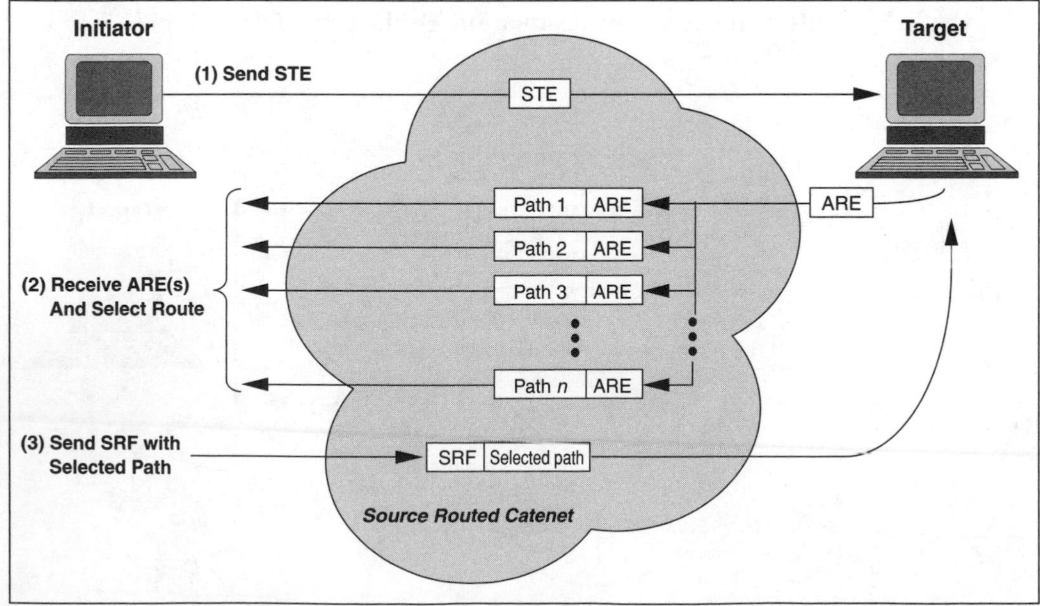

Figure 6.8 Route Discovery using STE request, ARE response.

6.5.1.2 Route Discovery Frames

The three steps in the procedure just outlined are reflected in the frames used for Route Discovery, as depicted in Figure 6.9.

The fields in Route Discovery frames indicate the following information:

Routing Information Indicator The RII is set to 1 for all Route Discovery frames. This ensures that these frames will be intercepted and acted upon by the source routing bridges in the catenet.

LLC DSAP/SSAP/Control Route Discovery frames use connectionless LLC-1 encapsulation, and comprise Unnumbered Information (UI) frames (LLC Control = 0x03). They are distinguished from other protocols by their unique LLC SAP value, 0xA6. This LLC SAP value implies that the remainder of the frame is formatted as shown in Figure 6.9 and described in the following text.

Version The current version number of the Route Discovery frame format is 1 (0x01).

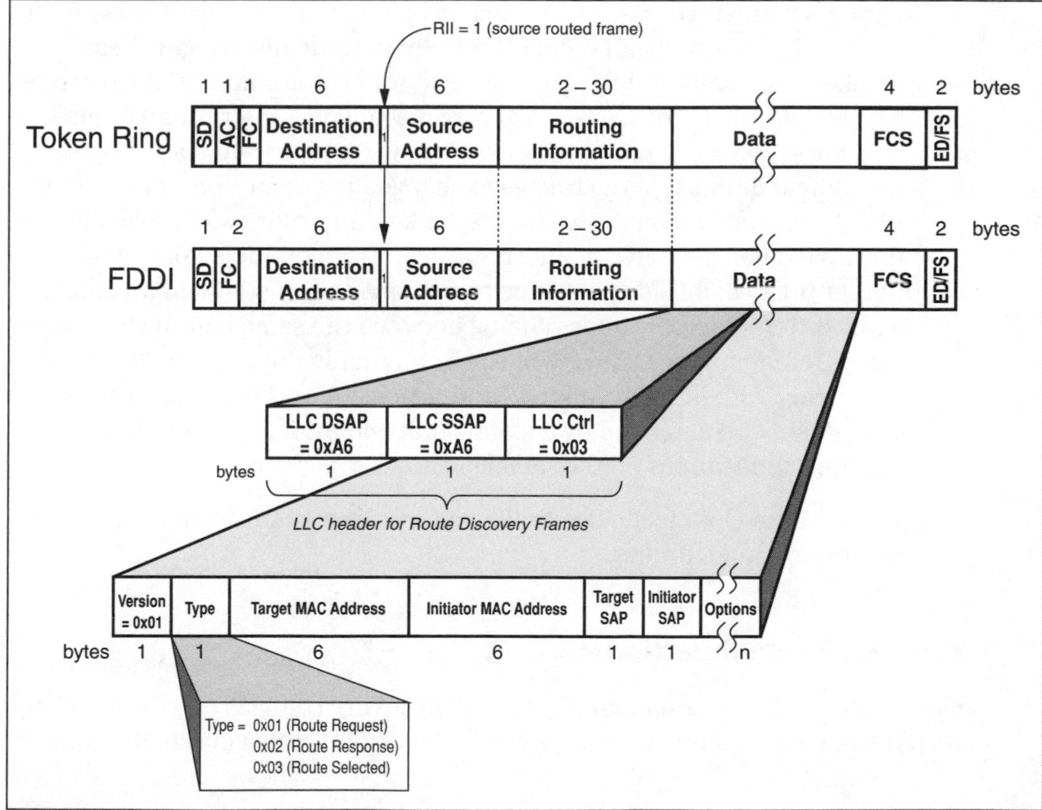

Figure 6.9 Route Discovery frame format.

Type Three types of Route Discovery frames are possible, corresponding to the three operations depicted in Figure 6.8:

- A *Route Request* (Type = 0x01) is sent by the initiator of the Route Discovery as a Spanning Tree Explorer.
- A *Route Response* (Type = 0x02) is sent by the target of the Route Discovery as an All Routes Explorer. The ARE frame(s) will propagate back to the initiator to indicate the available routes through the catenet.
- A *Route Selected* (Type = 0x03) frame is sent by the initiator to the target as a Specifically Routed Frame, indicating the selected route to use for the remainder of this session.

Target MAC Address/Initiator MAC Address These fields contain the 48-bit addresses of the target and initiator of Route Discovery, respectively. They are included in the Route Discovery frame to allow the underlying hardware to strip off the MAC header before delivery to the device driver.[14]

Target SAP/Initiator SAP These fields contain the Service Access Point (SAP) identifier of the LLC clients for which route discovery is being invoked. Normally, a single route is used for all communications between a given pair of stations, ensuring correct sequence order for all frames exchanged between those stations. However, proper application operation only requires that the frames exchanged between a pair of communicating applications on those stations be kept in order, rather than all frames exchanged between those stations (from multiple applications). Rather than establishing a source route for a pair of stations, we could allow different applications running between the same pair of stations to use different source routes. While not commonly done, the inclusion of the client SAP identifiers allows for this possibility. Performance could conceivably be improved by allowing link and bridge load-sharing among multiple applications on the same machines.

Options The Options field is available for future extensions to the Route Discovery frame format.

6.5.1.3 Route Selection

One of the stations participating in Route Discovery (typically the initiator) is responsible for selecting one of the available routes for use during the com-

[14] While not all hardware performs this operation, the inclusion of the MAC addresses in the LLC encapsulation allows for the possibility.

munication session. While this may sound like it should be a straightforward procedure, consider the plight of this station:

- It does not know in advance how many ARE frames (one for each available path) will be returning as a result of its Route Request. Indeed, if it did know, that would imply that the station knew the topology of the catenet without Route Discovery! The whole purpose of Route Discovery is to learn the number and nature of the available routes.
- Assuming it receives one Route Response (perhaps the first in a series), should it use that path or wait for a potentially better route?
- If it chooses to wait, how long should it wait?

The problem is very much like that of a tired commuter waiting for a bus. If a bus arrives at the bus stop, but there is no seat available, should the commuter take that bus (knowing she is in for a long, tiring, standing ride) or wait for another bus? The next bus might have a seat or—even better—might follow a shorter route to the destination (express service). However, our hapless commuter has no idea if there is another bus coming at all, how long the wait might be if there is another bus, or whether that bus (should it arrive) will have a seat available.[15]

To a certain extent, the answer depends on how important the commuter considers the seat to be. In an analogous manner, a route-selecting station must decide whether the first route is good enough or whether there is some important parameter that justifies waiting to see if there will be a better route (e.g., a larger MTU). There are two approaches to this problem:

1. *Take the first route.* This is by far the most popular approach. It avoids the issue of whether there will be any other responses at all. If any other Route Responses arrive, they can be discarded. It is also a practical approach. Even if there are other routes available, the station can assume that, by definition, the first response came along the path of least delay, at least at the instant in time when the Route Discovery procedure was invoked. Minimum delay is as reasonable a metric for route selection as any other. The commuter figures that it is better to get home earlier, even if it means standing on the bus.
2. *Take the first route that meets some specific criteria within a specified time window.* If some routing criterion is particularly important for this session, the station can allot a window of time in which it will wait for an available route that meets a minimum acceptable level of performance, based on that criterion. For example, the station may want to be

[15] For all the commuter knows, the next bus could be driven by a bomb-wielding terrorist with plans to storm the Las Vegas convention center during Networld+InterOp and demand that manufacturers stop building ATM LAN products. (No, I don't moonlight as a bus driver.)

sure that the selected route has no more than a specified number of bridge hops, or that the MTU is at least some minimum level.

Of course, the station cannot wait forever for an acceptable route. At some point, it may have to accept a substandard path or inform the requesting application that an acceptable route is not available.

Virtually all commercial source routing implementations simply take the first Route Response and ignore all others. This requires the least complexity and work on the part of the driver (the device driver, not the bus driver), and has been shown to work acceptably for a wide range of applications [WONG87].

In theory, a station should be able to select one route (e.g., the first response) and save any additional routes learned at a later time for possible future use. This action could allow a station to switch to an alternate route in the event of failure of a link or bridge along the active path. However, the procedure would impose considerable additional complexity. Not only would the device driver need to save the additional routes, but some mechanism would be needed to detect route failure during a session and to maintain proper frame order while switching to an alternate route in mid-session.[16] As a result, common practice does not include the caching of alternate routes. The failure of a source routed path results in the disruption of a communication session. The application (or user) will generally need to initiate a new session, which will invoke Route Discovery to learn a (currently available) route.

6.5.1.4 Issues in Route Discovery

Route Discovery is a necessary evil for the proper operation of source routing. However, there are a number of issues related to its use:

- *Session disruption.* The result of Route Discovery is that a single route is selected for station-to-station communications through the catenet. As stated earlier, the failure of a single bridge or ring in this active path will generally cause disruption of the communication session in a manner visible to the end user. Users may receive an explicit error message (e.g., "Session Terminated: Path Lost to Server") or simply a premature stop to an activity in progress. The user will usually need to manually restart the activity, invoking another Route Discovery procedure.
- *Frame explosion.* Route Discovery implies the use of All Routes Explorer frames, either from initiator to destination or vice-versa (depending on the Route Discovery algorithm in use). ARE frames "explode"; a single transmission request by a station performing Route Discovery can result in a large number of frames appearing on the destination station's ring. These frames all appear closely separated in time;

[16] This is a problem similar to that of transferring traffic flows among aggregated links, as discussed in Chapter 9, *Link Aggregation.*

we get a potential torrent of ARE frames all at once. If there are a lot of paths in the catenet, this can cause significant congestion.[17]

While most catenets don't have extremely large numbers of possible paths, it is not uncommon for many stations to be performing Route Discovery at the same time, which effectively creates the same situation. The failure of a single ring or bridge may disrupt a large number of concurrent sessions with a given server. When that link or bridge subsequently recovers, many users will be trying to re-establish their communication sessions with that server. This can create a short-term flood of Route Discovery and ARE frames.

- *Unpredictable load distribution.* One of the goals of source routing is to use all of the available link and bridge capacity in the catenet. Ideally, communications load should be evenly distributed across the available paths. However, for any given communication session, all of the load follows a single source route. That route is selected based on information provided only at the moment that Route Discovery is performed. A station selects a path typically based on a single received Route Response frame, and can use it for a session that lasts hours or more.

  Using this method, there is no assurance that load will be evenly distributed. Even assuming that the first received Route Response indicates the path of lowest delay:

  - The information is valid only at the instant the ARE frame(s) propagate through the catenet. There is no assurance that this path will be the path of least delay for any length of time.
  - It is not load that is being distributed, but sessions. Unless all sessions offer the same rate of traffic flow and last for the same length of time, the actual load distribution among the available paths is unknown. To the extent that different user sessions comprise different levels of traffic, the load distribution may be quite unbalanced.
  - Once established, there is no mechanism for shifting a session to an idle or lightly loaded path.

While source routing does work in practice, it is important to realize that it may not achieve all of its stated goals and incurs its own set of problems.

6.5.2 Station Operation

In this section, we consider the details of operation of source routing within a participating end station.

[17] In theory, on a maximally-configured catenet (14 rings end-to-end, with 15 bridges on each ring), a single ARE frame will be replicated 15^{14} times (2.9×10^{16}) on the destination station's ring. Even at 100 Mb/s, it would take over 5,000 years to transmit this many 70 byte Route Response frames.

6.5.2.1 Architectural Model of Source Routing

Within a station, the operation of source routing is intended to be transparent both to higher layer client protocols and applications and to the underlying LAN interface hardware. The device driver within each station is responsible for:

- Maintaining the route cache through the Route Discovery process
- Inserting appropriate source routing information on transmitted frames
- Stripping source routing information from received frames as depicted in Figure 6.10.

6.5.2.2 End Station Transmit Behavior

Each time a higher-layer client submits a frame for transmission, the source routing driver inspects the Destination Address. Frames sent to multicast destinations are sent as Spanning Tree Explorers (RII = 1, Routing Type = STE).

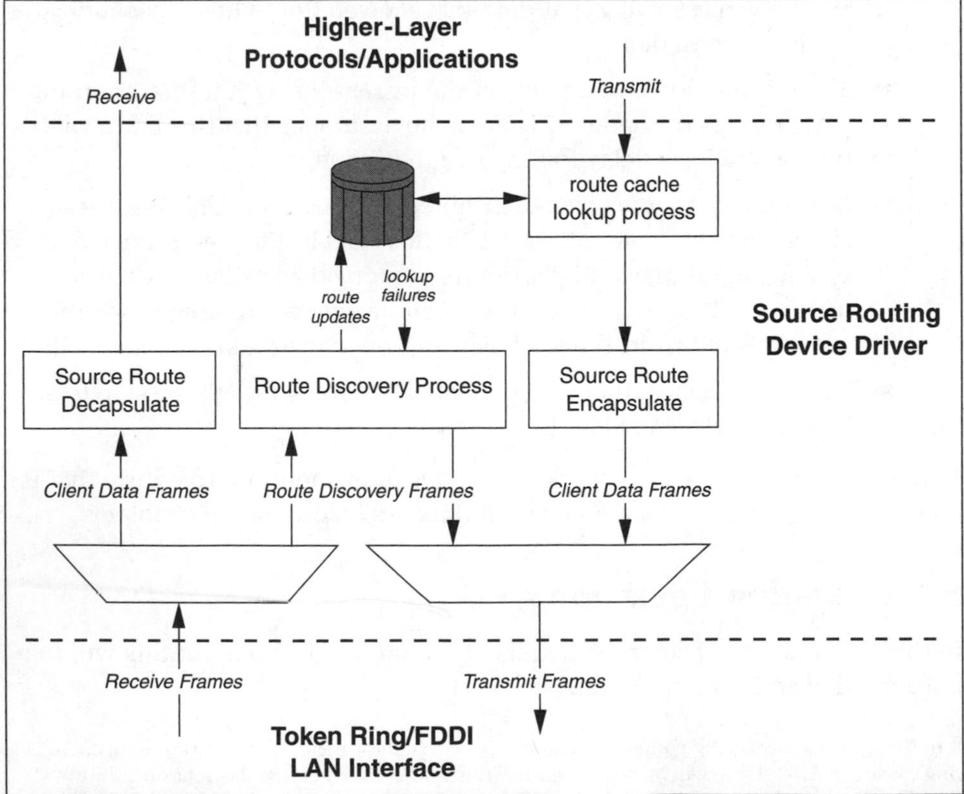

Figure 6.10 Model of source routing device driver.

For unicast traffic, the driver performs a lookup for a route to that destination in the local route cache. There are three possible outcomes:

1. The destination is known to be on the local ring, in which case no routing information needs to be inserted. (RII = 0)
2. The destination is known to be on another ring in the catenet, and a route to that station is present in the cache. The driver inserts the appropriate source route into the frame and submits it for transmission as a Specifically Routed Frame. (RII = 1, Routing Type = SRF)
3. The destination is unicast and not present in the route cache; that is, its location is currently unknown. In this case, the driver sends the frame as a Spanning Tree Explorer and invokes the Route Discovery process (if not already invoked from a prior transmission) to learn a route to this destination. (RII = 1, Routing Type = STE)

   Route Discovery need only be invoked once for a stream of frames sent to the same destination. The station will generate a Route Request and wait a specified time for the Route Response(s). If no responses are received, the process will generally retry the Route Request a few times before declaring that no route is available to the target. Frames sent before the Route Discovery process is completed are forwarded along the spanning tree.

The transmit process flow in a source routing end station is depicted in Figure 6.11.

6.5.2.3 End Station Receive Behavior

On reception, Route Discovery frames are separated from client data frames and sent to the Route Discovery process. Three types of Route Discovery frames must be handled:

- Route Requests trigger a Route Response (sent as an All Routes Explorer, RII = 1, Routing Type = ARE).
- Route Responses (from previously sent Route Requests) will cause the Route Discovery process to update its route cache based on the route selection criteria. If the cache is updated, the station sends a Route Selected frame to the sender of the Route Response as a Specifically Routed Frame (RII = 1, Routing Type = SRF).[18]
- Route Selected frames will cause the station to update its route cache; these frames indicate that the other station (that initiated route discovery) has selected this particular route for the instant session.

[18] Normally only the first Route Response will cause a change to the route cache, triggering a Route Selected frame.

Data frames have any routing information stripped and discarded within the device driver before passing them to the client protocol or application. The end station receive process flow is depicted in Figure 6.12.

6.5.3 Bridge Operation

Source routing bridges inspect and act upon only those frames that contain source routing information, as evidenced by the Routing Information Indicator. All other frames are ignored by the bridge; they will be seen only by stations on the local ring.

For those frames that do carry routing information, there are two cases a

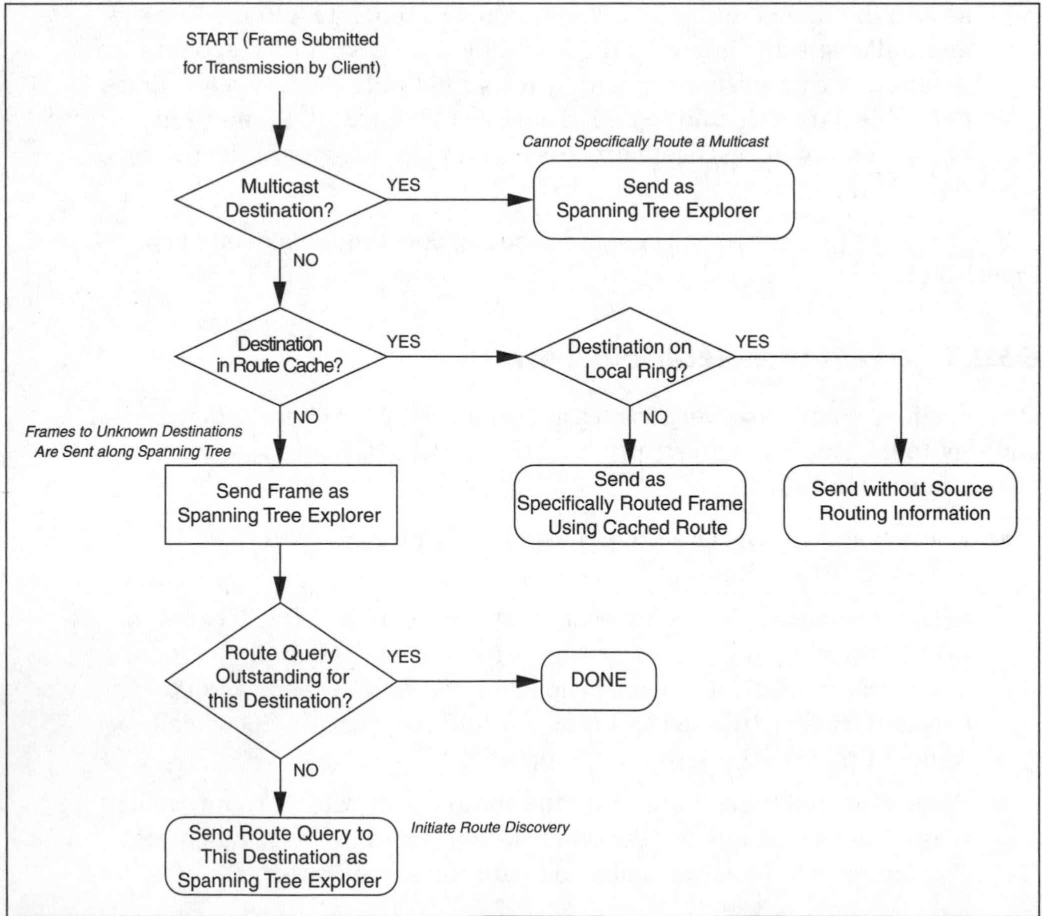

Figure 6.11 End station flow (transmit).

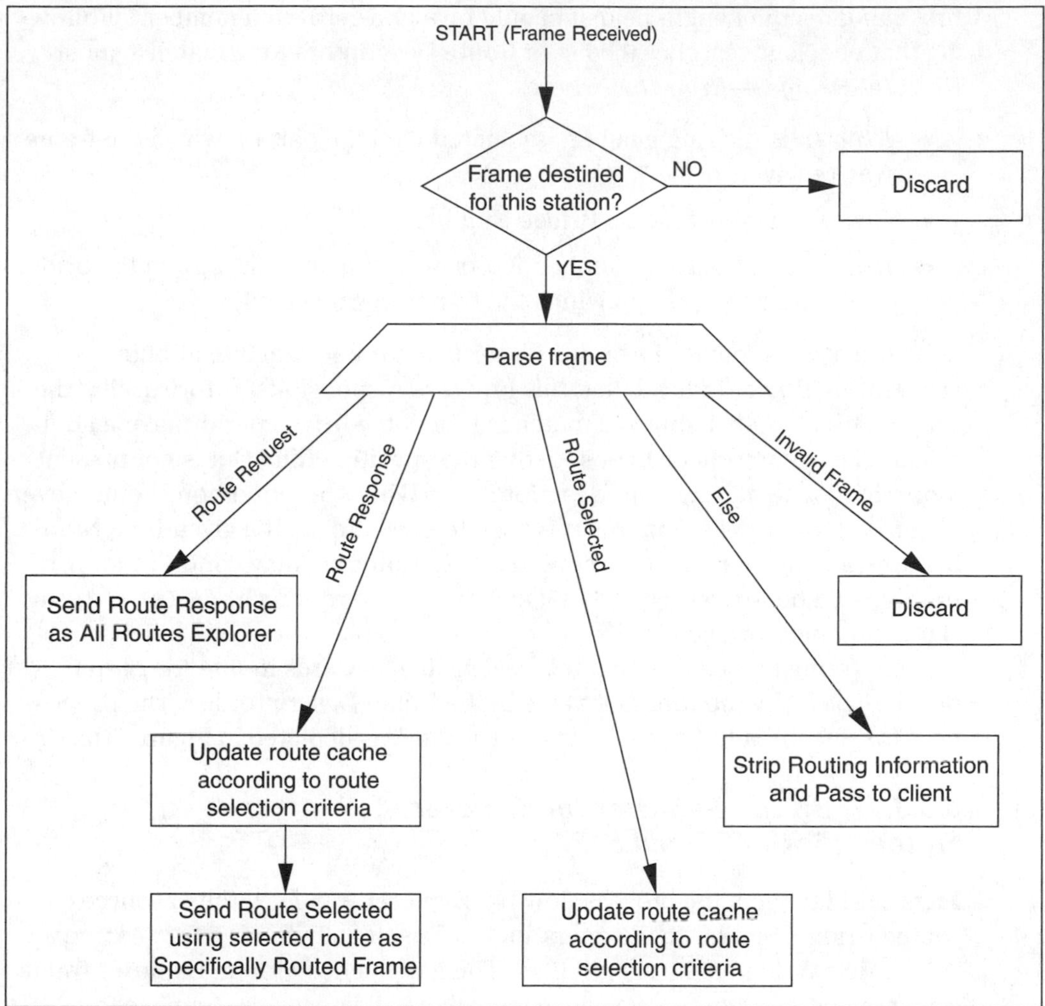

Figure 6.12 End station flow (receive).

bridge must deal with: (1) Specifically Routed Frames, and (2) Explorer frames.[19]

6.5.3.1 *Bridge Behavior for Specifically Routed Frames*

Specifically Routed Frames are signaled by setting the Routing Information Indicator to 1 and the Routing Type to 0b0XX. A bridge receiving such a frame

[19] Note that the first bit of the Routing Type field allows the bridge to easily separate source routed frames into these two classes. Specifically Routed Frames set this bit to 0; Explorer frames (both STE and ARE types) set this bit to 1.

first validates the Length field; it should be a non-zero even number.[20] Following that check, it searches the list of Route Descriptors for a match against *Ring In–Bridge #–Ring Out,* where:

- *Ring In* is the ring number associated with the port on which the frame was received
- *Bridge #* is this bridge's Bridge Number
- *Ring Out* is the Ring Number associated with another port on the bridge (other than the port on which the frame was received)

If no match is found, the bridge discards the frame, since the Route Descriptors do not indicate that this bridge is responsible for forwarding the frame onto any other ring. If a match is found, the bridge performs one additional consistency check to ensure that the specified Ring Out is not present more than once in the Route Descriptor list. While this condition should never occur under normal operation, it is wise to check for it. If a given Ring Number appears more than once, the Route Descriptor list may contain a loop; a frame could be forwarded endlessly by the source routing bridge(s), creating significant network congestion.

If the frame passes this final test, the bridge forwards it onto the output port indicated by the Ring Out value in the Route Descriptor list. The process flow for Specifically Routed Frames in a bridge is depicted in Figure 6.13.

6.5.3.2 Bridge Behavior for Explorer Frames (Both ARE and STE)

Figure 6.14 depicts the process flow for Explorer frames within a source routed bridge. Similar to the operation for Specifically Routed frames, the bridge first validates the Length field. The length check for an Explorer frame is somewhat more extensive, since the value will vary as the frame is forwarded through the catenet. In addition to ensuring that the value is even and non-zero, the bridge tests to make sure that it is less than the maximum allowed value of 30.[21] Optionally, bridges may discard frames whose Length is equal to 4, since this condition should never occur.

Additional consistency checks are made to ensure that the Direction bit has been properly set and that the last Ring Number in the Route Descriptor list properly reflects the ring from which the frame was received. Spanning Tree Explorer frames (RT = 11X) are discarded if the receiving bridge port is not part of the active spanning tree.

[20] This is also a simple check to perform in hardware. To meet these criteria, all that is required is for at least 1 bit of the field to be non-zero and the least significant bit to be 0.

[21] Bridges may invoke an implementation-specific maximum that is less than 30. Many source routing bridges limit the Length field to a maximum value of 18, implying no more than seven bridge hops between stations.

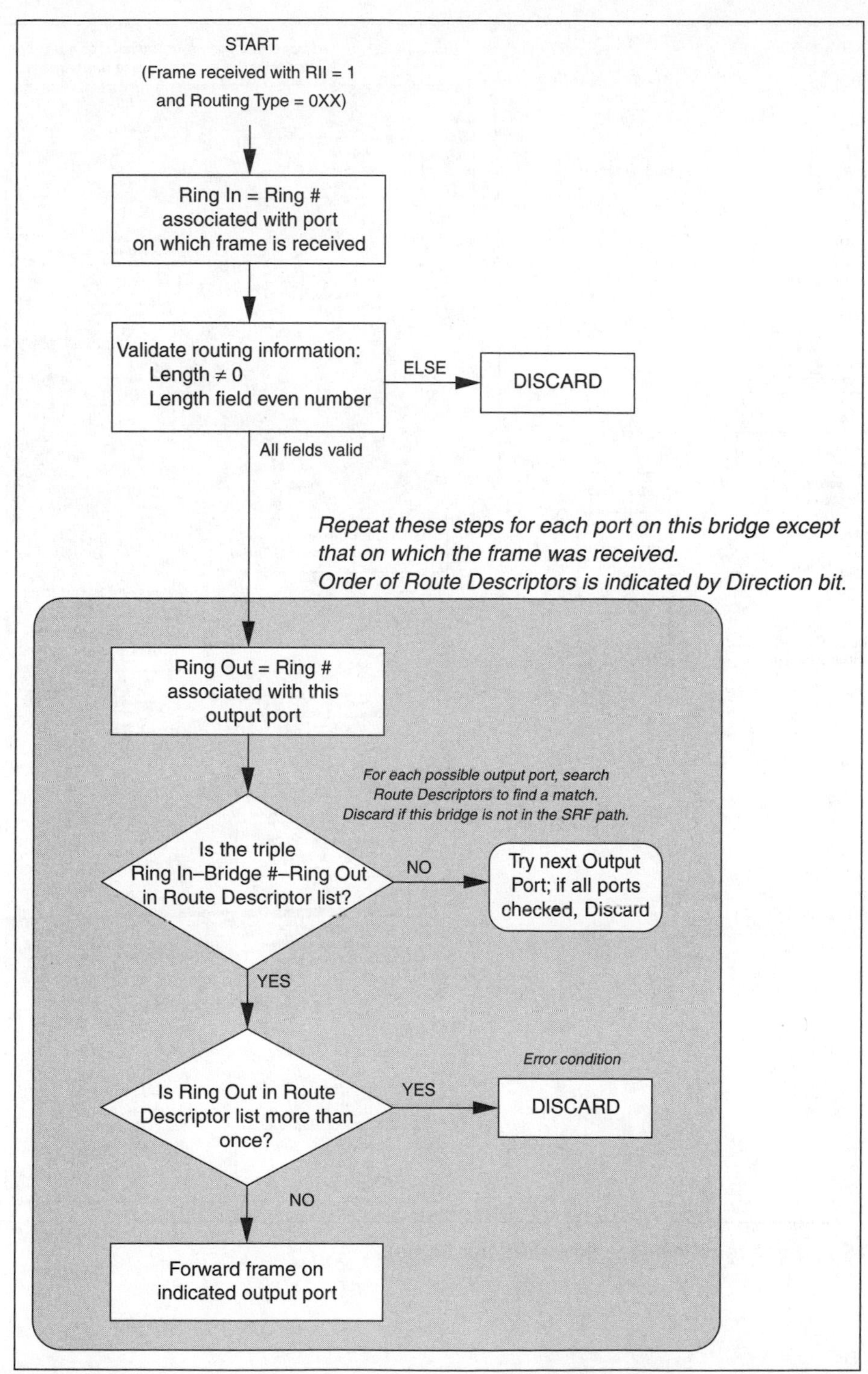
START
(Frame received with RII = 1
and Routing Type = 0XX)
Ring In = Ring #
associated with port
on which frame is received
Validate routing information:
Length ≠ 0
Length field even number
ELSE
DISCARD
All fields valid
Repeat these steps for each port on this bridge except
that on which the frame was received.
Order of Route Descriptors is indicated by Direction bit.
Ring Out = Ring #
associated with this
output port
For each possible output port, search
Route Descriptors to find a match.
Discard if this bridge is not in the SRF path.
Is the triple
Ring In–Bridge #–Ring Out
in Route Descriptor list?
NO
Try next Output
Port; if all ports
checked, Discard
YES
Error condition
Is Ring Out in Route
Descriptor list more than
once?
YES
DISCARD
NO
Forward frame on
indicated output port

Figure 6.13 Source routing bridge flow (Specifically Routed Frames).

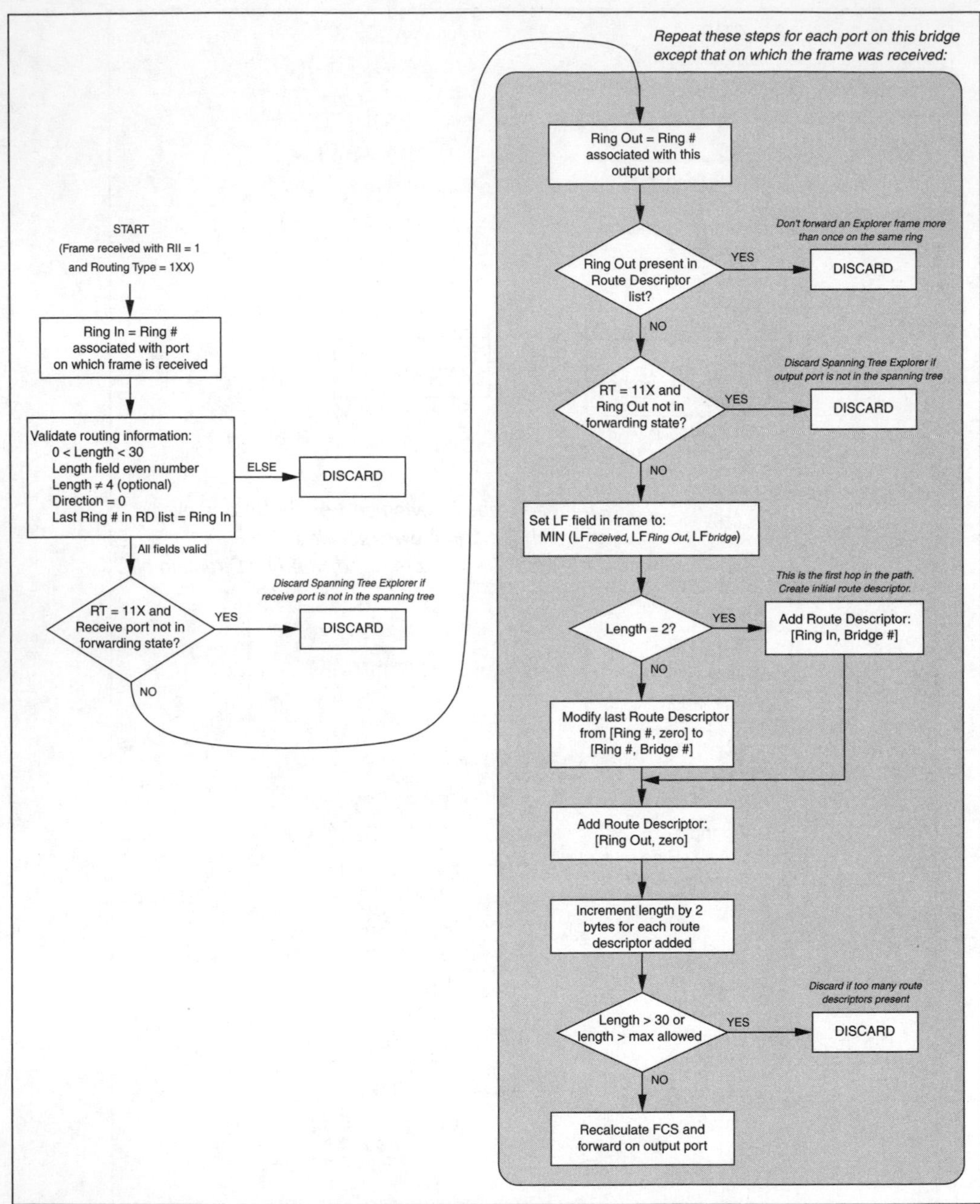

Figure 6.14 Source routing bridge flow (Explorer frame).

Explorer frames will normally be forwarded onto all ports except the one on which the frame was received, unless:

- The frame has already appeared on the ring associated with that port, as evidenced by the Ring Number already appearing in the Route Descriptor list. A given Explorer frame is never sent on the same ring more than once.
- The output port is not part of the active spanning tree, and the frame is a Spanning Tree Explorer.

For each frame to be generated on an output port, the bridge adjusts the Longest Frame (LF) bits as needed. The encoded value is either left the same as it was in the received frame, or reduced if the MTU of the output port is smaller than indicated by the received LF field or if the bridge is incapable of handling frames that large.

If the Length field is equal to 2, this means that there are no Route Descriptors present; the instant bridge is the first hop in the source routed path. In this case, the bridge must insert the first Route Descriptor, indicating the Ring In and Bridge Number associated with this bridge and the port on which the frame was received. If there are already Route Descriptors present, the Length field will be greater than 2, and the last Bridge Number will be 0 (indicating the last hop). In this case, the bridge puts its own Bridge Number in place of this 0 value. The bridge then appends a new Route Descriptor containing the Ring Number associated with the output port and a Bridge number of 0. It increments the Length field by 2 for each Route Descriptor created (4 for the first hop, 2 for each additional hop) and discards the frame if it now exceeds the maximum limits.

If everything is still acceptable, the bridge calculates a new FCS for the frame and forwards it on the appropriate output port.

6.6 Interconnecting the Source Routed and Transparently Bridged Universes

If the network environment comprises a pure, source routed catenet, and all of the end stations and bridges follow the principles and algorithms dictated by source routing, the system should behave as expected. In particular, if there is an operational physical path present between any pair of end stations, those stations should be able to communicate using source routing. Similarly, if the catenet comprises a set of stations and bridges operating according to the rules of transparent bridging, we should also expect to be able to communicate among all stations in a manner consistent with that bridging method. Each bridging method is valid and self-consistent.

SOURCE *ROUTING* IS PROPERLY NAMED

Consider some of the behavioral characteristics of a source routed network:

- End stations are aware of the presence of source routing bridges.
- End stations can exchange frames across multiple links only by explicitly sending them through named bridges.
- Transmitted frames are modified to include routing instructions.
- End station software is required to effect frame delivery across multiple links beyond that required to deliver frames across a single link.
- The algorithms support operation across an arbitrary underlying topology, including simultaneous use of links that form a physical loop.

These characteristics are much more descriptive of devices operating at the Network layer than of a Data Link bridging scheme. While source routing is positioned as an alternative style of bridging, in reality it constitutes a "lightweight" Network layer protocol. Source routing bridges and end stations operate more like participants in a routed internetwork than like their counterparts in a transparently bridged catenet.

Source routing operation differs from traditional Network layer operation in two obvious ways:

1. Network protocols usually place the burden of forwarding decisions on the router rather than the end station. However, even IP provides the option of allowing end stations to specify the path to be taken by a routed packet in a manner very similar to source routing; in fact, it is even called the IP source routing option.
2. Network protocols usually place the burden of topology discovery on the routers rather than the end stations, typically in the form of a separate routing protocol (e.g., RIP or OSPF). Source routing instead uses Route Discovery on a session-by-session basis for this purpose.

Looked at in this manner, it is clear that source routing constitutes a (very simple) Network layer protocol. This is the root cause of most of the problems incurred when trying to interconnect transparently-bridged catenets and source routed ones; the source routed catenets aren't really operating at the Data Link layer in the manner that the transparently bridged ones are, and seamless interoperation is impossible.

Why is source routing characterized as a bridging method rather than as Network protocol? The answer has more to do with politics than technology. Remember from the discussion in Section 6.3.3 that the IBM LAN architecture comprised high level applications communicating directly with the Data Link

layer; the architecture included neither a Network nor a Transport layer protocol. This doesn't mean that the functions of those layers were not needed, just that those layers did not exist in the IBM architecture. The typical connection-oriented Transport function was subsumed into the Data Link (in the form of LLC-2), and the internetwork routing function of the Network layer was implemented as source routing.

If it had wanted to be strictly correct architecturally, IBM could have proposed source routing as a new Network Layer protocol and submitted it for standardization. However, the official charter of IEEE 802 limits its scope to entities operating at the Data Link layer and below. IBM could not reasonably embark on a Network layer protocol activity within that organization. In the United States, the standards body responsible for dealing with Network layer protocols was (and is) the American National Standards Institute (ANSI). However, it would have been futile to propose source routing as a national or international Network layer protocol standard; a fully-approved standard already existed (ISO CLNP) that incorporated all of the functionality of source routing and more. The committee would have rejected the proposal as completely unnecessary.

Seifert's Law of Networking #11

Architectural purity goes out the window when purchase orders come in the door.

Thus, IBM and other Token Ring adherents chose to call source routing a method of bridging and force-fit it into the Data Link so that it could be officially sanctioned by the IEEE 802 committee, regardless of architectural positioning.

Real problems arise when, in the same catenet, some stations use source routing and others expect bridges to operate transparently. There is an absolute schism between the two schemes:

- Frames sent transparently always have the Routing Information Indicator in the source address field set to 0. A source routing bridge acts like a "brick wall" to transparently bridged frames; it intercepts and examines only those frames whose RIIs are set equal to 1 and discards all others. Thus, transparent traffic will not pass through a source routing bridge.
- Similarly, a transparent bridge is a "brick wall" to source routed frames. Frames whose RIIs are set to 1 are discarded by a transparent bridge. This prevents source routed frames from ever appearing on an Ethernet (or some other LAN technology) where they are not permitted.
- Source routing end stations always perform Route Discovery prior to each communication session. If Route Discovery fails (i.e., one or more valid routes are not presented to the initiating station), the station will not be able to open the session. The concept of transparent bridging is

foreign to a source routing end station; it does not understand the idea that some bridges may be able to deliver frames without the sending station inserting a route to that destination in each frame. In addition, Route Discovery requires that the target destination participate in the discovery protocol. Route Responses must be sent to back to the initiator to complete the prerequisite set-up procedure, even if the communicating stations are on the same ring.

- Conversely, end stations in a transparently bridged catenet never perform Route Discovery. Frames are sent with the expectation that bridges will forward them as necessary to reach their intended destinations. A transparently bridged end station will never initiate or respond to Route Discovery requests.

Consider the mixed environment depicted in Figure 6.15. Communications can occur normally among all of the stations within each bridged domain. For example, Token Ring stations T1 to T4 can all discover routes and communicate among themselves using source routing. Similarly, Ethernet stations E1 to E4 can communicate using transparent bridging.

However, communication is not generally possible between the domains. Regardless of the fact that there exists a physical path through a set of transparent bridges, none of the Token Ring stations will be able to initiate communications with stations on an Ethernet:

- Transparent bridges TB1, TB2, and TB3 will not forward any source routed traffic, including any initiating Route Requests generated by stations on the Token Rings.[22]
- Even if they did, no Ethernet station would respond to a Route Request; the discovery algorithm would fail to provide a route for any Token Ring station, and communications could not proceed.

In theory, communications should be possible between some of the Ethernet and Token Ring stations shown in Figure 6.15. For example, Ethernet frames from station E1 will propagate transparently to stations T1 and T5. However, the Token Ring stations would not normally be designed to handle this case; the communications will appear as unicast traffic for which no Route Discovery was invoked. Depending on the implementation of the source routing device driver in the Token Ring stations, this may be considered an error condition. Even so, the communications must be initiated by the Ethernet station, and both stations must be prepared to deal with the bit-ordering, MTU, and Frame Status bit problems discussed in Chapter 3.

Note that in Figure 6.15, not only can't we communicate between Token Ring and Ethernet devices, we can't communicate from Token Ring-to-Token

[22] Even if they were source routing bridges, they would not be allowed to forward source routed traffic, since the RII must always be 0 on an Ethernet.

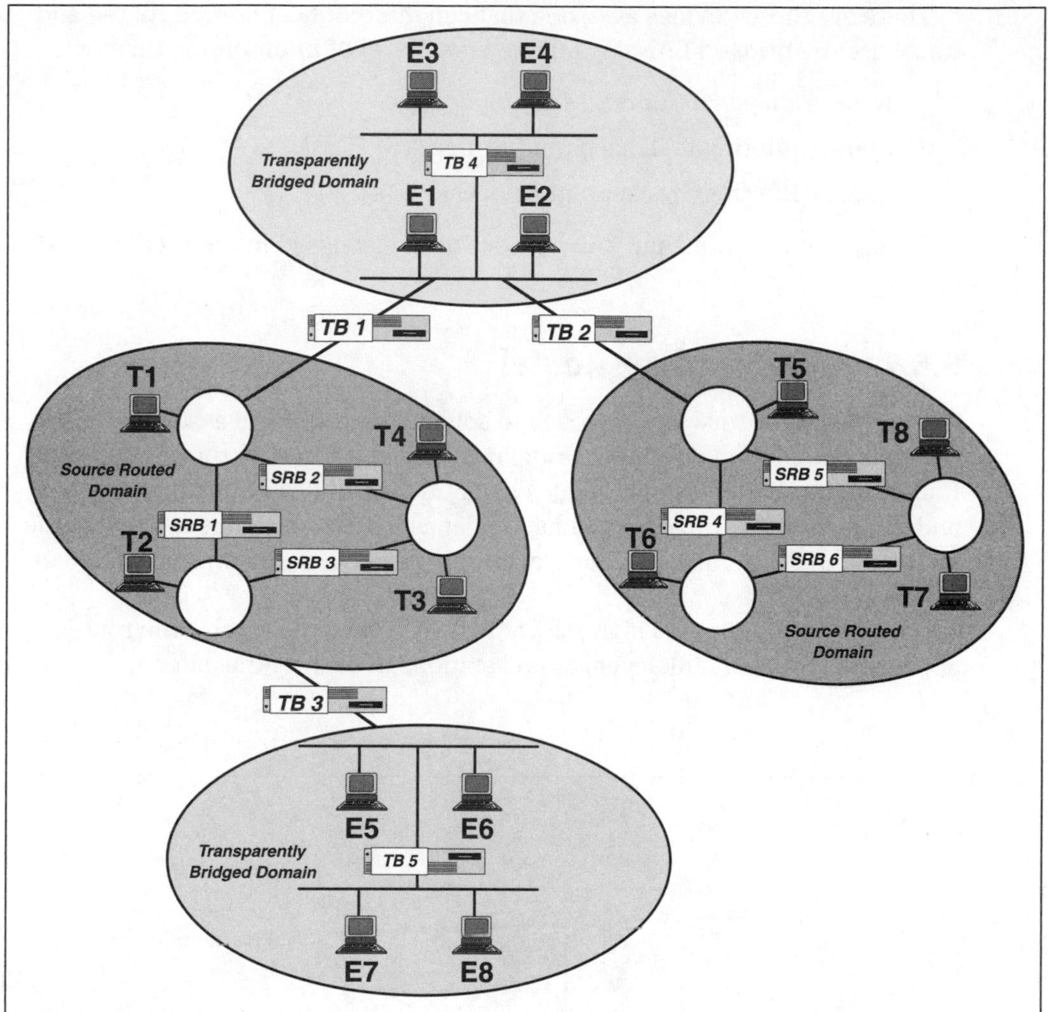

Figure 6.15 A mixed catenet.

Ring device or from Ethernet-to-Ethernet device across a dissimilar network. Transparent bridges TB1 and TB2 will block all Route Discovery traffic between Token Ring stations T1 to T4 and T5 to T8. Similarly, the intervening source routing bridges will block all transparent communications between Ethernet stations E1 to E4 and E5 to E8.

If the purpose of including bridges TB1, TB2, and TB3 was to allow Token Ring and Ethernet stations to intercommunicate, clearly this goal has not been accomplished. In fact, those three bridges serve no useful purpose in this catenet. It is not possible to achieve Token Ring-to-Ethernet communications using either the pure source routing or pure transparent bridges discussed up to now.

There are three devices available that can interconnect source routed and transparently bridged LANs to achieve some level of intercommunication:

1. Network layer Routers.
2. Source Routing-to-Transparent Bridges (SR-TBs).
3. Source Routing/Transparent Bridges (SRTs).

Each has its benefits and drawbacks, and is discussed in the sections that follow.

6.6.1 Don't Bridge—Route!

The most straightforward approach to solving the problems associated with catenets comprising dissimilar bridging methods is to avoid the issue entirely. Rather than trying to build a single catenet that includes both source routed and transparently bridged domains, we can isolate each bridge method within its own domain and use Network layer routers between them, as depicted in Figure 6.16.

Since they operate at a higher layer in the protocol hierarchy, the routers appear (at the Data Link layer) as end stations in each of the catenets to

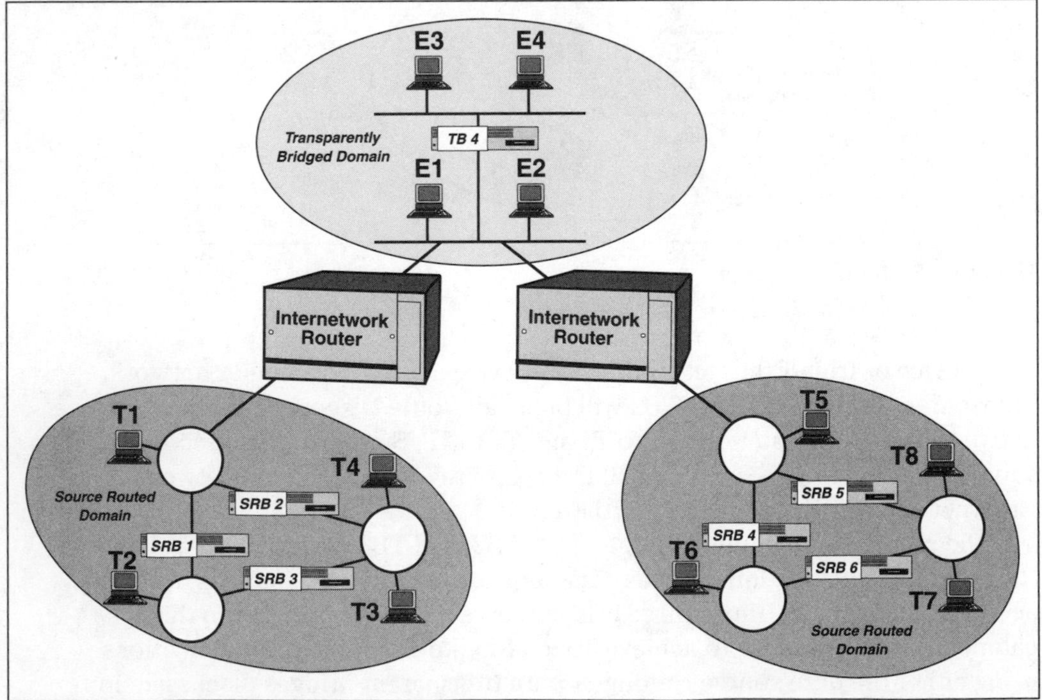

Figure 6.16 Routing between bridged domains.

which they connect. On their Token Ring ports, they participate in source routing and can communicate with any other station in the source routed domain. On their Ethernet ports, they operate in the transparent manner expected in that environment.

Rather than having a single heterogeneous catenet comprising multiple bridge types, we have three separate, homogeneous catenets interconnected by the routers. Stations in the separated catenets can communicate with each other by sending packets to the appropriate router, using Network layer mechanisms for internetworking. Note that this solution also solves the bit-ordering problem associated with mixed Big Endian/Little Endian catenets. Since address resolution messages (ARP and AARP) don't propagate through routers, we avoid virtually all of the problems associated with the encapsulation of Data Link addresses in higher-layer protocol fields (see Chapter 3).

The only downside to using routers is that there must be some Network protocol operating in the end stations. If the stations are using IP, IPX, AppleTalk DDP, or some other routable protocol at the Network layer, using routers is the preferred approach. If applications are using Data Link services directly without a Network protocol (e.g., over a NetBIOS interface to the Data Link, as depicted in Figure 6.2), interposing a router between the catenets will *prevent* communications. DEC LAT, NetBIOS/NetBEUI, and similar systems that communicate exclusively at the Data Link layer are simply not routable. If peer communications cannot be achieved at the Data Link, then communication is not possible for these applications.

It is therefore good practice to avoid the use of such non-routable protocols and applications; using routers to isolate dissimilar catenets is the preferred solution to the interoperability problems associated with mixed source routed/transparently bridged domains. Only when routing is not an option should users consider the hybrid approaches discussed in the following sections.

6.6.2 The Source Routing-to-Transparent Bridge (SR-TB)

The first device developed to allow Data Link layer communication between stations in dissimilar catenets was known as a Source Routing-to-Transparent Bridge, or SR-TB.[23]

An SR-TB translates between source routed and transparently bridged operation. A simplified block diagram of its operation is shown in Figure 6.17. From the Ethernet perspective, the SR-TB looks like a transparent bridge; it operates in promiscuous mode on the Ethernet port and forwards frames to the Token

[23] The first commercial SR-TB was the IBM 8209 (later superseded by the IBM 8229), which was imitated by many network equipment manufacturers. SR-TB functionality can usually be configured as a software option on most modular internetworking platforms today, although it is not often used anymore.

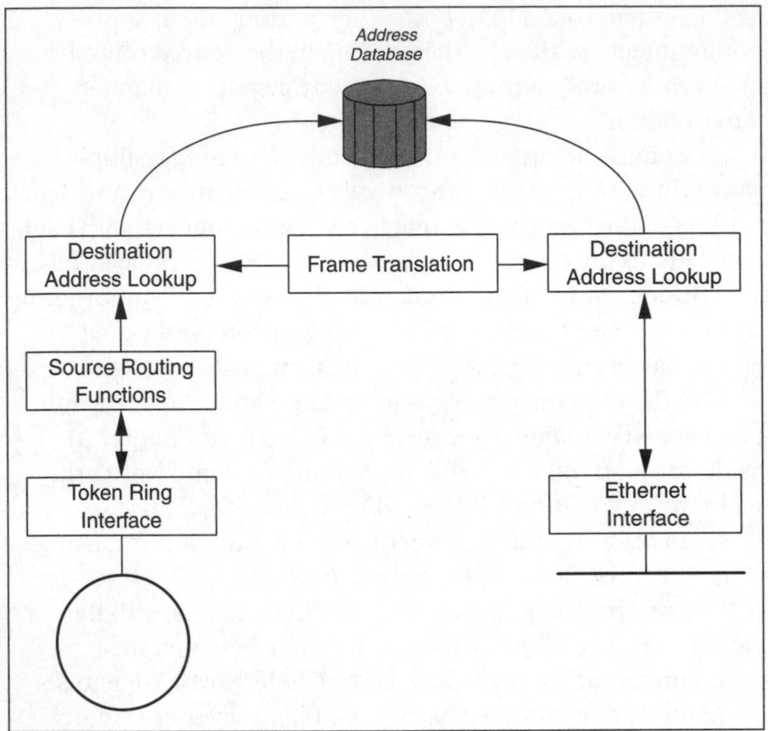

Figure 6.17 SR-TB simplified block diagram.

Ring port when appropriate. The only change from normal transparent operation is that the SR-TB must use source routing when forwarding frames onto the Token Ring. From the perspective of the Token Ring environment, the SR-TB does not behave as a source routing bridge; in particular, it does not act upon Explorer frames by updating the Route Descriptor list. In fact, the SR-TB behaves somewhat more like a source routing end station that relays frames to the Ethernet port as a proxy for all devices in the transparently bridged domain. In this regard, the SR-TB maintains a route cache for all known stations on the Token Ring port, and can initiate Route Discovery (if necessary) to learn routes needed to forward frames received from the Ethernet.

Figure 6.18 depicts the operation of an SR-TB, assuming that the bridge in question interconnects a single Token Ring (source routed) port and a single Ethernet (transparently bridged) port.[24]

Multicast traffic is always forwarded to the other port. Multicast frames are always sent transparently on the Ethernet, and as Spanning Tree Explorers on the Token Ring.

Unicast frames received on the Ethernet port are discarded if the address

[24] While it is possible to build SR-TBs with more than two ports, most common commercial implementations use exactly the configuration described.

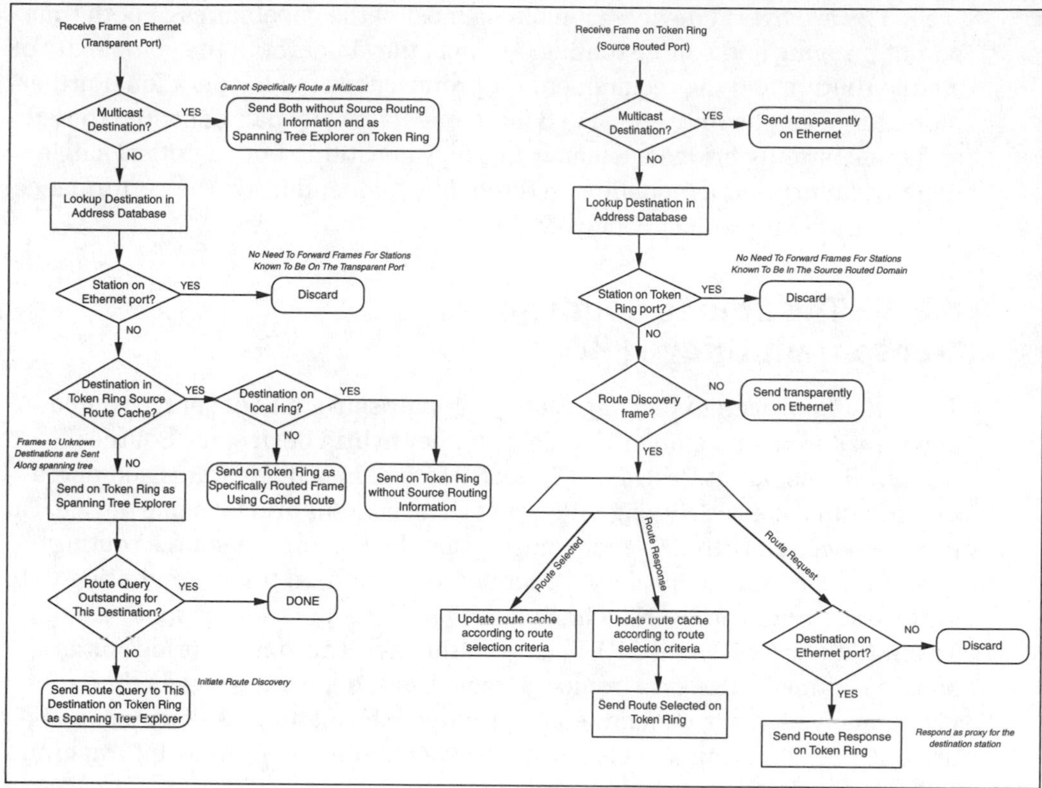

Figure 6.18 SR-TB flow.

database indicates that the destination is known to be reachable on the Ethernet. If not, the SR-TB consults its route cache to see if it already knows a source routed path to reach this destination on the Token Ring. If so, the SR-TB forwards the frame either without routing information on the local ring or using a list of Route Descriptors, as indicated by the route cache. If the destination is not in the route cache, the SR-TB forwards the frame as a Spanning Tree Explorer and initiates Route Discovery exactly like an end station.

Unicast frames received on the Token Ring port are similarly discarded if the address database indicates that the target destination is known to be reachable on the Token Ring. If not, the SR-TB forwards the frame onto the Ethernet, unless it is a Route Discovery frame.

The SR-TB behaves exactly like an end station with respect to Route Responses and Route Selected messages, updating its route cache as appropriate. In the case of a Route Request, the SR-TB checks the address database to see if the target destination is known to be on the Ethernet port. If so, the SR-TB responds to the Route Request as a proxy for the Ethernet station. Thus, Route Discovery can succeed even though the actual target does not participate in the discovery protocol.

SR-TBs are hybrid devices, combining most of the capabilities of both transparent bridging and source routing. As such, they incur both the complexity of source routing and the requirement for promiscuous mode operation. Furthermore, there can be only one SR-TB interconnecting any pair of source routed and transparently bridged domains; this may constitute both a critical single point-of-failure and a limitation on throughput, depending on the performance of the particular product deployed.

6.6.3 The Source Routing/ Transparent Bridge (SRT)

The other approach to building catenets comprising a mix of source routed and transparent end stations requires another hybrid device, the Source Routing/Transparent Bridge (SRT). An SRT combines the features and operation of both a source routing bridge and a transparent bridge in one device. On ports associated with LAN technologies that do not support source routing (e.g., Ethernet ports), the device operates as a standard transparent bridge. On ports associated with LAN technologies that do support source routing (e.g., Token Ring or FDDI), the SRT behaves either as a transparent bridge or as a source routing bridge on a frame-by-frame basis, depending on whether a given received frame contains source routing information. As depicted in Figure 6.19, this determination is made by inspection of the Routing Information Indicator in the Source Address field.

Unlike the SR-TB, an SRT does not translate between the two bridge methods. An SR-TB can take a source routed frame received on a Token Ring, strip

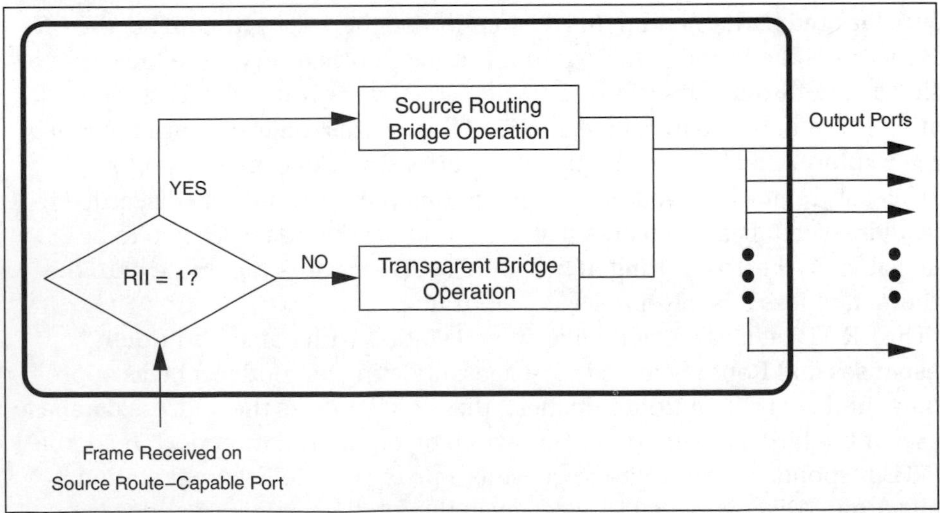

Figure 6.19 SRT operation on a source route–capable port.

off the routing information, and forward the frame transparently onto an Ethernet port. An SRT bridge cannot do this; within the SRT, frames are processed either by the source routing bridge module or by the transparent bridge module. A source routed frame will never be forwarded from a Token Ring or FDDI port to an Ethernet port.

Thus, the SRT bridge provides source routing services among those LANs that support source routing, and transparent bridge services among all ports to which it connects. (Source routing is supported only on Token Ring and FDDI; transparent bridging is supported on all LAN types.)[25] The SRT bridge participates in the Spanning Tree protocol along with standard transparent bridges to achieve a loop-free topology for transparently bridged frames. Figure 6.20 depicts a catenet comprising a mix of pure transparent bridges (TBs), pure source routing bridges (SRBs), and source routing/transparent bridges (SRTs).

Whether communication is possible between any given pair of stations in this catenet depends on:

- *The ability of the end stations to use a common bridging method.* Since SRTs do not translate between bridging methods like SR-TBs do, they cannot enable communication between a pair of dissimilar end stations. Stations on an Ethernet can communicate only by sending frames transparently; they are incapable of source routing. In theory, stations on a Token Ring can send frames either transparently or by using source routing. However, many commercial implementations support only source routed operation.

  Lacking an SR-TB to perform the translation, intercommunication between Token Ring and Ethernet stations will be possible only if the Token Ring station(s) supports and uses the transparent bridge method.

- *The nature of the bridges in the path between a given pair of end stations.* There must exist an active path through the catenet that supports the type of bridging being employed by the end stations. SRBs support only source routing and TBs support only transparent bridging; SRTs support both. Source routing will be possible if the path between the stations contains exclusively SRBs and/or SRTs. Transparent communication will be possible if the path contains exclusively TBs and/or SRTs.

  In the example shown in Figure 6.20, transparent communication is possible among all stations except those in the shaded area (T6, T7, and T8). These three stations are accessible only through the legacy, pure source routing bridges SRB2, SRB3, and SRB4. These stations are in an isolated, source route–only domain.

[25] From the earlier philosophical discussion, if source routing is a lightweight Network layer protocol, then an SRT can be considered a bridge/router. When received frames use the supported Network protocol (source routing), they are routed appropriately. If not, frames are bridged transparently.

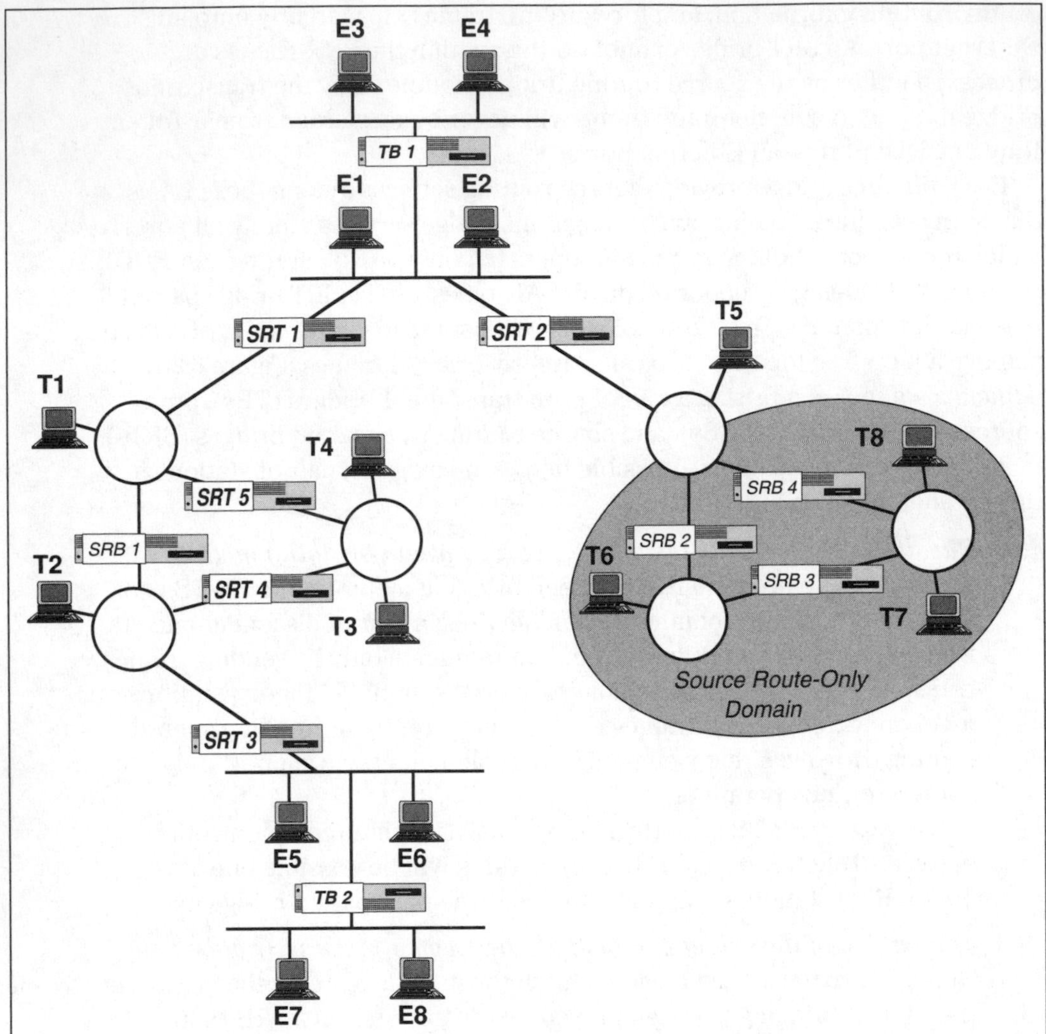

Figure 6.20 Mixed transparent, source routed, and source route/transparent bridged catenet (TB, SRB, SRT).

- *The nature of the LANs in the path between a given pair of end stations.* Token Ring stations T1 to T4 can communicate either transparently or by using source routing; however, these stations cannot use source routing to communicate with Token Ring stations T6 to T8, even though the path between them comprises SRBs and SRTs exclusively. This is because the only path between the two sets of Token Rings goes through an Ethernet, where frames are forbidden to carry native source routing information.

SRTs can be used to interconnect Token Ring and Ethernet LANs; however, they provide station-to-station intercommunication between the two LAN types only if the Token Ring stations are willing and able to send frames transparently. Many legacy Token Ring devices support only source routing; the use of SRTs will not enhance these stations' ability to communicate across dissimilar LANs. A change would be required to the device drivers in all of the legacy Token Ring devices to take advantage of the capabilities of SRTs.

The purported advantage of SRT bridges is that they can be deployed anywhere in a catenet employing both source routing and transparent bridges; they interoperate with both types of devices and never reduce the available connectivity. However, they don't provide for communication between the classic, pure source routed Token Ring environment and transparently bridged Ethernets. Any pure source routing bridges must be removed from the path between communicating end stations, and the Token Ring device drivers must be updated to allow transparent operation.

6.7 IEEE Standards and Source Routing

There is no IEEE standard for a pure source routing bridge. Considerable work was done in this area within the IEEE 802.5 (Token Ring) Working Group, but the project was never completed, and no draft was ever approved or officially published.

The only mention of source route bridging within the IEEE LAN standards is in the form of the SRT bridge discussed in Section 6.6.3. SRT bridging was incorporated into the IEEE 802.1D bridge standard in 1993, as the result of a joint IEEE 802.1/802.5 Task Force effort.[26] Thus, all standards-compliant bridges must include transparent bridge capability, along with the Spanning Tree Protocol. This is the "T" part of the SRT bridge. In a standards context, source routing is an optional enhancement to a transparent bridge.

Of course, pure source routing bridges are available from many suppliers, and have been widely deployed in Token Ring LANs; they are much more common than their officially-approved SRT counterparts. Source routing in its pure form is specified by IBM, an organization that, at least in the Token Ring world, is more important than the IEEE.

6.8 The Future of Source Routing

By the late 1990s, Token Ring networks were rapidly declining in popularity. Few users were installing new enterprise-wide networks based on Token Ring technology. While there is still a large installed base of legacy Token Rings, many users are migrating to higher-speed, lower-cost Ethernet technology.

[26] I was a member of that joint Task Force.

The Token Ring marketplace has become a maintenance business; manufacturers are supplying products to support the installed base and to ease the migration to other technologies.

Since source routing is intimately tied to the deployment of Token Ring technology, its use will similarly decline in volume and importance over time. In many cases, it is easier to migrate existing Token Ring LANs to Ethernet technology than to deal with the problems of intercommunication between source routed and transparently bridged catenets.

Advanced LAN Switch Concepts

CHAPTER

7

Full Duplex Operation

The popular LAN technologies all provide two important characteristics:

- *Full connectivity.* Stations on a LAN see themselves as directly connected to all other stations on the same LAN.
- *High speed.* Communication between stations is fast; the communications channel provides more capacity than any single station requires in the steady state.

Traditionally, LANs provided a means for multiple devices to share a common high-speed communications channel. The key word was *share;* in addition to providing connectivity, LAN technology offered a way to take an expensive resource (the high-speed channel) and spread its cost and capacity among multiple stations. As such, stations expected to be able to use the channel only intermittently, when it was not being used by other stations. With a shared common channel, it was generally not possible to both transmit and receive at the same time; traditional LANs all operated in *half duplex* mode, with one station transmitting at any given time.

The use of dedicated media connections and low-cost switches changes the channel architecture in such a way that it becomes possible for a station to transmit and receive simultaneously. In this chapter we look at the concept of full duplex LAN operation.

7.1 Why a MAC?

Why is a MAC algorithm needed at all? Remember, MAC stands for *Media Access Control.* The purpose of a MAC is to allow multiple stations to decide among themselves which one gets to use the channel at any given time when each has data to transmit. Such a procedure is necessary when multiple stations share a common underlying physical channel and can all offer traffic simultaneously. That is, a MAC is needed only when there is a possibility that two or more devices may wish to use a common communications channel; the MAC algorithm provides a set of rules by which the devices negotiate access to that shared channel.

But if there is no common, shared channel, then there is no need for a MAC algorithm at all! Consider a point-to-point link with separate paths for communicating in each direction (e.g., RS-422 over twisted pair, as shown in Figure 7.1).

Assuming that the receiver at each end is always enabled, either device can transmit to the other at any time. There is no need for any sort of arbitration for use of the channel, since there is never more than one device wishing to transmit on a given wire pair. Note that there are two independent communications channels here, one in each direction between the two stations. Such a channel can simultaneously support communication in both directions, and is referred to as a *full duplex channel.*[1]

Historically, we have tended to think of LAN technologies in terms of the MAC algorithm employed, for example, Ethernet (CSMA/CD), Token Ring, or Token Bus, and so on. The MAC algorithms differentiate these technologies based on how each one negotiates access to a common shared channel. But if we have no shared channel, there is no reason to use any of these access methods. We may still have a LAN, but there is no access control.

In the old days, much of what constituted LAN design consisted of designing the access control algorithm. LANs were all shared-medium communications channels, and LAN behavior was determined to a great extent by the access control method employed. A comparison of Ethernet to Token Ring usually consisted of a discussion of the merits of CSMA/CD versus token passing as a channel arbitration method. Neither Ethernet nor Token Ring were originally designed to support full duplex operation. In fact, the original Ethernet specification stated explicitly:

[1] Strictly speaking, a full duplex channel means a single communications medium that can be used for transmission and reception at the same time. What is shown and described here is properly called a *dual simplex* channel; there are two communications media (two separate wire pairs), each of which is used for unidirectional communications. The facts of the case notwithstanding, virtually every LAN switch manufacturer uses the term *full duplex* to describe this environment, and therefore so will I.

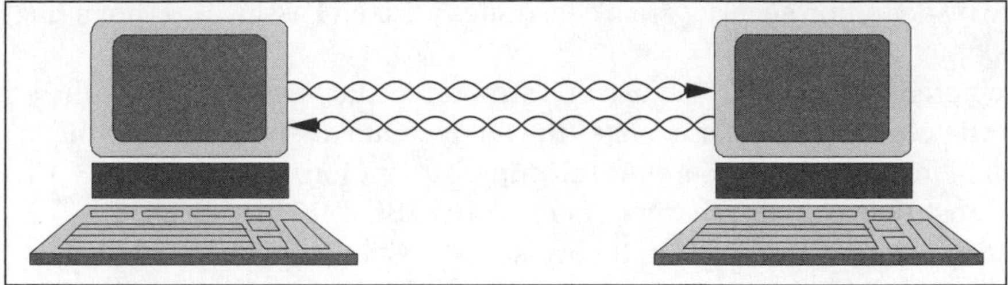

Figure 7.1 Point-to-point communications.

> "The following are *not* goals of the Ethernet design:
>
> . . .
>
> *Full duplex operation:* At any given instant, the Ethernet can transfer data from one source station to one or more destination stations. Bi-directional communication is provided by rapid exchange of frames, rather than full duplex operation." [DIX80]

The underlying channel in the original Ethernet design was a shared coaxial medium. It was incapable of supporting full duplex operation, and the system design did not try to overcome this limitation.

7.2 Full Duplex Enablers

Two factors are responsible for enabling LANs to operate in full duplex mode:

1. The use of dedicated media, as provided by the popular structured wiring systems deployed today.
2. The use of microsegmented, dedicated LANs, as provided by switches.

7.2.1 Dedicated Media

Ethernets migrated from using coaxial cable (10BASE5 or 10BASE2) to using structured wiring with twisted pair in the early 1990s, with the development of 10BASE-T [IEEE98e, Clause 14]. The higher-speed versions of Ethernet (Fast and Gigabit Ethernet) developed during the 1990s support only dedicated media connections both for twisted pair and optical fiber. There are no commercial shared-medium implementations of Ethernet at data rates above 10 Mb/s.

Interestingly, the underlying channel for Token Ring LANs has always provided dedicated connections between each station and a central hub [IBM82]. Initially these connections were made with shielded twisted pair (STP), and then later with unshielded twisted pair (UTP), at data rates of 4, 16, and later 100 Mb/s. It is simply not possible to build a Token Ring using a shared-medium channel; by definition such a system constitutes a Token Passing Bus (not a ring) [IEEE90c].

As depicted in Figure 7.2, the use of a structured star-wired system with hubs at the center of the star changes the fundamental assumption that the underlying medium cannot support full duplex operation. Unlike coaxial cables, most twisted pair Ethernet systems (10BASE-T, 100BASE-TX, 1000BASE-T, etc.) can, at least in theory, support simultaneous bidirectional communications, as there are separate paths (wire pairs) for communication in each direction. Interestingly, while Token Ring wiring systems have always supported the possibility of simultaneous bidirectional communications, only recently have commercial products become available that enable the system to be used in this fashion.

Even if the channel is capable of supporting bidirectional communications, a LAN deploying a shared-access hub at the center of the star (e.g., an Ethernet repeater or Token Ring Multi-Station Access Unit) uses this channel in a half duplex mode; at any given time, only one station can transmit a frame on the LAN without interference. Multiple simultaneous transmission requests must arbitrate for the channel using the MAC algorithm (e.g., CSMA/CD or token passing) and are resolved in the normal way (i.e., collision and retry or waiting for a token). But the migration to dedicated media at least enables the possibility of using the channel in a full duplex fashion.

Table 7.1 indicates which of the standard LAN systems are capable of supporting full duplex operation.

Figure 7.2 Dedicated media.

Table 7.1 Full Duplex Media Support

STANDARD DESIGNATION	MEDIA TYPE	FULL DUPLEX CAPABLE?
Ethernet		
10BASE5	50Ω thick coaxial cable	No
10BASE2	50Ω thin coaxial cable	No
10BASE-T	2 pairs Category 3/4/5 UTP, or STP	Yes[1]
10BASE-FL	2 optical fibers (62.5 μm)	Yes[1]
10BASE-FB	2 optical fibers (62.5 μm)	No[2]
10BASE-FP	2 optical fibers (62.5 μm)	No[3]
10BROAD36	75Ω coaxial cable	No
100BASE-TX	2 pairs Category 5 UTP, or STP	Yes
100BASE-FX	2 optical fibers (62.5 μm)	Yes
100BASE-T4	4 pairs Category 3 UTP	No[4]
100BASE-T2	2 pairs Category 3/4/5 UTP	Yes
1000BASE-SX	2 optical fibers (62.5/50 μm)	Yes
1000BASE-LX	2 optical fibers (62.5/50/9 μm)	Yes
1000BASE-CX	2 pairs STP	Yes
1000BASE-T	4 pairs Category 5 UTP	Yes
Token Ring		
4 Mb/s	2 pairs Category 3/4/5 UTP, or STP 2 optical fibers (62.5 μm)	No[5]
16 Mb/s	2 pairs Category 4/5 UTP, or STP 2 optical fibers (62.5 μm)	Yes
100 Mb/s	2 pairs Category 5 UTP, or STP, 2 optical fibers (62.5 μm)	Yes[6]

[1] While the channel design supports full duplex, the transceiver must be specifically configured for full duplex operation; the looping back of transmitted data onto the receive lines that is normally implemented in half duplex mode must be disabled.
[2] 10BASE-FB requires a synchronous repeater and cannot operate in full duplex mode regardless of the media type.
[3] 10BASE-FP uses a passive hub and cannot operate in full duplex mode regardless of the media type.
[4] 100BASE-T4 uses two of its pairs in an interfering, bidirectional mode and cannot support full duplex operation.
[5] While the channel theoretically supports full duplex, the IEEE standard does not specify full duplex operation at 4 Mb/s.
[6] Full duplex is the only mode of operation supported for Token Ring at 100 Mb/s.

7.2.2 Dedicated LAN

The use of dedicated media systems allows us to deploy switching hubs (i.e., bridges) rather than repeaters at the center of the star-wiring system. While attractive due to all of the advantages discussed in Chapter 4, *Principles of LAN Switches* (e.g., increased capacity), the use of a switch marks a fundamental architectural change to the LAN. Whereas with a repeater all of the devices connecting to the hub share the available channel and have to arbitrate for access, with a switching hub each of the attached devices has a dedicated channel between itself and the hub.

A switching hub (unlike a repeater) has a MAC entity for each of its ports. Architecturally, each of the connections to the switching hub constitutes a distinct LAN, with access to each LAN arbitrated independently of all others. A repeater with *n* ports constitutes a single LAN; a switch with *n* ports constitutes *n* LANs, one for each switch port, as depicted in Figure 7.3.

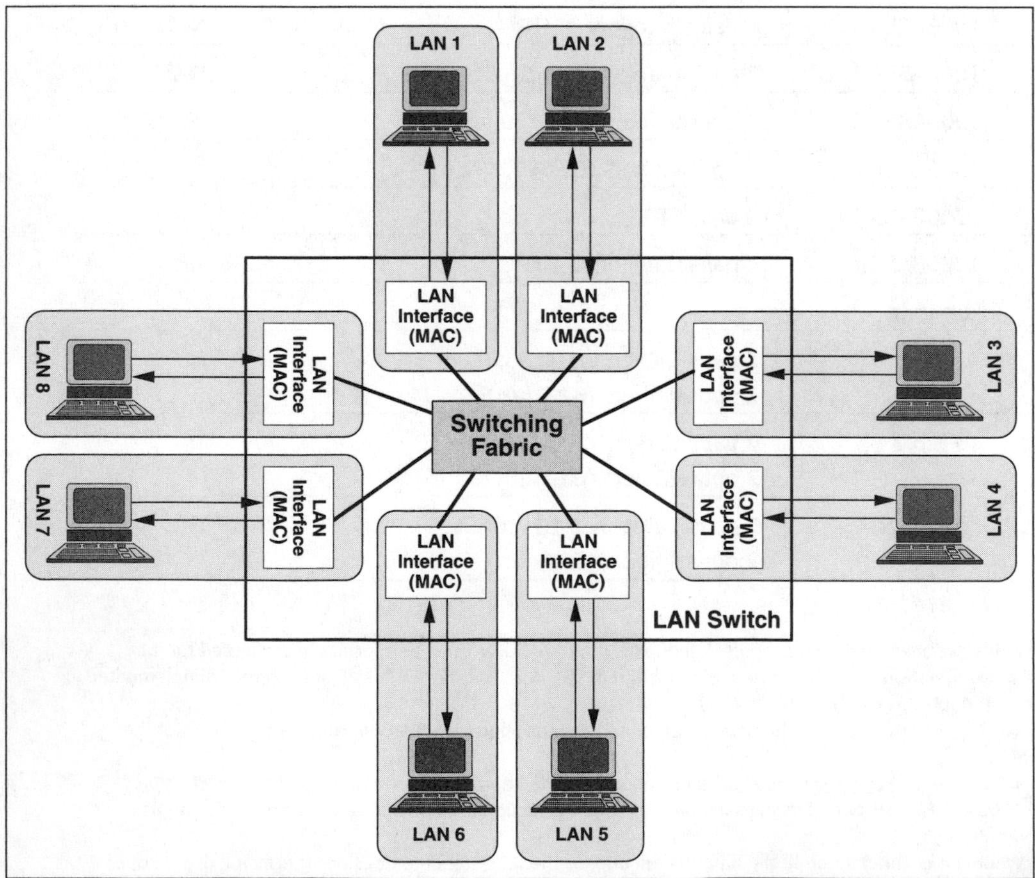

Figure 7.3 Switched LAN architecture.

In the case of a microsegmented switched LAN, each port comprises a two-station network composed of the attached device and the switch port itself. If we consider that two-station LAN in isolation, we can see that it appears exactly the same (architecturally) as the simple RS-422 connection shown in Figure 7.1. Each device has a private, independent channel to the other device; there is no possibility of contention for the use of the underlying communications channel.

Just providing a full duplex–capable media and topology is not sufficient to achieve full duplex operation. Unless we also modify the behavior of the LAN interfaces in the switch and the attached devices, we cannot use the channel in any manner other than the normal shared-LAN mode. This is because the LAN interface does not know that the channel is now dedicated for its private use. We must essentially disable the access control mechanism inherent in the LAN interface.

7.3 Full Duplex Ethernet

In the scenario depicted in Figure 7.3, we can modify the behavior of the Ethernet MAC controller in both the switch and the attached devices to take advantage of their unique situation. We need to:

- Disable the Carrier Sense function as it is normally used to defer transmissions. That is, the reception of data on the receive channel should not cause the transmitter to defer any pending transmissions. A normal (half duplex) Ethernet interface will withhold its own transmissions in order to avoid interfering with transmissions in progress under control of the carrier sense signal.
- Disable the Collision Detect function, which would normally cause the transmitter to abort, jam, and reschedule its transmission if it detects a receive signal while transmitting.
- Disable the looping back of transmitted data onto the receiver input, as is done on a half duplex channel.

Neither end of the link needs to defer to received traffic, nor is there any interference between transmissions and receptions, avoiding the need for collision detection, backoff, and retry. In this environment, we can operate the LAN in full duplex mode; stations can both transmit and receive simultaneously, as depicted in Figure 7.4.

7.3.1 "Ethernet Is CSMA/CD"

The very term *Ethernet* has come to mean that class of LANs that use CSMA/CD as their MAC algorithm. The CSMA/CD MAC is considered the most

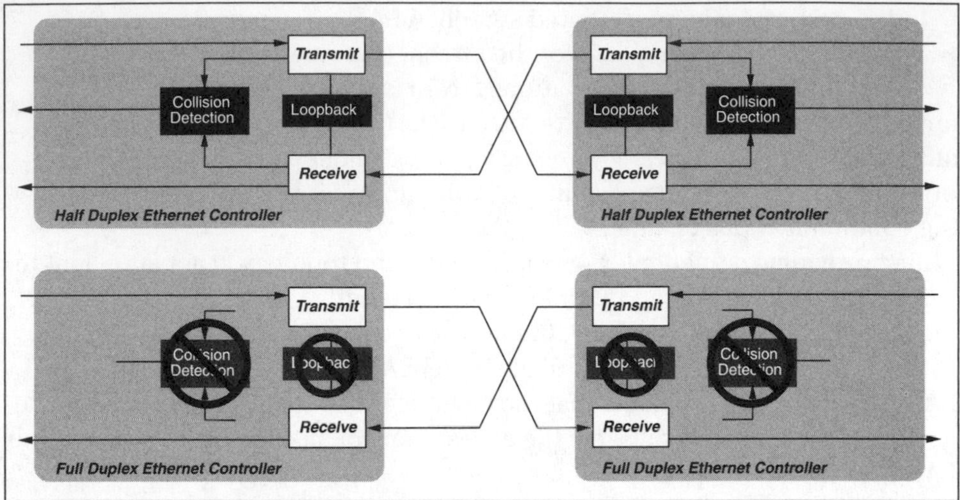

Figure 7.4 Half and full duplex Ethernet MAC.

important conceptual development of the original Xerox work [METC76]. It provided a communications channel that can be efficiently arbitrated among multiple devices with an extremely simple algorithm without requiring a central controller.[2] However, higher-layer protocols and applications operate completely unaware of the underlying MAC arbitration; they do not see, care to see, or need to see the channel access method in use. Their only concern is the ability to exchange messages across the channel in the form of Ethernet frames. That is, the ability of an application or protocol to use an Ethernet has nothing to do with the CSMA/CD algorithm; it has only to do with the knowledge of the Ethernet frame format. CSMA/CD may be the "essence of Ethernet" to LAN systems designers, but to applications it is only the exchange of Ethernet frames that is significant.

Full duplex Ethernet eliminates Carrier Sense, multiple access, and collision detection—all of the elements of CSMA/CD. However, it carries the same Ethernet frames as its half duplex sibling. Therefore, from the perspective of higher-layer protocols, it is still an Ethernet. The higher layers are unaware of the change to full duplex operation (other than a possible performance improvement).

[2] In fact, very little else was preserved in the transition from the original Xerox laboratory work of the mid-70s to the 10 Mb/s commercial Ethernet specified in 1980 and later standardized in IEEE 802.3. The cabling system, transceiver design, signaling methods, and frame formats, and even the FCS algorithm, were all changed, but the CSMA/CD access method remained (although the details of the algorithm itself were not even preserved).

7.3.2 Full Duplex Ethernet Operating Environment

There are three conditions that all must be met in order to use an Ethernet in full duplex mode:

- *There can be only two devices on the LAN.* That is, the entire LAN must comprise a single point-to-point link. A microsegmented switching hub environment meets this criterion on each of its ports. In addition, the special case of a simple, two station interconnection with no switch (Figure 7.5) can also support full duplex operation.
- *The physical medium itself must be capable of supporting simultaneous transmission and reception without interference.* Table 7.1 lists the media types that can support full duplex operation.
- *The network interfaces must be capable of operating in, and configured to use, full duplex mode.* Many legacy interfaces cannot operate in full duplex mode; they simply were not designed with such a possibility in mind. While the modifications required to make the MAC operate in full duplex mode are trivial, it is generally not possible to retrofit an existing, half duplex–only device to operate in full duplex mode.

Full duplex operation is not possible with traditional repeater hubs, as the use of repeaters implies shared medium access. Even if a switching hub is used, there can be only one device connected to a switch port operating in full duplex mode (microsegmentation). A shared hub cannot be connected to a port of a switch and still have that port operate in full duplex mode.

Full duplex Ethernet was standardized as part of the IEEE 802.3x supplement to the existing standard [IEEE97]. Other than the considerable editorial changes required to provide for two distinct operating modes in the standard, the significant changes were to the Pascal code that is used for the formal definition of the Ethernet MAC. In full duplex mode, the code disables the defer

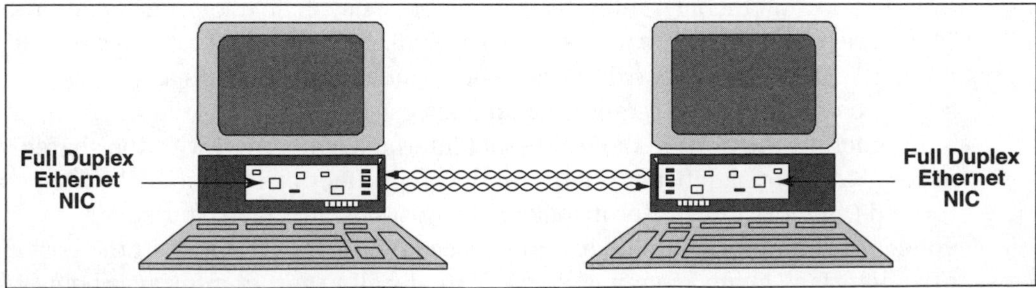

Figure 7.5 Two station LAN.

and collision detect functions and allows simultaneous transmission and reception without interference.

7.3.3 Subset of Half Duplex Operation

A "full duplex Ethernet MAC" is actually trivial (some would say nonexistent!). A station neither needs to defer to other traffic in the traditional manner (Carrier Sense), nor does it need to detect simultaneous transmissions (collision detect). That is, full duplex Ethernet is CSMA/CD without the CS, the MA, or the CD! In reality, with all possibility of contention removed, we no longer have any real need for a MAC. A full duplex Ethernet device doesn't use any MAC algorithm; a station in this mode may transmit at will, with no consideration of interference by other stations. The only properties that a full duplex Ethernet has in common with its half duplex counterpart are the Ethernet frame format and the encoding/signaling method used on the physical medium.

> ***Full Duplex Ethernet:***
>
> **No CS, no MA, and hold the CD!**

Of course, supporting the Ethernet frame format does imply some important functionality, including address decoding and checksum (FCS) generation and verification, which are required in both full duplex and half duplex mode devices. However, full duplex Ethernet is a proper subset of half duplex Ethernet operation. Full duplex operation requires no additional functionality to be built into an interface; it simply disables functionality needed for half duplex operation. This implies that, despite providing performance improvements and application enhancements, full duplex capability should not increase the cost of an Ethernet interface.

The standard [IEEE97] allows manufacturers to build conformant interfaces that can operate in half duplex mode only, full duplex mode only, or both. In theory, a "full duplex mode only" interface could be built and sold for less than a half duplex–capable interface. In practice (at least at 10 Mb/s and 100 Mb/s), a "full duplex mode only" interface would not be usable in a lot of installations. There are tens of millions of existing legacy interfaces that operate only in half duplex mode. To coexist with these devices (including repeaters as well as some existing switches) requires half duplex capability.

In practice, the portion of an Ethernet interface concerned with the shared-access MAC is insignificant relative to the other functions that must be performed (memory and buffer management, host bus interface, statistics collection, etc.), so including half duplex capability does not impact the cost of an interface in any meaningful way. Virtually all Ethernet interfaces being designed and built today (at 10 Mb/s and 100 Mb/s) are capable of both half and full duplex operation. Gigabit Ethernets are deployed exclusively in full duplex mode, because the use of CSMA/CD at 1000 Mb/s leads to impractical distance restrictions and unnecessarily reduced performance.[3]

7.3.4 Transmitter Operation

A full duplex transmitter may send a frame any time there is a frame in its transmit queue, following two simple rules:

1. The station operates on one frame at a time; that is, it finishes sending one frame before beginning to send the next pending frame.
2. The transmitter enforces a minimum spacing between frames (the same as for half duplex operation). This interframe gap allows receivers some minimum "breathing room" between frames to perform necessary housekeeping chores (posting interrupts, buffer management, updating network management statistics counters, etc.).

7.3.5 Receiver Operation

The receiver in a full duplex interface operates identically to one in half duplex mode:

1. When a frame begins to arrive, the receiver waits for a valid Start-of-Frame Delimiter and then begins to assemble the Data Link encapsulation of the frame.
2. The Destination Address is checked to see whether it matches an address that the device has been configured to accept, and any frames not so destined are discarded.
3. The FCS is checked, and any frame deemed invalid is discarded.
4. The frame length is checked, and all frames shorter than the minimum valid length (512 bits for all Ethernets) are discarded. In a half duplex Ethernet LAN, any fragment that is the result of a collision is guaranteed to be shorter than this minimum length; thus, discarding such frames ensures that collision fragments are not improperly perceived to be valid frames. In full duplex mode there are no collisions, so it is not possible for collision fragments to appear. Nonetheless, this step does not cause any problem or damage, and Ethernet maintains the 512-bit minimum

[3] While the inclusion of half duplex operation would not add significantly to the cost of the product, it is simply an unnecessary complexity that can be avoided completely in a Gigabit Ethernet interface. In fact, design verification and conformance testing of the half duplex MAC algorithm implementation is usually more work than the actual design. A full duplex only design thus has a shorter time to market.

frame length constraint even for full duplex operation (see the following text for further discussion).

5. The receiver passes up to its client (i.e., higher layer protocols or applications) all frames that have passed the previous tests. The order of executing the preceding validity tests is not critical and may vary with different implementations.

7.3.6 Ethernet Minimum Frame Size Constraint

Commercially-available Ethernet existed in its "half duplex only" incarnation for over 15 years before the networking environment could support (and the standards recognized and legitimized) the use of full duplex mode. Because of this history, there is a huge installed product base (and knowledge base) surrounding half duplex Ethernet. In order to allow a peaceful coexistence between the half and full duplex modes, we chose to retain a certain amount of baggage from half duplex Ethernet in the full duplex version.

In half duplex mode, it is necessary to enforce a minimum valid frame length that is at least as long as the worst-case round-trip propagation delay of the network plus the time to transmit the 32-bit jam signal. This ensures that a station will always be transmitting when a collision is detected on a frame; if a station were allowed to send frames shorter than this minimum, such frames could experience collisions without the transmitter being aware of them. The transmitter would not reschedule these (corrupted) transmissions, severely degrading network performance.

All standard Ethernets use a minimum frame length of 512 bits from the Destination Address to the FCS inclusive. While there is no need for a minimum frame length in full duplex mode, retaining this restriction allows device drivers and higher-layer software to treat both flavors of Ethernet (full and half duplex) identically.

Also, consider what would happen in a switched environment where some of the switch ports were operating in half duplex mode (with the minimum frame length constraint) and others were operating in full duplex mode (with no minimum length constraint). If a short frame were received from a full duplex port and needed to be forwarded to a half duplex port, the frame would have to be either discarded or padded. Any padding would require a change to the FCS, reducing the robustness of error detection. In addition, if a short multicast frame were being forwarded to a combination of full duplex and half duplex ports, the same frame would take different forms and require different transmission times. This unnecessarily complicates switch design. Thus, maintaining the minimum frame length restriction in full duplex mode allows for seamless bridging between half duplex and full duplex Ethernets.

7.4 Dedicated Token Ring

Token Ring networks were not immune to the advancements being made in switching technology. The architecture depicted in Figure 7.3 applies independent of the MAC employed in the stations and switch. A Token Ring network can be microsegmented just as easily as an Ethernet LAN—it just costs more. During the mid-1990s, manufacturers began to provide Token Ring switch products, bringing the advantages of switching to the Token Ring community.

Similar to the evolution of Ethernet switches, there were two steps taken in the migration path:

1. *Implementation of microsegmentation through the use of switching hubs.* Just as in Ethernet, changing from a shared-LAN hub to a switch effectively converts each port on the hub device to a two-station LAN. However, this LAN still operates in a shared-access mode; in the case of a Token Ring switch, there is still a token rotating among the two devices on each LAN (the end station and the switch). The two devices share the available capacity by passing the token back-and-forth between themselves, as depicted in Figure 7.6. Since each switch port is dedicated to serving a single end station, this configuration is called *Dedicated Token Ring* (DTR).

   The main advantage of using DTR in half duplex mode is that it is fully compatible with existing Token Ring NICs and end stations. By changing just the hubs, we get a migration path from shared- to switched-LANs without having to change all of the attached stations.

2. *Elimination of the access control algorithm.* Once again, we have the opportunity to improve performance even further by noting that Token Ring LANs always use an underlying communications channel that has a separate transmit and receive path between the partner devices on the ring. Whether it was UTP, STP, or optical fiber, Token Ring LANs have always used dedicated media (unlike Ethernet, which originally used a shared-bus coaxial cable). If we change the access control algorithm in the attached devices, there is no reason why they cannot both transmit and receive at the same time, as depicted in Figure 7.7.

In the same way that Ethernet implements full duplex operation by eliminating CSMA/CD, Token Rings implement full duplex operation by eliminating the tokens. Stations operating in full duplex mode transmit at will (subject only to a minimum interframe spacing requirement). This mode is called *Transmit Immediate* (TXI). There are no tokens passed, and both stations on the two-station LAN can transmit simultaneously. A Token Ring LAN operating in full duplex mode:

> ***Full Duplex Token Ring:***
> **Look, Ma! No tokens!**

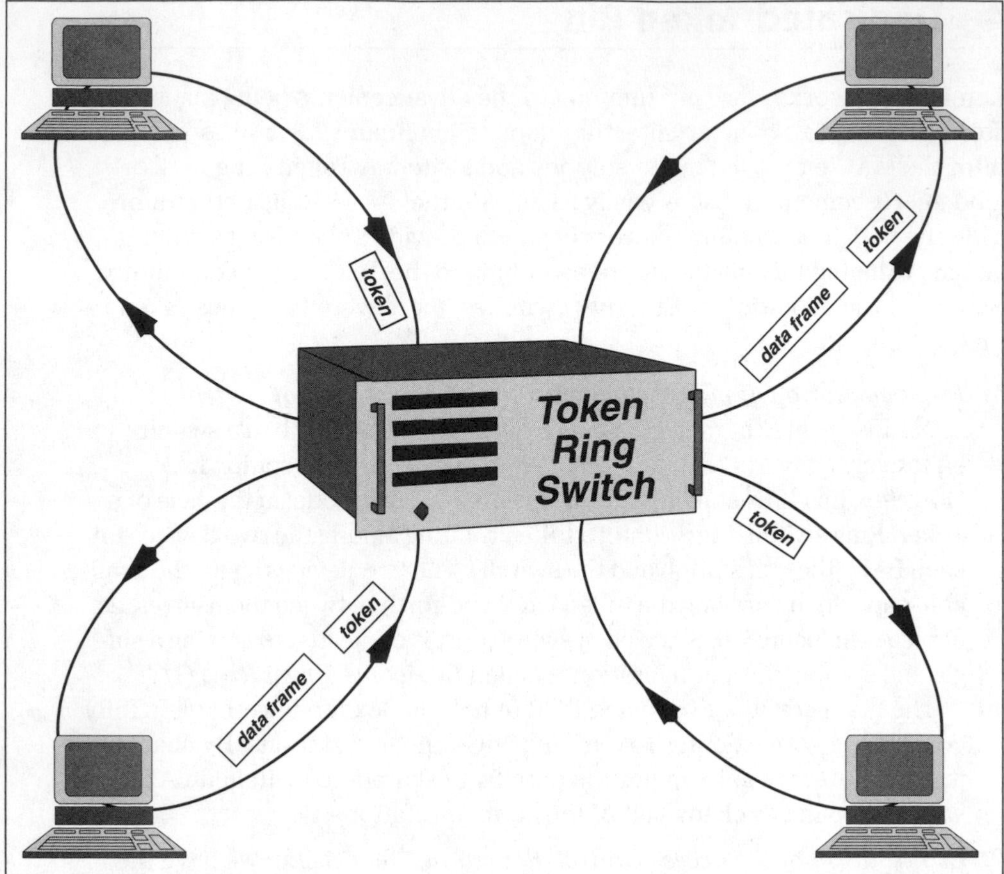

Figure 7.6 Dedicated Token Ring.

- Uses no token frames—the only frames used are for user data and network management.
- Eliminates the token priority mechanism and token reservation mechanism.
- Eliminates the Active Monitor function.
- Eliminates the Address Recognized, Frame Copied, and Error (A, C, and E) bit functions.
- Eliminates the loopback function—stations do not receive their own frames after the frame circulates the ring, as in half duplex mode.

In fact, the only real points of resemblance between a full duplex Token Ring and its half duplex sibling are the data frame format, the physical signaling, and the management functions. In 1998, the IEEE 802.5 Working Group

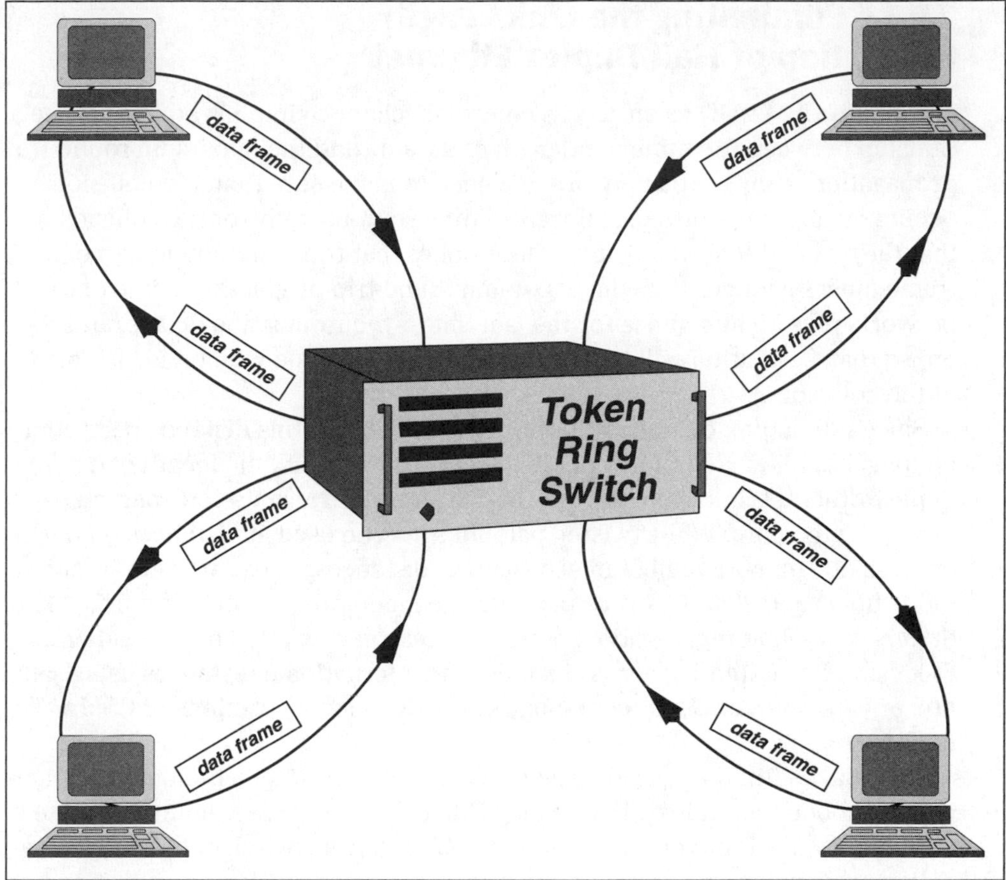

Figure 7.7 Full duplex Token Ring.

standardized both DTR and the TXI mode of operation for Token Ring, which together provide for full duplex operation [IEEE98f].

7.5 Implications of Full Duplex Operation

The use of full duplex mode has a number of important implications:

- Full duplex operation eliminates the link length restrictions of CSMA/CD.
- Full duplex operation increases the aggregate channel capacity.
- Full duplex operation increases the potential load on a switch.

7.5.1 Eliminating the Link Length Restriction of Half Duplex Ethernet

The use of CSMA/CD as an access control mechanism implies an intimate relationship between the minimum length of a frame and the maximum round-trip propagation delay of the network. We need to make sure that, if a collision occurs on any transmission, all transmitting stations know of the collision so that they can take proper action. This implies that the minimum length of a frame must be longer than the maximum round-trip propagation time of the network, plus an allowance for the jam time, synchronization delays, and so on, so that the station will still be transmitting the frame when it is informed of the collision.

Since full duplex operation does not use CSMA/CD, this distance restriction no longer applies. Regardless of the data rate of the LAN, the length of a full duplex Ethernet link is limited only by the physical transmission characteristics of the medium. While twisted pair links may be used at distances on the order of 100 m, optical fiber may be used at distances up to 2 to 3 km (multimode fiber) and 20 to 50 km or more (single mode fiber). With appropriate line drivers and signal regeneration, there is no reason why a full duplex Ethernet link cannot be extended across national and international distances using satellite, private fiber, or other technologies. The distance restrictions of CSMA/CD no longer apply.

This makes full duplex Ethernet especially attractive as a building and campus backbone technology. Full duplex Ethernet can be used at any supported data rate over kilometer-scale distances on switch-to-switch connections in a collapsed backbone.

Unlike Ethernet, Token Ring does not impose any strict architectural limit on the extent of a LAN. However, very long half duplex Token Rings networks may incur performance degradation, as the token rotation time increases with network propagation delay. Since full duplex Token Ring eliminates the token-passing algorithm, any such performance degradation vanishes. Stations do not wait for a token before transmitting, eliminating any concern about rotation times.

7.5.2 Increasing the Link Capacity

Clearly, a half duplex channel that could previously carry a maximum of *X* Mb/s can carry 2*X* Mb/s in full duplex mode, since it can carry data in both directions simultaneously. Unfortunately, this doubling of capacity occurs in a symmetrical manner. The most common bandwidth-intensive application on LANs today is bulk file transfer. File transfers move large amounts of data in one direction, but only small amounts (acknowledgments) in the other. The aggregate channel capacity may have increased, but the maximum data transfer rate from one device to another is still approximately *X* Mb/s. Since no widely-used traffic-intensive LAN applications use bandwidth in a symmetrical manner, the doubling of capacity does not directly double application throughput.[4, 5]

The capacity-doubling can be of benefit if there are multiple applications in use, some of which are intensively moving data in one direction while others are intensively moving data in the other. This would be rare in an end user's workstation, but more common in a server.[6] Since servers typically support many users and applications simultaneously, the probability that some applications will need to move data into the server at the same time others are moving data out of the server is much higher than for end-user workstations. Thus, full duplex operation is commonly used for server connections to a switch port. This also makes sense from a cost perspective; it may be prohibitively expensive to dedicate a switch port to every end user, but it is not unreasonable to dedicate switch ports to servers, since there are fewer servers. The servers can then be operated in full duplex mode and the end user workstations in the traditional half duplex mode. This is depicted in Figure 7.8.

Similarly to a server, a switch used as a collapsed backbone can benefit from the symmetrical increase in capacity. A collapsed backbone is a device used as the combining point for interconnected networks, as shown in Figure 7.9.

If the traffic distribution among groups is relatively uniform (i.e., there is no one group that is either a dominant source or sink of data), then the traffic through the switch ports on the collapsed backbone will be roughly symmetrical; traffic flow into and out of any given switch port will be approximately equal. Given this, the backbone switch can take advantage of full duplex operation to increase the channel capacity, since bandwidth usage is approximately symmetrical.

7.5.3 Increasing Switch Load

A switch supporting full duplex mode on any or all of its ports must deal with the possibility of increased data flow through the switch. The maximum aggre-

[4] In theory, a bidirectional video application could take advantage of symmetrical bandwidth, but this is not a common application on LANs today.

[5] Some suppliers market full duplex Ethernet as "20BASE-T" or "200BASE-T," but this is misleading as the maximum asymmetrical application throughput is not doubled.

[6] Appearances to the contrary, the most popular desktop operating systems (Windows 9x) are single tasking, single processor, and single threaded. Even though the user interface makes it appear that there are multiple tasks operating simultaneously (i.e., multiple open windows into separate applications), there is little parallelism or concurrency in operation. Servers, on the other hand, are by necessity multi-tasking, and often multi-processor and/or multi-threaded (UNIX, Windows NT, NetWare, and MacOS X). They can receive, transmit, and process data simultaneously, and thus achieve real benefits from full duplex operation.

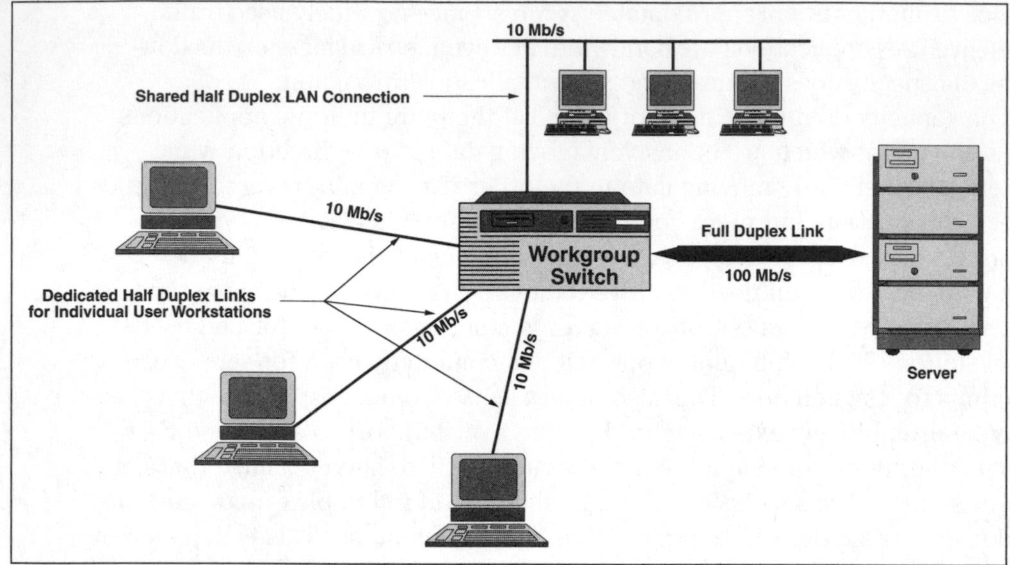

Figure 7.8 Full duplex server connection.

gate capacity required of a switch with n ports all operating at x Mb/s in half duplex mode would be:

$$\text{capacity}_{\text{agg}} = \frac{n\,x}{2}$$

since:

- A port can only be either transmitting or receiving at a given time, and not both (half duplex mode).
- All traffic flowing into the switch flows out as well (i.e., the switch is neither sourcing nor sinking significant traffic).

If the ports of the switch are operating in full duplex mode, then this maximum capacity requirement doubles, as the first disclaimer just given is no longer true. If a switch is to operate in a non-blocking fashion, then it must have double the internal switching capacity in order to support full duplex operation. This can affect the cost of a product and even the fundamental architecture employed. Of course, a switch designer may choose not to provide for non-blocking operation as a legitimate cost performance tradeoff. If the steady-state loads and network traffic patterns are such that the blocking nature of the switch would not normally come into play, then a blocking switch will provide equivalent performance to a non-blocking one at a lower cost. Clearly, it is more likely that a switch will be a potential blocking problem if its ports can operate in full duplex mode. The bottom line is that the use

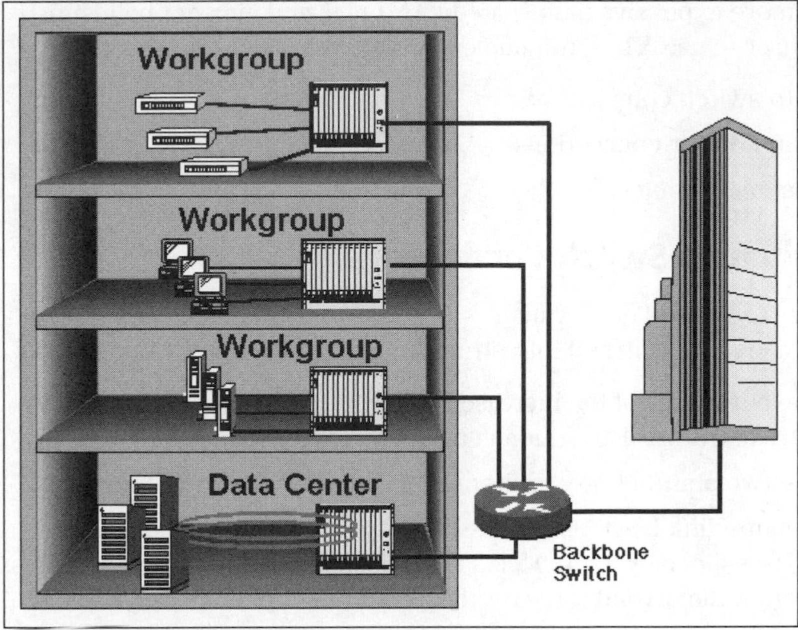

Figure 7.9 Switch used as a collapsed backbone.

of full duplex mode implies that a switch may have greater performance demands placed on it than if it only operated in half duplex mode.

A similar argument can be made for end stations, particularly servers, operating in full duplex mode. However, unlike switches, end stations rarely have large numbers of ports, and the doubling of the capacity to operate in full duplex mode is much less of a concern with low port densities.

7.6 Full Duplex Application Environments

Half duplex LANs have been in use for decades in every conceivable LAN application environment. No special conditions are required in order to use traditional half duplex LANs. They can operate on dedicated or non-dedicated media (e.g., twisted pair or coaxial cable), provide dedicated or non-dedicated bandwidth (switched or shared LAN), and are usable with any type of device with equal ease. Full duplex LANs are usable only in specific configurations that have both dedicated media capable of supporting simultaneous bidirectional communications, and exactly two devices on the LAN (microsegmentation).

While the use of dedicated media and switched LAN configurations meeting these requirements is rapidly increasing, there is still a huge installed base of legacy LANs that cannot currently support full duplex operation. In addition, switches are more expensive than shared LAN hubs, and may not be justified for general-purpose use. Thus, full duplex operation is most often seen in:

- Switch-to-switch connections
- Server and router connections
- Long-distance connections

7.6.1 Switch-to-Switch Connections

It makes sense to use full duplex mode where possible on connections between switches in a switched infrastructure. Switch-to-switch connections:

- Can take advantage of the increased capacity because of the generally symmetrical traffic distribution in a backbone environment.
- Meet the two-station LAN requirement of full duplex–mode operation.
- Often require link lengths in excess of those allowed by the use of CSMA/CD, especially for 100 Mb/s and 1000 Mb/s backbone applications. This is often the driving force for the use of full duplex mode in this application.

This makes this an obvious and popular application for deploying full duplex mode. Figure 7.10 depicts full duplex connections used in a switch-to-switch environment.

7.6.2 Server and Router Connections

Full duplex connections are also popular for connecting network servers to a LAN, particularly when connecting to a high-speed or backbone switch port. Network server connections:

- Can take advantage of the increased capacity because of their multitasking nature
- Are relatively low in number, and can therefore be justified (on a cost basis) in using dedicated switch ports, even at very high speeds

As traffic patterns tend to be from many clients to one server, server connections are often made to a high-speed full duplex port on a switch, with clients connected to lower-speed ports. This prevents the server port speed from becoming a point of network congestion. This was depicted earlier in Figure 7.8.

A router is simply a station connected to more than one network, whose purpose is to forward traffic among those networks. From a duplex mode perspective, there is no real difference between a switch and a router.[7] A router can be

[7] Of course, from an internetworking perspective there are huge differences, but these are unrelated to whether it is appropriate to use full duplex–mode interfaces.

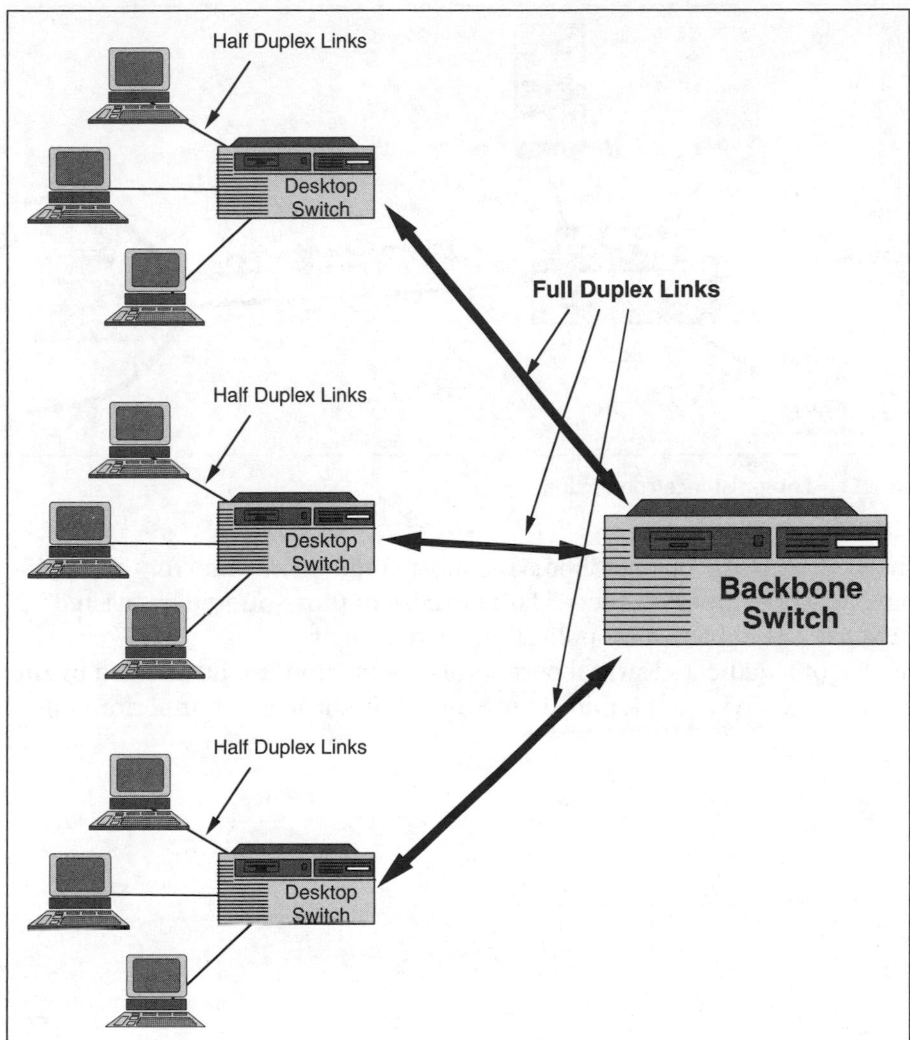

Figure 7.10 Switch-to-switch connections.

thought of as an internetwork server. As such, it becomes an ideal candidate for deployment of full duplex interfaces, for the same reasons just presented.

7.6.3 Long-Distance Connections

In some particular Ethernet environments, there may be a small number of end stations that need to be connected to a particular workgroup but that are physically separated beyond the limits of half duplex operation at the speed in use. To allow connection of such remote devices, a full duplex connection to a workgroup switch can be used, since full duplex eliminates the distance limi-

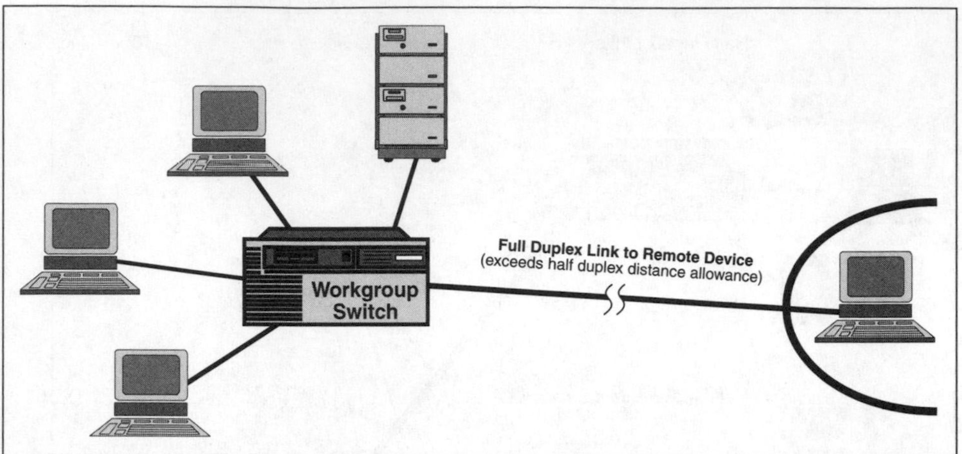

Figure 7.11 Long-distance connection.

tations of CSMA/CD. Optical fiber is the most common medium for this application, as it can support distances far in excess of those offered by twisted pair. Figure 7.11 depicts this application environment.

The use of a dedicated switch port in this application can be justified by the need for connectivity, not for any improvement in throughput or performance.

CHAPTER

8

LAN and Switch Flow Control

In this chapter we look at issues relating to frame loss, and the prevention of frame loss, within switches. Much of this discussion is also applicable to issues of frame loss within end stations, as the same solutions often can be applied to both problems.

The discussion is somewhat Ethernet-centric, for three reasons:

1. While a Token Ring LAN is itself connectionless, many Token Ring environments use a Logical Link Control protocol (i.e., LLC-2) that directly addresses the problem of frame loss within the Data Link by forcing a connection-oriented approach. LLC-2 sees much less use on Ethernet systems; the connectionless nature of Ethernet systems therefore makes frame loss more problematic.
2. Ethernet can address receiver overload on half duplex networks by applying backpressure (see Section 8.2.1). While theoretically a Token Ring station can backpressure the network by artificially delaying token release, such behavior is severely constrained.
3. The explicit flow control protocol discussed here was designed for, and is implemented solely on, Ethernet LANs.

The problems (and solutions) for switch flow control evolved directly from the development of Ethernet switches with full duplex interfaces. As such, the solutions tend to be Ethernet-specific.

8.1 The Need for Flow Control

Both LANs and LAN switches are connectionless in nature. Frames are sent between end stations on a single LAN or across a switched catenet on a *best-effort* basis. There is no concept of a virtual circuit, and no guarantee that any given frame will be successfully delivered either to its intended recipient or to any intervening switch. Frames are transferred without error to a high degree of probability, but there is no absolute assurance of success. More specifically, there are no mechanisms provided to:

- *Recover from frame errors.* There are no error control mechanisms that invoke retransmissions in the event of frame corruption within the Data Link layer. Any such error recovery is typically implemented within the Transport layer or the application itself.
- *Ensure that adequate resources (i.e., buffers) are available to receive frames.* Even if a frame arrives error free, there is no assurance that there will be a buffer available in which to store the frame.

In the event of a bit error, receiver buffer unavailability, or any other abnormal occurrence, a receiver simply discards the frame without providing any notification of the fact. This allows LAN interfaces to be built at very low cost; a connectionless system is much simpler to implement than a system that includes mechanisms for error recovery and flow control within the Data Link.

The probability of bit errors on LANs is extremely low. Ethernet specifies a bit error rate (BER) of 10^{-8} in the worst case[1] [IEEE98e, Clause 14]. A typical Ethernet in a benign (office automation) environment has a BER on the order of 1×10^{-12} or better. This translates into a frame loss rate (FLR) on the order of 10^{-8}, or 1 in 100 million.[2] This is low enough to be ignored at the Data Link layer and dealt with in higher-layer protocols or applications requiring reliable data delivery.

A lack of buffer resources can occur either at an end station or within a switch. In the case of an end station, buffer unavailability is most likely due to

[1] This is for copper media at 10 Mb/s. At 100 Mb/s and 1000 Mb/s, and with fiber media, the worst-case BER is orders of magnitude better.

[2] Frame loss rate can be calculated from bit error rate by:

$$FLR = 1 - (1 - BER)^n$$

where n is the number of bits in a frame, assuming a uniform distribution of errors across bits in the frame. The figure given in the text assumes the worst-case Ethernet frame length of 12,176 bits.

a mismatch between the capacity of the receiving station and that of the sending station and/or the LAN technology. In the case of a switch, buffer unavailability may additionally occur as a result of output port congestion and the pattern of traffic flowing through the switch, as depicted in Figure 8.1.

The loss of a frame due to buffer unavailability has the same effect (from the perspective of any higher-layer protocols or applications) as the loss of a frame due to a bit error. In both cases, the frame is not delivered to the intended recipient and the Data Link layer provides no indication of the event. The probability of frame loss due to buffer congestion can be much greater than that of bit errors, especially at high data rates and within switches.

Flow control refers to any mechanism that prevents a sender (or senders) of traffic from sending faster than the receiver is capable of receiving. Typi-

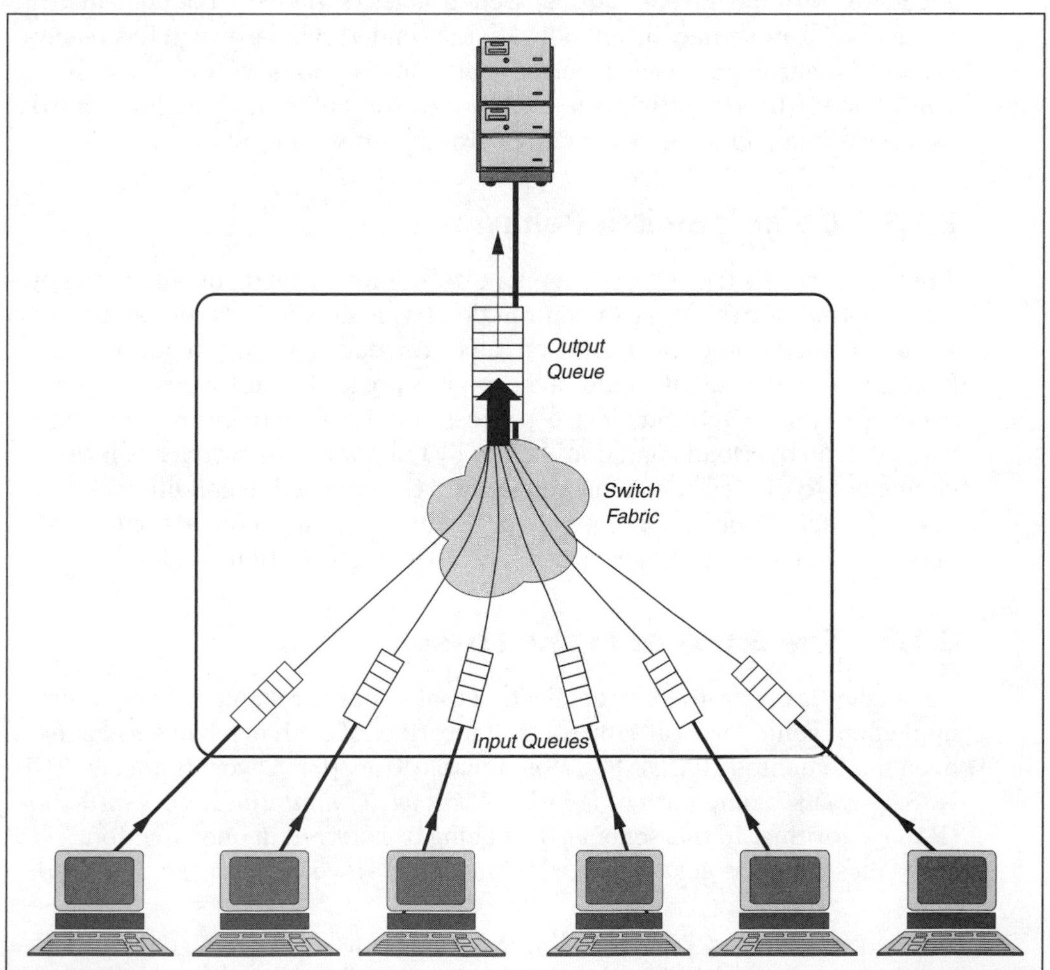

Figure 8.1 Switch congestion.

cally, this involves a feedback path from the receiver to the sender, where the sender's transmission rate is *throttled* based on buffer conditions at the receiver. Ideally, flow control should prevent frame loss due to receive buffer unavailability.

Flow control can be invoked at any (or more than one) layer of the protocol architecture. Most reliable Transport protocols (e.g., TCP) provide a means for end-to-end flow control across an internetwork of multiple links, switches, and/or routers. In this chapter we consider flow control mechanisms within a connectionless Data Link, and how these can be used to prevent unnecessary frame loss across either a single LAN or a switched catenet.

The original Ethernet design did not provide any means for flow control. When the network consists of end stations communicating across a single LAN, the mechanisms typically provided by higher-layer protocols are usually adequate. With the advent of transparent bridges (switches), the immediate receiver of a frame may be unknown to the sender; that is, a switch is receiving and forwarding frames on behalf of attached stations without those stations' knowledge or participation. Without a protocol to provide flow control, excessive frame loss can occur due to switch buffer congestion.

8.1.1 Default Switch Behavior

A switch receives frames on its input ports and forwards them onto the appropriate output port(s) based on information (typically the Destination Address) in the received frame. Depending on the traffic patterns, switch performance limitations, and available buffer memory, it is possible that frames can arrive faster than the switch can receive, process, and forward them. When faced with such an overload condition (hopefully temporary), a switch has little choice but to discard incoming frames until the congestion condition clears. Thus, the default behavior of a switch (or any device in a connectionless internetwork) is to discard frames when faced with a congestion condition.

8.1.2 The Effect of Frame Loss

Any higher layer protocol or application that requires reliable delivery must implement some form of error control. A variety of such mechanisms have been implemented [TANEN88]. Most reliable Transport Layer Protocols (TCP, NFS, etc.[3]) use some form of *Positive Acknowledgment and Retransmission* (PAR) algorithm. In this scheme, data being transferred in one direction between stations is acknowledged in the other. The originating station does

[3] While NFS is not strictly a Transport protocol, it is responsible for reliable message block delivery across a connectionless network.

not assume that the data has been successfully delivered until an acknowledgment has been received. If the acknowledgment is not received in some predetermined period of time, the originator assumes that the data has been lost en route (or the acknowledgment has been lost *etuor ne*[4]) and initiates a retransmission of the original data. In this manner, acknowledged, reliable end-to-end data communication can occur despite the possibility of frame loss in the underlying networks. The same mechanism is used to recover from frame loss regardless of the reason for the loss; remember that the predominant source of frame loss may be buffer congestion rather than bit errors.

A PAR protocol will operate correctly in the face of lost frames, but will incur a performance penalty in doing so. A lost frame will (in general) require that the higher layer protocol acknowledgment timer expire before retransmission is initiated. These timers must (at a minimum) be set to allow for the end-to-end propagation delay of the entire network, plus an allowance for processing time and delay variance. Typical protocols will use times on the order of seconds in order to operate across a large internetwork. Thus, depending on the Transport protocol, a single lost frame can incur the penalty of idling a data transfer for seconds.

This can have a devastating effect on throughput. Consider the case of NFS [RFC1094] operating over UDP and faced with a persistent underlying frame loss rate, as depicted in Figure 8.2. Because the loss of a single frame can cause NFS to halt (waiting for an acknowledgment) for seconds, the overall throughput degrades rapidly with the frame loss rate. For an NFS acknowledgment timer of 5 seconds, a 1 percent frame loss rate results in a performance degradation of almost 98 percent.[5]

It should be noted that with respect to flow control NFS over UDP is a rather primitive protocol. It was chosen as an example here specifically because it incurs rather devastating performance breakdown in the face of lost frames. Other protocols (notably TCP) can detect frame loss in the underlying network and respond by reducing their offered load and alleviating the congestion condition that may have caused the frame loss in the first place.

[4] That is, en route in the other direction (loud groan appreciated here).

[5] For a given frame loss rate (FLR), frame length (length) in bytes, data rate (rate) in bits per second, and acknowledgment timer (acktime), the performance degradation due to frame loss will be:

$$\text{degradation} = 1 - \left[\frac{(1 - \text{FLR}) \times \text{frametime}}{(\text{FLR} \times \text{acktime}) + \text{frametime}}\right]$$

where

$$\text{frametime} = \frac{\text{length} \times 8}{\text{rate}}$$

The graph in Fig. 8.2 is derived from this equation.

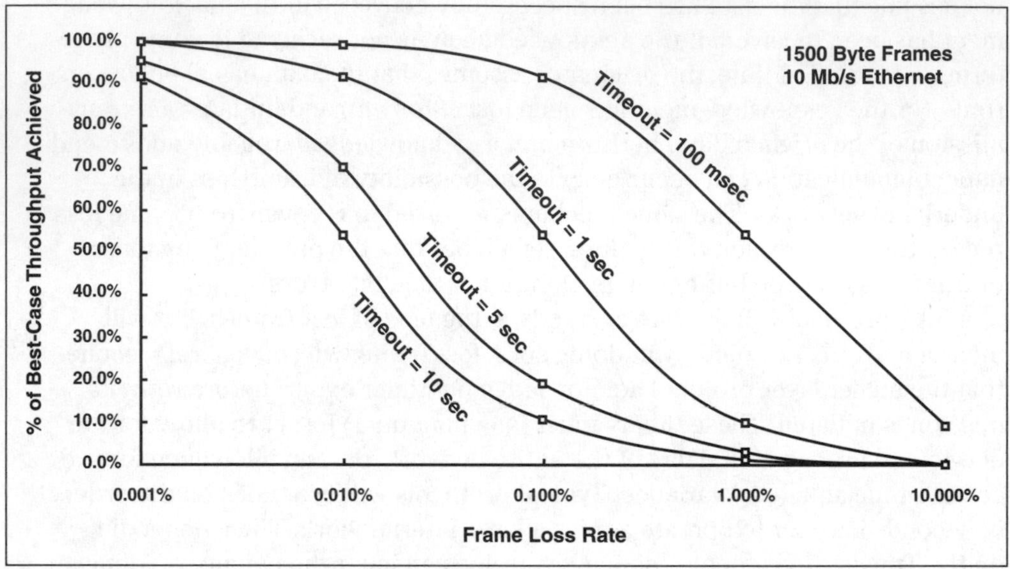

Figure 8.2 NFS throughput as a function of acknowledgment time and frame loss rate.

However, the message should be clear. While higher layer protocols can and do recover from frame loss, such loss should be considered a boundary or exception case, and not something that should be encouraged or allowed to occur unnecessarily. It would be better (in the NFS example just given) to throttle the underlying links so that only 10 percent of their capacity was available to the application, rather than letting them run at full speed and incur a 1 percent frame loss rate (due to buffer overflow).

Frame loss due to bit errors may be unavoidable, but we can design mechanisms to avoid unnecessarily discarding frames due to buffer congestion in switches and end stations.

8.1.3 End-to-End Flow Control

Reliable transport protocols usually provide a mechanism for end-to-end flow control; that is, they ensure that the originator of a data stream does not transmit when there are insufficient resources (e.g., buffers) at the receiver to process the data.[6] However, this only ensures that resources are available at the ultimate receiver of the data; a protocol operating solely between end stations cannot ensure that there are adequate resources available at every inter-

[6] In some protocols, the mechanism used for flow control may be the same as that used for error control; that is, an acknowledgment of data receipt indicates to the sender that it may continue sending. In other protocols (e.g., ISO TP-4 [ISO84]) the error and flow control mechanisms are decoupled.

vening switch or router to receive and process the data stream. An analogy can be made to highway traffic: The fact that there are adequate parking spaces (buffers) available for all patrons at the ballpark does not imply that the road to the ballpark can handle all of the traffic going there. Thus, end-to-end flow control does not guarantee that frames will not be discarded due to insufficient buffer memory in any intervening internetworking devices. If we need to solve a link buffer overflow problem, we must solve it within the link layer.

8.1.4 Cost-Performance Tradeoffs

If we design and implement a link flow control mechanism, this will incur additional complexity and therefore increase cost. This cost may not be justifiable in networks where high performance is not a major concern, for example 10 Mb/s desktop LANs. In this environment, not only is the impact of a performance degradation less significant, the probability of frame loss is lower, since it is not difficult to design switches that can process frame arrivals from multiple 10 Mb/s Ethernet ports at wire speed. However, as we increase the data rate and shift our focus from the desktop to backbone networks, the decision goes the other way. At gigabit and higher data rates, there is a much greater probability that a device can be overloaded by frame arrivals, especially a device with a large number of ports. In addition, we are already paying a premium for the higher speed LAN; if we do not address the frame loss problem, then we may not really be getting value from our increased expenditure.

The flow control mechanism discussed in Section 8.4 was developed as a result of the difficulties in switch design at 100 Mb/s; at higher data rates flow control becomes more of a necessity in order to provide good application performance at reasonable cost.[7]

8.2 Controlling Flow in Half Duplex Networks

If the ports connected to a switch are operating in half duplex (traditional, shared-LAN) mode, there are some tricks that a switch can play to try to improve performance both of the network and of the switch itself. These fall into two general classes of behaviors:

[7] While the flow control mechanism discussed in Section 8.4 is usable at any data rate, 10 Mb/s full duplex switches had been shipping for years, without flow control and without significant problems, before this protocol was designed.

1. *Backpressure.* To prevent buffer overflow from traffic arriving on its input ports, a switch can use the underlying access control method to throttle stations on the shared LAN and forestall incoming traffic.
2. *Aggressive transmission policy.* On the output side, a switch can empty its transmit queue in an expedited manner by using an access control algorithm more aggressive than that permitted by the standard. This effectively gives the switch priority over other traffic sources on its output ports.

8.2.1 Backpressure

On a CSMA/CD LAN, two methods are available to prevent switch input buffer overflow by manipulating the behavior of the MAC algorithm itself:[8]

1. *Force collisions with incoming frames.* On the surface, this appears to be a reasonable tactic. Like a horse flicking off an annoying fly with its tail, a forced collision will cause the sending station to reschedule the transmission of the frame for a later time (the fly will be back, but the horse gets some temporary relief). This does prevent the buffer overflow as intended. Unfortunately, there are some undesirable side effects:
   - The sending station(s) may be throttled too much, and the throughput of the system will actually be lower than the available capacity (i.e., there will be unnecessary idle time on the channel). This is because the collision will cause the end station to calculate an exponentially-increasing backoff. The station will select a time, initially in the range of 0 to 1 slotTimes,[9] but increasing to 0 to 1,023 slot times for later collisions. It is likely that switch input buffers will become available during this very long time, as the switch will be emptying its queue onto the output ports in the meantime. Even though the queue is so emptied, the channel will remain idle until the backoff timer expires. It seems a shame to waste bandwidth solely due to an inefficient backpressure algorithm.
   - In the event of sustained input buffer congestion, a station can experience 16 successive collisions on the frame at the head of its queue.

[8] The explanations in this section assume some familiarity with the Ethernet MAC algorithm. Readers unfamiliar with the terminology and behavior discussed here should see [SEIF98, Chapter 10], [SPUR97], [IEEE98e], or any good LAN reference text for a thorough discussion of the Ethernet half duplex MAC.

[9] A slotTime is the fundamental time unit of a half duplex Ethernet MAC. It is derived from the round-trip propagation delay and represents the minimum length of a frame as well as the quantum of retransmission for backoff purposes. Ethernet uses a slotTime of 512 bit-times at 10 and 100 Mb/s, and 4,096 bit-times at 1000 Mb/s.

Following the MAC algorithm, the station will discard such a frame and report it as an error to station management. To the higher layer protocols this appears as if the switch had discarded the frame. This has the same long-timeout and performance problems as discussed earlier, although only under sustained congestion conditions.

- Management counters and statistics will indicate very high numbers of collisions as well as higher numbers of *excessive collision errors*. While the statistics will be correct (strictly speaking), the interpretation by a human network administrator will likely be that there is some serious problem with the network. "Normal" Ethernets do not experience extremely high collision rates or large numbers of excessive collision errors; the latter events especially are indicative of systematic network problems requiring reconfiguration or repair.
- It takes some time for a device to generate a forced collision. Upon detecting an incoming frame that it wishes to backpressure, the device must then begin the process to initiate its transmission. Depending on the hardware implementation, it may take as much as a few byte-times or more before the collision is actually created. Unfortunately, there is no allocation in the system delay budget for this additional time. The slotTime is budgeted very carefully, and there is little or no margin, depending on the particular data rate and media employed [IEEE98e, Annex B]. Thus, the network designer must ensure that any switch using a forced-collision backpressure algorithm is not used in a network that is near the maximum allowable extent.

  Some switch designs have taken the forced-collision algorithm a step further and made it "smart." In one such algorithm, a collision is forced only if the incoming frame is destined for transmission on an output port whose buffers are already full; that is, collisions are forced selectively rather than on all incoming frames. This prevents unnecessarily backpressuring frames targeted for an otherwise uncongested port. However, this greatly increases the delay before the switch can invoke the forced collision; in order to make the decision whether or not to force a collision, the switch must receive the entire Preamble, Start-of-Frame Delimiter, and Destination Address, as well as perform its complete table lookup process to determine the target output port(s). This requires a minimum of 14 byte-times, a significant fraction of the total system delay budget (64 byte times). A network designer deploying a switch using such an algorithm must avoid all but the simplest network environments on all half duplex switch ports.

2. *Make it appear as if the channel is busy.* This uses the deferral mechanism rather than the collision backoff mechanism of the Ethernet MAC. As long as the station sees that the channel is busy (i.e., Carrier Sense is asserted) it will defer transmission, but it imposes no additional backoff delay, the frame remains at the head of the queue, and the frame is not discarded regardless of the duration of the deferral. This is a superior approach to the forced collision method. Using our earlier analogy, it is like the horse waving its tail anytime it doesn't want to be annoyed, rather than waiting for a fly to alight.

It is relatively simple to cause Carrier Sense to be asserted in the stations attached to a shared LAN; it requires only that validly-formed bits be present on the Ethernet connecting the switch to the station(s). The simplest approach is to generate Preamble onto the desired input port whenever the switch wants to throttle offered load in the face of congestion, as depicted in Figure 8.3. The end of the stream should never be a Start-of-Frame Delimiter.

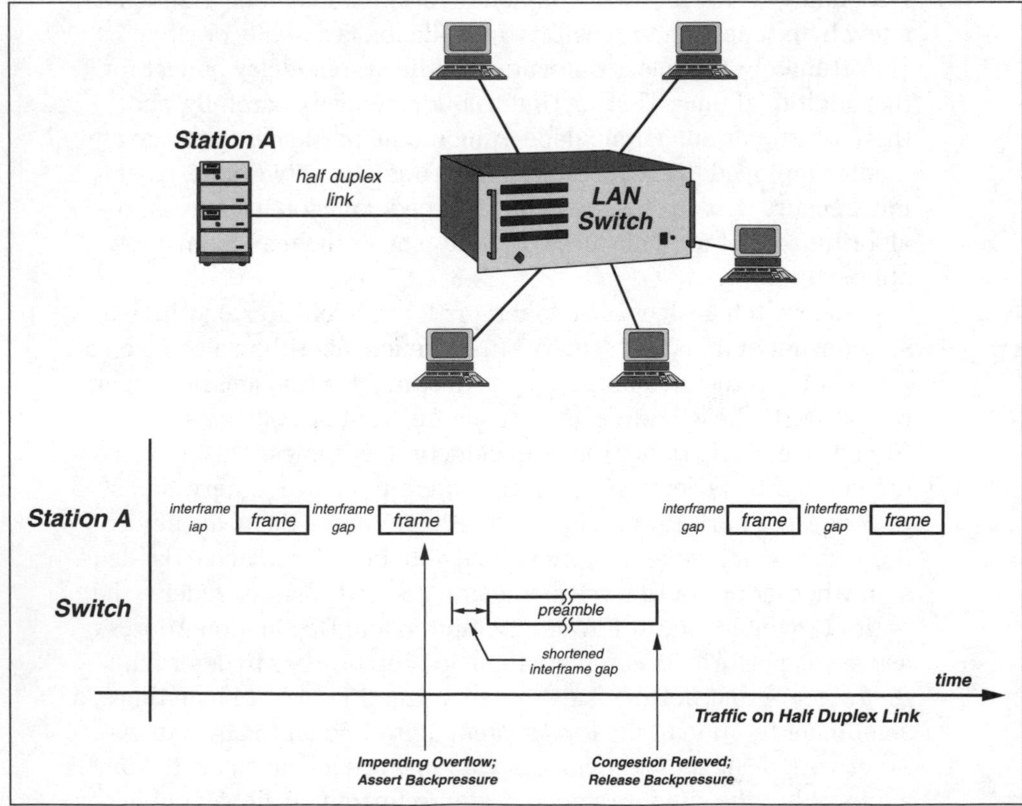

Figure 8.3 Forced Carrier Sense and microsegmentation.

This ensures that receiving station(s) will not interpret the stream as the start of a real frame.

Preamble can be sent in this manner for as long as necessary. It eliminates the forced collisions completely, and has no serious side-effects (believe it or not!). The only problem is that standard 10 Mb/s transceivers may assert *jabber control* (disabling their transmitter) if the Preamble is sent for longer than 20 ms. On 100 Mb/s and 1000 Mb/s systems, this is not an issue at all. In addition, stations that implement the excessiveDeferral management object of IEEE 802.3 should expect to see an increase in this statistic counter.

The use of false Carrier Sense is especially elegant in the case where there is only one end station connected to each switch port (microsegmentation). In this case, the only reason for input buffer congestion is the ability of the end station to offer more load than the switch can forward to its outputs. The false Carrier Sense algorithm will throttle this station perfectly. When the false carrier is dropped, the station will simply begin sending the frame at the head of its queue. There will be no collisions or backoff, even in the congested case.

There is a slight difference if there is more than one station connected to the switch port (shared LAN). When congestion occurs, Carrier Sense is asserted, and all stations will withhold transmissions. When the congestion clears, Carrier Sense is dropped. At this time, it is likely that more than one station has queued a frame for transmission. This guarantees a collision among those stations, at least for the first attempt. However, this is exactly what is expected in Ethernet. The stations will resolve their Ethernet congestion using the proper collision-detection and backoff method. (Buffer congestion has been resolved through the backpressure mechanism.) Thus, while collisions may be generated as an indirect result of the false Carrier Sense algorithm, these are normal and resolve properly.

A complete treatment of CSMA/CD backpressure algorithms and implementation issues can be found in [SEIF96].

In theory, backpressure mechanisms can be used on shared LANs using MAC algorithms other than CSMA/CD. In a token passing network, for example, a switch could hold the token for an extended period to forestall incoming frames. However, there are two problems with this approach that make it impractical:

- The token passing protocol is subject to strict time limits on the rotation period of the token. A switch cannot withhold token release for very long.
- Most Token Ring hardware provides no support for artificially delaying token release with any precision.

Thus, MAC algorithm backpressure is not used in LANs other than Ethernet.

8.2.1.1 Aggressive Transmission Policies

Backpressure provides a means of throttling arriving traffic by using either the collision or the deferral mechanism of the underlying MAC. It is also possible for a switch to manipulate the access control mechanisms to provide transmission priority on congested output ports.

8.2.1.1.1 Shortened Deferral

An Ethernet interface is expected to enforce a minimum spacing between transmitted frames, known as an *interframe gap*, equal to 96 bit times. The actual duration is a function of the data rate in use, and varies from 9.6 μs at 10 Mb/s to 96 ns at 1000 Mb/s. Receiving stations depend on there being some minimal breathing room between frames in order to perform any necessary housekeeping—interrupting a host, starting a DMA engine, updating buffer pointers and management statistics, and so on—that is required on a per-frame basis.

While senders are required to space frames a minimum of 96 bit times, receivers (especially on shared LANs) must be able to deal with spacing considerably closer than this, on the order of one-half, or 48 bit times. This is because the operation of repeaters in the network can shorten the interframe spacing as seen by a receiver.[10] The receiver in a typical interface can operate perfectly well with an interframe spacing of 40 bit times or less; some high-performance designs can operate with virtually no spacing at all.

Stations waiting to transmit are expected to wait out the interframe gap and then transmit. Due to normal circuit tolerances (e.g., clock frequency variation), it is possible that one station's interframe gap time will be slightly faster than that of another. The faster station will always begin its transmission slightly sooner than the slower station. If the deferral algorithm did not take this into account, the slower station would always hear the faster station before beginning its own transmission and defer. This would give the faster station an unintended priority; in the event of heavy offered load by the faster station, it could conceivably prevent the slower station from sending any traffic at all.

To account for this variation, a station waiting out an interframe gap makes an unconditional decision to transmit at some point in the deferral process, regardless of whether it hears another station after that point, as depicted in Figure 8.4. For transmissions that follow a reception, the decision is normally made at the two-thirds point, that is, after 64 bit times have elapsed. After this point, a station waiting to transmit will always transmit at the end of the interframe gap. However, if a station hears another transmission begin before the 64th bit, it will defer its own transmission.

[10] For a detailed analysis of this effect, see [IEEE98e, Clause 13] or [SPUR97].

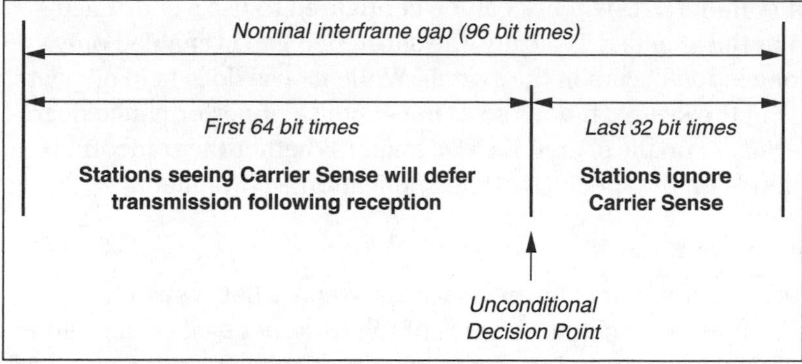

Figure 8.4 Two-part deferral process.

A device wishing to exert priority access can take advantage of this behavior. If the device begins to transmit with a shortened interframe gap (shorter than 64 bits), it will prevent other devices from attempting to transmit at the end of the interframe gap (assuming that they are following the normal rules). As with any tweak to a standard protocol, there are a few problems with this policy:

- It only works as intended if there is only one device on the shared LAN using the modified algorithm. If multiple devices are behaving aggressively with respect to interframe gap, they cancel each other's efforts, and collisions still result.
- A device using this algorithm needs to be careful not to shorten the interframe gap too much. If the gap is shortened below about 48 bit times, some receiving interfaces may not be able to receive back-to-back frames sent by the modified device. The receiving station may discard a frame because it could not get ready in time. As a result, the aggressive device has not achieved its purpose; it avoided discarding a frame in its own queue only to have it discarded anyway by the intended receiver.
- A device that consistently applies this aggressive behavior can prevent other stations from ever sending traffic. This will affect performance and application behavior for those stations.
- The modified policy violates the IEEE standard. The reason for the standard was to ensure fair access; this policy expressly tries to achieve an unfair advantage for its perpetrator. Depending on the implementation, it may not be possible to modify the deferral behavior with standard Ethernet controller ICs; designers may need to select from a subset of the marketplace or build their own controllers (typically within a larger ASIC).

A number of commercial switches can be configured to use a shortened interframe gap in this manner. Typically, the shortened gap is enabled only when buffer congestion occurs in the switch. While its use does help alleviate buffer overflow in the switch, it does so at the expense of performance degradation for other users on the shared LAN segment. Whether the tradeoff is acceptable depends on the specifics of the application environment.

8.2.1.1.2 Aggressive Backoff

Analogous to the backpressure approaches discussed earlier, a switch or other device can modify the characteristics of the Ethernet backoff algorithm to obtain an unfair advantage and to empty its output queue faster. A standard Ethernet controller, when faced with collisions, will select a rescheduling interval (backoff time) using the *truncated binary exponential backoff* algorithm. With this method, the backoff time for any retransmission attempt is a random variable with an exponentially-increasing range for repeated transmission attempts. The range of the random variable r selected on the nth transmission attempt of a given frame is:

$$0 \leq r < 2^k$$

where

$$k = \text{MIN}(n,\ 10)$$

Thus, the station starts with a range of 0 to 1 on the first collision encountered by a given frame and increases the range to 0 to 3, 0 to 7, 0 to 15, and so on, up to the maximum range of 0 to 1,023 when faced with repeated collisions encountered by the same frame. The backoff time is measured in units of the round-trip propagation delay of the channel, known as the slotTime. The range of the backoff variable is reset upon successful transmission of the frame, that is, there is no history maintained between frames.

If all stations use the same backoff algorithm, access will be fair when measured over long periods of time; that is, stations will share the available capacity equally. If a device wanted to unload its transmit queue in a hurry (e.g., when faced with impending buffer overflow), it could obtain an advantage by using a more aggressive algorithm. Modifications in commercial practice include:

- Selecting the random variable from a narrower range than specified by the standard (e.g., truncating at a ceiling of 2^4 rather than 2^{10} for multiple collisions)
- Using a linearly-increasing range rather than an exponentially-increasing range
- Always selecting 0 as the "random" variable

This last option is especially problematic. While it ensures that the device in question will always achieve the highest possible performance, it effectively locks out all other station accesses until the device in question stops using the aggressive policy. In addition, if there are ever two devices on the LAN using this same aggressive algorithm, they will encounter repeated collisions on every frame and never resolve their contention.

Many other modifications to the Ethernet backoff algorithm have been explored in an attempt to provide priority access for specific stations, including those in [PACE98] and [CHOU85].

The use of backpressure and/or aggressive transmission policies provides a form of *implicit flow control* for half duplex Ethernets. Stations are being prevented from sending frames and overflowing switch buffers, but they do not realize that it is the switch that is manipulating the MAC algorithm to this end. The affected stations are simply obeying the normal access rules for the network. The reduction in load on the switch is achieved without any explicit mechanism in the stations being throttled.

On a full duplex Ethernet, none of these schemes will work. A full duplex Ethernet interface does not detect collisions, and ignores Carrier Sense for the purpose of deferring its transmissions. A full duplex network therefore requires an explicit flow control mechanism to allow a switch to throttle a congesting end station. To achieve this, a standard mechanism (IEEE 802.3x) was developed for flow control of full duplex Ethernet [IEEE97].

8.3 MAC Control

Rather than define just a protocol for explicit flow control of full duplex Ethernet (that would have been too easy!), the IEEE 802.3x Task Force chose to specify a more generic architectural framework for control of the Ethernet MAC (MAC Control), within which full duplex flow control was the first (and currently, the only) operation defined. This allowed for future:

- Expansion of explicit flow control to half duplex networks
- Specification of alternative full duplex flow control mechanisms (besides the simple PAUSE function discussed later)
- Definition and specification of other functions (besides flow control)

While no such standard extensions of the MAC Control protocol have yet been developed, the architecture makes this a relatively easy task.

MAC Control is an optional capability in Ethernet. This avoided having to declare preexisting Ethernet-compliant devices to be noncompliant with a later revision of the specifications. Clearly, the use of flow control provides significant advantages in high-speed, full duplex switched networks, but an

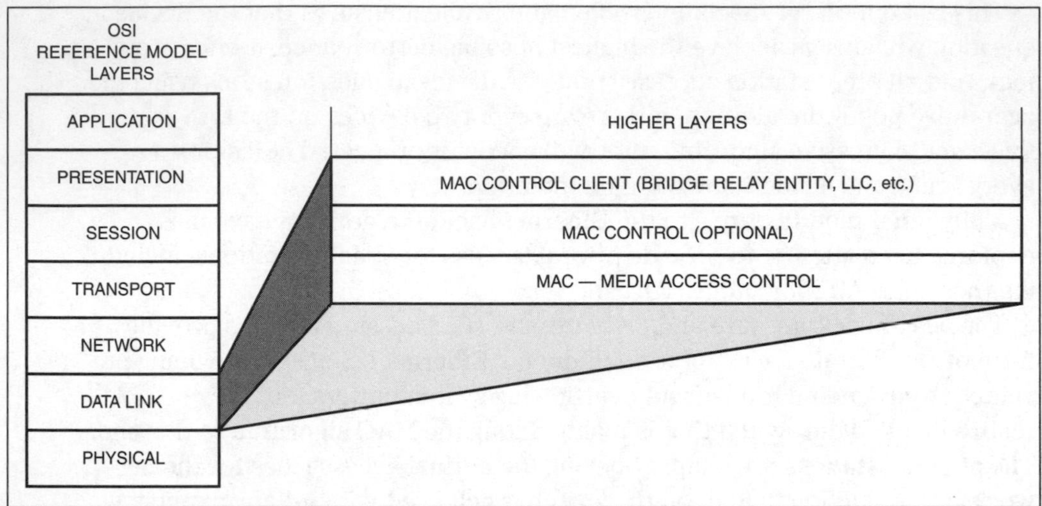

Figure 8.5 MAC Control architectural positioning.

implementor (and user) is allowed the choice of performance versus price. However, since the cost of implementation of the MAC Control protocol (specifically, the PAUSE function used for full duplex flow control) is extremely low (it can typically be implemented in hardware, in the Ethernet controller silicon itself), most vendors of full duplex Ethernet products implement this capability today, especially at 100 Mb/s and 1000 Mb/s data rates.

8.3.1 MAC Control Architecture[11]

Figure 8.5 depicts the MAC Control architectural layering.

MAC Control constitutes a sublayer of the Data Link; it is an optional function inserted between the traditional Ethernet MAC and the client of that MAC. That client may be a Network-layer protocol (e.g., IP) or the relay function implemented by bridges (switches) within the Data Link layer itself.

If the client of the MAC does not know about, or care to use, the functions provided by MAC Control, then the sublayer disappears; normal transmit and receive data streams pass from the MAC to and from its control-unaware client(s) as if the MAC Control sublayer were not there. MAC Control-aware clients (such as a switch desiring to prevent buffer overflow) can use the added capabilities of this sublayer to control the operation of the underlying

[11] Readers interested in reality, as opposed to architecture, may skip this section and go directly to the discussion of PAUSE operation in Section 8.4, with no loss of continuity.

Ethernet MAC. In particular, it can request that the MAC at the other end of a full duplex link cease further data transmissions, effectively preventing the impending overflow.

Upon request from a MAC Control-aware client, MAC Control can generate *control frames*, which are sent on the Ethernet using the standard underlying MAC. Similarly, an Ethernet MAC will receive MAC Control frames (generated by a MAC Control sublayer in another station) and pass them to the appropriate function within the MAC Control sublayer, as depicted in Figure 8.6. On the Ethernet, MAC Client (i.e., normal) data frames are thereby interspersed with MAC Control frames.

Prior to the invention of MAC Control, every frame transmitted on an Ethernet was a result of a request to transmit data by a higher layer protocol or application, and carried data relevant to that protocol or application. MAC Control introduces the concept of frames being generated and received (i.e., *sourced* and *sunk*) within the Data Link layer itself. This concept exists in

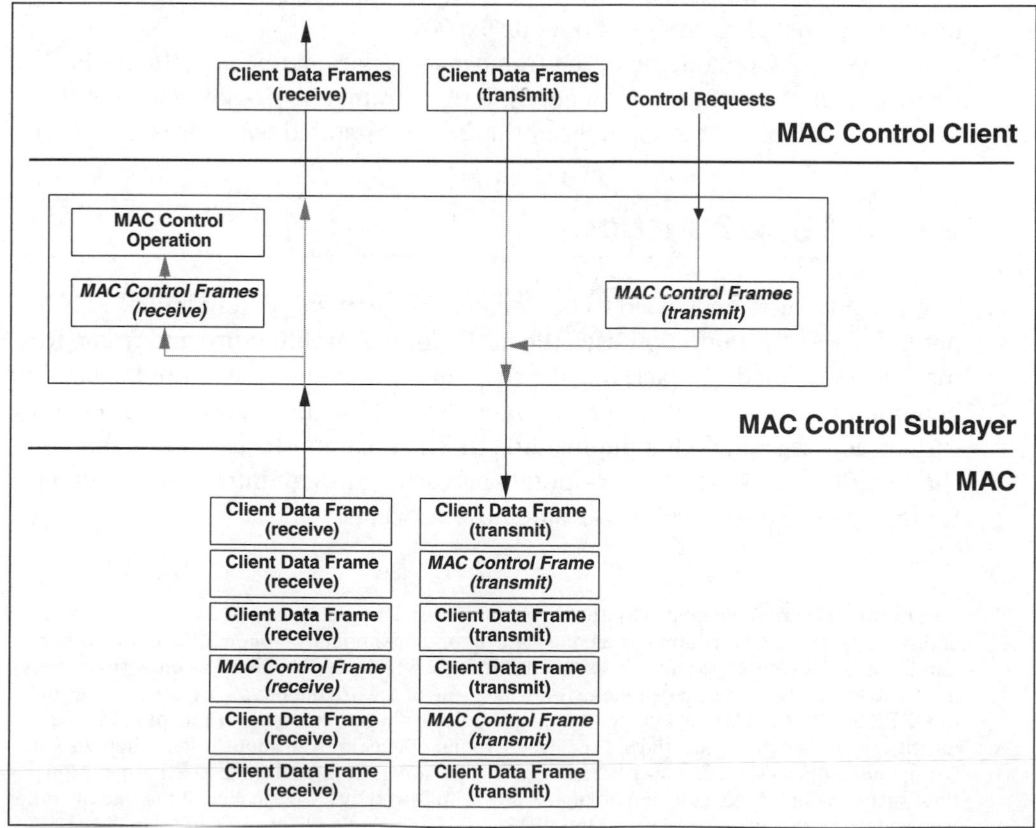

Figure 8.6 Client and control frames.

many other MAC protocols (e.g., IEEE 802.5 Token Ring and FDDI), but was new to Ethernet.[12]

8.3.2 MAC Control Frame Format

MAC Control frames are normal, valid Ethernet frames. They carry all the fields depicted in Chapter 1, *Laying the Foundation*, and are sent using the standard Ethernet MAC algorithms. Other than the unique Type field identifier (discussed later), MAC Control frames are unexceptional when transmitted or received on the network. All MAC Control frames are exactly 64 bytes in length, not including the Preamble and Start-of-Frame Delimiter; that is, they are minimum length Ethernet frames. Figure 8.7 depicts the generalized MAC Control frame format.

MAC Control frames are identified by a unique Type field identifier (0x8808) in the frame. This Type field has been reserved for Ethernet MAC Control.

Within the Data field of the frame, the first two bytes identify the MAC Control opcode, that is, the control function that is being requested by the frame. Currently, only one such opcode is defined (the full duplex PAUSE operation, discussed later). It is assigned opcode 0x0001.

Following the opcode field, the frame carries parameters specific to the requested opcode (if any are needed). If the parameters do not use all of the 44 bytes available, the remainder of the frame is padded with zeros.

8.4 PAUSE Function

The PAUSE function is used to implement flow control on full duplex Ethernet links. PAUSE operation uses the MAC Control architecture and frame format just described. (In fact, it is the only function ever implemented using that general-purpose architecture and frame format.) The operation is defined only for use across a single full duplex link; that is, it cannot be used on a shared (half duplex) LAN, nor does it operate across or through intervening switches. It may be used to control data frame flow between:

[12] For years, Ethernet advocates touted the simplicity of Ethernet as one of its key advantages, and the lack of any Control frames as one element of that simplicity. Token Ring, on the other hand, has always employed numerous Control frames, which can be viewed as either extremely powerful or overly complex, depending on which side of the argument you are on. As chair of the IEEE 802.3x Task Force, I presented the MAC Control protocol to the whole of IEEE 802 during one of its plenary meetings. I received a round of cheers from some Token Ring Working Group members as soon as they realized that we had added Control frames to Ethernet. "You finally saw the light!" was the immediate response, followed by "Now, just send the bits the other way and finish the job." (referring to the Big Endian/Little Endian controversy).

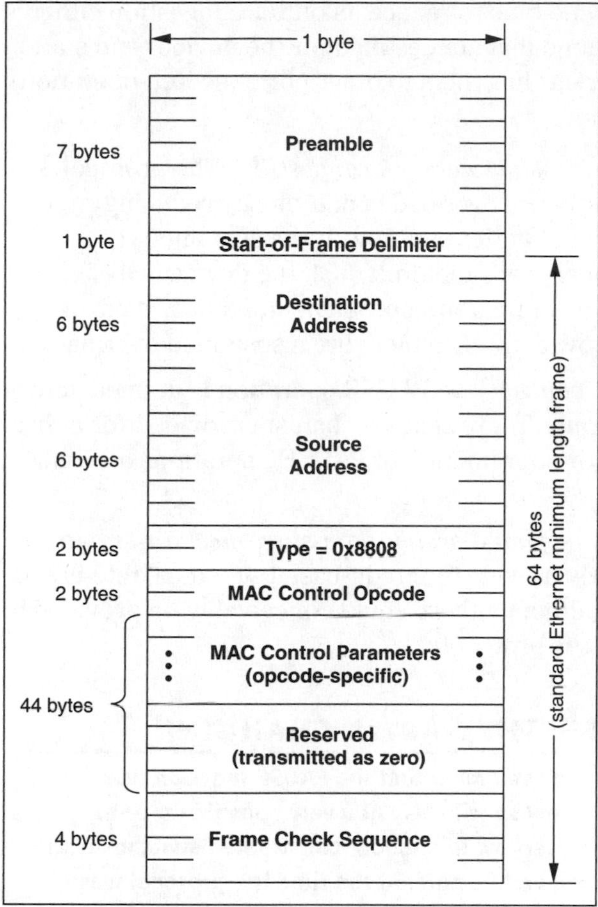

Figure 8.7 MAC Control frame format.

- A pair of end stations (i.e., a simple, two station network)
- A switch and an end station
- A switch-to-switch link

The PAUSE function is specifically designed to prevent switches (or end stations) from unnecessarily discarding frames due to input buffer overflow under short-term transient overload conditions. Consider a device designed to handle the expected steady-state traffic of the network, plus an allowance for a some time-variance of that load. The PAUSE function allows such a device to avoid discarding frames even when the short-term load increases above the level anticipated by the design. The device can prevent buffer overflow by sending PAUSE frames to its partner on the full duplex link; the reception of the PAUSE frame by the partner will cause the partner to stop sending data frames. This gives the first device time to reduce its buffer congestion either by processing frames in the queue that are destined for the device (end station operation) or by moving or forwarding them to other ports (switch operation).

The PAUSE function does not:

- *Solve the problem of steady-state network congestion.* The protocol is designed to alleviate temporary overload conditions by reducing inbound traffic in the face of buffer overflow. If the sustained (i.e., steady-state) traffic level exceeds that for which the device is designed, this must be considered a configuration problem, not a flow control problem. PAUSE-style flow control cannot cure a sustained overload.
- *Provide end-to-end flow control.* The PAUSE operation is defined across a single full duplex link only. There is no mechanism provided for either end-to-end flow control or coordination of PAUSE operations across multiple links.[13]
- *Provide any complexity beyond a simple stop-start mechanism.* In particular, it does not directly provide for credit-based schemes, rate-based flow control, and so on, although these could conceivably be provided in future enhancements to the protocol.[14]

THE TIMES, THEY ARE A CHANGIN'!

It is important to remember that the PAUSE function was designed for a very specific use at a very specific time—to prevent buffer overflow in memory-constrained switches with an input-queued architecture. At the time the protocol was devised (1995–1996), many low-cost switches used an input-queued approach and switch memory was relatively expensive. Reducing the cost of a switch usually meant reducing its memory capacity; using PAUSE-style flow control meant that such a switch could provide a good price performance mix and yet avoid frame loss under peak overload conditions. The PAUSE protocol is less useful today with lower-cost memory and the popularity of output-queued switches.

In addition, TCP (the most popular reliable Transport protocol in use) uses frame loss within the network as its indication of congestion. That is, TCP's end-

[13] Of course, it is possible to design a higher layer application or mechanism that performs this coordination, using the primitive PAUSE function as a tool for more complex flow controls, but the PAUSE function itself provides no such feature.

[14] During 1998–1999, a Study Group was formed within IEEE 802 with the express purpose of considering such enhancements. The group disbanded when its members came to the realization that there was no real benefit to be gained by modifying the protocol. It was one of the few times when a standards committee voted to disband and not to develop a new standard, an action very much like turkeys voting for Thanksgiving.

to-end flow control mechanism detects underlying frame loss and uses this information to throttle its flow. If switches prevent frame loss under congestion conditions, TCP will never recognize the congestion and will continue sourcing data into the network; in fact, TCP will see a lack of frame loss over time as an indication that it can *increase* the offered load, further exacerbating the congestion problem. If switches dropped an occasional frame, TCP would throttle back the offered load and alleviate much of the network congestion, eliminating the need to invoke PAUSE frames. This is the concept behind the Random Early Discard (RED) approach to flow control[15] [FLOY93]. Implementing Link-layer flow control on switches can actually interfere with the end-to-end flow control.

It is common to include PAUSE support in most switches, just as a data sheet checklist item, as it imposes little cost penalty to implement. However, in most environments, it is both common and reasonable practice to disable the function. The PAUSE function does remain useful for end stations that are unable to receive data at the sustained rate of the attached link (e.g., a server with a 1000 Mb/s interface).

8.4.1 Overview of PAUSE Operation

The PAUSE operation implements a very simple stop-start form of flow control.

A device (end station or switch) wishing to temporarily inhibit incoming data sends a PAUSE frame, with a parameter indicating the length of time that the full duplex partner should wait before sending any more data frames. When a station receives a PAUSE frame, it stops sending data frames for the period of time specified as the parameter in the frame. When this timer expires, the station resumes sending data frames where it left off.[16] PAUSE frames inhibit the transmission of data frames, but have no effect on the transmission of MAC Control frames (e.g., PAUSE frames from the other direction).

A station issuing a PAUSE may cancel the remainder of the pause period by issuing another PAUSE frame with a parameter of zero time. That is, newly received PAUSE frames override any pause operation currently in progress. Similarly, the issuing station can extend the pause period by issuing another PAUSE frame with a non-zero time parameter before the first pause period has expired.

Since the PAUSE function uses the standard underlying Ethernet MAC, there is no guarantee of frame delivery to the receiver. PAUSE frames could be corrupted by errors, and the receiver would not know that such frames were ever sent. The design of a PAUSE transmission policy (discussed later)

[15] While the term *Random Early Discard* accurately describes the action taken, some in the industry now call this operation *Random Early Detect*, which avoids having to explain to customers that, for their own good, you are randomly throwing away their packets.

[16] The use of a timer-based mechanism prevents the (unintentional) permanent disabling of another station from sending data frames.

must take this into account. For the formal, detailed specification of the PAUSE operation, refer to [IEEE97].

8.4.2 PAUSE Frame Semantics

A PAUSE frame contains all of the fields indicated in Figure 8.7. The Preamble, Start-of-Frame Delimiter, and Frame Check Sequence are the same as for all Ethernet frames, as discussed in Chapter 1. The remaining fields take the following values:

Destination Address This is the intended destination of the PAUSE frame. It always contains the unique multicast address reserved for PAUSE operation: 01-80-C2-00-00-01.

Why does a Destination Address need to be specified at all? Since the PAUSE function is defined only for full duplex links, clearly the target of the PAUSE is the station at the other end of the link! Even stranger, why is the destination specified to be a multicast address, since there can only be one other device on the link? The reasons are subtle, but important:

- In the event that a PAUSE frame is inadvertently sent on a shared LAN (through configuration error), the use of a specific multicast address ensures that the only stations that receive and interpret such frames will be those that actually understand the PAUSE protocol (i.e., the address is reserved for this purpose exclusively).
- The use of a multicast address relieves the sender of PAUSE frames from having to know the unicast address of its link partner. While this address is likely to be known by higher layer protocols, there is no need for the Data Link to be aware of it.
- The specific multicast address selected is a member of the special, reserved group of addresses that are blocked (sunk) by all standard bridges and switches (See Chapter 2, *Transparent Bridges*). Frames sent to addresses in this group are never forwarded onto other ports of a switch. This keeps PAUSE frames local to the single full duplex link on which they are relevant.[17]

Source Address This field contains the unicast address of the station sending the PAUSE frame. While it again seems unnecessary to specify a Source Address when the frame could only have been emitted by one device, including a Source Address provides:

[17] The default behavior of a switch with respect to multicast destinations is to forward them onto all ports except for the port on which the frame arrived. That rule is suspended for this reserved block of multicast addresses; frames with Destination Addresses in this block are never forwarded from one port of a switch to any other port. The reserved block includes all addresses in the range from 01-80-C2-00-00-00 through 01-80-C2-00-00-0F inclusive.

- Consistency with all other Ethernet frame types (i.e., the Source Address in all Ethernet frames contains the unicast address of the station sending the frame)
- Proper updating of management counters in monitoring devices (e.g., RMON [RFC1757]) that may be keeping track of frames generated on a per-station basis
- Ease in determining the sender if PAUSE frames are inadvertently emitted onto a shared LAN due to a misconfiguration

Type field The Type field contains the reserved value used for all MAC Control frames, equal to 0x8808.

MAC Control Opcode and parameters The MAC Control Opcode for a PAUSE frame is 0x0001.

The PAUSE frame takes a single parameter called the *pause_time*, a 2-byte unsigned integer value indicating the length of time for which the sender is requesting that data frames not be sent by the receiver. The time is measured in 512 bit-time increments; that is, the receiver should pause for a period of time equal to the pause_time multiplied by 512 bit-times at the data rate currently in use. The range of values for the pause_time is shown in Table 8.1.

The use of a data-rate-dependent parameter was chosen for two reasons:

- Specified in this manner, the PAUSE operation can be thought of as stopping the partner from sending a specified number of bits, regardless of data rate, rather than for a specified period of time. Since the original purpose of the PAUSE function was to allow memory-constrained switch implementations, an interface can be designed such that it emits PAUSE frames with a constant pause_time parameter when there is a constant number of bits of buffer remaining, regardless of the data rate. This can simplify some designs.
- In a half duplex Ethernet, the collision backoff counter measures time in increments of the slotTime, which is 512 bit-times for all data rates except 1000 Mb/s. Since the PAUSE function is only used on full

Table 8.1 PAUSE Timer Ranges

10 Mb/s	0–3.36 s (in 51.2-μs increments)
100 Mb/s	0–336 ms (in 5.12-μs increments)
1000 Mb/s	0–33.6 ms (in 512-ns increments)

duplex links, this counter (if implemented) is not needed for backoff timing, and can be used for PAUSE timing without change.[18]

8.4.3 Configuration of Flow Control Capabilities

It is important that the two partners on a full duplex link agree on whether they will be sending, and/or are capable of responding to, PAUSE frames. If a switch is betting on the fact that it can prevent buffer overflow by sending PAUSE frames, then it is important that the device at the other end of the link be capable of pausing properly. Since the PAUSE function is an optional feature, some form of configuration control is needed. This configuration can generally be accomplished in one of two ways: manually or automatically.

- Manual configuration implies that a human network administrator must properly configure the two ends of the link as desired. This would typically be done using some software tool (utility program) that can enable or disable various features and capabilities of the device. Such tools are typically vendor- or device-specific, but it may also be possible to use a generic tool (e.g., a standard network management station). While manual configuration is tedious and prone to error (those darn humans!), it may be the only configuration method possible for many devices.
- Some Ethernet physical media provide a mechanism for automatic negotiation of link parameters. When such a mechanism is available, it is clearly the preferred means of configuring the flow control capabilities of the full duplex link partners. On UTP cable, the Ethernet Auto-Negotiation protocol [IEEE98e, Clause 28] can be used to automatically configure the flow control capabilities of the link; 1000BASE-X provides an equivalent mechanism for gigabit optical fiber media. Table 8.2 indicates, for all full duplex capable Ethernet media, which configuration methods are possible.

Of course, the ability to automatically determine the capabilities of the attached devices and configure the link cannot make a device do something that it is not capable of. If a switch requires the ability to flow control the attached devices and that capability isn't there, then the switch must choose between working without flow control (and incurring the possibility of higher frame loss) or disabling the link entirely.

[18] When the PAUSE function was being designed, the slotTime was 512 bit-times for all varieties of Ethernet, and this benefit accrued across all data rates. The later change to a 4,096-bit slotTime for Gigabit Ethernet by the IEEE 802.3z Task Force eliminated some of this benefit.

Table 8.2 Flow Control Configuration Options

MEDIA TYPE	MANUAL	AUTOMATIC
10BASE-T	✔	✔
10BASE-FL	✔	
100BASE-TX	✔	✔
100BASE-FX	✔	
100BASE-T2	✔	✔
1000BASE-CX	✔	✔[1]
1000BASE-LX	✔	✔[1]
1000BASE-SX	✔	✔[1]
1000BASE-T	✔	✔[1]

[1] Auto-Negotiation of flow control is mandatory for all 1000 Mb/s media.

8.5 IEEE 802.3x Flow Control Implementation Issues

In this section we discuss a number of issues related to the implementation of Ethernet systems that support and use the PAUSE mechanism just described. Readers not interested in the low-level design of hardware and software for Ethernet interfaces can safely skip this section.

8.5.1 Design Implications of PAUSE Function

Flow control (specifically, the transmission and reception of PAUSE frames) imposes some new twists that did not previously exist for the design of Ethernet devices. Prior to flow control, all Ethernet frames transmitted by a given interface were submitted by a higher layer protocol or application. Similarly, all received frames were checked for validity and then passed up to the higher layer entity without the contents being inspected, interpreted, and acted upon by the Ethernet interface. This changes with the implementation of flow control, as the link interface can now generate PAUSE frames, and must inspect each incoming frame to determine if it is a PAUSE request from its link partner and act upon PAUSE requests. This raises some important issues in the design of Ethernet interfaces supporting the PAUSE function.

8.5.1.1 Inserting PAUSE Frames in the Transmit Queue

Without the PAUSE function, an Ethernet interface simply transmits frames in the order presented by the device driver. Since Ethernet has no concept of priority access (or user priority), a single-queue model can be used for the transmitter. However, the effective use of flow control requires that PAUSE frames be emitted in a timely manner.

A higher-layer application (e.g., the bridge relay function) will typically signal its need to assert flow control on the link due to an impending buffer overflow condition. If the PAUSE frame generated by this signal is simply inserted in the transmit queue like any other frame, its transmission will be delayed while waiting for all other frames in the queue to be transmitted. Depending on the size of the interface's transmit queue, flow control may not be asserted in time to prevent the buffer overflow, and the effort will be wasted.

Clearly, PAUSE frames must be given priority in transmission. In general, there is no need to have an actual transmit queue for PAUSE frames, since there can be only one outstanding flow control action in effect at any given time. In addition, the contents of the PAUSE frame are relatively fixed; the only field that may need to vary over time is the value of the pause_time parameter. An implementation can simply keep a well-formed PAUSE frame in a static buffer (or even hard-coded in logic) available for transmission upon request.

The transmission of a PAUSE frame cannot preempt a data transmission in progress. Therefore, the interface should (upon getting a signal to send a PAUSE frame) complete the transmission of any frame in progress, wait an interframe spacing, and then send the requested PAUSE frame. Following the end of the PAUSE frame, the interface can continue transmitting frames from the transmit queue in the normal manner, as depicted in Figure 8.8.

8.5.1.2 Parsing Received PAUSE Frames

An interface capable of being flow controlled must be able to inspect and parse the fields in all incoming frames to determine when a valid PAUSE has been received in order to act upon it. The following fields must be checked:

Destination Address This field must be checked for a match against either the well-known multicast address reserved for the PAUSE function (01-80-C2-00-00-01) or the unicast address of the port on which the frame is received. While (current) transmitters of PAUSE frames should never send to this unicast address, this provision in the receiver allows extension of the PAUSE function to half duplex MACs in the future.

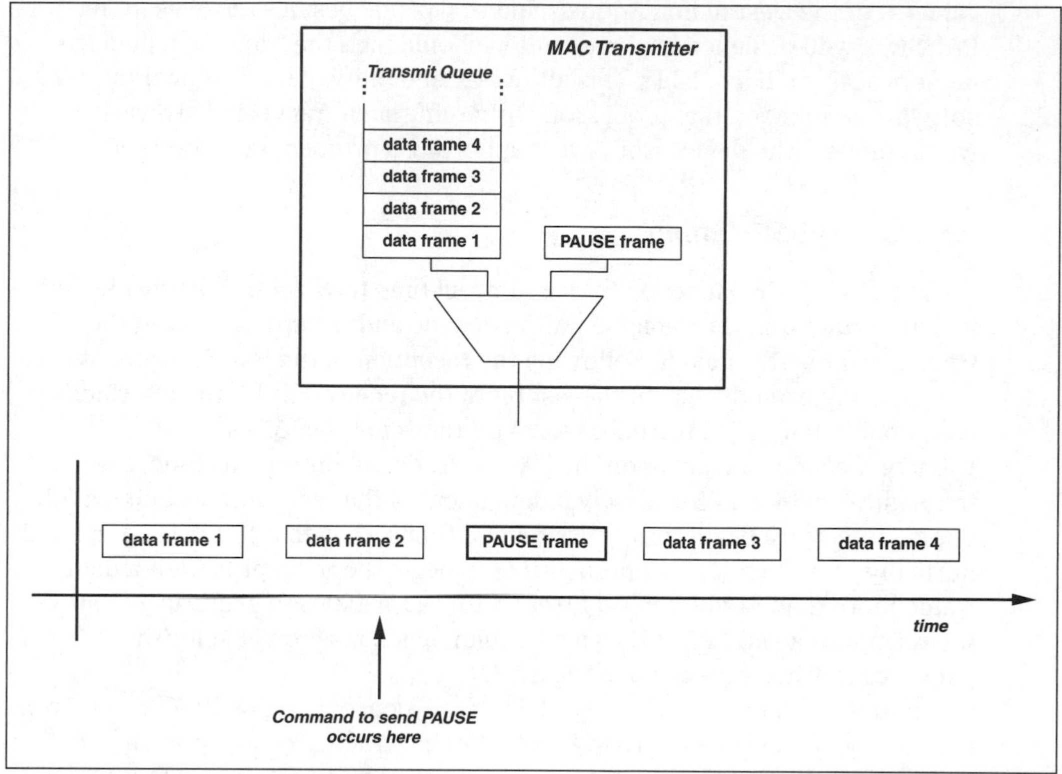

Figure 8.8 PAUSE frame insertion.

Type field This field must be checked against the reserved value for MAC Control frames (0x8808).

MAC Control Opcode This field must be equal to the value for the PAUSE function (0x0001).

Frame Check Sequence This must be the valid FCS for the received frame. Since the earlier fields may be parsed and checked before the reception of the FCS, some provision must be provided for ignoring an already-received-and-decoded PAUSE frame in the event of a subsequent FCS error.

> **Seifert's Law of Networking #17**
>
> If the hardware doesn't understand it, give it to the software.

Following the parsing and decoding, the receiver must extract the pause_time parameter from the frame and supply it to the logic that is performing the PAUSE function within the interface. PAUSE frames are not passed up to the device driver, but are absorbed within the interface.

In the event that a MAC Control frame (i.e., Type 0x8808) is received with a valid FCS but with some value(s) of the Destination Address and/or Opcode besides those used for PAUSE, a well-designed implementation should pass the frame to a management processor, if available. This allows extendibility of the protocol through software running on that processor. Discarding such frames in hardware would prevent the device from ever supporting a protocol upgrade.

8.5.1.3 PAUSE Timing

Because the PAUSE function is used for real-time flow control across the link, it is important that the implementation decode and act upon received PAUSE frames in a timely manner. Following the reception of the PAUSE frame itself (i.e., starting from the end of the last bit of the received FCS), the interface has a maximum of 512 bit times (1,024 bit times for 1000 Mb/s interfaces) to validate, decode, and act upon the PAUSE frame. If, during this time, the transmitter (which is completely independent of the receiver, this being a full duplex interface) begins transmission of a frame, then that frame is completed normally. However, it is not permissible to begin the transmission of a data frame more than 512 bit times (1,024 bit times for 1000 Mb/s interfaces) after the receipt of a valid PAUSE frame containing a non-zero value for the pause_time. This is depicted in Figure 8.9.

Without putting this upper bound on the response time of a PAUSE receiver, it would be impossible for a sender of a PAUSE frame to know how much additional data could be received before the flow would stop, and there would be no way to use PAUSE to effectively prevent buffer overflow.

8.5.1.4 Buffering Requirements

Since flow control operates on a full duplex link, and there is both a propagation delay and a response time delay between the link partners, sending a PAUSE frame cannot immediately stop the flow of data in the other direction (into the sender's receiver). Thus, the sender must allow for this additional data to be received, and send the PAUSE frame well before buffer overflow occurs. The maximum amount of data that could possibly be received following a request to the MAC Control entity to assert flow control (i.e., the amount of buffering required above the threshold for sending the PAUSE) is the sum of:

One maximum-length frame on transmit This is a frame from the sender's transmit queue that could have just been started when the flow control signal was asserted, and that cannot be preempted. It includes a maximum length Ethernet frame appended by a Virtual LAN (VLAN) tag of 4 bytes, plus Preamble, Start-of-Frame Delimiter, and interframe gap.	12,336 bits (1,542 bytes)

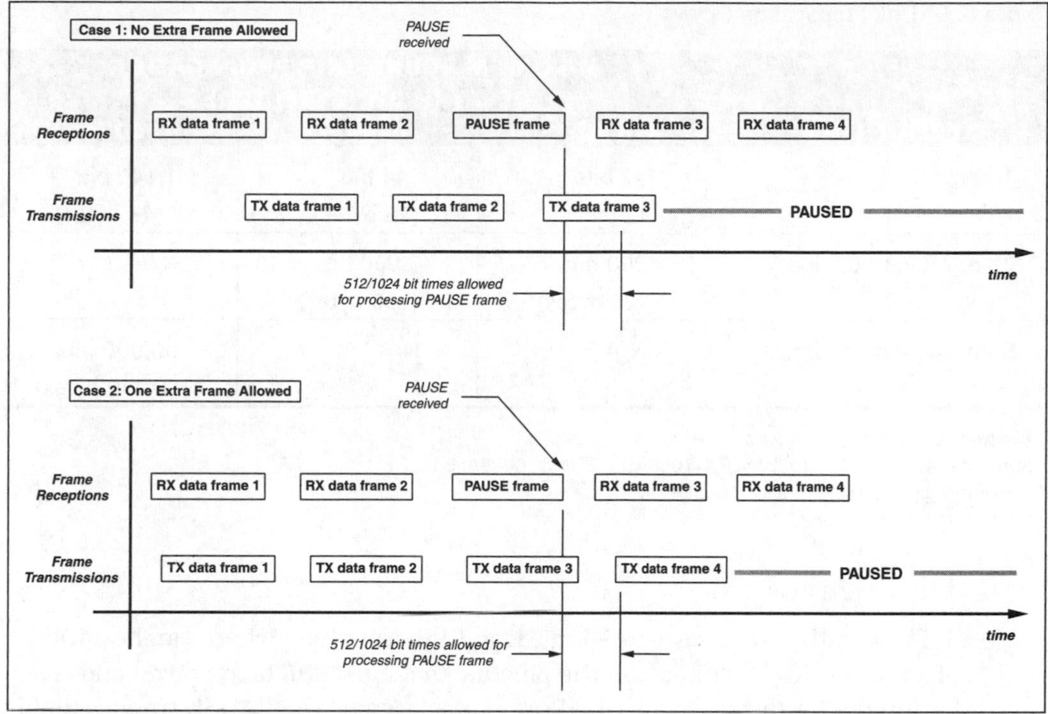

Figure 8.9 PAUSE timing.

One PAUSE frame time This is the PAUSE frame itself, including Preamble, Start-of-Frame Delimiter, and interframe gap.	672 bits (84 bytes)
The PAUSE frame decode time allowance The higher number is for 1000 Mb/s operation.	512/1,024 bits (64/128 bytes)
One maximum-length frame on receive This is a frame from the receiver's transmit queue that could have just been started when the PAUSE was decoded, and that cannot be preempted. The allowance is less than for the transmitted frame, since the Preamble, Start-of-Frame Delimiter, and interframe gap do not typically impact receive buffering.	12,176 bits (1,522 bytes)
The round-trip propagation delay of the link	See Table 8.3

The required buffering headroom is therefore about 3.2 Kbytes plus an allowance for the propagation delay of the link. This link allowance can be significant, as shown in Table 8.3.

Table 8.3 Link Propagation Delays

TYPE OF LINK	MAXIMUM ROUND-TRIP PROPAGATION DELAY IN BIT (BYTE) TIMES[1] 10 Mb/S	100 Mb/S	1000 Mb/S
100 m UTP[2]	12 bits (2 bytes)	114 bits (15 bytes)	1,140 bits (143 bytes)
2 km multimode fiber[3]	200 bits (25 bytes)	2,000 bits (250 bytes)	N/A
5 km singlemode fiber[4]	N/A	N/A	50,000 bits (6,250 bytes)

[1] Rounded up to the nearest bit or byte.
[2] Supported by 10BASE-T, 100BASE-TX, 100BASE-T2, and 1000BASE-T.
[3] Supported by 10BASE-FL and 100BASE-FX.
[4] Supported by 1000BASE-LX.

Thus, in the worst case (a 5 km Gigabit Ethernet link), there can be a total of about 9.5 Kbytes of data in the pipeline that must still be received and buffered after the assertion of a flow control signal. The PAUSE frame should stop the flow from the link partner after this time. The design of buffers and flow control threshold selection must take this delay into account to effectively use flow control to prevent frame loss. The use of non-standard, even longer single-mode fiber links further increases the buffering requirements for effective flow control.

8.5.2 Flow Control Policies and Use

The PAUSE mechanism provided for flow control of full duplex links is only a tool; the specification of the protocol defines what actions occur upon the sending or receiving of PAUSE frames, but it says nothing about when a device should assert flow control and when it should resume the flow. This section considers some of these *flow control policy* issues for practical implementations.

In a typical implementation, flow control is used to prevent input buffer overflow in a switch. This allows a switch to be built to accommodate average traffic levels without slowing throughput, while also preventing undesirable frame loss under short term overload conditions, all without incurring the cost of huge buffer memories to accommodate the overload case. The end result is a less expensive switch that performs perfectly well (from the user's perspective) under a wide range of traffic conditions.

8.5.2.1 Buffer Thresholds

A typical input-queued switch will have some amount of buffering available for each port, which holds frames until either the output port or the switching fabric itself is available to accept the frame, as depicted in Figure 8.10.

Depending on the traffic patterns and the total load offered to the switch, frames will experience a delay in this queue while waiting to be unloaded. During this time, additional frames are being received on the same port, causing the queue to fill further. A reasonable flow control policy would be to send a PAUSE frame (with a non-zero value for the pause_time) when the buffer fills up to a predetermined high-water mark, so that the switch can prevent frames from being dropped at the input due to buffer unavailability. While the link partner is throttled in this manner, the switch will be unloading frames from this queue and forwarding them out other ports of the switch. When the buffer empties below a predetermined low-water mark, the flow control can be canceled (by sending a PAUSE frame with a 0 value for the pause_time),

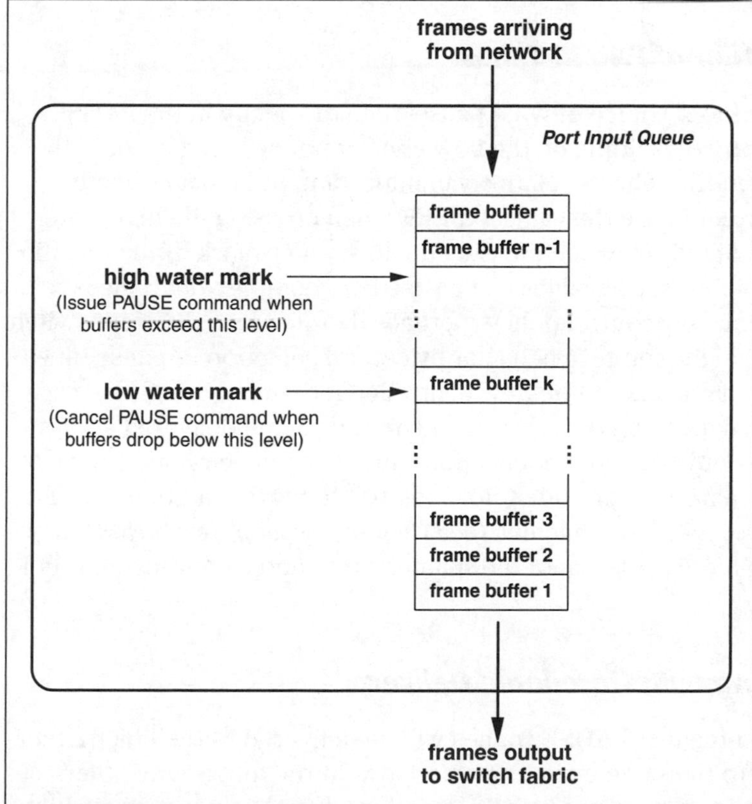

Figure 8.10 Input buffering.

and normal operation resumes. In this manner, the switch can be used at maximum capacity without discarding any frames.

As discussed earlier, the high-water mark should be set such that there is still sufficient buffering available above the mark to accommodate the additional traffic that may still be in the pipeline. This is a function of the data rate, media type, and length of the link. Similarly, to ensure that buffer starvation does not occur, there should be sufficient room below the low-water mark that incoming frames can arrive before the queue is completely emptied. Buffer underflow is less of a problem than overflow, since starvation will only cause a minor performance degradation (i.e., the switch could be temporarily idle, waiting for frames to arrive) rather than incurring an end-to-end recovery as would be needed in the event of a frame discard on overflow. The room required below the low-water mark is also less predictable, since it is a function of how fast the switch can empty the queue. This depends to a great extent on the specific switch architecture—whether there are output queues at all, the speed of the switching fabric between input and output queues, and the data rate of the output port(s).

8.5.2.2 Selection of PAUSE Times

The implementor has a choice of what pause_time to specify in the PAUSE frame. This can vary depending on the flow control policy being used. In the example just given, the value is relatively unimportant; in fact, a perfectly acceptable policy could use the value 0xFFFF when crossing the high-water mark and a value of 0x0000 when crossing the low-water mark. If the resulting behavior is acceptable, these values can be used; no complex heuristic is needed. A different flow control policy (perhaps dictated by a different switch implementation) might optimize behavior by careful selection of pause times.

It is important that a link not be flow controlled indefinitely. Higher layer protocols may be depending on at least some frames being delivered across the network, and could time-out connections, break virtual circuits, and so on, in the event of an extended period of flow control. In particular, timers in the Spanning Tree Protocol state machine (see Chapter 5, *Loop Resolution*) may time-out, causing a recalculation of the spanning tree and a consequent topology change.

8.5.2.3 Dealing with Unreliable Delivery

There is no guarantee that PAUSE frames will be delivered to the link partner. They are subject to the same error characteristics of the link as any other frame (although they should not be subject to loss due to buffer unavailability in a proper implementation). The sender of PAUSE frames can either deal with this explicitly (e.g., by implementing a policy of sending PAUSE frames multiple times) or by ignoring the problem and accepting that at some very low level (i.e., the inherent frame loss rate of the link) the flow control mechanism may not always work.

In any case, the worst that would happen if a PAUSE frame were not delivered is that flow control would not be asserted and frames would be discarded. This is no worse than the situation would be if flow control were not available on the link at all. Higher layer protocols and applications must already deal with the possibility of frame loss across a LAN; while performance may degrade significantly, correctness should still be maintained, and applications should behave (relatively) normally. Assuming that the PAUSE frame was lost due to a transient error, the system should quickly revert to proper operation (including flow control) on subsequent error-free transmissions.

In the event of the loss of a PAUSE frame intended to restart the flow (i.e., with a pause_time value of 0x0000), the result would be an unnecessary delay of one pause_time before frames could be sent across the link.[19]

8.6 Flow Control Symmetry

Flow control can be deployed either symmetrically or asymmetrically. In certain network configurations, it may be desirable to allow either device at the ends of a full duplex link to throttle the transmissions of the other; in other configurations it may be desirable to allow flow control in one direction only.

8.6.1 Symmetric Flow Control

Symmetric flow control makes sense when:

- Both devices must deal with a high statistical variance of frame arrivals (i.e., short-term transient overloads around some lower average traffic level)
- Both devices have similar buffer memory constraints (i.e., neither is inherently capable of absorbing the transients better than the other)
- The traffic pattern is relatively uniform (i.e., the traffic flows are not weighted heavily in either direction
- Neither device is the source or sink of much of the traffic

[19] This is one argument against using the value 0xFFFF for the pause_time, as discussed in Section 8.5.2.2. Fortunately, the worst delay (3.3 seconds) occurs on 10 Mb/s systems, where flow control is rarely needed or used.

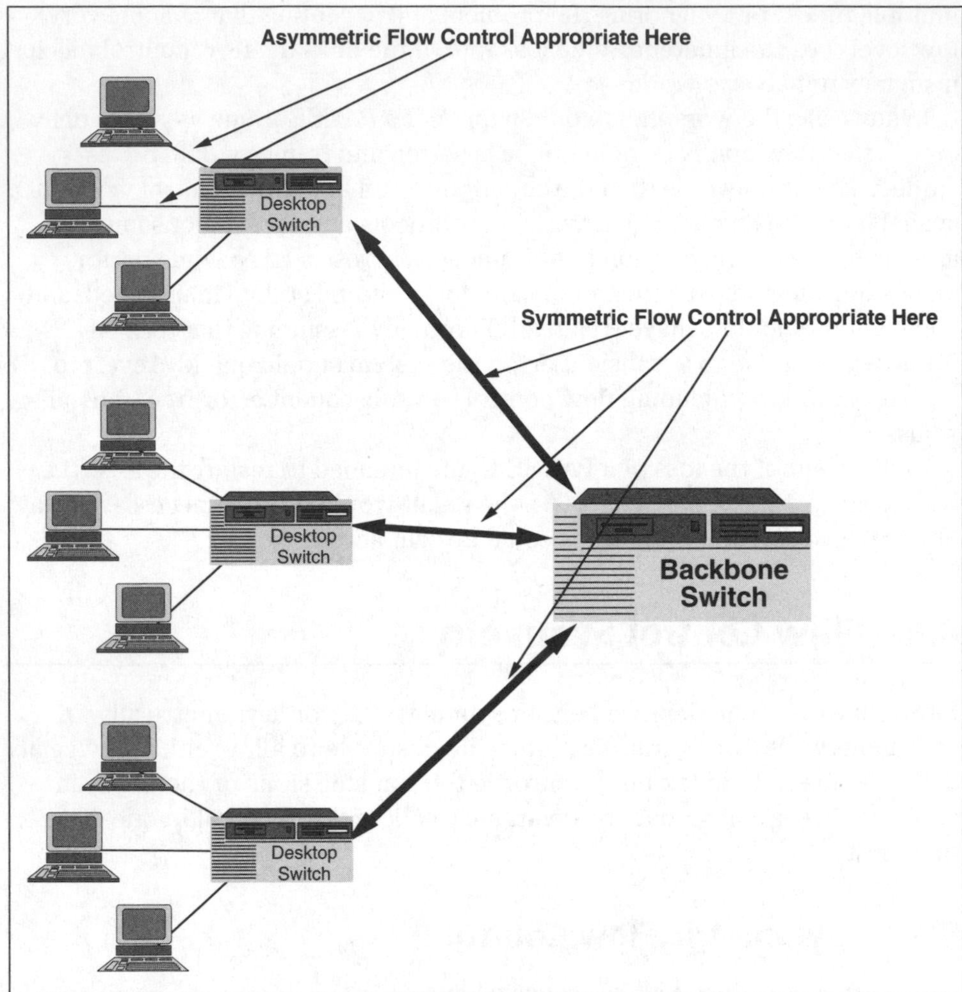

Figure 8.11 Symmetric and asymmetric flow control.

One common scenario meeting all of these conditions would be a switch-to-switch full duplex link, depicted in Figure 8.11.[20]

8.6.2 Asymmetric Flow Control

In some circumstances, it may be better to allow one of the link partners to throttle the other, but not vice-versa. The most common scenario for this would

[20] A router-to-router link would also meet all of these criteria, and would be a good candidate for symmetric flow control as well. The choice of a switch in this context is purely exemplary.

be when an end station is connected to an internetworking device (e.g., switch or router) through a dedicated full duplex link, as depicted in Figure 8.11.

There are two possible directions to the asymmetric flow control, and both have their uses:

- *The switch can throttle the station, but not vice-versa.* This is the most common application of asymmetric flow control. This allows a switch to push back directly on end stations when network congestion causes internal buffer overflow (or near-overflow). Since ultimately end stations are the source of all frames in the network, pushing back on the end stations reduces the congestion at the source. Within the end station, internal inter-layer flow controls (e.g., memory allocation mechanisms in the device drivers and operating system programming interfaces for higher layer protocols) will propagate the flow control right back to the application program where it belongs. Thus, a switch asserting flow control in this manner not only prevents its own internal buffers from overflowing, it actually reduces the total offered load to the network, effectively reducing or eliminating the true cause of the congestion.
- *The station can throttle the switch, but not vice-versa.* If the link capacity (i.e., data rate) is much greater than the ability of the attached station to process data, there is a possibility that frames will be dropped in the end station's interface controller due to link buffer overflow. This situation is unlikely in a 10 Mb/s Ethernet, but is a real concern at gigabit rates. Data may be coming in from multiple sources (especially in the case of a server) at a rate greater than the station's ability to process the data and free up link buffers. End-to-end flow control mechanisms, such as window advertisements in TCP, can prevent buffer overflow for a single data stream, but cannot necessarily prevent end station link overflow for multiple uncoordinated data streams. Asymmetric flow control allows the station to throttle the switch to prevent frame loss in this situation. In this manner, the end station is effectively borrowing buffer capacity in the switch for its own use. If the station can process data at wire speed, there is never a need for asymmetric flow control in this direction.

CHAPTER

9

Link Aggregation

A link is a link, that's *my* instinct,
And each of the links is distinct, I think.
But aggregate the links, and *blink*—
You'll see they work as one.

The frames source and sink, like any link,
But now you'll have bandwidth galore, I think.
And even with a failing link,
The load can shift around.

If statistics tell you that the network's running slow,
Use aggregated links to make the data really flow!

A link is a link, that's *my* instinct,
And each of the links is distinct, I think.
But aggregate the links, and *blink*—
You'll see they work as one!

If a LAN link between two devices supports some level of communications, then why not use two or more links and multiply the communications power? This is precisely the idea behind *link aggregation*—a method for using multiple parallel links between a pair of devices as if they were a single higher-performance channel.

Sometimes referred to as *trunking* or *bonding*, link aggregation allows us to increase the capacity and availability of the communications channel between devices (both switches and end stations) without changing or upgrading the underlying technology.[1] The concept is not particularly new; inverse multiplexers are commonly used in WANs to bond multiple slow-speed links together to form a higher-speed equivalent. Aggregation has been less commonly deployed in LANs because:

- In many cases, overall system performance is not limited by the LAN data rate.
- When the LAN data rate *is* a limiting factor, it is often less expensive to increase that data rate than to incur the complexity of aggregating multiple links.

However, there are some important situations where link aggregation makes sense, even for LANs. In this chapter we examine the benefits of aggregated links for those applications, as well as the technical issues that arise as a result of the use of aggregated links. Lastly, we look at the IEEE 802.3ad standard for vendor-interoperable link aggregation.

9.1 Link Aggregation Benefits

By taking multiple LAN connections and treating them as a unified, aggregated link, we can achieve practical benefits in many applications. In particular, aggregated links can provide:

Increased link capacity The total capacity of an aggregated link is the sum of the capacities of the individual links composing the aggregate. This is the primary reason most users deploy aggregation—to improve performance when a traditional individual link is a performance-limiting element or is overwhelmed by a sustained overload condition.

Incremental capacity increase While LAN technology offers a variety of data rates, the available options are usually separated by an order-of-magnitude improvement, for example 10 Mb/s, 100 Mb/s or 1000 Mb/s. Link aggregation can be used to fill in the gaps when an intermediate performance level is more appropriate; a factor of 10 increase may be overkill in some environments.

[1] The term *trunk* is widely used by both vendors and network administrators to refer to aggregated LAN links. However, this term can have other, conflicting meanings when used outside of an aggregation context; for example, it can also refer to any high-speed backbone link as well as a link that uses VLAN-tagged frames exclusively (see Chapter 11, *Virtual LANs: Applications and Concepts*). To avoid confusion, I use the term *aggregated link* in this chapter; this is consistent with the IEEE 802.3ad standard, as discussed in Section 9.5.

Higher link availability A properly-designed link aggregation scheme will prevent the failure of any single component link from disrupting communications between the interconnected devices. For links requiring high availability (e.g., backbone connections), this feature may be more important than the concomitant capacity increase. The aggregated link will *fail soft;* the loss of a link within an aggregation reduces the available capacity but does not disrupt communications entirely. Note that the Spanning Tree Protocol discussed in Chapter 5, *Loop Resolution,* also provides for high availability through the use of parallel links. However, unlike a spanning tree, link aggregation allows simultaneous use of all available paths. In addition, it may be possible to achieve faster switchover to the backup link(s) when using link aggregation. Since the Spanning Tree Protocol is designed for operation across a potentially complex catenet, its reconfiguration timers are set relatively long. Spanning tree recalculation can take tens of seconds or longer, with communications disrupted during this period. When properly implemented, reconfiguration of an aggregated link can often be accomplished in milliseconds.[2]

One of the benefits of using an aggregated link (as opposed to upgrading to a higher-capacity link technology) is that these improvements may be obtainable using existing hardware. A switch with 100 Mb/s-only ports can be coaxed to provide a higher effective link data rate with no equipment change. In some cases, it may not be possible to upgrade to higher native-speed links even if you want to. A bounded switch configuration may not have any facility for adding a high-speed uplink or for otherwise modifying the characteristics of its ports. A 1000 Mb/s interface may not be available for a particular model of server or router. In these cases, link aggregation may provide the only means of increasing the effective capacity without incurring a major hardware overhaul.

Of course, these benefits don't come for free:

- Additional LAN interfaces are needed at each end of the aggregation.
- Additional slots may be consumed in the devices being interconnected (e.g., server backplane slots or switch module slots).
- Additional complexity is required in the device drivers to support aggregated links.
- Controls (either manual or automatic) are needed to ensure that aggregations are properly configured and maintained.

Many network administrators have had the experience of upgrading network hardware (e.g., changing from 10 Mb/s NICs to 100 Mb/s NICs) and, in the end, seeing a performance improvement much less than the 10:1 ratio

[2] At the time of this writing, work is ongoing in IEEE 802.1 to modify the Spanning Tree Protocol to allow more rapid reconfiguration in catenets with certain topology characteristics.

implied by the hardware change (or perhaps no improvement at all!). Will an aggregated link actually provide a performance improvement commensurate with the number of links provided? This depends to a great extent on network traffic patterns and the algorithm used by the devices to distribute frames among the aggregated links. To the extent that traffic can be distributed uniformly across the links, the effective capacity will increase as desired. If the traffic and distribution algorithm is such that a few links carry the bulk of the traffic while others go nearly idle, the improvement will be less than anticipated. This is discussed in greater detail in Section 9.4.2.

9.2 Application of Link Aggregation

Figure 9.1 depicts a number of situations where link aggregation is commonly deployed. These include:

- Switch-to-switch connections
- Switch-to-station (server or router) connections
- Station-to-station connections

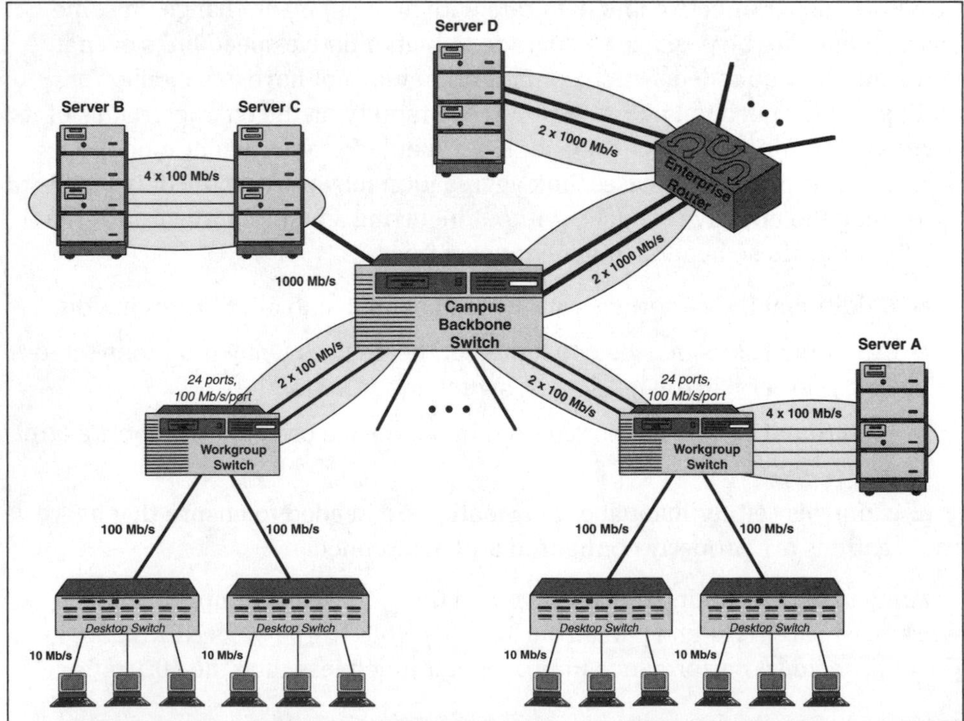

Figure 9.1 Aggregated links.

9.2.1 Switch-to-Switch Connections

In Figure 9.1, the capacity of each of the workgroup-to-campus switch connections has been increased by aggregating together two 100 Mb/s links, effectively creating a 200 Mb/s channel. Network availability has been increased as well; the failure of either of the physical links comprising the aggregate will not sever communications to the backbone. The capacity of the channel may be reduced in this case, but connectivity is not lost.

Note that the workgroup switches in this catenet are 24-port, 100 Mb/s-only devices, a common and popular configuration for bounded switches. These units have no high-speed uplink port for connecting to servers or backbone switches. By aggregating multiple links, we can create higher speed connections without a hardware upgrade. Aggregation thus implies a trade-off between port usage and additional capacity for a given device pair; link aggregation reduces the number of ports available for connection to other devices.

Of course, the switch itself must be designed to support link aggregation. Depending on the internal architecture (both hardware and software), a given switch may not be able to aggregate its links; this is a consideration that must be taken into account during the design of the switch (from the manufacturer's perspective) and in the purchasing decision process (from the user's perspective). Most modern switch designs support aggregation, especially if the device only supports a single link data rate.

9.2.2 Switch-to-Station (Server or Router) Connections

In Figure 9.1, server A is shown connected to a switch using four 100 Mb/s links. Most server platforms today can saturate a single 100 Mb/s link for many applications. Thus, link capacity becomes the limiting factor for overall system performance. In this application, we are using link aggregation to improve performance for the link-constrained station. By aggregating multiple links, we can achieve better performance without requiring a hardware upgrade to either the server or the switch. Aggregation on the server side can generally be achieved through software changes in the device driver for the LAN interface(s).

As stated earlier, link aggregation trades off port usage for effective link capacity. While it is common for high port-density switches to have some number of excess ports, it is rare for a server to have unused network interface cards (NICs). In addition, traditional single-port NICs use a server backplane slot for each interface; often a server configuration will have only a limited number of slots available for network peripherals. In response to this problem, a number of manufacturers offer multiport NICs specifically for use in servers. A typical product is depicted in Figure 9.2.

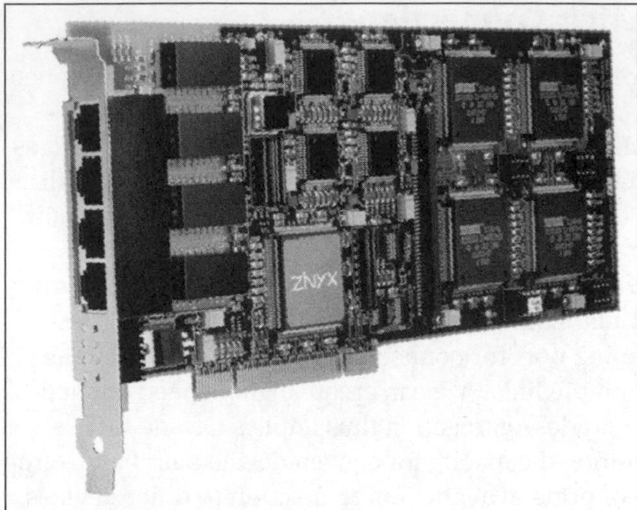

Figure 9.2 Multiport NIC.
Courtesy Znyx Corp.

The device driver supplied with the NIC will generally support either link aggregation among multiple ports or individual use of each NIC port (to allow a server to connect to multiple subnetworks in a non-aggregated manner).

Figure 9.1 also depicts multiple 1000 Mb/s links being aggregated between the campus switch and a high-performance enterprise backbone router. From the perspective of the switch, a Network layer router is simply an end station—not really different from a server.[3] As such, we can aggregate links between a switch and a router for the same reasons as in the switch-to-server case. One important difference arises regarding the choice of algorithm used to distribute frames among the links; this is discussed in Section 9.4.2.

In theory, links could also be aggregated between a switch and an end-user workstation; from a networking perspective this is the same as a connection between a switch and a server. However, such aggregations are rarely, if ever, used, because:

- Workstation performance is generally not link-limited.
- Network availability is less of a concern for an individual user connection (as opposed to a server or backbone link).
- A separate cable is needed from the user's workplace to the wiring closet for each physical link comprising the aggregate. Most buildings provide wiring capacity for typical network and telephone uses, but do not furnish each work location with lots of extra, unused wiring pairs that can be used for aggregated links. If higher speed access is required

[3] In a sense, a router can be considered a station providing Network layer routing services.

for a given user, it is probably less expensive to upgrade the LAN hardware than to pull additional wires.

9.2.3 Station-to-Station Connections

It is also possible to use aggregation directly between a pair of end stations, with no switches involved at all. Figure 9.1 depicts two servers (servers B and C) interconnected by an aggregation of four 100 Mb/s links. This high-speed connection may be useful for multiprocessing or server redundancy applications where high performance is needed to maintain real-time server coherence.[4]

As in the station-to-switch case, the higher performance channel is created without having to upgrade to higher-speed LAN hardware. In some cases, higher-speed NICs may not even be available for a particular server platform, making link aggregation the only practical choice for improved performance.

9.3 Aggregate or Upgrade?

Sometimes a network administrator has the choice either to upgrade the native link capacity or to use an aggregate of multiple lower-speed links. A typical case might be a network server with 100 Mb/s Ethernet capability; either the server (and the switch to which it is connected) can be upgraded to a 1000 Mb/s link, or multiple 100 Mb/s links can be aggregated.

Native link speed upgrades typically imply a factor of 10 capacity increase. In many cases, the device cannot take advantage of this much additional capacity. A 10:1 performance improvement will not be realized; all that happens is that the bottleneck is moved from the network link to some other element within the device. This is not necessarily a bad thing; it is just important to recognize that performance will always be limited by the weakest link in the end-to-end chain.

Depending on the point in the product maturity curve, link aggregation may be less expensive than a native speed upgrade and yet achieve the same performance level for the user. Consider a server with a computing performance ceiling commensurate with a network capacity of 400 Mb/s, based on processor, operating system, and application limitations. Since this device cannot process network-intensive applications faster than 400 Mb/s, there is no performance benefit to be gained by an upgrade to 1000 Mb/s compared with using a set of four aggregated 100 Mb/s links.

If the hardware cost of the 1000 Mb/s NIC and switch ports is less than 4 times that of the lower speed (100 Mb/s) connections, then it makes sense to upgrade to the higher speed, even if the server cannot immediately take full

[4] This configuration is sometimes called a *back-end network*.

advantage of the capacity provided. That is, if bandwidth is cheap, it doesn't hurt to have lots of idle excess capacity.[5] However, early in the product life-cycle of the higher-speed hardware, the reverse may be true. It may be less expensive to use four lower speed links if the lower speed hardware is mature and has achieved commodity pricing levels. This approach is especially attractive if NICs are available with multiple interfaces for a single backplane slot (i.e., a Quad or Octal NIC).

While the preceding discussion used an example of an upgrade from 100 Mb/s (the most common data rate for server LAN interfaces at the time of this writing), the same argument holds for upgrades from 1000 Mb/s or higher speeds. There is always a window in time when aggregated links are less expensive than a speed upgrade and will achieve equivalent user performance. In addition, if a system needs (and can take advantage of) link capacity beyond the highest data rate available, aggregation may provide the only means to improve performance while waiting for new technology to develop.[6]

9.4 Issues in Link Aggregation

Compared to some of the other advanced switch features discussed in this book (e.g., VLANs, Multicast Pruning, and Priority Operation), link aggregation is fairly straightforward. However, there are a few issues that we need to examine to fully understand the workings and limitations of aggregated links, including:

- Address assignment
- Transmission and distribution of frames across the links in an aggregation
- Constraints on the technologies employed in an aggregation
- Configuration management

9.4.1 Addressing

In a traditional, non-aggregated context, each network interface controller (NIC) has associated with it a globally-unique 48-bit MAC address. This address is used for two purposes:

1. As the unicast address for received frames (i.e., Destination Address comparison).
2. As the Source Address in transmitted frames.

[5] With respect to delay, this approach provides a distinct advantage.

[6] At the time of this writing, Gigabit Ethernet is the fastest commercially-available LAN technology. Many switches support aggregation of multiple Gigabit Ethernet links to achieve even greater performance while higher speed technology (e.g., 10 Gigabit Ethernet) is being developed.

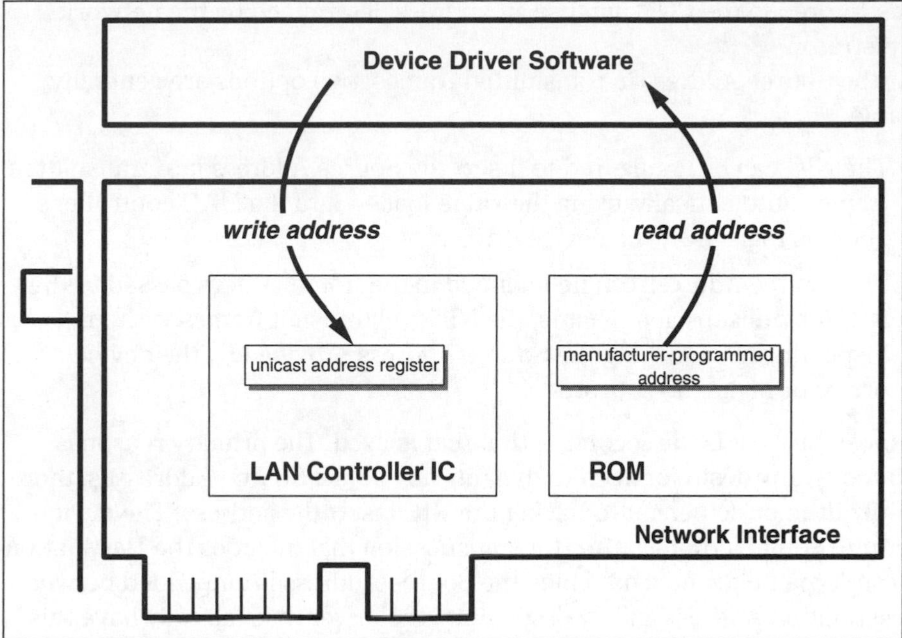

Figure 9.3 Configuring a traditional NIC address.

Figure 9.3 depicts the model of how this unique address is configured and used in a typical NIC application. The NIC includes both a MAC controller (either a discrete integrated circuit or a function embedded into a larger, system-level component) and a ROM containing the unique address. The ROM is programmed ("burned") with the address at the time the NIC is built; the manufacturer is responsible for ensuring address uniqueness.[7]

Upon initialization, the device driver normally reads the contents of the ROM and transfers the value to a register within the MAC controller. It is the value in that register that is actually used for comparison against unicast Destination Addresses during frame reception. That is, the controller itself is not pre-configured during manufacture with the unique 48-bit address; the device driver software loads this address into the controller at initialization time. The address loaded may be the same as the one read from the ROM, or it may be different, depending on the application. For example, the DECnet Phase IV protocol suite requires that the MAC address be configured in a manner compatible with the Network layer address; DECnet devices regularly ignore the

[7] While early NICs often used a discrete ROM dedicated to storing the address, many products today store the address in a larger memory that may contain diagnostic code, a bootstrap loader, and other software.

address stored in the ROM and use an address determined by the network administrator.[8]

For the Source Address in transmitted frames, two options are generally available:

1. The NIC can be configured to insert the Source Address into transmitted frames automatically, using the value loaded into the MAC controller's address register by the device driver.
2. The Source Address can be included in the frame buffers passed to the NIC for transmission. That is, the NIC will transmit frames without inspecting or modifying the Source Address provided by the device driver or higher-layer protocol.

In most cases, it is the second option that is used. The primary reason is unrelated to any desire or need to dynamically adjust Source Addresses; there is simply little or no benefit to having the NIC insert the address. The device driver must build a frame buffer for transmission that includes the Destination Address, Type field, and data. Since the Source Address is embedded between the Destination Address and the Type field, the driver must already have this field present in the buffer; it might as well put the right value there.

In an aggregation context, we want a set of aggregated links to appear to be a single link, with a single logical network interface. This is true both from the perspective of stations sending unicast frames to a device (i.e., as a destination for frames) and from the perspective of higher-layer protocols within the instant device that are sending frames to other stations (i.e., as a source of frames). That is, we want all of the network interfaces on an aggregated link to use the same address, rather than having a different address for each interface.

The NIC architecture just described easily supports this construct. For unicast Destination Address comparisons, the device driver can load the same address into the appropriate registers in the controllers of all NICs in the aggregation, as shown in Figure 9.4. The address used for the aggregation must still be guaranteed unique; the easiest way to accomplish this is to use the ROM-stored address of one of the NICs as the address for the entire aggregation. It doesn't even matter which NIC's address is used; since they are all unique, each one is unique.

For frame transmission, the task is even simpler. The device driver can disable automatic Source Address insertion in all NICs comprising an aggregation and use the common aggregation address as the Source Address by simply loading that value in the appropriate location in the transmit buffers.

[8] A device supporting both DECnet Phase IV and other protocols (e.g., IPX) may need to support multiple unicast MAC addresses in the same NIC—one for DECnet usage and one for use by the other supported protocols.

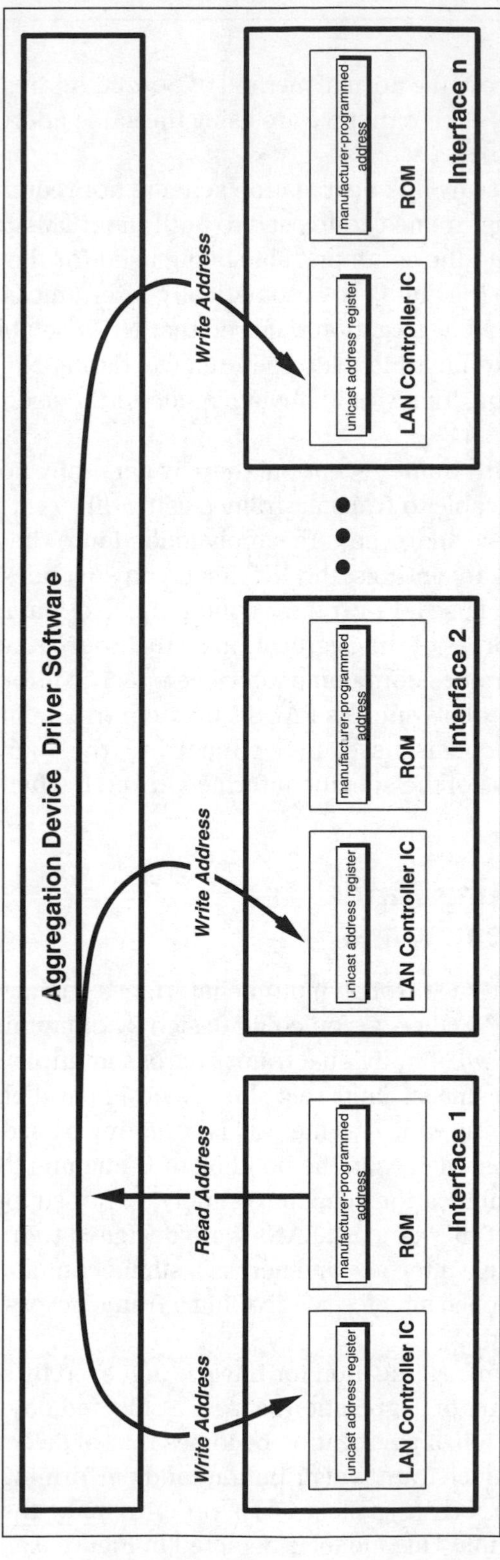

Figure 9.4 One address for all interfaces in the aggregation.

This is no different from the normal method of Source Address generation on non-aggregated links, except that we are using the same address across multiple physical interfaces.

It is important that any link aggregation scheme not require that NICs be able to receive unicast frames addressed to both the ROM-stored value for the individual NIC and the common value being used for the aggregation. Most NICs only have the ability to automatically filter unicast frames sent to a single address. If link aggregation required that NICs be able to receive unicast frames sent to multiple addresses, many existing NICs could not be used in an aggregation. This would obviate much of the usefulness of link aggregation.

Unlike the case with frame reception, there is generally no problem with requiring a NIC to be able to transmit frames using different Source Addresses. Since these addresses are simply loaded into the frame buffers by higher-layer software entities, the NIC itself can stay blissfully unaware of the actual value being used. For frames containing user data, the driver can use the common address of the aggregation as the Source Address in transmitted frames. For frames containing interface-specific information (e.g., link-constrained protocols such as PAUSE flow control and the Link Aggregation Control Protocol discussed in Section 9.5.8), the Source Address can be the unique address of the specific interface through which the frame is transmitted.

9.4.2 Distributing Traffic across an Aggregation

How do you send a frame through multiple interfaces and across multiple links simultaneously? In theory, you could design a communications channel that supported *striping* of individual frames across multiple links. Frames could be broken into smaller units (e.g., bits), sent in parallel, and reconstructed at the receiving end. This method is sometimes used when aggregating WAN technologies, such as in the bonding of B-channel ISDN lines. However, LAN communications channels simply do not support such subframe transfers; all of the standard LANs were designed to transfer complete frames through a single interface and across a single communications channel. There are no mechanisms for subdividing a frame across multiple LAN interfaces.

The result is that link aggregation for LANs is achieved by sending complete frames (the atomic unit of aggregation) across a selected physical link within the aggregation. The job of aggregation becomes that of selecting the link on which to transmit a given frame (distribution) and performing whatever tasks are necessary at the receiver (collection) in order to make the aggregation behave like a single link. This model is depicted in Figure 9.5.

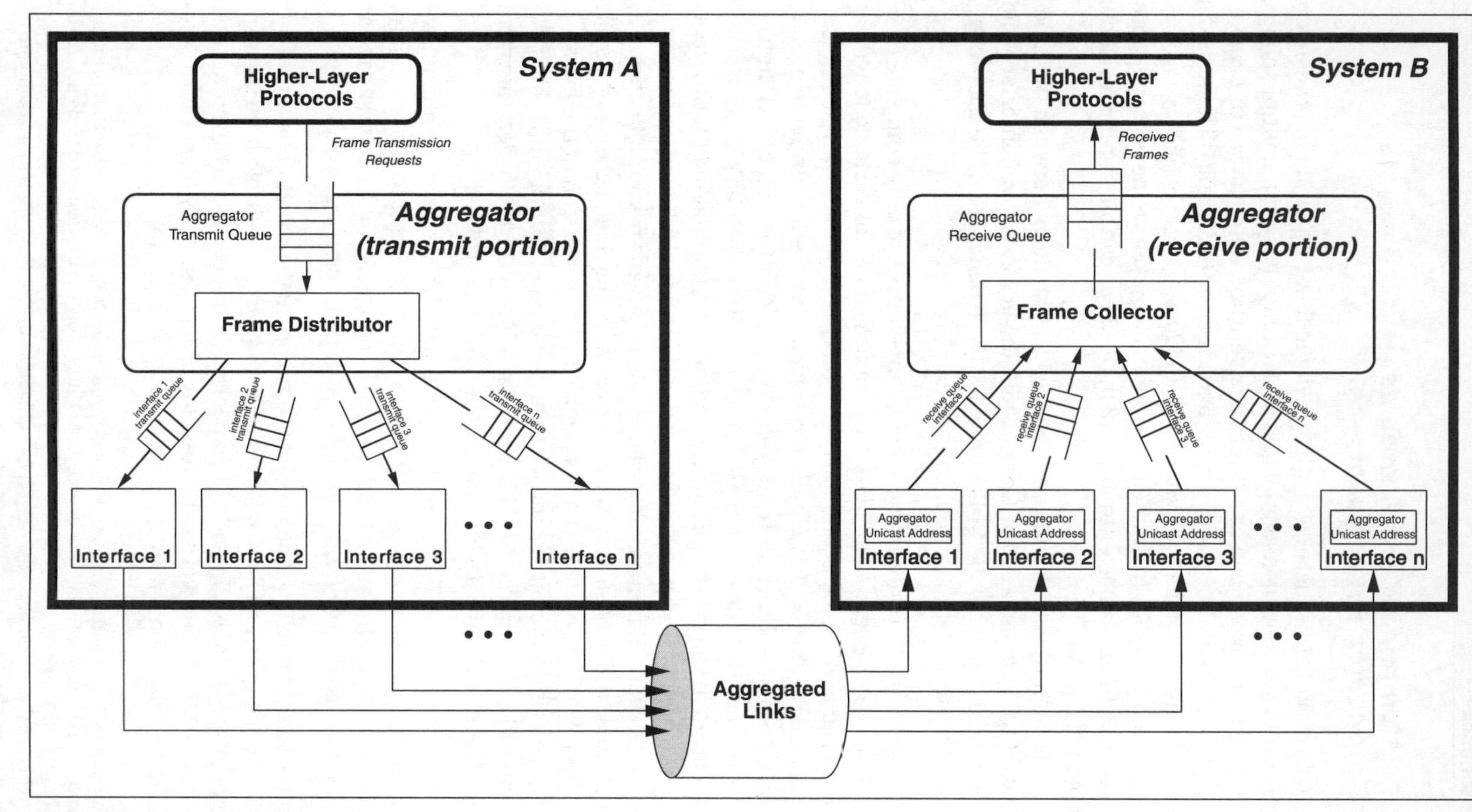

Figure 9.5 Link aggregation model.

9.4.2.1 Maintaining Link Invariants in an Aggregated Environment

The key to making this melange act like a single link is maintaining the link invariants. A traditional non-aggregated LAN cannot generate multiple copies of a single transmitted frame at a given receiver (non-duplication) or change the sequence of frames between sender and receiver (ordering). This was discussed in detail in Chapter 2, *Transparent Bridges*.

Non-duplication is fairly simple to enforce. As long as we never send more than one copy of any frame onto any link in the aggregation, duplicates should not appear at the receiver.

The ordering invariant is more of a challenge. The delay between the time the Distributor submits a frame for transmission across a given interface and the time it is delivered to the Collector can vary depending on the characteristics of the frame and the selected interface:

- Consider the situation depicted in Figure 9.6. Since only complete frames can be sent on any link, and frames can be of variable length, a long frame (e.g., a maximum length Ethernet frame with a 1,500-byte payload) sent on link A could be received *after* a short frame (e.g., a 64-byte minimum Ethernet frame) started at a later time on link B. In fact, more than 18 minimum length frames can be sent on link B (and received at the other end) before the single maximum-length Ethernet frame on link A is completely received. When multiple links are used in an aggregation, frames can arrive at the receiver's frame Collector in a different order from that in which they were queued at the sender's Distributor. We surely don't want to delay the transmission of the later frames while waiting for the first one to be received (or equivalently, withhold delivery) at the Collector just to preserve the order; this would negate most of the performance benefit of aggregation!
- The use of PAUSE flow control could temporarily suspend communications on a single link in the aggregation, unbeknownst to the Distributor.[9] Frames submitted at a later time on less-congested links could arrive at the receiver before frames queued for transmission on a paused link.

It appears that it will not be possible to replicate the exact behavior of a traditional, non-aggregated link. When distributed across multiple interfaces in an aggregation, frames can and will appear at the receiver in a different order from that in which they were submitted for transmission by higher-layer protocols and applications. What's a network architect to do?

[9] The full duplex flow control function (Chapter 8, *LAN and Switch Flow Control*), if present, lies architecturally below that of link aggregation. Unless specifically designed to do so, the Distributor and Collector may not be able to control PAUSE operation or even to determine if it is being invoked by some other entity. See Chapter 15, *Make the Switch!*, for a more complete discussion of integrated switch architecture.

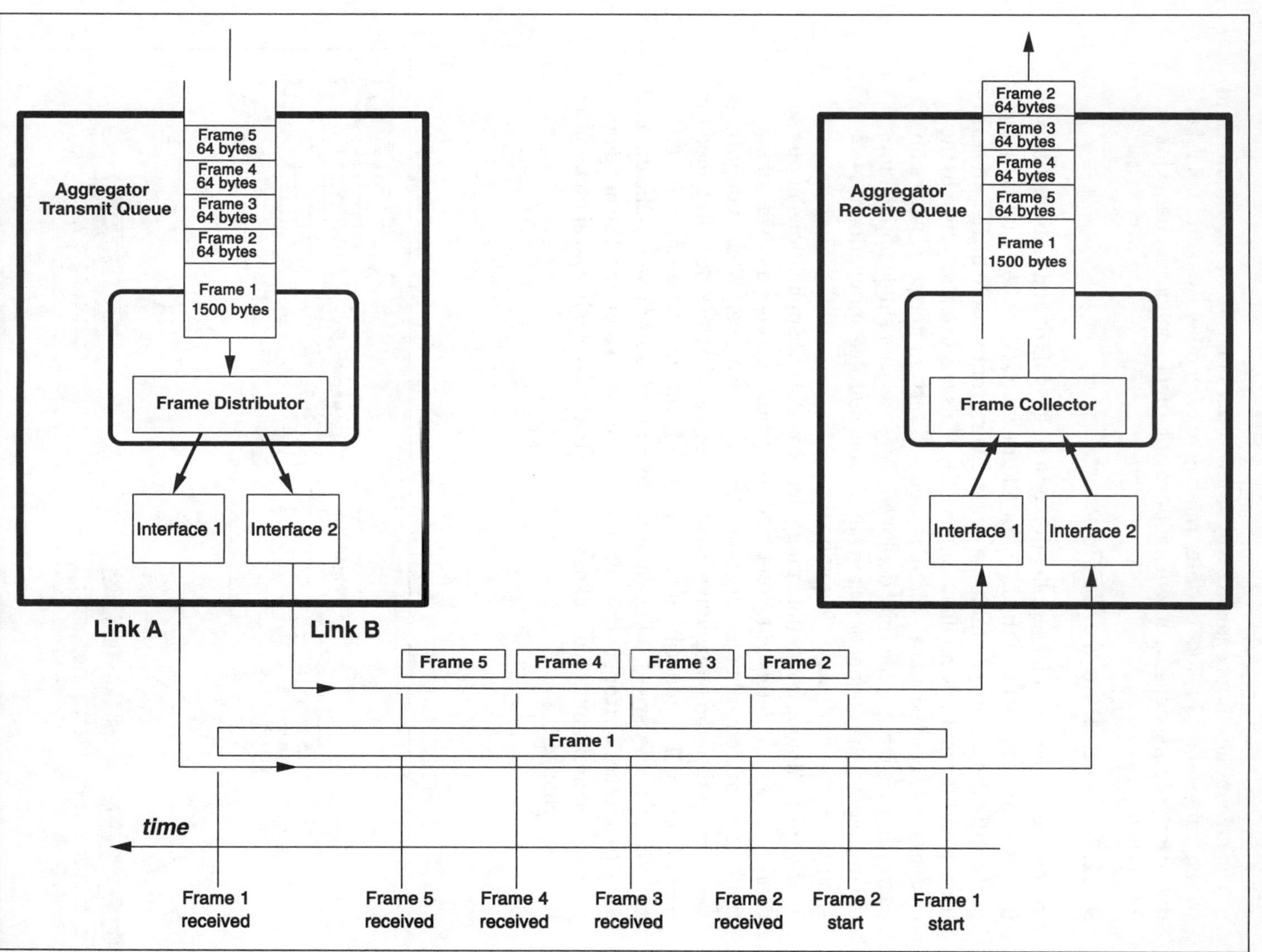

Figure 9.6 Frame mis-ordering.

The answer lies in recognizing why frame order needs to be maintained and which frames must be kept in order relative to each other. We can then relax the strict ordering constraint when it does not affect application behavior.

9.4.2.2 Separating Traffic Flows

In general, it is not a single application or a single pair of end stations that uses the entire capacity of the LAN for all time; the LAN is being used to support traffic flows between multiple station pairs, for multiple higher-layer protocols, and for multiple application benefits. This is particularly true in the case of LANs connected to switch, router, and server interfaces, where link aggregation is most commonly deployed. These are not single-application environments; the connections are supporting multiple application flows simultaneously, as depicted in Figure 9.7.

The traffic among communicating peer protocols or applications in one set of stations is completely independent of the traffic among other sets of stations, or even from other applications among the same set. What is important from the application perspective is that the order of frames be maintained for a given protocol or application among a set of communicating stations. It is not strictly necessary to maintain the order of frames from one application relative to another or from one set of stations relative to another. The applications and stations involved will never know that some higher-level meta-order has been changed.

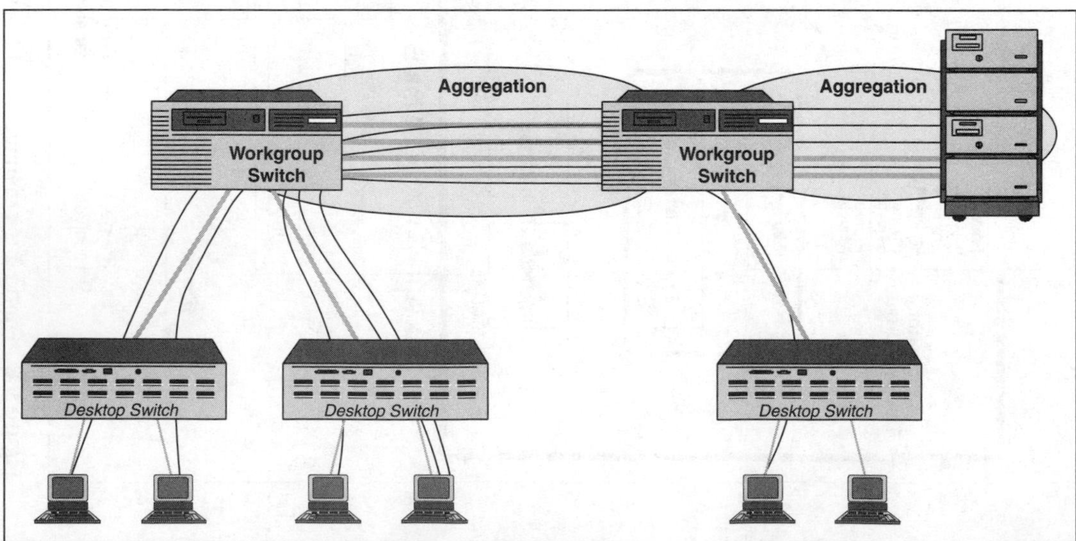

Figure 9.7 Multiple application flows through an aggregation.

In an aggregation context, we define a *conversation* as a set of traffic among which ordering must be maintained.[10] The Distributor's job then becomes obvious—all frames belonging to a given conversation must be transmitted across the same link within the aggregation. This will ensure proper ordering of frames for each conversation at the receiver. Different conversations can be assigned to different physical links, thus allowing the aggregation to carry traffic on all of its links simultaneously without creating an ordering problem for higher-layer protocols or applications. Of course, multiple conversations can (and generally, will) share the same physical link; there is no need to provide a physical interface for each anticipated conversation.[11]

By assigning any given conversation to a single physical link, we also simplify the job of the Collector at the receiving end. There is never a need to buffer or restore the proper frame order for frames arriving on any of the individual links. Frames arriving on any interface are simply delivered to the higher layer client(s) in the order received. Frames arriving on separate interfaces can be interspersed among each other in any convenient manner; no particular ordering relationship must be maintained among frames arriving on different interfaces since, through the action of the Distributor, they belong to separate conversations. (See Figure 9.8.)

Consider the alternative: If frames from a given conversation were distributed across multiple physical links in an aggregation, they could arrive at the receiver in the wrong order. Sequence information would need to be included with each frame so the Collector could restore the proper order before delivering frames to the client. By constraining the Distributor to assign a conversation to a single physical link, we avoid any need to add sequence numbers or to modify the frame format in any way.

An ideal aggregation system will distribute traffic as evenly as possible among the physical links comprising the aggregation. This behavior provides the maximum benefit from the aggregated capacity. The ability of the Distributor to achieve such uniformity is primarily a function of the distribution of the offered load among the active conversations. If a single conversation constitutes the bulk of the traffic, little benefit can be gained through aggregation, since that conversation's traffic must all pass across the same physical link.

9.4.2.3 Conversation Determination Aids the Realization of Aggregation

This brings us to the real question: What constitutes a conversation? How does a switch or end station participating in an aggregation decide which

[10] In other contexts, this concept is sometimes called a *flow*. However, *flow* is often used in both a looser as well as a much more restrictive sense (e.g., traffic passing between a specific pair of IP stations and TCP ports); hence the more specific term *conversation* is used here.

[11] In a non-aggregated context, all conversations are, by necessity, assigned to the one-and-only physical link available.

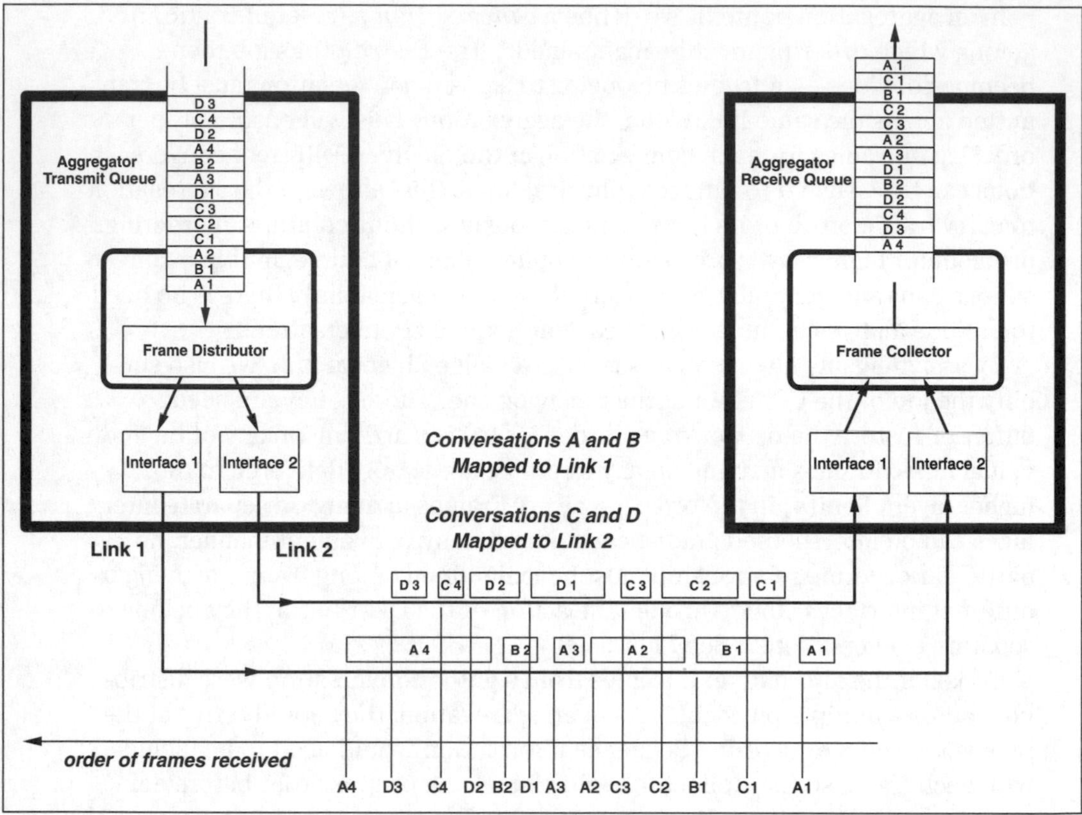

Figure 9.8 Conversations on an aggregation.

frames belong to a given conversation, and thus on which physical link those frames should be transmitted? The algorithm for assigning frames to a conversation depends on the application environment and the nature of the devices at each end of the link.

For example, in a switch-to-switch aggregation (as depicted in Figure 9.1 on page 358), a conversation may constitute the set of all frames with the same MAC Destination Address. This is a simple and effective distribution function in this environment; assuming that the switch is forwarding frames destined for a wide range of end stations, frames will be distributed relatively evenly across the set of aggregated links. However, if the aggregation is between a switch and a server (e.g., server A in Figure 9.1), this algorithm doesn't work well. All frames destined for the server carry the same MAC Destination Address, and will therefore be transmitted across the same physical link, eliminating any performance benefit. A more suitable distribution function in this case might be to assign frames to a conversation based on the MAC Source Address; if multiple stations are communicating with the server, their traffic will be appropriately distributed across the multiple links.

An important observation is that we don't have to use the same distribution function in both directions on the same aggregated set of links. Different algorithms make sense if the devices at the two ends of the link are different (e.g., a switch versus an end station). In the preceding example, distribution based on MAC Source Address is appropriate from the switch to the server, but not in the other direction; all traffic emanating from the server carries the same MAC Source Address. The server can use the MAC Destination Address for its distribution function. Using these approaches, frames exchanged between a pair of communicating devices (i.e., a client with its server and vice-versa) will traverse different physical links depending on the direction of transfer. Blocks of file transfer data from a server to a client will be carried on one physical link, while acknowledgments from the client to the server will appear on another.

It is also possible to use a concatenation of parameters for the distribution function. In the present example, both the switch and the server could assign frames to conversations (and hence, to physical links) based on a combination of MAC Source and Destination Address, rather than just the Source or Destination Address alone. This approach results in a consistent and more widely applicable distribution function at the expense of greater complexity (i.e., parsing and processing two 48-bit fields rather than one).

9.4.2.4 Mapping the Distribution Function to the Physical Link

Regardless of the particular distribution function employed, some operation must be performed to determine the link within the aggregation to which a given conversation will map. Using MAC addresses as an example, we can see that for aggregations comprising links in power-of-2 quantities (e.g., 2, 4, or 8 links), an appropriate number of bits can simply be extracted from the address to determine the port mapping, as depicted in Figure 9.9. When aggregating links in other quantities (e.g., three or five links), hash functions, modulo-*n* arithmetic, or other manipulations of the address bits can be used to map frames to physical links. Similar operations can be construed when the distribution function is based on frame fields other than MAC addresses, as discussed in Section 9.4.2.6. The mapping function itself is unimportant; all that matters is that conversations are distributed across all of the available links in as uniform a manner as possible, and that the calculation is simple to perform.

9.4.2.5 Conversations above the Data Link Layer

Some important cases arise when aggregating links between devices operating at layers of the network architecture above the Data Link. Consider the aggre-

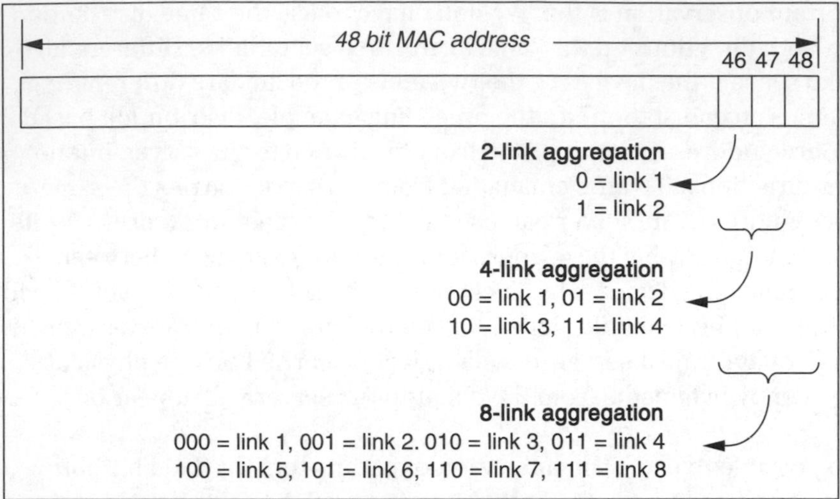

Figure 9.9 Mapping MAC addresses to physical links.

gation between server D and the enterprise router shown in Figure 9.1. The MAC Source and Destination Addresses will be the same in every frame exchanged between these two devices; any mapping of frames to conversations based on MAC addresses will not cause traffic to distribute across the aggregated links. The distribution function must use higher-layer protocol information. An appropriate function might be based on Network layer Destination Addresses (from the server to the router) or Network layer Source Addresses (from the router to the server).

The case of a station-to-station aggregation (servers B and C in Figure 9.1) is even more problematic. Not only are the MAC Source and Destination Addresses the same in all frames, but so are the Network layer Source and Destination Addresses (being those of the two servers). The frame distributor in this application needs to make its conversation mapping decisions based on information above the Network layer, for example TCP port numbers or possibly some application-specific fields.

Any device performing an aggregation (e.g., a switch, router, or server) must be capable of parsing frames to the depth and level of granularity appropriate for the distribution function being employed (e.g., MAC addresses, Network layer addresses, or higher).

9.4.2.6 Summary of Distribution Functions

Table 9.1 provides a summary of some important aggregation environments and the most common functions used to distribute frames among the aggregated links. Switches, routers, and end stations (servers) are considered both at the sending and receiving end of an aggregation; Table 9.1 lists those distribution functions that are most suitable, some that are feasible but less attractive, as well as some that are not feasible at all.[12]

9.4.2.7 Changing the Distribution

In the event of a change in the configuration (e.g., the addition or removal of a physical link from an active aggregation), the distribution mapping will generally need to change. Conversations previously assigned to a link that is no longer available will have to be reassigned to one of the links still remaining in the aggregation. Similarly, when a new link is added to an aggregation, we will want to shift some conversations to this link to take advantage of our new-found capacity. While the distribution function (e.g., that conversations are defined by Network Source Address) can remain unchanged, the mapping of a conversation to a given link (e.g., the bit selection or hash function) must change so that the function selects among all of the links (and only those links) that are physically present.

Even if there is no change to the physical connectivity, the Distributor may wish to change the mapping of conversations to physical links due to an imbalance in the offered load. The Distributor may notice that some links are heavily congested while others have excess capacity due to non-uniformity in the traffic patterns. It is perfectly reasonable for the Distributor to move some conversations from a congested link to an uncongested link to improve overall performance.[13]

Special care must be taken when transferring a conversation from one physical link to another so that the link invariants are maintained for the conversation. Clearly, the Distributor must not send any frames on both the original link and the newly-mapped link, to avoid duplication. Maintaining proper frame order is trickier:

- If we want to transfer a conversation from one active link to another active link (e.g., because a new link has become available), there may still be frames from that conversation in the transmit queue of the

[12] In addition to the parameters discussed in the text and shown in Table 9.1, frame distribution could also be based on VLAN association, as discussed in Chapter 11. For frames carrying VLAN tags, the VLAN identifier may be used to map the frame to one of the links in the aggregation. If VLAN tags are not present, the frame must be parsed more deeply to determine both the VLAN association and the conversation assignment; however, the same set of rules and mapping can be used for both purposes since, by definition, a conversation cannot cross VLAN boundaries.

[13] If this sort of *intelligent load balancing* is employed, care should be taken to avoid thrashing of the load. Conversation transfers can simply cause the congestion to shift to a different link, which may trigger additional conversation transfers; some residual level of imbalance must be tolerated or the distribution mapping will never converge to a stable state. Load shifts should only be performed when the imbalance exceeds an unacceptable level for some period of time. Hysteresis should be applied both in time and to the level of imbalance to avoid instability.

Table 9.1 Distribution Functions

SENDING DEVICE (DISTRIBUTOR)		RECEIVING DEVICE (COLLECTOR): SWITCH	ROUTER	END STATION
SWITCH	*Most suitable:*	MAC SA, DA, or SA/DA	Network SA, DA, or SA/DA	Network SA
SWITCH	*Possible to use:*		MAC SA, SA/DA[1,2]	MAC SA, SA/DA[2,3] Network SA/DA[2]
SWITCH	*Not feasible:*		MAC DA[4]	MAC DA or Network DA[5]
ROUTER	*Most suitable:*	Network SA, DA, or SA/DA	Network SA, DA, or SA/DA	Network SA
ROUTER	*Possible to use:*	MAC DA, SA/DA[1,2]		Network SA/DA[2]
ROUTER	*Not feasible:*	MAC SA[4]	MAC SA, DA, or SA/DA[4]	MAC SA, DA, or SA/DA Network DA[4,5]

SENDING DEVICE (DISTRIBUTOR)				
	END STATION	*Most suitable:* Network DA	*Most suitable:* Network DA	*Most suitable:* Higher-layer information (e.g., TCP port number)
		Possible to use: MAC DA, SA/DA[2,3] *Not feasible:* MAC SA or Network SA[5]	*Possible to use:* Network SA/DA[2] *Not feasible:* MAC SA, DA, or SA/DA[4] Network SA[5]	*Not feasible:* MAC SA/DA, or SA/DA[5] Network SA, DA, or SA/DA[5]

[1] Does not provide any benefit for router-to-router traffic passing through the switch-to-router aggregation.
[2] No benefit to using the concatenated SA/DA over a single address.
[3] Does not provide any benefit for router-to-station or station-to-router traffic passing through a switch-to-station aggregation.
[4] All traffic destined for a router or end station interface will have the same MAC Destination Address. All traffic emanating from a router or end station interface will have the same MAC Source Address.
[5] All traffic destined for an end station interface will have the same MAC and Network Destination Address. All traffic emanating from an end station interface will have the same MAC and Network Source Address.

originally-mapped interface, in transit across the link, or in a receive queue at the Collector side of the link. The Distributor must not send any frames belonging to this conversation onto the newly-mapped link until it is sure that all of the frames-in-process from the original link have been delivered to the higher-layer client protocol or application. A premature transfer could result in frame mis-ordering as seen by the aggregation client at the receiver.

- If we are transferring a conversation because the originally-mapped link is no longer in service (e.g., the link has failed or been configured out of the aggregation), we don't have to worry about any frames in the transmit queue or in transit on the link; if the link is out of service, they surely won't be delivered to the Collector. However, we still need to be concerned with frames that have been received but not yet delivered to the client. The Distributor must make sure these frames have been delivered before transmitting additional frames from this conversation onto the newly-mapped link.

There are two approaches to the problem of maintaining frame order during conversation transfer:

1. *Wait for a period of time longer than the worst-case delay for frame delivery across the link.* This is the simplest approach, and it works well, but it incurs two problems. First, the Distributor must have some idea of what value to use for the time delay. This is primarily a function of the device at the receiving end of the link (i.e., the size of its receive queues; whether it is a switch, router, or server; its processing performance, and so on). Either the Distributor must be manually configured with an appropriate time-out value, or network management must be able to interrogate the receiving device to determine the proper value.[14] Second, there will be a hiccup in throughput for conversations being transferred while waiting out the delay time. If conversations are not frequently moved, this effect will not be significant. Link configuration is usually not undergoing constant change, nor do links fail frequently (at least we hope not!). Thus, the occasional loss of performance due to the waiting time is not usually significant.

Seifert's Law of Networking #10
The solution usually creates another problem.

2. *Use an explicit protocol to determine exactly when frames can be sent on the newly-mapped link.* If a Distributor knows that it wants to trans-

[14] Typical values will range from milliseconds for high-performance servers to as long as a few seconds for some internetworking devices (switches and routers).

fer a conversation (or group of conversations) from one active link to a different active link, it can insert a special *Marker message* behind the last frame being sent from that conversation (or group of conversations) on the originally-mapped link. The Collector, upon seeing this Marker message, can send a response message back to the Distributor, as shown in Figure 9.10. When the Distributor receives the *Marker Response*, it knows that all of the frames from the conversation(s) in question have been properly delivered, and it can immediately begin sending frames associated with the conversation(s) onto the new link without further delay. This procedure can accelerate the conversation transfer time, which may be useful when the devices involved have highly-variable processing delays (i.e., the typical delay may be much shorter than the worst-case timeout value) and want to get the maximum performance benefit by shifting load as necessary. An aggregation between high-performance routers can fall into this category.

Of course, the Distributor and the Collector must cooperate for this method to work; the protocol must be designed into the link aggregation scheme itself. Also, this method will not work for a conversation being transferred due to a failed link; once a link fails, there is no path on which to send the Marker message. In this case, the Distributor must revert to the good-old-timeout strategy. The IEEE Link Aggregation standard (see Section 9.5) supports both an explicit marker exchange protocol and the timeout method of maintaining proper frame order during a conversation transfer.

The failure of a link can cause not only mis-ordered frames but frame loss as well. Any frames in the transmit queue or in transit across the link at the time of the failure may not be received at the other side. However, this poses less of an architectural problem than frame ordering. Higher layer protocols and applications must already account for occasional frame loss, since LANs generally provide only connectionless, best-effort delivery service. Link failure should occur infrequently enough so that these higher-layer recovery mechanisms are adequate.

9.4.3 Performance

An aggregation increases the overall capacity of the communication channel between the devices it connects. However, any given conversation is restricted to using only one of the aggregated links. Thus, while the total capacity of the channel will be equal to the sum of the capacities of the individual links, the maximum throughput for any given application will be limited to the capacity of the single link to which its conversation is assigned. To the extent that multiple applications map to the same conversation (e.g., a conversation may comprise all of the traffic between a pair of stations), and that mul-

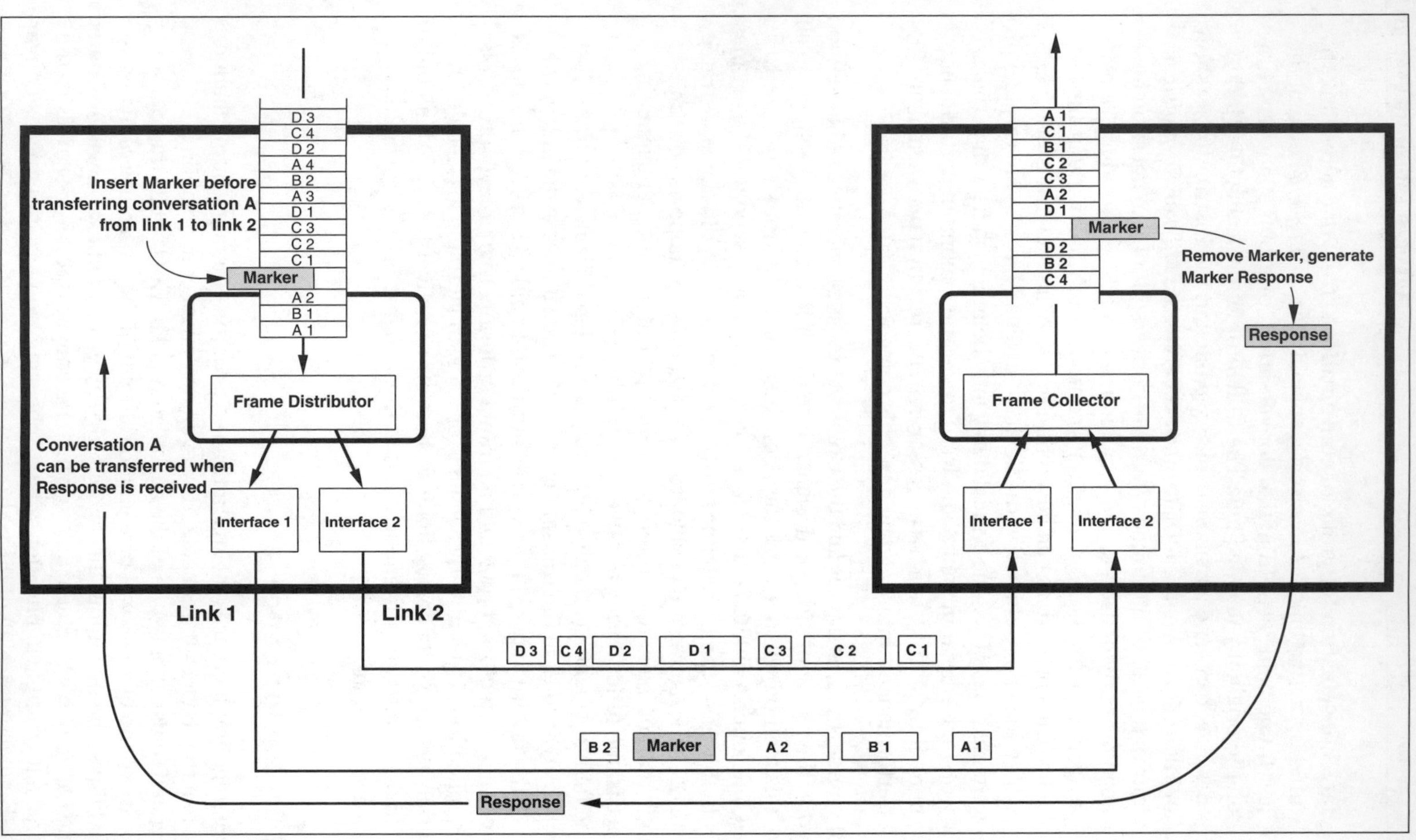

Figure 9.10 Marker and Marker Response.

tiple conversations map to the same physical link, the maximum throughput for an application will be further limited.

For example, if we change the connection between a server and a switch from a single 100 Mb/s Ethernet to an aggregation of four 100 Mb/s links, the server will have a total of 400 Mb/s of LAN capacity for use by the applications it supports. However, the throughput for a file transfer from that server to a client will be limited to 100 Mb/s maximum, regardless of whether any other applications are using the remaining 300 Mb/s of available capacity.

9.4.4 Technology Constraints (a.k.a. Link Aggravation)

Sometimes, you can ask for too much of a good thing.[15] A given switch may have a large number of ports, including both Token Ring and Ethernet technologies. Even within a given technology, there may be ports capable of 10 Mb/s operation and others capable of 100 Mb/s operation. While in theory it may be possible to provide a transparent aggregation comprising such dissimilar links, in practice any benefit gained is generally not worth the cost and complexity required to achieve these ends.

9.4.4.1 Mixing LAN Technologies in a Single Aggregation

The mind boggles at the thought of aggregating Token Rings or FDDIs with Ethernets. Such a configuration would require that frames be exchanged between aggregated link partners using two different frame formats, necessitating at least one set of translations.

Fortunately, there is no real demand for this type of aggregation. In practice, the user environments in which Token Ring is used tend to be separate from those where Ethernet predominates. While an organization may have some departments that use Token Ring and others that use Ethernet, it is virtually unheard-of to have a truly disparate technology mix within a department. As such, a switch supporting multiple technologies generally does so in order to bridge the gap between them (pun intended), as discussed in Chapter 3, *Bridging between Technologies.*

9.4.4.2 Mixing Data Rates in a Single Aggregation

Even if we restrict an aggregation to a single LAN technology, we still have the possibility of multiple data rates. Ethernet is supported at 10, 100, and

[15] This is especially true if someone else is paying for it.

1000 Mb/s,[16] and Token Ring at 4, 16, and 100 Mb/s. Can we aggregate a set of Ethernet or Token Ring ports operating at different data rates?

The problem is that, with conversations restricted to a single link, performance will vary from application to application depending on which applications are assigned to the faster or slower links. An allocation scheme could be devised such that high priority, traffic-intensive, or delay-intensive applications get mapped to the higher-speed links, but this presumes that there is a priori knowledge of the relative importance or performance requirements of the applications. Note that this knowledge would be needed not only in the stations that are actually running the applications in question, but in any intermediate switches that have implemented a mixed-speed aggregation through which these application conversations pass. As a result of this added complexity, neither the IEEE standard nor any commercial products support mixed-speed aggregations.

One possible reason for grouping a set of links with different data rates is to have the slower one(s) serve as a backup in the event of the failure of the faster one(s). However, we can achieve this end without aggregating the links; the Spanning Tree Protocol supports slower speed, hot-standby backup links, and will enable them if and when needed. Granted, the capacity of the backup links cannot be used in a spanning tree environment, but there is really little gain to be had; the slower links can typically carry only an order-of-magnitude less traffic.

9.4.4.3 Aggregation and Shared LANs

If the purpose of link aggregation is to increase capacity and availability, a more logical first step is to upgrade a shared-bandwidth LAN to one using switches with dedicated full duplex links. Once full duplex links are employed, aggregation becomes much simpler; the devices involved don't need to consider and account for link traffic from any stations other than themselves, and there is no problem with variable latency across a link due to MAC access delay.

9.4.5 Configuration Control

Much of the technical discussion up to this point has dealt with the principles underlying link aggregation in order to understand why we implement link aggregation the way we do. The actual operation of an aggregated link, once properly configured, is relatively straightforward and intuitive. The most difficult challenge is usually to ensure that the link configurations are such that aggregation can be deployed, and to detect and react to changes in the configuration that affect the aggregation.

To even consider creating an aggregation, a device must have multiple physical links that all use the same MAC technology and data rate. While a device

[16] Ethernet at 10,000 Mb/s is under development at the time of this writing.

will generally know the MAC technology of a given interface (the device driver must be aware of the nature of the interface in order to properly handle frames both for transmission and reception), the data rate and duplex nature of the link may change over time. Many Ethernet interfaces perform an Auto-Negotiation procedure upon initialization; the data rate and duplexity of the link will change depending on the capabilities and management configuration of the device to which it is attached. Thus, a given set of links may be aggregatable at one point in time (e.g., by having the same data rate) but not at another. The aggregation entity within each device must be made aware of both the static and dynamic interface characteristics in order to determine the aggregatability of its links.

Armed with the knowledge of which links in a system can potentially be aggregated, we must next ensure that a given set of links interconnects the same pair of devices before using the links as an aggregation. Figure 9.11 depicts a campus backbone switch with a large number of ports, and indicates which ones can be aggregated and which cannot. Only those links that meet the technology criteria *and* terminate in the same pair of devices are aggregatable.

If the topology and constitution of the network never changed, we could be finished with configuration control for aggregation once and for all. Fortunately for the continued employment of network administrators everywhere, networks are dynamic. Physical links can be added, be removed, fail, or have their termination points changed over time. Network devices (e.g., switches and stations) are often added, removed, and upgraded as well. Within a device, individual interfaces may be enabled or disabled for various reasons, or changed to meet the needs of the users. Any of these modifications can affect the ability of a set of links to be aggregated.

A device performing aggregation must:

- *Be aware of any changes that affect a link's ability to participate in an aggregation.* In particular, the device must know whether each of its links is enabled or disabled, its data rate and duplexity, and the status of the device at the other end of the link (which must cooperate for the aggregation to work).

- *Redistribute conversations when a new link is added or removed from an active aggregation.* Aggregation is only effective if conversations are distributed uniformly across the set of available links. When the number of links in an aggregation changes, the conversation-to-link mapping must generally change to accommodate the new configuration. The aggregating device must further implement an appropriate mechanism (either timeout or explicit marker exchange) to ensure that frame order is maintained when redistributing conversations, as discussed in Section 9.4.2.7.

In extremely simple environments comprising a limited number of aggregation-capable devices and a very stable topology, manual configuration controls may be acceptable. However, manual controls cannot adapt to changes

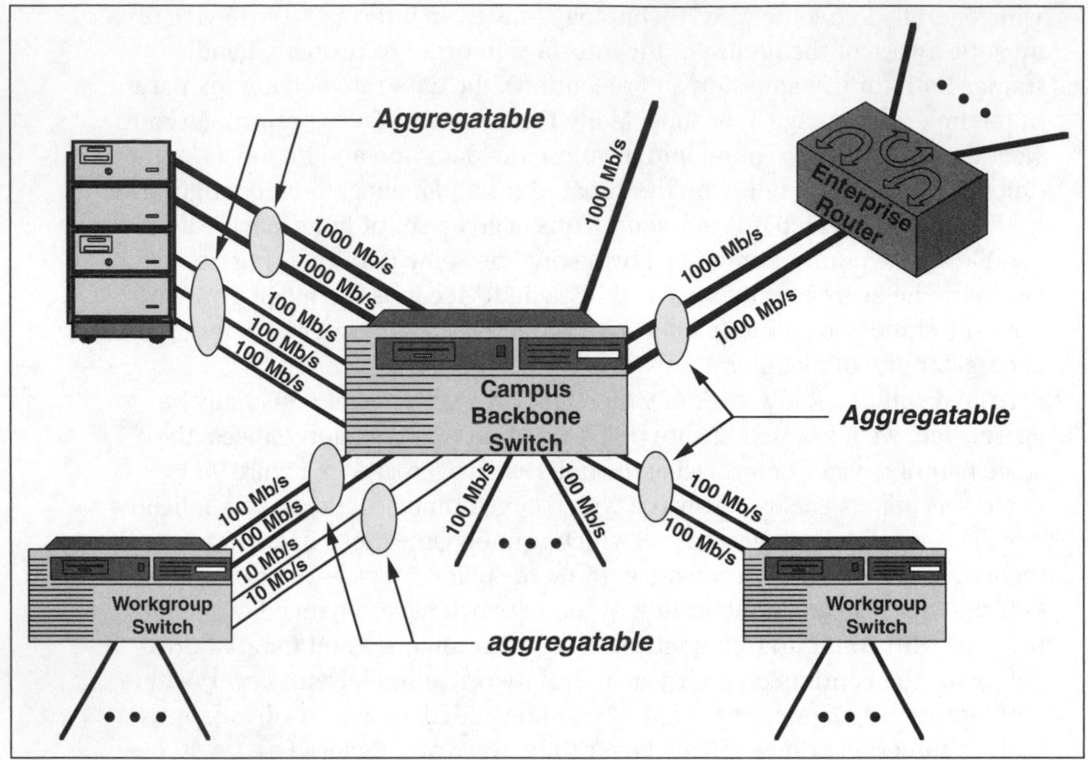

Figure 9.11 Link aggregation possibilities.

in topology or device configuration. Users generally want their networks to adapt quickly and automatically to a changing environment; increased availability is one of the primary reasons for using aggregated links in the first place.

Thus, some automatic means is required to detect and monitor link status and connectivity to ensure non-stop network operation when using aggregated links. Early commercial products supporting link aggregation used proprietary protocols to accomplish automatic configuration;[17] the IEEE 802.3ad standard specifies a vendor-interoperable Link Aggregation Control Protocol (LACP) specifically for this purpose (see Section 9.5.8).

Using link aggregation with an automatic configuration control protocol combines some of the best features of two worlds. As with the Spanning Tree Protocol, we can provide redundancy with automatic switchover in the event of link failure,[18] plus we get to use the capacity of all of the available links simultaneously.

[17] Cisco Systems designed the Port Aggregation Protocol (PAgP) for use with its Fast EtherChannel product.

[18] Properly implemented, a link aggregation control protocol should be able to shift conversations to an alternate link more quickly than the Spanning Tree Protocol.

9.5 IEEE 802.3ad Link Aggregation Standard

IEEE 802.3ad is the official standard for Link Aggregation[19] [IEEE99b]. The explanation of aggregation presented in this chapter is consistent with both the model of operation and the formal description in the standard. However the usual caveats apply—this chapter is not intended as a replacement for the standard and does not attempt to present all of the formal compliance requirements and specifications of the standard itself. Readers responsible for developing standards-compliant products can use this book as a guide, but should refer to the official documents for specific conformance requirements.

Initial presentations and discussions relating to link aggregation occurred at an IEEE standards meeting in November 1997. The IEEE 802.3ad Task Force first officially met in July 1998. By July 1999, a draft standard was ready for formal balloting; final approval of the standard is expected in March 2000.

9.5.1 Scope of the Standard

There is always a tradeoff to be made between specifying a standard with wide applicability and getting the work completed in a timely manner. Defined too narrowly, a standard has limited usefulness. Defined too broadly, it may take so long for the specifications to be agreed on that proprietary solutions (with a narrower scope) will become widely deployed, making the standard moot. IEEE 802.3ad specifies a method for vendor-interoperable link aggregation under the following constraints:

- The standard applies exclusively to Ethernet LANs; no provision is made for aggregation of Token Ring or FDDI LANs either to themselves or to Ethernets.
- Aggregation is specified independent of the data rate; it can be used at any standard Ethernet data rate. However, all links within an aggregation must be operating at the same data rate.[20]

[19] While at the time of this writing the standard is in the final stages of balloting and is not yet approved, no significant technical changes are anticipated. Every attempt has been made to ensure that the explanations presented in this book are consistent with the standard, but it is possible that some differences will creep in as both documents move toward publication. Since I am both the author of this book and the editor of the standard in question, I do have some say in the matter, but the reader is advised that orchestrating a standard is akin to herding cats—both activities are highly frustrating, with a mostly unpredictable outcome.

[20] During the early stages of the standard's development, we seriously considered supporting mixed-speed and even mixed technology and shared LAN aggregations. The (well-founded) conclusion of the group was that the complexity implied by such configurations would have delayed the standard by a year or more and provided no real benefit in practical user environments.

IEEE 802.3ad SETS AN EXAMPLE FOR THE UNITED NATIONS?

The development of IEEE 802.3ad proceeded in a fashion almost unheard of in network technology. With the exception of a mild political skirmish over which Working Group should be responsible for the standard (802.3 as opposed to 802.1[21]), there were surprisingly few differences of opinion among the committee members regarding the technical aspects of the standard itself.

Almost no discussion was needed about the operation of aggregation per se; there was general agreement about how a Distributor and Collector should behave, and that the specification of the distribution algorithm should be implementation-specific. Most of the work within the committee focused on defining the abstract architectural model, aggregation addressing model, and the Link Aggregation Control Protocol (LACP).

Even the LACP specification was a model of cooperation among industry rivals. The protocol itself was based on a proposal from Cisco Systems derived from the proprietary Port Aggregation Protocol (PAgP) used in Cisco's Fast EtherChannel product. Nortel Networks contributed additional material, while the formal state machines were developed, simulated, and tested primarily by committee representatives from 3Com.

The result of this general cooperation and mutual admiration society was a quickly-developed, technically-sound standard with immediate industry consensus. It's amazing what happens when everyone's goals are the same. When standards-wars occur, it usually indicates that the participants are operating at cross-purposes or that the standards arena is being used for political purposes; there are often no technical problems at issue.

- Aggregation is supported on full duplex, point-to-point links only.
- Only one multiple-link aggregation is supported between a pair of devices.[22]

While this may seem to be overly restrictive, the fact is that the majority of the target application environments for link aggregation fit under this umbrella. Most LAN backbone (i.e., switch and router) and high-performance server connections use full duplex Ethernet at a single data rate. Confining the standard to this subset of possibilities meant that the algorithms for distribution, collection, and control were greatly simplified, and the standard was completed in a relatively short time; all of the significant technical issues were resolved within one year from the official start of the project.

[21] This clash was resolved by having the standard developed under the 802.3 umbrella, but granting voting rights to 802.1 committee members as well. In reality, the standard was developed jointly by members of both groups working together, irrespective of the title on the cover of the document—yet another rare display of cooperation in the networking world.

[22] There can be any number of non-aggregated individual links between a pair of devices.

CISCO'S FAST ETHERCHANNEL

Prior to the development of IEEE 802.3ad, Cisco Systems developed and promoted its Fast EtherChannel product for aggregation of 100 Mb/s Ethernets.[23] First shipped in 1997, Fast EtherChannel allows up to eight full-duplex Fast Ethernet ports to be aggregated, for a total of up to 800 Mb/s of link capacity in each direction.

The model of aggregation used by Fast EtherChannel is virtually the same as that of IEEE 802.3ad. Fast EtherChannel also incorporates an automatic link configuration protocol that provides features similar to those of the Link Aggregation Control Protocol specified in the IEEE standard, although the two control protocols are not interoperable.

Cisco licensed Fast EtherChannel technology to a number of other equipment manufacturers; until the development of IEEE 802.3ad, it had become a de facto standard for link aggregation. However, Cisco also was an active participant in and contributor to the IEEE standard development; it is expected that the IEEE standard will see more widespread use in the future than Fast EtherChannel (particularly since it doesn't require a license from Cisco). There will continue to be an installed base of Fast EtherChannel products in field use for at least one more product generation.

It is important to note that, while the automatic aggregation control protocols differ between Fast EtherChannel and the IEEE 802.3ad standard, the data flow architecture, algorithms, and invariants are the same for the two systems. As a result, if the respective control protocols are disabled and the systems are properly (manually) configured, it should be possible to achieve interoperable link aggregation between existing Fast EtherChannel devices and IEEE 802.3ad standard-compliant ones.

9.5.2 Features and Benefits of the Standard

IEEE 802.3ad provides:

- *Increased bandwidth* by combining the capacity of multiple links into one logical link.
- *Linearly incremental bandwidth* by allowing capacity increments in unit multiples as opposed to the order-of-magnitude increases available through Physical layer technology.

[23] Fast EtherChannel is a direct descendant of EtherChannel, a method for link aggregation of 10 Mb/s Ethernets developed years earlier by Kalpana Corporation. It is no surprise that Cisco simply updated this scheme for Fast Ethernet, as Cisco had previously acquired Kalpana and many of the former Kalpana engineers now worked for Cisco.

- *Increased availability* through the use of multiple parallel links.
- *Load sharing* of user traffic across multiple links.
- *Automatic configuration* of aggregations to the highest performance level possible in a given topology and configuration.
- *Rapid reconfiguration* in the event of changes in physical connectivity.
- *Maintenance of the link invariants* (i.e., non-duplication and frame ordering) during both steady-state operation and (re)configuration.
- *Support of existing higher-layer protocols and applications* without change.
- *Backward compatibility* with aggregation-unaware devices.
- *No change* to the Ethernet frame format.
- *Network management support* in the form of management objects for configuration, monitoring, and control of aggregations.

The standard imposes a frame distribution philosophy that places all of the burden of maintaining the link invariants on the Distributor, rather than the Collector; that is, the Distributor must ensure that the frames from any conversation are transmitted over only one link within the aggregation. This yields three important results:

1. The link invariants are properly maintained.
2. The Collector is relieved of any requirement to resequence frames received on any interface.
3. Collector operation is the same regardless of the distribution function chosen.

As a consequence, the standard does not specify any particular distribution function. The Distributor can use whatever algorithm it deems appropriate to decide what constitutes a conversation for the application in which aggregation is being deployed.[24] Distributors in separate devices can use different distribution functions on their aggregated links; even within a single device, the Distributor for one aggregated link (e.g., a set of switch ports connected to a server) can use a different algorithm than the Distributor for another aggregation (e.g., from the same switch to another switch). Since the Collector is independent of the distribution function, implementations should be interoperable regardless of the algorithm used.

[24] There is an Annex to the standard that discusses the use of various possible distribution functions, but there is no requirement that an implementation use or conform to any of the algorithms discussed.

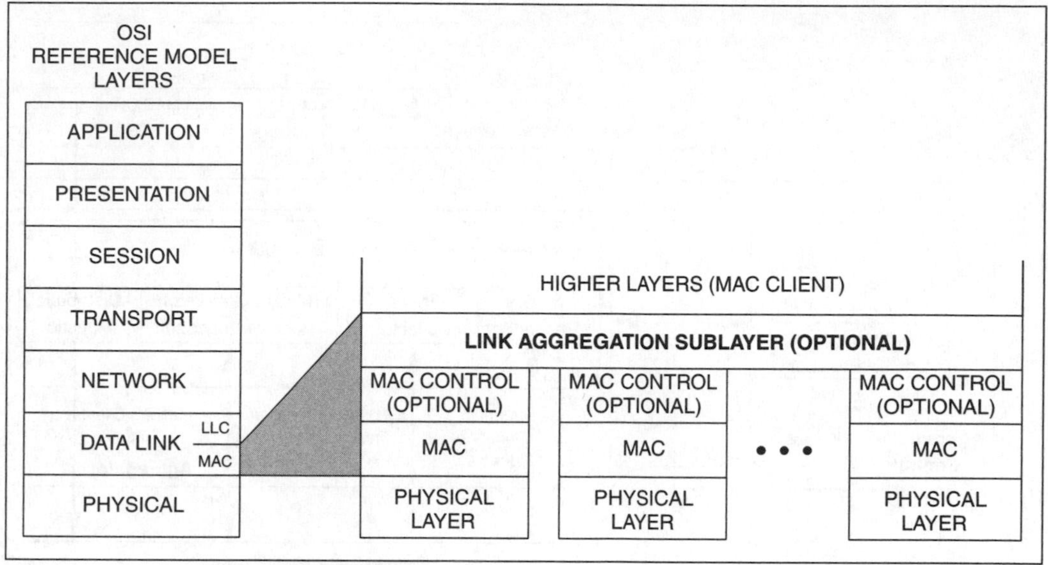

Figure 9.12 Link Aggregation architectural positioning.

9.5.3 Link Aggregation Architectural Model

As we keep adding new functionality to LANs, we need to find places to slip these features into the architectural model. Link aggregation distributes and collects frames to and from multiple MAC entities, yet appears to the higher layers of the architecture as if it were a single MAC. To accomplish this feat, we need to slide the aggregation function in between the existing interface between the MAC and its client. This is referred to as a *shim sublayer*—a new function fitted between existing protocol entities.[25] Link Aggregation constitutes an optional sublayer of the 802.3 MAC, as depicted in Figure 9.12.

The Link Aggregation sublayer comprises the Distributor, Collector, and other functions needed to perform aggregation; the internal architecture is shown in Figure 9.13.[26]

Link aggregation comprises the following modules:

[25] Full duplex flow control was also implemented as a shim between the Ethernet MAC and its client. Sometimes it seems as if we need to bring a large mallet to standards meetings to drive all of these shims into place. Unlike doorjambs, there always seems to be room in network architecture to slip in another shim without the entire structure becoming mis-aligned!

[26] For those readers who may have occasion to refer to the standard itself, the figure presented here is slightly simplified relative to the model provided in the official document. The main difference is that the model in the standard contains two parsers/multiplexers; one to separate out the control frames, and another to separate the marker messages from client data. I have combined those two into a single frame parser/multiplexer in Figure 9.13. The difference is an artifact of the way that standards are written; there is no functional difference between the two diagrams.

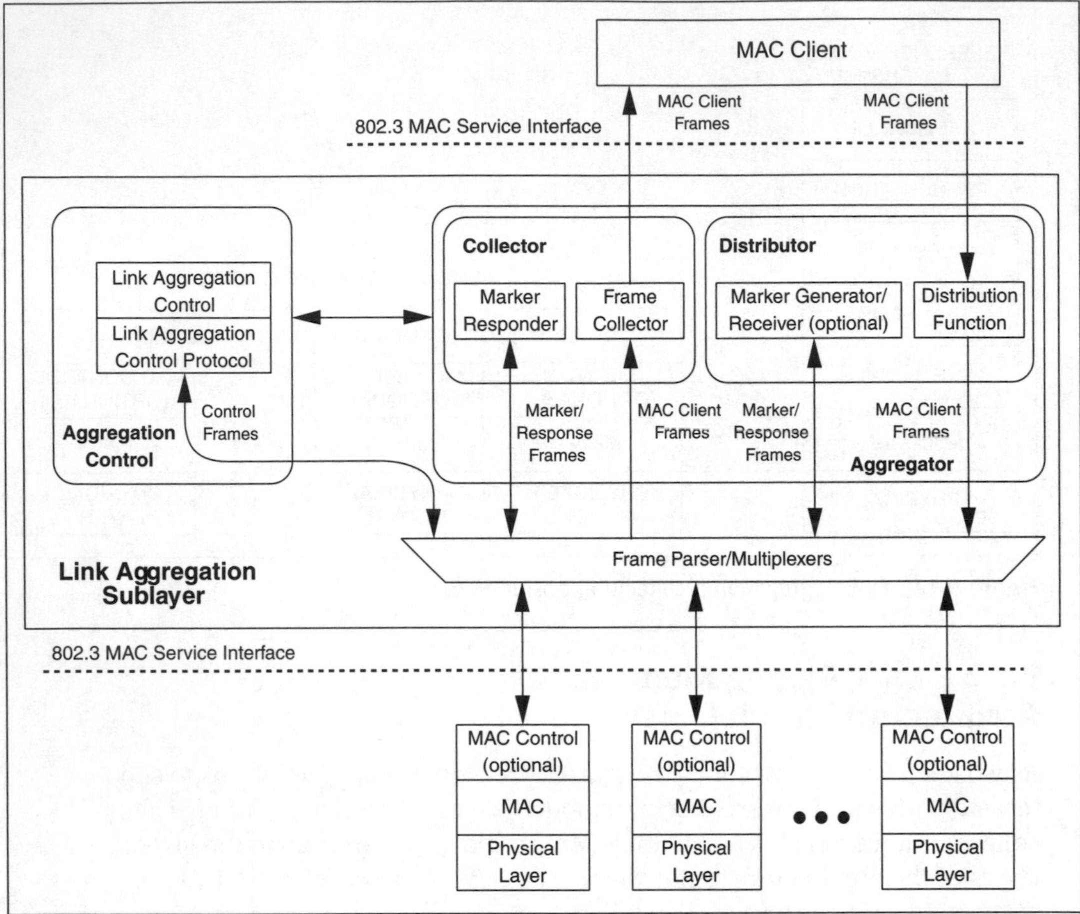

Figure 9.13 Link Aggregation sublayer internal architecture.

Distributor The Distributor accepts frames from the MAC client and submits them to one of the available physical interfaces (through a frame multiplexer, discussed later). The distribution function itself is implemented within this module. Each frame submitted by the client is associated with a particular conversation (based on the distribution rule in effect), mapped to one of the physical interfaces within the aggregation, and submitted for transmission on that link.

The distributor also incorporates a Marker Generator/Receiver. If the Distributor needs to move a conversation from one physical link to another, it can generate a Marker message at the appropriate place in the conversation stream and await a response from the Collector at the other end of the aggregation (see Sections 9.4.2.7 and 9.5.7). The Marker Generator/Receiver is optional; distributors may choose to use a simple timeout mechanism to move conversations rather than to implement the explicit Marker Protocol.

Collector The Collector processes two classes of frames received from the underlying interfaces (through the frame parser, discussed later). Marker messages (generated by a Distributor at the other end of the aggregation) are handled by the Marker Responder. This module generates an appropriate response message and submits it for transmission on the same link from which the Marker message was received. While the Marker Generator/Receiver is optional in the Distributor, the Marker Responder is mandatory; without it, the Marker Protocol would never work.

Frames other than those belonging to the Marker Protocol are passed up to the MAC client. Because the distribution function ensures that any given conversation maps to a single physical link, the Collector is free to gather frames from the underlying interfaces in any manner it chooses (round-robin, first-come-first-served, etc.), as long as it does not re-sequence frames received from any individual interface. This approach greatly simplifies Collector operation; no buffering, frame inspection, or sequence numbers are required to maintain proper frame order, regardless of the distribution function employed.

Frame parsers/multiplexers The frame multiplexer is more of a standards artifact than a functional module. All it does is accept frames from the various modules capable of submitting them for transmission (i.e., the Distributor, the Collector, and Aggregation Control) and pass them to the interface associated with the multiplexer. (A multiplexer is provided for each interface.)

The frame parser separates received frames into three groups and passes them to the appropriate module for each:

- Control protocol messages are passed to the Link Aggregation Control Protocol (see Section 9.5.8).
- Marker messages are passed to the Marker Responder.
- Marker Response messages are passed to the Marker Receiver (or, if the Marker Receiver is not implemented, to the MAC client via the Frame Collector).
- All other frames are passed to the MAC client via the Frame Collector.

Aggregation control This module implements the functionality required to bind together the underlying interfaces into an aggregation. This includes both the capabilities for manual control and management and the automatic Link Aggregation Control Protocol discussed in Section 9.5.8.

9.5.4 Binding Physical Ports to Aggregators

A system capable of link aggregation comprises some number of physical ports and some number of Aggregators, as shown in Figure 9.14. Physical

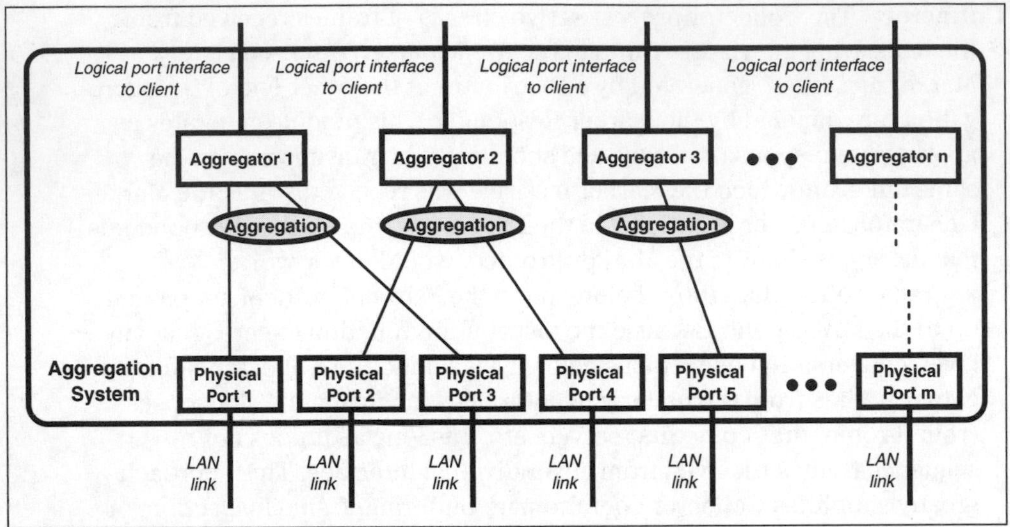

Figure 9.14 Aggregators and physical ports.

ports are determined by the hardware capabilities and configuration of the system. Aggregators are logical entities, and correspond to logical ports as seen by higher layer protocols and applications. An aggregation is created by *binding* one or more physical ports to an Aggregator.

An Aggregator with no bound ports appears to higher layers like an interface with a disconnected cable. An Aggregator bound to a single physical port operates like an individual (non-aggregated) interface. While this may appear to serve no purpose (why bother using aggregation for a single interface?), it allows for the possibility that the number of ports in an aggregation may change over time. The failure of one link in a two link aggregation results in a one-link aggregation, as opposed to the elimination of aggregation altogether. Like putting on a pair of pants one leg at a time, when connecting equipments, usually one link is attached at a time. A multiple-link aggregation can grow from a single physical connection as the network administrator connects the rest of the cables. An aggregation of a single physical port is therefore not treated as a special case. This approach provides uniformity and consistency of operation over a wide range of environments.

A system may contain any number of logical Aggregators. If the number of Aggregators is equal to the number of physical ports, then there will always be an Aggregator available to bind to each and every physical port in the event that no multiple-port aggregations are possible. If the number of Aggregators is less than the number of physical ports, it is possible that a physical link may be attached and operational, but not available to higher-layer protocols due to the lack of a logical interface through an Aggregator. This is not necessarily a problem, depending on the configuration. Figure 9.15 depicts a

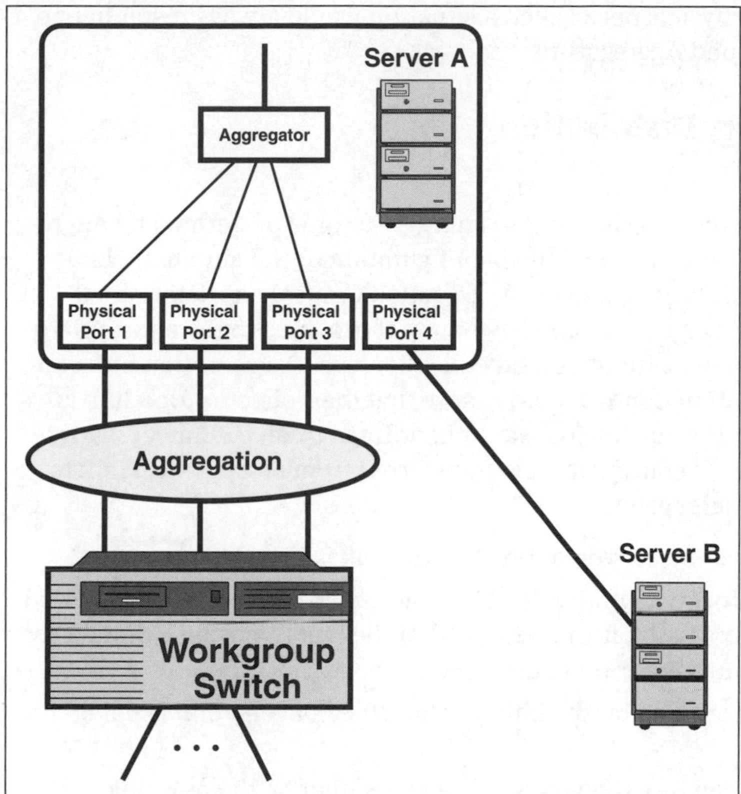

Figure 9.15 Restricting port usage.

server (server A) with four physical ports and a single Aggregator. This server is designed to support a single logical interface to the network; the server does not expect to be connected to two networks or two different devices simultaneously.

If one of the physical ports is incorrectly connected to the wrong device (server B instead of the workgroup switch), we don't want server A to use the rogue link for user data transfer. The server will try to aggregate as many links as possible for its connection to the workgroup switch, but does not support connections to multiple devices. Because only a single logical Aggregator is provided, the system is prevented from using the errant connection. When the network administrator moves the connection from server B to an appropriate port on the switch, the Aggregator in server A can now bind to the fourth port to achieve maximum performance from the links.

Of course, some devices (e.g., switches and routers) may be able to use as many connections to as many devices as are available. By providing as many logical Aggregators for the system as there are physical ports, we can ensure that all available capacity can be used. There is never a need to provide more

Aggregators than physical ports; such a situation would always result in one or more idle, unbound Aggregators.

9.5.5 Binding, Distribution, and Collection

The actual binding of physical ports to an Aggregator is performed by Aggregation Control, either through manual configuration or the automatic Link Aggregation Control Protocol. Once Aggregation Control has determined which links can be aggregated, and has bound those links to the appropriate Aggregator, the frame distribution and collection processes for that link can be started. Aggregation Control must ensure that the Collector for a link is enabled before the Distributor for that link, or frames can be unnecessarily lost. Similarly, when a conversation is transferred from one physical link to another within an aggregation:

- Distribution of the conversation onto the link is disabled.
- The Distributor waits until it is sure that frames-in-process have passed through the Collector at the other end of the link (by using a timeout or the explicit Marker Protocol discussed in Section 9.5.7).
- Collection is enabled on the link to which the conversation is being transferred.
- Distribution can be enabled for the conversation on the new link.

9.5.6 Addressing

Each physical interface has associated with it a unique 48-bit address. This address is used as the Source Address when transmitting frames that are constrained by design to remain on a single physical link. Both the Marker Protocol (used for moving conversations between aggregations, and discussed in Section 9.5.7) and the Link Aggregation Control Protocol are link-constrained, as is the full duplex flow control protocol (PAUSE) discussed in Chapter 8.

In addition to the addresses of the physical interfaces, each Aggregator has a unique 48-bit address associated with it (see Figure 9.14). Higher-layer protocols and applications see this as the address of the logical interface formed by the aggregation. For example, when running IP on an aggregated link, ARP would map the station's IP address to the 48-bit address of the Aggregator, as opposed to the addresses of the underlying interfaces. The Aggregator's address is used as the Source Address for all frames carrying MAC client (user) data, and as the Destination Address for all unicast traffic sent to the aggregation.

By convention, the Aggregator takes as its logical address the address of the lowest-numbered physical interface within the aggregation. However, this is not a requirement either for proper operation or of the standard. This practice simply avoids having to allocate addresses for logical aggregations in addition to those already assigned to physical interfaces.[27]

9.5.7 Marker Protocol Operation

The standard supports both methods of moving conversations among aggregations. Either a timeout can be used or the Distributor can send an explicit Marker message after the last frame in a conversation (or set of conversations) being transferred. When the Collector at the other end of the aggregation sends a Marker Response message, we can be sure that all frames-in-process for the conversation(s) have been received and that frame ordering will not be violated as a result of the transfer.

Marker/Marker Responses comprise 128-byte, fixed length Ethernet frames and are link-constrained. The Marker Protocol is one of a class of *Slow Protocols*, defined in the 802.3ad standard (the Link Aggregation Control Protocol is another Slow Protocol), intended for housekeeping functions or background tasks that do not demand high performance. So that they can be implemented in an inexpensive microprocessor, Slow Protocols are required to limit their transmissions to no more than five frames per second (hence the name). The standard allows for a maximum of 10 different Slow Protocols using the same Ethernet Type field, so a receiver should never see more than $10 \times 5 = 50$ Slow Protocol frames per second total.[28]

Figure 9.16 depicts the frame format for both the Marker and the Marker Response messages. The fields within the frame are as follows:

Destination Address Marker and Marker Response messages all carry the globally-unique multicast address 01-80-C2-00-00-02. This address is within the range of reserved addresses that bridges never forward, constraining any such frames to a single link. (See Chapter 2.)

Source Address The Source Address is the 48-bit address of the physical interface on which the Marker/Marker Response is being sent (not the address of the logical aggregation).

Ethernet Type The Ethernet Type value of 0x8809 identifies the frame as being a Slow Protocol.

Subtype and Version All Slow Protocols have a subtype value and version number in these positions in the frame. The Marker Protocol Subtype is 2, and the protocol version is 1.

[27] In particular, a server manufacturer does not need to obtain a block of addresses for Aggregator use when aggregating multiple NICs. Any one of the ROM-programmed addresses in the NICs can be used for the Aggregator address.

[28] Two of the 10 allotted protocols (Marker Protocol and LACP) are specified in 802.3ad; the remaining 8 possibilities are not yet defined or assigned.

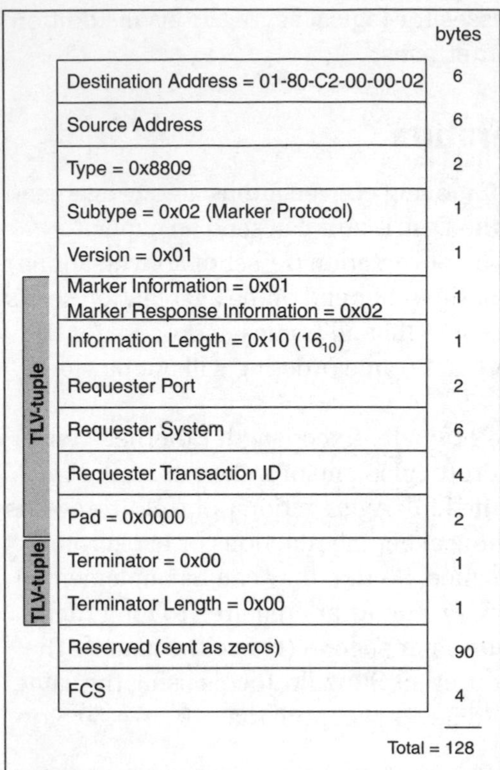

Figure 9.16 Marker/Marker Response message format.

TLV-tuples The Marker Protocol payload uses a common encoding format known as Type/Length/Value (TLV).[29] This format provides for generic encapsulation of lists of arbitrary data (TLV-tuples). The first field (Type) indicates the nature (syntax and semantics) of the data value(s) in this TLV-tuple, the second field is the length of the TLV-tuple in bytes, and the rest of the fields are specific to the Type value provided.

Marker/Marker Response Information Marker messages are Type 1; Marker Responses are Type 2. The TLV-type encoding is local to the subtype (in this case, the Marker Protocol). That is, other protocols with different subtype values can number their TLV-tuples 1, 2, 3, . . . , just like the Marker Protocol, without any conflict or ambiguity.

Length The length of the Marker/Marker Response information is 16 bytes, primarily to aid boundary alignment of transmit and receive buffers in memory.

[29] Both the Link Aggregation Control Protocol and the Generic Attribute Registration Protocol (GARP, discussed in Chapter 10, *Multicast Pruning*) use TLV encoding.

Requester Port This field contains the port number of the port through which the Marker message was sent. Note that this is a system-specific port number and not the 48-bit address of the physical interface associated with the port.[30] When sending a Marker Response, the responding device does not change the value in this field; that is, it always contains the port number of the initiator of the exchange (the requester). This both simplifies the implementation of the Marker Responder and aids in troubleshooting; the Marker Receiver can identify the port that emitted a Marker message, regardless of the port on which the response arrives.

Requester System This field contains the System Identifier of the device sending the Marker message. This is a globally-unique 48-bit value assigned by network management and used to uniquely identify a system participating in aggregation. As discussed in Section 9.5.8.1.2, this allows the automatic configuration protocol to determine that the same device is present at the other end of multiple links, which is a prerequisite for aggregation. As with the Requester Port value, the responding device does not change the value in this field; that is, it always contains the system identifier of the initiator of the exchange.

Requester Transaction ID This field contains an arbitrary value generated by the sender of the Marker message. Typically a device will increment a counter with each transmitted Marker message and put the counter value in this field. Again, the responder simply reflects back whatever value was received in the original Marker message. Thus the initiator of the exchange can associate a Marker Response with the marker that triggered it through the Transaction ID.

The TLV-tuple is padded out with zeros, both to allow for future enhancements to the protocol and to align the next TLV-tuple on a 32-bit boundary.

Terminator TLV-tuple List terminators are identified by a TLV-type value of 0 and a TLV-length of 0. This indicates that there are no more TLV-tuples in the frame.

Reserved The rest of the frame is padded out with zeros. This allows for future extensions to the Marker Protocol while maintaining a single fixed-length frame for all time.[31]

FCS This field carries the 32-bit check sequence common to all Ethernet frames.

[30] Port numbers will generally be the same as the interface index (ifIndex) value used in SNMP-based management systems (see Chapter 14, *Switch Management*).

[31] The Marker Responder, being an extremely simple entity, is especially amenable to implementation in hardware as a finite-state machine. The use of a fixed-length frame simplifies matters even further.

A Distributor may send a Marker message any time it wishes to mark a point in the stream of frames associated with a conversation or set of conversations. When it receives the Marker Response, the Distributor can safely transfer the conversation(s) to another link within the aggregation. Of course, there is always a possibility of frame loss due to errors, both for the Marker and the response, so the Distributor must be prepared to use a timeout mechanism in the event a response is not received. There is no requirement for a device to ever send Marker messages, or even to implement the capability to do so. However, all standards-conformant devices must implement the Marker Responder so that the protocol will work properly should a device choose to use it.

Implementation of the Marker Responder is quite simple. Upon receiving a Marker message, the only action required is to change the TLV type value from 1 to 2, insert the proper Source Address, and send the same message back onto the link on which the Marker message was received.

9.5.8 Link Aggregation Control Protocol (LACP)

The Link Aggregation Control Protocol is used to automatically configure and maintain aggregations among cooperating systems. While it is possible to institute manual controls and overrides to the protocol, most users will want to allow devices to automatically detect the presence and capabilities of other aggregation-capable devices and to adjust their behavior and configuration accordingly. LACP provides controls that allow network administrators to specify exactly which links in a system may be aggregated to which others.

9.5.8.1 LACP Concepts

LACP operates on a set of principles similar to those of the Spanning Tree Protocol (see Chapter 5):

- Devices advertise their aggregation capabilities and state information on a regular basis on all aggregatable links. Protocol partners on an aggregatable link compare their own configuration and state information with that of their partner and decide what action(s) to take.
- Aggregations are maintained in the steady-state by the regular, timely exchange of consistent state information between the partners. Should the configuration change (e.g., a link is moved by a network administrator) or fail, the protocol partners will time out and take appropriate action based on the new state of the system.
- LACP emits state information independently on each aggregatable link. Even within an aggregation, independent LACP messages are sent on each link to provide link-specific information to the partner system.

- There is no synchronization of LACP messages; partners on an aggregatable link send LACP messages autonomously.
- LACP messages are link-constrained; they are never forwarded by an internetworking device (switch or router).
- LACP can be overridden with manual controls if desired.

Seifert's Law of
Networking #19
Exchange state,
not commands.

Note that there are no aggregation commands issued by the protocol, nor is there any concept of request-and-response; LACP operates by periodically advertising up-to-date state information and expecting all participants to "do the right thing" based on their knowledge of the system state, both from their own configuration and from received protocol information. As a result, LACP is well-suited for use on connectionless LANs; no special care is needed in the protocol design to allow for occasional lost frames, since state updates occur on a regular basis.[32]

Information from received LACP messages is used to determine which physical ports to bind to which Aggregators and to control the operation of the Distributors and Collectors within each Aggregator as depicted in Figures 9.13 and 9.14. The protocol is typically implemented in software in each aggregation-capable device. Since the rate of LACP message exchange is quite low (one frame per second maximum in the steady-state), very little processing performance is demanded.[33]

The formal specification of the protocol is provided by a set of finite-state machines in the standard. Readers responsible for LACP implementation or interested in the low-level details of protocol operation should take a deep breath and ask themselves, "Why?" Should you ignore this advice, you can refer to the standard itself for the protocol details [IEEE99b].

9.5.8.1.1 Actor and Partner

On each aggregatable link, messages are sent between the LACP protocol entities within the two attached devices. Each device refers to itself as an *Actor* (i.e., the device taking action) and to the device at the other end of the link as its *Partner*. LACP compares Actor information (a device's own state) with Partner information (the advertised state of the other device) to determine what action(s) to take, if any. Of course, both devices are Actors and both are

[32] This is known as an *idempotent transaction*, since the resulting action taken by a device is independent of the number of times that it receives the same protocol information.

[33] The protocol is actually simple enough to allow hardware implementation. However, there is no performance benefit to be gained by this approach, since the timing constraints of LACP are quite lax.

Partners; the terms are only meaningful relative to the protocol entity within each device.

Thus, the Partner's Partner information constitutes the Partner's view of the Actor. LACP can compare the Partner's Partner information with its own state to make sure that the Partner has received the Actor's information correctly.

9.5.8.1.2 System IDs and Priority

We need to ensure that aggregations are created only among links that interconnect the same pair of devices. To this end, each device is assigned a globally-unique System Identifier; an Actor will only consider aggregating links when received LACP information indicates that the same system is the Partner for all links in the potential aggregation.

A System Identifier is a 64-bit (8-byte) field comprising a concatenation of a globally-unique 48-bit field and a 16-bit priority value, as depicted in Figure 9.17. System Identifiers follow precisely the same style and usage as Bridge Identifiers in the Spanning Tree Protocol.

A system will typically use the address assigned to one of its physical ports for the 48-bit unique portion of the System Identifier. Since all we care about is uniqueness, it doesn't really matter which of the available MAC addresses we use, although by convention we usually use the address of the lowest-numbered port.

In the same way that Bridge Identifiers are used in the Spanning Tree Protocol, a priority field is prepended to the 48-bit unique value so that a network administrator can control the relative numerical values of System Identifiers among devices (i.e., which ones are higher or lower than others) independent from that which would result if the network administrator depended solely on the 48-bit portion. Since MAC addresses (and their Organizationally-Unique Identifier component) are assigned by outside authorities in no particular order, the relative numerical interpretation of System Identifiers is uncontrollable unless the priority field is included.

A numerical interpretation of the System Identifier is used when the aggregation capabilities of a device need to be modified dynamically in response to received LACP information. To prevent partners from making simultaneous changes that could prevent convergence to a stable state, only the system with

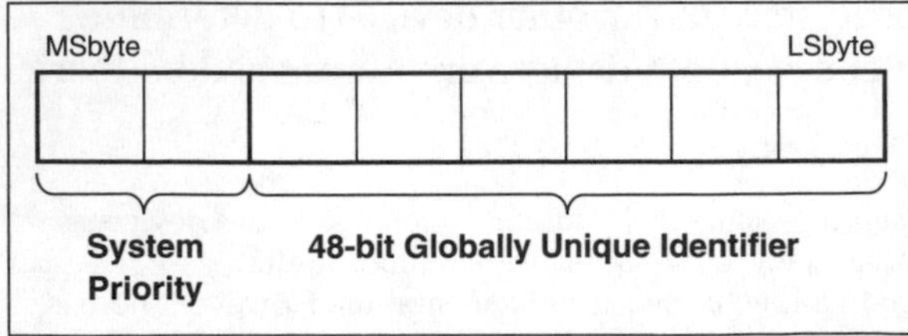

Figure 9.17 System Identifier.

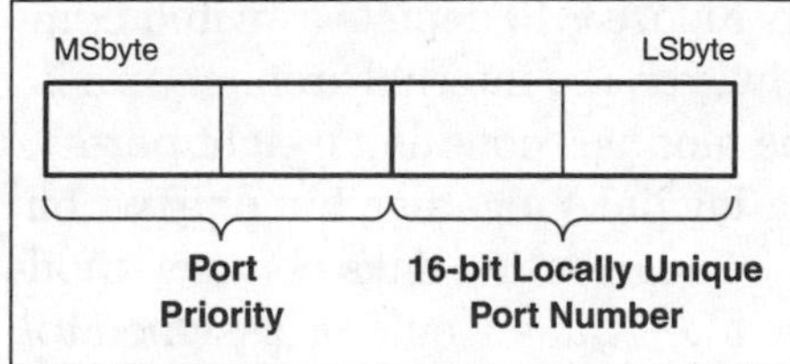

Figure 9.18 Port Identifier.

the numerically-lower System Identifier is allowed to make dynamic changes in its advertised aggregation capability.

9.5.8.1.3 Port Numbers and Priority

Each port that can be included in an aggregation is assigned a Port Identifier, as shown in Figure 9.18. Similar to the System Identifier, a Port Identifier concatenates a 16-bit port number with a configurable priority field.

Port numbers are locally-unique (to a device), and simply denote the number of the physical attachment. They are normally numbered from 1 to *N*, where *N* is the number of ports on the device.[34]

9.5.8.1.4 Identifying Aggregation Candidates

Just because an Actor recognizes (through LACP messages) that some set of links all terminate in the same partner system does not imply that the Partner is able and/or willing to aggregate them. Devices indicate their willingness to aggregate a set of links by assigning the same value to a *key* associated with each port. This is not a key in the cryptographic sense, but simply an administrative "handle" to stipulate which links can be aggregated with which others. Keys are arbitrary 16-bit values. They have no semantic meaning (i.e., the value itself is unimportant). A set of links that carry the same key can be aggregated by a partner system, should it be able to do so; links with different key values should never be aggregated together.

Keys are administratively assigned based on any of a number of factors:

- *Characteristics of the links.* Links that do not share the right set of characteristics are assigned different keys. For example, a set of 10 Mb/s ports may be assigned one key value, while a different value would be used for a set of 100 Mb/s ports on the same device, since these cannot be aggregated together. If the data rate of one of the links changes (e.g., due to reinitialization and Auto-Negotiation), the key for that link will generally change as well.

[34] Note that we learned our lesson from the Spanning Tree Protocol. The port number used for link aggregation is 2 bytes long rather than 1 byte (as in the Spanning Tree Protocol) to allow more than 255 links to be configured on a single system.

- *Physical limitations of the hardware.* Figure 9.19 depicts a switch comprising twenty-four 100 Mb/s ports; however, the internal architecture is such that the switch is built from three modules containing eight ports each. The switch is capable of aggregating links together, but only within the eight-port modules; it is incapable of aggregating links between modules. To reflect this situation, a different key value would be assigned to each of the three groups of eight ports.
- *User-controlled configuration restrictions.* A network administrator can arbitrarily limit the number of ports or the set(s) of specific ports that can be aggregated by assigning keys appropriately.

Of course, an administrator can choose to allow unlimited aggregation simply by giving the same key value to all ports on the device. With this key assignment, any links that can aggregate will aggregate, subject only to the aggregation abilities of the partners on each port.

Keys notwithstanding, any port can be identified as an individual port, never to be included in a multiple-port aggregation.

9.5.8.1.5 Active and Passive Operation

LACP provides two modes of operation:

- A port in *active mode* will generate LACP protocol messages on a regular basis, regardless of any need expressed by its partner to hear them.
- A port in *passive mode* will generally not transmit LACP messages unless its partner is in the active mode; that is, it will not speak unless spoken to.

By comparison, the Spanning Tree Protocol provides only an active mode; there is no provision for disabling protocol messages without disabling the protocol altogether. The inclusion of the passive mode in LACP allows us to

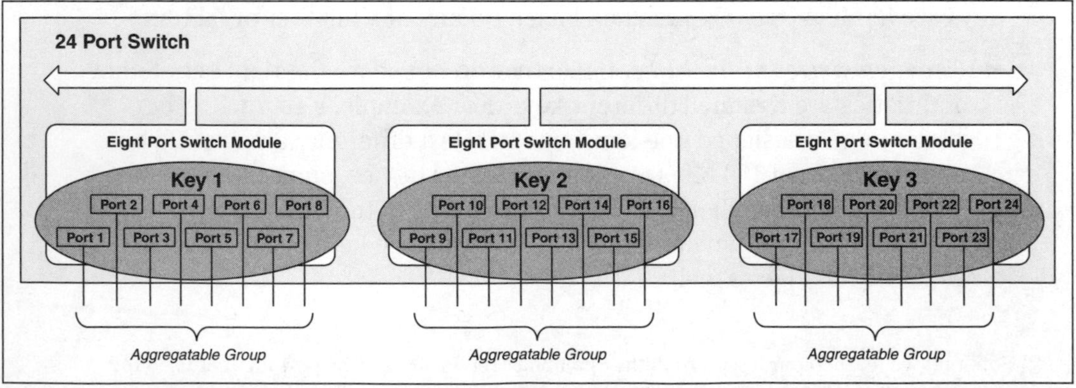

Figure 9.19 Hardware aggregation limitation.

dispense with LACP transmissions on a given link if it has been determined that the device at the other end does not implement the protocol (e.g., in the case of an aggregatable switch port connected as an individual link to an end station). There is already enough background clutter of periodic transmissions from other protocols (Spanning Tree, RIP broadcasts, IPX Service Advertisements, proprietary "hello" protocols, etc.). Customers often wish they could turn these transmissions off if they don't serve any purpose on a given link; LACP provides the capability to do exactly that.

If a port in passive mode is later connected to a partner that does send LACP messages, the passive port will generate LACP messages as well, ensuring proper automatic configuration. Passive mode doesn't mean disabled; it means "speak if spoken to."[35]

9.5.8.1.6 Periodic Transmission Frequency

LACP normally emits messages on a regular, periodic basis. A control is provided to adjust the frequency of those periodic transmissions to either once every second (fast rate) or once every 30 seconds (slow rate). The tradeoff is between having more background clutter of LACP messages and providing more rapid detection of link configuration changes and convergence to a new aggregation state.

Each Actor sets its transmission frequency as requested by its Partner. Since the Partner is the one that will time out if protocol updates are not received in a timely manner, the Actor must ensure that LACP messages are sent however often the Partner needs to see them. When there is doubt about the Partner's needs (e.g., during reconfiguration, when the Partner itself may be changing), the fast rate is used.

9.5.8.2 LACP Frame Format

Figure 9.20 depicts the format and content of LACP messages.

The structure of LACP frames follows the same model as that for Marker and Marker Response frames. Following the address, type, subtype, and version fields, the payload is organized into TLV-tuples. Each TLV-tuple comprises a set of information fields relevant to the Actor, the Partner, and the Collector of the device sending the frame. The semantics of the fields are as follows:

Destination Address LACP messages all carry the globally-unique multicast address 01-80-C2-00-00-02. This is the same value as used for Marker and Marker Response messages, so that only one multicast address is used by Link Aggregation.

[35] If two aggregation-capable ports connected to each other are both in passive mode, they will never discover their respective capability.

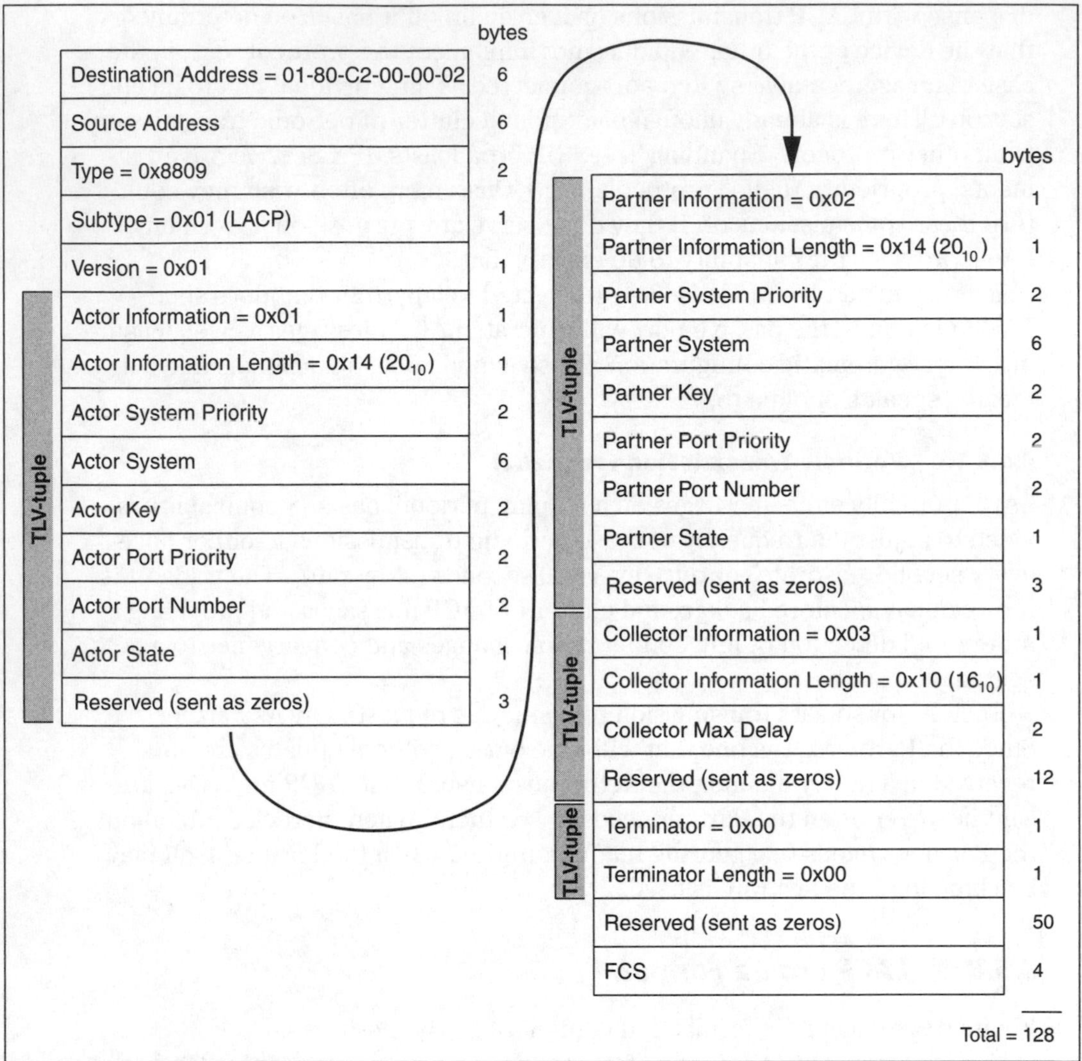

Figure 9.20 LACP frame format.

Source Address The Source Address is the 48-bit address of the physical interface on which the LACP message is being sent (not the address of the logical aggregation).

Ethernet Type The Ethernet Type value of 0x8809 identifies the frame as being a Slow Protocol.

Subtype and Version The Slow Protocol subtype for LACP is 2, and the LACP Protocol Version is 1.

Actor Information and Length Actor information is encoded into TLV Type 1 for LACP messages; the length of the Actor information is 20 bytes.

Actor System Priority and System These fields contains the 2-byte priority value and the 48-bit globally-unique identifier (the same value as is used for Marker messages) of the Actor, which are concatenated together to form the prioritized System Identifier.

Actor Key This field contains the key value associated with the port from which the LACP message is being sent.

Actor Port Priority and Port Number These fields contains the 2-byte priority value and the 2-byte Port Number of the Actor's port through which the LACP message is being sent.

Actor State This field indicates the state of the port from which the LACP message is being sent. The bits are encoded as shown in Table 9.2.

The TLV-tuple is padded out with zeros, both to allow for future enhancements to the protocol and to align the next TLV-tuple on a 32-bit boundary.

Partner Information and Length The Actor's view of the Partner information is encoded into TLV Type 2 for LACP messages; the length of the Partner information is 20 bytes. Normally, these fields are derived from Actor information in previously-received LACP messages. It is reflected back so that the original sender can confirm that the Partner correctly understands the current configuration and state.

Partner System Priority and System These fields contains the 2-byte priority value and the 48-bit globally-unique identifier of the Partner system, from the Actor's perspective.

Partner Key This field contains the key value that the Partner has associated with this port, from the Actor's perspective.

Partner Port Priority and Port Number These fields contains the 2-byte priority value and the 2-byte Port Number assigned by the Partner to this port, from the Actor's perspective.

Partner State This field indicates the Actor's view of the Partner's state for this port. The bits are encoded the same as for the Actor state, as shown in Table 9.2.

The TLV-tuple is padded out with zeros, both to allow for future enhancements to the protocol and to align the next TLV-tuple on a 32-bit boundary.

Collector Information and Length Collector information is encoded into TLV Type 3 for LACP messages; the length of the Collector information is 16 bytes.

Collector Max Delay This field indicates, in tens-of-microseconds, the maximum delay that the Frame Collector may incur between receiving a frame and delivery to the higher-layer client of the MAC. The first byte transmitted is the most-significant byte; the second byte is the least-

Table 9.2 State Information Bit Encoding

BIT	NAME	SEMANTICS	
0	Activity	0	Passive mode—port will emit LACP messages only if the partner system is doing so.
		1	Active mode—port will emit LACP messages on a periodic basis regardless of the partner's mode.
1	Timeout	0	Long timeouts are in use (90-second timeout corresponding to a 30-second transmission period).
		1	Short timeouts are in use (3 second timeout implying a 1 second transmission period).
2	Aggregation	0	Link cannot be aggregated with others (individual use only).
		1	Link can be aggregated.
3	Synchronization	0	Port is not currently bound to an appropriate aggregator (e.g., link is in transition due to a reconfiguration in progress).
		1	Port is bound to an appropriate aggregator.
4	Collecting	0	The Collector for this link is either disabled or may be in the process of being disabled.
		1	The Collector for this link is enabled and will not be disabled unless instructed to do so (by management or LACP).
5	Distributing	0	The Distributor for this link is disabled and will not be enabled unless instructed to do so (by management or LACP).
		1	The Distributor for this link is enabled or may be in the process of being enabled.
6	Defaulted	0	The device is using administratively-configured default Partner information.[1]
		1	The device is using Partner information from received LACP messages.[1]
7	Expired	0	The device's LACP receive state machine is not in the expired state.[1]
		1	The device's LACP receive state machine is in the Expired state.[1]

[1] These bits are not actually used by the protocol; they provide internal diagnostic state information about the LACP, which is useful for troubleshooting.

significant byte; the range is zero to 0.65535 seconds. This value can be used by the Partner to determine an appropriate timeout value when transferring conversations among links in an aggregation.

The TLV-tuple is padded out with zeros, both to allow for future enhancements to the protocol and to align the next TLV-tuple on a 32-bit boundary.

Terminator TLV-tuple List terminators are identified by a TLV-Type value of 0 and a TLV-length of 0. This indicates that there are no more TLV-tuples in the frame.

Reserved The rest of the frame is padded out with zeros. This allows for future extensions to the LACP while maintaining a single, fixed-length frame for all time.

FCS This field carries the 32-bit check sequence common to all Ethernet frames.

CHAPTER

10

Multicast Pruning

The default behavior for a switch is to flood all multicast traffic. When a switch receives a frame destined for a multicast address, it will normally forward the frame out all ports except the port on which it arrived. This ensures that all parties that might be interested in hearing that multicast frame do, in fact, hear it. If the level of multicast traffic is low, flooding provides for proper application operation without significantly increasing the traffic burden on the catenet. However, if there are applications using multicast in a traffic-intensive manner, the inefficiency of flooding becomes problematic. Flooding increases the traffic load on all active paths in the spanning tree, regardless of whether any given link is really needed to carry the traffic to those stations interested in receiving it.

In this chapter we look at mechanisms for restricting multicast traffic propagation within the catenet to only those links needed to ensure proper end-station application behavior.

10.1 Multicast Usage

I love multicast; it really is a wonderful and powerful mechanism. Networks have always incorporated the concept of station-to-station (unicast) addressing, and most multipoint networks also provide a means to send data to all stations at once (broadcast). Multicast is an important generalization of the multiple-recipient delivery concept; it provides the ability to send frames to any arbitrary set of devices.

Multicast, as it is currently used, was developed as an integral part of the original Ethernet system. A key enabler was the decision to use a globally-administered 48-bit address space. Generalized multicast addressing greatly increases the number of addresses needed. For a catenet of n devices, only n unicast addresses are needed (one per device), but the number of possible multicast groupings of n devices grows exponentially large. In a catenet comprising n devices, the number of possible distinct multicast groupings is:

$$\sum_{k=1}^{n} \frac{n!}{k!(n-k)!}$$

While in practice we never need quite that many distinct groupings, the use of multicast addressing generally requires that we provide for more unique addresses than there are devices in the catenet.[1] However, since we provisioned an address space with 2^{48} elements, it is considered unnecessary to carefully conserve addresses. We split the address space in half—half for unicast and half for multicast.

Unicast addresses denote a physical device or interface. In fact, they are often referred to as *physical addresses* for this reason. There is a 1:1 mapping between unicast addresses and devices. Multicast addresses, on the other hand, denote a logical group of devices. (In some early literature, they are even called *logical addresses*, although current usage favors the term *multicast* or *group address*.)

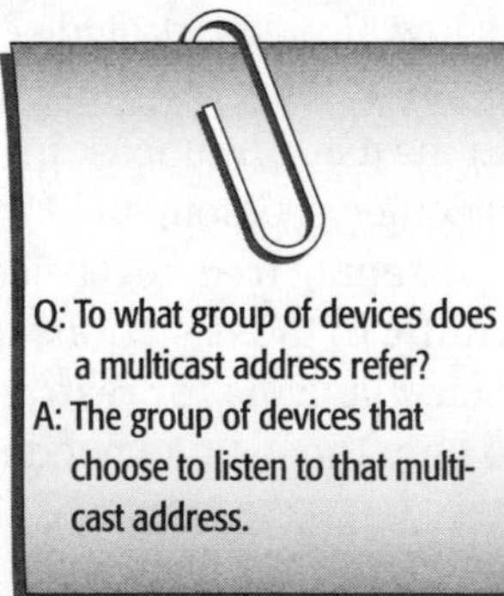

Q: To what group of devices does a multicast address refer?
A: The group of devices that choose to listen to that multicast address.

This sounds like a circular definition, but it is really the case. To understand this better, let's look at how multicast addresses are assigned and used.

[1] In theory, a catenet containing only 16 devices could exhaust the multicast address space with distinct groupings.

10.1.1 Who Assigns Multicast Addresses?

Globally-unique unicast addresses are assigned by the manufacturer of the networking device. Typically, this address is burned into a read-only memory or the interface controller itself. Device driver software can read this hard-wired address and configure the interface controller appropriately.[2]

Multicast addresses are assigned by higher-layer protocols or applications. (For the purposes of this discussion, such higher-layer entities are collectively referred to as *applications.*) If an application needs the ability to communicate with a group of devices running an identical (or cooperating) application, it can assign a multicast address for that purpose. In order to receive any such group-wide communication, applications must instruct their network interfaces to receive frames sent to this multicast address (in addition to their unicast address).[3] The *logical grouping* of devices is thus the set of devices that have been enabled to receive this particular multicast address. Some well-known examples include:

- The Spanning Tree Protocol uses a multicast address to define the logical group of all bridges that implement the protocol.
- AppleTalk uses a multicast address to denote "All AppleTalk devices," and an additional multicast for each AppleTalk zone containing members on a given catenet.[4]
- The Open Shortest-Path-First routing protocol (OSPF) uses a multicast address (at both Layers 2 and 3) to denote the set of all OSPF-enabled routers.

[2] In some application environments it is necessary to override the hard-wired value and configure the controller with a software-determined unicast address. (See Chapter 9, *Link Aggregation.*) Regardless, there is still a 1:1 mapping of unicast addresses to network devices, and the addresses are unique within the catenet.

[3] Such instruction is generally performed by a function call to the device driver for the network interface. The driver registers the particular multicast as one of interest to a client application within the device, and passes frames received with this destination to the application that made the address registration. The driver understands what facilities (if any) are provided by the underlying hardware for filtering of multicast traffic, and configures the interface hardware appropriately. If necessary, the driver performs some (or all) of the multicast filtering itself in software. A network interface will therefore receive frames sent to its unicast address, the broadcast address, and any multicast address(es) enabled by higher layer entities.

[4] The first incarnation of the AppleTalk protocol suite—AppleTalk Phase 1—was designed specifically for use on Apple's proprietary LocalTalk technology [APPL90]. LocalTalk lacks a generalized multicast capability; it supports only unicast and broadcast addressing. As a result, AppleTalk Phase 1 used broadcast extensively for its advertisement, name binding, and zone information exchanges. When AppleTalk began to be used on Ethernet LANs, this extensive use of broadcasting sometimes resulted in noticeable network performance degradation; all of the stations on the Ethernet (including those that were not using AppleTalk protocols at all) had to receive, parse, and actively discard all of the AppleTalk broadcast traffic. AppleTalk Phase 2 eliminated this problem by using the generalized multicast capability available on Ethernet and other IEEE 802 LANs; as a result, the AppleTalk Phase 2 protocols are not supported on legacy LocalTalk links.

Note that in all cases there must be an identical or cooperating application running in each receiving device in the multicast group. It is meaningless to define a logical grouping of devices that do not have an application in common—the application defines the method and semantics of any group-wide communications. It does no good to send frames to a defined set of devices unless all of the devices understand the meaning of the contained information.

The simplest and most common method of multicast address selection is to have it done by the designer of the higher-layer application. For the Spanning Tree Protocol, the address was selected from the OUI belonging to the IEEE 802.1 Working Group itself (01-80-C2-xx-yy-zz); AppleTalk multicast addresses were selected from an OUI belonging to Apple Computer (09-00-07-xx-yy-zz); OSPF multicasts map to an OUI used for Internet-standard protocols (01-00-5E-xx-yy-zz). Of course, if the designer wants the application to interoperate with implementations built by others, then any such address selection must be made public knowledge. In the case of the Spanning Tree Protocol, this was done through the publication of the IEEE 802.1D standard; for AppleTalk, through publication of the AppleTalk protocol specifications [APPL90]; for OSPF, through the publication of the OSPF standard [RFC2178].

It is also possible to have a multicast address assigned dynamically at the time an application is invoked. There are multicasting applications that are invoked only sporadically and whose logical grouping changes with each invocation. A good example would be a network videoconferencing application. We would like to be able to use multicast techniques to distribute voice and video traffic among a group of conference members (all of whom are running the cooperating conference application), but the parties involved will surely change from conference-to-conference. There is no easy way to pre-ordain the multicast address to be used by any arbitrary group of conference attendees, nor do we want to use a single multicast address for all possible conferences. One solution is to provide a conference server, which can, upon request from the conference application, create the conference, connect all of the parties, and assign a unique multicast address for this particular conference from a pool of addresses available to the conference application. When the conference is over, the address can go back into the pool.[5] The pool range would likely be assigned by the designer of the conference application, but the particular multicast address used for a given conference would be dynamically assigned at the time the application is invoked.

Thus, multicast groups define a logical grouping of devices on an application basis, not on a physical basis. There is no reason to assign a multicast address to the engineering department (or the fourth floor) unless there is some application that needs to make such a distinction and that application is actually running on every machine in the engineering department (or on the

[5] The conference attendees can go back into the pool, too, but they need to shower first.

fourth floor). This is why multicast addresses are associated with and assigned by application designers, not network administrators.

When it comes to multicast, many people, including some network architects and product designers, simply don't *get it.* The idea of a globally-unique address that identifies a common process within multiple computers, as opposed to a fixed set of the computers themselves, is not intuitive. Most people immediately understand the idea of unicast and broadcast, but it takes some thought to understand the power of generalized multicast.

Ethernet has had multicast capability since its commercial inception, but some protocol suites simply ignored the facility. (Most of the multicast-enabled protocol suites, including DECnet and AppleTalk Phase 2, came from network architects who *did* get it.) In particular, many of the support protocols in IP, such as ARP and RIP, use the broadcast address rather than a protocol-specific multicast. There is no excuse for this. ARP was designed specifically for Ethernet; its use of broadcast is not a historical artifact. As a result, devices that don't even use IP have to receive and process all of the ARP and RIP traffic just to figure out that they should discard it.

Token Ring adopters further contorted the concept of multicast by implementing *Functional Group Addressing* (discussed in Chapter 3, *Bridging between Technologies*), where individual bits in the address map to fixed functions. Again, this is an example of network architects unable (or unwilling) to grok the multicasting concept.

Multicast provides an elegant way for applications to communicate without burdening any machine not currently running that particular application. Until the application instantiates itself on a computer, the network interface can ignore all traffic destined for the multicast address(es) particular to that application. Coupled with a good implementation of multicast filtering in the interface hardware, multicast provides incredible flexibility and efficiency.

In fact, with proper use of multicast techniques, there is never, ever a valid reason to send frames to the broadcast address. Broadcast can be eliminated from the architecture. We considered not defining a broadcast address in the original Ethernet design, but left it in (for political and historical reasons) with a disclaimer: "The use of broadcast is expressly discouraged" [DIX80, DIX82]. Broadcast places a burden on every station in the catenet, regardless of whether it understands the message being sent. If you want to send a message to every station on the catenet that can understand it, just define a multicast for that purpose. There are 2^{47} of them to choose from! Don't waste your time sending messages to stations that can't understand them.

Some early Ethernet hardware didn't do a very good job of multicast filtering, so multicast didn't provide much of a performance benefit over broadcasting. However, this is no excuse for using the broadcast address instead of a multicast; multicast is never worse than broadcasting. Using broadcast is just dumb design.

10.1.2 Application Use of Multicast

To understand the nature of the multicast distribution problem better, let's look at the purpose(s) for which applications use multicasting and the implications of the default switch behavior for multicast traffic.

Historically, multicasting has been used mostly for two classes of applications:

1. *Support protocols.* Multicast is widely used for many network support functions; these are often referred to as *background tasks* or *housekeeping functions.* The Spanning Tree Protocol, AppleTalk Name Binding Protocol (NBP), and the bulk of routing protocols (e.g., OSPF) all fall into this category. Multicasting is perfectly suited for these functions, as each has a need to communicate with all currently-active instantiations of a given protocol without knowing their individual addresses or even how many devices are listening to the transmissions.

2. *Service advertisements.* An application that provides a network service needs some way to inform all of its potential clients that the service is available. Manual configuration of each client with the address of the server:

   - Is both tedious and error prone
   - Cannot accommodate a service application that is moved from one machine to another
   - Cannot easily take into account which of multiple servers may actually be available at any given time

   As depicted in Figure 10.1, multicasting allows clients to dynamically determine if a service is available (from one or more servers). Once the service is invoked, client-server communication usually proceeds using unicast addressing; the service advertisement provides the client with the current address of the server.

   Examples of service advertising include the NetWare Service Advertisement Protocol (SAP) and DEC's Local Area Transport (LAT) protocol. In the case of SAP, NetWare clients can automagically build a list of available servers and make their connection choice appropriately. In the case of LAT, terminal servers can learn which (if any) host computers are available for opening a user session. Multicasting makes the operation flexible and dynamic.

An important factor for both support protocols and service advertisements is that the absolute level of traffic offered is quite low. A bridge using the

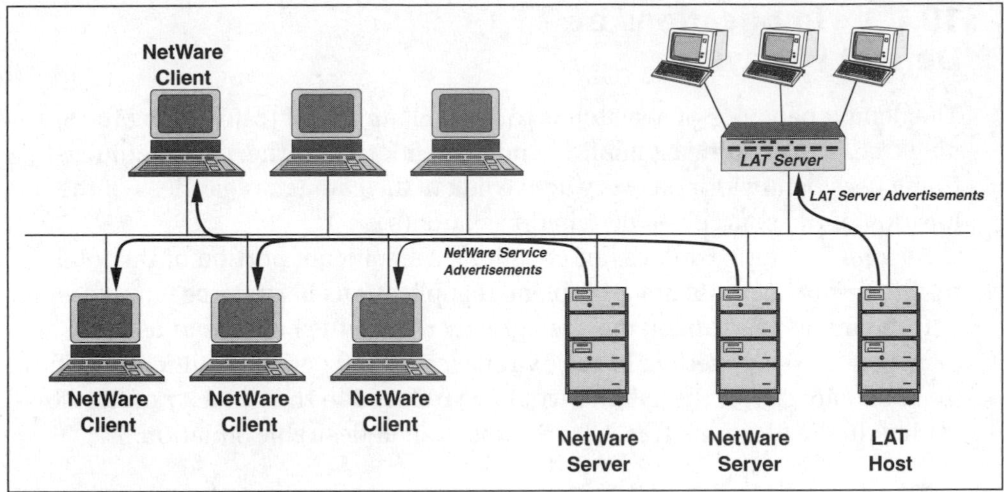

Figure 10.1 Server multicasting.

Spanning Tree Protocol will emit a BPDU once every 2 seconds (default); even on a 10 Mb/s LAN this constitutes a mere 0.003 percent of the available capacity. Service advertisements are usually made even less frequently, on the order of tens-of-seconds between messages. Even adding together all of the various support and advertisement protocols, multiple bridges and servers, and so on, the multicast traffic load is relatively light. It rarely constitutes more than a few percent of the capacity of a LAN.

An interesting phenomenon occurs when we increase the capacity of the LAN (which we seem to do more and more often these days). Unlike unicast traffic, the multicast load does not tend to increase. A Spanning Tree Protocol-enabled bridge emits messages once every 2 seconds, regardless of the data rate of the link. Similarly, routing protocols and service advertisements generate traffic in the mode of "x frames per second," independent of data rate. Thus, the percentage of capacity used by the multicast traffic actually decreases linearly with LAN capacity; one Spanning Tree message every 2 seconds constitutes 0.00003 percent of the capacity of a Gigabit Ethernet link.

The flooding problem is therefore not associated with any historical use of multicast. We are not especially concerned with increasing switch complexity to improve efficiency for the tiny fraction of load offered to the catenet by service advertisement traffic. Of greater concern is new applications that may use multicast in a traffic-intensive manner. Network-based videoconferencing, on-line training, and other applications using multicast delivery of stream video have the potential to source megabits-per-second *per stream*. With many simultaneous streams present, multicast traffic could constitute the bulk of the network traffic.

10.1.3 Implications of Default Behavior

The default behavior of a switch is to flood all multicast traffic along the spanning tree. Thus, multicast implies a multiplication of traffic; every multicast frame uses bandwidth on every active link in the catenet, regardless of the location of the source and destination station(s).

As long as multicast does not constitute a significant portion of the total traffic, this behavior is not a problem. If applications begin to use multicast in a traffic-intensive manner, they can greatly reduce the benefits of using switched LANs altogether. In the extreme case (100 percent multicast traffic), the total capacity of the catenet would be reduced to the capacity of the slowest link in the spanning tree. Clearly, this is an undesirable situation.

10.2 Trimming the (Spanning) Tree

Ideally, we would want multicast traffic to traverse only those links in the catenet that either:

- Have stations directly attached that want to receive the particular multicast
- Are needed to reach some station(s) that wants to receive that multicast traffic

Propagating multicast traffic on any other links is simply wasteful.

Note that unicast traffic is propagated perfectly (according to these two principles) by the natural action of the learning and forwarding algorithms in switches. By learning the relative location (port mapping) of each unicast address, switches can forward traffic onto only those ports actually needed to reach a particular station. As depicted in Figure 10.2, unicast traffic flows on the minimum subset of the spanning tree needed to deliver the frame from source to destination.

Wouldn't it be great if this happened automatically for multicast as well? Well, too bad, it can't. The problem is that there is no way for a switch to determine which stations need to receive which multicast groups by simply inspecting the traffic. Multicast addresses are never used as Source Addresses, so they cannot be learned like unicasts. If we want to restrict the unnecessary propagation of multicast traffic, we will have to do something different.

One possibility is to manually configure the switches with the mapping of multicast addresses to switch ports. Unfortunately, this suffers from all of the usual drawbacks of manual configuration methods. In addition, it precludes the use of dynamic multicast address assignment.

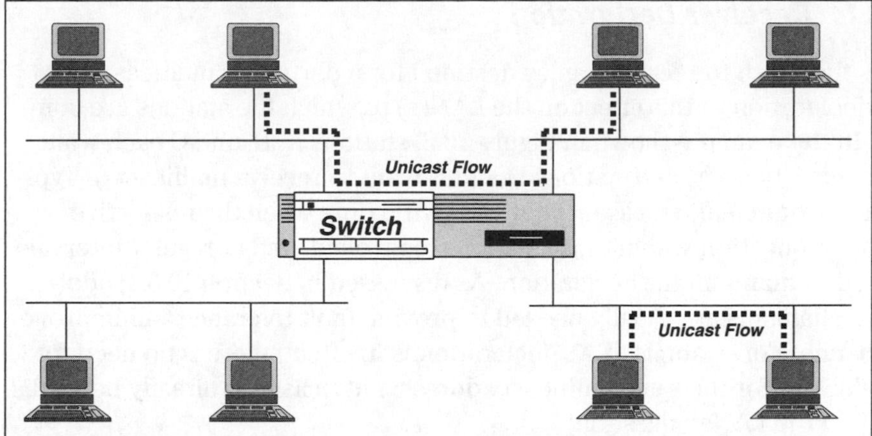

Figure 10.2 Unicast flows on a subset of the spanning tree.

The solution is to add an explicit protocol mechanism for multicast address registration. Devices that need to hear a particular multicast address can declare that requirement; stations and switches in the catenet can use this information to learn the location of all devices that need to receive a given multicast address. Once these locations are learned, traffic can be restricted to just those paths between the source(s) and destination(s) associated with each multicast address. We can prune the spanning tree to the minimum subset required for communication.

Seifert's Law of Networking #16
Solutions to network problems usually involve the invention of a new protocol.

10.2.1 The Weekend Networker's Guide to Tree Pruning

The design of a protocol mechanism for dynamic multicast pruning comprises four factors:

1. Receiver declaration to the local LAN.
2. Registration of the declaration in any switches or multicast traffic sources directly connected to that LAN.
3. Propagation of the registration across the catenet.
4. Source pruning in the absence of any receivers.

Let's look at each of these in greater detail.

10.2.1.1 Receiver Declaration

Stations that wish to receive frames destined for a particular multicast must send a declaration to this effect on the LAN(s) to which the stations are connected. In the example shown in Figure 10.3, stations A, B, and C each want to receive multicast x, and stations D and E want to receive multicast y. Typically, they would make their declarations at the time when the respective receiving application within those stations is invoked, and at regular intervals as needed to maintain the declaration. As discussed in Section 10.3.1, additional mechanisms are usually needed to provide fault tolerance and improve performance. For example, if A's declaration is in effect, there is no need for C to also declare for the same multicast address; multicast x is already being distributed on the LAN in question.

An interesting question is: What should be the Destination Address for these declaration messages? We would like the declaration to be received by all devices that are capable of transmitting multicast traffic onto the LAN, so that they can know which traffic needs to be sent here and which does not. This is a perfect application for a multicast address. We can (and do) assign a multicast address to be used for the purpose of multicast address declaration—a fitting tribute!

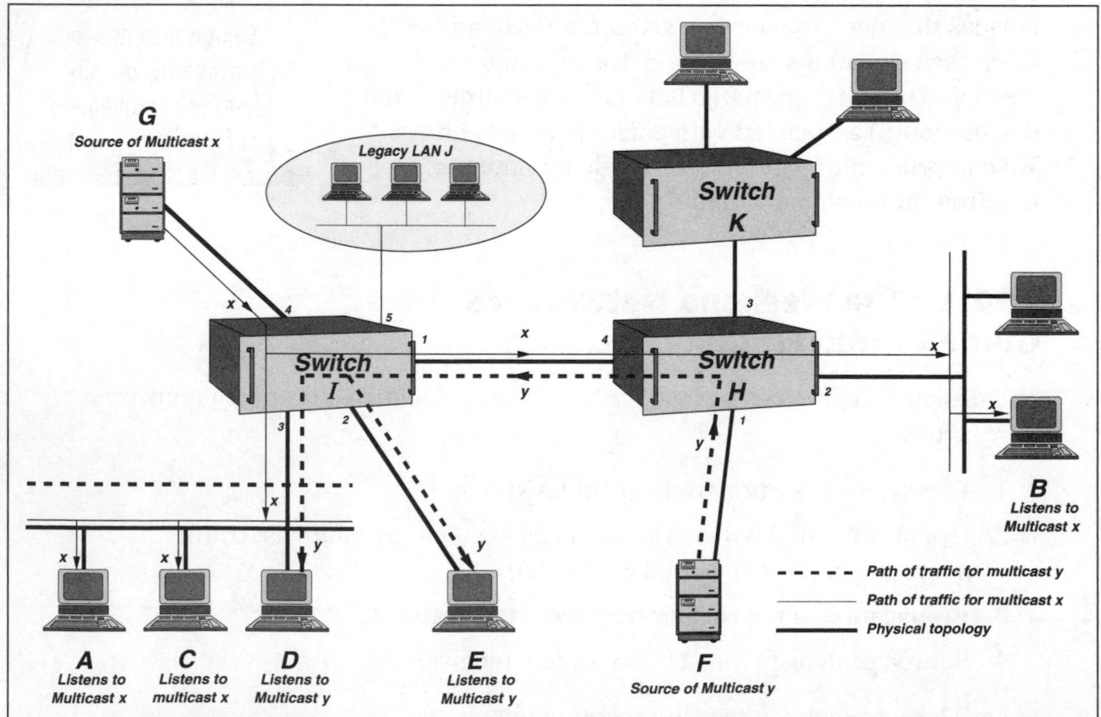

Figure 10.3 Multicast traffic flow.

Note that only the recipients of multicast traffic need to declare their desires. Any station can send traffic to a multicast address without prior notice; switches will forward the traffic along the spanning tree pruned to those branches needed to reach the declared recipients.

10.2.1.2 Registration of the Declaration

Devices that are capable of sourcing or forwarding multicast traffic onto the LAN will receive any declarations made by intended receivers, as just discussed. (They must enable reception of the multicast-registration address for the registration application they contain.) In the example, switches H and I will hear receiver declarations, as will stations F and G, which are devices that will be the source of multicast stream traffic (e.g., video delivery servers).

Upon hearing valid declarations, those devices would *register* the need for those multicast addresses to be heard on the ports where the declarations were heard. For example, switch H knows that it should forward traffic for multicast x onto port 2, but not onto ports 1 or 3, since there was no declaration for x on those ports.

It is important that switches not forward the multicast declaration messages if they are participating in this registration protocol. If they flooded the declarations, it would always appear that there were potential end-station receivers for that multicast address on every link in the catenet, which would defeat the purpose of the pruning protocol. Such action would also be inefficient in that there would be multiple declarations made on every LAN for every station wishing to hear a multicast. Switches sink (and interpret) the declaration messages, and issue new declarations on other ports as needed for proper operation.

Torresi's Law

The only reason God was able to create the universe in six days was because He didn't have to worry about the installed base.
Enzo Torresi

10.2.1.3 Propagation of the Registration

Once registered, switches need to propagate the registration so that any intervening switches know of downstream receivers and so that sources of multicast traffic know that there are potential receivers in the catenet. They propagate the registration by making their own declarations for all registered multicast addresses. In the example, switch I will, after registering station A's declaration for multicast x, issue a declaration for x on all of its other ports. Thus, station G (the source of traffic for multicast x) will learn that there is a potential receiver for its multicast stream, and can proceed with transmissions.

One problem with this scheme is that it presumes that all of the devices that need to hear and send multicast traffic are aware of, and have implemented, the registration protocol. Unfortunately, while that might be true sometime in the future, we invariably need to deal with a huge installed base of products that have either not been upgraded with this capability or are incapable of being so upgraded. Legacy devices don't advertise their need to hear multicast traffic; they simply assume that all multicasts will be flooded and that they can choose to listen to whatever addresses they want. If there are pockets of legacy devices in the catenet, then the switches to which they are connected need to recognize this fact and act accordingly. In the example, port 5 of switch I is connected to a legacy LAN, and has been configured to know this. As a result, switch I must *forward all multicasts* onto port 6, regardless of the fact that there were no declarations made by devices on that port.[6] As it was before we started trying to prune the tree, there is no way to determine which, if any, devices on that legacy port need to hear which (if any) multicast traffic. Darn.

10.2.1.4 Source Pruning

One final optimization can be made. If we know that there are no devices listening to a given multicast address, then there is no reason for any station to ever send traffic to that address. Multicast traffic sources can prune themselves out of the tree. In the example, assume that stations D and E are powered down (and for now, let's ignore the legacy LAN on port 6). D and E's declarations for multicast *y* will ultimately expire, and switch I will de-register multicast *y* and stop propagating the registration information. Once this happens, station E (the source of traffic for multicast *y*) will know that there is no one listening anymore. It can stop the multicast transmission until someone else declares a need to hear that multicast address. It is as if a television station could tell that there was nobody watching the show and turned off its transmitter.[7]

10.2.2 IEEE 802.1p

It should be obvious that, to be useful, any explicit multicast registration protocol must interoperate among different vendors' equipment. If each manufacturer used its own protocol, the benefits of multicast pruning would only accrue to that manufacturer's equipment. This is of little value to the network administrator with a large, heterogeneous catenet.

An IEEE 802 Task Force was formed in 1995 to address the concerns of vendors implementing switches targeted at multimedia environments. The primary focus of the Task Force was on:

[6] An optimization can be made that only forwards those multicasts that have not been registered using the new protocol. See Section 10.3.2 for further discussion of this mechanism.

[7] I suspect that, if we had such a mechanism for television broadcasts, a lot of transmitters would be turned off (especially during pledge week on PBS).

- Priority traffic handling in switches
- A standard mechanism for explicit multicast address registration and pruning, to optimize catenet use for traffic-intensive multicasting applications

The resulting standard is known as IEEE 802.1p.[8] Chapter 13, *Priority Operation*, discusses the issues related to priority traffic handling within switches. In the sections that follow, we look at the GARP Multicast Registration Protocol (GMRP) included as part of IEEE 802.1p.

10.3 GARP Multicast Registration Protocol (GMRP)

GMRP is the industry-standard protocol that incorporates all of the concepts discussed in Section 10.2.1. The name of the protocol itself has an interesting story:

When the IEEE Task Force first defined the protocol, it was called the *Group Address* Registration Protocol, with the acronym GARP. As the name implied, it provided for explicit registration of multicast addresses across the catenet. During the development of IEEE 802.1p, a second project was started to work on Virtual LANs (VLANs), ultimately creating the IEEE 802.1Q standard. During the work on IEEE 802.1Q, it was recognized that an equivalent protocol was needed for declaration and registration of VLAN membership. Rather than design two completely independent protocols, a *Generic Attribute* Registration Protocol (also abbreviated GARP) was devised; this general-purpose protocol could be used to register multicast addresses, VLANs, and any other connectivity or membership-style information. Thus, the meaning of the GARP acronym changed from being a multicast-specific protocol to being a generic protocol.[9] The multicast registration protocol became GMRP, and the VLAN registration protocol became GVRP. (If you can't figure out what GVRP stands for, you will have to wait until Chapter 12, *Virtual LANs: The IEEE Standard.*)

GMRP is a GARP Application, as depicted in Figure 10.4.

[8] IEEE 802.1p was never published as a standalone document. The work of the Task Force was rolled into a revision of the base IEEE 802.1D (MAC Bridge) standard and published as [IEEE98a].

[9] A similar acronym-transformation occurred in my neighborhood. I live in a very rural, mountainous area in Northern California that has a large concentration of redwood trees. The region in which my home is located was designated a Timber Preservation Zone (TPZ), which prescribes limits on how much commercial logging can be conducted. As a result of various economic and political changes, my home is still in a TPZ, but now TPZ stands for Timber Production Zone. Same abbreviation, different meaning.

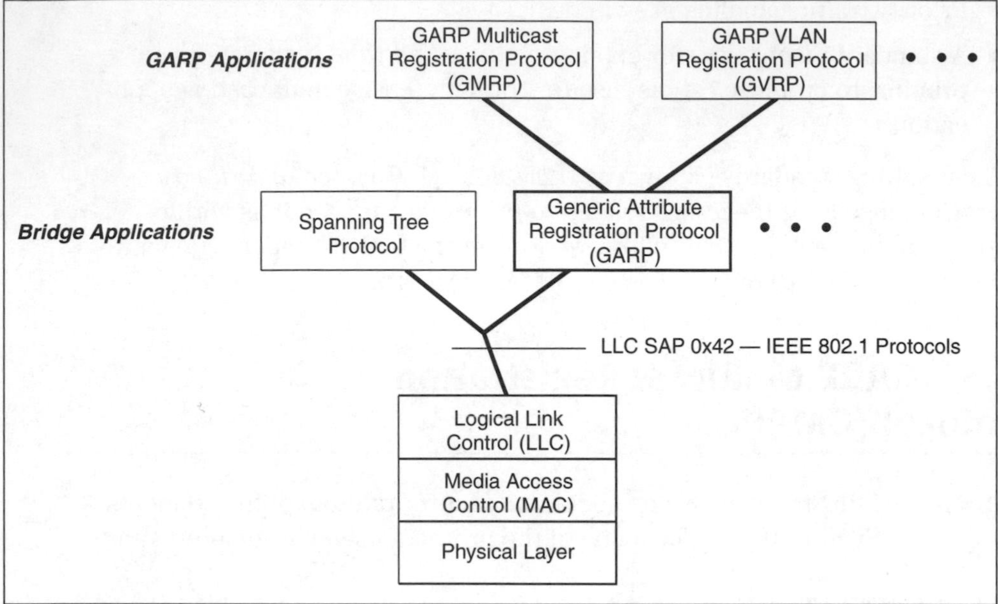

Figure 10.4 GARP architecture.

10.3.1 Generic Attribute Registration Protocol

GARP is a general-purpose protocol that supports a specific class of applications within bridges and switches. In particular, it defines a subset of the spanning tree that contains devices interested in a given network commodity, referred to as an *attribute.* GARP operates on the following general principles:

- Devices declare their desire for a given attribute (e.g., a multicast address) by making a *declaration.* Declarations are made by issuing a *Join* command using GARP (GARP commands are called *events* in the formal protocol). Declarations can be withdrawn by issuing a *Leave* command.
- There is no need for every interested device to issue a declaration. If a device hears others declaring the same attribute, it can assume that registration will occur without additional declarations.
- Devices (e.g., switches) enter a *registration* for an attribute on a given port when they hear a declaration for the attribute on that port. Deregistration of the attribute occurs when all devices that have made a

declaration have withdrawn it, or equivalently, when the registering device clears out old, stale registrations (known as *garbage collection*).

- Registrations are propagated along the spanning tree as declarations on other ports of the registering device.

GARP defines three classes of participants:

1. An *Applicant* can make declarations as well as be aware of declarations from others. An end station that is both a source and receiver of multicast traffic will typically be in this class.
2. An *Applicant-Only* can make declarations on its own behalf, but is not aware of the declarations of others. An end station that is only a receiver of multicast traffic will typically be in this class. Since it is unaware of others' needs, it is incapable of source pruning, making this an appropriate class of behavior for a source of multicast traffic.[10]
3. A *Registrar* can register declarations made by Applicants (and Applicants-Only).

A switch must implement both the Applicant and Registrar classes of operation.

Figure 10.5 depicts the fields in a GARP protocol exchange.

The fields of a GARP protocol exchange have the following meanings:[11]

Destination Address (DA) GARP exchanges use a multicast Destination Address from a range specifically reserved for the purpose. Each GARP application is associated with a specific address selected from this range, as shown in Table 10.1. Thus, different uses of GARP (e.g., GMRP or GVRP) are distinguished by the DA in their GARP protocol exchanges. Since the only intended usage of GARP is for declaration and registration of attributes among devices in a catenet, there is no need for unicast exchanges; all GARP exchanges carry a multicast Destination Address.

Note that while the range of addresses reserved for GARP seems similar to the range of addresses reserved for link-constrained protocols (i.e., 01-80-C2-00-00-00 through 01-80-C2-00-00-0F, as discussed in Chapter 2, *Transparent Bridges*), there is a key difference. GARP exchanges are not necessarily constrained to a single link. Bridges should never forward

[10] The standard defines a special subset of the Applicant-Only class, called a *Simple Applicant*. Simple Applicants don't even listen to others' declarations, much less register them. As such, they can make superfluous declarations of attributes that have already been registered. While the Simple Applicant reduces the complexity of the Applicant state machine, it is inefficient and not recommended practice.

[11] The example shown uses an Ethernet frame for the MAC encapsulation. GARP exchanges on Token Ring of FDDI LANs would use the appropriate MAC encapsulation for those LANs.

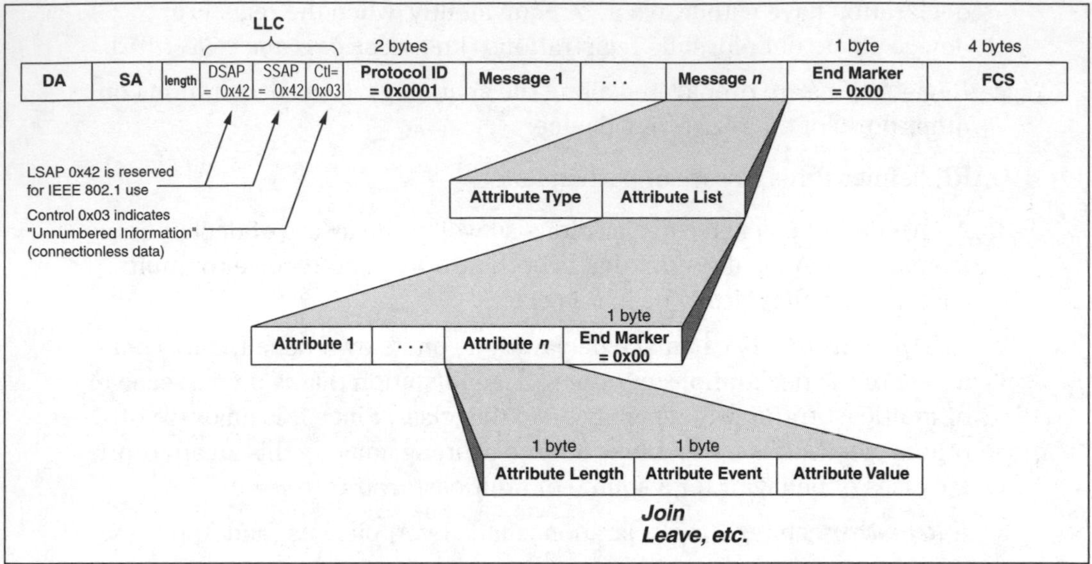

Figure 10.5 Format of a GARP protocol exchange (Ethernet Encapsulation).

spanning tree BPDUs, full duplex PAUSE messages, or Link Aggregation Control messages (all of which use DAs in the link-constrained range). Bridges may or may not forward GARP messages, depending on the specific GARP applications they support. If a bridge does not support a particular GARP application, then it must transparently forward any GARP exchanges for that application; otherwise, other bridges that are aware of the GARP application in question would never see the declarations being made. If a bridge is GARP-aware for a given application, then it should sink and process all GARP exchanges for that application, and not forward them transparently. The bridge may, as a result of receiving GARP protocol information, initiate a new GARP protocol exchange (e.g., prop-

Table 10.1 GARP Application Addresses

ADDRESS	GARP APPLICATION
01-80-C2-00-00-20	GARP Multicast Registration Protocol (GMRP)
01-80-C2-00-00-21	GARP VLAN Registration Protocol (GVRP)
01-80-C2-00-00-22 through 01-80-C2-00-00-2F	Reserved for future use

agating a multicast registration), but this is not the same as transparently forwarding the original message.

Source Address (SA) The Source Address in a GARP exchange always carries the unicast address of the device issuing the GARP message.

Length field When using Ethernet encapsulation, GARP exchanges use the length-interpretation of the Ethernet Length/Type field and native LLC encapsulation.[12]

LLC header All GARP exchanges carry an LLC Destination and Source Service Access Point (DSAP and SSAP) of 0x42 (the value assigned for IEEE 802.1 use), and a control value of 0x03, indicating connectionless data exchange.

Protocol ID Note that the LLC DSAP/SSAP in a GARP exchange is the same value used for the Spanning Tree Protocol (STP, see Chapter 5, *Loop Resolution*). The first field following the LLC header in the STP is also a Protocol Identifier, which is assigned the value 0x00 for the STP. For GARP use, the Protocol Identifier is assigned the value 0x01. Thus, we are able to differentiate STP messages from GARP exchanges unambiguously, even if the address information has been removed by earlier protocol parsing.

GARP messages A GARP exchange carries a variable number of generic messages. There is no explicit indication of the number of variable length messages contained in a single exchange; the end of the message list is indicated by an *End Marker*, which has the value 0x00. GARP protocol processing is performed on a message-by-message basis until the messages in a given exchange are exhausted.

Each message comprises an *Attribute Type*, which is specific to the particular GARP application sending the message, and a list of attributes of the indicated type (*Attribute List*). An example of an Attribute Type would be "Specific Group Membership Information" for GMRP declaration; the Attribute List would then contain the list of specific multicast addresses being declared.

Similar to the messages themselves, the Attribute List comprises a variable number of variable-length generic attributes.[13] There is no explicit indication of the number of attributes contained in a single message; the end of the attribute list is indicated by an End Marker, which has the value 0x00.

[12] The depiction in Fig. 10.5 does not show the use of VLAN-tagging. If a GARP exchange was VLAN-tagged, then there would be a Type field indicating the VLAN tag followed by the VLAN tag control information. Following these fields would be the Length field discussed here. See Chapter 11, *Virtual LANs: Applications and Concepts*, and Chapter 12 for a complete discussion of VLAN tagging.

[13] Which is why it is called the Generic Attribute Registration Protocol in the first place!

Each Attribute consists of three elements:

1. The *Attribute Length*, which is 1 byte long, indicating the number of bytes in the Attribute field, including the Length field itself.
2. The *Attribute Event*, which is a 1 byte long generic "command code" indicating the action to be taken relative to the value (e.g., Join or Leave a multicast group).
3. The *Attribute Value* specific to the Attribute Type (for example, the value of the 48-bit multicast address being declared).

Table 10.2 lists the currently-defined values for Attribute Events. Attribute Types and Values are specific to particular GARP applications; GMRP-specific uses are discussed in Section 10.3.2.[14]

The protocol is clearly quite general, and can be used to support a variety of applications requiring explicit registration of various functions. The protocol is also fairly complex, in great part due to the need to provide for proper operation under a variety of error and boundary conditions (e.g., lost GARP exchanges; stations and bridges coming and going over time; etc.) No attempt has been made here to provide a complete specification of GARP—that specification alone consumes 72 pages of the official standard, not including any application-specific issues! Implementors should refer to the standard [IEEE98a] for the formal specification. The standard includes both a state machine formalization and reference C code for GARP.

10.3.2 GMRP Use of GARP

GMRP uses the GARP protocol mechanisms to declare and register the needs of end stations and switches to hear multicast addresses. Like any GARP application, GMRP defines both a GARP application address and a set of application-specific attribute types.

GMRP Application Address The Destination Address in all GMRP exchanges carries the value 0x01-80-C2-00-00-20, as indicated in Table 10.1.

GMRP Attribute Types GMRP defines two Attribute Types:

1. *Specific Group Membership Information.* This Attribute Type is used to declare, register, and propagate the need to hear specific multicast addresses. The Attribute Value(s) for this Attribute Type are 48-bit multicast addresses. Specific Group Membership is encoded in the Attribute Type field as 0x01.

[14] GVRP-specific uses are discussed in Chapter 12.

Table 10.2 GARP Attribute Events

ATTRIBUTE EVENT	USAGE
0x00	**Leave All** Announcement by a device that all of its registrations (for all attribute values in this application) are about to be de-registered unless someone indicates continued interest by issuing a new Join. Used to clear out old, stale registrations (garbage collection).
0x01	**Join Empty** Used to declare an attribute, where the declarer has not currently registered the attribute from anyone else (i.e., a declaration into what is perceived as an empty group).
0x02	**Join In** Used to declare the attribute, where the declarer has currently registered the attribute from someone else (i.e., a declaration into what is perceived as an non-empty group).
0x03	**Leave Empty** Used to withdraw a registration for a group that is perceived to be empty.
0x04	**Leave In** Used to withdraw a registration for a group that is perceived to be non-empty.[1]
0x05	**Empty** Used to state a desire to hear declarations for a given attribute without actually declaring the attribute (e.g., a multicast source that will transmit a stream only if someone is listening)

[1] Leave Empty and Leave In are kept separate within GARP for possible future protocol modifications. The treatment of these two events is identical in the formal specification.

2. *Group Service Requirement Information.* It is not realistic to expect to be able to upgrade an existing catenet from all GMRP-unaware devices to all GMRP-aware devices at once. There will invariably be a period when the catenet will contain pockets of legacy devices that do not understand GMRP. Existing devices expect to see all multicast traffic without having to explicitly ask for it. The applications running on these legacy devices will not operate correctly unless the multicast traffic is propagated in a manner consistent with the "old way." To support the migration from legacy equipment to GMRP-aware equipment, GMRP provides a means to register a general service requirement for multicast address propagation.

Two types of service requirements are supported:

- *Forward All Multicast.* Indicates a need for full legacy-style support. If a declaration is made for this service (typically by a bridge connected to a legacy segment, such as bridge I in Figure 10.3), then all GMRP-aware devices will know that all multicast traffic must be propagated to the device making the declaration. This declaration effectively disables multicast pruning between any multicast source and the device making this service declaration. While unfortunate, it is sometimes needed to provide true legacy-system support.
- *Forward All Unregistered.* Allows some multicast pruning capability while still providing legacy-system compatibility. Let's assume that we are using GMRP for its intended purpose, that is, to reduce catenet utilization for traffic-intensive multicast applications. By definition, these are non-legacy applications, and can be assumed (or designed) to use multicast addresses that do not conflict with any legacy multicast use. (For example, we would not use the "All AppleTalk Devices" multicast address for some new conferencing application, even if we intend to run the application over the AppleTalk protocol suite.) Thus, we can keep the traffic-intensive multicast addresses separate from the legacy multicast addresses. GMRP declarations and registrations will only be made for these new multicast addresses by the

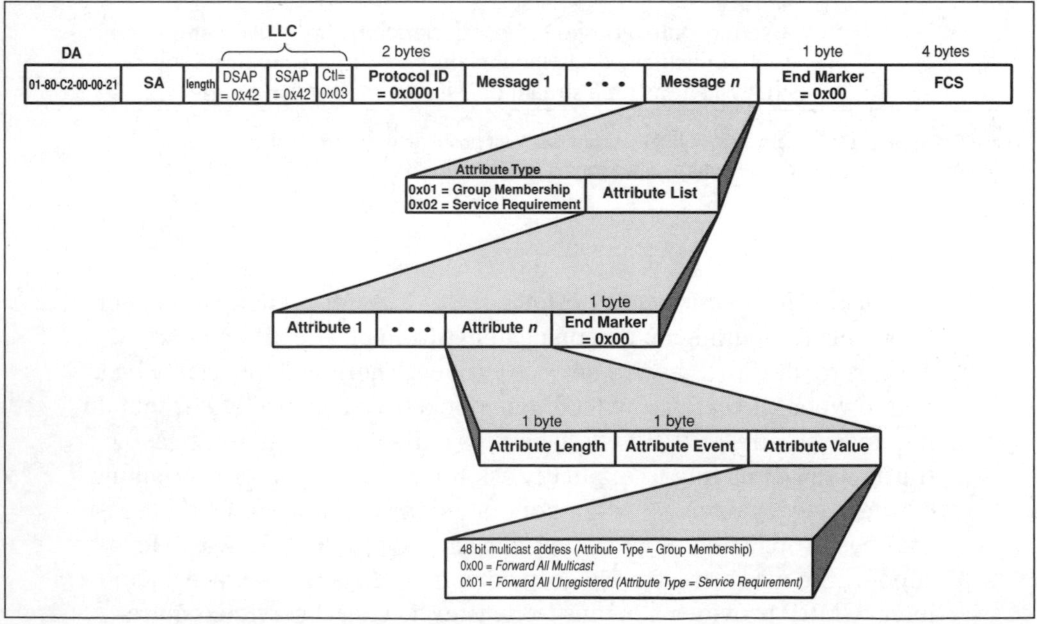

Figure 10.6 GMRP protocol exchange format.

devices hosting the new, traffic-intensive applications. As a result, we don't need to forward all multicast traffic to legacy segments—only that traffic that is not registered with GMRP, that is, the traffic using the legacy multicast addresses. A *Forward All Unregistered* declaration performs this function. Only the low-utilization legacy multicast traffic must be flooded; traffic-intensive multicast traffic can be pruned by GMRP.

The *Group Service Requirement* is encoded as 0x02 in the Attribute Type field. *Forward All Multicast* is encoded as Attribute Value 0x00; *Forward All Unregistered* is encoded as Attribute Value 0x01.

Figure 10.6 depicts the format of GMRP protocol exchanges.

CHAPTER

11

Virtual LANs: Applications and Concepts

Up to now, we haven't had much trouble figuring out what a LAN was.[1] Even though we haven't explicitly stated it, we have a mental image of a LAN as a collection of stations, cables, hubs, and related equipment configured to support communications within a local area. A LAN allows direct Data Link layer communications among the application processes running within those stations attached to the LAN.

A typical medium-to-large organization may have many LANs in place to support large numbers of users and network applications. Each user is typically attached to a single physical LAN; the set of devices connected to a given LAN is defined by the limitations of the equipment employed (e.g., the number of ports on a hub) and the cable connections configured by the network administrator (i.e., which devices are connected to which hubs or shared media segments). Once the LAN is installed and configured, its extent is fixed; changing the LAN configuration (i.e., the set of devices and applications that appear on a given LAN) requires a change to those physical connections that created the LAN. The logical connectivity of the LAN is equal to its physical connectivity.

[1] I can't imagine how you could get to Chapter 11 without having at least *some* idea!

Virtual LAN (VLAN) technology allows us to separate the logical connectivity from the physical connectivity. Users are still connected via physical cables to physical wiring devices, but the connectivity view from the station or application perspective is no longer restricted to the bounds of this physical topology. That is, the set of stations or applications that can directly communicate as if on a common LAN can be controlled through software configuration of the switches and/or the end stations in the catenet. The LAN is virtual in that a set of stations and applications can behave as if they are connected to a single physical LAN when in fact they are not.[2]

To achieve this flexibility, we must use switches rather than shared-bandwidth (repeater) hubs for our device interconnections. Furthermore, the switches need to be *VLAN-aware;* they must include a set of features and capabilities beyond those of the VLAN-unaware switches considered up to now. It is these additional capabilities that allow us to configure the logical connectivity as appropriate for the user's application environment. As will be discussed, even greater power can be unleashed by making the end stations themselves VLAN-aware. Fortunately, we can provide most of the advantages of VLANs through incremental changes in the infrastructure; it is not necessary to change all of the devices at once to achieve substantial VLAN benefits.

The chapter is divided into two sections, each with its own unique focus:

- *Applications of VLANs.* In this section, we take the view of the network planner and user to see how VLAN technology can be used to provide added benefits in practical networks.
- *VLAN concepts.* Here we explain the technical foundations of VLANs: VLAN-awareness, VLAN tagging, frame distribution within VLANs, VLAN mapping rules, and architectural layering. It is the application of these concepts that allows us to achieve the application benefits discussed in the first section.

Chapter 12, *Virtual LANs: The IEEE Standard,* explores the technical details of the industry standard for VLAN operation and behavior.

11.1 Applications of VLANs

In this section, we examine both some popular as well as some more exotic, emerging applications of VLAN technology. The focus here is on the benefits and capabilities provided to the network planner/administrator and to the

[2] A *virtual entity* is one that can be treated as if it exists, even though it doesn't (e.g., virtual memory). The converse is a *transparent entity;* this is something that can be treated as if it isn't there, even though it is (e.g., a Transparent Bridge).

users. At this point, we consider just the operational effects and not how the technology provides these capabilities.

11.1.1 The Software Patch Panel

In the early 1990s, 10BASE-T quickly became the LAN technology of choice. Sales and network deployment levels exploded much faster than anticipated by the market analysts and many corporate product planners. Within a few years, virtually all new Ethernet installations used 10BASE-T's star-wired twisted pair cabling scheme rather than the multidrop coaxial cable bus arrangement popular in the 1980s.

Why did everyone glom onto this new system so wholeheartedly? Contrary to popular belief, it was not because 10BASE-T was less expensive. (It wasn't.) While the twisted pair cable itself may be less expensive per unit length than coaxial cable, the star-wired nature of 10BASE-T implies that a lot more cable is needed. Structured wiring systems provide a *home-run* from every workplace to the central wiring hub; a dedicated cable is provided from every user to the wiring closet. This uses a lot more cable than if all users simply tap into a single, common shared medium. In addition, 10BASE-T mandates the use of an active hub device that is not required in coaxial Ethernet, further increasing the cost.[3]

The reason why 10BASE-T became so popular was that its structured star-wiring system allows the wiring closet to become a centralized, controllable focal point for configuring and managing the network. In practice, LANs used for office automation applications are constantly in a state of flux; people and equipment are being moved, added, and changed on an ongoing basis. With the coaxial cable system, such changes often required rewiring, or at a minimum, disruption of the network during periods of reconfiguration. With the centralized wiring center, connections between equipment on the LAN are made by patch-cord interconnections on a wiring panel or punch-down block. Thus, moves/adds/changes can be achieved simply by changing the patch cord interconnections without rewiring or network down-time.

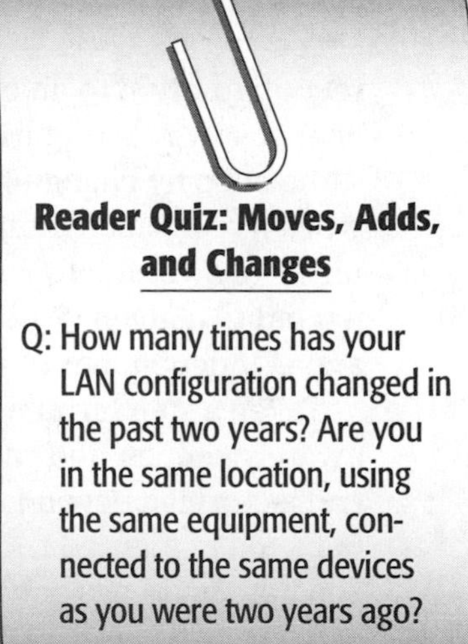

Reader Quiz: Moves, Adds, and Changes

Q: How many times has your LAN configuration changed in the past two years? Are you in the same location, using the same equipment, connected to the same devices as you were two years ago?

If we replace the shared-bandwidth wiring hubs from the original 10BASE-T system with VLAN-aware switches, we can take the concept of easy LAN

[3] A two-station 10BASE-T Ethernet does not require a hub, but was not a particularly interesting configuration when 10BASE-T first became popular.

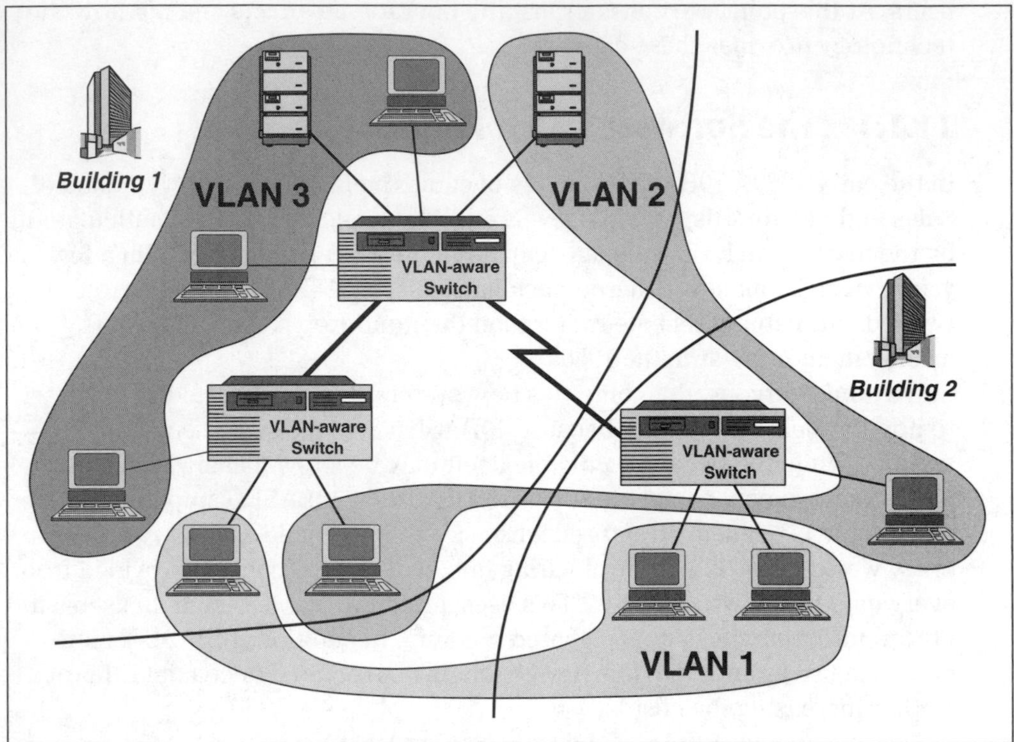

Figure 11.1 Creating VLANs across multiple switches.

reconfiguration to an even higher level. Rather than implementing moves/adds/changes by reconfiguring patch cords in the wiring closet, we can achieve the same ends by changing the VLAN associations of the switch ports using network management software. The use of VLANs allows us to partition a single physical switch into a set of *virtual switches*, where the set of devices connected to a given virtual switch is controlled by the mapping of switch ports and is independent of the physical packaging of the (single) switch.[4]

Taken a step further, if all of the wiring concentrators in the catenet are VLAN-aware switches, and can be consistently managed as a group, logical workgroups can be formed beyond the limits of the individual switches themselves. As depicted in Figure 11.1, VLANs can be created across multiple switches, even in separate buildings or geographically-dispersed regions. A catenet so comprised can be viewed as if all of the users were connected to a single wiring closet. Any arbitrary set of users, servers, and other equipment can be configured as a closed group (i.e., a VLAN); the connectivity is the same as if their patch cords were connected to the ports of a switch dedicated to that workgroup alone.

[4] And, in the process, we can further reduce the muscle tone of network administrators by allowing them to avoid that walk to the wiring closet and do even more of their jobs without leaving their soft, cushy, ergonomically-designed chairs.

Of course, the performance may not be the same as if the members of the workgroups were really in the same physical location, connected through a single dedicated switch. Traffic propagating through multiple switches, sharing LAN and possibly slower-speed WAN link capacity, will by necessity incur greater delay and lower throughput than if it traversed a dedicated LAN. However, the increase in configuration flexibility can be phenomenal and worth the performance penalty (if any).

The use of VLANs to build such *software patch panels* was both the first and the easiest application to be implemented with VLAN technology.[5] This particular application requires only simple, port-based VLAN capabilities, as discussed in Section 11.2.3.1 (although the task of designing and implementing software to manage the configuration is not trivial).

The scenario described here reflects what is possible; what you will actually get with a given set of switches depends on the limitations of the particular vendor's implementation. You do not reach Paradise by the dashboard light, nor achieve Nirvana through purchase orders (especially those within the purchase authorization limits of lower-level managers). The flexibility obtained from a commercial set of VLAN-aware switches will be a function of the features implemented in the devices, the limitations of those features (numbers of VLANs, permitted configurations, etc.), and the capabilities of the management software provided with the product.

11.1.2 LAN Security

When using a shared-bandwidth (non-switched) LAN, there is no inherent protection provided against unwanted eavesdropping. Indeed, this is often used as a generic complaint against shared LANs; any user can, using software on a conventional personal computer, capture and inspect every frame on the LAN, regardless of the intended destination. Commercial network monitoring tools are sold for precisely this purpose. In addition to eavesdropping, a malicious user on a shared LAN can also induce problems by sending lots of traffic to specific targeted users (i.e., overloading their network interfaces and LAN software with huge amounts of spurious traffic, resulting in performance degradation, undesired behavior, or system crashes) or the network as a whole (using spurious broadcasts). The only cure is to physically isolate the offending user.[6]

A conventional switched LAN provides some natural protection against casual eavesdropping. A user on a given switch port will hear only that traffic

[5] Surprise, surprise. Designers rarely implement the most complex functions in the first incarnation of new products, regardless of the usefulness of such features. Competitive pressures invariably force vendors to sacrifice functionality for time-to-market; additional capabilities are added later, after market share and an installed base of users are established.

[6] Often, such physical isolation involves permanent removal from the building and the employment roster.

intended for destinations on that particular switch port. In a microsegmented environment (i.e., one user per port), that traffic will comprise only:

- Unicast traffic intended for the attached user
- Unicast traffic for destinations whose port mapping is unknown
- Multicast traffic

Thus, it is not possible to capture or inspect much of the interesting traffic, that is, transactions and data exchanges among other users. An eavesdropper can still hear all of the multicast traffic, but this does not commonly contain sensitive information.[7] However, it is still possible for our malicious colleague to disrupt operations with unsolicited traffic. A conventional switch will forward both unicast and multicast traffic to the appropriate port(s); we can impede listening but not transmitting.

By creating logical partitions to the catenet with VLAN technology, we further enhance the protections against both unwanted eavesdropping and spurious transmissions. As depicted in Figure 11.2, a properly implemented port-based VLAN allows free communication among the members of a given VLAN, but does not forward traffic among switch ports associated with members of different VLANs. That is, a VLAN configuration restricts traffic flow to a proper subset of the catenet comprising exactly those links connecting members of the VLAN. This isolation accrues both to unicast and multicast traffic. The switch in Figure 11.2 knows that station Y is reachable through port 5. Were the switch a conventional VLAN-unaware device, it would naturally forward any traffic destined for station Y to port 5. However, with the VLAN configuration shown, the switch only forwards traffic to port 5 that belongs to VLAN 3. Since traffic from station X originates in VLAN 1, it cannot propagate across the boundary. The VLAN configuration is providing traffic isolation, even among ports on the same switch. This is true for multicast and unknown unicast traffic as well. While a conventional switch forwards all multicast and unknown unicast traffic to all ports except that on which the traffic arrived, a properly-configured VLAN-aware switch will forward such traffic only to those ports (except for the arrival port, of course) that contain members of the VLAN associated with that traffic.[8]

Thus, we have enhanced our protection against malicious or curious users. Users can eavesdrop only on the multicast and unknown unicast traffic within

[7] As discussed in Chapter 10, *Multicast Pruning*, most multicast traffic today comprises service advertisements and network housekeeping functions. If and when LAN multicast video and audio conferences become popular, the assumption that most multicast traffic is innocuous may change.

[8] Some commercial products are less-than-ideal when it comes to isolating traffic for unknown unicast destinations between VLANs. The result is known as a *leaky VLAN*, as some of the traffic (notably the exception or boundary cases) sometimes appears outside the intended scope.

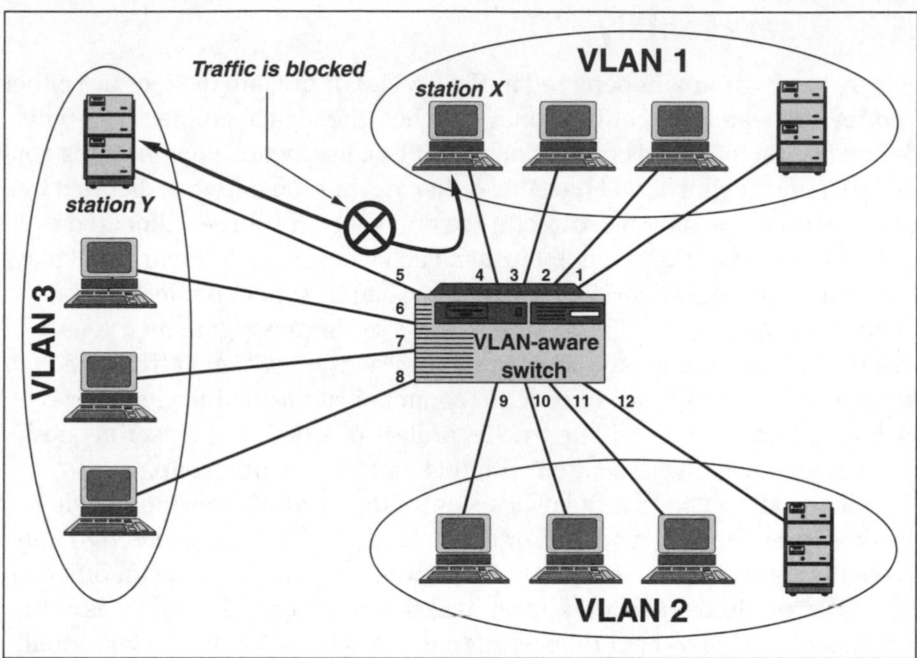

Figure 11.2 VLAN traffic isolation.

their own VLAN; presumably the configured VLAN comprises a set of logically-related users (e.g., a company department). It is no longer possible to eavesdrop on traffic from other departments. Similarly, while it is still possible to inject malicious traffic, such traffic should only propagate among switch ports within a single VLAN, and thus any network disruption is localized. Of course, this improvement in security is achieved through a reduction in connectivity; it is no longer possible to communicate directly (i.e., at the Data Link layer) between stations in disjoint VLANs, even though they are connected to a common switched catenet. (Communication can still be achieved at Network layer through a router.)

It should be emphasized that there is no such thing as total electronic security. While VLAN technology can isolate traffic as described, such mechanisms will not prevent all security attacks. VLAN isolation simply makes the intruder's job more difficult, and will prevent intrusions only from those attackers who are unwilling to expend the effort necessary to break the level of protection provided.

Reader Quiz: Network Security
Q: Do you usually secure the latch on the door of a stall in a public restroom?
Q: Do you think this would stop anyone who really wanted to get in?

11.1.3 User Mobility

Consider the environment depicted in Figure 11.3. If the hub devices are either shared-LAN repeaters or conventional switches, the logical connectivity will be defined by the physical connections. That is, a user whose computer is connected to a port on hub 1 will have his or her view of the network dictated by that connection. The user will directly see only those resources allocated to that workgroup (e.g., the server). Further, each workgroup in Figure 11.3 may comprise a separate Network layer entity (e.g., an IP subnet or NetWare/IPX network) with its own local Network layer address assignments. A user connected to hub 1 must have a Network layer address assigned from the local network address space in order to communicate using the given Network-layer protocol. This will be true regardless of whether the user in question is, in fact, logically associated with that particular workgroup.

It would be more useful if the user's view of the network was independent of the physical connection point. For example, if our friend connected to hub 1 was really a member of workgroup C, but was temporarily using an office in building 1, it would be nice if it appeared to that user that he or she was actually connected to his or her home workgroup. Providing for such user mobility with VLAN technology conveys some important benefits:

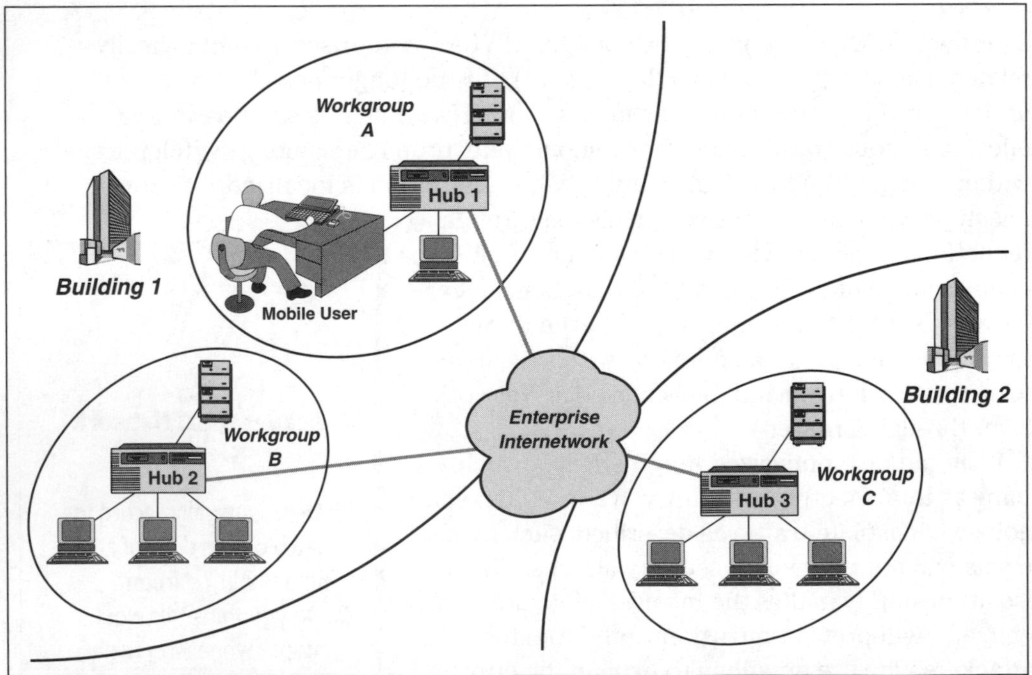

Figure 11.3 Workgroups defined by physical connectivity.

- Each user's view of the network can stay consistent regardless of physical location; the available servers, printers, and so on remain the same. Such consistency can make life much easier for users, since they do not have to deal explicitly with their own mobility.
- Network layer addresses may not need to be changed based on physical location in the organization.
- User privileges can be constrained to a minimum set of appropriate resources. In the conventional (non-VLAN) environment of Figure 11.3, mobile users will typically need to be granted access privileges on every LAN to which they might physically connect, just to make it possible to reach their "home" servers. For example, we might have to give a mobile user an account on the local server for workgroup A to allow him or her remote access to the home server (C).

VLANs can accommodate such transparent user mobility. By defining a VLAN based on the addresses of the member stations, we can define a workgroup independent of the physical locations of its members. Unicast and multicast traffic (including server advertisements) will propagate to all members of the VLAN so that they can communicate freely among themselves; traffic for other VLANs (i.e., other workgroups) will be isolated. The resulting logical connectivity can be as depicted in Figure 11.4.

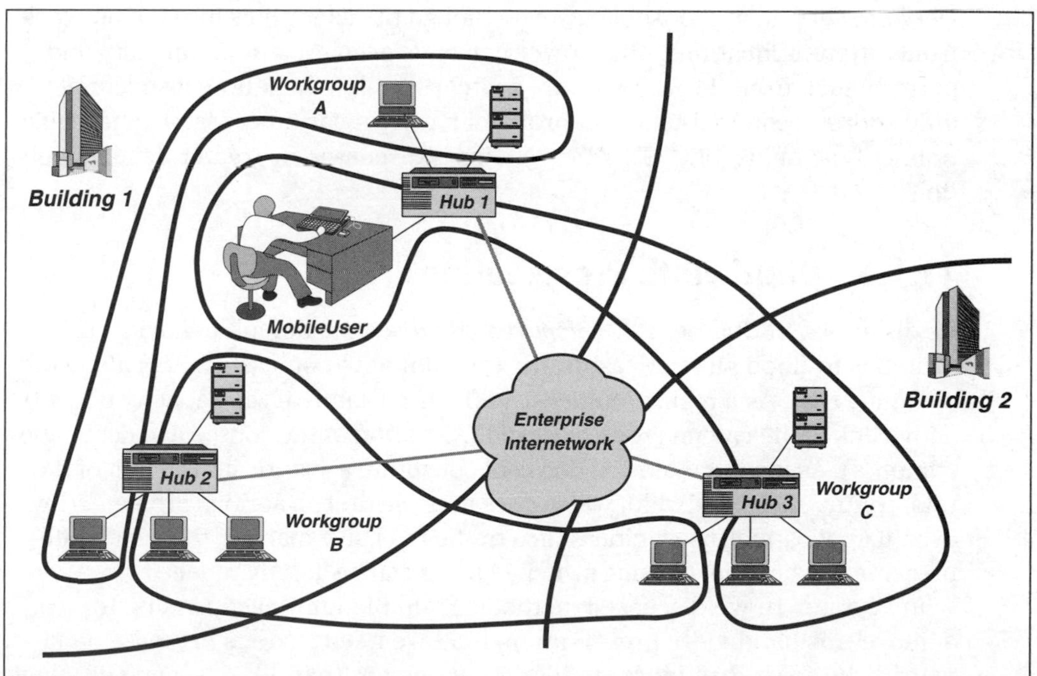

Figure 11.4 Workgroups defined by logical connectivity.

This mobility can be extended to multiple floors, buildings, and even geographically-dispersed locations, although of course performance may suffer as a result of traffic forwarding across multiple LANs and/or slower-speed WAN connections. Again, this is a tradeoff among performance, cost (of the switches), and flexibility.

As discussed in Section 11.2.3, providing user mobility in this manner imposes greater performance requirements on the VLAN-aware switches than the simple software patch-panel or security applications described earlier. Those simpler applications required the switch to determine VLAN membership solely based on the switch port on which frames arrive; for a mobility application, the switch must inspect (at a minimum), in real time, the Source Address of every frame to determine the VLAN to which it belongs.

It is possible to achieve even greater flexibility for users running multiple protocol suites on their computers (e.g., IP, AppleTalk, and NetWare/IPX). The logical connectivity can be a function not only of the station address, but of the protocol encapsulated by the frame. A user may have a different view of the network (different logical connectivity) for applications running over each of the different protocols; the resources available to AppleTalk applications may be different from those available to IP applications, and so on. However, each of those multiple views can be kept consistent (for that user) independent of physical location within the organization. This is an incredibly powerful mechanism. AppleTalk printers and zones remain consistent, as do NetWare servers and IP subnets, even though the user plugs into the network from different locations. This power demands even greater complexity and performance from the VLAN-aware switches, which must now inspect not only addresses in real-time, but protocol types (in various possible encapsulations—Type fields, LLC, SNAP, etc.). This is discussed in greater detail in Section 11.2.3.3.

11.1.4 Bandwidth Preservation

As discussed in Chapter 2, *Transparent Bridges*, the default behavior of a switch is to flood all multicast traffic (and unknown unicast traffic) along the spanning tree. As a result, multicast traffic uses some of the capacity of every active link in the catenet, regardless of the location of the source and destination station(s). As long as multicast does not constitute a significant fraction of the total traffic, such bandwidth waste does not constitute a serious problem. However, if applications use multicast in a traffic-intensive manner, the bandwidth-preservation benefits of using switched LANs can be greatly reduced.

In Chapter 10 we discussed methods of simple multicast pruning to achieve this bandwidth preservation. If all we need to do is preserve bandwidth, Multicast Pruning is simpler to implement than VLANs, and sufficient for the purpose. However, if we are deploying VLAN technology for any other purpose (e.g., mobility), we get much of the benefit of bandwidth preservation as an added bonus, with no additional effort required. A properly-implemented VLAN will restrict multicast and unknown unicast traffic to only those links necessary to reach members of the VLAN associated with that multicast (or unknown unicast) traffic. That is, VLAN operation subsumes multicast pruning. It is also possible to deploy both mechanisms: VLAN technology will isolate traffic between logically separated workgroups, and multicast pruning can be used to further preserve bandwidth within a VLAN in the face of multicast-intensive traffic among specific VLAN-member stations or applications.

As discussed in Chapter 12, the protocol used for automatic configuration of VLANs (the GARP VLAN Registration Protocol, GVRP) provides capabilities similar to those of the protocol used for automatic multicast pruning (GMRP, discussed in Chapter 10).

VLANS ARE NOTHING NEW

It is interesting to note that while there is a great deal of current activity and interest in VLANs from vendors, users, and the standards community, the concepts are not really new. The AppleTalk protocol suite has always included the idea of a logical grouping of users, known as an AppleTalk *zone,* which is completely orthogonal to the Network-layer organization (i.e., zone identifiers do not correspond to network identifiers). Zone membership allows users the capability to access resources within the zone, regardless of their physical location. The AppleTalk suite includes a number of support protocols to allow seamless operation of zones across an internetwork, including the Zone Information Protocol (ZIP), which performs a function nearly identical to that performed by GVRP. In a very real sense, an AppleTalk zone is a Network-layer Virtual LAN.

11.2 VLAN Concepts

If a catenet is a set of stations that are able to communicate transparently at the Data Link layer, then a VLAN can be seen as being a proper subset of the catenet. A VLAN comprises a set of stations (defined by the VLAN association rules in effect) together with the links and switches needed to interconnect them. A station may be a member of multiple VLANs, depending on the VLAN association rules, the capabilities of the stations and switches deployed, and the nature of the protocols and applications operating within the station.

From the previous section, we can see that VLAN technology can provide real end user benefits. In this section we look at the technical and operational aspects of VLANs that are needed to achieve these benefits. To this end, we consider four important mechanisms:

- VLAN tagging
- VLAN awareness
- VLAN association rules
- Frame distribution

But before we begin, let's examine something even more basic:

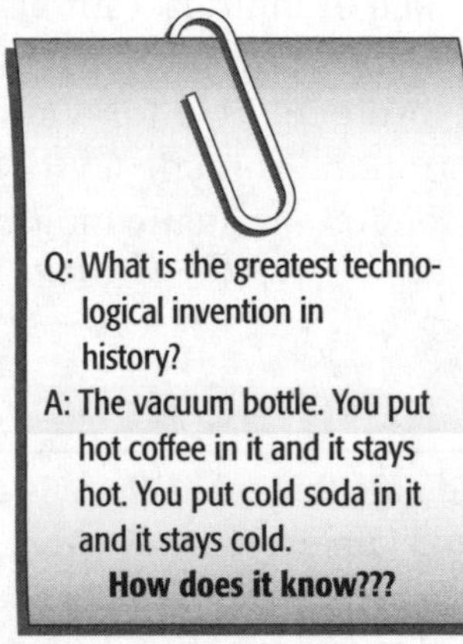

Q: What is the greatest technological invention in history?
A: The vacuum bottle. You put hot coffee in it and it stays hot. You put cold soda in it and it stays cold.
How does it know???

As we can see from the various VLAN applications described earlier (and many more that will become evident), a VLAN is a logical grouping of entities in a catenet, but there is no restriction on the nature of the entities so grouped. A VLAN can comprise a set of logically-related stations (e.g., a distributed workgroup), a set of Network-layer protocol entities (i.e., an IP subnet or IPX network), a set of high-level application entities (e.g., a LAN videoconference), and so on. Clearly, we don't want to have to design different types of VLAN-aware devices (switches and end stations) for different applications. So the question becomes, "How do the VLAN-aware devices know what the logical relationships are, so that frames can be properly distributed to achieve the desired behavior?"

The answer is that, like the vacuum bottle, they don't know. More importantly, they don't have to know. All that is needed to make VLANs work is for the logical relationship to somehow be manifested in the contents of the frames sent by the entities involved. That is, stations and switches simply look at frames and classify a frame as belonging to a particular VLAN based on a set of VLAN association rules. While the rules are clearly a result of some desired application behavior, VLAN-aware devices don't need to know the reason for the rules, but just need to apply the rules and classify every frame as belonging to one VLAN or another. Two important observations can be made as a result of this approach:

1. *From the perspective of the VLAN-aware devices, it is* frames *that belong to a VLAN, and not stations, protocols, or applications.* As always, we are dealing with a connectionless catenet; each frame is handled indepen-

dently of all others. A device associates each frame with a given VLAN on a frame-by-frame basis and makes decisions (e.g., frame forwarding) based in part on that association. In Section 11.2.3 we discuss various possible VLAN association rules that can be used to achieve different application behaviors. Depending on the rule(s) in place, frames transmitted by a given station may all be classified into the same VLAN or into different VLANs. That is, a station does not belong to a VLAN, its frames do.

2. *A given frame is associated with a single VLAN.* There must be a 1:1 mapping of frames to VLANs. Depending on the applications it is running, a station may be a member of multiple VLANs, but the mapping of a frame to a VLAN must be unambiguous.

In the sections that follow, we will be discussing various methods of mapping frames to VLANs, making forwarding decisions, and so on. It is important to remember that, from the perspective of the VLAN-aware devices in the catenet, all VLAN-related associations, mappings, and resulting behaviors are on a *frame* basis.

11.2.1 Playing Tag on Your LAN

How can you tell which LAN(s) a frame is on? In a traditional (non-VLAN) environment, this is a trivial problem. If a frame is on a given LAN, then it is on that LAN; there is no ambiguity as to which LAN the frame is on. A protocol analyzer connected to a LAN can display all of the frames present on that LAN.

In a VLAN environment, however, a frame's association with a given VLAN is *soft;* the fact that a given frame exists on some physical cable does not imply its membership in any particular VLAN. VLAN association is determined by a set of rules applied to the frames by VLAN-aware stations and/or switches.

There are two methods for identifying the VLAN membership of a given frame:

- *Parse the frame and apply the membership rules.* This is sometimes referred to as *implicit tagging.* A frame's VLAN association can always be inferred by inspecting the frame contents and applying the complete set of VLAN association rules for the catenet. Typically, this form of VLAN determination is made by an edge switch (see Section 11.2.2.2.1); the forwarding behavior of the switch is, in part, determined by the resulting VLAN association of the frame.

- *Provide an explicit VLAN identifier within the frame itself.* This is known as *explicit tagging* (or sometimes just *tagging*). A VLAN-aware end station or switch can declare the VLAN association through the use of a predefined tag field carried within the frame.

11.2.1.1 Implicit Tags

The name notwithstanding, there are no tags involved with implicit tagging.[9] An implicitly tagged frame is a normal, unmodified frame as emitted by any conventional end station or switch. The VLAN association is implied by the frame contents and is a function of the VLAN rules particular to the application environment. As discussed in detail in Section 11.2.3, the VLAN association may be a function of:

- Data Link Source Address
- Protocol type
- Higher-layer network identifiers (e.g., IP subnet)
- Application-specific fields, and so on

In a VLAN environment, all frames sent by VLAN-unaware end stations are considered implicitly tagged. Being VLAN-unaware, the end stations don't know about VLAN associations; such associations are implied by the contents of the frames they send. They may be processed in the conventional manner by VLAN-unaware switches, or in a VLAN context by VLAN-aware switches. Any such VLAN-aware switch operating on an implicitly tagged frame must first make the proper VLAN association from the frame contents. Once done, that switch may forward the frame with an explicit VLAN tag (if the frame is being forwarded into a VLAN- and tag-aware domain) or without an explicit tag (i.e., the same way the frame arrived).

Implicit tagging requires that the VLAN association be determined by applying the set of VLAN rules every time the frame is processed by a VLAN-aware switch. If there are no explicit tags provided, each VLAN-aware switch in the path between the source and destination(s) must independently determine the VLAN association from an application of the rules. Besides requiring repetitive, superfluous, redundant processing, the implication is that every switch must know the complete set of VLAN association rules in force in the entire catenet. Depending on the application environment, this could be hundreds or even thousands of rules, applied to various fields in the frame (including higher-layer application-specific fields). This is a heavy burden to place on every switch; this workload can be significantly reduced by making the VLAN association just once, then explicitly tagging the frame with the resulting value.

11.2.1.2 Explicit Tags

An explicit tag (usually just called a *VLAN tag*) is a predefined field in a frame that carries (at a minimum) the VLAN identifier for that frame. Figure 11.5

[9] There is also no lobster in Cantonese lobster sauce.

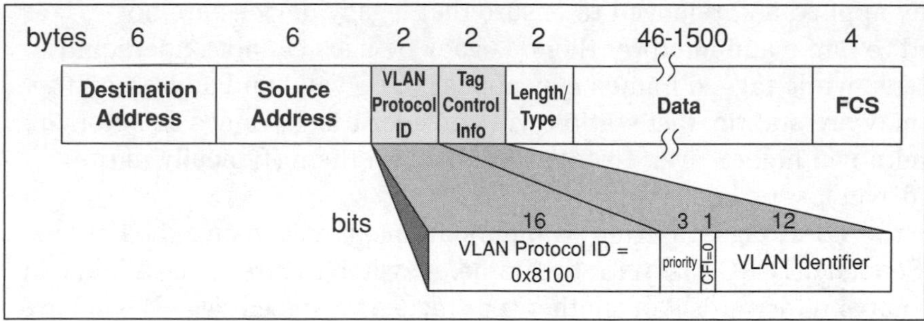

Figure 11.5 VLAN-tagged Ethernet frame.

depicts a VLAN tag in an Ethernet frame. (The figure here provides just one example of a tagged Ethernet frame; see Chapter 12 for the complete description of all of the fields and options in the IEEE standard VLAN tag.)

VLAN tags are always applied by a VLAN-aware device; this may be a VLAN-aware end station sending natively-tagged frames or an edge switch that receives untagged frames, applies the VLAN association rules, and forwards the frames with a tag. (See Section 11.2.2.2 for a discussion of edge and core switches.) The advantage of applying the tag is that any VLAN-aware device that receives the frame does not need to re-apply the (possibly hundreds of) application rules in force to determine the VLAN association—the VLAN identifier is right there, staring it in the face!

VLAN-tagging provides a number of benefits, but also carries some disadvantages, as summarized in Table 11.1.

A number of performance benefits accrue to the use of tags, primarily to the VLAN-aware switches in the catenet. On the downside, tags must be

Table 11.1 VLAN Tagging

ADVANTAGES	DISADVANTAGES
+ VLAN association rules only need to be applied once	– Tags can only be interpreted by VLAN-aware devices
+ Only edge switches need to know the VLAN association rules	– Edge switches must strip tags before forwarding frames to legacy devices or VLAN-unaware domains
+ Core switches can get higher performance by operating on an explicit VLAN identifier	– Insertion or removal of a tag requires recalculation of the FCS, possibly compromising frame integrity
+ VLAN-aware end stations can further reduce the performance load of edge switches	– Tag insertion may increase the length of a frame beyond the maximum allowed by legacy equipment

carefully applied and removed to ensure that legacy devices are not required to parse and interpret them. Legacy devices cannot understand VLAN tags; while tagged frames may appear to be valid and addressed to a VLAN-unaware station, that station will consider those frames as belonging to an unknown higher-layer protocol and discard them (typically in the device driver).

Since the VLAN tag is inserted within the frame, it will change the Frame Check Sequence (CRC value) for the frame. A switch that receives a frame in one format and forwards it in another (i.e., tagged versus untagged) will have to recalculate the FCS. Depending on the implementation, this may expose the frame to undetected errors within the switch itself, as discussed in Chapter 3, *Bridging between Technologies*.

Finally, a tag adds a few bytes to the frame; if a station sends an untagged, maximum-length frame, a switch inserting a tag on that frame will have to forward a frame that is longer than the legacy maximum allowed. This was considered a serious issue during the development of the IEEE VLAN standard.[10]

The detailed operations of tag insertion, removal, and frame field mapping are discussed in Chapter 12.

11.2.1.3 VLAN-Awareness and Tag-Awareness

A device must be VLAN-aware in order to be capable of dealing with VLAN tags (i.e., tag-aware). In the case of an end station, there is no way to distinguish between VLAN-awareness and VLAN-unawareness unless the station transmits and receive tagged frames. Thus, it is meaningless to consider a VLAN-aware end station that is not also tag-aware.

However, tag-awareness is not a strict requirement for VLAN-aware switches; a switch can be VLAN-aware without being tag-aware. For example, a VLAN-aware switch can be designed that accepts only untagged frames, determines all VLAN associations by applying the application rules, and forwards all frames untagged. Such a device would be VLAN-aware but incapable of inserting, removing, or interpreting VLAN tags.

Some early VLAN-aware switches behaved in precisely this manner. The most common application was when the VLAN association rule was based solely on the switch port on which the frames arrived, as described in Section 11.2.3.1. With such a simple VLAN association rule, no real-time frame inspection is required, and tagging imparts no performance benefit. Applications for such port-based VLANs are discussed in Section 11.2.3.7. Modern VLAN-aware

[10] To keep your blood pressure in check until you reach that discussion, you can rest assured that this is more of a theoretical problem than a practical one. Virtually all legacy commercial devices can tolerate the slightly-longer frames produced by a VLAN-tagging switch.

switches capable of applying more complex VLAN rules are usually capable of inserting, removing, and interpreting VLAN tags.

11.2.2 VLAN-Awareness

Clearly, both end stations and switches exist today that are blissfully ignorant of the capabilities, functional requirements, and power of VLANs. These devices operate perfectly well in the environments for which they were designed; not every network application requires the use of VLANs. Even in a catenet where VLAN technology provides some advantage, it is not always necessary for every device to implement VLAN capability in order to receive the desired benefits.

11.2.2.1 What It Means to Be VLAN-Aware

A VLAN-aware device understands that there is a mapping function occurring between the physical connectivity and the logical connectivity; it understands and can deal with subsets of the switched catenet. It can therefore change its behavior or make decisions based on the VLAN context, including:

- *Making frame forwarding decisions based on the VLAN association of a given frame.* A VLAN-aware switch can make its frame forwarding decision (i.e., onto which port(s) to forward or not forward a frame) based not only on the destination address in the frame, but also on the VLAN to which the frame belongs. In contrast, a VLAN-unaware switch makes its decisions based solely on the contained address information.
- *Providing explicit VLAN identification within transmitted frames.* A VLAN- and tag-aware station or switch can provide additional information in a frame that indicates the VLAN to which the frame belongs (i.e., a VLAN tag). A tag-aware switch may also remove a tag from a frame before forwarding it to VLAN- or tag-unaware devices. VLAN tags can only be understood by tag-aware devices; tag stripping is needed to ensure that a tag-unaware device never has to parse and interpret a VLAN-tag.

11.2.2.2 VLAN-Aware Switches

The fundamental concepts of VLANs arise from the use of switches. In a shared-LAN environment, the idea of logical connectivity as being something separate from physical connectivity is moot. Since shared-LAN hubs distribute frames to all stations regardless of the contents of the frame, no benefit accrues from associating a frame with only a subset of the devices; all of the stations will see all of the frames regardless of any such logical associations.

A switch provides mechanisms for traffic isolation and LAN segmentation. As such, it can partition traffic, forwarding frames onto only those links needed to interconnect the source and destination(s) indicated by the frame's address fields. A VLAN-aware switch can provide traffic isolation based not only on the addresses within the frames, but on a pre-determined logical connectivity. A VLAN-aware switch will forward frames only within the boundaries of the defined logical connectivity (i.e., the VLAN). Frames intended for destinations outside the VLAN will be blocked; similarly, frames arriving from outside the VLAN will not be accepted by the switch for forwarding into an inappropriate VLAN.

A VLAN-aware switch makes a VLAN association for every arriving frame. It must determine to which VLAN the frame belongs in order to make its switching decisions. As discussed in Section 11.2.3, this decision may be based on explicit VLAN identification provided by a tag or may be made implicitly by applying a set of VLAN association rules to the frame contents. It is precisely the application of the VLAN association rules that defines the extent of the VLAN. Using our analogy, the rules define the subset of the catenet that composes the VLAN.

A catenet employing VLAN technology will typically be separated into two parts:

- A VLAN-unaware domain
- A VLAN-aware domain

VLANs are a fairly recent phenomenon in the LAN marketplace; most devices, especially the hundreds-of-millions of end stations in the world, are VLAN-unaware. In order to allow a smooth migration to VLAN-based networks, we cannot reasonably require that all of the devices in the catenet be VLAN-aware before we can achieve any of the benefits of the technology. The number of devices that are at or near the leaves of the catenet (e.g., end stations and desktop switches) is huge; the number of devices within the interconnection backbone is much smaller (e.g., campus and enterprise switches). Thus, it is common to partition the catenet between these leaf devices and backbone devices, as depicted in Figure 11.6. By deploying VLAN capability just within the backbone, we can achieve much of the benefit with the least amount of equipment disruption. Over time, as end stations become VLAN-aware, additional VLAN-related benefits can be achieved by increasing the scope of the VLAN-aware domain.

With this partitioning in mind, VLAN-aware switches fall into two classifications: edge switches and core switches.

11.2.2.2.1 Edge Switches

Edge switches connect at the boundary between the VLAN-unaware domain (comprising end stations and/or VLAN-unaware switches) and the

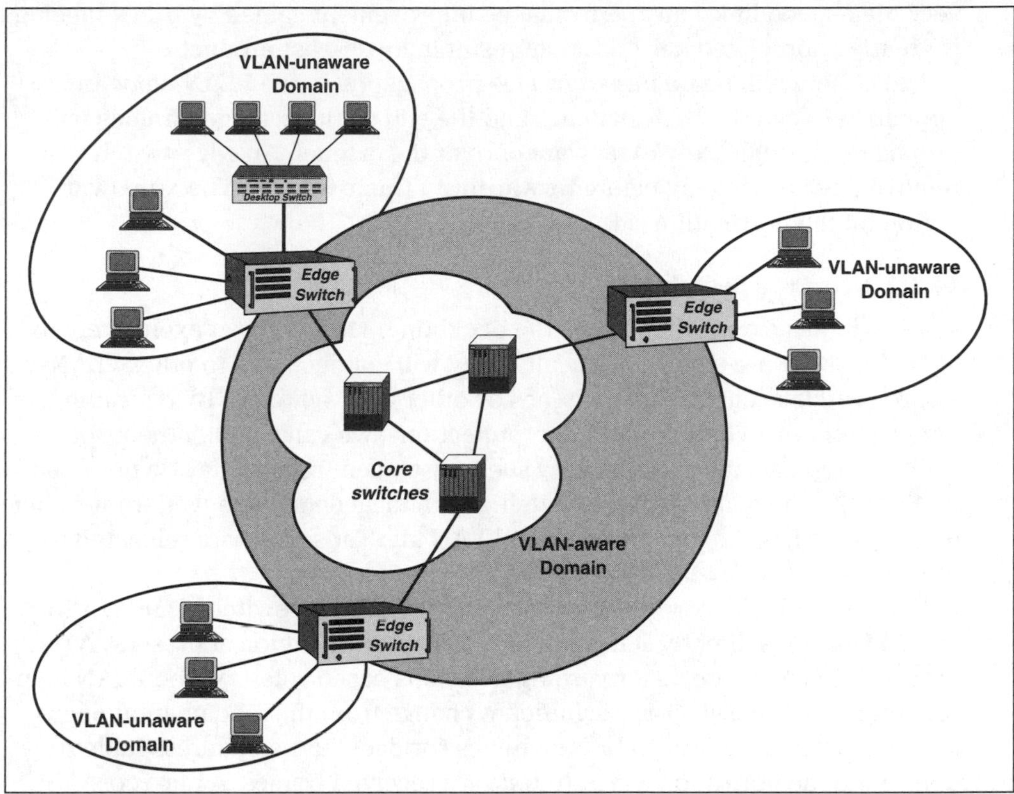

Figure 11.6 VLAN-aware and VLAN-unaware domains.

VLAN-aware domain (backbone). It is at this edge that the VLAN association rules are applied. No devices in the VLAN-unaware domain will be sending frames with explicit tags indicating the VLAN association (how can they—they are VLAN-unaware!); the edge switches must determine VLAN associations by inspecting every frame and applying the set of pre-determined rules.

The rules themselves are determined by the requirements of the application environment. Using either proprietary or industry-standard network management tools, edge switches are programmed with the classification rules for associating a frame with a given VLAN. As discussed in Sections 11.1 and 11.2.3, the association may be determined by switch port, Source Address, protocol type, or higher-layer information contained within the frame, as required by the application.

Once these rules are applied, an edge switch can tag (with an explicit VLAN identifier) those frames that must traverse the backbone through the core switches. As will be seen, this greatly simplifies the operation of the core switches. Core switches see concentrated backbone traffic and often attach to very-high-speed links; any performance improvement gained by VLAN tagging is greatly appreciated here, as it can result in lower-cost products.

Thus, there will be no tagged frames propagating in the VLAN-unaware domain between the edge switches and the end stations; tagged frames will propagate through the VLAN-aware core of the catenet. An edge switch will remove any inserted tag before forwarding a frame into the VLAN-unaware region on the destination side.

11.2.2.2.2 Core Switches

Core switches exist solely within the backbone. They connect exclusively to other VLAN-aware devices. Typically, they will connect only to other VLAN-aware switches, either edge switches or other core switches. By restricting core switches to VLAN-aware interconnections, we can simplify their operation. In a typical environment, they see only tagged frames; they do not need to deal with the complexities of parsing both tagged and untagged frames, nor do they ever have to add or remove a VLAN tag. Those jobs are relegated to the edge switches exclusively.

Furthermore, if a core switch connects only to other switches and not to any end stations directly, it never needs to deal with station addresses. A pure core switch can make its forwarding decisions based solely on the VLAN identification in the tag! This is a significant change from the fundamental operation of a switch; traditional LAN switches (bridges) use an address table to determine the port(s) on which to forward received frames. A pure core switch does not even need the address table.[11] What it does need is a table that maps VLAN identifiers to the set of ports that are needed to reach all of the members of that VLAN, as depicted in Figure 11.7.

When a frame arrives, the core switch determines the VLAN association by looking at the explicit identifier in the VLAN tag and performs a table lookup to determine which port(s) connects to members of that VLAN (indicated by a 1 in the "use" column for each port); the core switch then forwards the frame onto all indicated ports except the one on which the frame arrived. While this sounds remarkably similar to the operation of a traditional VLAN-unaware switch with respect to 48-bit addresses, there is one significant difference: The VLAN identifier space is much smaller than the 48-bit address space.

As discussed in Chapter 12, IEEE 802.1Q-standard devices use a 12-bit VLAN identifier. That is, there are only 4,094 possible VLANs in a given

[11] While in theory a pure core switch will not require a traditional address table as described, this precludes allowing any direct VLAN-unaware end station connections to the switch in question. In practice, a product that can't support such end station connections would have a rather limited market; as a result pure core switches are rare. Products designed for a switched VLAN backbone generally provide at least some edge switch functionality. However, the concepts presented in this section are still valid; the use of VLAN tagging can greatly improve the performance of core switches, at least for those frames that are tagged.

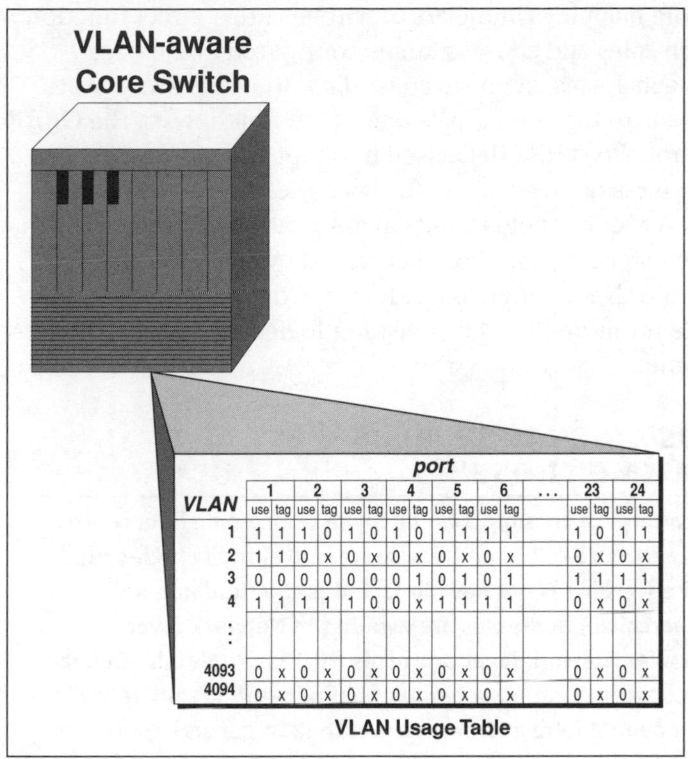

VLAN	port 1		2		3		4		5		6		...	23		24	
	use	tag	use	tag	use	tag	use	tag	use	tag	use	tag		use	tag	use	tag
1	1	1	1	0	1	0	1	0	1	1	1	1		1	0	1	1
2	1	1	0	x	0	x	0	x	0	x	0	x		0	x	0	x
3	0	0	0	0	0	0	0	1	0	1	0	1		1	1	1	1
4	1	1	1	1	1	0	0	x	1	1	1	1		0	x	0	x
:																	
4093	0	x	0	x	0	x	0	x	0	x	0	x		0	x	0	x
4094	0	x	0	x	0	x	0	x	0	x	0	x		0	x	0	x

Figure 11.7 VLAN table lookup.

catenet.[12] Thus, the lookup process can use a simple, brute-force approach; no fancy performance-enhancing mechanisms are needed (e.g., hash tables or binary searches). The VLAN identifier can be used directly as an index into a table of VLAN entries; the memory requirement is relatively benign and is independent of the number of stations in the catenet. The depth of the table can be fixed at 4,094 entries. The width is a function of the number of ports that the switch can support. A minimum of 2 bits are needed for each port—1 to indicate whether frames associated with the given VLAN should be forwarded out this port (the use bit), the other to indicate whether frames for this VLAN on this port should be sent tagged or untagged (the tag bit). Some additional bits are generally needed for control functions (e.g., table aging and validity, not shown in Figure 11.7). The memory requirement is therefore on the order of tens-of-kilobytes, even for switches with large numbers of ports.

As with the VLAN association rules in the edge switches, the VLAN-identifier-to-port mapping is configured through network management. However, it should not require additional human intervention to configure the core

[12] The values 0x000 and 0xFFF are reserved, reducing the maximum number of VLANs from 4,096 to 4,094.

switches; the VLAN table mappings in the core switches are a direct function of the VLAN association rules and address tables configured in the edge switches. Automatic mechanisms can be used to allow the edge switches to indicate their VLAN needs to the core; this is one of the functions of the GARP VLAN Registration Protocol (GVRP), discussed in Chapter 12.

A 12-bit VLAN identifier is quite adequate for even the largest networks. Remember that this identifier connotes a logical association of devices in a single catenet. Multiple catenets (e.g., those separated by Network layer routers) can re-use the VLAN identifier space. Rarely would a network administrator need to provide for more than 4,094 distinct logical groupings of users within a single flat catenet.

PLUS ÇA CHANGE, PLUS C'EST LA MÊME CHOSE[13]

The concept of creating a hierarchy of addressing in order to reduce the size of the address space and simplify high-speed internetworking is not new. In fact, it is the fundamental reason why flat (non-hierarchical) addresses are avoided in Network-layer protocols.[14] All of the popular Network-layer protocols (IP, IPX, AppleTalk, DECnet, etc.) divide their address space into at least two parts: a network identifier and a station identifier. The key benefit derives from the fact that, in general, there are many fewer networks than there are stations.

Within the internetwork core, high-speed routers need only inspect the network identifier portion to determine the appropriate path on which to send a packet. It is only at the edge of the network that routers must look at the station address and map this to a particular port.[15]

The logical hierarchy we have created, where edge switches deal with station addresses and core switches deal exclusively with VLAN identifiers, is exactly analogous to the network and station identifier hierarchy used at Network layer, and exists for the same reason—to improve the cost performance tradeoff in the high-speed core devices.

11.2.2.3 VLAN-Aware End Stations

In order to provide VLAN capabilities in the catenet, at least some of the switches must be VLAN-aware. VLAN association rules can be applied at

[13] Translation: You can teach a dog new tricks, but he won't do them when guests are watching.
[14] IP multicast addresses do not have such a hierarchy; their address space is a flat 28 bits. This factor makes it difficult to design IP multicast routing algorithms that work well in both small and large IP internetworks.
[15] In the case of IP, edge routers also generally need to use an Address Resolution Protocol (ARP) to map the Network layer station identifier to a Data Link address. Within the core, ARP is not needed on a packet-by-packet basis, since core routers don't normally connect to end stations directly.

edge switches to achieve the desired application behavior transparently to the end stations. This allows us to migrate from a traditional to a VLAN-aware catenet by upgrading just the switches and not the end stations. Since there are generally fewer switches than end stations, this is the path of least pain.

However, there are limits to what can be achieved without involving the end stations in the VLAN decisions. Without VLAN-awareness, all frames emitted by an end station will be, by definition, untagged; they carry no explicit VLAN identification. Any VLAN classification must be made implicitly by the edge switches in the catenet, as described earlier.

If the end stations themselves are VLAN-aware, they can explicitly include VLAN identification in transmitted frames by applying a tag before the frame is ever sent out. This provides a number of important advantages:

- VLANs can be used for highly application-specific functions. Besides just using VLANs for workgroup traffic isolation or station mobility, particular applications within the end stations can use VLANs for narrow purposes. For example, a set of stations may negotiate a dynamically-created VLAN for the purpose of carrying on a short-term audio or video conference; the conferencing application in the end stations can tag the frames for that particular conference with a unique VLAN identifier. In practice, such conferencing applications will likely use multicast destination addressing, making the use of VLANs particularly attractive as it provides multicast traffic isolation for bandwidth-intensive applications. VLAN-aware switches will forward the frames to just the members of the conference by simple inspection of the VLAN tag. No complex parsing of application protocols is needed to achieve the desired functionality.
- A VLAN-aware end station can use a single physical LAN interface as multiple, independent logical interfaces. Different protocol suites or applications within a station can have unique logical connectivities; the world-view of the catenet for each application within the station can be different. Each can be a member of its own VLAN; the frames it sends will propagate only to members of that same VLAN. Each VLAN may even use a different Source Address for the same physical LAN interface.[16]
- In the extreme case, if all frames carry VLAN tags, there is no need for edge switch functionality; all switches can make their decisions solely on the VLAN tag information (i.e., every switch becomes a core switch).

[16] There are ways to achieve these same ends without the use of VLANs; however, they usually require the use of implementation-specific modifications to device drivers or protocol stacks. A proper implementation of generic VLAN capability in an end station would make such capability universal and clean.

This simplifies the implementation of high-performance switches. Of course, this state can only be achieved if all end stations are VLAN-aware and tag all frames. It is unlikely that this situation will ever occur in practice. There will always be some legacy devices or applications that do not need VLAN capability.

In a traditional LAN, stations send frames to target destinations through a given physical LAN interface; the assumed connectivity is that provided by the physical LAN. In a VLAN-aware end station, frames are sent to destinations through a physical interface using a selected VLAN connectivity. That is, the station can use the physical infrastructure in different ways, depending on the needs of the application(s). In the simplest (traditional) case, all applications within the station use the same logical connectivity; this is the equivalent of having a single VLAN associated with the station. Not much benefit is gained by making the end station VLAN-aware in this environment; a simple port-based VLAN association in the switch to which the end station is connected can achieve the same result.

However, if different applications can benefit from different connectivity patterns, VLAN-awareness in the end station allows the connectivity to change on a frame-by-frame basis. For example:

- Independent protocol stacks within a device can have different views of the catenet. IP applications can see an arbitrary set of devices as being within their subnet; AppleTalk applications can see a completely different set of devices as being within their AppleTalk network; and so on. There is no need to try to reconcile the connectivity requirements of separate protocols in a multi-protocol end station.
- A single device can connect to multiple Network layer entities (e.g., IP subnets) through the same physical port. Each network would have its own VLAN identifier in the catenet. This allows simple implementation of so-called *one-armed routers*, as discussed in Section 11.2.3.5.
- Bandwidth-intensive applications (e.g., video streams) can be assigned to their own VLANs for maximum bandwidth conservation. When the VLAN identification is applied in the end station, not even the local desktop switch needs to distribute this traffic unnecessarily to disinterested ports.

11.2.2.4 He Looks Around, Around, He Sees VLANs in the Architecture, Spinning in Infinity . . .

All of this power comes at a price. Currently there are no mechanisms provided in standard desktop operating systems, standard LAN device drivers, end sta-

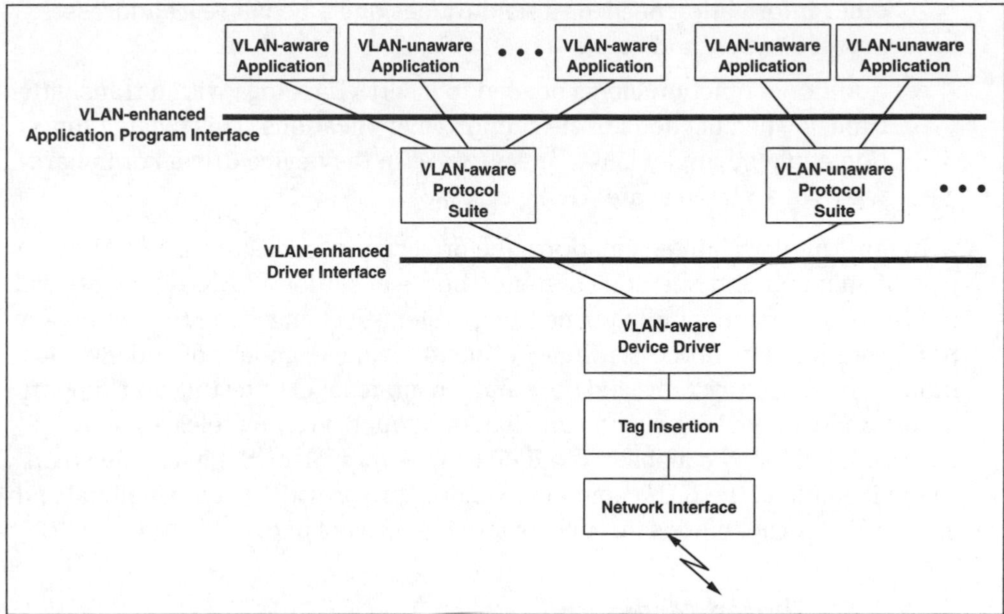

Figure 11.8 End station VLAN architecture support.

tion protocol stacks, or applications themselves for including VLAN identification. It is one thing to want to allow an application to explicitly identify its frames as belonging to a given VLAN. It is another to provide the software support to make this possible. As shown in Figure 11.8, there are a number of architectural changes needed to make VLAN-awareness a reality in end stations:

- Applications themselves need to be written (or re-written) to be VLAN-aware. For example, a conferencing application would need to specify a VLAN in the messages it passes to the protocol stack.[17]
- Application Program Interfaces (APIs) to the protocol stacks need to be enhanced to support the passing of VLAN information to and from applications.
- Protocol suites (TCP/IP, NetWare/IPX, etc.) need to be enhanced to support passing VLAN information to and from both VLAN-aware applications and the underlying network device drivers.
- Device drivers for LAN interfaces need to be changed to allow a client (an application or protocol stack) to specify a VLAN in addition to all the

[17] Alternatively, a shim layer could be added between an existing VLAN-unaware application and a VLAN-compatible protocol stack. The shim would insert the appropriate VLAN information for the application involved. However, this is admittedly a short-term kludge, justified only by its ability to provide VLAN-awareness for existing applications.

other information needed to send frames on its behalf (e.g., addresses, protocol types, and data).

- Additional functionality is needed to insert VLAN tags within transmitted frames when needed for the supported applications. This tagging function could be implemented in software (in the device driver) or in hardware (in a VLAN-aware NIC).

In most modern implementations, the drivers, protocol stacks, and APIs are part of an integrated operating system. Thus, end station VLAN-awareness will not become common until the operating system(s) changes to provide this support. This is a slow process, primarily due to the huge amount of code within modern operating systems and the commensurate level of testing and support associated with making significant changes. It may be a few release cycles before native VLAN capability is added to Windows, MacOS, Linux, and so on. In the meantime, the LAN equipment vendors are providing some minimal end station VLAN capabilities through proprietary drivers and applications.

11.2.2.5 Shared Media and VLAN-Awareness

VLAN-awareness doesn't provide any real benefit within a shared-LAN environment. In a shared-LAN, all stations see all traffic regardless of Destination Address, much less VLAN identification. Thus, any VLAN benefits (traffic isolation, bandwidth preservation, etc.) are lost here. As depicted in Figure 11.9, even if all of the end stations connected to VLAN 1 are VLAN-aware, and are

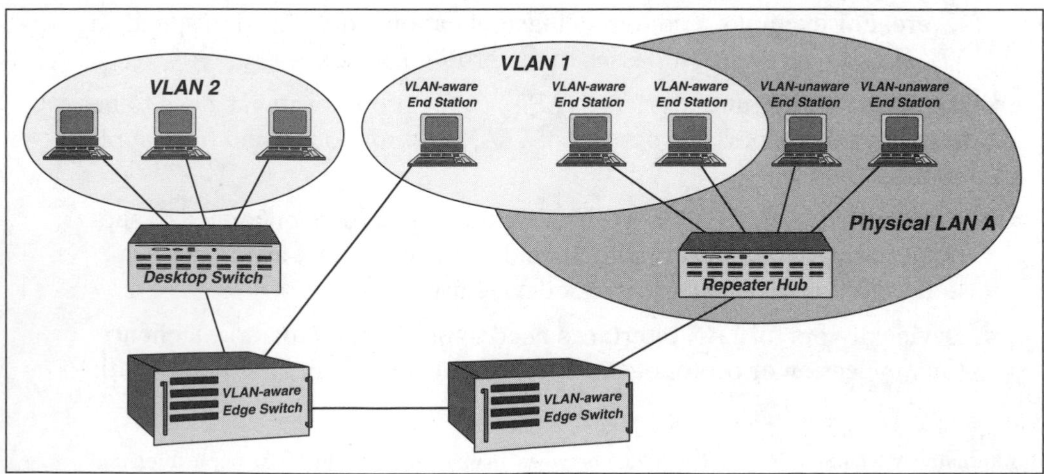

Figure 11.9 Shared media and VLANs.

emitting tagged frames, there is no way to prevent these frames from appearing at all stations on (physical) LAN A, regardless of their VLAN associations. We cannot prevent unwanted eavesdropping or reduce bandwidth utilization on LAN A through VLAN technology.

11.2.2.6 Non-VLAN-Aware Switches and End Stations

If you bought any network equipment before 1995, either station attachments or switches, it was probably VLAN-unaware. If you now want to implement VLAN capability in your network, does this mean that you have to throw out all of your existing equipment and buy new stuff?[18] Fortunately, the answer is no.

Just because a switch is VLAN-unaware doesn't mean that it cannot coexist in a catenet where VLANs have been deployed. Clearly, such devices cannot be used as either edge or core VLAN-aware switches, since they will be incapable of tagging, untagging, or interpreting tags in a VLAN-tagged frame. However, they can operate perfectly well in a VLAN-unaware domain of the catenet (see Figure 11.6).

Also, because of the way VLAN tagging is defined (see Section 11.2.1.2), a VLAN-unaware switch can process a VLAN-tagged frame in the traditional manner, that is, based solely on the addresses in the frame. The VLAN tags are transparent with respect to the traditional frame format.[19] Thus, while the legacy equipment cannot deal with the VLAN information explicitly, it will not consider such frames as malformed or in error. From the perspective of any VLAN-aware switches and end stations, legacy switches are transparent.

Legacy end stations cannot transmit frames with VLAN tags, nor will they be capable of properly interpreting tagged frames. Thus, while they can coexist in a catenet where VLANs have been deployed, they must always be in a VLAN-unaware domain. Any tagged frames destined for such an end station (tagged either by a VLAN-aware end station or an edge switch) must have their tags stripped off by an edge switch before delivery. This is generally assured by proper configuration of the catenet by the network administrator.

11.2.3 VLAN Association Rules (Mapping Frames to VLANs)

From the perspective the VLAN-aware devices in the catenet, the distinguishing characteristic of a VLAN is the means used to map a given frame

[18] If you are a network equipment salesperson, I know what *you* want the answer to be!
[19] The one minor exception is the issue of exceeding the maximum frame length with a tagged frame, as discussed in Chapter 12. In practice, this is rarely, if ever, a problem.

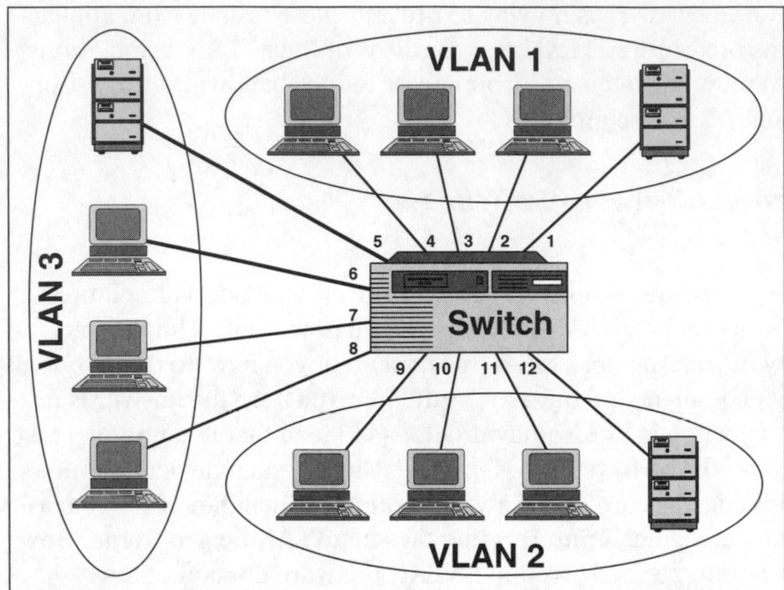

Figure 11.10 Port-based VLAN mapping.

to that VLAN. Note that, in the general case, it is individual frames that map to a given VLAN, as opposed to a device (or a switch port) that maps to a VLAN.[20]

In the case of a tagged frame, the mapping is simple—the tag contains the VLAN identifier for the frame, and the frame is assumed to belong to the indicated VLAN. That's all there is to it. In the absence of an explicit tag, a VLAN-aware switch must use a rule (or set of rules) to determine the VLAN to which the frame belongs. The set of rules will be a function of the type of behavior that we wish the VLAN to exhibit; presumably this is determined by the application for which we are deploying VLAN technology.

In theory, there are an infinite number of possible VLAN-mapping rules, depending on the specific application environment. In practice, a number of common rule-sets have been implemented in commercial products and have seen widespread practical application.

11.2.3.1 Port-Based VLAN Mapping

The simplest implicit mapping rule is known as *port-based VLAN mapping.* A frame is assigned to a VLAN based solely on the switch port on which the frame arrives. In the example depicted in Figure 11.10, frames arriving on ports

[20] For some sets of VLAN association rules, the mapping may actually reduce to the latter case. However, in general, we cannot make this simplification.

1 through 4 are assigned to VLAN 1, frames from ports 5 through 8 are assigned to VLAN 2, and frames from ports 9 through 12 are assigned to VLAN 3.

Stations within a given VLAN can freely communicate among themselves using either unicast or multicast addressing. No communication is possible at the Data Link layer between stations connected to ports that are members of different VLANs. Communication among devices in separate VLANs can be accomplished at higher layers of the architecture, for example, by using a Network layer router with connections to two or more VLANs.

Multicast traffic, or traffic destined for an unknown unicast address arriving on any port, will be flooded only to those ports that are part of the same VLAN. This provides the desired traffic isolation and bandwidth preservation. The use of port-based VLANs effectively partitions a single switch into multiple sub-switches, one for each VLAN.

Port-based VLANs were the first type available in commercial products, primarily because they are the easiest to implement. It is not necessary to parse and inspect frames in real-time to determine their VLAN mapping; regardless of their contents, all frames received on a given port will be assigned to the same VLAN. Port-based VLANs are appropriate for software patch-panel, switch segmentation (using a high port-density switch as if it were a number of smaller switches), and bandwidth preservation applications. As discussed in Chapter 12, port-based mapping is the default behavior specified by the IEEE VLAN standard.

11.2.3.2 MAC Address-Based VLAN Mapping

Moving from the simplest rule to a more complex mapping, many commercial products are capable of assigning a frame to a VLAN based on the MAC Source Address in the received frames. Using this rule, all frames emitted by a given end station will be assigned to the same VLAN, regardless of the port on which the frame arrives, as depicted in Figure 11.11. This is an appropriate rule for a mobility application; a station's VLAN membership is tied to its address, not the port through which the device connects to the switch. Assuming that all of the switches understand the address-based mapping, if a station is moved to another switch port (including a port on another switch), its frames still propagate exclusively among the members of its assigned VLAN. A virtual workgroup is thus created for the set of addresses assigned to each VLAN.

In order to determine the VLAN associated with a given frame, the switches must parse and inspect the Source Address and perform the VLAN mapping in real-time—a task not demanded of a port-based VLAN switch. However, the task is not as onerous as it may seem; a conventional switch needs to perform an address table lookup for Source Addresses anyway as part of the learning process. The same lookup process that is used to learn the port mapping for

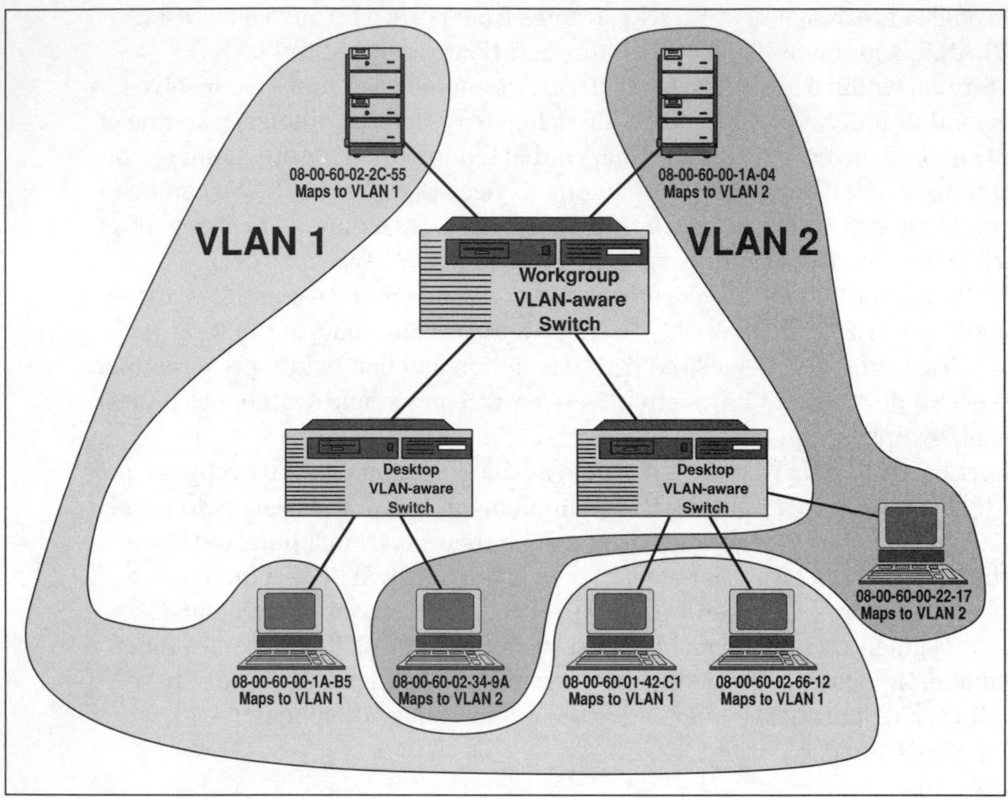

Figure 11.11 MAC address–based VLAN mapping.

the station can be used to determine the VLAN mapping, assuming that the switch can learn at wire-speed. Since address-based VLAN mapping does not impose any major architectural change on a switch design, it is the second most-common form of VLAN implementation in commercial products (after port-based mapping).

An interesting problem arises if a switch using address-based VLAN mapping receives a frame from an unknown Source Address. Since the switch is using the Source Address to determine the VLAN membership, the switch therefore does not know the VLAN to which this frame belongs.[21] Should it forward the frame to the intended destination(s) or not? The decision reflects a tradeoff between ease of connectivity and VLAN security. Strict enforcement of the VLAN rule mandates that the frame should not be forwarded; such

[21] Note that this case never occurs if the switch uses a port-based mapping rule (either solely or as a secondary rule applied when the MAC address rule cannot resolve the VLAN membership). A frame cannot arrive at the switch without having come through a known port!

action protects the integrity of the VLAN. This is one mechanism for providing the security features described in Section 11.1.2; unknown stations (such as an intruder's portable computer) cannot access services on the catenet. However, many commercial products are not so strict in their operation; they may forward traffic from unknown sources to the port determined by the Destination Address (including flooding traffic to all ports in the case of an unknown or multicast destination) as if it were all a conventional, VLAN-unaware switch. This provides open connectivity, at least until the switch learns the VLAN mapping for that particular address (through management).

A switch could also combine address-based VLAN mapping with port-based mapping into a more complex rule. For example, we may define the rules to permit access to a given VLAN by unknown Source Addresses, but only from specific ports. This could allow guest access to limited resources (a *guest VLAN*) only from specific locations (e.g., a guest center). Guest users could not easily access VLANs reserved for other purposes, nor could they defeat security by finding an empty office and connecting a portable computer.

11.2.3.3 Protocol-Based VLAN Mapping

Both the port-based and the MAC address-based VLAN mapping rules discussed earlier result in all frames from a given station being associated with the same VLAN. Under both of these rules, the VLAN can be thought of as comprising a set of devices: those devices connected to the appropriate switch ports or those devices with certain addresses.

We can instead use a VLAN mapping that associates a set of processes within stations to a VLAN rather than the stations themselves. Consider a catenet comprising devices supporting multiple protocol suites, as depicted in Figure 11.12. Each device may have an IP protocol stack (supporting IP applications, such as Internet access), an AppleTalk protocol stack (supporting AppleTalk applications), an IPX protocol stack (supporting NetWare applications), and so on.

If we configure VLAN-aware switches such that they can associate a frame with a VLAN based on a combination of the station's MAC source address and the protocol stack in use, we can create separate VLANs for each set of protocol-specific applications. As depicted in Figure 11.13, the stations in the catenet will have a different view of the network depending on the application being used. The grouping of stations in a given IP subnet can be different from the grouping for the IPX network as well as that for the AppleTalk network.

The flexibility afforded by such a protocol-based VLAN mapping is much greater than that of the simpler rules discussed earlier. In the configuration shown in Figure 11.13, station 3 provides its user with an NFS client running

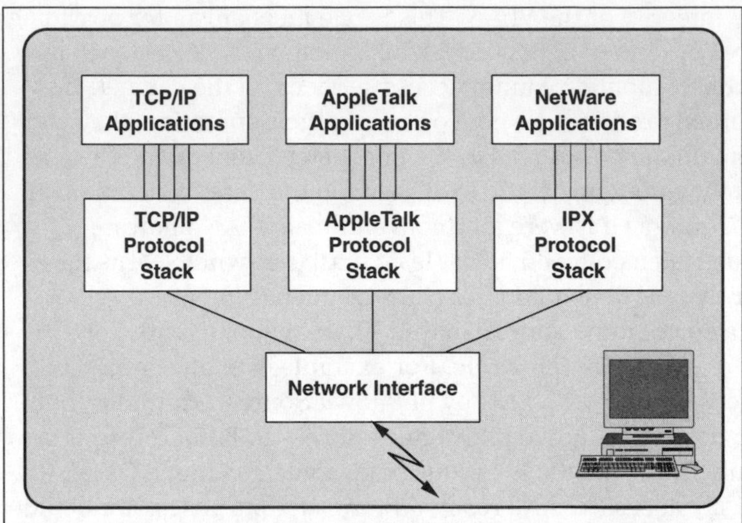

Figure 11.12 Multiple protocol stacks in an end station.

over IP as well as a NetWare client and AppleTalk peer services. Station 4 is a server providing NFS-over-IP and NetWare-over-IPX application services. Station 3 will be unable to directly access the NFS server application running on server 4 since they are on separate IP subnets (A and B). However, station 3 *can* use NetWare application- and file-sharing services provided by that same device, since they are within the same IPX network (Y). In addition, every station in the catenet can use the AppleTalk-based printer (station 5), as the entire catenet is in a single common VLAN from the perspective of the AppleTalk protocol.

Note that protocol-based VLAN mapping allows a station to be a member of multiple VLANs, depending on the number of protocols it supports. This is the more general case; a VLAN is not necessarily an association of *devices*, but an association of *processes* running within the devices. The fact that a port-based or address-based VLAN mapping rule reduces this generality to become a set of devices is due to the simplicity of those rules.

The VLAN-aware switches in this environment have to perform considerably more work to determine the VLAN mapping for a given frame. The VLAN mapping is a function of both the Source Address and the encapsulated protocol. It is not a trivial matter to determine the protocol being used; remember that there are a number of different possible encapsulations and protocol type identification methods. As discussed in Chapter 3, *Bridging between Technologies* (see Figure 3.3, Table 3.2, and the accompanying text), at least three

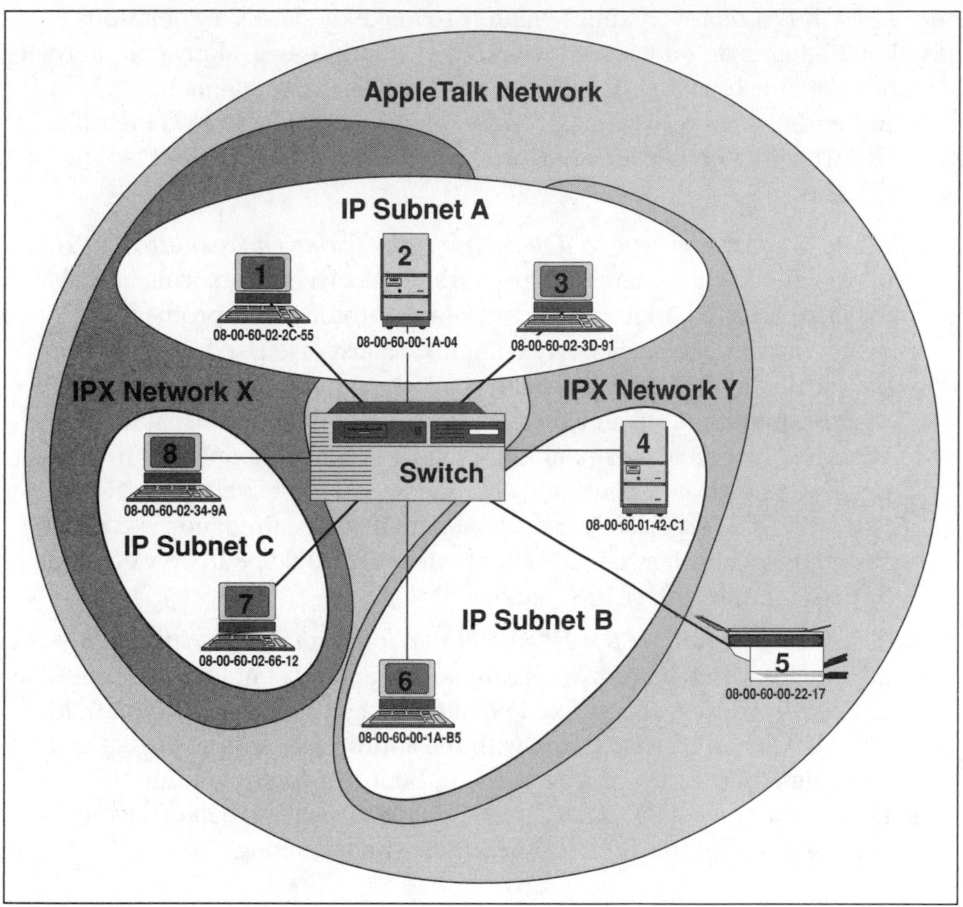

Figure 11.13 Protocol-based VLAN mapping.

encapsulations are possible on Ethernet frames alone. A protocol-determining switch must parse all of the possibilities to unambiguously determine the encapsulated protocol type, especially in a mixed IP/IPX/AppleTalk environment. The Appendix provides a decision tree formulation of a parser that can discriminate among IP, IPX, AppleTalk, DECnet, LAT, and NetBIOS protocols. This parser can be easily implemented in hardware-based logic; it has been designed into the ASICs used in some commercial switches supporting protocol-based VLAN mapping.

11.2.3.4 IP Subnet-Based VLAN Mapping

Using the MAC address-based VLAN mapping described earlier, VLAN associations were created among groups of devices based upon their MAC Source

Addresses. It is a relatively simple matter to make the VLAN associations based on higher-layer addresses instead of MAC addresses. Many commercial switches are able to create IP subnet-based VLANs in this manner.

IP addresses contain two parts: a subnet identifier and a station identifier.[22] A VLAN-aware switch needs to perform two operations to create IP subnet-based VLANs:

1. *Parse the protocol type to determine if the frame encapsulates an IP datagram.* In the general case of a frame received on an arbitrary LAN encapsulating an arbitrary Network-layer protocol, the problem of protocol-type parsing is fairly complex, as just discussed. However, in the particular case of IP-over-Ethernet, the protocol parsing problem is greatly simplified. On an Ethernet, IP datagrams always use native Ethernet Type field encapsulation; thus it is a fairly simple job to inspect this fixed-position, 2 byte field and compare it to the value for IP (0x0800) [RFC1123]. No conditional parsing is required, nor is it necessary to inspect other fields in the frame, as it would be if we were trying to detect AppleTalk or IPX packets.[23]
2. *Examine and extract the IP subnet portion of the IP Source Address in the encapsulated datagram.* Again, this is a fairly simple procedure. The IP Source Address is in a fixed position within the Ethernet data field. The switch can be configured with the appropriate subnet mask for the environment (i.e., which bits of the IP Source Address contain the subnet identifier as opposed to the station identifier) and can easily determine the subnet to which a given frame should belong.[24]

[22] Strictly speaking, the subnet identifier is either an IP network identifier or a catenation of an IP network identifier and a subnet field, but for the purposes of creating Data Link layer VLANs, we can consider everything except the station identifier to be subnet identification. The distinction is more properly treated in a book on IP than one on switches; interested readers are referred to [COME95] for more information.

[23] There is one esoteric boundary condition where this simple parsing method does not work. If the catenet contains end stations directly connected to FDDI LANs, and there are bridges interconnecting the FDDI LANs to Ethernet LANs that do not implement the recommendations of IEEE 802.1H [IEEE95a], then it is possible for IP datagrams to appear on the Ethernet using SNAP encapsulation. The IP standards do not require stations to be able to receive such frames (although it is recommended that they do so [RFC1123]). Many commercial products ignore this boundary condition. If it does arise in the field, the network administrator must either restrict the IP subnet-based VLANs to exist only within the physical Ethernet LANs in the catenet or replace the bridges interconnecting the FDDI and Ethernet LANs with devices that implement the IEEE 802.1H recommendations. IEEE 802.1H specifies a method of transforming SNAP encapsulated FDDI frames to native Ethernet Type field encapsulation for IP datagrams.

[24] For a simple implementation, it must be assumed that fixed-length subnet masks are in use. If variable-length masks are deployed, the problem of determining the subnet identifier becomes more difficult, as there may be multiple known subnet identifiers that match the given Source Address; the switch must then select the match with the longest resulting subnet identifier.

Once it is known that a given frame carries an IP datagram belonging to a given subnet, the switch can propagate the frame as needed within the confines of the subnet to which it belongs. Thus, Data Link layer VLANs can be created that automatically map to Network layer entities (subnets). The assignment of an IP address to a device will automatically place that device in a VLAN appropriate for that subnet.

If a device with a given IP address moves within the VLAN-aware catenet, the boundaries of its IP subnet can automatically adjust to accommodate the station's address. This is a powerful mechanism; without IP subnet-based VLAN mapping, a device that moves within the physical organization must generally get a new IP address assigned at each location, either through manual administration and reconfiguration or through some automated, dynamic address assignment {e.g., the Dynamic Host Configuration Protocol (DHCP) [RFC1531]}.

The resulting configuration can operate as shown in Figure 11.14. Each IP subnet corresponds to a single VLAN, which may span multiple switches. The switches treat intra-subnet traffic as being on a common LAN; that is, stations within a subnet can communicate among themselves at the Data Link layer. No Data Link layer communication is possible between subnets.

Protocols other than IP are switched in the conventional manner. Depending on the capabilities of the switch, alternative VLAN association rules may be applied to the non-IP traffic (e.g., port-based or MAC address-based VLAN mapping).

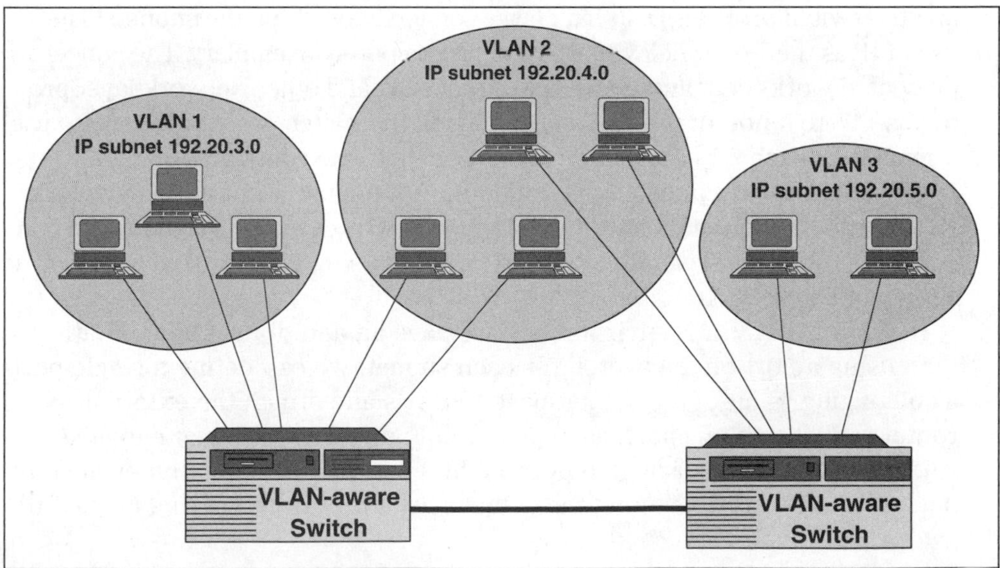

Figure 11.14 IP subnet-based VLANs.

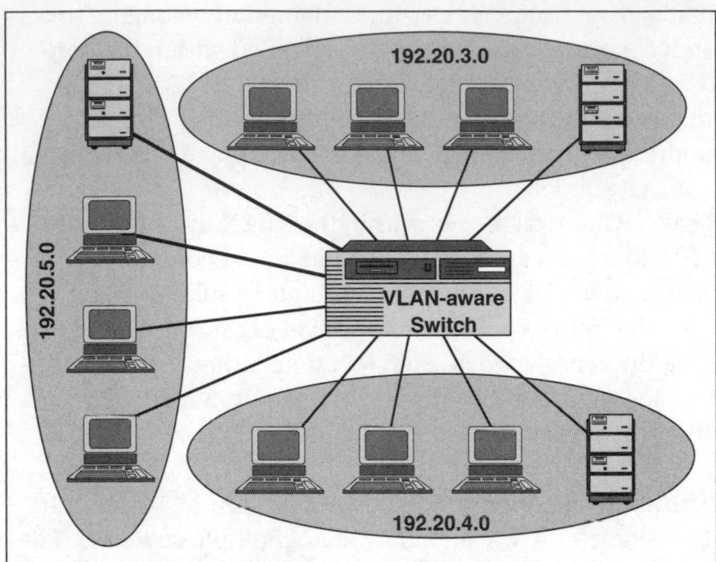

Figure 11.15 IP subnets.

11.2.3.5 A VLAN Phenomenon: The One-Armed Router

Consider the configuration depicted in Figure 11.15. In this scenario, a VLAN-aware switch has partitioned the attached stations based upon their Network layer address, for example IP subnet. Each subnet is mapped to a unique VLAN, and the switch provides Data Link layer connectivity within the subnet. (The use of IP as the Network-layer protocol here is purely exemplary. The concept presented works equally well for IPX, AppleTalk, and other Network-layer protocols.) Were it not for the VLAN capability of the switch, we would need to use a separate switch for each subnet to achieve the same configuration.

By definition, any inter-subnet communication must occur at the Network layer through a router. In a traditional (non-VLAN) case, this would mean connecting a router between the separate switches using a port on each switch, as shown in Figure 11.16.

However, in a VLAN environment, we have an additional choice. Rather than using a port on the switch for each subnet, we can define a single port as belonging to all of the subnet-based VLANs and attach the external router to just this one port, as depicted in Figure 11.17. This *one-armed router* treats the single switch port as three logical ports, one on each subnet, and routes traffic among the subnets as appropriate.[25] Using normal IP

[25] A similar situation can arise with the use of multiple subnets on a single shared medium LAN. Only one router port is needed for all of the subnets using the shared medium.

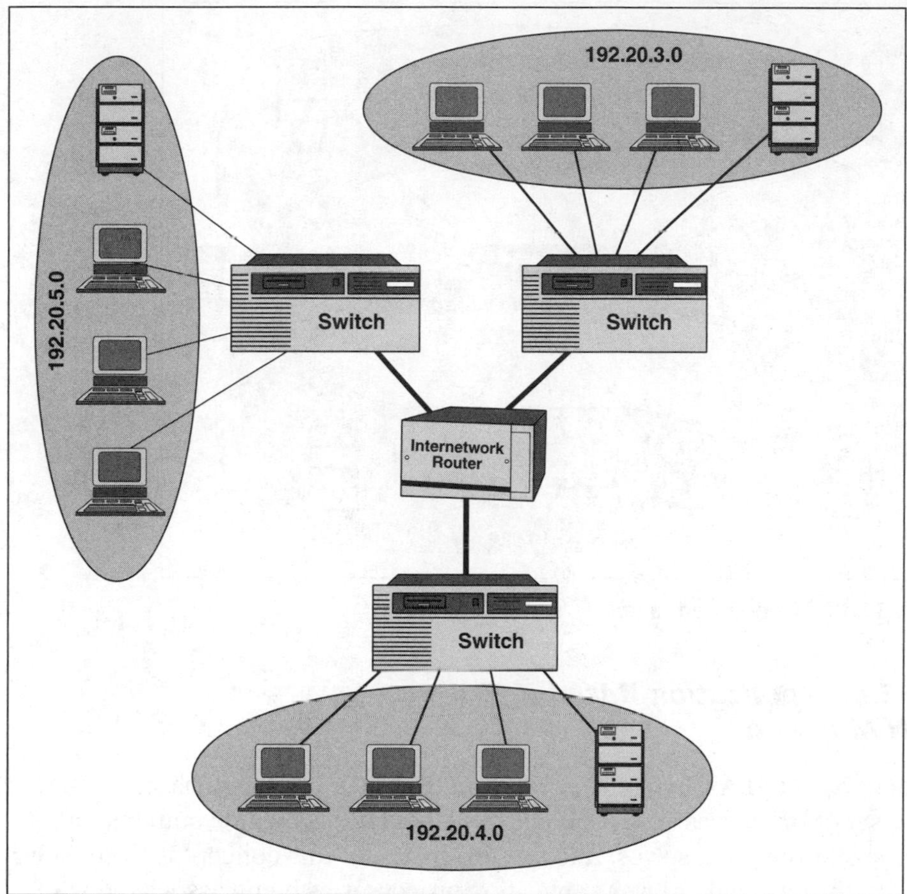

Figure 11.16 Conventional router interconnection.

conventions, the router will have three IP addresses on this one port—one for each subnet.

In addition, there is no architectural requirement that the routing device be physically separate from the switching device; this is a product decision based upon the cost, performance, and features appropriate for some set of target customers. It is perfectly reasonable to integrate the routing function into the same physical device that performs the switch function to produce a so-called switch/router (or *swouter*). This is a common, commercially-available implementation.[26]

[26] It could be argued that, since the router doesn't even use a single external switch port, that it is completely armless.

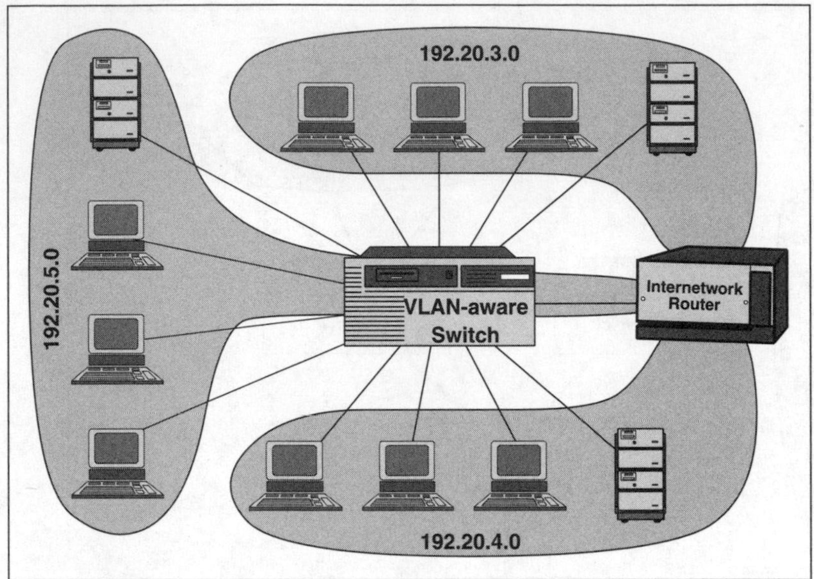

Figure 11.17 One-armed router.

11.2.3.6 Application-Based VLAN Mapping

Protocol-based VLAN mapping introduced the concept of associating a VLAN with a set of processes (i.e., protocol implementations) within stations rather than the stations themselves. A logical extension of this concept is to consider a set of arbitrary higher-layer application processes as being associated with a VLAN, rather than just Network-layer protocol implementations.

Figure 11.18 depicts a VLAN mapping that combines frames exchanged among a set of common applications within end stations in the catenet. The applications so associated could provide audio or video conferencing, collaborative groupware (e.g., group document preparation), or any other application requiring many-to-many communications.

There are two significant issues that arise in this environment that we did not encounter previously:

1. *Determining the application solely from the frame contents can be a daunting task for a switch.* In order to associate an untagged frame with an application-based VLAN, a switch must parse the frame sufficiently to determine the application that actually generated the frame. In general, this is an incredibly complex task. The application may be encapsulated within numerous higher-layer protocol possibilities, for example:
   - TCP or UDP over IP

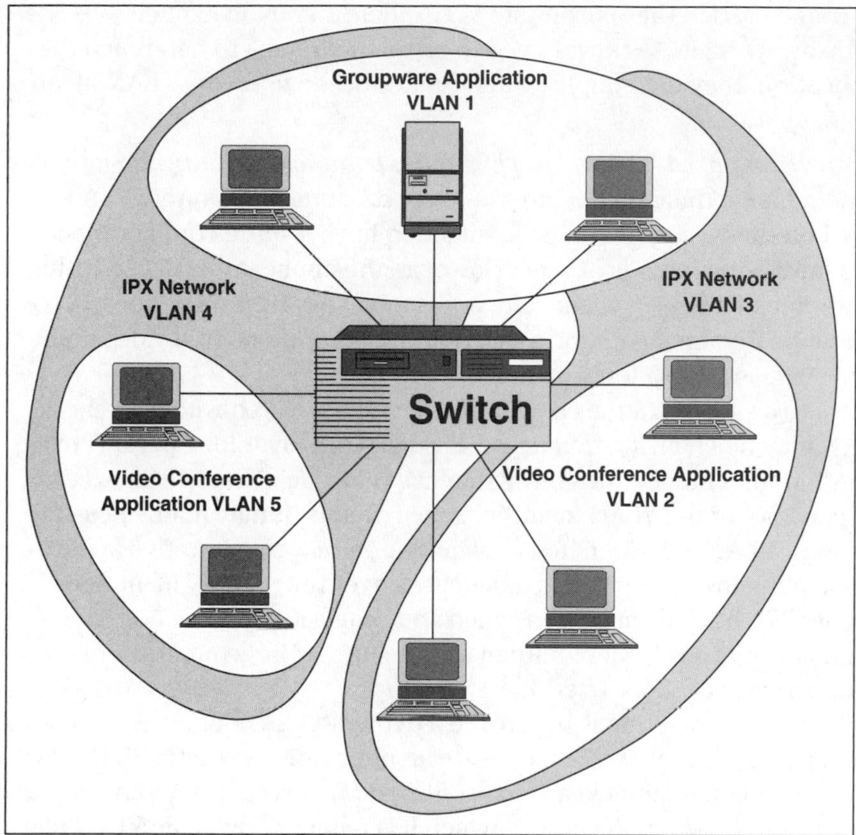

Figure 11.18 Application-based VLAN mapping.

- ATP or ADSP over DDP (AppleTalk)
- SPX over IPX (NetWare)
- NetBIOS over LLC

In order to determine the application encapsulated by a given frame, a switch would need to understand the frame format for every possible encapsulation of every possible protocol stack in use in the catenet—a formidable task! In practice, parsing an untagged frame to determine the application is an unreasonable burden to place on a switch.[27] As a result, the use of such application-based VLANs typically requires that the end stations be VLAN-aware and that they send tagged frames expressly for this purpose. The application itself (through an API in a VLAN-aware operating system protocol stack, see Section 11.2.2.4) would ensure that

[27] This is precisely the task performed by a network protocol analyzer, which captures, decodes, and displays hundreds of different protocol and application formats.

the frame carried the appropriate VLAN identifier in an explicit tag. The VLAN-aware switches never need to parse the frames to determine the application; they can simply switch frames based upon the VLAN identified in the tag.

2. *Application-based VLANs may be highly transient in nature.* Stations do not change their MAC addresses or port connections often; VLANs based on these entities can be assumed to have a static configuration over fairly long periods of time. However, the applications in use within a station can change dynamically over much shorter time periods. A collaborative document-editing session may last for an hour; a video conference may last only a few minutes.

   Thus, the set of stations and applications associated with a given VLAN may be changing frequently. Furthermore, over long periods of time, the total number of VLANs that may have been in use can exceed the capacity of the VLAN identifier space; that is, it may not be possible to assign VLAN identifiers to an instantiation of a collaborative application in a manner that ensures uniqueness over time. VLAN identifiers will need to be dynamically assigned and re-used, to relieve both the administrative assignment burden and to support large numbers of collaborative applications over time.

   The obvious solution is to provide a dynamic VLAN-allocation server. When an application wishes to create an application-specific VLAN (for example, when it initiates a video conference), it requests a VLAN identifier assignment from the server, which has a pool of dynamic VLAN identifiers available for this purpose. The VLAN is created for the duration of the application instantiation and is then returned to the common pool for re-use. This is exactly analogous to the way dynamic IP addresses are assigned by a DHCP server.[28]

11.2.3.7 The Rules Follow the Application

By now, the power and flexibility of VLANs should be becoming apparent. In fact, one of the problems is that VLAN technology is in some ways too flexible; as in the case of software with too many features and options, it can be difficult to figure out exactly how to use it.[29] VLANs can be created based on almost any desired relationship—ports, addresses (at various protocol layers), protocol types, applications, and so on.

[28] At the time of this writing (mid-1999), no such application-based VLAN-mapping stations, switches, or dynamic-assignment servers are available. This capability should emerge as end stations become VLAN-aware. It is expected that the VLAN-assignment server will be incorporated as a process in general-purpose LAN servers or into the VLAN-aware switches themselves.
[29] Software designers, especially those in the Pacific Northwest, take note!

In many cases, the range of possible VLAN association rules will more likely be limited by the capabilities of the VLAN-aware switches, rather than the users' real application needs. Thus, what people actually do with VLANs is whatever their equipment is capable of; for the most part, this consists of port-based, MAC address-based, and IP subnet-based configurations. It doesn't matter what the user really wants to do with VLANs—this is all that the equipment can do. However, as technology advances (in particular, as VLAN-aware end stations become commonplace), the VLAN configuration focus will shift away from equipment limitations back to the users' needs. At this point, users need to determine the reasons (if any) that they are deploying VLANs; this will dictate the appropriate VLAN association rules to be used. Table 11.2 summarizes the rules, applications, and issues presented in this section.

Seifert's Law of Networking #2
The application determines the network.

Table 11.2 VLAN Association Rules Summary

VLAN ASSOCIATION RULE	TYPICAL APPLICATION	COMMENTS
Port-based	Software patch panel	Simplest to implement
	Switch segmentation	Supported by all VLAN-aware switches
	Simple security and bandwidth preservation	
MAC address-based	Station mobility for all protocols and applications	Performance demands are comparable to those of a VLAN-unaware switch
IP subnet-based	IP subnet mobility	Especially useful in an integrated switch/router (swouter)
Protocol-based	Protocol-dependent access control	
	Mobility in a multiprotocol environment	
Application-based	Dynamic groupware environment	Generally requires VLAN-aware end stations
	Fine-grained bandwidth preservation	

Table 11.3 Frame Forwarding Rules Summary

DESTINATION ADDRESS	VLAN-UNAWARE SWITCH BEHAVIOR	VLAN-AWARE SWITCH BEHAVIOR
Known unicast	1. Determine the output port associated with the Destination Address from the address table. 2. If the associated output port is different from the port on which the frame arrived, forward the frame to the associated output port. 3. Otherwise, discard the frame.	1. Determine the VLAN associated with the received frame. 2. Determine the output port associated with the Destination Address from the address table. 3. If the associated output port is different from the port on which the frame arrived, *and* is a member of the VLAN associated with the received frame, forward the frame to the associated output port. 4. Otherwise, discard the frame.
Unknown unicast and multicast	1. Flood the frame to all ports except the port on which the frame arrived.	1. Determine the VLAN associated with the received frame. 2. Flood the frame to all ports that are members of the VLAN associated with the received frame, except the port on which the frame arrived.

11.2.4 Frame Forwarding

Let's go back to those golden days of yesteryear. Do you remember the frame forwarding rules for a conventional (non-VLAN) switch?[30] A traditional switch will forward traffic based on the Destination Address in received frames as follows:

- If the destination is a known unicast address, compare the port associated with that address to the port on which the frame was received. If

[30] I hope so. Otherwise, go back and read Chapter 2 again. Try not to forget them before you get back here, or you will find yourself in an infinite loop.

the ports are the same, discard the frame; otherwise, forward the frame onto the associated port.

- If the destination is a multicast or an unknown unicast address, flood the frame onto all ports except the one on which the frame was received.

A VLAN-aware switch adds another dimension to the analysis. For each frame, the VLAN association must be determined either explicitly (from the VLAN identifier in a tag) or implicitly (from a set of VLAN association rules). The forwarding behavior is then a function of both the Destination Address and the VLAN association, as summarized in Table 11.3.

CHAPTER 12

Virtual LANs: The IEEE Standard

In Chapter 11, *Virtual LANs: Applications and Concepts*, we examined VLANs from the perspective of application usage and technical concepts. In this chapter we look at the technical details of the IEEE 802.1Q standard.

IEEE 802.1Q [IEEE98d] is the official industry standard for virtual bridged networks (this is standards terminology for a catenet comprising VLAN-aware switches). The standard itself closely mimics the IEEE 802.1D standard from which it was derived, but does not replace that earlier document; IEEE 802.1D [IEEE98a] is still the controlling document for VLAN-unaware switches. Much of IEEE 802.1Q comprises extensions to the concepts and architecture provided for VLAN-unaware devices rather than reinventing the canons of switched catenets altogether. In some cases, no changes at all were made to the 802.1D standard in order to provide for VLAN-aware operation; for example, IEEE 802.1Q makes no changes to the Spanning Tree Protocol, it simply points the reader to the IEEE 802.1D document for the protocol and compliance requirements. Much of the material in IEEE 802.1Q is literally copied from IEEE 802.1D and augmented to provide the necessary support for VLAN functionality.

This should not be taken to imply that a VLAN-aware switch can be built by making some simple modifications to an existing VLAN-unaware design. Nothing could be further from the truth. Support of VLAN capability implies some fundamental changes to switch architecture, particularly with respect to the structure and operation of the lookup tables (called the *filtering database* in the standard) and the application of VLAN behavioral rules at both the input and output ports.

Development of the standard followed a pattern typical within IEEE 802:

- Identification of a significant market opportunity (i.e., VLAN technology)
- Recognition that a standard was needed for vendor-interoperable implementations
- An organizational turf battle to decide which group would get the right to develop the standard[1]
- Lots of meetings in nice locations around the world[2]
- Lots of draft documents and technical compromises
- Voting, vote resolution, and a final standard

Initial presentations and discussions at an IEEE standards meeting occurred in July 1995. The IEEE 802.1Q Task Force first officially met in March 1996. By June 1998, a draft standard was ready for formal IEEE balloting, with final approval achieved in December of that year. A total of 11 drafts were produced before the final standard was published.

The conceptual material presented in Chapter 11, combined with the details of the IEEE 802.1Q standard provided here, should give the reader a good understanding of the purposes, the applications, and many of the implementation details of VLAN-aware products. However, the usual caveats apply—this book is not intended as either a replacement or a "companion document" to the standard, and does not attempt to present all of the formal compliance requirements and specifications of the standard itself. Readers responsible for developing standards-compliant products can use this book as a guide, but should refer to the official documents for specific conformance requirements.

For the sake of reading simplicity, I use the terms *Q-compliant* and *D-compliant* throughout the rest of this chapter to refer to a device that is compliant with IEEE 802.1Q or IEEE 801.D, respectively. Similarly, I drop the *IEEE* moniker and use the terms 802.1Q and 802.1D to refer to the standards themselves. Both of these practices align with common industry usage.

[1] In this specific case, the issue was whether VLANs fell under the existing scope of the IEEE 802.1 Working Group or whether VLANs constituted a wholly-new dimension requiring the formation of a new Working Group. Since the final standard is designated IEEE 802.1Q, you can figure out who won this battle.

[2] During the course of the standards development process, meetings were held in Maui (twice); Montreal (twice); La Jolla, California (twice); the Netherlands; Vancouver, British Columbia; and other places. Not bad work if you can get it.

12.1 Overview and Scope of the Standard

Like most communications standards, 802.1Q provides both the architecture and a minimally-required set of functions needed to support the target applications. Q-compliant switches can be built that provide all of the application behaviors and benefits discussed in Chapter 11: traffic isolation, ease of moves/adds/changes (software patch panels), and so on. However, the standard itself is more of a toolbox than an implementation guide. The architecture and functionality specified supports an almost unlimited range of potential VLAN applications—including all of the ones we have examined and more—yet there are no recipes provided to build any particular application feature and no requirement to support any specific application environment. This approach (which is the same one used in most network standards) provides for interoperability among vendors without restricting their ability to provide products with different capabilities for different market segments. In addition, such flexibility provides the hooks to support future application environments not yet conceived.

In this spirit, the standard shows how any set of VLAN association rules is applied and processed within a switch, but does not mandate the use of any particular rule; that is left to the equipment vendors, presumably based on the application needs of their customers.

CORRECTING A COMMON MISCONCEPTION

The 802.1Q standard specifies a default behavior that is port-based; that is, in the absence of any other implementation-specific rules, a Q-compliant switch associates an untagged received frame with a VLAN identifier based on the port on which the frame arrived. Since this port-based behavior is the only VLAN association rule even mentioned in the standard, and is specified as the default, many users (and vendors) believe that 802.1Q supports only port-based VLANs. This is a wholly incorrect conclusion. The critical missing link is that the default behavior is taken only when a given implementation provides no other set of association rules. If a product can always apply some other rule to a frame (e.g., based on MAC Source Address), then the standard-specified default behavior is never invoked and does not apply. Contrary to popular opinion, the use of VLAN association rules other than port-based mapping is not outside the scope of the standard.[3]

[3] There was actually an obscure phrase buried in a detailed specification subclause in a late draft of the standard that would have precluded the use of rules other than port-based mapping, but it was removed before final approval and publication.

802.1Q provides for backward compatibility with existing D-compliant bridges and VLAN-unaware end stations. A catenet can be built using an arbitrary mix of VLAN-aware and VLAN-unaware switches. The VLAN-unaware switches are transparent from a VLAN perspective; that is, they process and forward frames based solely on contained MAC addresses, regardless of whether the frames contain a VLAN tag. Legacy D-compliant switches see tagged frames no differently from untagged ones, by virtue of the way that the tags are inserted into the frames (see Section 12.3). A D-compliant switch comprises a proper subset of the functionality of an 802.1Q VLAN-aware switch. If a portion of the target environment is such that VLAN-awareness is either unnecessary or inappropriate, D-compliant switches can be deployed in lieu of Q-compliant ones in the same catenet.

It is interesting to note that, as a standards document, 802.1Q applies to VLAN-aware *switches* only. It contains no specifications regarding VLAN-aware end stations, although by implication Q-compliant switch behavior will to a great extent determine what a VLAN-aware end station must do to avail itself of the VLAN features of the catenet. For example, an end station cannot use a tag format different from that used by the switches! At the time of this writing, however, there is no formal specification of the operation of VLAN-aware end stations; this is perhaps one of the reasons why such capability is not widely implemented. Work is ongoing (both in the commercial marketplace and the standards community) to define the requirements for interoperable VLAN-aware end station behavior.

12.2 Elements of the Standard

802.1Q provides, at a minimum, all of the functionality, features, and capabilities of 802.1D. Thus, the standard provides:

- An architecture for transparent bridging among an arbitrary number of ports attached using any MAC technology that supports 48-bit globally-unique addresses (Ethernet, Token Ring, FDDI, etc.)
- An architecture for a filtering database, that is, a data structure that allows the bridge to know the mapping of devices to ports
- The algorithms for filtering and forwarding frames among the ports, based on the contents of the filtering database
- The algorithms for learning and aging entries in the filtering database
- Optionally, the capability to support multicast pruning and priority operation, as discussed in Chapter 10, *Multicast Pruning*, and Chapter 13, *Priority Operation*, respectively[4]

[4] Just like a D-compliant device, a Q-compliant bridge can implement either or both multicast pruning and traffic class expediting; these functions are orthogonal to its VLAN capabilities.

- A specification for the Spanning Tree Protocol to prevent active loops in the catenet
- A standard set of objects [Management Information Base (MIB)] for vendor-interoperable management of bridges

To support the VLAN-related operations of a switch, 802.1Q extends the 802.1D functionality in a number of areas:

Filtering database A D-compliant filtering database only provides the means to map 48-bit addresses to ports. This was all that was needed for basic bridge operation. For 802.1Q, the filtering database concept must be expanded to also include means to map addresses to VLANs and VLANs to ports.

Frame tagging 802.1Q provides a method for tagging frames with explicit VLAN identification. As discussed earlier, this VLAN tag allows one device to map a frame to a given VLAN based on a set of association rules and other devices to operate based on that VLAN association without having to know the rules used. In addition to defining the standard tag format(s), 802.1Q specifies how tags are inserted and/or stripped as frames propagate in and out of a VLAN-aware switch.

Priority operation 802.1Q provides support for priority encoding of VLAN-tagged frames. While this is not really a VLAN issue, it was a relatively simple matter to provide the "hooks" in the VLAN tag to signal priority. One side benefit is that this mechanism allows Ethernet frames to carry priority information. Native Ethernet frames have no means for an application to indicate frame priority; when using VLAN-tags, priority can be encoded within a field provided in the tag. This is discussed further in Chapter 13 and Section 12.3.2.

Dissimilar LAN encapsulation A method is provided to encapsulate Token Ring and FDDI frames within Ethernet frames (and vice-versa). The encapsulation eliminates any need to change the Little Endian or Big Endian nature of the encapsulated frames; natively encoded frames can be transported across dissimilar LANs. In addition, support is provided for carrying Token Ring Source Routing information in an Ethernet frame. The primary purpose is to allow Ethernet backbones to interconnect legacy source-routed Token Ring LANs without having to modify existing Token Ring devices. This function eases the migration from Token Ring to Ethernet technology.

Automatic distribution of VLAN configuration information A protocol is provided for automatic distribution of VLAN membership information among VLAN-aware switches and end stations. The GARP VLAN Registration Protocol (GVRP) allows VLAN-aware switches to automatically learn the mapping of VLANs to switch ports without having to individually configure each switch, and allows end stations to register their VLAN membership(s). This mechanism ensures that frames propagate correctly to all members of a given VLAN in the catenet. GVRP provides the primitive functions necessary for dynamic creation and destruction of VLANs.

Switch management The 802.1Q standard provides a formal definition for a set of managed objects associated with VLAN-aware switches. As with most IEEE 802 standards, management is officially optional; however, user needs, product requirements, and competitive market considerations render the idea of an unmanaged VLAN-aware switch curious at best. Only the most cost-competitive market segments can tolerate the deployment of unmanaged switches. Switch management is discussed in Chapter 14.

In the sections that follow, we look at these issues in greater detail.

12.3 Tag and Frame Formats

In Chapter 11 we discussed the purpose and use of VLAN tags. In this section we examine the details of the 802.1Q tag format and how it is encapsulated in the various LAN technologies of interest.

An 802.1Q VLAN tag comprises three elements:

- The *VLAN Protocol Identifier* (VPID) field identifies the frame as being VLAN tagged; that is, it is used to differentiate tagged frames from untagged frames.
- A *Tag Control Information* (TCI) field comprises the essential ingredients of the VLAN tag.
- An optional *Embedded Routing Information Field* (E-RIF) allows Source Routing information to be embedded within the VLAN tag for transport across LANs that do not support native Source Routing.

Each of these fields is described in detail in the following text. Following those explanations, we will show how these three fields are inserted into Ethernet, Token Ring, and FDDI frames.

12.3.1 VLAN Protocol Identifier

The VLAN Protocol Identifier (VPID) is a 2-byte field with a value of 0x8100. When present, it indicates that the frame is VLAN tagged and that the next 2 bytes in the frame contain the Tag Control Information. Depending on the type of LAN, the VPID field is encoded in one of two ways:

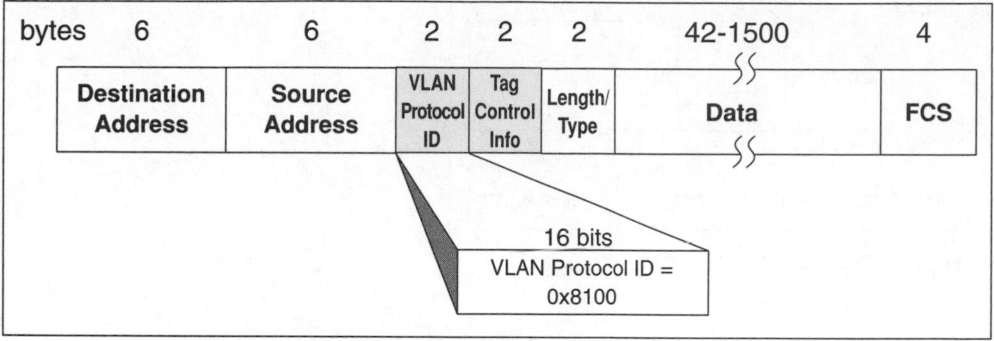

Figure 12.1 VLAN Protocol Identifier on Ethernet.

Ethernet LANs On an Ethernet, the VPID is used as a protocol type; that is, when the Ethernet Type field (following the Source Address) contains the VPID value, the frame carries a VLAN tag and the next 2 bytes contain the Tag Control Information, as depicted in Figure 12.1.

Non-Ethernet LANs Only Ethernet supports the use of a native Type field for protocol identification. On non-Ethernet LANs, the VPID must be encapsulated using LLC/SNAP format, as shown for a Token Ring frame in Figure 12.2.

12.3.2 Tag Control Information Field

Regardless of LAN type, VPID encoding, or the presence of optional embedded Source Routing information, all VLAN tags carry a 2-byte Tag Control Information (TCI) field, depicted in Figure 12.3.

The fields are used as follows:

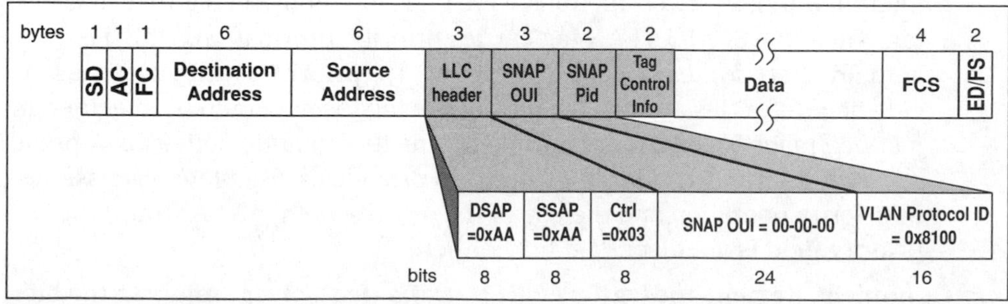

Figure 12.2 VLAN Protocol Identifier in LLC/SNAP format.

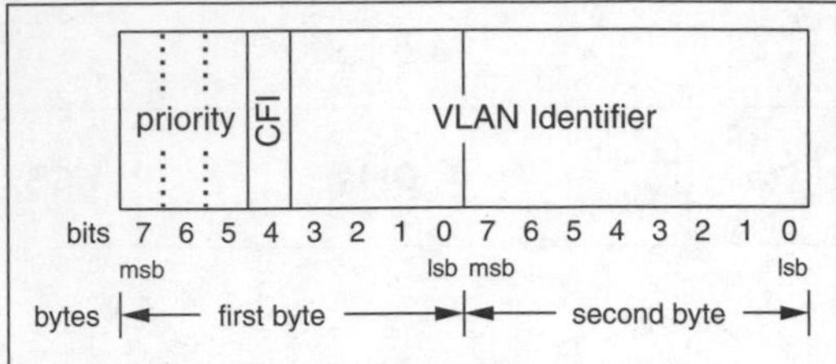

Figure 12.3 Tag Control Information field.

Priority This is a 3-bit field that indicates the user priority of the frame. It can take any value from 0 (0b000) to 7 (0b111). Bit 5 of the first byte is the least-significant bit of the priority field; bit 7 is the most-significant bit.

The priority field is actually unrelated to the use of tags for VLAN identification; it is not there for VLAN purposes at all. The priority function is simply getting a free ride on the VLAN bandwagon. This is primarily a result of the arbitrary separation of the priority function of IEEE 802.1p (the revision to 802.1D that provided for multicast pruning and traffic class expediting) and 802.1Q. The traffic class expediting function is much easier to implement if frames carry explicit user priority information, in much the same way that VLAN-aware switches can benefit if frames carry explicit VLAN identification. By including this information in the frame itself, we relieve the switches of the burden of having to determine frame priority by parsing the frame contents and applying a set of priority rules.

Some LAN technologies have the native ability to carry user priority information (e.g., IEEE 802.4 Token Bus); others (such as Ethernet) don't have this capability. Therefore, it made sense to provide the means to add explicit priority information to frames for use in those technologies without native priority support. However, it seemed unreasonable to provide two types of tags, one for priority information and another for VLAN identification; the two functions were therefore combined into a single tag. Thus, the 802.1Q VLAN tag carries priority information, which is actually there for the benefit of IEEE 802.1p (priority-aware) switches. A side benefit of this approach was that the tag format could be specified in just one place (802.1Q), rather than having its semantic definitions spread out over multiple standards. Chapter 13 provides a complete discussion of priority operation and the use of the priority field in VLAN tags; the priority field is not discussed further here.

Canonical Format Indicator (CFI) *Canonical format* refers to the bit-ordering (Little or Big Endian) of the bytes within a frame. Data within

Ethernet frames is normally sent using canonical (Little Endian) bit order; Token Ring frames normally send data using non-canonical (Big Endian) bit order. This difference in bit-ordering can be important for higher layer protocols, especially when the encapsulated data contains MAC addresses. Higher layer protocols [e.g., the Address Resolution Protocol (ARP), as used in IP and AppleTalk] interpret the bit order of these embedded MAC addresses according to the native order of the LAN technology through which frames are received. As discussed in Chapter 3, *Bridging between Technologies*, if frames are being bridged from a dissimilar technology, the bit-ordering of the embedded addresses may be incorrect and the higher layer protocols will not work properly. The CFI bit was intended to indicate whether embedded MAC addresses are in canonical or Big Endian bit order; this allows transportation of frames across LANs using dissimilar bit order without loss of meaning.

The CFI bit is perhaps the most incorrectly-named bit in the history of networking. The CFI does not, in fact, always indicate whether embedded MAC addresses are in canonical format or not. Worse, the sense of the bit is reversed from normal conventions (0 means canonical format, and 1 means non-canonical format). Furthermore, the semantics of the CFI bit are a function of the underlying LAN technology, as indicated in Table 12.1.

WHAT THE HECK IS GOING ON?

Why would anybody consciously choose a name for a bit that has such a bizarre relationship to its meaning and purpose? As sometimes occurs in standards development, political considerations can have odd effects.

What is now the CFI bit began its life with a different name and interpretation. In early drafts of 802.1Q, this bit was called the Token Ring Encapsulation (TREN) bit. In this formulation, the bit (if set to 1) indicated two things: that the frame contained embedded Source Routing information, and that embedded MAC addresses were in Big Endian bit order. Thus, the name of the bit really reflected its purpose; a device would set this bit when it was encapsulating a Token Ring frame into an Ethernet frame (Source Routing information, Big Endian bit order, and all).

The problem was that calling the bit TREN it made Token Ring handling seem like an exception condition—a special case. In addition, there was no clear way to indicate that a frame carried embedded Source Routing information yet had its data in Little Endian format, a condition that could conceivably occur if Token Rings were being used as backbones among Ethernet LANs. Thus, the use and intent of the TREN bit made Token Rings appear to be second-class citizens.

Table 12.1 Interpretation of the CFI Bit

	CFI = 0	CFI = 1
Ethernet	1. The VLAN tag is not extended to include embedded Source Routing information 2. Any embedded MAC addresses are in canonical (Little Endian) format	1. The VLAN tag is extended to include embedded Source Routing information 2. The endian-ness of any embedded MAC addresses is determined by a bit in that embedded Source Routing information field
Token Ring	Embedded MAC addresses are in canonical (Little Endian) format	Embedded MAC addresses are in non-canonical (Big Endian) format
FDDI using native Source Routing[1]	Embedded MAC addresses are in canonical (Little Endian) format (same interpretation as for Token Ring)	Embedded MAC addresses are in non-canonical (Big Endian) format (same interpretation as for Token Ring)
FDDI without native Source Routing[1]	1. The VLAN tag is not extended to include embedded Source Routing information 2. Any embedded MAC addresses are in canonical (Little Endian) format (same interpretation as for Ethernet)	1. The VLAN tag is extended to include embedded Source Routing information 2. The endian-ness of any embedded MAC addresses is determined by a bit in that embedded Source Routing information field (same interpretation as for Ethernet)

[1] FDDI frames can carry Source Routing information natively. This is indicated by setting the Routing Information Indicator (the first bit of the Source Address) equal to 1.

The fact is that, as a practical matter in switched LANs today, Token Rings *are* second-class citizens.[5] They are present in ever-decreasing numbers, and user emphasis is on migration to Ethernet. That the original TREN bit supported Token Ring migration to switched Ethernet backbones better than the other way around was a Good Thing™, not a design flaw.

However, Token Ring advocates do also participate in standards meetings and have voting rights. In order to allow the standard to proceed smoothly to completion, the name of the TREN bit was changed to the less-incriminating *Canonical Format Indicator,* and the meaning was changed to decouple the Source Routing extension from the bit-ordering. Unfortunately, this left us with a dichotomy between the name and the semantics of the CFI bit.

[5] No offense is intended to Token Ring users or advocates—I am just telling it like it is. Token Ring equipment is less widely available and more expensive than Ethernet equipment for the same level of performance.

VLAN Identifier This field contains the 12-bit VLAN identifier—the explicit indication of the frame's VLAN association. A total of 4,096 (2^{12}) values are theoretically possible, but 2 have special meaning, reducing the maximum number of VLANs in a catenet to 4,094:

- The value of all ones (0xFFF) is reserved and currently unused.
- The value of all zeros (0x000) indicates a *priority tag*—the tag not being used to indicate VLAN association, but solely to signal user priority on a LAN that does not have any such native capability. This is the case discussed earlier, where priority signaling is getting a free ride on the VLAN tag. A device that wishes to indicate priority without invoking VLAN mechanisms uses the VLAN tag format with a VLAN identifier of 0. As discussed in Section 12.4.1.2, a priority-tagged frame is treated the same as an untagged frame from the perspective of a VLAN-aware switch.

12.3.3 Embedded Routing Information Field

Depending on the underlying LAN and the value of the CFI bit, a VLAN tag may include an optional Embedded Routing Information Field (E-RIF), as depicted in Figure 12.4.

The fields of the E-RIF are defined as follows:

12.3.3.1 Route Control Portion

Routing Type This field indicates the type of Source Routed frame being employed, as encoded in Table 12.2. Note that bit 5 (denoted with the value X in the table) is always transmitted as a 0 and ignored on receipt.

This encoding is somewhat different from the encoding of the Routing Type field employed when using native Source Routing on Token Ring

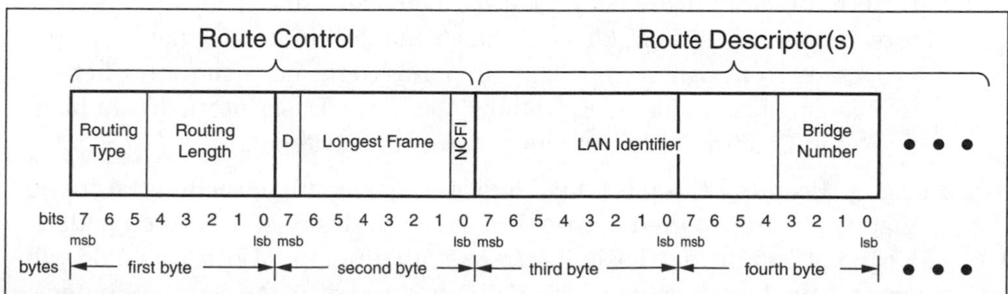

Figure 12.4 Embedded Routing Information field.

Table 12.2 Routing Type Field Interpretation

ROUTING TYPE			
BIT 7	BIT 6	BIT 5	INTERPRETATION
0	0	X	Specifically Routed Frame; used when relaying an untagged, natively Source Routed frames from a Token Ring or FDDI onto an Ethernet or FDDI for Source Routing using tagged format with embedded Source Routing.
0	1	X	Transparently Bridged Frame; used when relaying an untagged transparently bridged frame from a Token Ring onto an Ethernet or FDDI using tagged format. A frame carrying this Routing Type has no Route Descriptors attached; the length of the E-RIF field is exactly 2 bytes.
1	0	X	All Routes Explorer Frame; used for Route Discovery in a Source Routed catenet.
1	1	X	Spanning Tree Explorer Frame; used to propagate frames along the Spanning Tree in a Source Routed catenet.

and FDDI LANs (see Chapter 6, *Source Routing*). Bridges supporting both native, untagged Source Routed frames and VLAN-tagged frames using embedded Source Routing must be able to convert between the two sets of interpretations of this field.

Routing Length This 5-bit field indicates the length of the E-RIF field in bytes, including both the Route Control portion and all Route Descriptors. The value of the Routing Length is always an even number in the range of 2 to 30 bytes, depending upon the number of Route Descriptors. Bit 4 is the most-significant bit of the length, and bit 0 the least-significant.

Direction This single bit field signals the direction in which Route Descriptors are processed. A value of 0 indicates that the Route Descriptors are processed from left-to-right; a value of 1 indicates that they are processed from right-to-left. This simplifies frame construction when exchanging frames between stations; the Route Descriptors do not have to be shuffled for the reverse path through the catenet.

Longest Frame This 6-bit field indicates the length of the longest frame that can be transported across the catenet in this Source Routed path. In a catenet comprising dissimilar LANs with different MTUs, this field will contain the lowest value of the MTU for any LAN in the Source Routed path. The value is determined during Route Discovery and is encoded in this field using a method that allows it to represent MTU values from 516 bytes to more than 59,000 bytes. The details of the encoding are provided in Chapter 6 and [IEEE98a]; the most important point to remember is that the field does not contain a numerical byte value, nor can the actual byte value for the MTU be determined by a simple calculation from the bits in this field.

Non-canonical Format Indicator (NCFI) Here is where the other shoe drops. Remember the Canonical Format Indicator (CFI) from the Tag Control Information field? For certain values of the CFI bit on certain LAN technologies, determination of the endian-ness of embedded MAC addresses was deferred to a bit in the E-RIF field. This is that bit. However, in the style of the CFI bit, the sense of the NCFI is also reversed from normal conventions. When the NCFI is used to signal the endian-ness of embedded MAC addresses, a value of 0 indicates Big Endian format; a value of 1 indicates Little Endian format.[6]

12.3.3.2 Route Descriptor Portion

LAN Identifier and Bridge Identifier These fields provide the sequence of LANs and bridges through which a Source Routed frame is to be passed between the source and destination. There will be as many Route Descriptors as necessary (up to a maximum of 14) to deliver the frame, as determined during the Route Discovery process (see Chapter 6).

SOURCE ROUTING, VLANS, AND LITTLE TOES

It should be clear that support for Source Routing in a VLAN-aware catenet complicates matters considerably. The fundamental differences in architecture between Source Routing and Transparent Bridging have produced a design that contains myriad special cases resulting from all of the various combinations of native versus embedded Source Routing, Big versus Little Endian bit-ordering, and tagged versus untagged frames. Add to that the fact that Ethernets never use native Source Routing, Token Rings almost always use native Source Routing, and FDDIs sometimes do and sometimes don't use native Source Routing, and you get an

[6] Dear Reader: I protested long and loudly about the ludicrous encoding of the CFI and NCFI bits during the development of the 802.1Q standard. I even submitted a disapproval vote based in part on this issue, but alas, I was just one voice against a standards juggernaut.

environment where it is almost impossible to enumerate all of the combinations, much less make them all work.

While for political reasons a standard must attempt to cover all of the bases, a commercial product need only support those environments that customers really deploy. Fortunately, these comprise a subset of the available options, and 802.1Q was optimized for the more common cases.

For example, the mechanisms of 802.1Q make it relatively straightforward to transport Source Routed Token Ring frames from the periphery of the catenet across a transparently bridged, VLAN-aware Ethernet core (to the extent that such a process can ever be straightforward!). The reverse case (i.e., one with a VLAN-aware, Source Routed Token Ring core) is somewhat problematic. In fact, a network planner who wants a predominantly Source Routed catenet will probably not use 802.1Q-style VLANs at all, as they eliminate much of the usefulness of Source Routing. One of Source Routing's goals is to use multiple simultaneously-active paths through a catenet, yet 802.1Q propagates frames only along a spanning tree. At the time of this writing, a project is currently under way within the IEEE 802.5 (Token Ring) Working Group to define VLAN usage in a true Source Routed catenet, but the characteristics and behavior of such a catenet are not currently well understood.

The saving grace of all of this confusion is that the marketplace is speaking loud and clear. Ethernet is the preferred LAN technology, and VLAN-aware transparently bridged catenets are preferred over Source Routing. Source Routing will become the "little toe" of networking—like the one on your foot, it had a use at one point in our evolution, but nobody remembers what it was, and it will probably disappear in a few generations.

12.3.4 Tagged Ethernet Frames

Figure 12.5 depicts the format of a tagged Ethernet frame for the case where there is no embedded Source Routing information (CFI = 0). This is the most common case of a VLAN tag on an Ethernet.

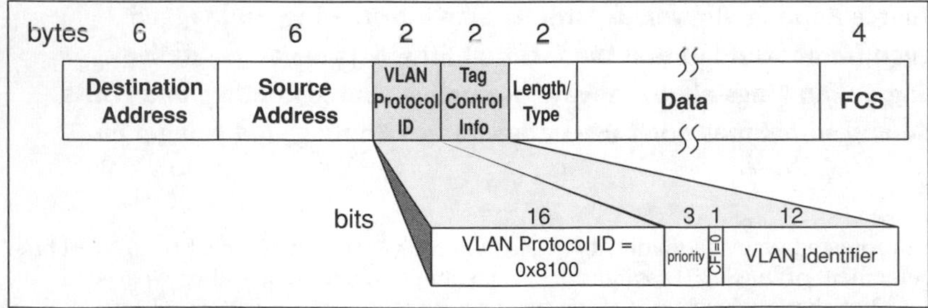

Figure 12.5 Tagged Ethernet Frame (no embedded Source Routing).

The Destination and Source Address fields are unchanged from their use in an untagged frame; they indicate the recipient(s) and sender of the frame, respectively.

A tagged frame is indicated on an Ethernet by a Type field value equal to the VLAN Protocol Identifier (0x8100). The presence of this field signals that the next 2 bytes contain the Tag Control Information, as depicted in Figure 12.5. Following the Tag Control Information is the original Ethernet Length/Type field (i.e., the field that would represent the length or type value if the same frame contents were being sent untagged). That is, the VLAN tag is inserted between the Source Address and the Length/Type field relative to an untagged frame.

The decision to use an Ethernet Type field (rather than an LLC or SNAP identifier) to indicate VLAN tagging was made deliberately. It is much simpler to parse and decode a single 16-bit Type field value than to deal with the Length, LLC DSAP/SSAP/Control, and SNAP fields, as would be necessary if LLC/SNAP encapsulation were used. This simplification reduces the cost of the hardware required to implement a VLAN-aware Ethernet switch.

The problem is that Ethernet is alone among LAN technologies in supporting a native Type field. As a result, we need to use a different encapsulation format for tagged frames on other technologies (as shown in Figure 12.2). That is, VLAN tagging is optimized for the Ethernet case; tag parsing in an Ethernet-only switch is simpler than in any other technology. The tradeoff is greater complexity when switching between dissimilar LAN technologies; such a switch must deal with at least two types of tag formats, translating among them as needed.

Figure 12.6 depicts how an untagged Ethernet frame is converted to a tagged frame, and vice-versa.

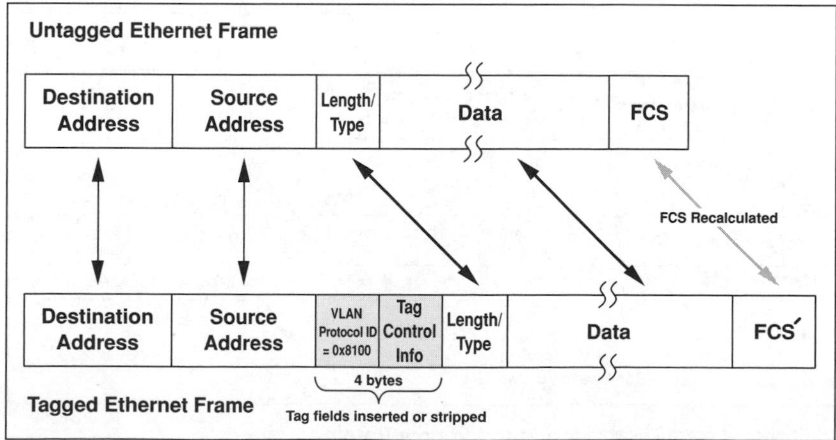

Figure 12.6 Mapping between tagged and untagged Ethernet frame formats.

Regardless of whether the original, untagged frame used Type or Length encapsulation, the resulting tagged frame always uses a Type field, indicating that the Tag Control Information follows in the next 2 bytes.

A very important factor is that the original Length/Type field is offset from its untagged position in the frame by exactly 4 bytes—there are no variable length or optional fields present before the Length/Type field. This greatly simplifies hardware parsing of the frame; no conditional operations are required, and the protocol type can be easily extracted.

Since the VLAN tag modifies the portion of the frame protected by the Frame Check Sequence, the FCS must be recalculated for the modified frame both upon insertion and stripping of the tag.

Figure 12.7 depicts a tagged Ethernet frame that carries embedded Source Routing information in an E-RIF field. This would typically be used to transport Source Routed Token Ring frames across an Ethernet backbone.

Note that the fact that such a format exists does not imply that VLAN-aware devices on an Ethernet must support Source Routing. There are three interesting cases to consider:

1. *VLAN-aware Ethernet end stations.* Ethernet has never supported native Source Routing. As a result, traditional (VLAN unaware) Ethernet end stations do not know how to deal with Source Routed frames. Such frames will be discarded, either by the NIC or the device driver, if they are ever received. There is no reason for new VLAN-aware Ethernet end stations to support Source Routing either. The inclusion of the E-RIF field in the 802.1Q VLAN tag was only to support transportation of Source Routed frames (sent and received by Token Ring stations at the periphery) across an Ethernet backbone, not to enable speaking to Ethernet end stations using Source Routing. It is perfectly permissible

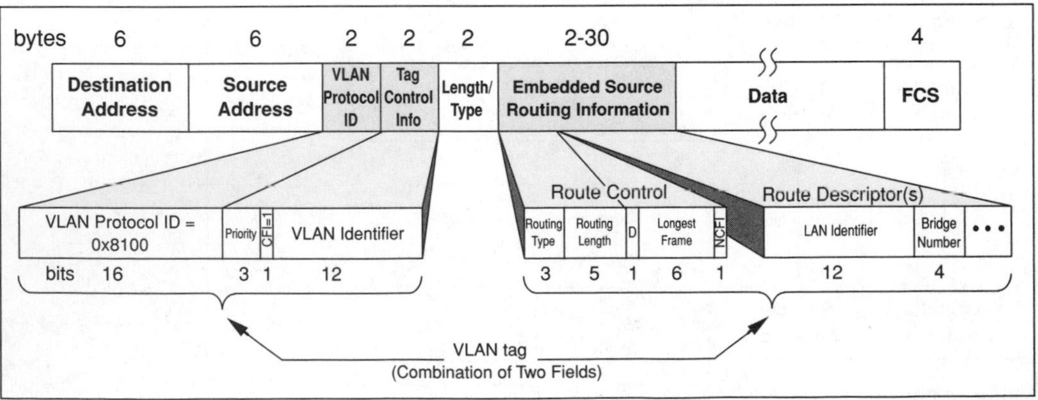

Figure 12.7 Tagged Ethernet frame with embedded Source Routing.

for an Ethernet end station to discard any frames containing an E-RIF field. Support for embedded Source Routing in Ethernet stations is not required by the standard.[7]

2. *VLAN-aware switches equipped solely with Ethernet ports.* With regard to handling of the E-RIF field, a VLAN-aware, Ethernet-only switch has a number of possibilities to deal with, depending on whether frames are arriving in tagged or untagged format and whether they are being forwarded in tagged or untagged format. These cases are enumerated in Table 12.3.

   As can be seen from Table 12.3, the complexities of embedded Source Routing do not have any material effect on the implementation (and hence the cost) of an Ethernet-only switch. This is important considering the volumes and cost sensitivity of these products. A switch only needs to interpret the E-RIF field when a frame is forwarded onto a non-Ethernet LAN—a situation never encountered by an Ethernet-only switch.

3. *VLAN-aware switches supporting dissimilar LAN technologies.* It is only in this case that the E-RIF field must be parsed and interpreted by a switch. Depending on the combination of input and output port technology, and on whether the attached LANs support native Source Routing, the switch may need to implement the Source Routing algorithms as well as translate frame formats between embedded and native Source Routing.

Table 12.3 Handling of E-RIF in an Ethernet-Only Switch

	FORWARD UNTAGGED	FORWARD TAGGED
Receive Untagged	This is the same behavior as a VLAN-unaware switch. Untagged frames on an Ethernet never carry native Source Routing or E-RIF fields.	Since the received frame will never contain native Source Routing information, the forwarded frame will never need to have an E-RIF field.
Receive Tagged	Since the forwarded frame cannot carry native Source Routing information, the E-RIF field can be ignored (and discarded).	The forwarded frame will include the E-RIF field from the received frame, but the switch does not need to examine or modify it during frame processing. All decisions can be made examining the contained addresses by and Tag Control Information.

[7] And, in my opinion, should be discouraged, to prevent the proliferation of Source Routing onto Ethernet LANs.

12.3.5 Flash! Ethernet MTU Increases by 4 Bytes!

As discussed in Section 12.3.4, the VLAN tag (including the VPID and TCI fields) constitutes an additional 4 bytes that can be inserted into an untagged Ethernet frame. Ethernet, like all LAN technologies, supports frame transmission and reception up to some maximum length; for pre-VLAN Ethernet, this was 1,518 bytes (not including preamble). What happens if we insert a VLAN tag into a maximum-length untagged Ethernet frame? Clearly, we get a frame that is longer than the maximum—the use of 802.1Q VLAN tags could force the tagging device to violate the IEEE 802.3 standard!

This was considered a serious problem during the development of the 802.1Q standard. If there were a lot of devices in the field that could receive or transmit only the specified maximum, and not a byte (or 4 bytes) more, then we would be faced with a huge installed base of devices that could not interoperate in a VLAN-aware environment. Note that, even if we don't expect these legacy devices to ever be VLAN-aware, we need them to be able to handle VLAN-tagged frames. Existing VLAN-unaware bridges are expected to forward tagged frames transparently based on the contained address information. Otherwise, tagged frames could not pass through a VLAN-unaware domain of the catenet.

The standards committees (both 802.1Q and 802.3) struggled with this problem and considered three alternative solutions:

1. Leave the 802.3 frame limit intact, and take the 4 bytes needed for the VLAN tag from the data portion of the frame. That is, we could reduce the data payload field from 1,500 to 1,496 bytes maximum, in which case the VLAN tag would not cause the frame to become longer than the existing 802.3 specification allowed.

   The problem with this approach is that, to make it work, all of the existing higher layer protocol software (e.g., all of the IP protocol stacks running over Ethernet) would need to be modified so that they knew not to try to send 1,500 bytes of data per frame. This was considered untenable at best.

2. Increase the maximum length of the Ethernet frame to support the added 4 bytes of the VLAN tag. This would solve the problem for VLANs, but it:

   - Required that the 802.1Q Task Force convince the IEEE 802.3 Working Group to modify the Ethernet standard. Believe it or not, this is not a trivial matter. IEEE 802.1Q was responsible for defining the standard for VLAN operation, but had no authority to make changes to IEEE 802.3.

- Incurred the possibility of incompatible legacy devices discussed earlier.

3. Ignore the problem (i.e., define a VLAN tag that requires an extra 4 bytes, don't change IEEE 802.3 to explicitly support it, and hope that the vendor community does the right thing).

In the end, we chose the second option (although for a long time it appeared that the third option would win). In 1998, the IEEE approved supplement IEEE 802.3ac [IEEE98g], which increased the maximum length of an Ethernet frame by 4 bytes to 1,522 bytes (not including Preamble).[8] Of utmost importance, it was clearly stated in the standard that the added length was to be used specifically and exclusively for the VLAN tag. Without this restriction, higher layer protocols could conceivably use the added 4 bytes for data, putting us right back where we started—adding a VLAN tag to this (4 byte longer) data would violate the length limit again.

So what about all those legacy devices that can't handle the longer frames? It turns out that there aren't any. While in theory someone could have built a device that strictly enforced the original upper length limit, this was never done in practice. During an informal investigation of the Ethernet marketplace, the standards committees were unable to find a single device that had a problem with a 4-byte-longer frame. Many devices that used dynamic memory allocation for their frame buffers could support much longer frames than needed for VLAN operation (in some cases, 10 Kbytes or more). Devices that use fixed-length frame buffers could typically support either 1,536 byte frames (0x0600, a nice round number) or 2-Kbyte frames (an even nicer, rounder number, but a little less efficient for memory utilization); both of these values are commonly used to simplify the memory architecture of commercial Ethernet devices. As long as we didn't try to increase the frame size beyond 1,536 bytes, there would be no real problem in the field.

Note that we only need to consider the 4 bytes added by the VPID and TCI fields, and not the optional E-RIF fields. Source Routing on a Token Ring LAN is performed by the end stations, which are already aware that Route Descriptors reduce the amount of payload that can be put into the Data field of the frame. So any allowance for the E-RIF field can come out of the Data field and does not require increasing the maximum frame length. The MTU of the catenet is learned by the Source Routing end stations as part of the Route Discovery process; the device drivers (and hence, higher-layer protocols) must already be able to modify their maximum data payload as a result.

[8] I was the editor of the IEEE 802.3ac standard.

VLANS AND ARCHITECTURAL LAYERING

Didn't we all learn that the beauty of architectural layering was that you could make changes in one layer without having to make changes in other layers? Why did the specification of VLANs (above the Ethernet MAC layer) require changes to be made to the underlying MAC (increasing the maximum frame length)?

The answer is that 802.1Q VLANs don't follow strict layering guidelines. If they did, the VLAN tag information would have been encapsulated within the Data field of the Ethernet frame, just as occurs with IP, TCP, and other layered protocols. A strictly-layered client of the Ethernet would simply accept the limitations of the underlying LAN (the maximum frame supported).

There are a few reasons why 802.1Q did not use a strictly-proper layered approach. From a hardware implementation perspective, it is important to be able to extract tag information with a minimum of effort and delay. Because it puts the TCI field immediately after the VPID field, a VLAN-aware device does not need to buffer and parse fields embedded within the data payload portion of the frame. This significantly reduces the cost and complexity of VLAN-aware switches. Second, we want to be able to apply VLAN-awareness in a manner *transparent to existing protocols and applications.* By slipping VLANs in as a shim layer (between existing layers such as Ethernet and IP), we can provide VLAN capability for existing applications without changing those applications. (We can also choose to change the applications to become VLAN-aware, for added benefits.)

By inserting VLAN tag information into the frame (rather than encapsulating it), we make it much easier to transform between the tagged and untagged versions of a frame. This eases the migration from legacy VLAN-unaware devices and applications to a VLAN-aware future.

12.3.6 Tagged Token Ring Frames

Figure 12.8 depicts a tagged Token Ring frame. Since Token Ring does not support a native Type field, the VLAN Protocol Identifier uses LLC/SNAP encoding, as discussed in Section 12.3.1. Similarly to the case with Ethernet, the VLAN tag information is inserted following the Source Address in the frame.

Note that VLAN-tagged Token Ring frames never carry embedded Source Routing information (E-RIF field). This is because all Token Ring implementations support native Source Routing (see Chapter 6). If a frame is being Source Routed, the Routing Information Indicator (the first bit of the Source Address) will be set equal to 1 and routing information will be inserted between the Source Address and the VLAN tag (or the Data field, if the frame is untagged). Because there is never an E-RIF field, and therefore no NCFI bit present, the CFI bit takes a different interpretation on Token Ring LANs, as shown in Table 12.1.

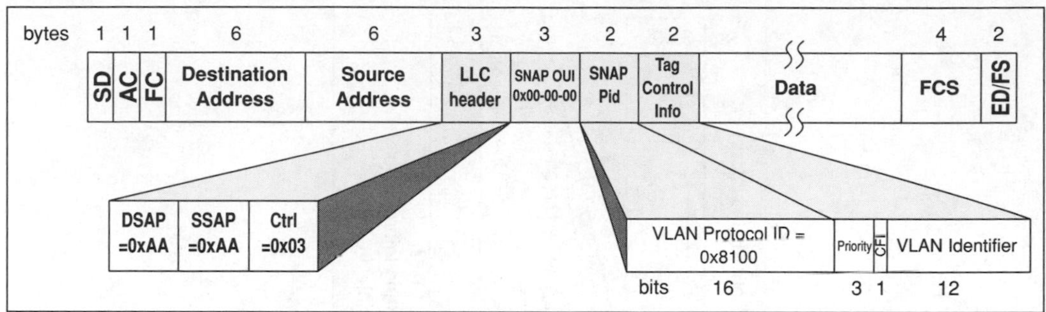

Figure 12.8 Tagged Token Ring frame.

12.3.7 Tagged FDDI Frames

Figure 12.9 depicts a tagged FDDI frame. Like Token Ring, FDDI does not support a native Type field, and the VLAN Protocol Identifier uses LLC/SNAP encoding as discussed in Section 12.3.1.

While Token Ring LANs and devices invariably support native Source Routing, this is considered an optional feature for FDDI products. Some FDDI devices support it and some do not. As a result, both native and embedded Source Routing is supported on FDDI. This results in two forms of VLAN tag usage:

- If native Source Routing is being used, the frame format is similar to that of Token Ring; the Routing Information Indicator is set equal to 1, routing information is inserted following the Source Address, there is no E-RIF field in the VLAN tag, and the semantics of the CFI bit are the same as for Token Ring.
- If embedded Source Routing is being used, the frame format is similar to that of Ethernet, except that the VLAN Protocol Identifier must be encoded using LLC/SNAP. The E-RIF field is present, and the semantics of the CFI and NCFI bits are the same as for Ethernet.

12.3.8 VLAN Tags on Other LAN Technologies

It is also possible to include 802.1Q VLAN tags on LANs other than Ethernet, Token Ring, and FDDI (e.g., on an IEEE 802.11 Wireless LAN), although these three are the only technologies explicitly discussed in the 802.1Q standard. Since no LANs other than Token Ring and FDDI support native Source Routing, the tag format is straightforward. If a native Type field is available, the tag uses Ethernet-style encoding and semantics; if not, the tag uses FDDI-style

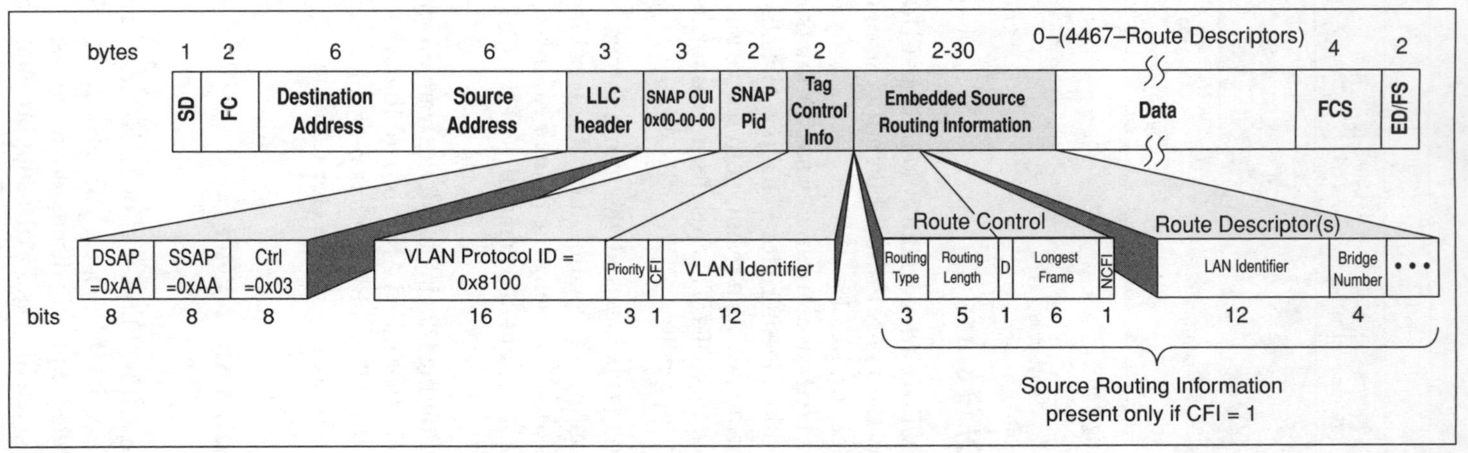

Figure 12.9 Tagged FDDI frame.

encoding and semantics. The tag is inserted between the end of the technology-specific MAC header information and the data payload.

12.3.9 A Word on Bit and Byte Order

Many people, including network equipment designers, get confused about bit and byte orderings.[9] VLAN tags are especially nasty, as the same fields can be sent on dissimilar LANs that use different bit orders (e.g., Ethernet versus Token Ring).

The ordering rules are actually fairly simple. The first byte is sent first, the second byte second, and so on. In any frame format diagram, bytes are always enumerated from left-to-right or from top-to-bottom (depending on the orientation of the diagram).[10] In general, when a multi-byte field with numerical significance is being sent, the most-significant byte is sent first.

Within each byte, the bit-ordering is dependent on the underlying LAN technology. Ethernets operate in Little Endian bit order; bytes are sent least-significant bit first to most-significant bit last (or least-significant nibble first to most-significant nibble last, in the case of Fast Ethernet). Token Rings operate in Big Endian bit order; bytes are sent most-significant bit first to least-significant bit last.

With bit and byte ordering, an example is always best. Looking at how the Tag Control Information field in Figure 12.3 would be sent on an Ethernet, the bit order would be as shown in Table 12.4.

Everybody got it now?[11]

12.4 IEEE 802.1Q Switch Operation

We can understand all of the application environments, define all of the VLAN association rules, and specify frame and tag formats all we want, but ultimately a real-life VLAN-aware switch has to implement all this stuff. Figure 12.10 depicts a model of the operational flow of frames through a VLAN-aware switch.

[9] I get more than a few phone calls from people "just making sure" they have the ordering correct. The most common time to do this is just before committing to silicon on a new part; the price of being wrong can be weeks or months of delay in the development schedule.

[10] I have never seen anyone, even those who use Hebrew as a native language, order their bytes from right-to-left!

[11] And if you guessed that this table, enumerated down to the bit level, was included here because one of my consulting clients almost blew it, you were absolutely correct! Design review is a wonderful concept.

Table 12.4 Tag Control Information Bit Ordering on Ethernet

First bit sent	Bit 0 of the first byte (the ninth bit of the VLAN identifier)
Second bit sent	Bit 1 of the first byte (the tenth bit of the VLAN identifier)
Third bit sent	Bit 2 of the first byte (the eleventh bit of the VLAN identifier)
Fourth bit sent	Bit 3 of the first byte (the twelfth bit of the VLAN identifier)
Fifth bit sent	Bit 4 of the first byte (the CFI bit)
Sixth bit sent	Bit 5 of the first byte (the LS bit of the Priority field)
Seventh bit sent	Bit 6 of the first byte (the middle bit of the Priority field)
Eighth bit sent	Bit 7 of the first byte (the MS bit of the Priority field)
Ninth bit sent	Bit 0 of the second byte (the first bit of the VLAN identifier)
Tenth bit sent	Bit 1 of the second byte (the second bit of the VLAN Identifier)
...	...
Sixteenth bit sent	Bit 7 of the second byte (the eighth bit of the VLAN Identifier)

A switch comprises some number of physical port interfaces that can be used both to receive and transmit frames. The fundamental job of a VLAN-aware switch is to receive frames and decide, on a frame-by-frame basis:

- Onto which port(s), if any, to forward the frame
- Whether forwarded frames should be transmitted in tagged or untagged format

To achieve these ends in a VLAN context, the switch must maintain state information for each VLAN that indicates which ports attach to LANs that are needed to reach members of that VLAN. This set of ports, known as the *member set*, is determined by the VLAN association rules in effect. Ports in the member set for a given VLAN can be expected to receive and transmit frames belonging to that VLAN; ports not in the member set should generally not be receiving and/or transmitting frames for that VLAN. The member set for a VLAN may be configured by a human administrator or, more likely, learned dynamically through an automatic mechanism such as the GARP VLAN Registration Protocol discussed in Section 12.4.5.

For each frame received from a physical port, the switch performs a three-stage process comprising a set of *ingress*, *progress*, and *egress* behaviors. In the descriptions of these processes that follow, the only frames being discussed are those that are actually subject to switch processing. For the sake of clarity, we will assume that control frames (PAUSE flow control, Spanning Tree BPDUs, etc.) are handled separately. In Chapter 15, *Make the Switch!*, we

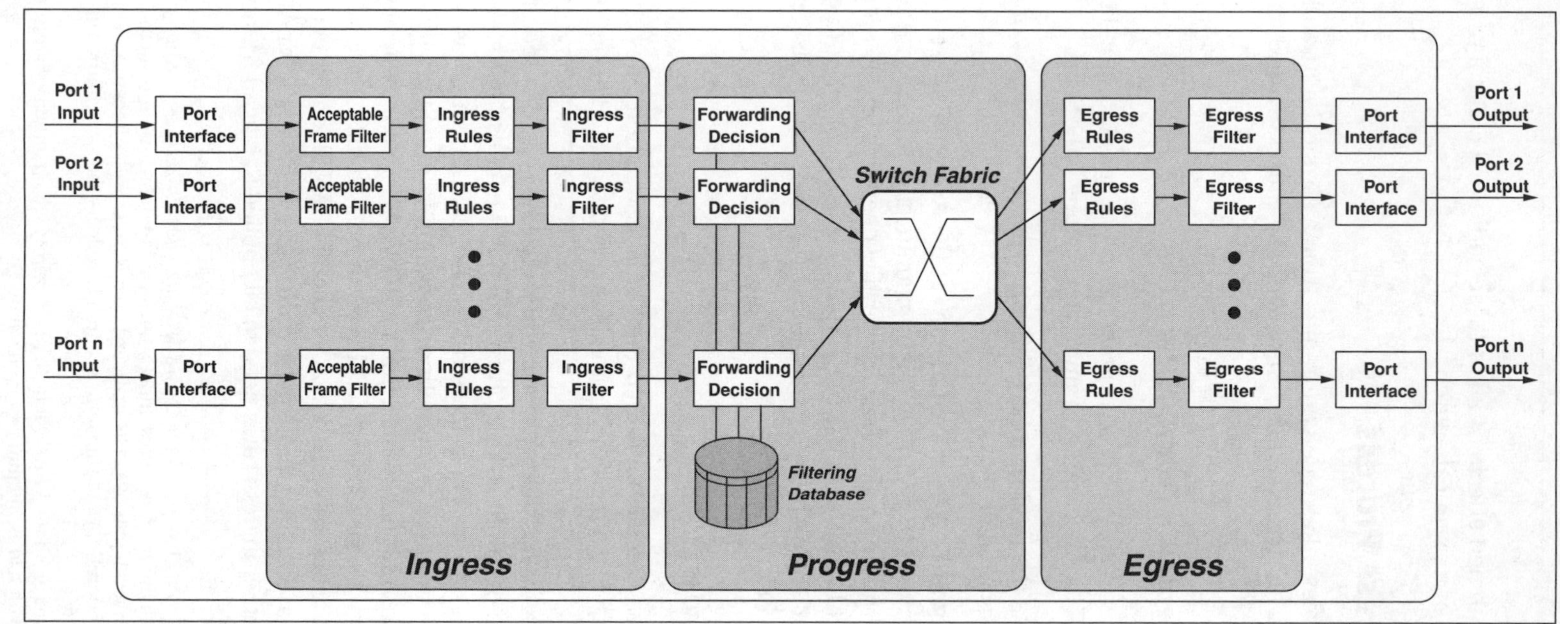

Figure 12.10 IEEE 802.1Q switch operation flow.

consider the combined effects of all of these additional control processes on the architecture of a practical switch.

12.4.1 Ingress Process

The ingress process takes received frames from a physical port and performs three operations: an *Acceptable Frame Filter*, the *Ingress Rules*, and an optional *Ingress Filter*.

12.4.1.1 Acceptable Frame Filter

A control parameter called the *Acceptable Frame Types* is applied to every received frame. The Acceptable Frame Types can be either:

Admit All As the name implies, this value passes all frames on to the Ingress Rules module.

Admit All Tagged A core switch can set the Acceptable Frame Types to Admit All Tagged to avoid having to examine any untagged frames. As pure core switches make their forwarding decisions solely on the value of the VLAN Identifier in the tag, it makes sense to block untagged frames from further switch processing; untagged frames can be discarded at the Acceptable Frame Filter.

12.4.1.2 Ingress Rules

It is in the Ingress Rules module that the VLAN association rules are applied to received frames.[12] Each received frame is mapped to exactly one VLAN in this module.

The VLAN association rules are arbitrary, based on the desired application behavior and the capabilities of a given product (i.e., most switches support only a limited set of possible ingress rules). Typically, the Ingress Rules are determined and configured by a network administrator using network management software, and distributed among the VLAN-aware switches in the catenet by automatic means (e.g., GVRP, as discussed in Section 12.4.5).

If the received frame contains a VLAN tag, the VLAN identifier in the tag determines the VLAN association; that is, the frame is assigned to the VLAN indicated by the tag.[13] No other ingress rules need to be applied to tagged frames.

[12] Throughout this book, I have used the term *VLAN association rules* as a synonym for what the 802.1Q standard calls the *Ingress Rules*, mostly because I find the former term more useful and descriptive of their overall purpose. The standard uses *Ingress Rules* because it is solely concerned with switch operation, and this term accurately reflects the association rules from the switch's point of view.

[13] The only exceptions are if the VLAN Identifier is all zeros, which indicates a priority tagged frame, or all ones, which is an invalid, reserved value.

The VLAN association rules are applied to all untagged frames. 802.1Q specifies a default port-based Ingress Rule in the absence of any other configured rules. A *Port VLAN Identifier* parameter (PVID) is assigned to each port. Frames that are not associated with a VLAN by application of other rules are assigned to the PVID as a last resort.

Note that the ingress rules (including the port-based default) are applied to both untagged and priority-tagged frames (tagged frames with a VLAN identifier of all zeros). As a result, a VLAN-aware switch will never transmit priority-tagged frames. Priority tagged frames are always mapped to some non-zero VLAN value (at worst, the PVID) by the Ingress Rules module. If and when such frames are transmitted through an output port, they may be tagged with the assigned (non-zero) VLAN identifier or sent untagged if appropriate for that port. Priority-tagged frames are transmitted only by VLAN-unaware end stations with priority capability.

12.4.1.3 Ingress Filter

Following the application of the Ingress Rules, the Ingress Filter can be configured to discard any frame associated with a VLAN for which that port is not in the member set. Enabling this filter provides a validation check on incoming frames; frames will be submitted for forwarding only if they properly belonged on the LAN on which they were received (from the perspective of the switch applying the filter). If the Ingress Filter is disabled, we can create so-called *asymmetrical VLANs* in which frames can be received on certain ports but not sent out those same ports. By appropriately manipulating the member sets, Ingress Rules, and Egress Rules (discussed in Section 12.4.3.1), we can configure a VLAN for one-way communication.

12.4.2 Progress Process

A switch makes frame forwarding decisions based on the contents of its filtering database. The progress process comprises this forwarding mechanism, the mechanisms required to maintain the database, and the database itself.

12.4.2.1 Forwarding in a VLAN-Aware Switch

In a traditional VLAN-unaware switch, the filtering database maps frames to output ports based solely on the Destination Address in received frames; database entries are created and updated by a learning process based solely on received Source Addresses. (This is the address table mechanism discussed in Chapter 2, *Transparent Bridges*.) In a VLAN-aware switch, the mapping of frames to output ports is a function of both the Destination Address and the

VLAN mapping for each frame. The filtering database must therefore reflect this more complex, multidimensional organization.[14]

The result of the forwarding process is that frames are transported through an (implementation-dependent) switch fabric and queued for transmission on the appropriate output port(s) as determined by their destination MAC address and VLAN identifier.

12.4.2.2 Maintaining the Filtering Database

The filtering database in a traditional VLAN-unaware switch is maintained by a combination of a learning process based on Source Addresses plus a table aging mechanism. In addition, some table entries may be permanent and/or statically configured, as discussed in Chapter 2.

A VLAN-aware switch incorporates all of this base functionality from its VLAN-unaware sibling. Beyond this, a mechanism is needed to learn the port member sets for each VLAN, that is, the switch needs to know the mapping of VLANs to ports to ensure that frames are forwarded only within the VLAN-specific subset of the catenet. As with the address mapping, static VLAN entries may be configured by a human network administrator. Dynamically-learned VLAN mappings are created and maintained by a new protocol specifically designed for this purpose—the GARP VLAN Registration Protocol (GVRP), discussed in Section 12.4.5.

The 802.1Q standard subsumes all of the functionality for multicast pruning, as discussed in Chapter 10. Address entries in the filtering database can reflect either multicast or unicast destinations. Unicast destinations are learned by inspection of Source Addresses; multicast entries can be learned through the GARP Multicast Registration Protocol (GMRP). In a VLAN-aware switch, multicast address entries in the database are associated with a VLAN the same as unicast entries, that is, multicast propagation can be controlled on a per-VLAN basis. For example, a VLAN-aware switch using protocol-type based VLAN associations can propagate broadcast traffic through different sets of ports depending on whether the frames encapsulate an IPX packet or

[14] I have chosen not to burden the reader with an extensive discussion of the architecture and operation of the filtering database. While this consumes a large portion of the 802.1Q standard, it is of interest primarily to product developers. The architecture, database structure, and operations specified in the standard are appropriate for the formalized description of a Q-compliant switch. However, the requirements placed on a compliant product are solely on the observed external behaviors; the internal implementation of the filtering database in a commercial product need not (and likely will not) be identical to that presented in the standard. In particular, the partitioning of the database between hardware and software elements will vary from product to product, based on cost, performance requirements, and the designer's preferences. Because of this, any detailed discussion of the operation of the filtering database from the 802.1Q standard will provide little benefit to anyone.

an IP datagram. IPX-based service advertisements will propagate within the IPX-specific VLAN subset of the catenet; IP-based Address Resolution and Routing Information Protocol messages will propagate within the IP-specific subset, which can comprise a different set of ports.

802.1Q supports unicast address learning in two ways:

- Specific groups of VLANs can be identified as a *Shared VLAN Learning* (SVL) set. Within this set, any address-to-port mapping deduced by the learning process will be learned simultaneously for all VLANs in the group, regardless of the VLAN association of the frame from which the address was learned. With this method, a device transmitting frames into multiple VLANs with the same Source Address need be learned only once for all VLANs within the SVL set.
- Alternatively, groups of VLANs can be identified as an *Independent VLAN Learning* (IVL) set. The learning process will record address-to-port mappings within this set only for the specific VLAN associated with the received frame from which the address was learned.

The most common implementations provide either (1) one address database for all VLANs (all VLANs are in a single SVL set), or (2) a separate address database for each VLAN (all VLANs can be configured into a global IVL set, providing VLAN-specific learning). The latter implementation is the most flexible; any arbitrary group of VLANs can be combined into an SVL set by replicating the address information across the set. However, a more complex data structure is required, as well as a larger memory space. The decision whether to support SVL, IVL, or a combination of SVL and IVL learning is a function of the target application environment, the memory structure for the filtering database, and product cost.

12.4.3 Egress Process

The progress process moved frames from their respective input ports to the appropriate output port(s) as determined by the contents of the filtering database. Lastly, we apply an egress process to make the final decisions with respect to whether and how to transmit frames through the output port. The egress process comprises two operations: an Egress Rules module and an Egress Filter.

12.4.3.1 Egress Rules

To tag, or not to tag—that is the question.[15] Given the choice, 'tis nobler to send tagged frames rather than untagged; the tag provides additional informa-

[15] My apologies to the Bard.

tion to the receiver (the VLAN Identifier, priority, etc.) with nothing taken away. A tag is pure icing on the cake. However, for a given VLAN on a given output port, a switch can send frames containing VLAN tags only if the following condition is met:

Every device that is a member of that VLAN and directly connected to that port must be tag-aware.[16]

The reasoning behind this rule is simple; we must never send tagged frames into an environment where one or more of the intended receivers won't be able to interpret the tag. It's that darn installed base problem again! Figure 12.11 depicts a few combinations of tag-aware and tag-unaware devices on various switch ports, and indicates where tagged frames may be sent in accordance with the egress rule stated earlier.

The tagging decision for a given port is made on a VLAN-by-VLAN basis. We may send tagged frames for some VLANs, and untagged frames for others, through the same port, but on any given port, all frames associated with a given VLAN will be transmitted the same way. We do not need to consider the tag-awareness of devices that are not members of the particular VLAN for which we are making the tagging decision. Even though there may be tag-unaware devices attached to a switch port, we can still send tagged frames associated with VLANs that do not include the tag-unaware devices as members, since the tag-unaware devices will not have to receive and interpret these frames.

12.4.3.2 Egress Filter

Like a hockey goaltender, the Egress Filter is the last defense against sending inappropriate frames on an output port. The filter discards frames for either of two reasons:

1. The output port is not in the member set for the VLAN associated with this frame (as determined by the Ingress Rules). That is, the filtering database indicates that the destination station is reachable through this port (or the frame contains a multicast or unknown unicast destination and is being flooded), but it is known that no members of this VLAN should be reachable through this port.

   It would seem that this is an error condition that should not occur; there is an apparent mismatch among the filtering database, the Ingress Rules, and the VLAN associations of the output port. However, this situa-

[16] "Directly connected" means either attached to the physical LAN or reachable through legacy VLAN-unaware bridges.

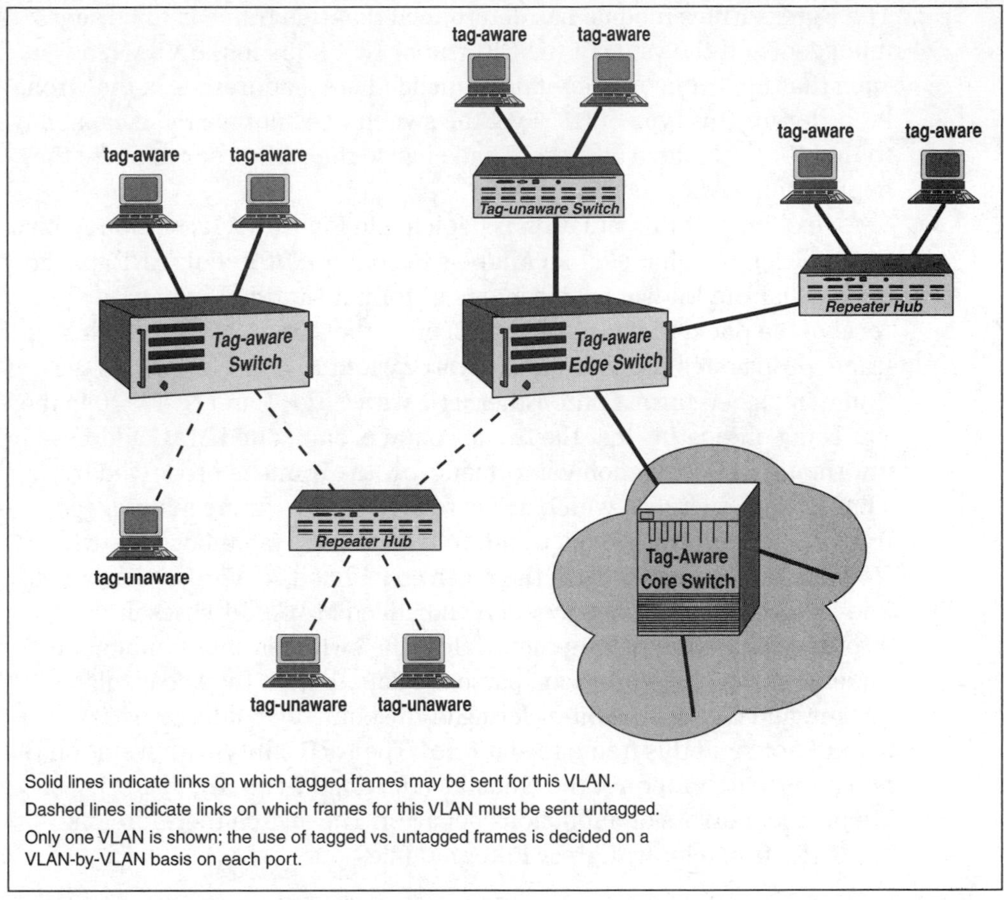

Figure 12.11 The egress tag rule in action.

tion can easily arise when the switch is using Shared VLAN Learning (SVL) among some set of VLANs. In an SVL-based switch, MAC address information in the filtering database is common among the SVL set. As a result, the progress process may attempt to forward frames to an output port for a MAC address that was learned from a VLAN to which that output port does not belong; we use the Egress Filter to ensure that such frames are not actually transmitted out that port. Within an Independent VLAN Learning (IVL) set, the filtering database is independent for each VLAN and this "error" will not normally occur.[17]

[17] Within an IVL set, this situation may still arise if static filtering entries exist for some address that is inconsistent with the member set for a given VLAN.

2. The Egress Rules module has determined that this frame is to be sent untagged, and the value of the CFI and/or NCFI bits in the VLAN tag is such that the frame may contain embedded MAC addresses in the wrong bit order for this type of LAN, yet the switch does not have the capability to find the embedded addresses and change their bit order to make the application work properly.

   An example of this situation is depicted in Figure 12.12. station A, on a Token Ring LAN, has sent an Address Resolution Protocol (ARP) packet in its usual Big Endian (non-canonical) format. station B wants to receive the packet (stations A and B are in the same IP subnet). This frame propagates through VLAN-aware switch X, which forwards the frame in tagged format onto Ethernet 1 with CFI = 1 and NCFI = 0 in the VLAN tag, indicating that the frame contains embedded MAC address information in non-canonical format. Now the frame is processed by VLAN-aware switch Y, which wants to forward the frame in untagged format onto Ethernet 2, since station B is a legacy tag-unaware device. However, from the values of the received CFI and NCFI bits, the switch knows that the frame may contain embedded MAC addresses in the wrong bit order for an Ethernet. Unless the switch is smart enough to understand the ARP protocol, parse the data field of the encapsulated packet, and correct the bit-ordering of the embedded addresses, it should not send this frame to station B. The ARP entity within station B will incorrectly interpret the embedded MAC addresses, causing possible protocol errors or anomalous behavior. The switch therefore discards the frame in the Egress Filter module.

Once the Egress Rules and Egress Filter are applied, the egress process can make any necessary transformations to the frame, including:

- LAN technology-specific changes (e.g., MAC header formats)
- Insertion of a new tag or stripping of a received tag
- If possible, and if the switch is capable of doing so, re-ordering the bits in embedded MAC addresses depending on LAN technology and the values of the CFI and NCFI bits in a received tag
- Recalculation of the FCS

12.4.4 System-Level Switch Constraints

A Q-compliant switch must obey many of the same system-level restrictions as legacy D-compliant devices, including the following:

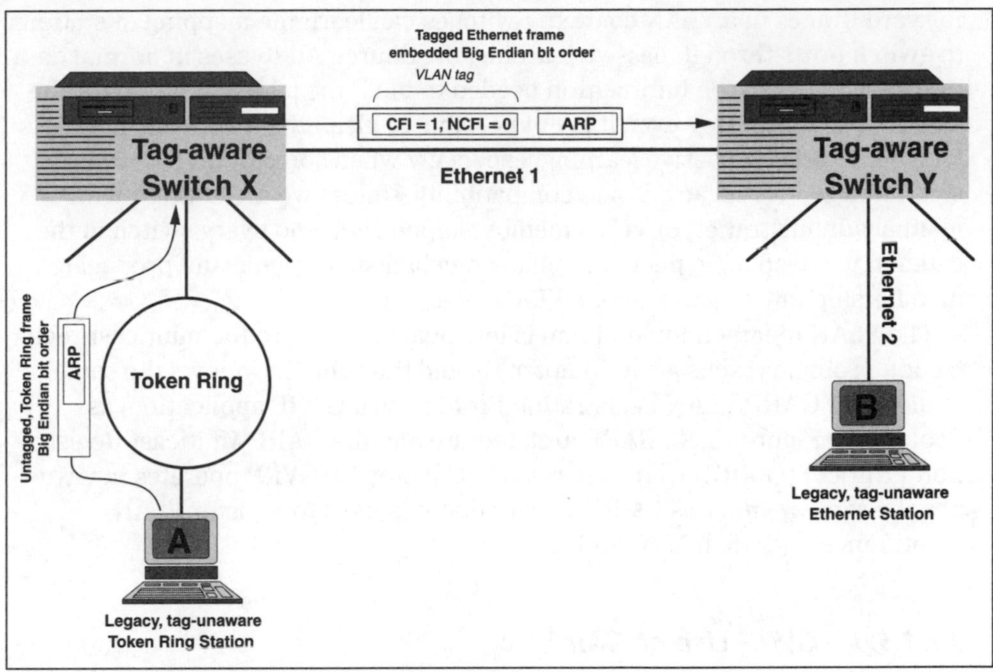

Figure 12.12 Egress filtering due to incorrect bit ordering.

- Frames with an invalid FCS (CRC error) are discarded upon receipt.
- Frames sent to any of the multicast addresses reserved for link-constrained protocols are sunk by the switch and not forwarded (see Chapter 2).
- The switch must put an upper bound on transit delay, i.e., frames cannot be delayed indefinitely within the switch waiting for transmission.
- The Spanning Tree Protocol port state determines whether a given port may be used for receiving or forwarding frames. (See Section 12.6 for a discussion of the use of the Spanning Tree Protocol in VLAN-aware switches.)

12.4.5 GARP VLAN Registration Protocol (GVRP)

In all of our discussions above about VLAN-aware switch operation, we assumed that a switch knew which ports were in the member set for each VLAN in use. Without this knowledge, it is not possible to properly filter and forward frames in a VLAN context. Switches can learn the mapping of stations to switch ports through passive learning; the Source Addresses in normal data frames provide all the information needed to build the address portion of the filtering database. However, it is not possible to glean the mappings of VLANs to switch ports by passive learning, especially when some or all frames are sent untagged for legacy device compatibility. Unless we are content with manual administration of VLAN membership in each and every switch in the catenet, we need an explicit, automatic mechanism to signal and propagate membership information among VLAN-aware devices.

The VLAN membership problem is identical in nature to the multicast registration problem discussed in Chapter 10, and the solution follows the same model. The GARP VLAN Registration Protocol is a GARP application, as depicted in Figure 12.13. GARP architecture and the GARP Multicast Registration Protocol (GMRP) were discussed in Chapter 10. GVRP operates in virtually the same manner as GMRP, except that it is used to register VLAN identifiers rather than MAC addresses.

12.4.5.1 GVRP Use of GARP

GVRP uses the GARP protocol mechanisms to declare and register the needs of VLAN-aware end stations and switches to receive frames belonging to spe-

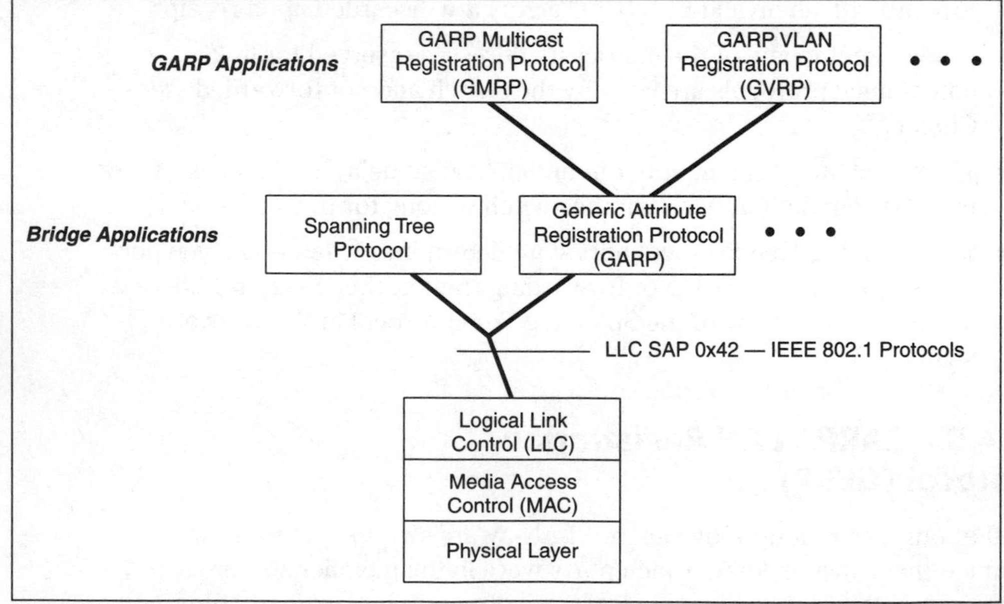

Figure 12.13 GARP architecture.

cific VLANs. Like any GARP application, GVRP defines both a GARP application address and a set of application-specific attribute types.

GVRP Application Address The Destination Address in all GVRP exchanges carries the value 0x01-80-C2-00-00-21 (see Table 10.1).

GVRP Attribute Types GVRP defines only one attribute type: VLAN Identifier Information. This attribute type is used to declare, register, and propagate the need to hear frames belonging to specific VLANs. VLAN Identifier Information is encoded in the Attribute Type field as 0x01. The Attribute Value(s) for this attribute type are 12-bit VLAN identifiers encoded into a 2-byte field using the same bit positions for the VLAN Identifier as are used in the Tag Control Information field of a VLAN tag.

Figure 12.14 depicts the format of GVRP protocol exchanges.

12.5 Multicast Registration and VLAN Context

It is possible (in fact, likely) that a VLAN-aware device implementing GVRP will also be capable of multicast pruning and will include GMRP as part of its operation. As discussed in Chapter 10, GMRP allows switches to restrict multicast propagation to a proper subset of the spanning tree. For a catenet comprising both GMRP- and VLAN-aware devices, 802.1Q extends GMRP capability to support separate multicast registrations within each VLAN. That is, rather than just restricting multicast propagation relative to the catenet as a whole, a combined GMRP/VLAN-aware device can restrict multicasts to a subset of a VLAN (which is already a subset of the catenet). This permits more fine-grained control than would otherwise be possible.

12.6 VLANs and the Spanning Tree

As discussed in Chapters 2 and 6, it is critical that active loops not be present in the catenet. Loops in the topology can cause catastrophic proliferation of multicast traffic and will prevent the filtering database from converging to a steady state. As a consequence, we impose a tree structure on the topology of the catenet, using the Spanning Tree Protocol to determine and maintain the tree automatically.

VLANs are no different from physical LANs in this regard. Since the operation of a switch within a given VLAN context is essentially the same as that of a VLAN-unaware bridge in a traditional catenet, we need to ensure that no loops are present in the active topology of the VLAN. To this end, 802.1Q spec-

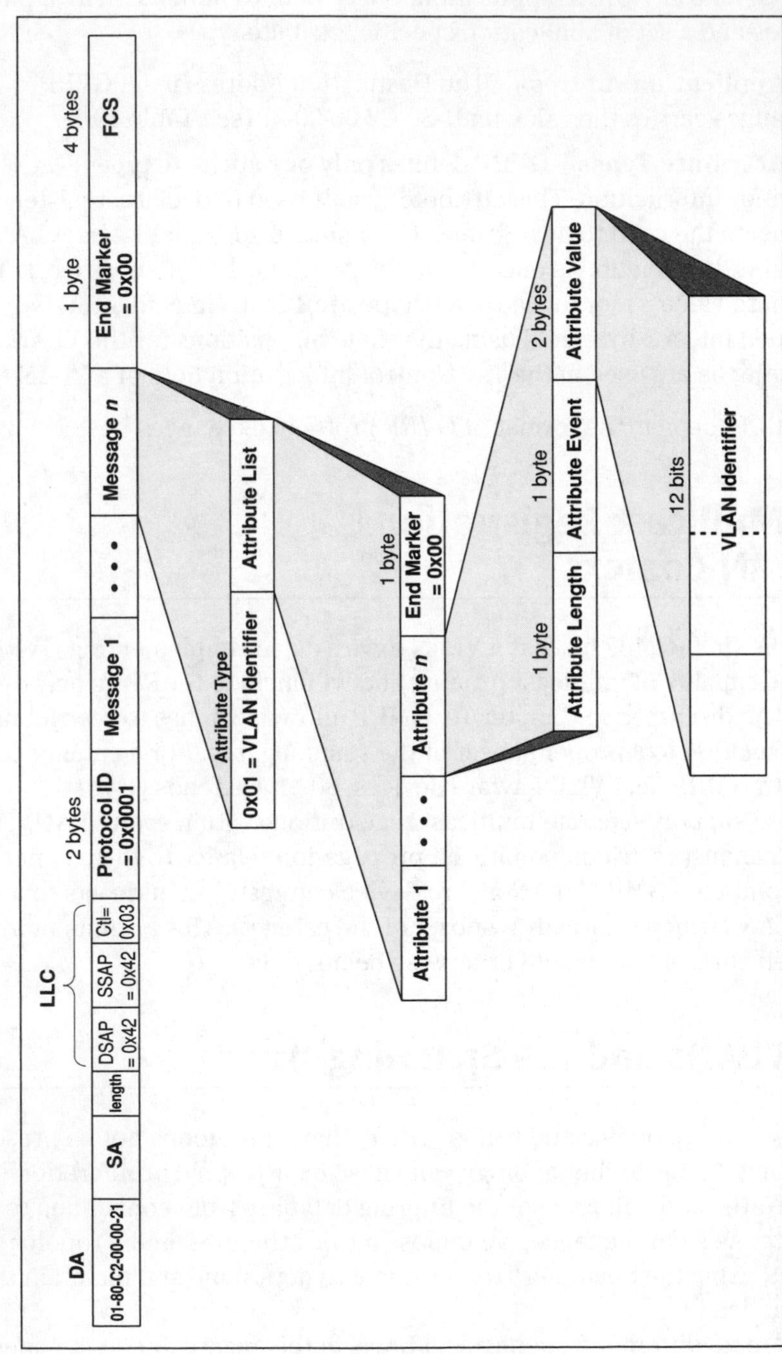

Figure 12.14 GVRP protocol exchange format.

ifies the use of the identical Spanning Tree Protocol as that of 802.1D; in fact, 802.1Q simply points implementors to the relevant section of 802.1D, and does not restate the protocol itself.

The Spanning Tree Protocol defines a single tree structure interconnecting all physical LANs in the catenet. Since a VLAN constitutes a proper subset of the catenet, traffic for a given VLAN will only propagate along a subset of the spanning tree—the precise set of links needed to reach all members of the VLAN, as depicted in Figure 12.15. In the figure, it can be seen that the loop in the topology has been resolved by disabling one of the links (the dotted line); all traffic flows along the solid-line paths indicated. However, traffic for a given VLAN (e.g., VLAN 1) does not need to propagate beyond a subset of the total spanning tree. Such behavior is ensured by the normal action of the VLAN-aware switches; due to the operation of their filtering databases and egress filters, they will not forward (or flood) traffic onto ports that are not in the member set for a given VLAN.

In a VLAN-unaware environment, a single spanning tree for the entire catenet makes sense, as multicast and unknown unicast traffic must propagate to all stations in the catenet. However, the situation changes when we consider VLANs. What we need to do is to make sure that no loops are present

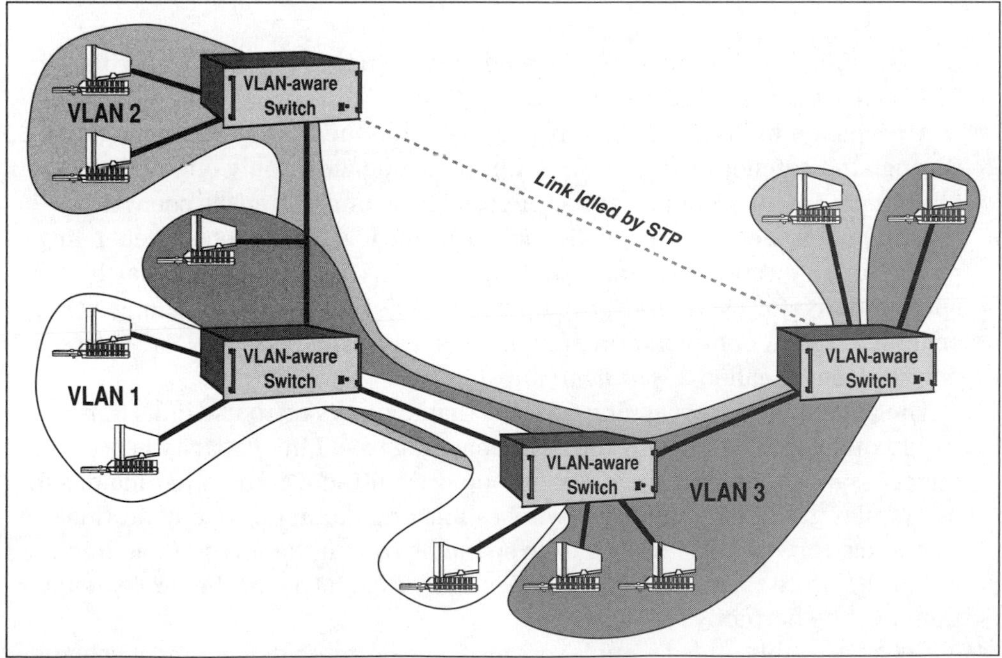

Figure 12.15 VLANs across a spanning tree.

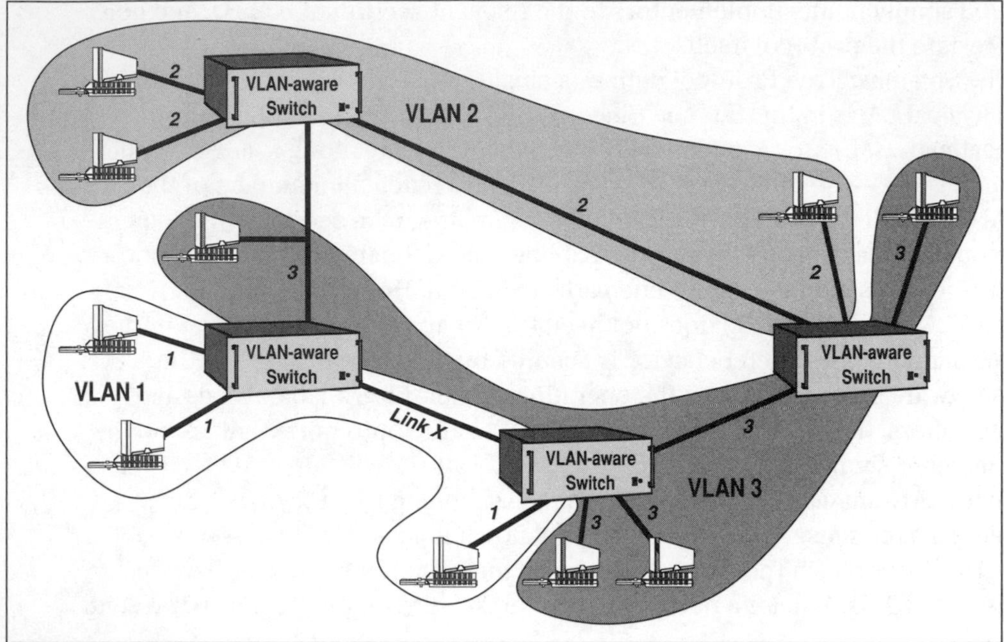

Figure 12.16 A spanning forest.

in the traffic flow for any VLAN. It is not strictly necessary that traffic for all VLANs use the same links.

As depicted in Figure 12.16, it is possible to define multiple spanning trees through the catenet, with each VLAN propagating along only one of the spanning trees. The maximum number of possible spanning trees is equal to the maximum number of possible distinct paths through the catenet. Depending on the topology and the number and types of VLANs in use, there may be one spanning tree for each VLAN, or multiple VLANs may propagate along a single spanning tree. A configuration of multiple spanning trees in a VLAN-aware environment is called a *spanning forest.*

The advantage of a spanning forest is that it allows us to use links that would otherwise be idled by a classic spanning tree. Link capacity is not unnecessarily wasted in the name of loop prevention. On the other hand, a forest implies greater complexity. Switches must maintain port state information (blocking, forwarding, etc.) for each spanning tree in the forest. In addition, either the protocol itself must be replicated for each tree or the implementation must be perfectly re-entrant.

Because of this added complexity and the risk to the development schedule, the 802.1Q Task Force chose to specify a single spanning tree for the entire catenet rather than try to work out the details of a vendor-interoperable standard for a spanning forest. However, numerous vendors already provide (proprietary) support in their VLAN-aware switches for multiple spanning trees, and the IEEE 802.1 Working Group has begun a project to add support in 802.1Q for spanning forests (IEEE 802.1s). A standard is expected to be approved sometime in 2001.

CHAPTER

13

Priority Operation

Up until now, our switches have dealt with all user traffic equally; there was no preferred treatment given to one group of users or type of traffic over others. In this chapter we look at the mechanisms used to prioritize traffic flow through a switch.

13.1 Why Priority?

What's wrong with being fair? Why should some users or applications receive preferred treatment?[1] If the performance of the catenet is acceptable for all applications under all traffic conditions, then there really is no reason to invoke priority mechanisms. This is both the desired and the typical case. Since LAN bandwidth and switch capacity are relatively inexpensive, overprovisioning is a common and acceptable solution to most LAN performance concerns. Of course, application needs increase over time, and it is impossible to overprovision to the extent of supporting worst-case transient situations. It is important to remember that Priority operation adds complexity to switches; there is no need to pay for this complexity unless there is an application performance benefit to be gained.

[1] In particular, why is *my* traffic always afforded low priority and everyone else's given precedence??!!

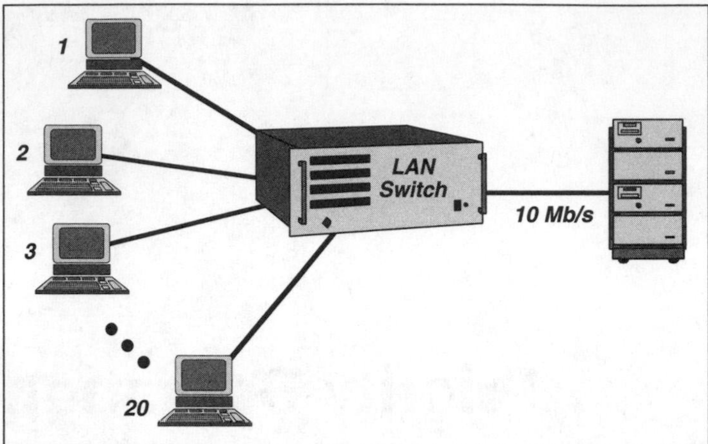

Figure 13.1 Inadequate capacity.

There are two situations to consider:

1. *The catenet (or some subset of it) cannot handle the steady-state traffic load offered by the attached users and applications.* This situation can occur if some link or switch in the catenet has inadequate capacity to support the desired application data flows. In the situation depicted in Figure 13.1, if the 20 workstations shown each move an average of 5 Mb/s of data to the server during an eight-hour business day, the 10 Mb/s capacity of the server port is simply inadequate. Even if we increased the capacity of the server port to 100 Mb/s, a steady-state problem would still exist if the switch did not support wire-speed operation at the higher data rate.

   No traffic prioritization policy will help in this situation. The network is simply unable to support the intended application. The only solution is to add capacity to the network (or send some workers home).[2]

2. *The catenet has sufficient capacity to handle the steady-state traffic load, but not short-term peak loads.* In a typical network the offered load varies significantly both over time and as a function of which links we are observing. Process control networks may have predictable traffic load with little variance over time, but most traditional data communications environments experience very bursty traffic patterns.[3] While the catenet needs to be designed to handle the long-term average load with ease, it is not possible to design the network to support the absolute

[2] If a *train station* is the place where the train stops, then what is a *work station??*

[3] Experimental work has shown that most data communication traffic is not only bursty, but self-similar; that is, it appears bursty regardless of the averaging interval that is used to measure the traffic [LELA94].

worst-case possible traffic over long periods. Given that the catenet is never a fully-connected mesh, there are always links that must carry load from multiple stations. Similarly, there are devices (e.g., servers) that naturally congregate traffic from multiple devices, making it impossible to design for the theoretical worst-case.

Offered load may temporarily exceed capacity due to:

- Applications generating varying amounts of traffic over time
- Traffic patterns (sources and destinations) changing over time

Thus, there can be times when the traffic load will exceed the capacity of some link or switch, regardless of the design of the catenet.

When the short-term load exceeds the available capacity, switches must buffer frames until the capacity becomes available to forward them onto the appropriate ports. The network's response to short-term overload is therefore to add delay. Buffering is used to smooth out peaks in the offered load to the level where the catenet is capable of handling them. This is where priorities can help. If it can be determined that some traffic streams are more important (in particular, more sensitive to the delay imposed by buffering), then these streams can be given preferential treatment (priority) over less critical traffic. Thus, priority provides a means to ride-through transient overload conditions without adversely impacting the performance of time-sensitive applications.

Seifert's Law of Networking #18

If everyone uses high priority, no one actually gets it.

Note that this policy works only if the overload condition is short-term. If the overload is sustained, giving priority to any traffic stream will delay some other stream indefinitely; with inadequate sustained capacity there is never an opportunity to catch up. Similarly, the policy only works if the volume of priority traffic is less than the capacity of the congested link or switch. Not all traffic streams can be given priority.

13.2 LAN Priority Mechanisms

Many LAN technologies provide internal mechanisms that support one or more forms of Priority operation. These priority mechanisms fall into two classes:

- *Access priority.* In a shared-bandwidth LAN, multiple stations are capable of requesting use of the underlying physical medium at the same time. Shared LANs therefore impose some form of Medium Access Control (MAC) protocol to allow the stations to arbitrate for the use of the physical channel when there are multiple simultaneous access requests.

Access priority mechanisms allow one station to obtain preferred access to the LAN over others. Thus, the MAC algorithm is unfair to the extent that some stations have priority over others. Access priority may be *static* (i.e., priority is granted to a station for all time, regardless of the nature of its traffic flow) or *dynamic* (a station's priority changes over time, possibly on a frame-by-frame basis, as a function of the needs of the applications running on the device).

In a full duplex environment, access priority is meaningless, since each device has unfettered access to the channel at all times.

- *User priority.* User priority is unfortunately a misnomer. It doesn't refer to the priority of one (human) user of the network over another, but to the priority assigned to a given frame (or stream of frames) by the application sourcing those frames within a station.

Thus, access priority indicates the preferential treatment given to one station over another to transmit a frame on a shared LAN; user priority indicates the preferential treatment afforded to one frame over others across the entire catenet. If the LAN to which a station is connected supports multiple access priorities (e.g., Token Ring), then a requested user priority within the station may map to a specific access priority on the LAN, as supported by the hardware.[4] That is, if an application assigns a high priority to some frame, that frame may be transmitted preferentially on the attached LAN. However, this is a local issue, relevant only to the particular device and LAN in question; that is, access priority is a local optimization for expediting transmission on shared-bandwidth LANs. A frame may traverse a catenet containing many different types of LANs, some of which support access priority and some which do not. The access priority may vary as the frame is transmitted on the links in the catenet, but the user priority is maintained from end-to-end.

13.2.1 Token Ring Priority Mechanisms

IEEE 802.5 Token Rings provide both access and user priority mechanisms, with eight levels of each. Figure 13.2 depicts how these priority levels are indicated in the relevant portion of the Token Ring frame. Access priority is effected by changing the priority level of the token.[5] Stations may only use a

[4] The fact that a LAN allows multiple priorities does not mean that all (or even any) of the network interfaces connected to that LAN must support multiple priorities. A given product may support only one access priority (which simplifies implementation), the entire set of allowed priorities, or any number in between.

[5] The field shown in Figure 13.2 as *access priority* is called the *token priority* in the formal standard.

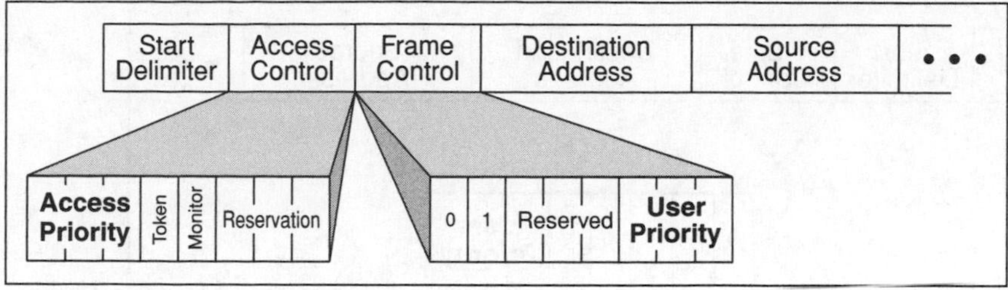

Figure 13.2 Token Ring priority mechanisms.

token to transmit if their requested access priority equals or exceeds the current priority level of the token. The token priority level can be raised or lowered through a *token reservation* scheme, which uses the *reservation bits* in the Access Control field. The complete specification of the access control method can be found in [IEEE98f]; a more understandable explanation is provided in [CARL98].

When sending user data (indicated by the 0b01 in the first 2 bits of the Frame Control field), the user priority is indicated by the last 3 bits of the Frame Control field. For both access and user priority, 0 indicates the lowest priority and 7 indicates the highest.

13.2.2 FDDI Priority Mechanisms

Although it is a token-passing system, FDDI does not implement the token priority and reservation scheme used in Token Ring. Thus, there is no access priority mechanism in FDDI.[6]

As indicated in Figure 13.3, FDDI provides for user priority indication in a manner similar to Token Ring. When user data is being sent (indicated by the 0b0101 in the first 4 bits of the Frame Control field[7]), the user priority can be signaled in the last 3 bits of the Frame Control field.[8]

[6] FDDI supports the concept of synchronous bandwidth. When enabled, this allows stations to pre-reserve a fraction of the available capacity for guaranteed use by the device. Thus, it provides a form of access priority to those stations reserving synchronous bandwidth. However, very few commercial FDDI products support this mechanism; its use is restricted to highly-specialized applications.

[7] The value 0b0101 actually indicates asynchronous user data with 48-bit addresses, but this is the only form of user data commonly conveyed on an FDDI network.

[8] The standard [ISO89a] does not actually say that this field is used for user priority. It simply says that user data frames can be sent with these bits set to any value (0 through 7) but does not indicate what the values mean. In common usage, they are used for user priority signaling.

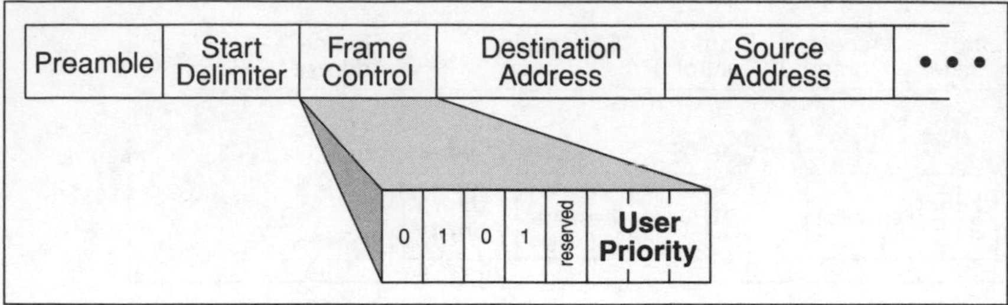

Figure 13.3 FDDI priority mechanism.

13.2.3 Ethernet Priority Mechanisms

Ethernet has no native mechanisms to support either access priority or user priority. This was intentional. The lack of priority provides:

- *Simplicity.* Ethernet interfaces don't need any logic to assert or manage multiple priority levels. In the old days, when circuitry directly related to the cost of a product, this provided a competitive advantage.
- *Fairness.* All stations and traffic receive equal and fair treatment across the LAN. This was a stated design goal of the original Ethernet design [DIX80].

That said, vendors have implemented numerous priority schemes on Ethernet, both for access and for user priority. All of these are non-standard, but most of them can interwork (more or less) with existing standard Ethernet interfaces in typical configurations. In fact, the whole idea of most of these schemes is to provide priority for the modified device(s) over the existing standard interfaces.

For Ethernet access priority, some of the methods employed include:

- *Shortened interframe gap.* By shortening the gap between back-to-back transmissions, a station can assert its signal on the LAN before that of other standard-compliant interfaces. The intent is to cause Carrier Sense to appear on the network and force other stations to defer to the pending transmission. In order for this scheme to work, the interframe gap must be shortened to less than two-thirds of the nominal gap (i.e., less than 64 bit-times); otherwise, standard-compliant interfaces will ignore the earlier signal assertion and not defer to the modified station.

  This scheme only provides priority when transmitting back-to-back (consecutive) frames; the second frame will receive the priority treatment.[9] Of course, there will be no priority relationship among multiple modified devices. That is, there are only two levels of priority provided—modified and unmodified.

- *Modified backoff algorithm.* The use of a more aggressive backoff algorithm than that specified in the standard can give a device effective priority over its standard-compliant brethren. When a collision occurs, the device using the more aggressive algorithm (i.e., shorter average backoff time) will be more likely to transmit its frames sooner than the other station(s) involved in the collision.

  This priority mechanism only works in a statistical-average sense; on any given frame, there is still some probability that the standard algorithm will select a lower random number than the modified algorithm, unless the modified algorithm always selects a value of 0.[10]

- *Loooong Preamble.* Another modification (read: kludge) involves sending frames with very long Preambles, approaching (or, in some cases, exceeding) the slotTime of the network. When a very long Preamble is sent, standard-compliant interfaces will experience a collision (and backoff) if they transmit at the same time as the modified device. The modified device(s) ignores collisions during the lengthened Preamble. Once the other stations back off, the modified device can then terminate the Preamble and continue with its frame transmission unimpeded. There is a slight performance penalty, since any such prioritized transmission will require a long Preamble with its concomitant higher overhead.

  An interesting twist on this approach is that devices can implement multiple levels of priority by using different elongated Preamble lengths. The longer the Preamble, the higher the priority, as depicted in Figure 13.4. In the figure, station D has the lowest priority, being an unmodified, standard device. Devices A, B, and C are modified, with B being the highest priority, A the next highest, and C the lowest of the modified devices. The priority is effected by lengthening the Preamble; only the highest-priority device will complete its Preamble, not detect a collision, and send its frame.

[9] Depending on the implementation of the interframe gap in the standard-compliant devices, this scheme may not even work under this condition. According to the standard, it is permissible for a station to always make an irrevocable transmission decision at the beginning of the interframe gap, rendering the length of the gap moot and canceling any priority effect. However, the standard recommends dividing the interframe gap into two portions (first two-thirds and second one-third), in which case the priority scheme works as described. Most interfaces implement the two-part interframe gap recommendation.

[10] The implications of this approach are discussed in Chapter 8, *LAN and Switch Flow Control.*

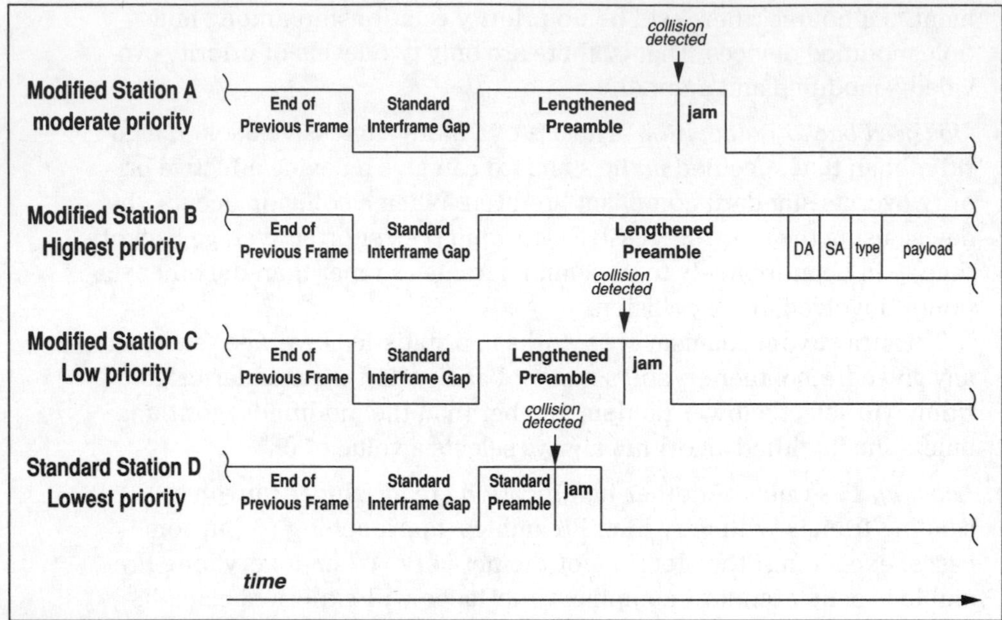

Figure 13.4 Ethernet access priority through Preamble elongation.

All of the access priority schemes described can be implemented through manipulation of the MAC algorithm; they do not require any changes to the frame format on Ethernet. This is not the case for user priority. Signaling user priority requires that somewhere in the frame there has to be some bit(s) that indicates the priority of that frame to the recipient, but no field was reserved for this purpose in Ethernet. This has not stopped some folks from trying to do it anyway.

There is one rarely-meaningful bit in an Ethernet frame. In general, Ethernets always use globally-administered addresses; local address administration is most often found in Token Ring environments. Thus, the Global/Local address bit (the second bit of the address) in an Ethernet frame is usually set to 0. One vendor has proposed an approach that uses this bit in the Source Address field to signal user priority: if the bit is 0, it is a standard default priority frame. If the bit is set to 1, it indicates a high priority frame, as depicted in Figure 13.5 [PACE96].

This scheme has never been widely accepted or implemented. It requires that both the sender and receiver of such priority-encoded frames understand the modified format; the scheme is therefore not easily integrated into an

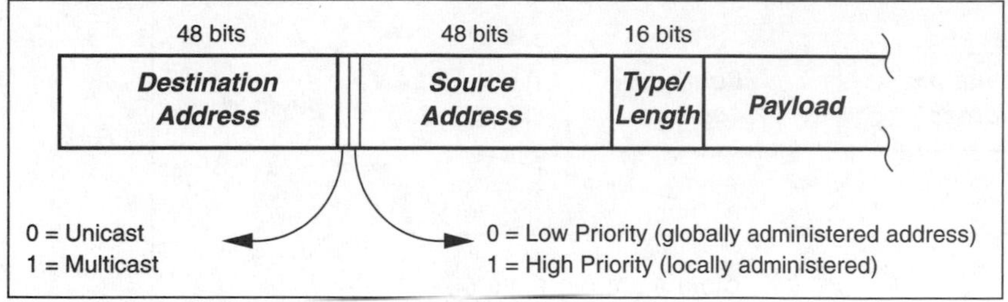

Figure 13.5 User priority encoding in Source Address.

existing catenet. It also requires that users not use locally-administered addresses on Ethernet; while this is normally the case, there are exceptions.[11]

Conceivably, someone could signal user priority within the Ethernet Type field as well. Rather than reserving a single value for a given protocol, a user might reserve a range of values, for example OxA000 through 0xA007. The different values could be used to signal priority levels for that protocol. In fact, there would be no way to know whether someone had already done this.[12] Of course, it would only work for the protocol so defined. It would not be possible to implement IP or IPX priority levels using this scheme without modifying all of the existing IP or IPX devices on the network.

DISCLAIMER

I have described these various methods of achieving access priority on Ethernet for informational purposes only, as many of these have actually been implemented in commercial products. However, a little knowledge can be dangerous. I am not advocating or recommending the use of any of these schemes in commercial products, nor do I mean to imply that any of them work well. Each approach has its limitations and drawbacks, and may cause anomalous behavior in some configurations. Don't try this at home. Your mileage may vary. Batteries not included.

[11] In addition, a few globally-administered OUIs have been assigned from the locally-administered address space. That is, some vendors have OUIs that appear to constitute locally-administered addresses. These assignments were made by Xerox Corporation for the original Ethernet. At that time, there was no concept of locally-administered addressing; all addresses were globally assigned, so there was no conflict. The IEEE 802 committee added the (dubious) feature of locally-administered addresses years later, when there were already a fair number of devices in the field using the original Xerox address assignments. Strangely, one of these conflicting assignments was to 3Com Corporation, the proponent of this user-priority signaling scheme! The proposed PACE priority signaling would not work with some of 3Com's own equipment.

[12] If you have done something like this, send me an e-mail. Seriously, I'd like to know.

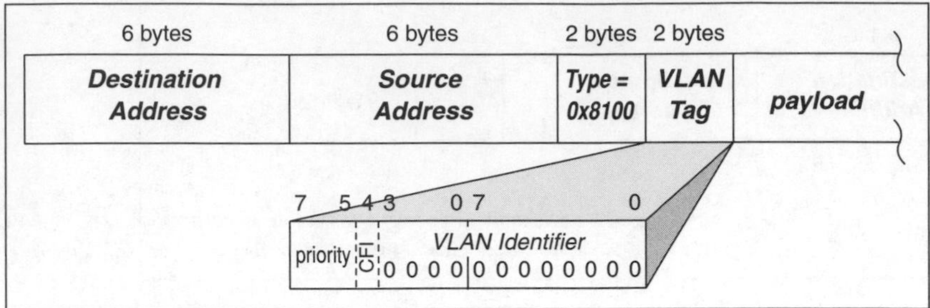

Figure 13.6 Priority-tagged Ethernet frame.

13.3 VLAN and Priority Tagging

In Chapter 11, *Virtual LANs: Applications and Concepts*, and Chapter 12, *Virtual LANs: The IEEE Standard*, we discussed the use of Virtual LAN (VLAN) tagging to explicitly indicate the VLAN association of a given frame. A VLAN tag contains both a VLAN identifier and a priority value indicating the user priority assigned to the frame. Through the use of tags, a device can signal user priority on LANs (such as Ethernet) that provide no native priority support. It is possible to perform this feat even if the device in question does not support VLANs. The special case of a tagged frame carrying a VLAN Identifier of all zeros is not, strictly speaking, a VLAN tag. It is referred to as a *priority tagged frame,* and is depicted in Figure 13.6. VLAN identifier 0x000 is specifically reserved for this purpose.[13]

While Figure 13.6 depicts a Priority-tagged Ethernet frame, tags (both VLAN and priority) can be used with any LAN technology. Thus, they are the most general method for explicit priority indication.

13.4 Getting into the Priority Business

Let's explore a fundamental question regarding the use of priority in switched catenets:

At what point do we classify and differentiate traffic based on priority?

There are two parts to the problem:

1. Assigning a priority to a given frame or stream of frames.
2. Providing preferential treatment across the catenet based on the priority assignment.

[13] While extensively discussed and permitted by the standard [IEEE98d], Priority tagging in this manner is not common. Since the complexity of implementing tagging for priority is not significantly less than that of implementing tagging for VLANs, most devices that insert tags do so in a VLAN context and use a non-zero value for the VLAN Identifier.

In general, priority classification is more difficult once we are removed from the application and end station sourcing the traffic. That is, if an application itself is priority-aware, it can indicate its requested user priority in all of the traffic that it originates. There is no need to infer the priority from the contents of the frame. If an application (or the end station on which it is running) is not priority-aware, then priority-enabled switches will have to determine the desired priority by inspecting each frame's contents and applying some set of administrative rules. This operation can impose a considerable performance penalty in switches, especially if such classification must be performed millions of times each second.

The sooner in the end-to-end communication process we make the priority classification, the sooner we can provide preferential treatment, and the easier it becomes to implement high performance priority-enabled switches. Once a priority determination is made, the frame can be tagged with that priority, and all devices "down the line" do not need to know the policy rules that were applied; they can simply act on the indicated priority.

The implication is that, ideally, applications within the end stations should make the priority decision and emit tagged frames from the outset. Unfortunately, virtually no end station today (either client or server) is capable of dealing with application priorities or VLAN-style tags.[14] This is only because application-specific VLANs and the use of VLAN tags are relatively new. In order to use priority mechanisms:

- Applications will have to be modified to request a specific priority when transmitting information, or alternatively, applications will need have their priority assigned by administrative policy. The operating system and protocol stack will also have to be modified to request a specific priority based on that assignment.
- Application Program Interfaces (APIs) in the internal protocol stacks will have to be modified to support such priority requests.
- Protocol implementations (e.g., IP code) within the end stations may have to be enhanced to provide multiple queues for prioritization.
- Operating system code (in particular, network devices drivers and NIC APIs) will have to be modified for network priority and tag handling.
- Network interfaces themselves may need to be changed to support priority queuing and tags.

[14] In theory, Token Ring and FDDI-attached stations could assign frame priorities using the native signaling methods available on those LANs. However, few operating systems, protocol stacks, or APIs within those systems provide any means for priority signaling from the higher-layer applications themselves. That is, the devices are capable of signaling priority, but there is no means provided for an application to ask for such signaling. Perhaps more important, virtually no applications are designed to ask for priority, even were it available for use.

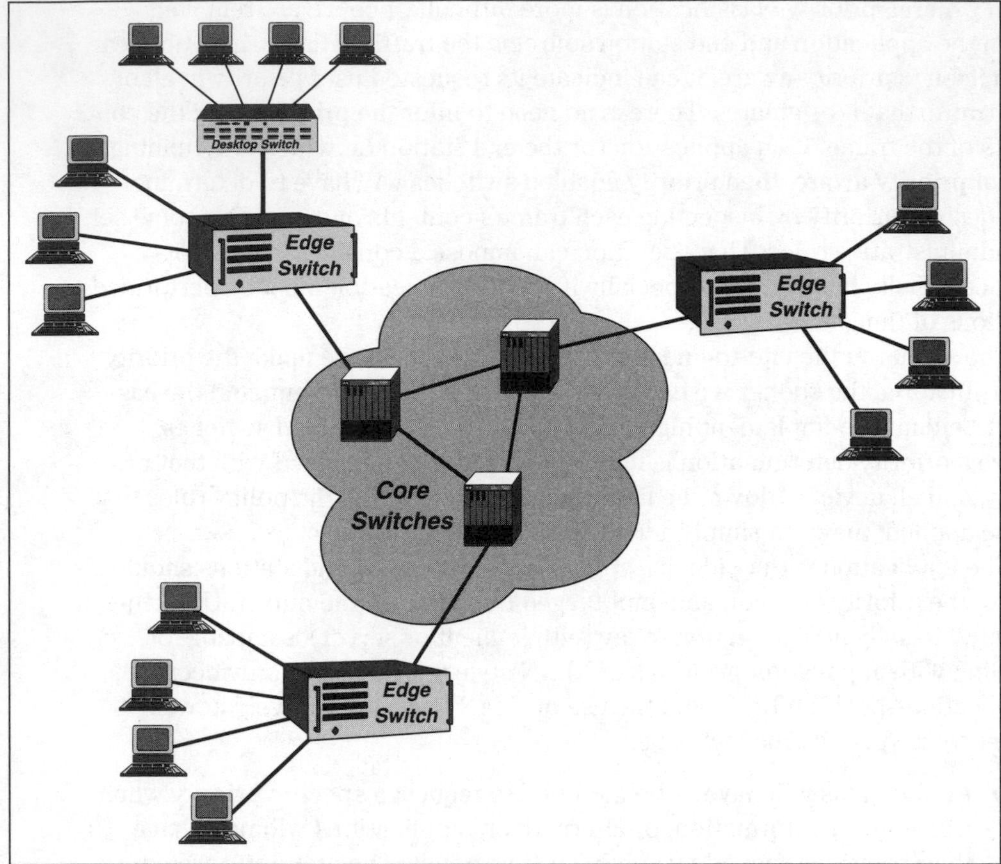

Figure 13.7 Edge and core switches.

This is a lot of changes.[15] Ultimately, it is believed that end stations will become priority and tag-aware, but this will take considerable time to permeate the installed base. In the meantime, it is the switches that will make the priority decision, and if appropriate, tag frames.

As discussed in Chapter 11, we can separate switches into two classes, as depicted in Figure 13.7:

- *Edge switches.* These sit on the boundary between the priority-unaware world and the priority-aware core. They provide attachments for end stations either directly or through legacy priority-unaware desktop switches.
- *Core switches.* These typically provide backbone interconnections between the edge switches.

[15] The same changes are needed to make the end stations VLAN-aware as well as priority-aware.

In the absence of end station priority-awareness, edge switches can make the determination of frame priority and tag frames appropriately. Similarly, edge switches can strip these tags before forwarding frames to priority-unaware receiving devices. This has a number of benefits overall:

- The policy for assigning priority can be administered through management of the edge switches exclusively. This reduces the number of devices that must be so manipulated and decreases the probability of policy incoherency across the catenet.
- The core switches can be freed from having to make a priority determination based on rules applied to the frame contents. They can determine priority by simply parsing the tag. As tags comprise simple semantics at a fixed offset in an Ethernet frame, hardware implementation of priority determination becomes straightforward. Since the core switches typically carry aggregated traffic from multiple workgroups (possibly millions of frames per second), high performance at lower cost can be achieved by reducing their workload.

We thus improve overall performance by separating the task of priority determination from that of high-performance switching. The edge devices (typically connecting small numbers of devices operating at lower data rates) accept responsibility for priority determination, and the core devices concentrate on high-speed switching.

13.5 Priority Operation in Switches

In this section we consider how a switch deals with frame priority.

If we don't invoke any priority mechanisms, the operation of a switch is quite straightforward. When frames arrive on a port, the switch makes its filtering/forwarding decision and determines onto which port(s) the frame should be forwarded. A single-queue model can be used for both input and output ports, as depicted in Figure 13.8. Frames are operated on and forwarded in a first-come first-served manner.

In this scenario, the switch does not attempt to determine priority and handles all frames equally.

13.5.1 The Ordering Invariant—Redux

Switches, being Data Link layer internetworking devices, must maintain the ordering invariant. Before we considered priority, this invariant was posited as a constraint on the order of frames between any Source-Destination Address pair. However, the actual invariant is that ordering must be maintained on the

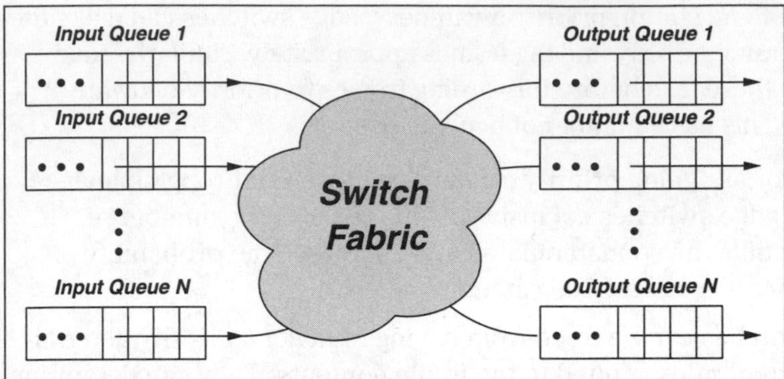

Figure 13.8 Single-queue model.

flow between any Source-Destination Address pair for frames of a given user priority [ISO95]. If there is no concept of user priority (e.g., in an old-fashioned Ethernet environment), this invariant requires us to maintain strict order for all frames sent between each address pair. However, if we allow frames to have an associated user priority, then we need only to maintain the order for those frames assigned to a given priority level. The order of frames between the same pair of stations does not have to be maintained across different priority levels.

This makes perfect sense; the whole idea of priority is to allow frames that are deemed more important to "jump ahead" of lower-priority frames in the queue. If ordering cannot be so changed, priority becomes meaningless and doesn't provide any performance benefit.

Most early bridges and switches did not provide for any form of priority operation. This is primarily because the vast majority of such devices only supported native Ethernets, where there was no obvious means of determining or signaling user priorities. As applications requiring priority treatment were developed along with methods of priority signaling on Ethernet (e.g., with tags as discussed in Section 13.3), the implementation of priority mechanisms in Ethernet switches quickly followed. Token Ring switches have almost universally employed priority mechanisms, since Token Ring has always inherently supported priority signaling.

13.5.2 IEEE 802.1p

The original standard for LAN switches supported the concept of priority for those ports with native user priority mechanisms, namely Token Ring and FDDI [IEEE90a, IEEE93a]. However, that standard did not:

- *Support priority operation on Ethernet.* Ethernet provides no native mechanism for indicating either user or access priority; switches built to the earlier standard had to treat all Ethernet traffic without regard to precedence.
- *Allow reordering of frames between Ethernet ports.* With no means of signaling priority on Ethernet, a standard-compliant switch could not use even an implicit means of priority determination to change the order of frames transmitted at the output. Essentially, priority was banned on Ethernet ports.
- *Provide for priority regeneration.* Proper operation of priority mechanisms (for those ports supporting native priority) required that the user implement a consistent set of priority semantics throughout the catenet.

A project was begun in 1995 to address the concerns of vendors implementing switches targeted at multimedia environments. In particular, the problems of Priority operation and the use of multicast mechanisms for delivery of voice and video stream data were to be addressed by this project, dubbed P802.1p. At the inception of the project, there was not yet any activity within the standards community regarding VLANs or the use of the tags to signal priority.

While P802.1p was under way, a second project (P802.1Q) was begun to address the standardization of the wide range of incompatible VLAN-capable switches being offered in the marketplace. As anyone interested in building switches would naturally be concerned with both priority operation and VLANs, the two standards were developed by the same IEEE 802.1 Interworking Task Force. Both standards had the same chair, editor, and participating membership. The developers would meet in the same room and at the same time. It was very hard for anyone outside the task force (and even for many within the task force) to recognize that these were separate projects developing separate standards.

Not surprisingly, there is a great deal of overlap and interdependence between the two standards. In the end, P802.1p was folded into the existing IEEE 802.1D standard as a revision of that work and published as [IEEE98a]. This work addressed the issues of priority determination, regeneration, and mapping to classes of service. In addition, P802.1p addressed the problems of multicast stream traffic and included the standard for the GARP Multicast Registration Protocol (GMRP) and the Generic Attribute Registration Protocol (GARP) itself (see Chapter 10, *Multicast Pruning*).

IEEE 802.1Q was published as a completely separate document from IEEE 802.1D [IEEE98d]. IEEE 802.1Q is a standalone specification for VLAN-capable switches. As such, it includes all of the basic bridge/switch requirements from IEEE 802.1D (forwarding operation, Spanning Tree Protocol, etc.) plus all of the VLAN requirements (e.g., tagging and traffic isolation). Thus, while a VLAN-unaware, IEEE 802.1D/p-compliant switch can use VLAN-style tags to signal priority (as discussed in Section 13.3), the specification for the Priority tag is part of the IEEE 802.1Q standard, not IEEE 802.1D/p. It is very confusing indeed.

The primary reason for the confusion was the IEEE standards process itself. Every standards project must have a specific set of objectives and deliverables defined in a Project Authorization Request (PAR). The Task Force must either deliver the standard specified in the PAR or return the PAR and disband.[16] The PAR for P802.1p did not allow the Task Force to work on VLANs or tagged frames. When the VLAN PAR was initiated at a later date, it was not allowed to address the priority or multicast pruning issues already covered by the P802.1p PAR. Worse, the existence of the two PARs meant that two standards had to be developed—one for each PAR. There was no easy procedural method for combining two PARs once the projects had begun. The only way to combine the two groups would be to disband both and start a new, combined project. Besides abandoning the considerable progress already made within P802.1p, the political problem here is that any such new project would be open to fresh debate as to its goals and objectives. Similarly, a new chair and editor would be elected to run the group. All of this could both delay the final standard and change the balance of power in the task forces. So the participants chose to keep the PARs intact and the standards separate, but to do the actual work jointly.

13.5.3 Switch Process Flow for Priority Operation

The forwarding process (i.e., Bridge Address Table lookup) determines the output port(s) onto which a given received frame will be forwarded. For non-priority-enabled switches, this is the only mechanism needed. However, if a switch is implementing some form of traffic prioritization, then a series of additional steps must be taken to implement the priority mechanisms. The data flow for traffic prioritization can be modeled as a three-step process, as depicted in Figure 13.9.

1. On receipt of a frame, the switch must determine the priority of that frame, either from explicit priority information provided in the frame itself (tag bits or user priority identification specific to the LAN technology) or implicitly from the frame contents and a set of administrative policy rules.
2. Knowing the priority of the frame, the switch must map that priority to one of a set of Classes of Service available at each output port on which

[16] PAR modifications are possible, but impose a bureaucratic procedure not significantly easier than generating a new PAR.

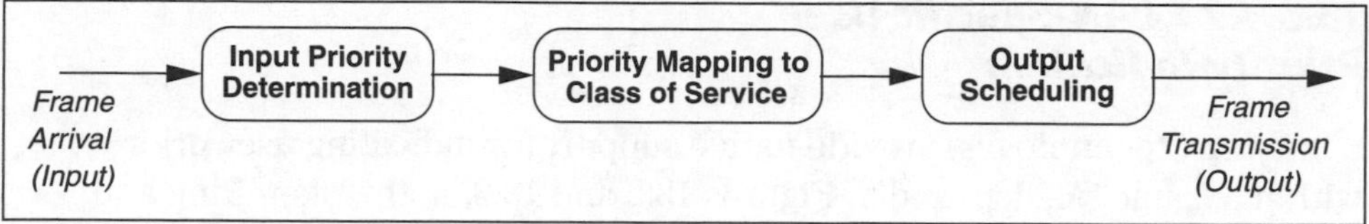

Figure 13.9 Priority process model.

the frame is to be forwarded. Typically, each service class identifies a particular output queue on each port.

3. For a set of multiple output queues, the switch must apply some scheduling algorithm to transmit frames from those queues according to the needs of the classes of service that they represent.

Each of these operations are discussed in detail in the following sections.

Note that it is only user priority that we are concerned with here. User priority indicates the precedence requested by the end station (typically by some application within that end station, through an API). The access priority may vary as the frame is transmitted across the links in the catenet, but the user priority should be consistent from source to destination end station.

13.5.4 Determining Frame Priority on Input

With respect to priority operation, the first job of the switch is to determine, on a frame-by-frame basis, the priority that should be associated with each frame. This can be done in a number of ways, depending on the features that have been implemented in other switches in the catenet, the attached end stations, and the nature of the underlying LAN technologies.

13.5.4.1 Tag, You're It!

If a received frame carries a VLAN or priority tag (see Section 13.3), the tag header carries a priority value for the associated frame in the range of 0 to 7. In this case, the job of the switch is simple—the priority of the frame is the priority indicated in the tag. The switch can assume that whatever device put the tag on the frame (either the originating end station or some intervening switch) applied a set of rules that associated the frame with the indicated priority. No further work is needed to validate the frame priority for a tagged frame.

13.5.4.2 LAN-Specific User Priority Indication

Some LAN technologies provide native support for indicating user priority within a frame. As depicted in Figures 13.2 and 13.3, both Token Ring and FDDI LANs include means for directly indicating user priority within the frame without resorting to an additional tag.[17] Similar to the tag method, eight levels of priority are supported in both of these technologies. If a tagged Token Ring or FDDI frame indicates a different value of user priority in the native user priority field versus that in the tag, the priority field in the tag should override the native priority indication in the frame.

13.5.4.3 Implicit Priority Determination, or "Whose Clues Do You Use?"

Ethernet has no native means to indicate frame priority. In a priority-scheduling Ethernet switch, the question becomes, "What priority should be assigned to a frame received with no tag?" Typically, the switch in question will be an edge device, as discussed in Section 13.4. Edge devices attach end stations to a backbone. Since the vast majority of end stations today (1) use Ethernet as their LAN technology and (2) do not insert tags on outgoing frames, edge devices must often deal with implicit priority determination as a matter of course.

The priority assigned to untagged Ethernet frames becomes a matter of administrative policy. That is, the network administrator can decide which classes of traffic should be assigned to the available priority levels. Such a determination can be made on the basis of various factors:

- Certain protocols may be prioritized over others. For example, AppleTalk and LAT traffic may be given priority over IP traffic, since the former protocols are somewhat more delay sensitive than IP. The switch would need to inspect the protocol Type field in the received frame (in its various possible encapsulations) to determine the priority.
- Within a protocol suite, certain applications may be given priority over others. For example, in the TCP/IP suite, an administrator may choose to prioritize Telnet over HTTP (due to its latency-sensitive response time), HTTP over FTP (interactivity versus bulk data transfer), and so on. That is, the performance of the applications can be optimized through priority assignment. The switch would need to inspect the application identifier (in this case, the TCP port number) to determine the frame priority.

[17] Some other LAN technologies (such as IEEE 802.4 Token Bus [IEEE90c]) also provide native indications of user priority. However, few modern switches support Token Bus or any LAN technologies other than Ethernet, Token Ring, and/or FDDI.

- Specific higher-layer applications may be given priority independent of protocol. Network management might be given the highest priority, and real-time interactive voice/video applications may be given precedence over lower-priority traditional data communications.
- Specific users or devices might be given priority over others, as indicated by the device Source Address.

The number and nature of such administrative policies is virtually endless. In practice, the policies implemented will be limited by the feature set of the specific devices deployed in the catenet. Some products may be able to implement extremely sophisticated policy rules by examining multiple higher-layer protocol fields within the frame; others may only be capable of simpler frame parsing methods.

For frames that do not meet any of the specific administrative rules, a default priority is assigned by the switch. This is usually a low (often, the lowest available) priority.

13.5.4.4 Priority Regeneration

The IEEE 802.1p and Q standards provide for *priority regeneration*. Its use is best explained by example. Consider the situation in Figure 13.10.

Figure 13.10 shows three independently-administered departmental catenets, with native priority mechanisms implemented in each one. The network administrators of those three catenets have chosen equivalent priority policies: Network management has been given the highest priority, interactive voice/video services have been given a moderate priority, and all other traffic has been given a default (lower) priority. The service behavior of all three catenets will be identical. However, the absolute values of the priorities chosen for high, medium, and low priority are different in each department.

If we now interconnect the three departments, there will be an imbalance among the service levels provided to users from the three departments. In the example, interactive applications from department B (at priority 6) will get better performance across the catenet than those of department A (at priority 4) simply because of the specific priority values chosen by the local administrators. Priority regeneration allows us to map locally significant priorities to a globally-significant value, thus creating consistent priority semantics across the departments. In the example, the priority regeneration tables for each of the three ports map the local department priorities to the same levels: management to priority 7, interactive services to priority 6, and a default of priority 0. Thus, priority regeneration allows an easy means of migrating and merging existing priority-enabled LANs into a larger catenet without having to change all of the local administrative policies at once.

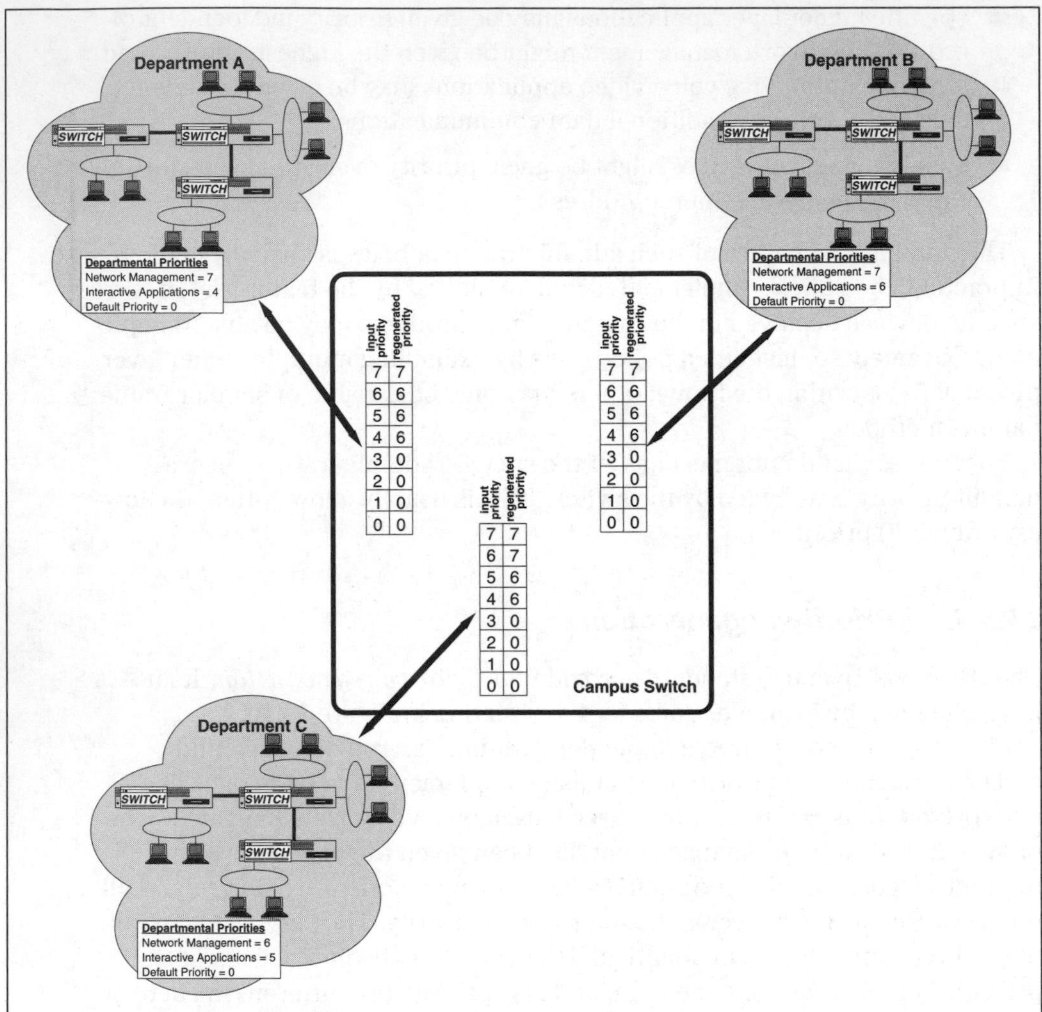

Figure 13.10 Priority regeneration.

Priority regeneration is only used when explicit priority is indicated in received frames through a native priority field. When determining priority implicitly (through inspection of the frame contents), there is never any need to regenerate the derived priority. We can simply set our administrative priority determination rules to be the same on all of the affected ports. Put another way, unless the priority is explicitly indicated in the received frame, we have no way of even knowing what the departmental priority policy is, so there is no need to remap it for global significance.

Note that priority regeneration can be used not only to equalize service levels among the departments but to change or override the local administrative policy. For example, we might want to regenerate priorities to give specific users or applications higher priority than their peers on other ports of the switch. As always, this is an issue for network administration policy-setting.

13.5.5 Mapping Input Priority to Class-of-Service

Once we assign a priority to each received frame, we must map that priority to one of the Classes of Service supported by the switch. Each service class identifies a set of traffic for which the switch can provide some differentiated level of performance relative to the other classes. Typically, each Class of Service is associated with a transmission queue on a given output port. All traffic for a given output at the same Class of Service will be handled first-in-first-out in the same queue. Differentiated service between classes is provided by putting traffic into different queues and applying preferential treatment to the higher Classes of Service.

A device may support different numbers of service classes for different ports. Thus, the mapping of priority to Class of Service is done on a port basis.

13.5.5.1 Class of Service versus Quality of Service

There is a fundamental difference between the concepts of *Class of Service* (CoS) and that of *Quality of Service* (QoS). While both terms are often used in a rather free and loose manner (i.e., taking on whatever meaning the user wants), most network architects would define QoS as a guarantee that a network makes to an application in terms of providing a contracted level of service throughout the application session.

Using the QoS approach, an application would request (either explicitly through a session setup mechanism or implicitly through the nature of the application itself and the associated administrative policy) a certain level of service prior to using the network. The network would reserve the appropriate resources (e.g., memory buffers and channel capacity) for the duration of that application session. If the needed resources were not available, the application would be so informed, and it could choose not to run until the resources became available or to run with a lower QoS guarantee. Thus, QoS implies a connection-orientation and reservation of network resources to provide a guarantee of a minimum level of service. Additional protocol mechanisms (e.g., RSVP [RFC2205]) are generally needed to request and reserve the needed resources.

CoS is much simpler. The network provides a higher level of service to those applications operating at a higher priority, but no explicit guarantees are made. The highest priority class will get the best available service, but there is no guarantee that this will meet any specified minimum level. CoS is much easier to implement, as the switch does not need to retain state information about each application flow. Priorities are assigned to each received frame on a frame-by-frame basis. The switch provides the best available service by putting the higher-priority frames in the queue associated with the higher CoS. Memory does not need to be reserved, nor does channel capacity. No additional protocol mechanisms are required to reserve resources or set up application sessions.

If bandwidth is expensive, then QoS-style approaches may make sense. QoS allows specific applications to perform correctly when network resources are scarce. The fundamental QoS assumption is that resource reservation mechanisms are necessary to achieve proper operation in the typical case; that is, there is insufficient capacity for all users to do what they want at the same time, and capacity must be explicitly allocated over time.

The CoS approach assumes that network capacity is adequate for all applications on average, but that short-term transient conditions may cause temporary congestion. CoS (simple priority) provides a way for time-critical applications to get the best possible service at times of transient overload. Priority pushes the important traffic to the head of the queue so that performance is not degraded when congestion is present, but it is assumed that this is a temporary situation created by the statistical nature of traffic arrivals and traffic patterns. In a LAN environment, we can overprovision the capacity of the links to make this capacity assumption valid at a relatively low cost. Higher capacity LANs are constantly becoming available at lower and lower prices. Thus, in a switched catenet, it is invariably simpler (and therefore less expensive) to provide excess capacity and use a CoS approach to cover the instances when transient overloads occur than to invoke complex QoS mechanisms.

Seifert's Law of
Networking #14
No one needs
a QoS guarantee
when they
have enough
bandwidth.

13.5.5.2 How Many Queues Do You Chueues?

The number of priority levels and Classes of Service to be supported has been a subject of great debate over the years.[18] Historically, those technologies that provide native priority support have provided for eight levels of priority (both user priority and access priority). However, in practice, all eight levels have rarely (if ever) been used.[19]

[18] As usual, such debates result in the consumption of both lots of meeting time within the standards committees and of lots of beer at the bar (after the meeting).

[19] Token Bus systems have never implemented more than four levels of user priority. In historical Token Ring systems, virtually all user traffic is sent at the same priority (priority 6), with only management traffic being afforded precedence (priority 7).

Table 13.1 IEEE 802.1p Priority Recommendations

PRIORITY	TRAFFIC TYPE
7 (highest)	Network management
6	Voice
5	Video
4	Controlled load
3	Excellent effort
0 (default)	Best effort
2	Spare (undefined)
1 (lowest)	Background

There are two points on which most everyone agrees:

1. You need at least two levels of priority. (This should be self-evident!)
2. No one knows what they would do with more than eight levels of priority.

The most common implementations use either two levels (high and low), eight levels (cover all bets), or a compromise somewhere in between. The issue is the complexity of the memory data structures, particularly when the switch is being implemented in hardware.

The IEEE 802.1p standard defines eight levels of priority and suggests how they might be used as shown in Table 13.1.

The highest priority is given to management. This is important; when there are problems in the network, it is critical that the management commands issued to (hopefully) resolve the problem override any other traffic that may be causing the problem. Voice traffic is given priority over video, since voice traffic is generally more sensitive to latency and jitter. *Controlled load* refers to applications that have specific minimum steady-state bandwidth requirements but no special sensitivity to delay or jitter. *Excellent effort* just means "better than best effort" (seriously).[20]

The lowest priority is earmarked for background tasks (e.g., file server backups). Interestingly, this level is not the default; the default (priority 0) is considered more important and is given a higher precedence. The reason for this is backward compatibility. In the absence of priority mechanisms, all traf-

[20] Historically, the term *best-effort* service has come to mean "whatever we can do without any special mechanisms." Thus, native Ethernet provides best-effort service for all applications. Best-effort is therefore synonymous with connectionless datagram service. Given this definition, the definition of *excellent effort* becomes clearer; it is a connectionless datagram service with a higher priority than that afforded traditional best-effort traffic.

fic is considered to be at the default priority (0). Even on those LANs that have native priority mechanisms, priority 0 is generally used as the default priority for all best-effort traffic. Once we implemented eight levels of priority in our catenet, it became inappropriate to designate "best effort" (which was our earlier default behavior) as the worst class of service available! We recognized that some applications are of lower priority than the default, and we allocated two levels for this purpose. It looks weird, but it makes (some) sense.

ONE MAN'S OPINION

My personal belief is that the right number of priorities is three:

1. **The highest priority is for network management.**
2. **The middle priority is for time-sensitive or expedited service.**
3. **The default (low) priority is for everything else.**

Additional levels just add complexity with no great benefit. It is an extremely rare case when fine-tuning of priority levels with tiny granularity provides any real advantage in a LAN environment. If the channel has lots of excess capacity (the desired situation), then priority doesn't matter much. Everyone gets acceptable (fast) service regardless of priority.

The only reason for providing priority is to deal with the case of transient traffic congestion or overload, in which case you want to give a momentary preference to the more critical traffic streams. If the catenet is congenitally overloaded, you need to reconfigure it, not add priority levels.

13.5.5.3 Default Priority Mappings

Frames arrive and are assigned a priority (presumably in the range of 0 to 7). This priority is regenerated (if appropriate) and then mapped to a Class of Service associated with an output queue. The number of Classes of Service (i.e., output queues on a port) supported by a switch may be different from the number of priority levels, and different for each port. For example, a switch may be able to understand VLAN-tagged priorities in the range of 0 to 7, but may only provide four queues on each output port. We would need to map the eight levels of frame priority to one of the four Classes of Service provided. The IEEE 802.1p standard defines a set of recommended mappings of user priority to Class of Service as shown in Table 13.2.

Table 13.2 shows, for a frame at a given user priority level (numbered 0 to 7 in the left column) and a given number of Classes of Service (numbered 1 to 8 from left to right across the top of the remaining columns, and typically the same as the number of output queues available), which Class of Service the

Table 13.2 IEEE 802.1p Recommended Priority Mappings to Class of Service

	NUMBER OF CLASSES OF SERVICE (OUTPUT QUEUES) PROVIDED							
USER PRIORITY	1	2	3	4	5	6	7	8
0 (default)	0	0	0	1	1	1	1	2
1	0	0	0	0	0	0	0	0
2	0	0	0	0	0	0	0	1
3	0	0	0	1	1	2	2	3
4	0	1	1	2	2	3	3	4
5	0	1	1	2	3	4	4	5
6	0	1	2	3	4	5	5	6
7	0	1	2	3	4	5	6	7

frame should be assigned. If the queues are numbered 1 to 8, a frame in CoS 0 would be put into queue 1, CoS 1 into queue 2, and so on.

Some observations:

- If only one Class of Service is provided, all frames go into the same queue, regardless of priority (column labeled 1).
- If two Classes of Service are provided, the four lower priorities map to the lower class and the four higher priorities map to the higher class (column labeled 2).
- If eight Classes of Service are available, the port priorities map exactly as shown in Table 13.2 (column labeled 8).
- The default priority (priority 0) is given some level of preferential treatment in any implementation supporting four or more Classes of Service (columns labeled 4 through 8).

13.5.6 Output Scheduling

Once the frames are placed into the output queues associated with the various Classes of Service supported for a given port, we need to schedule the transmissions appropriately for the desired priority behavior. In the nonpriority case this task is trivial; with a single output queue, we simply transmit frames first-in-first-out (FIFO). With multiple queues, we need to decide which algorithm we will use to select the appropriate queue at any given time. For each queue, we maintain the FIFO approach; this ensures that ordering is maintained within each priority level.

13.5.6.1 Scheduling Algorithms

Many different scheduling algorithms are possible. Each provides different behavior, with a different set of performance tradeoffs. In this section we consider two of the most popular algorithms:

- Strict priority
- Weighted fair queuing

The queue model is depicted in Figure 13.11. For a given output port, there is a queue associated with a given Class of Service, and frames are placed into a queue by the switch on the basis of the priority determined at the input port and the mapping of the priority to the Class of Service, as discussed in Sections 13.5.4 and 13.5.5. The scheduling algorithm selects the next queue from which to remove a frame.

13.5.6.1.1 Strict Priority

Using strict priority, the scheduler always dequeues the next frame from the highest-priority nonempty queue. Strict priority, as the name implies, interprets priority literally; higher priority queues will always be served before lower priority queues. From an implementation perspective, strict priority is the easiest policy to implement.

The downside of strict priority is that, by taking the priority policy literally, it puts the burden of proper behavior on the administrator setting that priority policy and on users and applications not taking advantage of it. A strict priority policy allows a single high priority application to completely starve lower priority applications. If a high priority user offers more load than the capacity of the output port, no frames will be transmitted from the lower priority

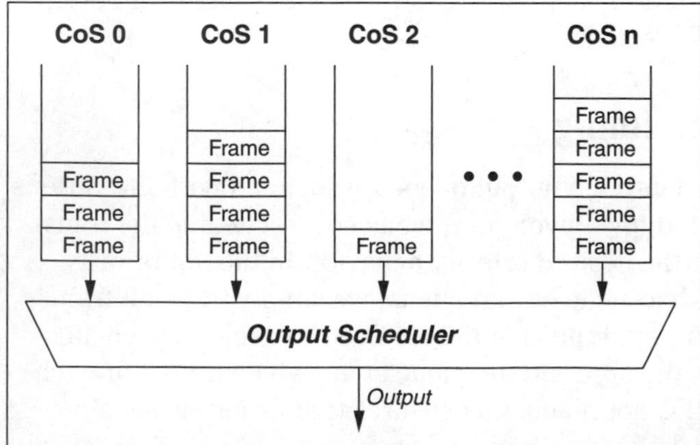

Figure 13.11 Output queue model.

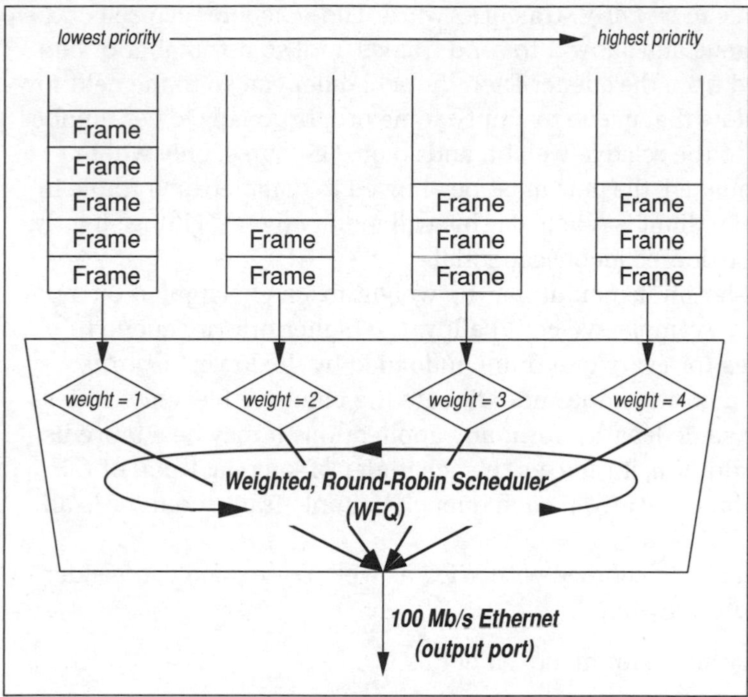

Figure 13.12 Weighted fair queuing.

queues. In the extreme case, all frames in lower priority queues will be discarded due to exceeding the transit delay bounds of the switch.[21]

13.5.6.1.2 Weighted Fair Queuing

An alternative approach is to give precedence to higher priority queues, but not to the complete exclusion of the lower priority queues. The most common application of this approach is known as *weighted fair queuing* (WFQ). A *weight* is assigned to each queue; higher priority queues are given greater weight than lower priority queues, as depicted in Figure 13.12. The output scheduler then uses a round-robin algorithm tempered by the indicated weight.

Weights are generally assigned relative to the proportion of the bandwidth allocated for each queue. That is, if all queues have traffic to send, the available bandwidth will be divided among them by the ratio of their weights. In the example of Figure 13.12, under congestion conditions, the highest priority queue will receive 40 percent of the channel capacity, the second highest priority 30 percent, the third 20 percent, and the lowest 10 percent. Note that priority is achieved without starving any of the lower priority queues.

[21] Of course, this situation will only arise if the offered load exceeds the capacity of the output port on a sustained basis. As discussed in Section 13.5.5, LANs are normally overprovisioned to avoid exactly this situation.

Implementation can be fairly straightforward. The scheduler can select the highest priority queue and allow it to send frames until some number of bits have been emptied from the queue. Then the scheduler can go to the next lowest priority and allow that queue to empty some proportionally lower number of bits in relation to the relative weight, and so on. Of course, only whole frames can be dequeued; the port must be allowed to complete any frame in progress once the bit limit is reached. This will modify the weighting slightly, but is generally considered inconsequential.

For an even easier implementation, the weighting can be applied on a per-frame basis. In the example, we could allow the higher priority queue to unload four frames for every one frame unloaded by the lowest priority queue. While this algorithm does not allocate the bandwidth evenly (unless all frames are the same length), for many applications it may be a more useful approach. In addition, it relieves the scheduler of keeping track of the bandwidth used (bits sent) from each queue. A simple frame counter is all that is needed.

Strict priority can be combined with WFQ as well. For example, consider my ideal three-queue situation:[22]

- A top priority queue for management use
- A middle priority queue for time-sensitive applications
- A low priority queue for everything else

We can allow management to have strict priority; management frames should always be sent if there are any in the queue. Between the middle and low priorities, we can use a WFQ policy to accelerate the performance of the time-sensitive flows.

13.5.6.2 Indicating the Priority in Transmitted Frames

In addition to sending frames from the various CoS queues, we need to decide both if and how we wish to indicate the user priority in the transmitted frames. On input, we made a priority determination and possibly remapped that priority to a globally-consistent set of semantics (priority regeneration). On output, we have three choices:

1. *Signal the user priority in a VLAN-style tag.* We can make life easier for the next switch in the path if we include the priority value in a VLAN

[22] No sane network architect would recommend a four-queue approach, unless he or she had perfect enunciation skills!

or priority tag. This relieves the next device from having to make an implicit priority determination from a set of administrative rules, which is generally a more difficult task than simply taking the priority value from the appropriate field in the tag. The tagging approach requires that the output port (and presumably, the next device receiving the frame) support tagged frames.

In general, it is appropriate to use tags when the next device to receive the frame is another switch as opposed to an end station; that is, tags are generally used within the core of the catenet, but are stripped at the edge devices that connect to end stations. This is because most end station implementations (at least today) don't support tags. In some cases it may not be possible to tag frames even within the core of the catenet if that core contains legacy switches that do not support tags. However, if it is known that tags are supported in the target environment, then they should be used. There is no disadvantage other than backward compatibility.

2. *Signal the user priority in a LAN-specific manner.* If the output port does not support tags, but supports native indication of user priority, then this method can be used to signal the priority. Native priority support is provided in Token Ring and FDDI, but not Ethernet.
3. *Don't signal user priority.* On Ethernet ports without tag support, there is little choice but to send the frame with no indication of the priority determined by the sending switch. The next device to receive the frame will need to determine the priority through implicit means, if it cares about priority at all.

Table 13.3 Mapping of User Priority to Access Priority on Token Ring

USER PRIORITY	DEFAULT	LEGACY (ALTERNATE)
0	0	4
1	1	4
2	2	4
3	3	4
4	4	4
5	5	5
6	6	6
7	6	6

13.5.6.3 Mapping User Priority to Access Priority at the Output Port

If the output port is a shared Token Ring, we have one more arrow in our quiver. We can, if we wish, allow the user priority to map to one of the eight access priorities provided. The highest priority (level 7) is generally reserved for critical management operations and ring maintenance. In addition, some early implementations only supported four of the allowed eight priority access levels. The IEEE 802.1p standard thus provides two allowable mappings of user priority to access priority, as indicated in Table 13.3.

CHAPTER

14

Switch Management

Up to now, the discussions have concentrated on the technical aspects of switch operation and implementation, along with the features, applications, and performance trade-offs that must be considered when selecting switch products for deployment in an enterprise internetwork. However, as depicted in Figure 14.1, these issues are just part of a continuous process that constantly attempts to ensure that the network meets the organization's needs in the face of both changing technology and user application requirements.

As important as product features are to the behavior of an enterprise network, the network administrator must constantly:

- Monitor network performance to ensure that all links and devices are operating as intended by the design
- Tune the network for optimum performance by adjustment or reconfiguration of device parameters
- Isolate and repair failed links, devices, subsystems, and software components
- Plan for changes and/or upgrades to the network to meet the needs of new and growing application requirements

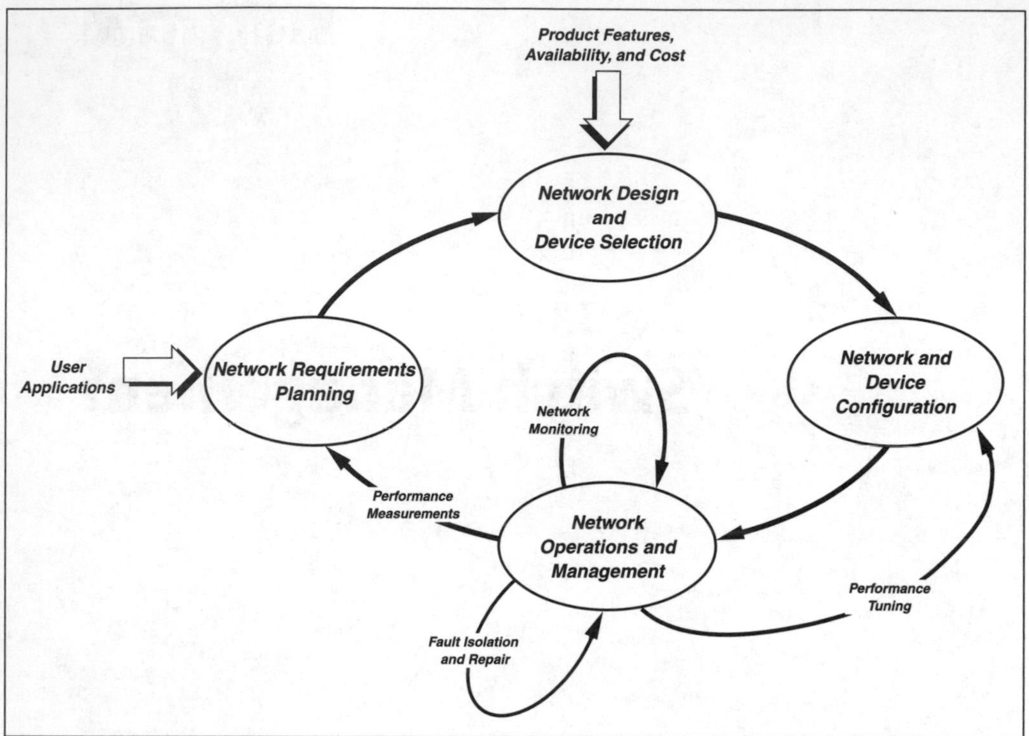

Figure 14.1 Network design and operation cycle.

This chapter looks at how the need to support these network management requirements is reflected the design of LAN switches. The chapter is not intended as a primer or a treatise on network management or as a troubleshooting guide for switched LANs; those subjects are sufficiently important and complex to justify many bookshelf-meters of their own.[1] In particular, network troubleshooting tends to be very product- and diagnostic tool-specific; there is little advice that would be generally useful across the broad spectrum of switches, application environments, and network management tools in use. Readers in need of a good introduction to network management principles and protocols should refer to [TERP94], [ROSE96], [PERK98], or similar works. Some of the best troubleshooting information actually comes from the manufacturers' product literature and user groups; network administrators can get the benefit of thousands of hours of other people's time and effort in identifying and solving difficult device-specific problems.

[1] I find bookshelf-meters a useful measurement of the importance or interest level in a given subject. As one who rarely throws out a book, the extent of my total reading can be calculated in bookshelf-meters per year.

14.1 The Simple Network Management Protocol (SNMP)

When internetwork technology itself was new, product success (and along with it the success of the manufacturer of the product) was tied primarily to the operational features and performance characteristics of the networking equipment. As most organizations were not yet critically dependent on the proper operation of their networks, management and fault-detection capabilities were often ignored in favor of having more bells-and-whistles to list on the competitive data sheet. If network management capability existed at all within a product, it was often added as an afterthought. Any such management features would invariably be vendor- or even product-specific; there was no reason to provide common interoperable network management across equipment from multiple vendors.

During the early 1980s, most networks were relatively small in extent by today's standards. In many cases, a single vendor could supply virtually all of the networking equipment used by a given customer. With the growth of large enterprise networks and the Internet during the late 1980s, it became impossible for any single vendor to provide the breadth of products needed. Manufacturers began to specialize in particular product classes, and large networks would always comprise a mix of equipment—NICs, hubs, bridges, routers, and so on—from different suppliers. As a result, mixed-vendor networks became the rule rather than the exception.

Along with this equipment mix came a plethora of proprietary network management tools needed to independently configure, maintain, and monitor each vendor's products in a heterogeneous network.[2]

Nowhere was this problem more evident than in the burgeoning Internet itself. By its very nature, the Internet comprises a geographically-dispersed set of equipment from many different suppliers. Worse, there is no single place where the entire network can be configured and/or controlled; the Internet is a highly distributed system. Without any common management tools, it

[2] During this period, I had the opportunity to work with a large multi-national company that had an extensive internal enterprise network. The network management center was in a room measuring approximately 10 × 25 m, filled with nothing but dozens of logically-independent proprietary management tools for each vendor's products. Row after row of network management stations from Ungermann-Bass, IBM, Cabletron, AT&T Paradyne (and many others I have since forgotten) were lined up, each with a management staffer staring intently at a screen. Each of the systems worked differently, and each required specialized training to use properly; most of the personnel were knowledgeable about only a subset of the equipment. That is, not only were the management systems not interoperable, the people were not interchangeable as well. Fault isolation often required many people's combined effort, coordinated across multiple management systems providing conflicting information. It was a consultant's dream come true.

became virtually impossible to detect, isolate, and repair problems as they arose.

As a result of the increased consumption of analgesics on the part of Internet technical staff, a project was initiated to develop a network management system that could be used across multiple vendor platforms. The Simple Gateway Monitoring Protocol (SGMP) [RFC1028] was developed to allow vendor-interoperable monitoring capability for IP routers. From the success of this experiment, the protocol was expanded and refined into the Simple Network Management Protocol (SNMP) [RFC1157]. While SNMP is designed to allow management of a wide range of devices, much of the early deployment focused on internetworking products (bridges and routers).

SNMP is one of the great success stories of networking. Unlike many whiz-bang product features pushed by manufacturers (i.e., solutions in search of a problem), SNMP provided an answer to a real end-user need. As a result, it became the industry standard for internetwork management virtually overnight. During the early 1990s, SNMP supplanted almost every vendor-proprietary network management system. Combined with the success of the TCP/IP protocol suite (of which it is a part), SNMP was deployed in lieu of the international-standard Common Management Information Protocol (CMIP) [ISO89c] of the ISO protocol family. The SNMP protocol itself is specified in [RFC1157]; many other standards define the data structures used and manipulated by the protocol. Those specific to switch management are cited in the relevant sections that follow.

14.1.1 SNMP Concepts

For the purpose of our discussion, we need to remember some important concepts embodied by SNMP, as depicted in Figure 14.2:

- Manager/agent architecture
- Management Information Base (MIB)
- The SNMP protocol

14.1.1.1 Manager/Agent Architecture

Unlike most of the protocols we have discussed in this book, SNMP operates asymmetrically; commands are typically issued by a network management station (sometimes called a *network manager*) and are responded to by a network management agent within each managed device (switch, router, etc.).

In normal operation, the network manager automatically polls each agent at regular intervals, extracting the contents of the local device's management information database and combining it with that of all other devices into a

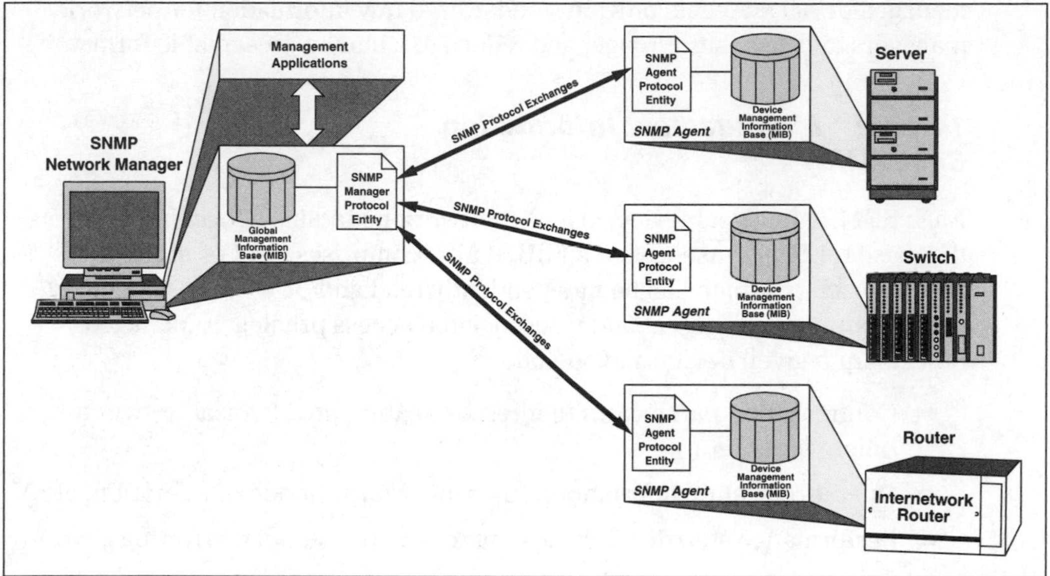

Figure 14.2 SNMP operation.

common global data store. Typically, the individual management agents provide a myriad of primitive, raw information about each device's internal state and performance. Network management applications running on the management station can assimilate and correlate the information gathered to provide a more human-usable presentation of the state of the network, including:

- Network maps indicating connectivity, topology, and device status (up, down, initializing, etc.)
- Network load displays, that is, current and historical utilization levels on each link
- Error logs indicating device and/or link failures and time of occurrence
- Performance reports

Network management agents are designed to be as simple as possible. Since there are many more agents than managers, and agents must often be implemented in low-cost embedded systems (e.g., desktop switches), it is important to keep the required agent complexity at a minimum; this optimizes the total system cost. All of the management complexity is shifted to the network manager—typically a high performance workstation dedicated to the task of network monitoring and management.

From the (human) network administrator's perspective, the management features and capabilities that are available are much more a function of the network management station and its resident applications than of the agents in the managed devices. Agents provide standardized raw information for network managers to digest, sift through, and reduce to a human-presentable format.

14.1.1.2 Management Information Base (MIB)

Each SNMP-manageable device in the network maintains a local information database for SNMP use, called a MIB. A MIB comprises a set of *managed objects*, each of which can be independently read and/or written, depending on the nature of the object and its associated access privileges. Managed objects for a given device may include:

- Configuration parameters (addresses, feature enable/disable switches, timer values, etc.)
- Operational state information (interface status, mode of operation, etc.)
- Performance statistics (frame counters, byte counters, error logs, etc.)

MIBs are hierarchical in nature; the MIB for a given manageable entity subsumes the MIBs for its subset components. Thus, to the extent that a given device comprises multiple functions—a switch will typically include some number of network interfaces, a bridge relay entity, a remote monitor entity, and so on—the MIB for that device will include the MIBs for each of its components. This organization is depicted in Figure 14.3.

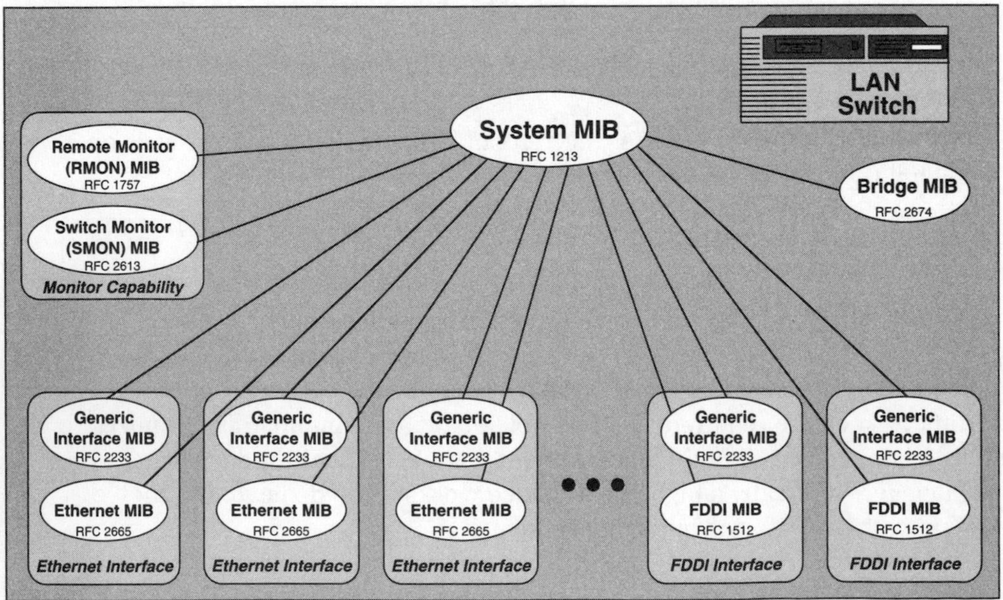

Figure 14.3 MIB hierarchy for a typical switch.

The nature and semantics of the managed objects within a given device's MIB are specific both to the functions the device performs and the implementation of the MIBs for those functional entities.

14.1.1.2.1 Standard MIBs

Rarely can we perform fault diagnosis or gain any real insight into the operation of a network by inspecting the management information from just a single device. Often, we need to compare counters and error statistics from a number of devices in order to determine if and where a problem may exist. Thus, it is important that devices use a consistent set of semantics for common management information, so that the comparisons are meaningful. For example, if two devices on a single LAN segment used a different definition of *error*, one device might indicate that there were no errors while the other may show a significant number of errors. Which one is correct? By their independent definitions, they both are, but this does not help the network administrator trying to track down a problem.

Seifert's Law of
Networking #13
A man with a watch knows what time it is.
A man with two watches is never sure.

To avoid this problem, we define industry-standard MIBs for many of the common manageable entities within a device. Examples of standard MIBs include:

- Ethernet, Token Ring, and FDDI interfaces (and many other technologies)
- Bridges (including VLAN and priority operation)
- IP, UDP, TCP, and so on (protocol entities)

There is even a defined MIB for a coffee pot! [RFC2325][3]

Standard MIBs are typically documented in Internet RFCs. The list of standard MIBs is both long and constantly changing. Table 14.1 lists those standard MIBs that are particularly relevant to the management of switches as discussed in this book. Of course, by the time you read this, some of these may be updated or rendered obsolete, but this list should provide a good starting point. As new switch features become standardized, standard MIBs will be developed, published, and added to the list.[4]

14.1.1.2.2 Proprietary MIBs

If vanilla were the only flavor of ice cream that people wanted, there would be no Baskin-Robbins, Ben and Jerry's, or [*insert your favorite specialty ice*

[3] Actually, the MIB is for a "Drip-Type Heated Beverage Hardware Device."

[4] At the time of this writing, the MIB for Link Aggregation is being developed and prepared for standardization (see Chapter 9, *Link Aggregation*).

Table 14.1 Switch-Relevant MIBs

RFC	DESCRIPTION
1213	Basic MIB for any system comprising a TCP/IP protocol stack
1493	Transparent Bridge
1512	FDDI interface
1513	Token Ring Remote Monitoring extensions
1525	Source Routing Bridge
1748	Token Ring Interface
1749	Token Ring Source Routing extensions
1757	Remote Monitoring
2074	Remote Monitoring protocol identifiers
2233	Generic Interface
2613	Remote Monitoring in switched LANs
2665	Ethernet Interface
2674	Bridges with priority, multicast pruning, and VLAN capability

cream distributor here]. While it is possible to build successful commercial products that provide just a minimal, standards-compliant implementation of a given function, such products tend to be low-cost commodity devices with little need for additional features (e.g., Ethernet repeater hubs). In the higher-priced, higher-performance product space, most vendors constantly try to add features and value beyond the minimum set prescribed by the standards. This is not a Bad Thing™ per se; it is the essence of competition. To the extent that these value-added features help customers achieve their business objectives, they are useful regardless of their lack of standardization. A standards-development effort can be justified only for those products and features with the broadest market potential; the lack of an industry standard should not be interpreted to mean that a given product or feature should be avoided.

Seifert's Law of
Networking #10
Proprietary is not a four-letter word.

SNMP provides mechanisms for proprietary extensions to the standard MIBs, so that common tools can be used to manage the nonstandard aspects of a product. Again, such extensions are not evil; they are simply the means by which we can use the standard protocol (SNMP) and management platform to manage product-specific features.[5]

Proprietary MIBs are generally published by the respective equipment manufacturers; there is no value to keeping these MIBs secret—if they were not publicly available, customers could not use them unless they were embedded into a vendor-specific network management station.[6]

14.1.1.3 The Simple Network Management Protocol (SNMP)

Everyone accepts that you need *some* protocol for network management. What makes SNMP so popular is the first word—*Simple*. It is SNMP's simplicity that allows the implementation of management capability without a huge impact on either product cost or development time.[7]

While designed with network management in mind, SNMP is actually a generic idempotent transaction protocol. It allows for the exchange of arbitrary information between a requester and a responder. In normal use, the requester is a network management station, the responder is an agent within each device being managed, and the information being exchanged comprises the managed objects composing each device's MIB, but this is an artifact of the typical use of the protocol and not the protocol itself.

The architectural positioning of SNMP is depicted in Figure 14.4.

[5] While proprietary MIBs can provide useful extensions to the standard, it is important that systems be designed such that they can be managed at the level of the standard MIBs (i.e., without extensions) if desired. Thus, it is important that system designers not store standard MIB objects solely within a proprietary MIB data structure, as this would make them inaccessible from a network management station that supported only the standard MIB structure. A proprietary MIB should either (1) include only the non-standard objects (to be used in conjunction with the standard MIB) or (2) replicate the entire standard MIB together with the proprietary extensions (so that a network management station could choose to traverse either the standard MIB or the proprietary MIB, depending on its capabilities).

[6] "Publication" of a vendor- or product-specific MIB is generally accomplished by (1) providing the MIB to those companies manufacturing popular network management platform products so that it can become part of their standard software distribution, (2) including the MIB in machine-readable form with the product distribution so that it can be loaded into an existing network manager station, or (3) making the MIB available on a publicly-accessible site on the World Wide Web.

[7] Indeed, the failure of SNMP Version 2—the intended replacement protocol for SNMP—to achieve any significant commercial acceptance is due primarily to the increased complexity of that protocol. Despite the real benefits it offered for management security and handling of dynamic equipment changes, developers were unwilling to accept its increased costs in terms of memory requirements, code complexity, and time to market. Rather than using the protocol's official name (SNMPv2, implying an improvement over the first-generation of SNMP), many people in the industry call it "NMP"—SNMP without the simplicity.

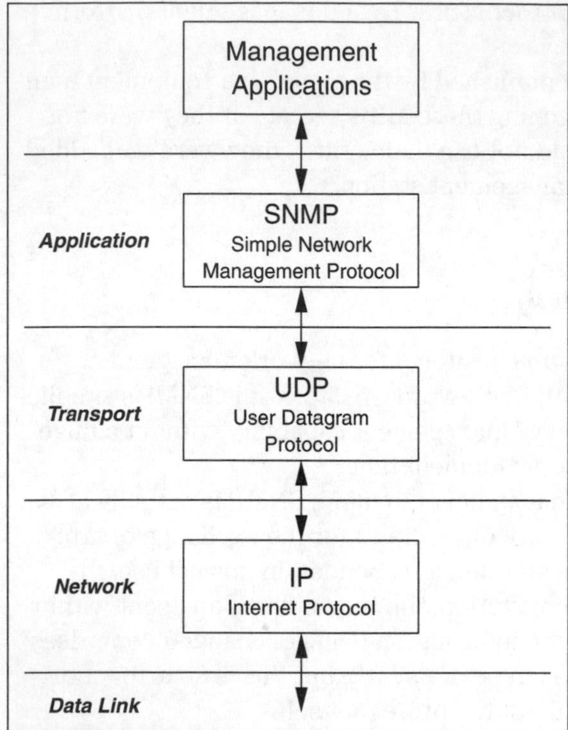

Figure 14.4 SNMP layering.

Some important characteristics of SNMP include:

- *Connectionless operation.* SNMP does not invoke any reliable transport mechanisms. There is no call setup or teardown, no flow control, and no retransmission mechanisms invoked by the network or SNMP to recover from errors. (See Chapter 1, *Laying the Foundation*, for a discussion of connectionless network operation.) As a result, SNMP can operate over the User Datagram Protocol (UDP) and does not require the more complex Transmission Control Protocol (TCP).
- *Stateless agent operation.* Not only does SNMP avoid the complex state machines of TCP, there is little state information maintained within the SNMP protocol itself. From the perspective of the network management agent, SNMP transactions are handled independently of all others. Thus, SNMP agent implementations do not have to maintain internal records reflecting the history or sequence of operations taken over time. No special procedures are required to synchronize requester state with responder state. This lack of state also eases management continuity in the event of the failure and restart of either a network manager or a managed device. There is no need to determine what the management process was

doing before the change occurred; management exchanges can proceed without concern for past history, with no loss of correctness.

- *Idempotency.* The objects in standard SNMP MIBs are defined such that successive interrogations of the same object will supersede the information received from any previous interrogations. For example, the standard byte, frame, and error counters are defined to be cumulative over time. If a given SNMP transaction encounters a transmission error, there is no need to take explicit action to recover from the error and retrieve the lost information. Later interrogation of the same counter (on the next polling cycle) will provide a new, up-to-date value that includes all of the information that would have been received had the previous transmission been successful. It is the careful definition of managed objects in this manner that allows SNMP to use connectionless, best-effort underlying service.[8]

In keeping with the idea of protocol simplicity, SNMP supports only five operations, listed in Table 14.2.

Table 14.2 SNMP Operations

SNMP OPERATION	DIRECTION	DESCRIPTION
Get Request	Manager → Agent	Requests that the management agent return the current value of a specified managed object.
Get-Next Request	Manager → Agent	Requests that the management agent return the current value of the next managed object in the MIB.
Set Request	Manager → Agent	Requests that the management agent set a specified managed object to the value provided.
Get Response	Agent → Manager	Provides the response to a Get, Get-Next, or Set Request. The value provided is the current contents of the MIB object after the operation that triggered the response.
Trap	Agent → Manager	Provides unsolicited notification of significant events (link enable/disable, device reset, etc.).

[8] Note that this would not be the case if, for example, error counters recorded only those errors seen since the last interrogation—that is, if counters were cleared and reset at each transaction. Under this non-idempotent scenario, it would be necessary to make sure that every response was properly received by the requester, or an incorrect view of the device would result. Furthermore, any such clearing of counters would make it difficult to monitor a device from multiple network management stations unless some mechanism was added to inform all of the management stations any time a counter was cleared.

14.2 Network Monitoring Tools

Troubleshooting problems within a single computer can be difficult, but at least all of the potential problem-causing elements are physically located in the same place and are available for inspection and examination. In a network of interconnected computers, this is no longer true. Application, communication, and performance problems can occur as a result of misbehavior from a large number of interacting devices distributed over a wide geographical area. Traffic appearing on a single LAN can comprise interspersed application communication streams from a variety of different systems. A problem in one device (e.g., an internetwork router or LAN switch) can affect many different users in ways that are almost unpredictable. Troubleshooting a network is thus considerably more complex than troubleshooting a single computer system, and demands tools that can observe the totality of network activity rather than the activity of any single device.

One important weapon in the network troubleshooter's arsenal is the *protocol analyzer*.[9] As depicted in Figure 14.5, a protocol analyzer is a device that can monitor the traffic activity on a given LAN. By receiving and inspecting all LAN frames, the protocol analyzer can:

- Collect network performance statistics, including utilization, frame rates, errors, and so on.
- Capture specific frames based on a set of administrator-configured criteria, for example frame to/from specific stations, frames encapsulating data from selected higher-layer protocols or applications, frames containing errors, and so on.
- Generate alarms based on a set of administrator-configured criteria, including utilization or error levels, specific frame sequences indicating a problem, and so on.

Protocol analyzers are especially useful for tracking down intermittent or rarely-occurring problems. Rather than having to store and evaluate the thousands or millions of frames that may traverse a LAN during the business day and tediously pore over them in search of a particular sequence of events, the protocol analyzer can be configured to look for the problematic sequence, store and record the relevant data, and alert the administrator that the anticipated event has occurred.

By definition, a network protocol analyzer must operate in promiscuous-mode; it must be able to observe and inspect all of the traffic on the LAN and

[9] A protocol analyzer is often called a network *sniffer*, although strictly speaking Sniffer is a trademark of Network Associates (formerly Network General), which makes protocol analysis products under this name.

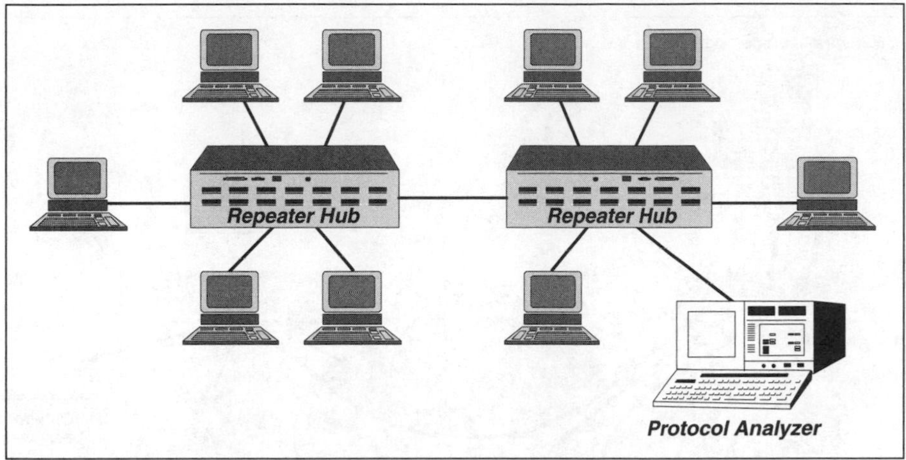

Figure 14.5 Monitoring a LAN using a protocol analyzer.

apply the pre-programmed test criteria against the received frames. Similarly, to be truly effective, the protocol analyzer must operate at wire-speed; it must be capable of at least inspecting (if not storing) all of the traffic without exception. A network troubleshooting tool that misses portions of the traffic is not especially useful; the missed frames could be the one-in-a-million event that you were looking for.

Traditionally, protocol analyzers are built around standalone computer systems with one or more network interfaces; often, the computer is a portable (laptop) machine for operator and deployment convenience. When a problem is surmised, the network administrator can connect the protocol analyzer to the suspect LAN, configure it as necessary for the problem being evaluated, and wait for results. Upon notification, the network administrator can peruse the collected data on the protocol analyzer to decide the appropriate action(s) to take.

A typical enterprise network can often comprise tens or hundreds of physically separate LANs. It is inconvenient (not to mention expensive) to deploy a traditional protocol analyzer and human operator to monitor multiple LANs simultaneously. In response to this problem, Remote Monitoring (RMON) devices were developed that could perform the same set of tasks as a traditional protocol analyzer, yet were not implemented using a traditional general-purpose computer system and did not require a local human operator. As depicted in Figure 14.6, RMON probes can be deployed on each LAN; the probes report their analysis results back to a centralized network management station using SNMP.

Thus, RMON probes provide distributed, programmable protocol analysis. Rather than requiring the administrator to physically go to the LAN being

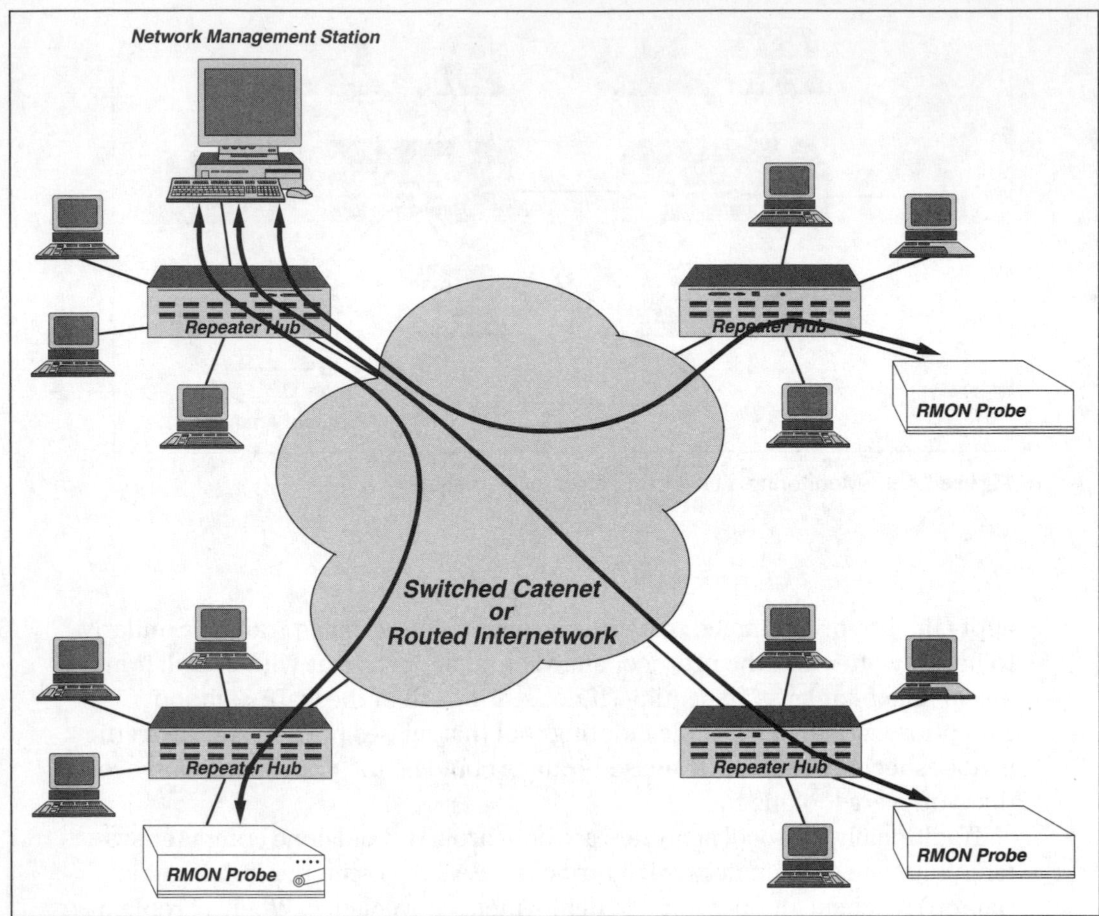

Figure 14.6 RMON probe deployment.

monitored, the RMON probe provides local monitoring and remote reporting. A single human administrator (or management application) can simultaneously evaluate the data collected from multiple probes both to provide ongoing performance monitoring and to determine the cause of problems that span multiple LAN segments.

RMON is not separate from SNMP management; in fact, RMON simply comprises a set of SNMP MIBs. An RMON probe is a device that implements one or more of the RMON MIBs (see Section 14.2.2), along with the SNMP protocol itself. It uses SNMP to receive instructions from, and report results to, an SNMP network manager.

14.2.1 Protocol Analysis in a Switched LAN

On a shared-bandwidth hub, all of the traffic appears on every port of the hub, regardless of which stations are reachable through a given port or the content of the frames being repeated. As a result, a standard promiscuous-mode network monitor (either a local protocol analyzer or an RMON probe) should function properly when attached to any port of the hub.

When a LAN switch is used in place of a shared-bandwidth hub, devices connected to a given switch port will see only that traffic destined for stations that may be reachable through that particular port, that is, known unicast destinations, unknown unicast destinations, and multicast destinations. Multicast and unknown unicast traffic may be further restricted due to the operation of multicast pruning and/or VLAN filtering by the switch (see Chapter 10, *Multicast Pruning;* Chapter 11, *Virtual LANs: Applications and Concepts;* and Chapter 12, *Virtual LANs: The IEEE Standard*). Thus, as a result of normal switch operation, it is no longer possible to monitor all of the traffic by attaching a promiscuous-mode device to a single port.

Three alternatives are commonly used to address this problem:

- Port mirroring
- Switch mirroring
- Internal RMON probe

We look at each of these options in the sections that follow.

14.2.1.1 Mirror, Mirror on the Switch, Which Is the Port that's Got the Glitch?

While it may not be possible to see all of the traffic traversing a switch by looking at only one of its ports, it is possible for a switch to replicate the traffic from any single port onto another port, as depicted in Figure 14.7.

Through appropriate management configuration of the switch, one port is selected as a *Mirror Port* and another as the *Monitored Port.*[10] The normal rules for traffic forwarding through the switch are suspended for the Mirror Port. Instead, the traffic presented to the Mirror Port by the switch becomes the same as the traffic on the Monitored Port; that is, the Mirror Port reflects the Monitored Port's traffic. The normal switch forwarding rules remain in effect for the Monitored Port; that is, traffic is replicated (not diverted) to the Mirror Port. Port mirroring is a commonly-available feature that allows a pro-

[10] The Switch Monitor standard [RFC2613] calls the Mirror Port a *Copy Port.*

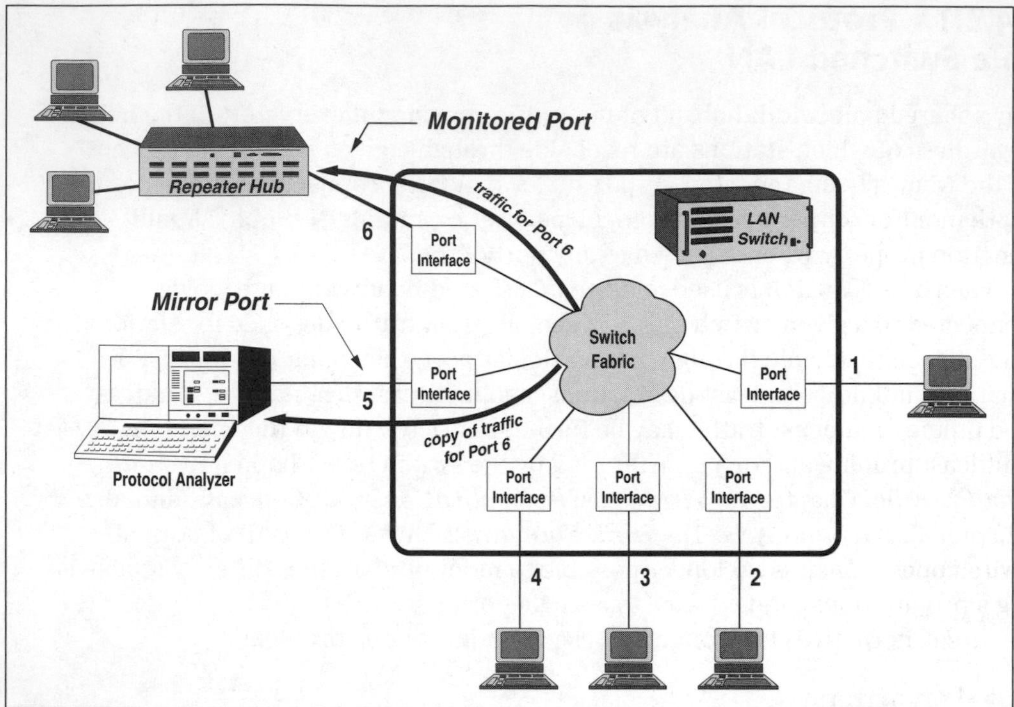

Figure 14.7 Port mirroring.

tocol analyzer to be used in a switched LAN environment; a protocol analyzer connected to a Mirror Port can observe the traffic on any Monitored Port selected by the network administrator. Because it is not defined by any industry standard, the exact behavior of a port mirror is highly implementation-dependent.

Most switches that support port mirroring allow only one port mirror to be enabled at any given time. In some implementations, the Mirror Port must be a fixed port dedicated for network management use; in others, any port may be selected as a Mirror Port under configuration control.

In most cases, a network administrator will want a protocol analyzer connected to the Mirror Port to see the same frames that it would have seen had it been connected to the Monitored Port; that is, the Mirror Port should reflect the traffic exiting the switch through the Monitored Port. Some switches additionally provide the capability to mirror either the incoming or the outgoing traffic from the Monitored Port. That is, the traffic presented to the protocol analyzer can be either the traffic being received by the switch from the Monitored Port or the traffic being sent out the Monitored

Port by the switch. This capability may be useful in certain fault isolation scenarios.[11]

In general, port mirroring is appropriate only for use with a local protocol analyzer as opposed to an RMON probe. RMON probes must be able to perform SNMP protocol exchanges with a network management station. Since the switch does not use the normal frame forwarding rules for the Mirror Port but instead mirrors traffic from the Monitored Port, SNMP commands from the network management station will not reach the RMON probe, and it will not be able to respond.[12]

To avoid frame discard, the data rate of a Mirror Port should be at least the same as the data rate of the Monitored Port. Most switch implementations require that the two ports be operating at exactly the same data rate; port mirroring often uses a special data path through the switch that does not include buffer memory, that is, the mirroring does not take place through the normal switch fabric and frame store. The switch may take the data as it is being presented to (or received from) the Monitored Port and simply present it simultaneously to the selected Mirror Port. The Mirror and Monitored Ports are in lock-step synchronization and must therefore operate at the same data rate.

14.2.1.2 Switch Mirroring

In an attempt to overcome the limitations of port mirroring, some switches provide the capability for the Mirror Port to reflect not just the traffic from a single Monitored Port, but all of the traffic being forwarded by the switch. That is, the switch can be configured such that when a frame is forwarded to

[11] At least one commercial switch provides the capability to mirror both the incoming and outgoing traffic from the Monitored Port simultaneously onto a single Mirror Port. Obviously, a port mirror operating in this mode cannot support sustained full duplex wire-speed operation; the sum of the incoming and outgoing traffic cannot be greater than the outgoing capacity of the Mirror Port, or frames will be discarded. In addition, the same frame-to-frame timing relationships cannot be maintained for all frames on the Monitored and the Mirror Ports; incoming and outgoing mirrored traffic is interleaved onto the Mirror Port. Still, this mode can be useful for debugging many common problems, especially those involving high-layer protocol exchanges. A Mirror Port used this way will see both the actions and reactions of the higher-layer protocol in the correct order.

A switch operating in this mode may append proprietary tag information onto the frames so that the protocol analyzer can separate the incoming from the outgoing traffic in the combined mirrored stream of data.

[12] Note that nothing has been said about the switch's behavior with respect to incoming traffic from the Mirror Port. Port mirroring itself is nonstandard; the behavior of a port mirroring switch with respect to traffic arriving on a Mirror Port is quite implementation-specific. Some switches may ignore all traffic arriving on this port; others may forward it appropriately. Even if a switch correctly forwards traffic arriving on the Mirror Port, an attached RMON device will not gain much benefit from this behavior; the SNMP commands from the management station will still not be forwarded to the RMON device, unless the management station just happens to be connected through the Monitored Port.

A REFLECTION ON MIRRORS

Port mirrors allow a protocol analyzer to be used to monitor the activity of any port in a switch. The problem with the use of mirrors is that the network administrator must know in advance which port he or she wants to monitor. When tracking down particularly insidious network problems, it is often not known which device is causing the observed problem symptom(s).

In a shared LAN environment, a protocol analyzer sees all of the traffic from all of the devices; anomalies can often be discerned by collecting and inspecting this traffic. In many cases, the device being affected by a problem is not the one that is causing it. Port mirrors do not help much to determine which device may be causing a problem; in particular, they are not capable of showing protocol interactions between devices attached to separate switch ports.

Once the source of a problem is known, a port mirror may help a network administrator to identify the specific nature of the problem and the remedial action to be taken. A mirror may also be used to look for an intermittent problem on a known device. However, it is not a general solution for network fault isolation.

any port(s) on the switch, it is also forwarded to the Mirror Port. This so-called *switch mirroring* capability avoids the problem of having to know in advance which port should be mirrored, since all ports are mirrored simultaneously. As a variation of switch mirroring, some switches allow a network administrator to configure the Mirror Port to reflect a subset (i.e., some, but not all) of the ports on the switch.

As usual, the solution comes with its own set of problems:

- On a switch with even a moderate number of high-speed ports, the traffic load presented to the Mirror Port can easily exceed the capacity of that port. In the worst-case, the load offered to the Mirror Port will be the sum of the capacities of all other ports of the switch combined. Under severe or sustained Mirror Port overload conditions, some frames will have to be dropped and will not be observable by a monitoring device attached to the Mirror Port.
- Mirror Port congestion can be alleviated somewhat by using a high-speed (uplink) port for the mirror. Even so, such uplink ports are usually only 1 order-of-magnitude greater in data-carrying capacity than the other (station attachment) ports of the switch. If there are more than 10 attachment ports, then Mirror Port overload can still occur, although the statistical probability is lower than if the Mirror Port had the same capacity as the attachment ports. For example, a common switch configuration may provide 24 or more 100 Mb/s attachment ports and two 1000

Mb/s uplinks. Even if one of the uplinks is used as a Mirror Port, sustained, heavy traffic load on the attachment ports can still swamp the available capacity (not to mention the addition of traffic received from the other 1000 Mb/s uplink port).

Also, it is generally expensive to dedicate a high-speed uplink port on a switch for monitoring purposes; such use eliminates its availability for a more traditional connection to a server or backbone network.

- Unlike a port mirror, a switch mirror configuration must include buffer memory for the Mirror Port. Even if the combined average traffic being directed to the Mirror Port is within that port's capacity, at any instant in time the switch may be forwarding multiple frames simultaneously. Only one frame can be forwarded onto the Mirror Port at a given time; the other frame(s) must be temporarily buffered. Similarly, if the Mirror Port uses a high-speed uplink, buffer memory is needed to perform any necessary speed conversion; switch mirroring cannot operate in a lock-step manner like a port mirror.
- As a result of the required buffer memory and the need to interleave frames from multiple ports onto the Mirror Port, a monitoring device attached to the Mirror Port will not observe the same frame-to-frame timing relationships that were present in the original traffic stream(s). When tracking down certain classes of faults, these timing relationships can sometimes provide important clues to device or protocol failures.

Despite all of its shortcomings, switch mirroring can be useful, especially if the offered load on the switch is relatively light. A switch mirror can help to isolate a problem to a particular port; once the investigation is narrowed in this way, a port mirror can be used for further investigation. In addition, a switch mirror can operate properly with either a local protocol analyzer or an RMON probe, as long as the switch properly forwards traffic received from the device attached to the Mirror Port. SNMP commands emanating from the management station will arrive at the RMON probe regardless of the relative location of the manager, since all switch traffic is replicated onto the Mirror Port.

While the operation of both port and switch mirrors is not formally standardized, [RFC2613] specifies standard methods for managing (i.e., configuring) mirrors in those products where they are implemented.

14.2.1.3 Look within Yourself for the Truth

Both the port mirror and switch mirror attempt to modify switch behavior so that an external protocol analyzer or RMON probe can be used in a manner similar to a shared hub. While these approaches to network monitoring are better than nothing at all, they cannot resolve the fundamental difference between a shared and a switched LAN environment.

The idea behind protocol analyzers and RMON probes is that these devices can monitor all of the traffic and allow application software and network administrators to make inferences about the status of the network from the collected data. When a shared hub is used, all of the traffic is observable at any of the hub ports. In a switched LAN environment, there is no single external port that ever carries all of the combined traffic of the catenet. The only place where all of the traffic passing through a switch can be seen and monitored is within the switch itself.

The obvious solution is to embed RMON capability within the switch. This is the approach taken by most modern switches, especially high-end products where the additional cost of the monitoring capability can be justified. Between the extremes of a full-blown RMON implementation and no management capability at all, there is a wide range of possibilities for switch implementors to trade off features and user benefits for added cost and complexity.

14.2.2 RMON Capabilities and MIBs

Remote monitoring encompasses a wide range of facilities, as reflected in the set of managed objects defined for RMON (i.e., the RMON MIB). As the complete MIB for a device implementing all of the standardized features composing RMON is quite extensive, RMON functionality is broken down into nine distinct groups, each of which can be optionally included in an RMON-compliant device. However, if a given RMON group is included in a product, all of the MIB objects within that group are considered mandatory.[13]

The nine RMON groups are:

Ethernet Statistics Group

Ethernet History Group[14]

Alarm Group

Host Group

HostTopN Group

Matrix Group

Filter Group

[13] While the MIB information presented here is applicable to both standalone and embedded RMON probes, the discussions that follow focus more on the issues related to embedded RMON probes in a LAN switch.

[14] A Token Ring Statistics Group and Token Ring History Group is also defined for RMON probes intended for use on Token Ring LANs [RFC1513]. The discussion here considers only the Ethernet Statistics Group, as this is the more common implementation.

Packet Capture Group

Event Group

Most embedded RMON probes within LAN switches implement only a subset of this total RMON capability. The most common practice is to support only four RMON groups: Ethernet Statistics, Ethernet History, Alarm, and Event. As will become obvious from the discussions in the sections that follow, this practice minimizes the requirement for specialized hardware. These four RMON groups can be provided from a basic set of counters defined by the Ethernet Statistics Group. All of the remaining objects in the four-group set can be derived by software manipulation of these primitive statistics. Additional hardware support (at additional cost) is generally needed to implement RMON functionality beyond these four groups.

14.2.2.1 Ethernet Statistics Group

This group defines a set of standard performance statistics for each Ethernet interface being monitored. Ethernet Statistics is the most widely supported and implemented of the standard RMON groups. While the standard [RFC1757] specifies a rather arcane list of raw statistics, application software can assimilate this low-level data to provide considerable insight into the utilization of the LAN, the load distribution, and the level and nature of errors.

Table 14.3 provides a summary of the statistics included in the Ethernet Statistics Group.[15]

The frame-based statistics shown in Table 14.3 are maintained in either a 32-bit counter (for Ethernets operating at 10 or 100 Mb/s) or a 64-bit counter

IMPLEMENTOR ALERT! IMPLEMENTOR ALERT!

It is interesting to note that some of the managed objects specified for RMON are similar, but not precisely identical, to the objects specified for basic SNMP use on an Ethernet interface, that is, for interface management irrespective of RMON [RFC2233]. For example, the ifInOctets counter of SNMP counts the total number of bytes received in valid frames only and includes framing bytes in the count. The RMON object etherStatsOctets counts bytes in all frames (both valid and invalid) and does not include framing bytes. While both objects are received byte counters, they are obviously not the same; depending on the implementation, separate hardware counters and registers may be needed to support both the basic SNMP and RMON MIBs.

[15] Readers interested in the detailed definition and specification of the managed objects should refer to [RFC1757].

Table 14.3 Ethernet Statistics Group MIB Objects Summary

RMON FORMAL OBJECT NAME	DESCRIPTION
etherStatsDropEvents	Count of the number of times 1 or more frames were dropped due to lack of resources in the RMON probe (e.g., buffers exhausted or performance limitation exceeded).
etherStatsOctets[1]	Total bytes received, not including framing bytes. Used as a measure of overall LAN utilization.
etherStatsPkts[1]	Total frames received, including those with errors.
etherStatsBroadcastPkts	Total valid frames received with a Destination Address equal to FF-FF-FF-FF-FF-FF.
etherStatsMulticastPkts	Total valid frames received with a multicast Destination Address (not including broadcast).
etherStatsCRCAlignErrors	Total frames received with a valid length (64–1,518 bytes) and an incorrect value for the Frame Check Sequence.[2]
etherStatsUndersizePkts	Total frames received with a length of less than 64 bytes but with a valid Frame Check Sequence. Often referred to as *runt frames.*
etherStatsOversizePkts	Total frames received with a length of more than 1,518 bytes but with a valid Frame Check Sequence.[2] Often referred to as *giant frames.*[3]
etherStatsFragments	Total frames received with a length of less than 64 bytes and an invalid Frame Check Sequence. Such frames are normally the result of collisions.
etherStatsJabbers	Total frames received with a length of more than 1,518 bytes and an invalid Frame Check Sequence.[2]
etherStatsCollisions	The best estimate of the total number of collisions observed.
etherStatsPkts64Octets	Total frames received with a length of exactly 64 bytes, including those with errors. Often referred to as *tinygrams.*
etherStatsPkts65to127Octets	Total frames received with a length of between 65 and 127 bytes inclusive, including those with errors.
etherStatsPkts128to255Octets	Total frames received with a length of between 128 and 255 bytes inclusive, including those with errors.
etherStatsPkts256to511Octets	Total frames received with a length of between 256 and 511 bytes inclusive, including those with errors.
etherStatsPkts512to1023Octets	Total frames received with a length of between 512 and 1,023 bytes inclusive, including those with errors.
etherStatsPkts1024to1518Octets	Total frames received with a length of between 1,024 and 1,518 bytes inclusive, including those with errors.[2]

[1] The RMON MIB specification uses the terms *Octets* and *Pkts* (packets) to refer to bytes and frames, respectively.

[2] At this time, the RMON MIB specification does not take into account the additional 4 bytes that may be present in a VLAN-tagged frame. Many tag-aware switch implementations modify the semantics of this object appropriately.

[3] Giant frames between 1,519 and 1,522 bytes (which are valid if they contain a VLAN tag) are sometimes referred to as *baby giants.*

(for Ethernets operating at higher data rates, for example Gigabit Ethernet). Byte-based statistics are maintained in 32-bit counters at 10 Mb/s, and in 64-bit counters at the higher data rates. In general, each of these statistics counters may need to be updated on a frame-by-frame basis in real time. Since the frame arrival rate on an Ethernet can theoretically be as high as about 1.5 million frames per second (at 1000 Mb/s, see Chapter 2, *Transparent Bridges*), these counters invariably require hardware assistance.[16] Typically, such statistics counters are implemented within the port controller itself; it is standard practice today for network interface silicon to provide all of the low-level counters needed to support both the basic SNMP Interface and the RMON statistics MIBs.

14.2.2.2 Ethernet History Group

The Ethernet History Group builds directly from the raw Ethernet statistics just discussed to provide the capability to present those statistics as a histogram over time. Network management software can configure control objects in the History Group to collect and sum Ethernet statistics over a sequence of discrete time intervals called *buckets.* Both the number of buckets and the time interval associated with each bucket are configured prior to running a histogram. The maximum number of buckets that can be supported, and the resolution and range of the time interval, are implementation-dependent; typical RMON probes can support hundreds or thousands of buckets and sampling intervals as short as 1 second.

Ethernet histograms include the first 11 objects from the Ethernet Statistics MIB (etherStatsDropEvents through etherStatsCollisions inclusive), as shown in Table 14.4.

[16] For a switch supporting RMON capability simultaneously on a large number of Ethernet ports, the hardware implications can be considerable. There are 17 Ethernet statistics in the group, each requiring a 32-bit (or 64-bit) counter. A 24-port, 100 Mb/s Ethernet switch chip would therefore need at least [(16 statistics × 32 bits) + (1 statistic × 64 bits)] × 24 ports =) 13,824 counter bits. Depending on the semiconductor design practices used, this would require on the order of 50,000 to 75,000 NAND gate-equivalents. This is just for the RMON statistics group; many other management objects and counters may be required for other groups and for SNMP support other than RMON.

A number of approaches to reducing the hardware requirements have been implemented in practice. The most common is to have the hardware maintain shorter counters than the 32 or 64 bits required by the standard; for example, reducing the counter length to 16 bits halves the hardware required in the example given. The full 32- or 64-bit version of the counter is maintained by software. The RMON driver can poll the shorter hardware-maintained counters on a regular basis and update the software-maintained counter appropriately. Alternatively, the hardware can generate an interrupt upon overflow of the shorter counter; the driver can use this interrupt to increment the software version of the counter by 2^{16} (65,536). At 100 Mb/s, a 16-bit valid-frame counter can overflow at most once every 440 ms; this is easily within the response time of any well-designed software driver.

Table 14.4 Ethernet History Group MIB Objects Summary

etherHistoryDropEvents	etherHistoryFragments	etherHistoryCRCAlignErrors
etherHistoryPkts	etherHistoryCollisions	etherHistoryOversizePkts
etherHistoryMulticastPkts	etherHistoryOctets	etherHistoryJabbers
etherHistoryUndersizePkts	etherHistoryBroadcastPkts	etherHistoryUtilization

Each of the objects has the same meaning as its counterpart in the Statistics Group; as used here it is simply a time history of the same information.[17] That is, the History Group includes an entry for each of these specified MIB objects for each time bucket in the histogram.

One additional object was added to the History Group—etherHistoryUtilization. This is the best estimate of the overall LAN utilization over a time bucket in hundredths of a percent. This object can be derived from the other Ethernet statistics as:[18]

$$\text{Utilization}_{\%}$$

$$= \frac{[\text{etherStatsPkts} \times (\text{interframe gap bits} + \text{Preamble bits}) + (\text{etherStatsOctets} \times 8)] \times 100}{\text{sampling interval} \times \text{data rate}_{\text{bits/second}}}$$

$$= \frac{[\text{etherStatsPkts} \times (96 + 64) + (\text{etherStatsOctets} \times 8)] \times 100}{\text{sampling interval} \times \text{data rate}_{\text{bits/second}}}$$

Implementation of the Ethernet History Group is really quite simple. At the beginning of each sampling interval (time bucket), RMON software samples and stores the value of each of the relevant Ethernet statistics. At the end of the sampling interval, the software again samples each of the relevant statistics, determines the amount by which each counter has incremented during the time bucket, and stores this difference in the Ethernet History MIB object for that statistic and time bucket. Finally, it calculates the utilization for this particular bucket and stores that as well.

Note that no new hardware counters are required to support the Ethernet History Group beyond those already implemented for the Ethernet Statistics Group. The Ethernet History Group can be implemented completely in software. This is especially true as the minimum resolution of the time interval is 1 second—a relatively long time by software standards.

Depending on the processing power available, a switch may be able to implement the Ethernet History Group simultaneously on multiple ports. The

[17] The complexity of maintaining a time history of the frame length distribution provided by the last six Statistics Group objects was not justified by its usefulness and is not part of the standard.

[18] The equation provides a utilization estimate in percent; the actual RMON MIB object is defined as hundredths of a percent, that is, 100 times the value calculated from the equation.

performance demand placed on the management processor will increase linearly with the number of such concurrent histograms.

14.2.2.3 Alarm Group

The Alarm Group provides a mechanism for defining thresholds above which an SNMP Alarm Event is declared. For example, a network administrator may want to know if and when the utilization of a given LAN exceeded some unacceptable level over a given averaging period. By using the specified averaging period as the time bucket interval for the Ethernet History Group, an alarm threshold can be set against the value of etherHistoryUtilization. The action taken upon crossing the specified alarm threshold is determined by the corresponding entry in the Event Group, discussed in Section 14.2.2.9.

As in the case of the History Group, alarms do not generally imply additional hardware support. RMON software can generate the appropriate alarms and events based upon the crossing of user-defined rising and/or falling thresholds for a wide variety of parameters, including:

- Error counters
- Multicast traffic levels
- LAN utilization

14.2.2.4 Host Group

The Host Group allows an RMON probe to maintain a list of the stations observed on the LAN along with a set of statistics for each of these stations.[19] A table of stations is built from the Destination and Source Address fields of validly received frames. For each of the stations in the table, the Host Group maintains the counters shown in Table 14.5.

Note that while these counters are similar to some of the Ethernet Statistics counters discussed in Section 14.2.2.1 and listed in Table 14.3, there is an important difference. Within the Host Group, these counters are maintained on a per-station basis, whereas in the Statistics Group they reflect the operation of the interface as a whole. Thus, there is much more information that must be collected and maintained for Host Group support than for the basic Ethernet Statistics Group.

All of the counters in Table 14.5 may need to be updated in real time on a frame-by-frame basis. In a switch, there will generally be a large number of ports, and the possibility of hundreds or thousands of stations in the catenet. As such, it is generally impractical to implement the Host Group using soft-

[19] *Host* is an IP-style term meaning *station*.

Table 14.5 Host Group MIB Objects Summary

RMON FORMAL OBJECT NAME	DESCRIPTION
hostInPkts	Count of valid frames for which the station was the destination of the frame.[1,2]
hostOutPkts	Count of valid frames for which the station was the source of the frame.[1,2]
hostInOctets	Total bytes contained in valid frames transmitted to the station as a destination, not including framing bytes.
hostOutOctets	Total bytes contained in valid frames transmitted from the station as a source, not including framing bytes.
hostOutErrors	Count of invalid frames (i.e., those containing errors) for which the station was the source of the frame.
hostOutBroadcastPkts	Count of valid frames for which the station was the source of the frame and the destination address was FF-FF-FF-FF-FF-FF.
hostOutMulticastPkts	Count of valid frames for which the station was the source of the frame and the destination was a multicast address (not including broadcast).

[1] The RMON MIB specification uses the terms *Octets* and *Pkts* (packets) to refer to bytes and frames, respectively.
[2] *In* and *out* are with respect to the station, as opposed to the switch or the RMON probe.

ware alone; there needs to be some hardware assistance in order to maintain meaningful (i.e., correct) values for these counters in a switch.

Aiding the implementation of the Host Group, a switch (unlike an end station) already needs to keep track of the stations present on the LAN. This is the essence of the Bridge Address Table used to make forwarding decisions within the switch (see Chapter 2), with one difference: the address table used for forwarding purposes is built from just the Source Addresses in received frames. The Host Group requires that statistics be maintained for stations appearing either as the source or destination in received frames.

For normal (i.e., unmanaged) operation, a switch does not need to keep byte and frame statistics counters at all, much less on a per-station basis. This is an added burden imposed by the Host Group and impacts the hardware required for RMON support.

There are two common approaches to implementation of the Host Group:

1. A brute-force approach can be used to maintain, within the switch silicon itself, the set of specified counters for some maximum number of stations.

Assuming the use of 32-bit counters, this imposes the need for ($7 \times 32 =$) 224 counter bits per station entry. To support as few as 100 stations in the Host Group would require more than 22,000 counter bits. If the number of stations observed exceeds the storage limitation within the switch, older station entries may be discarded on a least-recently-used (LRU) basis.

2. A second approach commonly used is to extract the raw information needed for the Host Group within the switch itself, but to offload the collection and storage function to either an external processor or a hardware accelerator chip. The complete set of Host Group statistics can be derived from a vector of information extracted from each received frame, comprising:

   - The Destination Address (6 bytes)
   - The Source Address (6 bytes)
   - The number of received bytes in the frame (11 bits for the maximum Ethernet frame length of 1,522 bytes)
   - A flag indicating whether the frame was valid or invalid (a 1-bit error indicator)

   A switch already needs to parse and extract all of this information in order to perform its switching function. Host Group support implies providing a means whereby this vector can be passed to an external RMON processing function, as depicted in Figure 14.8.

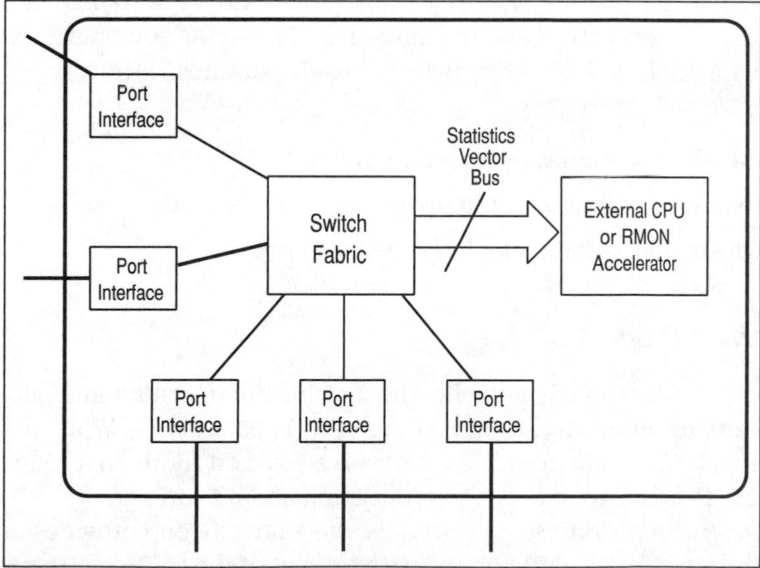

Figure 14.8 Host Group information vector extraction.

Using this vector-extraction approach, any switch can support the RMON Host Group for an arbitrary number of active stations in the catenet. The statistics themselves can be kept in low-cost general-purpose RAM, as opposed to internal storage within the switching silicon. Typically the vector is passed across an interface dedicated for the purpose. For a switch comprising 24-ports of 100 Mb/s Ethernet, the maximum bandwidth demand placed on this dedicated interface would be:

$$\text{Vector bus bandwidth} = \text{vector length} \times \text{frame rate}_{max} \times \text{number of ports}$$
$$= 14 \text{ bytes} \times 148{,}809.5 \text{ frames/second} \times 24\text{-ports}$$
$$= 50 \text{ Mbytes/second}$$

which is well within the capacity of a 32 bit, 33 MHz PCI bus or equivalent. The Host Group statistics for a catenet of 64K stations fits within a single 1 Mbyte RAM.

14.2.2.5 HostTopN Group

Just as the Ethernet History Group is created through manipulation of Ethernet Statistics Group objects, the HostTopN Group provides a compilation of Host Group statistics from some number of stations (*N*) presented in order of a given statistic over a specified time interval. This function can generally be implemented through software; there is no additional hardware required to implement the HostTopN Group beyond that required for the Host Group.

A network administrator can select *N* (the number of stations included in the list), the time interval of interest, the Host Group statistic to use, and the start time for the sampling period. The driver software records the change in the specified statistic(s) over the sampling interval and presents a list of the *N* stations with the maximum recorded increase. Thus the administrator can easily determine:

- The top 10 senders of frames over the last minute
- The top 5 senders of frames containing errors in the last 24 hours
- The top 20 destinations for traffic over the past hour

14.2.2.6 Matrix Group

The Matrix Group provides what is arguably the most useful information of all for network capacity planning and resource (e.g., server) positioning. While the Host Group collects traffic statistics for each observed station (both on a frame and byte basis), the Matrix Group collects information about traffic on the basis of Source Destination Address pairs; that is, the Matrix Group provides a view not just of the quantity of traffic on the network but of the traffic patterns. From the information collected, a network administrator can determine which stations are communicating with which others, and for each communicating pair, the number of frames, bytes, and errors that passed between them.

Table 14.6 shows the MIB objects included for each Matrix entry. Figure 14.9 depicts an example of the logical organization of this information as a traffic matrix.

As depicted in Figure 14.9, the matrix is effectively a cross-tabulation of all network traffic. It tells you exactly which stations are communicating with which others, and the number of frames, bytes, and errors for each such pairing.

Note that the Matrix Group does not require any additional primitive information beyond that needed for the Host Group; it simply provides a different organization and presentation of the same raw data. However, this does not mean that implementation of the Matrix Group follows naturally from an implementation of the Host Group. The data storage requirement for the Host

Destinations

Sources	08-00-60-00-00-12	08-00-60-00-00-47	08-00-60-00-00-75	08-00-60-00-00-93	08-00-60-00-00-33	08-00-60-00-00-32	• • •
08-00-60-00-00-12	0 0 0	1102 75678 0	407 25788 1	3 855 0	8845 81543 2	0 0 0	
08-00-60-00-00-47	45 6650 0	0 0 0	35 5723 0	0 0 0	0 0 0	0 0 0	
08-00-60-00-00-75	9572 22198 0	6683 19156 0	0 0 0	0 0 0	345 20666 0	0 0 0	
08-00-60-00-00-93	245 11522 1	0 0 0	0 0 0	0 0 0	46 8192 0	577 33278 4	
08-00-60-00-00-33	1066 65966 0	0 0 0	8841 90496 0	7777 78466 0	0 0 0	6123 79413 0	
08-00-60-00-00-32	203 8192 0	0 0 0	0 0 0	12 672 0	155 11000 0	0 0 0	
• • •							

Legend: Frames / Bytes / Errors

Figure 14.9 An example of the matrix.

Table 14.6 Matrix Group MIB Objects Summary

RMON FORMAL <NONE>OBJECT NAME	DESCRIPTION
matrixSDSourceAddress	The Source Address of the Source-Destination Address pair to which this entry applies.
matrixSDDestinationAddress	The Destination Address of the Source-Destination Address pair to which this entry applies.
matrixSDPkts	Count of frames (both valid and invalid) sent from the source to the destination.[1]
matrixSDOctets	Total bytes contained in all frames transmitted from the source to the destination, not including framing bytes.[1]
matrixSDErrors	Count of invalid frames (i.e., those containing errors) transmitted from the source to the destination.

[1] The RMON MIB specification uses the terms *Octets* and *Pkts* (packets) to refer to bytes and frames, respectively.

Group increases linearly with the number of active stations in the catenet; that is, the memory required is directly proportional to the number of stations for which statistics are being kept. To support the Matrix Group, the memory required increases at a greater rate; depending on traffic patterns, the storage requirement increases exponentially with the number of active stations, with the exponent in the range of 1 to 2.[20] For example, in a catenet comprising 100 stations, each of which communicates bidirectionally (two-way) with 10 other stations, a total of ($100 \times 2 \times 10 =$) 2,000 of the 10,000 (100^2) possible matrix entries will be non-zero. Since each matrix entry implies 192 bits of storage, the total requirement is 384,000 bits (48 Kbytes). A catenet of 64K stations similarly communicating would require 30 Mbytes of storage to keep the full set of matrix statistics.

14.2.2.7 Filter Group

The Filter Group allows a network administrator to examine each frame, perform a pattern match of selected bytes within the frame against a predeter-

[20] If all traffic is to/from a single station, for example one server, then the Matrix Group maintains the linearly-increasing storage requirement of the Host Group. In this case, the Matrix would be non-zero for only one row and one column. If traffic is uniformly distributed (i.e., every station communicates with every other station), then the matrix is non-zero in every cell, and the memory requirement increases with the square of the number of active stations. Most practical networks will fall somewhere in between these two extremes.

mined sequence, and direct any such matched frames to be captured (by the Packet Capture Group) for further analysis.

Some primitive protocol analysis tools attempt to capture and store all of the frames present on a LAN, but they quickly become memory constrained. A total capture of a heavily-loaded 100 Mb/s Ethernet for even a minute may require hundreds of megabytes of storage. The intent of the Filter Group is to provide a more intelligent capture mechanism where the only frames stored are the ones that are likely to be of interest, having passed one or more qualification tests (i.e., filters). Thus, a network administrator tracking down a difficult problem may be able to capture:

- Frames sent between a particular pair of stations using a particular high-layer protocol (e.g., HTTP exchanges between a client and server)
- Frames emanating from a particular station that contain errors (e.g., FCS mismatch or invalid length), and so on

Historically, the Filter Group has been implemented using software on both protocol analyzers and standalone RMON probes. As the filter criteria can be quite arbitrary (variable length and position of filter bytes, arbitrary match and mask values, etc.), it has been difficult to provide hardware assistance in a cost-effective manner. As a result, performance can suffer; many standalone RMON probes are incapable of performing frame filtering at wire speed on high-speed LANs. As the number and complexity of the filters being applied increases, the ability of a software-based RMON probe to keep up with sustained, heavy traffic typically degrades further.

Since switches generally interconnect large numbers of high-speed LANs, the Filter Group has historically not been implemented in embedded RMON probes. The performance demands far exceed the ability of software-based approaches using practical embedded processors.

Advances in silicon technology are making it possible to build general-purpose frame filters in hardware. Using either reconfigurable logic [e.g., embedded Field-Programmable Logic Arrays (FPGAs)], dedicated communications processors, programmable state-machines, or similar methods, it is becoming possible to apply sets of arbitrary frame filters against millions of frames per second. As this technology matures, next-generation switches may implement the RMON Filter Group in embedded probes [CIAM98].

14.2.2.8 Packet Capture Group

The Packet Capture Group is used in conjunction with the Filter Group. While the Filter Group specifies the test criteria to be applied against received frames, the Packet Capture Group manages and manipulates the memory buffers used to store those frames that pass through the specified filters.

14.2.2.9 Event Group

The Event Group allows a network administrator to specify the action(s) to be taken upon the occurrence of various RMON-related events. Actionable events may include the successful capture of a frame meeting specified filter criteria, the crossing of a threshold specified within the Alarm Group, and so on. For each such event, RMON software may generate an Event Log entry, issue an SNMP Trap notification, or both. The Event Group presents little implementation difficulty and no additional hardware implications.

14.2.3 RMON Support for Virtual LANs

A standalone RMON probe provides remote monitoring capability for a single LAN. An RMON implementation within a switch may provide monitoring capability for multiple LANs, that is, for each of its ports.

From the perspective of the network user or administrator, a Virtual LAN is a LAN. The fact that a VLAN comprises an arbitrary subset of the catenet is not apparent or relevant to the user; a user's application has access to resources on a given VLAN exactly as it would if that VLAN were instead a physical LAN segment. In the same way that we might put a traditional RMON probe on a physical LAN, we ideally might want to put an RMON probe on each Virtual LAN to monitor its behavior.

The implications for this approach to RMON implementation in a VLAN-aware switch are staggering. Conceivably, the switch would need to provide support for many of the RMON groups (e.g., Host, HostTopN, and Matrix) on a per-VLAN basis rather than on a per-port or per-switch basis. For a switch supporting hundreds or thousands of VLANs, the memory and performance requirements grow quite rapidly.

14.2.4 Levels of RMON Support

Obviously, most switches do not implement all of the RMON capabilities discussed here. There are a range of possible implementations commensurate with a cost benefit tradeoff. At the low end of the spectrum, a switch may simply provide Ethernet Statistics on a per-port basis; software can be used to provide the Ethernet History, Alarm, and Event Groups based on the underlying Ethernet statistics, either for a single port at a time or for all ports simultaneously. If more features (and a higher price) are justified, the Host and HostTopN Groups can be implemented for one port at a time, for the switch as a whole, or on a per-VLAN basis. The Matrix, Filter, and Packet Capture Groups can provide additional management capability, but imply additional hardware support and software performance demands.

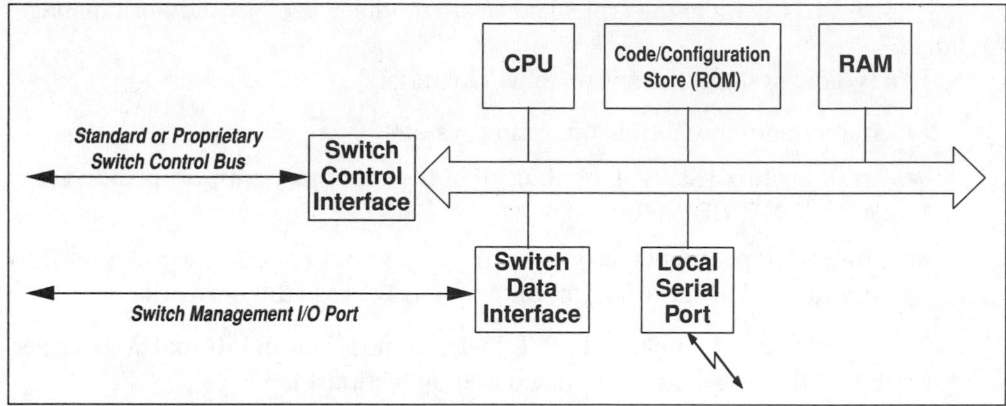

Figure 14.10 Embedded management platform.

14.3 Internal Switch Management Platforms

As discussed in Chapter 4, *Principles of LAN Switches*, most high-performance switches today implement the real-time address lookup and frame forwarding functions in dedicated hardware; this is the only practical way to achieve wire-speed operation on large numbers of high-speed ports at a reasonable cost. There is generally no processor or software involvement in the actual switching process.

While it may not be used for real-time operations in the fast-path of the switch, most switches incorporate an embedded processor to perform myriad necessary housekeeping functions. Network management is simply one of these routine functions relegated to the embedded housekeeping processor. Figure 14.10 depicts a typical embedded processor platform capable of supporting management operation.

A CPU is needed, along with memory for storage of both the management code and the MIB data structures.[21] The code store is usually implemented in non-volatile memory; EEPROM or Flash ROM is typically used. This allows the management capability to be available upon device initialization, without the need for either code download or a local mass storage device (i.e., disk), while still allowing code modifications, bug fixes, and minor upgrades without a hardware change.

A serial port is normally provided for initial device configuration, secure out-of-band management, and code modifications, as discussed in Section 14.4.2.

[21] Popular CPU platforms for embedded switch housekeeping include the MIPS and MIPS-like RISC processors, ARM, and the Motorola PowerPC.

Figure 14.11 depicts the typical software modules used by network management.

In a typical system, the software will include:

- An embedded real-time operating system
- An IP protocol stack, including all of the necessary support protocols (ARP, ICMP, UDP, etc.)
- The SNMP protocol entity, including the ASN.1 encoder/decoder used to format the MIB information for exchange across the network

Many systems also include TCP, Telnet, and possibly an internal Web server, for non-SNMP management, as discussed in Section 14.4.

As shown in Figure 14.4, SNMP operates as a client of UDP. Therefore, a switch must include UDP and IP in order to support SNMP. This is true even if the switching function operates exclusively at the Data Link layer (i.e., a Layer 2 switch). Network layer (e.g., IP) and higher-layer protocols must be incorpo-

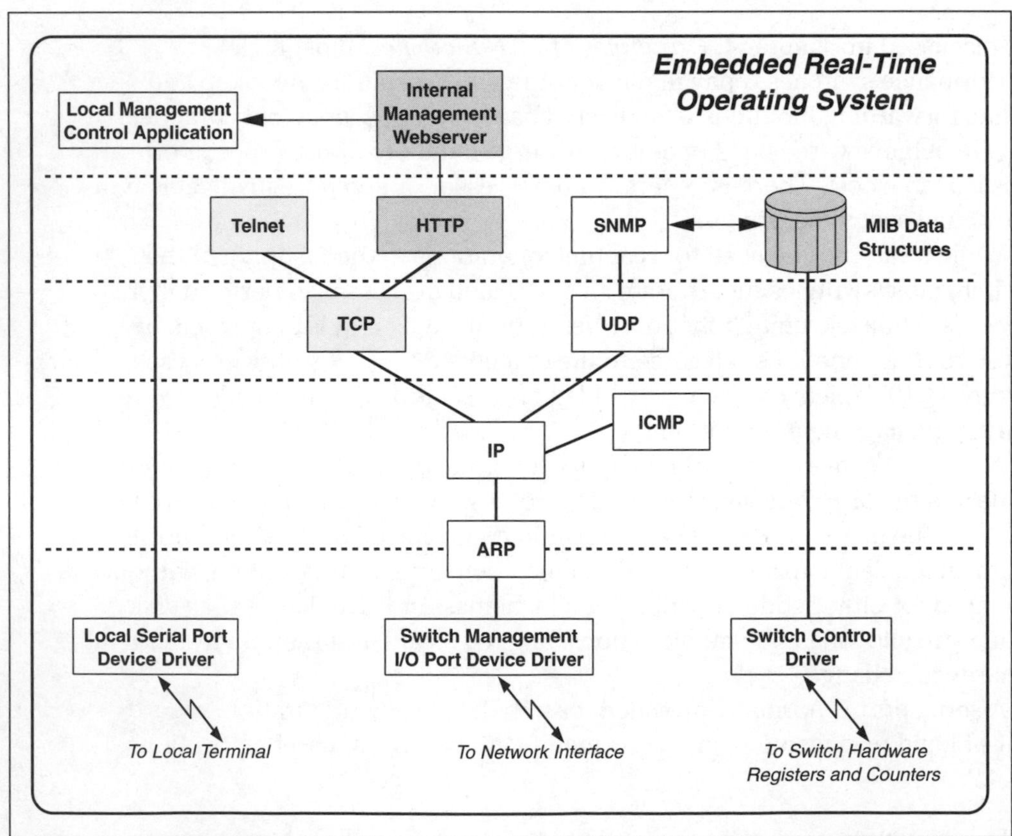

Figure 14.11 Embedded management software block diagram.

rated just to support standard management, even though those protocols are unnecessary for the primary purpose of the device (i.e., Layer 2 switching).

Fortunately, the performance demands of the management system are relatively light. The implementation of IP/UDP/SNMP and their related support protocols do not need to be capable of high-performance operation. In particular, the IP implementation can be optimized for end-station operation. Just because a high-performance Layer 2 switch includes IP code does not mean that it must support internetwork routing; the presence of Network layer functionality does not imply that the device has become a Layer 3 switch.

In most practical implementations, a single embedded processor platform (hardware and software) is shared for use by all of the housekeeping functions required. Network management comprises one set of processes running on this platform. Depending on the features and capabilities provided by the switch, management may be sharing the processing platform with the Spanning Tree Protocol, the GARP Multicast Registration Protocol, the Link Aggregation Control Protocol, and so on.

14.4 Non-SNMP Management

SNMP-based network management applications are by far the most popular means to monitor performance, and these applications can both detect and isolate faults on a continuing basis in a operational network. However, SNMP-based systems do have their limitations:

- Given its lack of security, most network administrators are unwilling to use SNMP for online configuration (and reconfiguration) of operating parameters in the switches and routers in their networks. SNMP does provide a mechanism that would allow such actions (i.e., the SET command); however, only a community name is needed to authorize the SET operation. Worse, the community name (and every other SNMP-related field) is transmitted in plaintext; it is a fairly straightforward matter for a malicious user to capture the appropriate community name value and use it to issue unauthorized configuration changes.[22] Improper switch or router configuration can cause serious network disruption.

  For this reason, many products incorporating SNMP management agents either don't provide SET support at all or have a means to statically disable the feature. This avoids the problem of lax security under SNMP, at the expense of eliminating the use of SNMP for device control.

[22] As in *Consumer Reports'* tests of the efficacy of locks, I will tell you what can be done, but not how to do it!

- The standard SNMP MIBs include those management objects that are common to all devices in a given class; however, most real-world products include a wide range of features that go beyond these basic necessities. Configuration and control of these device-specific features is by its very nature manufacturer and product-specific. While it is possible to design proprietary SNMP MIBs that include all of the objects needed to configure each particular product, it is usually simpler to avoid using SNMP altogether for device configuration, especially given the security limitations just discussed.
- SNMP is an *in-band* management mechanism; that is, it functions as an application on the network, running above the IP protocol. Proper operation of SNMP presumes that the network itself is operational; if a device is not reachable on the network (because of link or device failure), it will not be possible to communicate with that device using SNMP. An alternative out-of-band communications path is needed to effect whatever changes are required to restore service.

Thus SNMP is used extensively for monitoring purposes, but rarely for device control.

14.4.1 Internal Web Servers

The widespread growth of the World Wide Web and the ubiquitous availability of Web browser software provides an alternative to traditional SNMP-based management. If a managed device is equipped with an internal Web server as depicted in Figure 14.11, it becomes possible to communicate management and internal state information to any computer equipped with an appropriate browser. Security can be achieved through the use of password controls and encrypted exchanges; while not perfect, this is still superior to the access security provided by traditional SNMP-based systems.

The information exchanged between the internal Web server and the manager's browser may be the same as that provided by SNMP. The intent of a Web-based approach is to allow simpler management tools, better security, and a more user-friendly interface, not to change the semantics of the management information. If the MIB data structure is kept consistent in both the network management station and the management agent, higher-layer applications running on the management station should be able to use this information in the same manner as if the underlying transport mechanism used SNMP. It is the information that matters, not how it got there.

Historically, one of the driving forces for SNMP-based management was to reduce the resource demands made on the managed device; an SNMP agent entails considerably less complexity, code, memory, and CPU performance than a Web server. However, as memory and processing costs decrease, this argument disappears. In addition, specialized hardware (Web-server-on-a-chip) for embedded systems applications is becoming increasingly common and is already being widely deployed in internetworking products.

Note that, like traditional SNMP-based management, the Web-based approach operates in-band; its use presumes that the network and the device being managed are minimally functional. When a network manager is trying to isolate a network fault, this presumption may fail; the network cannot always be depended upon for the exchange of management information.

14.4.2 Out-of-Band Management

The simplest management mechanism is to connect a local terminal to a port on the device specifically provided for this purpose, as depicted in Figure 14.12.

Historically, the local terminal has been a dumb ASCII device connected to an RS-232 serial port on the switch. In practice, a computer emulating an ASCII terminal is often used. The switch being managed provides a command-line user interface through an internal ROM-based program residing on the management module. The user can, through the command-line interface, interrogate the device to determine its current configuration and change the

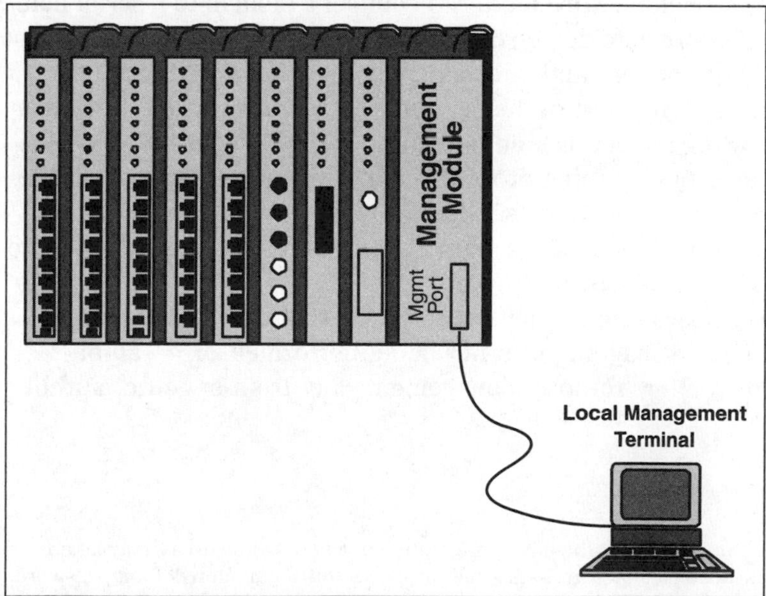

Figure 14.12 Local terminal for device configuration.

configuration as needed. Password-based access control is used to prevent unauthorized (re-)configuration.

Modern implementations of this local management method commonly use a computer with a browser interface for the local terminal, communicating with the internal Web server in the management module (see Figure 14.11). The traditional RS-232 port is replaced by an Ethernet for faster rendering of the browser displays. The graphical interface is an improvement over the older command line-style interaction for the human administrator, but there is no significant difference in operation from the perspective of the device being managed. It is simply a different method of supplying and displaying the device's operational parameters.

Whether a dumb terminal or a browser interface is used, this form of device management assumes that the human administrator is local, with physical access to the device being managed. Combined with password controls, this provides a reasonable level of access security.[23]

The management communications channel in this configuration operates out-of-band, that is, the local management port is different and separate from that used for network communications. The ability to perform management operations therefore becomes independent of the integrity or operational condition of the network. In some cases, local management may be the only method of effecting device reconfiguration to cure a network problem. In general, the use of a local management port is required to initially configure a device being installed on a network.

It is a relatively straightforward matter to connect a modem to a serial management port to allow remote device configuration. Note that the management communication is still out-of-band; the modem connection is dedicated for management use and is not part of the network that is transporting user data. In addition to allowing remote user administration, it is also possible for a device manufacturer, system integrator, or outside support service to provide remote diagnostic and management services through this dial-in modem port. Indeed, some vendors will not offer a support contract unless the capability to remotely access their products is provided.

For security purposes, the modem can either be physically disconnected when remote management is not being performed or a call-back unit can be used to allow remote management only from specific, authorized locations.

[23] In the special case of initial, out-of-the-box configuration of a new switch, there may be no password security, as most manufacturers ship their products with a common default password. It is assumed that the person doing the initial configuration is authorized to do so; this person can (and should) change the default password to prevent unauthorized access in the future.

14.4.3 Management by Telnet

Telnet is an application service that provides remote terminal access through a TCP/IP-based internetwork. A station running the Telnet client application provides its user with a virtual terminal connected to the remote station partner running the Telnet server application. Thus, Telnet can provide the same management capability as a locally-attached terminal; the difference is that the operations can be performed in-band across the network rather than through a physically separate management port.

The advantage of this approach is that it can provide much greater management capability than normally available through SNMP-based systems; any management operation that can be performed locally can be performed remotely using Telnet. The disadvantages are:

- *Telnet offers less security than an out-of-band system.* By using the end-user data network, malicious or rogue users can make attacks on the management system from anywhere in the organization. In contrast, an out-of-band system requires either local physical presence or knowledge of the proper modem access mechanisms (i.e., telephone numbers). The only real control provided by a Telnet-based system is the use of passwords; however, these are normally sent unencrypted and are thus subject to interception by a network monitoring device.

- *The network itself must be operational.* As is the case with any in-band system, the use of Telnet presumes that the network is functional at least to the point of being able to access, open, and maintain a connection with the managed device. Similarly, Telnet requires that the device being managed be at least nominally functional. Thus, it is not usually possible to use Telnet for fault isolation and repair; Telnet access is used mostly for performance monitoring (statistics inspections) and relatively benign configuration updates.

- *Telnet requires that the device being managed support TCP.* Architecturally, Telnet is a client of TCP. It uses TCP's connection-oriented services, including end-to-end error and flow control. For a device to be manageable through Telnet, it must include an instantiation of TCP along with the Telnet service itself, as depicted in Figure 14.11. While the Telnet application itself makes few demands with respect to memory and performance, the same is not true for TCP. TCP is normally one of the larger code modules in the protocol suite. In contrast, SNMP-based systems operate over UDP rather than TCP; a system supporting Telnet may require additional memory (ROM) and therefore cost more.

Despite its shortcomings, most enterprise-class switches support remote management through Telnet, although a network administrator may choose to disable this capability for security purposes.

14.4.4 Reach Out and Ping Someone

SNMP-based network management stations, internal Web servers, and local terminals can all provide huge volumes of raw information about the current operational state of a managed device. When performing initial device configuration or troubleshooting a particularly obscure performance anomaly, this level of detail is often necessary. Most of the time, however, the network should be running smoothly. Often, all that is needed to provide a high degree of confidence that network integrity is being maintained is a basic connectivity check.

The Internet Control Message Protocol (ICMP) provides a very simple mechanism for a network station to send an Echo message and for the targeted device to issue an Echo Response as a reply. The application program typically used to invoke this mechanism is called *ping.*[24]

Pinging a device actually provides a network administrator with a lot of information.[25] A successful sequence of received responses to ICMP Echo Requests indicates:

- The target device is powered on and its internal CPU, memory, and protocol stack are functional.
- At least one network interface on the target device is operational.
- There is an operational path between the pinger and the pingee, including any switches, routers, and links.

The administrator may not learn the current level of offered load or any other detailed statistics, but a successful ping and the absence of user complaints says that there are probably no catastrophic problems at the moment, which is pretty good information considering the simplicity of the mechanism being used.

Carl Malamud [MALA93] tells the story of Jun Murai, a network administrator in Japan who developed a useful tool called the *Phone Shell.* This was a UNIX-based application that could accept input in the form of Dual-Tone

[24] Many people confuse the echo mechanism with the program that invokes it. Ping allows a user to specify the parameters of an echo test (e.g., the number of attempts and the length of the messages sent). It then makes the appropriate function calls to transmit ICMP Echo messages and to look for Echo Responses in return. Ping then displays the result to the user. Strictly speaking, there is no ping message in ICMP.

[25] You know you are becoming a true networker when you start using words like *ping* as regular verbs.

Multi-Function (DTMF) tones (the 12 keys on a standard telephone keypad) instead of a keyboard. The tones could be used to invoke specific pre-programmed scripts upon command from any telephone. As Jun explained, "I can go to the bar and drink beer. I go to a phone and ping my routers, and if they are still working, I go back and drink more beer." Compared with sifting through piles of statistics, this is clearly the preferred method of network management.

CHAPTER

15

Make the Switch!

Up to now, we have considered the various facets of switch operation only in isolation; that is, the issues related to flow control, Multicast Pruning, VLANs, Priority Operation, and so on were treated independently of each other. This chapter shows how many of the concepts and mechanisms that have been discussed up to now can be integrated into a complete switch architecture. Since the operation of these switch functions has already been discussed in depth in earlier chapters, no detail is provided here; the focus of this chapter is on how the various functional elements are combined in practical switches.

The approach taken is to walk through a hypothetical switch from input port to output port. At each stage, we look at the operations that must be performed, and in particular, the order in which actions must be taken to achieve the desired end results. To get the maximum benefit from this process, we assume that our switch is fully-featured; that is, in addition to the basic functionality of a transparent switch, we consider the implications of:

- IEEE 802.3x Flow Control
- IEEE 802.3ad Link Aggregation
- IEEE 802.1p Multicast Pruning
- IEEE 802.1Q Virtual LAN support

WARNING FOR READERS WHO DO NOT REGULARLY ENJOY MYSTERY NOVELS!

In a good mystery story, the pleasure comes from following the tale as the author weaves it—from beginning to end in a linear fashion. Circuitous routes, flashbacks, and digressions (if appropriate) are provided by the author, not by having the reader jump from chapter to chapter in nonsequential order.

Many people (myself included) read technical literature with the goal being to glean useful information rather than to be entertained.[1] Unlike a mystery novel, it often makes sense to start reading a technical book at the end, going back to earlier chapters only as needed to fill in the gaps that were not understood.

Please resist this temptation here. The discussions contained in this chapter presume that you have read (and, I hope, understood) most of the previous chapters. Many of the concepts and much of the terminology from prior chapters is used here without introduction or explanation, as that would require restating most of the contents of the entire book within this one chapter.

- IEEE 802.1p/Q Priority Operation
- Network management

Of course, many switches implement only a subset of these capabilities, either for the switch as a whole or for particular ports (e.g., not every switch port will be part of an aggregation). Those functions that are not implemented just simplify the design.

It is impossible to discuss in one chapter all of the possible permutations and design considerations for LAN switches. By necessity, I have narrowed the scope to what I believe are the important issues that affect and have driven modern switch architectures. In particular:

- The emphasis of the discussion is on the operations performed by the switch to achieve proper data flow from input to output port(s). In any practical switch there will also be numerous control paths among the various modules to communicate state information, policies, table updates, and so on. As these tend to be quite implementation-specific, they are not discussed in great detail here.
- While the operations discussed are those of a Layer 2 switch (transparent bridge), the architecture and data flow could also be generalized to support Network layer routing (Layer 3 switching). The only significant

[1] When I want an uproarious fun time, I read patent specifications and IEEE network standards. I need to get out more.

changes will be an increase in the complexity and organization of the Classification and Lookup Engines (see Sections 15.2.4 and 15.2.6) and an increase in the workload relegated to the housekeeping processor subsystem (see Section 15.1.2).

- While no particular LAN technology is presumed for the various port interfaces, there is no discussion of:
  - Source routing as used on Token Ring and FDDI LANs
  - Handling of embedded source routing information in VLAN tags
  - Big Endian/Little Endian conversions
- A commercial switch may, of course, use a different architecture or model than the exemplary one given here, although the functions performed must necessarily be similar. In some products, some functional modules may be combined (e.g., VLAN input filtering may be performed by the Lookup Engine rather than as a separate block, as discussed in Sections 15.2.5 and 15.2.6).

Figure 15.1 depicts the architecture of our hypothetical switch from a very high-level viewpoint. Following a discussion of embedded housekeeping functions, this chapter then delves into greater detail on:

1. The path from where frames are received on the attached LANs to the point where the switch has decided to which output port(s) the frame should be transferred (input flow).
2. Switch fabrics—the mechanisms by which frames are transferred among the multiple ports of a switch.
3. The path between the switch fabric and the (possible) transmission of frames onto the LAN ports (output flow).

15.1 Keeping House

In the early days of internetworking, many bridge and router products implemented the majority of their functionality through software executed on an embedded microprocessor. While this may have been adequate for devices supporting small numbers of ports at relatively low data rates, it is rarely the approach taken today. The time-critical operations in the data path of a modern switch are invariably performed by dedicated hardware.

However, there is still a need for an embedded microprocessor in a hardware-based switch, except in the most basic, cost-driven, unmanaged desktop devices. While all of the fast path functions may be performed by specialized hardware, there are still myriad background processes, support functions, network management, and control protocols that are neither necessary nor practi-

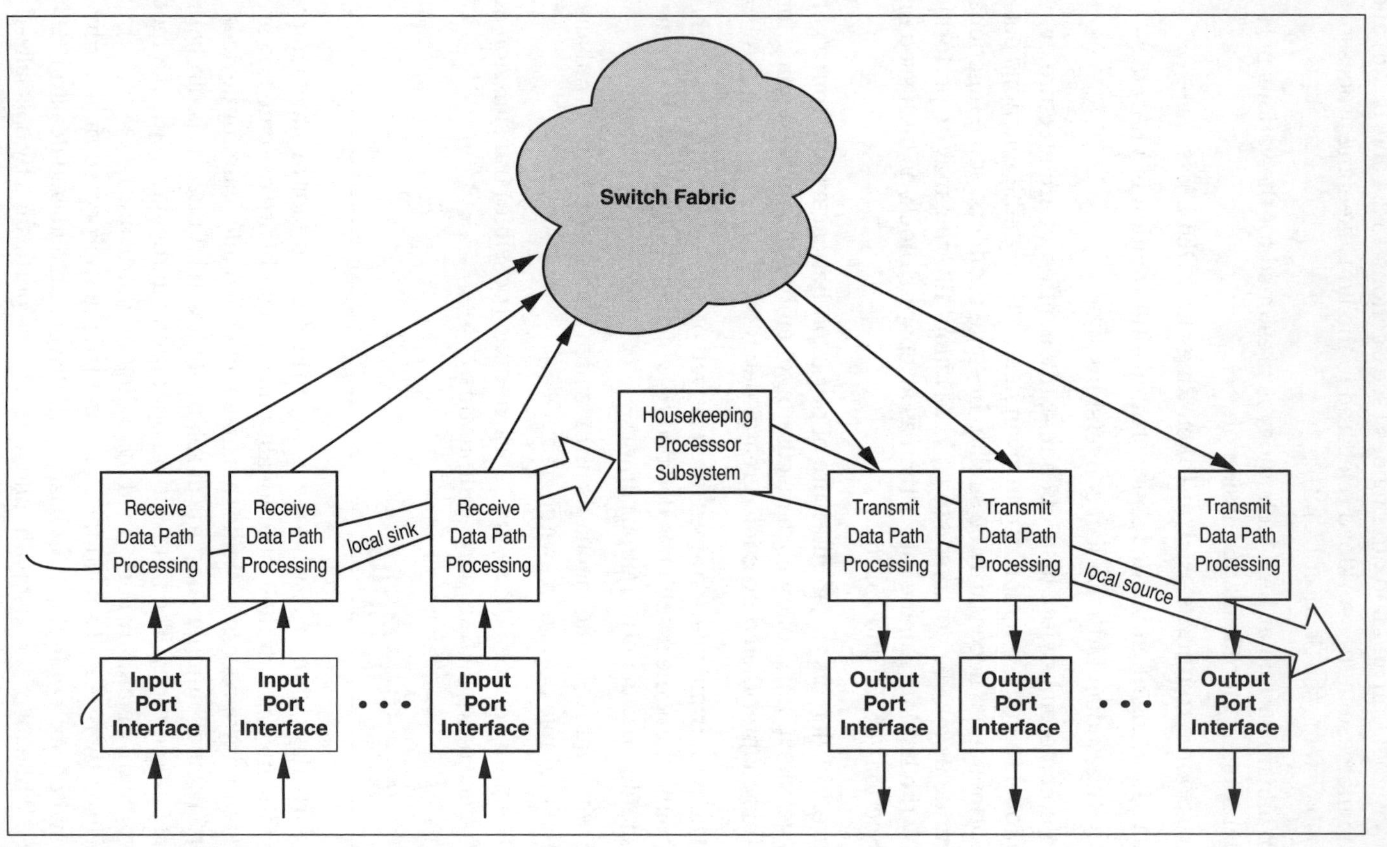

Figure 15.1 High-level block diagram.

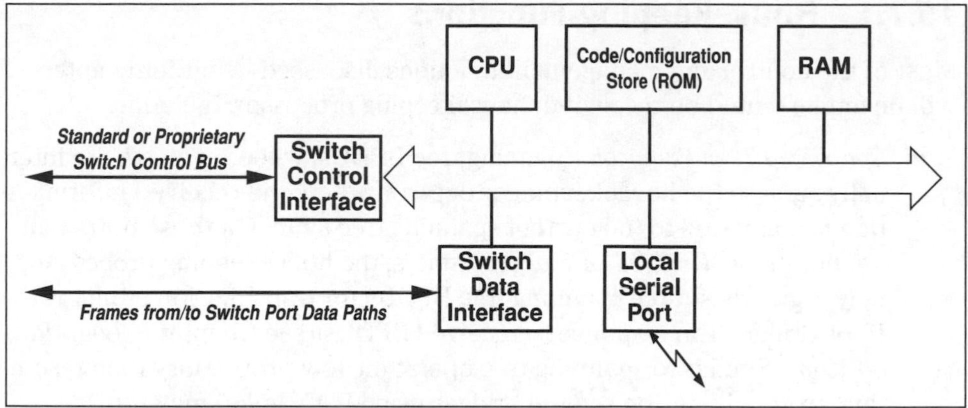

Figure 15.2 Housekeeping processor subsystem.

cal to implement in dedicated hardware. In general, this *housekeeping processor* is used for all switch functions that are not in the typical fast path of the data flow.

Figure 15.2 depicts a common configuration for the housekeeping processor subsystem. The system includes a standard microprocessor (CPU) along with memory for storage of both the operational code and frame buffers. The code store is often implemented in nonvolatile memory; EEPROM or Flash ROM is typically used.[2] This allows the housekeeping capability to be available upon device initialization without the need for either code download or a local mass storage device (i.e., disk), while still allowing code modifications, bug fixes, and minor upgrades without a hardware change. Volatile storage for frame buffers and other data structures is provided in Dynamic RAM (DRAM). A serial port is normally provided for initial device configuration, secure out-of-band management, system debug, and code modification download (see Chapter 14, *Switch Management*).

There must also be some means to move data (typically frame buffers) between the switch's ports and the housekeeping subsystem, both for reception and transmission. This *switch data interface* is generally implementation-specific. It may vary from a Direct Memory Access (DMA) channel between the port memory and the housekeeping RAM to a proprietary internal bus structure. The *switch control interface* similarly allows the housekeeping processor to directly control the underlying hardware in an implementation-specific manner (switch fabric control registers, port configuration registers, etc.).

[2] Typically, the operational code is transferred from ROM to RAM during device initialization for performance reasons.

15.1.1 Housekeeping Functions

Most of the control and management functions discussed in earlier chapters will be implemented on the switch housekeeping processor, including:

- *Spanning Tree Protocol.* Spanning tree BPDUs, when received, are internally sunk to the housekeeping processor, where the received information is compared to the current spanning tree state. On those ports that are not in the *disabled* or *blocking* states, the housekeeping processor may regularly source spanning tree BPDUs for transmission either as the Root Bridge or in response to received BPDUs (see Chapter 5, *Loop Resolution*). Similar to spanning tree operation, any proprietary loop resolution protocol (e.g., on remote bridges using WAN links) may be implemented in the housekeeping processor as well.
- *Link Aggregation Control Protocol (LACP).* The protocol used to automatically configure and maintain aggregated links was specifically designed to make relatively low performance demands, so that it can be executed in software on an embedded microprocessor. LACP messages received on any switch port are passed to the protocol entity running on the housekeeping processor; messages are similarly sourced as needed on the appropriate output ports. Note that LACP must be able to source frames onto a particular physical link within an aggregation rather than to the aggregation as a whole; that is, it inserts frames into the physical port queues rather than the aggregated port queues, as discussed in Section 15.4.2.
- *Marker Protocol.* When transferring conversations among physical links within an aggregation, the switch may accelerate the transfer through the use of the Marker Protocol discussed in Chapter 9, *Link Aggregation.* The housekeeping processor may be used to insert Marker messages into the frame stream as necessary. As discussed in Sections 15.2.3 and 15.4.3, the Marker and Marker Response mechanisms are somewhat more time-sensitive than some other control protocols. For that reason, high-performance switches that anticipate a need to perform frequent and/or rapid conversation shifts may implement the Marker functions either in dedicated hardware or in a separate microprocessor.
- *Enabled GARP Applications.* Depending on the features supported by the switch, one or more GARP applications may be in operation (e.g., GMRP or GVRP; see Chapter 10, *Multicast Pruning*, and Chapter 12, *Virtual LANs: The IEEE Standard*). Frames encapsulating messages for enabled GARP applications will be sunk to the housekeeping processor. Frames containing messages for GARP applications that are either not implemented or not currently enabled will be forwarded through the switch fabric without processor intervention. The differentiation

between the two sets of messages is made through appropriate configuration of the Classification Engine, discussed in Section 15.2.4.

- *Network Management.* All of the management software discussed in Chapter 14 will generally be implemented on the housekeeping processor, including:
  - The TCP/IP protocol stack as needed
  - The SNMP protocol implementation and MIB data structures
  - Telnet
  - Any internal Web server functions
  - Local serial port functions and user interface, and so on
- *Internal Diagnostics and Maintenance.* Generally, there will be a variety of implementation-specific functions that are performed on the housekeeping processor, including:
  - Device initialization
  - Power-on self test
  - Diagnostic and debug routines
  - ROM code update capability, and so on

A switch implementing Network layer routing capability may have another entire set of non-fast-path housekeeping functions to perform in addition to those just listed. Routing protocols (e.g., RIP or OSPF), IP control protocols (e.g., IGMP and ICMP), and even IP options processing could be delegated to the housekeeping processor, although these may significantly increase the processing burden and affect system performance.

As noted in Section 15.2.2, the Ethernet flow control function (i.e., PAUSE mechanism as discussed in Chapter 8, *LAN and Switch Flow Control*) must generally be implemented in hardware due to its severe timing constraints.

15.1.2 Implementation and Performance (or, It's Tough to Find a Good Housekeeper)

Historically, a number of popular embedded CPUs have been used as housekeeping processors. During the early-to-mid-1990s, the Intel i960 family was widely used. Recent implementations have favored the MIPS and MIPS-like families of RISC processors, ARM, and the Motorola PowerPC. All of these are available in a wide variety of configurations, processing powers, and costs, allowing the housekeeping subsystem to be closely tailored to fit the needs of a particular switch implementation.

Considered individually, none of the functions just discussed imposes a substantial processing burden. However, the performance demands of all of the functions combined can be significant. Depending on the number and complexity of the features implemented (in particular, the presence of Network layer routing capability), the number of switch ports, and the anticipated frame arrival rate, it may be necessary to use multiple housekeeping processors to distribute the workload.

15.2 Switch Data Receive Path Functions

Figure 15.3 depicts the path followed by data received from a given input port. The sections that follow examine each of the logical blocks within the receive path.

15.2.1 Port Interfaces (Receive)

The Media Access Control (MAC) and Physical Layer receiver (PHY) comprise the traditional network interface functions. On the receive side, the PHY takes the electrical or optical signals from the medium and decodes them into a bit, nibble, or byte stream as appropriate for the particular technology in use. The PHY will generally be different for different media (e.g., twisted pair or optical fiber) and different technologies (e.g., data rate and LAN type). The MAC performs the necessary framing and validity checking to reconstruct properly-formed frames from data stream presented by the PHY.

Typically, the receiving MAC will compute the Frame Check Sequence (FCS) value in real-time while receiving data from the PHY. In the event of an invalid FCS, the MAC will discard the frame. Other than possibly incrementing an error counter for management purposes, there is no need for a switch to continue to process a frame received in error.[3] The receiving MAC will normally maintain most of the real-time port-based statistics counters discussed in Chapter 14 (e.g., RMON Ethernet statistics).

The receiving MAC must store incoming frames in a local buffer. If the switch uses a shared-memory fabric (see Section 15.3.1), it may be possible to store the frame just once into a common buffer pool and avoid having to perform any buffer copy operations between input and output port(s). In this case,

[3] In the special case of a cut-through switch, a frame containing an FCS error may still be processed and forwarded. As discussed in Chapter 4, cut-through operation is rarely used today, as it requires that the input and output ports operate at the same data rate. Unless all of the switch's ports operate at the identical rate, it cannot be known whether cut-through forwarding is appropriate until the address table lookup operation is complete. In store-and-forward mode, a switch can transfer frames among ports operating at any data rate and can always discard frames containing FCS errors.

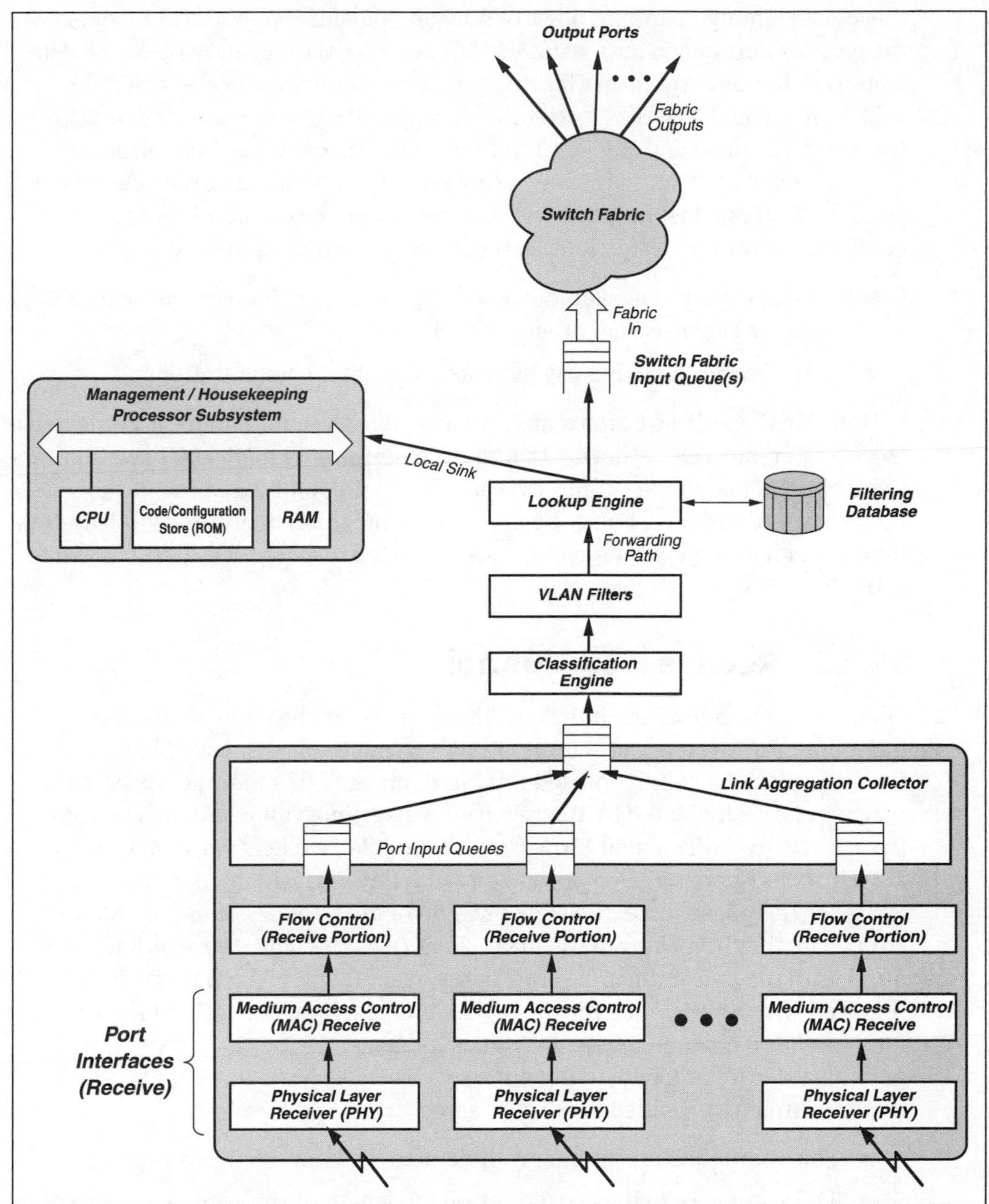

Figure 15.3 Switch input data flow (receive path).

the switch simply maintains a list of outstanding buffer pointers and adjusts the various port queue data structures rather than actually moving frame data from port to port. With other fabrics (e.g., crosspoint matrices, see Section 15.3.3), it is usually necessary to provide a frame buffer memory for each port (or group of ports) and transfer the frame data across the switch fabric.

Historically, PHY and MAC devices were built as individual packaged components with one instantiation per integrated circuit (IC). Modern silicon capability allows both horizontal and/or vertical integration, that is:

- PHY devices are available in quad, hex, octal, and denser configurations, both for Ethernet and other technologies.
- MAC devices are similarly available in multiple instantiations.

Both MAC and PHY devices are also available as semiconductor cores that can be integrated into a device that may be performing additional switch functions besides just the MAC and PHY interfaces. Depending on the nature of the target end product, it may be possible to integrate an entire switch system onto a single IC (system-on-a-chip), as discussed in Chapter 4, *Principles of LAN Switches.*

15.2.2 Receive Flow Control

On the receive side of the interface, the flow control module inspects the incoming traffic stream in search of PAUSE frames, as discussed in Chapter 8. Upon receipt of a validly-formed PAUSE command, this module updates the pause timer as indicated by the received pause_time value and provides control signals to the Transmit Flow Control module (see Section 15.4.4) as appropriate. For example, upon receipt of a PAUSE frame with a non-zero value for the pause_time, the transmit side of the interface must be told to stop accepting frames from the MAC client (e.g., the Link Aggregation Distributor) until the pause timer expires; in the event that a PAUSE frame is received with a zero value for the pause_time, the transmit side of the interface can be re-enabled to accept frames for transmission. The functions of parsing, interpreting, and acting upon received PAUSE frames are invariably implemented in dedicated hardware, since:

- The operations are simple, well-defined, and bounded in nature.
- There are very tight restrictions on the length of time between reception of a PAUSE frame and the halting of the transmit frame flow (512 bit times for 10 Mb/s or 100 Mb/s interfaces, 1,024 bit times for 1000 Mb/s interfaces).

Of course, since link flow control is defined only for Ethernet, the Receive Flow Control module will not be present on a Token Ring or FDDI interface.

In those cases, all frames would be delivered directly from the receiving MAC to the Link Aggregation Collector or Classification Engine.

15.2.3 Link Aggregation Collector

If multiple physical interfaces are being aggregated into a single logical interface, this module implements the frame collection function. The Collector gathers frames received from each of the underlying physical interfaces and presents a single, combined stream to the Classification Engine. As discussed in Chapter 9, the Collector does not need to take any special action to ensure proper frame order among frames received from each of the physical interfaces; the operation of the Distributor on the transmitting side of the link ensures that each conversation comprising a set of frames among which frame order must be maintained is mapped to a single physical link in the aggregation.

The Collector also includes the implementation of the responder portion of the Marker Protocol; this function may be implemented as a finite state machine or as software on a conventional microprocessor.[4] Depending on the design of the particular switch, the general-purpose housekeeping processor may be used to generate Marker Responses, although care must be taken to ensure very rapid response times. Typically, the Distributor at the other end of the aggregated link is waiting for a Marker Response before shifting one or more conversations from one physical link to another in the aggregation (see Section 15.4.3). To the extent that Marker Responses are delayed, communications from those conversations will be stalled.

In general, the Link Aggregation Control Protocol (LACP) will be implemented in the housekeeping processor, as its operation is much less time-critical than that of the Marker Protocol. LACP frames always use a multicast Destination Address within the reserved range for link-constrained protocols; the Classification Engine will flag these for local sink to the housekeeping processor, as discussed later.

15.2.4 Classification Engine

Depending on the level of features and sophistication provided in a product, the Classification Engine can be one of the more complex and performance-intensive elements of a switch. This module takes the stream of received frames from an input port and parses them as needed to generate a vector of classifications based on various criteria and administrative policies. In particular, the Classification Engine may be used to implement:

[4] The design of the Marker Protocol was intentionally kept simple to facilitate a pure hardware implementation at reasonable cost.

- Local sinking of reserved multicast addresses
- The VLAN Ingress Rules
- Priority assessment

Each of these are discussed in the sections that follow.

15.2.4.1 Local Sinking of Reserved Multicast Addresses

Frames with Destination Addresses in the range reserved for link-constrained protocols (01-80-C2-00-00-00 through 01-80-C2-00-00-0F; see Chapter 2, *Transparent Bridges*) must be identified and flagged to ensure that they are not forwarded to any other output ports through the switch fabric. Typically these frames will contain spanning tree BPDUs, Link Aggregation Control PDUs, and similar protocol messages, and must be locally sunk to the housekeeping processor. Note that while Ethernet flow control also uses one of these reserved multicast addresses, PAUSE frames will be sunk and acted upon by hardware within the Receive Flow Control module (see Section 15.2.2) and will not normally be passed to the Classification Engine.

15.2.4.2 VLAN Ingress Rules

These are the rules used to associate a given frame with the VLAN to which it belongs. In a VLAN-aware switch, every frame must be classified as to VLAN membership.

As discussed in Chapter 11, *Virtual LANs: Applications and Concepts*, there are two ways to determine the VLAN to which a frame belongs. If the frame carries a VLAN tag, then the task of the Classification Engine is trivial; the VLAN identifier contained in the tag tells the switch the VLAN to which the instant frame belongs.[5] Of course, the Classification Engine must parse the frame to determine whether it does indeed contain a tag. On an Ethernet, this implies a comparison of the Type field against the VLAN Protocol Identifier (0x8100). On a Token Ring or FDDI, the VLAN Protocol Identifier is encapsulated by LLC and SNAP, as discussed in Chapter 12.

If the frame is untagged, then its VLAN membership must be determined by applying the set of VLAN association rules to the contents of the frame. Depending on the capabilities of the switch and the nature of the administrative policies being applied, the implicit mapping of a frame to a VLAN could be quite complex. VLAN membership could be based on MAC addresses, proto-

[5] Note that if the VLAN identifier in a tag is 0x000, the frame is considered to be priority tagged rather than VLAN tagged, as discussed in Chapter 12. In this case, the VLAN membership must be determined implicitly from the frame contents just as if the frame carried no tag at all.

col types, Network layer address information, or even TCP ports and higher layer application data, either individually or in various combinations. As a result, the Classification Engine may need to:

- *Parse multiple fields in the frame.* The VLAN membership may be based on a catenation of MAC address, protocol type, or other information taken in combination.
- *Perform serial, conditional parsing.* It may be necessary to first parse the frame to determine the higher-layer protocol type and then look at different fields deeper in the frame depending on the encapsulated protocol. For example, VLAN membership may be based on IP subnet information for those frames comprising IP packets and on IPX network identifiers for those frames containing IPX packets. The parsing must be done serially and conditionally, as the second qualifier will have a different syntax and be in a different position in the frame for each encapsulated protocol.
- *Deal with variable length fields.* Depending on the protocol and the fields of interest, the Classification Engine may need to calculate field offsets into the frame in real-time as a function of parsed information. For example, if an IP datagram contains options, the IP protocol header will be variable in length. An inspection of any fields positioned after the IP header will require a variable offset.
- *Perform extensive comparisons and/or table lookups to determine the VLAN mapping.* Depending on the VLAN association rules, the Classification Engine may need to compare MAC addresses, protocol types, or other parsed information against a stored database of mappings. This implies some form of lookup mechanism and local memory store accessible by the Classification Engine.

Regardless of the complexity or the set of policies in place, the end result is the assignment of a single VLAN Identifier to each frame in the range of 1 through 4,094.[6] If multiple policies are in place (e.g., application-, MAC address-, and port-based VLAN association rules), a priority order must be established by policy; for example, an application-based VLAN mapping (if present) may take priority over a MAC address-based mapping that also renders a match. In the absence of a match of the frame's contents against any stated administrative policy, the default VLAN for the input port is used; that is, port-based VLAN mapping is used only if no other rules apply to a given frame.

[6] Note that if a frame arrives in priority-tagged format (i.e., with a VLAN Identifier of 0x000), it will be assigned a non-zero VLAN Identifier by the Classification Engine. Ultimately, the frame will be forwarded on the appropriate output port(s) either untagged or tagged with the non-zero value. That is, priority-tagged frames never propagate through a switch without a change to the VLAN identifier; an IEEE 802.1Q-compliant switch will never emit a priority-tagged frame.

15.2.4.3 Priority Assessment

In addition to categorizing each frame according to VLAN membership, the Classification Engine also determines a user priority value for each frame, typically in the range of 0 to 7. As discussed in Chapter 13, *Priority Operation*, the priority value may be:

- Extracted from a VLAN or priority tag (if present)
- Indicated by LAN-specific priority signaling (e.g., the native user priority field in a Token Ring or FDDI frame)[7]
- Determined implicitly from the frame's contents

From an implementation perspective, the latter case poses the most difficult task, as it implies parsing the frame and comparing the results against a set of policies in a manner similar to implicit VLAN classification.

15.2.4.4 Do It Once and Save the Results

The Classification Engine performs all of the frame parsing and field comparisons needed to determine the salient characteristics of the frame from the switch's perspective. As a result of this processing, the switch can know:

- If the frame must be link-constrained (see Section 15.2.4.1)
- The VLAN identifier associated with the frame (see Section 15.2.4.2)
- The priority assigned to the frame (see Section 15.2.4.3)
- The port on which the frame arrived (by virtue of the physical port or Aggregator that passed the frame to the Classification Engine)
- The time at which the frame arrived (by applying a timestamp upon receipt of the frame)
- Whether the frame was tagged or untagged upon receipt (from the VLAN and priority parsing processes)
- Whether the frame data payload is in canonical or non-canonical bit order (from the tag contents or the nature of the underlying physical port)
- Whether the frame carries a unicast or multicast destination, and so on

Once all of this information is collected, it makes sense to record the classification results along with the frame, so that other switch modules can simply inspect the classification vector rather than having to re-inspect the frame to determine its characteristics before taking appropriate action(s). Thus, most

[7] In the case of such a natively-signaled priority, priority regeneration may also be used to map locally-assigned priorities to globally-significant values.

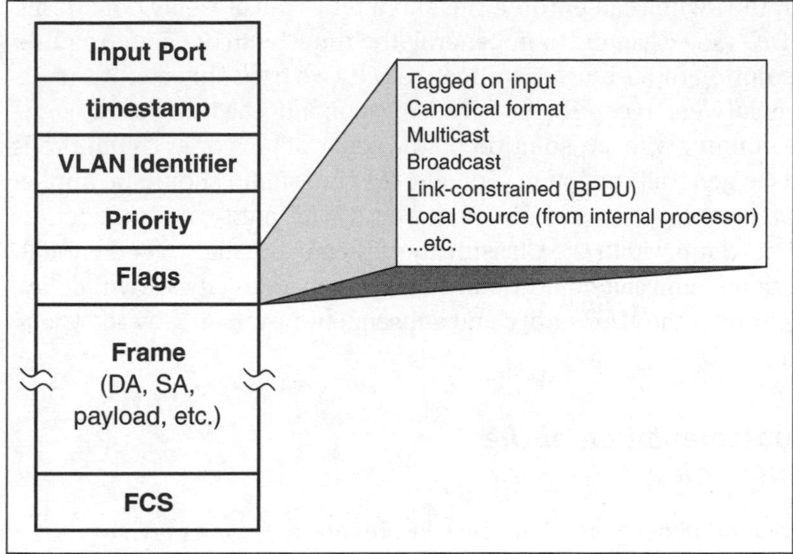

Figure 15.4 Internal switch header.

switches create an *internal switch header* for each received frame that is carried along with the frame during subsequent processing. The header is stripped prior to actual transmission through any output port; thus, the format of the switch header does not have to conform to any particular standard. It can be tailored to the specific needs and implementation of a given switch. Figure 15.4 depicts a hypothetical internal switch header.

Depending on the implementation, the internal switch header may actually be stored along with the frame contents (as depicted), or it may instead be associated with a queue entry for the frame; that is, the frame contents themselves may be stored separately from the header and linked with a buffer pointer.[8]

The timestamp is used so that the switch can determine the transit delay of a frame between reception and possible transmission through an output port.

[8] In Chapter 12 we discussed the theoretical problem of increasing the maximum length of an Ethernet frame to accommodate the 4-byte VLAN tag, and noted that no existing products were found that were unable to handle longer frames, as long as they weren't made too much longer. In practice, the limitation on how many bytes could be added to the frame before implementations would fail was a function of the length of practical internal switch headers. Many switch designs used (and still use) fixed-length buffers of 1,536 bytes (0x0600, a nice, round number), which includes both the frame itself and the internal switch header. Given the need to store a 1- or 2-byte port number, a 1- or 2-byte timestamp, 2 bytes of VLAN identifier and priority, a byte or so of flags, and perhaps a few bytes of buffer memory pointer(s) within this 1,536-byte buffer along with the Ethernet frame, the "threshold of pain" for an increased frame length was somewhere around 1,526 to 1,530 bytes maximum. Thus, we were able to increase the maximum Ethernet frame length from 1,518 (untagged) to 1,522 bytes (tagged), but could not have accommodated a much longer VLAN tag.

In this manner, the switch can enforce the Maximum Transit Delay constraint of IEEE 802.1D/Q (see Chapter 2). In general, the timestamp does not require either high resolution or absolute significance (i.e., we care only about the time difference between reception and transmission, not the time-of-day). Thus, a simple counter with a resolution on the order of tens or even hundreds-of-milliseconds is generally adequate. Ideally, the timestamp should be applied when the frame actually arrives at the input port's MAC entity; in practice, applying the timestamp within the Classification Engine is usually good enough. If desired, the timestamp can be normalized with respect to any known delay between reception by the MAC entity and subsequent processing by the Classification Engine.

15.2.4.5 Implementation of the Classification Engine

The performance demands placed on the Classification Engine may vary greatly, depending on:

- The nature of the classification rules supported (in particular, the allowable VLAN Ingress and Priority Rules)
- The data rate of the attached port
- The number of ports that may be aggregated prior to classification

In the simplest case (e.g., a core switch), the Classification Engine may only see VLAN-tagged frames from a single port. With no implicit rules to be applied, the task of the engine is fairly easy; simply parse the tag and extract the relevant fields (e.g., VLAN Identifier and Priority). These functions could be implemented in hardwired logic, as little flexibility is needed.[9]

On the other hand, an edge switch supporting multiple aggregated 100 Mb/s and/or 1000 Mb/s ports may have to deal with a large and complex set of VLAN and/or priority assignment rules. A simple hard-coded logic function will generally not provide either the capabilities or the flexibility required. In addition, wire-speed operation at 1000 Mb/s implies the ability to handle nearly 1.5 million frames per second.

As a result, the Classification Engine becomes a large and critical part of an edge switch designer's job. Some of the approaches taken to engine design include:

- *Hard-coded logic.* If the VLAN and priority rules are restricted to simple algorithms (e.g., port-based, MAC address-based, and/or protocol-type-based), the Classification Engine can still be implemented in fixed-

[9] This is one of the key justifications for the use of tags and the concept of core switches. High performance can be achieved with very little complexity at low cost.

function logic; that is, circuitry can be designed specifically to parse and extract information from the relevant predetermined frame fields. Wire-speed operation at relatively low cost is achieved at the expense of low rules complexity. Many switches take this approach.

- *Classification Processors.* If greater rules flexibility is required, a microprocessor can be used to parse and analyze frames under program control. The exact fields inspected and the actions taken become a function of software running on this Classification Processor.

  As often happens, we are presented with a three-way tradeoff. A microprocessor-based approach can provide lots of flexibility, but the performance will not equal that of a pure hardware-based solution for the same cost. We must either use a lot of processing power (through faster or multiple processors) at a greatly increased cost, or live with a lower level of performance (either slower port data rates or non-wire-speed operation).

  Seifert's Law of Networking #15

  Cost, Performance, Features. Pick two out of three.

  A number of specialized *network processors* are now available that are tailored specifically for Classification Engine and similar purposes. They often include multiple RISC processors, embedded control memory, and optimized high-speed data paths for switch applications.

- *Programmable state machines.* While a microprocessor approach is extremely flexible, the performance of a software-based engine can sometimes be inadequate, especially for very high port data rates (e.g., 1000 Mb/s or greater). However, a standard embedded microprocessor may provide more flexibility than is actually needed. The Classification Engine must parse and compare frame fields at high speeds against a set of pre-programmed rules, but it does not need many of the arithmetic or data manipulation features provided by a general-purpose processor. As a result, some high-performance switch designs have implemented parse-and-compare engines as programmable, finite-state machines, rather than using a traditional microprocessor.

  Ultimately, the set of VLAN and/or priority rules can be expressed as a sequence of bit strings and offsets that are compared against a received frame's contents. Rather than using software, you can design configurable hardware that is optimized for such arbitrary pattern matching in fixed and/or variable-position fields. The amount of logic required is much less than for a general-purpose microprocessor; as a result, optimized performance can be achieved at a lower cost than a pure software-based solution. The programmable-state machine may be implemented in traditional logic, as a programmable microengine (essentially a specialized microprocessor with a highly-restricted instruction set), or even as an embedded Field Programmable Logic Array (FPGA).[10] In most cases, embedded memory (typically SRAM) is used to store the rules set.

On a 1000 Mb/s Ethernet link, complete frames can arrive every 672 ns in the worst-case. Even dedicated logic would have difficulty applying a multitude of rules within this time limit. Thus, regardless of the approach taken, most designs resort to some form of pipelined processing for the application of multiple rules in sequence. Pipelining allows much more time for classification processing; however, it increases the absolute delay (latency) for all processed frames. That is, we can classify many more frames-per-second by setting up an assembly line and performing a variety of rules tests on multiple frames in parallel, but each frame experiences greater delay as it proceeds through the pipelined process before being forwarded by the switch.

It is especially important that the pipeline delay be bounded and within reasonable limits; that is, we cannot use an arbitrarily long pipeline to solve the problem of classification processing performance. Consider the plight of a high-priority frame belonging to a time-sensitive application flow (e.g., interactive voice traffic). We must make sure that the frame does not get excessively delayed while we attempt to determine its priority. Conceivably, we could exceed the delay allowance before we even get to switch the frame! Such delay considerations inevitably place an upper bound on the number of rules that may be applied to a given frame.

15.2.5 VLAN Filters

The VLAN Filter module implements the two VLAN input filters discussed in Chapter 12.

Acceptable Frame Filter A core switch may choose to admit for forwarding only those frames carrying an explicit VLAN tag and to discard untagged frames.[11] As shown in Figure 15.4, the switch header usually has a flag bit indicating whether a frame was tagged when it was received; the Acceptable Frame Filter need only inspect this flag and take the appropriate action.

Note that, regardless of the switch's policy with respect to forwarding untagged frames, frames whose Destination Address is in the reserved multicast range must still be locally sunk regardless of whether they are tagged or not; for example, a core switch must still implement the Span-

[10] One example of an early specialized Classification Engine is 3Com's Flexible Intelligent Routing Engine (FIRE) [CIAM98]. Many other approaches are expected in emerging high-performance switch designs.

[11] Discarded untagged frames may additionally be counted for network management purposes.

ning Tree Protocol, whose frames may be untagged.[12] Thus, the BPDU flag bit in the switch header (indicating that the destination was in the reserved multicast range), if set, overrides the VLAN Acceptable Frame Filter; BPDUs must always be passed to the local housekeeping processor.

VLAN Ingress Filter Under administrative control, a switch may be willing to accept (or reject) frames when the port on which a frame was received is not in the member set for the VLAN to which the frame belongs. When set to reject, a VLAN becomes symmetric; frames will be accepted only from ports on which the switch is also permitted to emit frames for this VLAN. Asymmetric VLANs can be created by accepting frames from ports where the switch is prohibited from sending frames for the given VLAN.

Figure 15.5 depicts a flowchart for the combined set of VLAN filters. In the preceding discussion we described the filters as comprising a separate, discrete module. Practical implementations may integrate these functions into the Lookup Engine, discussed in Section 15.2.6.

15.2.6 Lookup Engine

The Lookup Engine is the heart of the switch forwarding process. This module must decide what to do with frames that have successfully passed through all of the prior collection, classification, and VLAN Filter operations. The result of the lookup will be a set of output ports to which a given frame should be passed for further processing and possible transmission.

Table lookup is performed against the filtering database. This dynamically-maintained database contains the current mapping of Destination Addresses and VLANs to the port(s) through which the target recipient(s) are reachable. Note that for a switch supporting IEEE 802.1p multicast pruning, the filtering database will include both unicast and multicast destination mappings. Frames being sent to unicast destinations should map to a single output port in the absence of a lookup failure; frames being sent to multicast destinations will map to one or more output ports.

15.2.6.1 Generating the Output Vector

As depicted in Figure 15.6, the Lookup Engine takes as its input the Destination Address in the received frame, the VLAN to which that frame belongs, and the flag bits in the internal switch header, and provides as an output a vec-

[12] While an implementation of multiple spanning trees (spanning forest) may use tagged BPDUs, a switch may still need to deal with untagged BPDUs to support legacy devices capable only of using a single spanning tree.

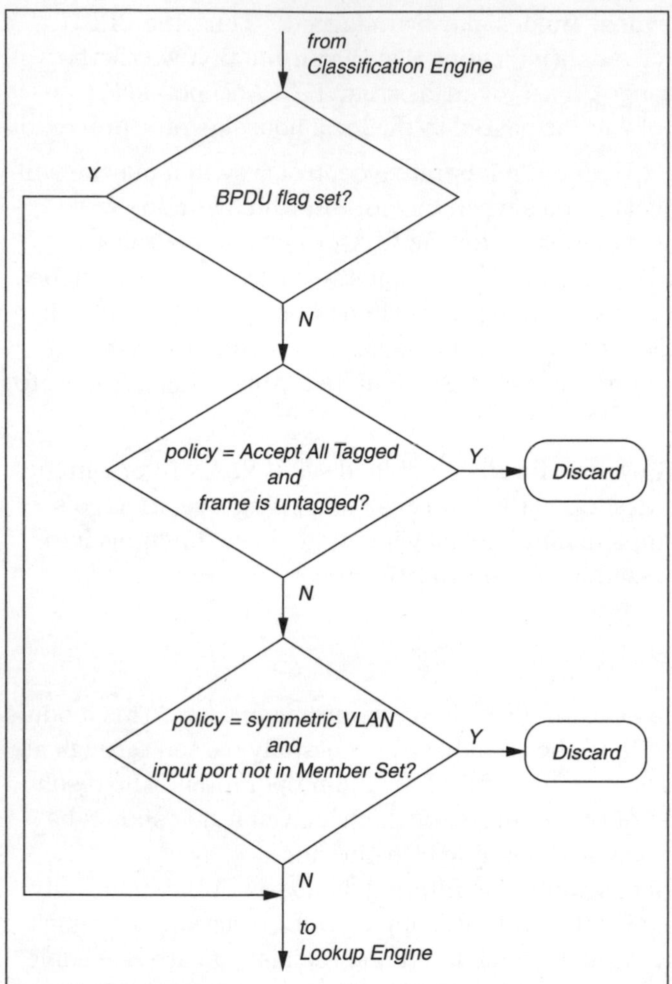

Figure 15.5 VLAN filter flow.

tor of ports to which this frame must be forwarded.[13] The Destination Address is in a known location within the frame buffer (typically the first field in the frame); the VLAN identifier and flag bits are stored in the internal switch header, as determined by the Classification Engine.

In Chapter 2 we discussed the operation of the table lookup process for a VLAN-unaware bridge. In that case, only the Destination Address was needed to determine the appropriate output port(s); the lookup decision was not tem-

[13] This describes the lookup process for a Layer 2 switch. In a Layer 3 switch (i.e., a router), the lookup is generally more complex, being a function of protocol type, network and/or subnet identifiers, and so on. In addition, the result may need to include not only the output port vector but information about whether the target destination is locally or remotely connected and next-hop routing information.

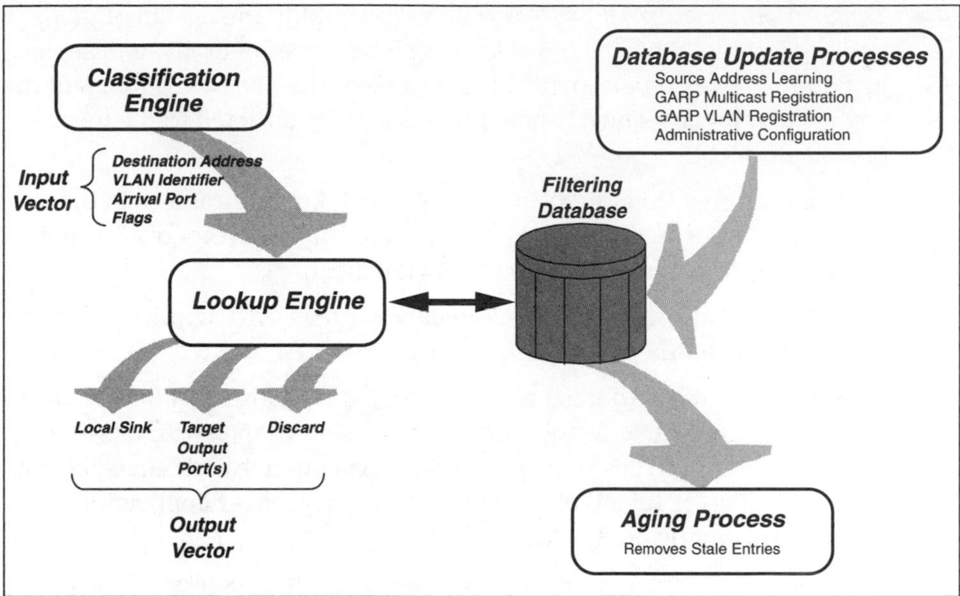

Figure 15.6 Filtering Database processes.

pered by VLAN membership information. In a VLAN-aware switch, we must consider the VLAN membership when determining the port(s) on which to forward each received frame; we cannot send a frame onto ports that are not in the member set for the VLAN associated with that frame.

Depending on the contents of the filtering database, the output port vector may be:

- *A single output port.* This will be the typical case for a frame when:
  - The Destination Address is a known unicast and the port from which the database entry was learned is in the member set for the VLAN to which the received frame belongs.
  - The Destination Address is a known multicast, it is known that only the one port is needed to reach all devices listening to that multicast, and that port is in the member set for the VLAN to which the received frame belongs.
- *Multiple output ports.* A frame may be forwarded to multiple output ports if the Destination Address is a multicast or an unknown unicast; the frame will be directed to all ports in the member set for the VLAN to which the received frame belongs (except the port on which the frame arrived).

- *The local housekeeping processor port.* To simplify the design of the Lookup Engine, the local housekeeping processor generally appears as just another port on the switch; that is, one of the possible outputs of the engine is to locally sink a frame. Frames may be directed to the local processor port if:
  - The Classification Engine has determined that the frame is in the range of addresses reserved for link-constrained protocols (as indicated by a flag bit in the internal switch header).
  - The Destination Address is associated with a GARP application that is enabled on the switch (e.g., GMRP or GVRP).
  - The Destination Address is equal to the MAC address of one of the switch's ports; that is, the frame is being sent to the switch itself as an end station. These frames may encapsulate network management traffic (SNMP, Telnet, etc.) or any other higher-layer application that may be running on the switch.[14]
  - A lookup failure occurs. The housekeeping processor can be used to handle lookup exception conditions, for example receiving a frame that belongs to a VLAN unknown to the switch.

  In some cases it may be appropriate to forward a frame to the local housekeeping processor in addition to one or more output ports of the switch. This might occur when a frame carries a multicast Destination Address and the local housekeeping processor is participating in the higher-layer application or protocol to which that multicast address maps.

- *No output port.* In some cases it is appropriate for the Lookup Engine to discard a frame without even sending it to the housekeeping processor. For example, in a switch using pure Independent VLAN Learning (IVL), if a frame is received with a known unicast Destination Address but with a VLAN association different from the one to which that destination is known to belong, the frame should be discarded. In lay terms, someone is trying to send a "red frame" to a "blue station." Regardless of the fact that the destination is known, the VLAN is incorrect, and the frame should not be forwarded.

Note that a frame will never be forwarded out the same port from which it arrived. This would violate the non-duplication invariant of the Data Link.

[14] Note that this case allows the housekeeping processor to be used for Network layer routing in what would otherwise be a pure Layer 2 switch. Many switches provide such a software-based routing capability. While the performance may not equal that of a device optimized for routing, the feature can provide Network layer connectivity in cases where performance is not critical.

15.2.6.2 Maintaining the Filtering Database

As discussed in Chapter 2, the filtering database in a simple bridge can be maintained just by Source Address learning and the aging function. A full-featured switch needs to learn not only the port mappings for each known unicast source, but the mapping of registered multicast addresses as well as the port member set for each VLAN.

As such, the filtering database is maintained by a variety of processes as depicted in Figure 15.6:

- Static database entries are created and modified under human administrator control, through network management.
- Dynamic unicast entries are learned by inspection of the Source Address in received frames.
- Multicast entries are learned through the GARP Multicast Registration Protocol (GMRP, see Chapter 10).
- Port VLAN mappings are maintained through a combination of administrator control and the GARP VLAN Registration Protocol (GVRP, see Chapter 12).

As discussed in Chapter 12, address learning may be performed independently for each VLAN (Independent VLAN Learning), or for multiple VLANs in the same data structure (Shared VLAN Learning).

15.2.6.3 Lookup Implementation

The implementation of the Lookup Engine is usually highly product- and vendor-specific. Depending on the complexity of the lookup operation and the number and data rates of the ports being supported, the Lookup Engine may incorporate:

- Content-addressable memory (CAM), providing almost instantaneous search and update capability through specialized associative storage (see Chapter 2).
- Pseudo-CAM, that is, using a standard memory (typically SRAM) together with a finite-state machine that emulates the operation of a CAM. Pseudo-CAMs generally provide both lower cost and lower performance when compared to true CAMs.
- Embedded microengines providing flexible, programmable lookup under software control.
- A combination of methods, for example a small CAM for a most-recently-used-entry cache, with a microprocessor-based fallback in the event of a cache miss.

Lookup Engines are generally modeled in one of two ways:

1. *Centralized Lookup.* In this model, a single engine is used to perform the table lookup for all frames received from all ports, as depicted in Figure 15.7. While the burden placed on this engine is the sum of the lookup requirements from all ports combined, there need only be one engine for the entire switch, reducing overall cost. Due to the performance limitations of a single engine, this approach is used primarily with switches comprising moderate numbers of ports with relatively low data rates (e.g., 10/100 Mb/s Ethernet desktop and workgroup switches). A centralized lookup model is most appropriate when a shared-memory or shared-bus switch fabric is present (see Sections 15.3.1 and 15.3.2).
2. *Distributed Lookup.* If a single Lookup Engine is incapable of keeping up with the frame arrival rate of all ports on the switch combined, it is usually necessary to provide a separate Lookup Engine for each port or group of ports, as depicted in Figure 15.8. While the cost will generally be greater than for a single Lookup Engine, this approach provides for greater and more scalable performance levels. The power of the combined Lookup Engines grows along with the number of ports deployed on the switch. In addition to the added cost, the switch designer must

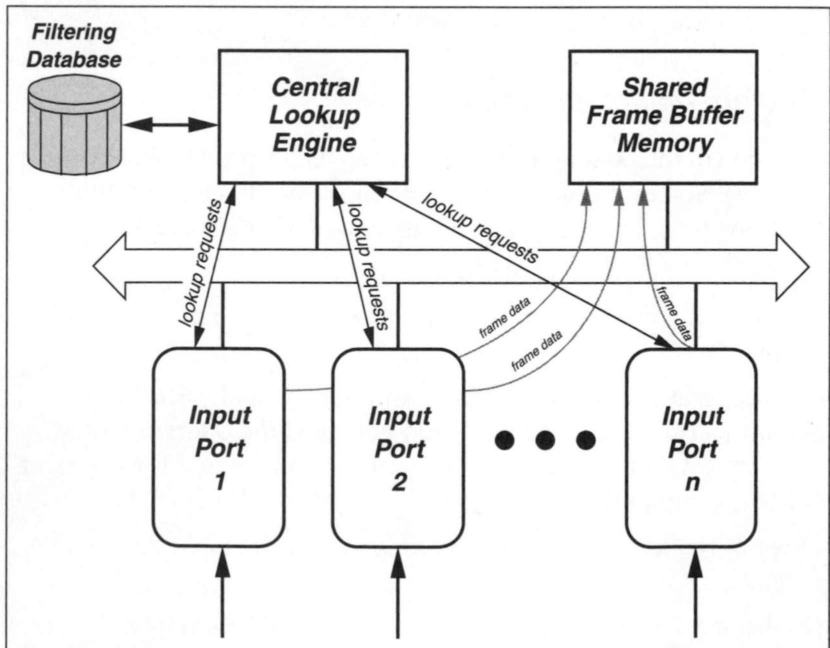

Figure 15.7 Centralized Lookup Engine.

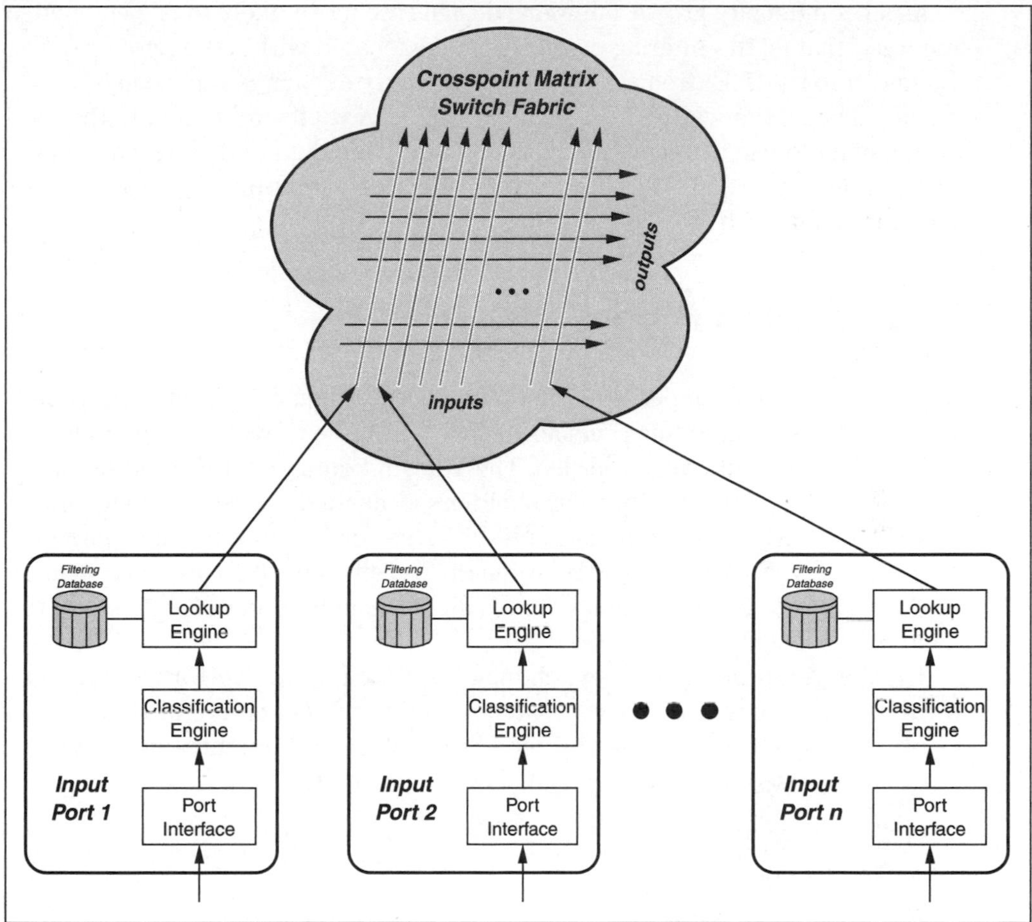

Figure 15.8 Distributed Lookup Engine.

solve the problem of properly distributing and maintaining the contents of the filtering database so that the Lookup Engines operate in a coherent manner. Normally, this implies the presence of a control data path to distribute database updates among the port interfaces.[15]

The filtering database itself is most commonly implemented in high-speed RAM, external to the Lookup Engine itself. Depending on the memory bandwidth required by the Lookup Engine, the memory interface may be a conventional address/data bus or may use acceleration techniques such as Double Data-Rate (DDR) or Rambus technology.

[15] A PCI bus is often provided for this purpose.

As silicon density grows, emerging designs are more likely to use embedded memory; that is, the filtering database can be located within the Lookup Engine chip itself. Extremely high-speed memory exchange rates can be achieved since the width of the memory can be virtually unlimited. Rather than having to use a conventional 32- or 64-bit wide data path, internal memory widths can be 256, 512, or more bits, effectively multiplying the available memory bandwidth.[16]

15.3 Switch Fabrics

The Receive data path performs all of the necessary qualification, classification, and table lookup functions needed to determine to which output port(s) a given frame should be forwarded. The Transmit data path takes these forwarded frames, applies additional qualifiers as needed, implements any prioritization and distribution policies, and sends the frames onto the appropriate output(s). A *switch fabric* sits between the Receive and Transmit data paths; its function is to transfer frames among all of the input and output ports of the switch.

The design of the internal switch fabric is critical to the performance of a switch. While a comprehensive treatment of this subject could fill its own book, in this section we look at three switch fabric architectures that have been widely used in commercial LAN switch products:

- Shared memory
- Shared bus
- Crosspoint matrix

Each approach reflects a distinct method used to move frames from input to output ports, and has its own set of characteristics, limitations, and design issues.

15.3.1 Shared Memory

A shared memory architecture entails the lowest level of both design and implementation complexity, and usually provides the lowest-cost solution in those products where it can be used. As a result, it is the most popular approach to fabric design in LAN switches. The primary limitation of a shared

[16] External memories are rarely practical in such wide organizations, since the number of pins required on both the memory and Lookup Engine devices would increase their cost prohibitively. By embedding the memory, we eliminate the pin restriction. A 512-bit wide, 8 ns SRAM can provide 64 Gb/s of raw memory bandwidth; this is the equivalent of a 64-bit wide external memory with a 1000 MHz clock.

memory switch fabric is the memory bandwidth; the speed at which data can be moved into and out of the shared memory will place an upper bound on both the number of ports in the switch and the data rates that can be supported on those ports.

15.3.1.1 Shared Memory Fabric Operation

A shared memory fabric uses a single common memory as the exchange mechanism for frames between ports, as depicted in Figure 15.9. Frames arriving through an input port's Receive data path are stored in the shared memory, where they can be assigned and channeled into the Transmit data path of the appropriate output port(s). Ideally, frames might be deposited directly from the receive port interface into the shared memory; in practice there is usually some amount of per-port memory required in the Receive data path where frames are stored temporarily during reception and classification. However, the bulk of the system memory is in the common buffer pool.

Initially, all of the frame buffers in the shared memory are unused; they begin their life in the pool of free buffers. Free buffers are assigned to frames as they arrive from the various input ports. Depending on the results obtained from the Lookup Engine, frames in the shared memory are linked into the appropriate output queues for the ports onto which they will be forwarded. These output queues represent the stream of frames to be processed in the Transmit data path (see Section 15.4). Frame discard is effected by returning a buffer to the free pool.

There are a number of advantages to a shared memory approach:

- Using a single large memory rather than individual buffer memories for each port lowers the total memory (and memory control logic) cost.
- The task of moving frames from one port to another becomes trivial. As shown in Figure 15.9, each port's output (transmit) queue comprises a linked list of buffer pointers representing frames stored in the shared memory. To move a frame from an input port to an output port simply entails linking a pointer to the appropriate frame buffer into the target output port's queue.
- The Lookup Engine can be implemented either as a single, common engine for all ports or in a distributed manner, with each port performing lookups for its own received frames. This is a function of the performance demands being placed on the Lookup Engine (see Section 15.2.6). Other fabric architectures (e.g., crosspoint matrices, see Section 15.3.3) make the use of a common Lookup Engine problematic.
- Lookup on a given frame may be completed before the frame is stored in the shared memory, or alternatively, frames may be stored while the lookup operation is performed in parallel. That is, a frame may be stored

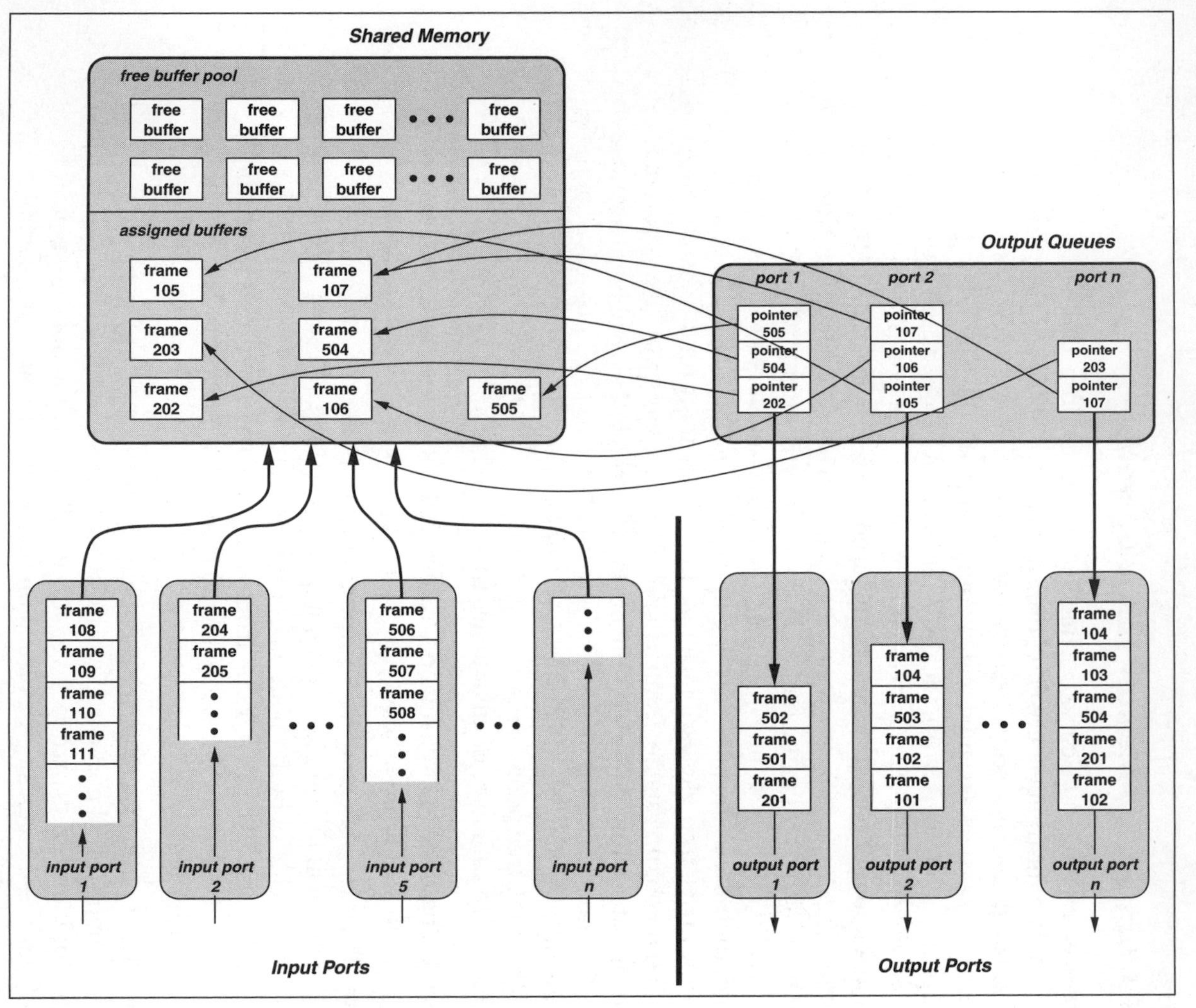

Figure 15.9 Shared memory architecture.

before the switch knows what to do with it; its buffer pointer can be linked to the appropriate output queue(s) once the Lookup Engine completes its work.

15.3.1.2 Multicasting in a Shared Memory Architecture

A shared memory fabric facilitates the ability to move frames from an input port to multiple output ports. Since the common memory is accessible from all ports, there is no need to perform multiple transfers or to provide special data paths for multicast traffic. Each frame buffer can be provided with a Transmit Port Map, as depicted in Figure 15.10.

The Lookup Engine determines the port(s) onto which the frame should be forwarded for transmission. If a frame is destined for more than one output port (e.g., it is a multicast or unknown unicast frame), the appropriate bit for each target output port is set to 1 in the Transmit Port Map. When the output port Transmit data path no longer needs a copy of the frame in the shared memory (either because it has completed transmission or because it has copied the frame into a local port buffer), it clears the bit for its port in the Transmit Port Map and checks whether there are any bits still set. Once all of the bits in the Transmit Port Map are clear, the frame buffer can be returned to the free pool.

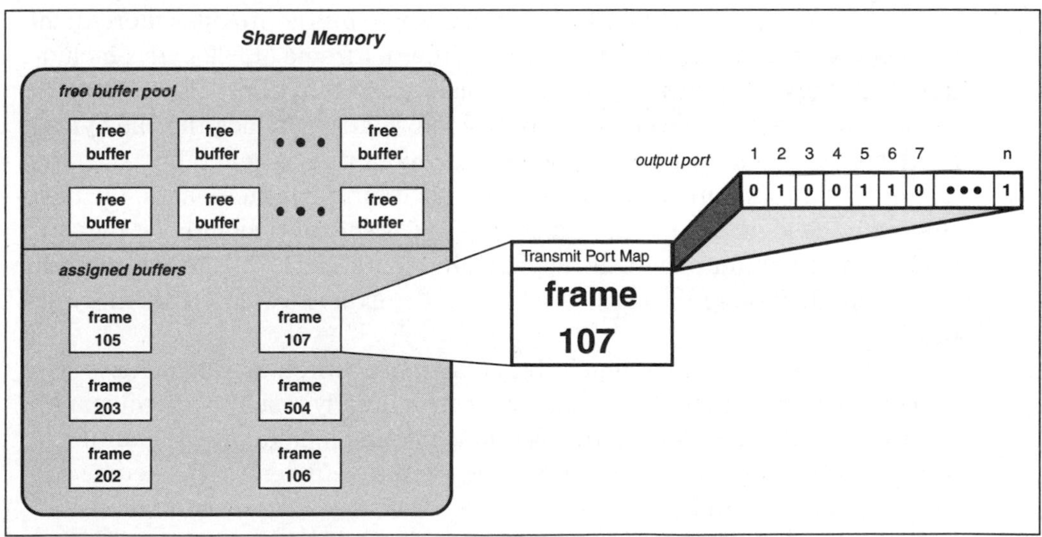

Figure 15.10 Transmit Port Map.

15.3.1.3 Buffer Organization

The shared memory is organized as a sequence of frame buffers (including any memory in the free buffer pool). However, there is no strict requirement that a given frame must be stored in one contiguous block. Frame buffers may be either contiguous or discontiguous. Each approach has its own set of advantages and disadvantages, as discussed in the following text.

15.3.1.3.1 Contiguous Buffers

The design of the memory interface and control logic is much simpler when buffers are contiguous. A contiguous buffer can be identified by a single pointer representing the location of the start of the frame. A Direct Memory Access (DMA) engine used to move frames into and out of the shared memory can work from this single buffer pointer; there is no need to scatter or gather frame fragments into disjoint portions of the shared memory.

The greatest simplicity occurs when the frame buffers are both contiguous and of fixed length. Using this scheme, the entire shared memory can be preallocated into distinct, numbered frame buffers. There is never any need to provide complex dynamic memory allocation when taking this approach. However, each fixed-length buffer must be large enough to store a maximum-length frame; to the extent that the received frames are smaller than the maximum possible length, the efficiency of memory utilization will drop. Thus, there is a clear tradeoff between the cost of the memory and the cost of the memory interface logic.

One common approach used in Ethernet switches is to allocate fixed-length contiguous buffers of 2,048 (2K) bytes. A 2-Kbyte buffer provides more-than-adequate storage for a maximum-length Ethernet frame (1,522 bytes, including VLAN tag), plus the internal switch header, Transmit Port Map, and any implementation-specific memory control information. In fact, the 526 bytes available for this internal overhead is much more than is generally necessary; however, if a round number (in binary) is used for the buffer length, the memory interface logic can use the frame number as the most-significant bits of each memory buffer pointer, as depicted in Figure 15.11. This represents a further simplification of the hardware logic at the expense of lower memory utilization.

While it is possible to design a shared memory switch fabric that uses variable-length contiguous buffers, this will generally result in a significant increase both in memory interface complexity and memory fragmentation. As a result, if the system cannot tolerate the memory efficiency afforded by contiguous, fixed-length buffers, designers generally opt for a discontiguous buffer allocation scheme, since this provides both higher memory utilization and variable-length buffer support without incurring significant memory fragmentation problems.

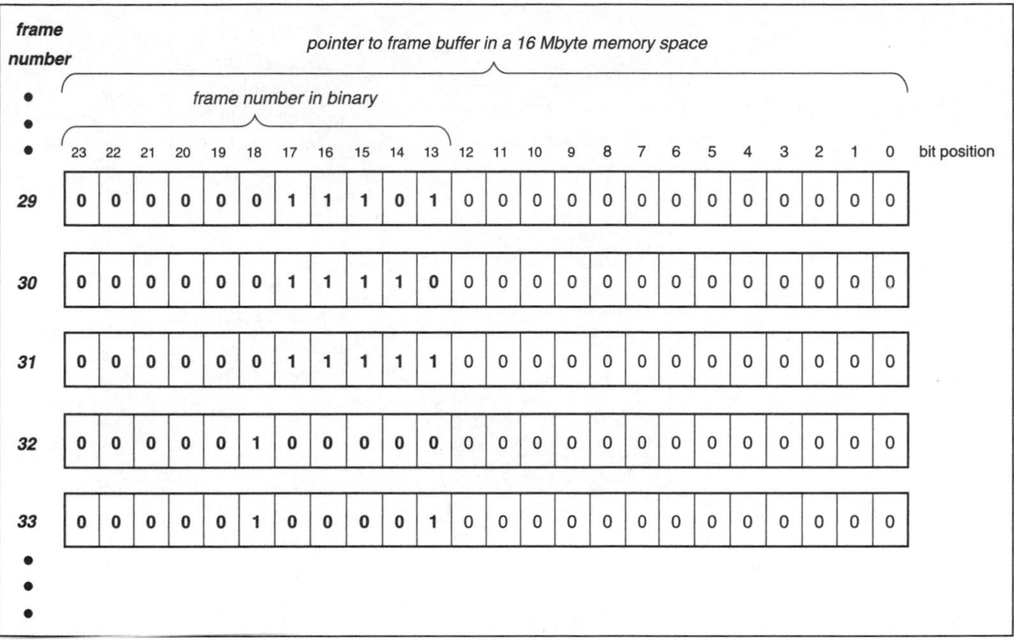

Figure 15.11 Using frame numbers as buffer pointers.

15.3.1.3.2 Discontiguous Buffers

Rather than storing a frame in a single block of memory, the use of discontiguous buffers allows a single frame to be stored as a series of frame segments scattered throughout memory. Thus, the start of a frame is identified by a single buffer pointer, but that pointer only indicates the first of the frame's possible segments. The entire frame is referenced by traversing a linked-list of buffer pointers, as depicted in Figure 15.12.

The linked list of memory pointers may be stored either in the output queue data structure (as shown in Figure 15.12) or within the frame data buffer segments themselves by having the end of each data buffer segment provide either the next memory pointer or a flag indicating the end of the linked chain.

Each frame segment can be variable in length; usually there is some minimum value supported by the hardware, with the total length of each segment being some multiple of this minimum. A discontiguous variable-length buffer approach uses memory much more efficiently than any fixed-length buffer scheme. In the worst case, the amount of memory allocated that goes unused is one minimum-length buffer less 1 byte, rather than a maximum frame.[17]

A linked-list buffer scheme can handle much larger frames than a fixed-

[17] It is common practice to use a 64-byte minimum segment length when using a discontiguous buffer approach in an Ethernet switch, since this is the length of the minimum Ethernet frame. The larger the minimum length of a segment, the fewer links will be required for a given frame, at the expense of somewhat reduced memory efficiency.

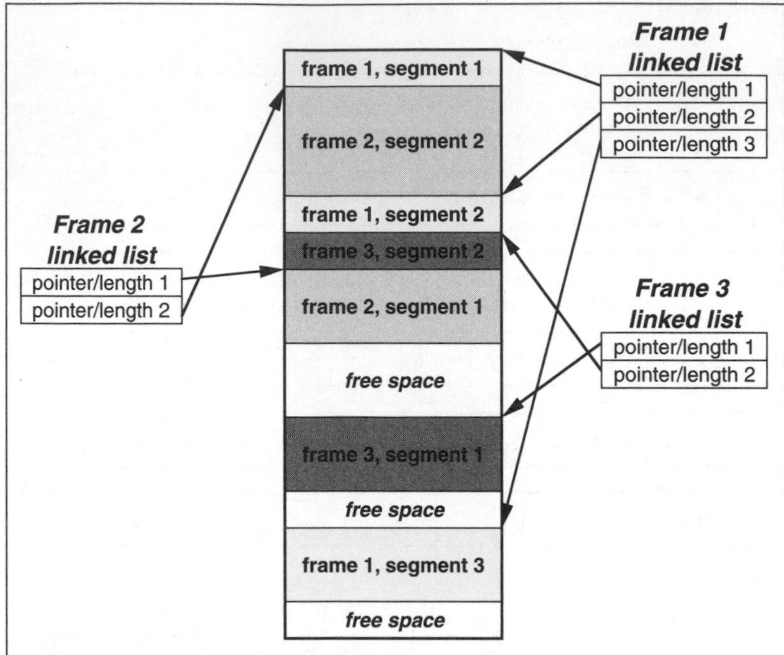

Figure 15.12 Discontiguous buffer pointers.

length approach without sacrificing memory efficiency. Token Ring and FDDI LANs can support longer frames than can Ethernets; while the memory inefficiency of using fixed-length buffers is often tolerated for 1,522-byte Ethernet frames, an increase in memory interface complexity may be justified for the 18-Kbyte frames used in some Token Ring systems.

WHAT'S THE BIG DEAL ABOUT MEMORY ORGANIZATION?

In most computer contexts, we gladly accept greater complexity in the memory data structures in exchange for better efficiency. Why are we so concerned over the organization of the buffers in switch memory?

A computer program can easily manipulate complex memory data structures; other than requiring additional care and thought in the coding of the program, there is no cost impact associated with the implementation of discontiguous, variable-length buffers as linked-list queues in software. For performance reasons, high-speed switches cannot implement the shared memory data structures in software. All of the buffer manipulation and queue management must be performed by dedicated hardware—typically a set of finite-state machines—within the switch. Any complexity imposed on the organization of the memory buffers results in more complex and expensive logic for the memory interface. Thus, there is a real cost tradeoff between memory efficiency and data structure complexity that must be addressed by the switch fabric designer.

15.3.1.4 Memory Bandwidth Limitations

Quite simply, if a system *can* use a shared memory switch fabric, then it probably *should* use a shared memory fabric. A shared memory architecture is usually the simplest and lowest-cost solution available to the switch designer. Given this conclusion, why would any switch designer not choose a shared memory approach?

Since all frames must pass through the single, common shared memory, the speed of the memory interface will ultimately limit the capacity of the switch. For example, consider a memory system with a 32-bit wide data path, using 10 ns synchronous static RAM (SSRAM) and a 100 MHz clock. Each frame must pass across the memory interface at least twice—once when written from the input port and once when read into the output port.[18] This effectively halves the available memory bandwidth. Even in the best case of streaming data (i.e., 10 ns memory access times can only be achieved for multiple sequential reads or writes of data, not for individual random accesses) the aggregate switch capacity is limited to:

$$32 \text{ bits} \times 100 \text{ MHz} \div 2 = 1.6 \text{ Gb/s}$$

In practice, we cannot get the full benefit of data streaming through synchronous RAM; the actual performance improvement due to streaming will be a function of the design of the messaging system used to move frame data into and out of the memory. Typically, the usable memory bandwidth will be on the order of 50 to 70 percent of the maximum. Furthermore, to prevent unbounded queuing delays, the effective memory bandwidth should be undersubscribed by a factor of at least 30 percent. This results in a usable non-blocking switch capacity on the order of 35 to 50 percent of the raw memory bandwidth, or about 550 to 800 Mb/s in the example just given.

Assuming full to duplex operation on all ports, this capacity is adequate for a 10 Mb/s switch with a port count of 24 to 48 or more, or even a 48-port 10 Mb/s switch with two 100 Mb/s uplinks.[19] The switch cannot provide non-blocking operation for more than eight 100 Mb/s ports. Thus, the design example given is appropriate only for desktop or small workgroup switch applications.

15.3.1.5 Increasing the Memory Bandwidth

A number of approaches can be taken to increase the memory bandwidth so that a shared memory fabric can be used for higher-performance switches:

[18] Multicast traffic may have to be read into multiple output ports, as discussed in Section 15.3.1.2.

[19] If the ports are operating in half duplex mode, the design can either support more ports or provide additional margin for non-blocking operation.

- *Use the fastest memories available.* Clearly, faster memory products will allow the system designer to use higher clock speeds without incurring wait states. However, there is always a physical limit to the speed of semiconductor RAM, based on currently available technology. In addition, the fastest memories are always the most expensive, negating some of the benefit of using a shared memory architecture.
- *Use a wider memory data path.* While the memories themselves may be clock-rate limited, the total memory bandwidth can be increased by widening the data path. As more bits can be transferred in a single clock cycle, the memory bandwidth will increase proportional to the width of the memory interface. In our example, changing to a 64-bit-wide data path would double the memory bandwidth. This would allow the fabric to support a non-blocking 100 Mb/s workgroup switch with 12 to 16 ports.

  Standard memory products are typically designed for use in 16-, 32-, or 64-bit-wide data paths. In addition, advances in memory technology tend to be directed toward achieving greater memory density, that is, stuffing more and more memory into each chip. The smallest SSRAM memory chip configurations today provide about 1 megabit of depth for each bit of width. Thus, a 64-bit-wide memory cannot generally be built with less than 8 Mbytes of total capacity (64 Mbits). If more memory bandwidth is needed, you can go to a 128- or 256-bit-wide data path; however, this will double or quadruple the total memory size (to 16 or 32 Mbytes) as a consequence of using standard memory chips. In many cases, the result is higher memory bandwidth, but with more total memory than is actually needed by the switch. Since conventional memory products are not optimized for such wide-yet-shallow memory arrays, you end up having to pay for more memory than you really wanted just to get a faster path.
- *Use non-traditional memory.* Rather than taking the brute force approach of simply widening the data path of a conventional memory array, there are alternative memory designs that provide higher interface bandwidth, including:
  - *Synchronous Graphic RAM (SGRAM).* Like LAN switches, graphic display subsystems often need memory configurations that are wider and shallower than traditional computer memories. Some semiconductor manufacturers provide specialty SGRAMs with this desirable characteristic. While they are occasionally used in LAN switches, they are more expensive than conventional RAMs due their lower volume and limited market.
  - *Rambus Dynamic RAM (RDRAM).* Designed for use in high-performance PCs, workstations, and servers, RDRAM supports clock speeds of 600 MHz and more across the memory interface. Again, this

higher-performance memory comes at a higher price, although RDRAM has the capability of extending the use of shared memory switch fabrics to much higher-end switch products.

- *Use embedded memory.* Even if you are willing to pay for a 32 Mbyte, 256-bit-wide SSRAM array to achieve a 4 to 6 Gb/s switch capacity, the sheer number of pins required to connect the memory array to the rest of the switch logic becomes problematic. Much of the cost of the custom-designed and manufactured ASIC devices used in high-performance switches is related to IC packaging requirements. If more than 256 pins are needed just to connect to the memory (there are a lot of arbitration, control, and power signals needed in addition to the memory data path lines), this will significantly increase the cost of the switch.

  An increasingly attractive alternative is to embed the memory within the switch ASIC itself. If the memory is internal rather than external, no pins (or their associated pads) are required. In addition, internal logic can be clocked much faster than external memories, due to lower lead inductance and reduced drive currents. Embedded memory data paths of 512 bits or more can be achieved at little or no cost penalty.

  For example, an 8 ns, 1,024-bit-wide embedded SRAM has a raw memory bandwidth of 128 Gb/s! Even if this bandwidth cannot be used with perfect efficiency, such an array could easily support a non-blocking campus-class switch with 16 to 24 Gigabit Ethernet ports. In addition, the memory size can be tailored to the exact requirements of the switch; there is no need to stay within the strictures of merchant memory chips. Of course, embedded memory comes with its own set of problems:

  - Large embedded memories can take up much of the available die space of an ASIC. SRAMs in particular are space-intensive; DRAM takes less space, but can generally run only at much slower clock speeds.
  - Embedded memory is more expensive bit-for-bit than merchant memory chips.
  - Not all semiconductor manufacturing processes can support embedded memory, which may limit the available suppliers.

Problems notwithstanding, as semiconductor densities increase and embedded memory becomes more of a commodity technology, this approach will become increasingly attractive for new switch designs and will extend the use of shared memory architectures to even higher levels of performance. Even when it is impractical to use for the switch fabric itself (due to the large amount of memory typically required), embedded memory may be used for the output port queue data structures or the internal storage required by the Lookup and/or Classification Engines (see Sections 15.2.4 and 15.2.6).

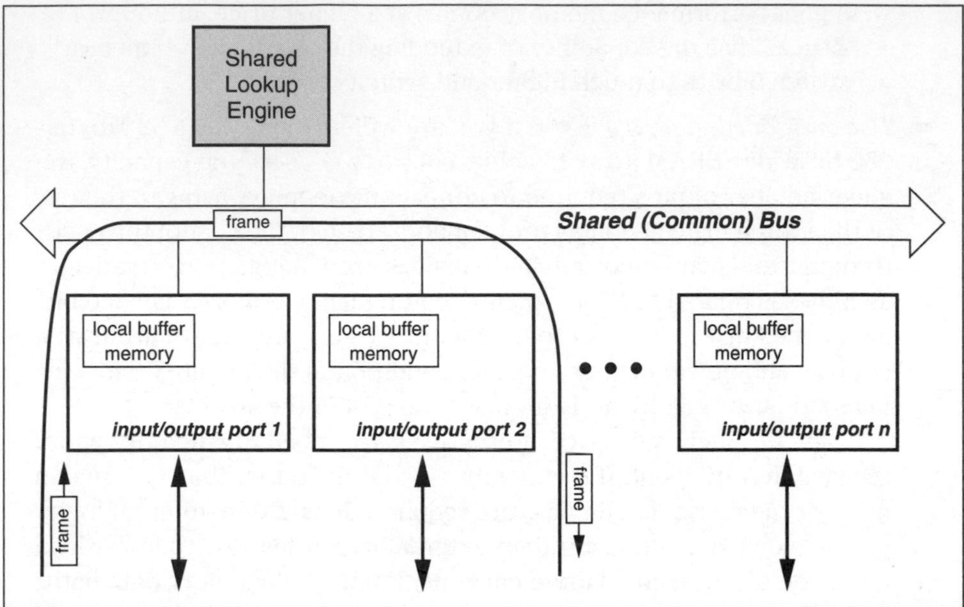

Figure 15.13 Shared-bus architecture.

15.3.2 Shared Bus

In the old days, memory was much slower than it is today, and most embedded processor systems were designed around 16-bit-wide internal data paths. In that environment, the available switching capacity of a shared memory fabric would be quite limited, typically on the order of about 150 Mb/s.[20] Thus, shared memories were practical only in 10 Mb/s switching systems with low port densities (15 or fewer ports for non-blocking operation). If a switch comprised a greater number of ports, or ports operating at higher data rates, it was usually necessary to change the fabric design.

A shared bus architecture (depicted in Figure 15.13) uses a common bus as the exchange mechanism for frames between ports, rather than a common memory. Each port (or small group of ports) has its own memory, both for input and output queues, depending on the design. The main advantages of this approach are:

- A shared bus can often provide higher bandwidth than an older-style shared memory. For example, a 32 bit, 33 MHz PCI has a theoretical maximum capacity of slightly over 1 Gb/s—more than 7 times the 150

[20] This is for a system using 25 ns SRAM and a 16-bit data path, after allowance for overhead, undersubscription, and two memory operations (write/read) per frame.

Mb/s available from the preceding example. Proprietary buses can be used to achieve even higher capacities through the use of wider bus widths or faster clocks. A 1-Gb/s shared bus architecture can support a moderate number of 100 Mb/s ports (typically eight) and/or a very large number of 10 Mb/s ports.

- A shared bus is accessed only once per transaction (rather than once in, once out as in the shared memory case), so the effective capacity is doubled relative to the shared memory approach.
- Shared bus fabrics provide a natural mechanism for multicast transfers; it takes the same amount of time and bus capacity to transfer a frame to a single output port or to multiple output ports.
- A shared bus architecture can support either a distributed Lookup Engine (i.e., one engine on each interface) or a shared, common engine, depending on the performance demands of the system. A shared engine can be connected either to the same bus as is used for data transfers (as depicted in Figure 15.13) or to a separate, dedicated control bus. In the former case, some bus capacity is used to transfer header information to the Lookup Engine (and lookup results back to the requesting interface); this capacity cannot also be used for data transfers. The latter case imposes the greater cost and complexity of providing two bus structures.

The disadvantages of a shared bus architecture include:

- *A separate memory is needed for each port (or group of ports).* As there is no common, shared memory among ports, each interface module must provide local memory for both input and output-queued frame storage. The memory on each interface must be sized for the anticipated worst-case load through the port. Depending on traffic patterns, some of the ports may become memory-starved while ample free buffers are available on other port interfaces. When all of the frames shared a common buffer pool, memory could be used more efficiently; that is, the statistical nature of load distribution allows a shared memory to support more traffic for a given memory capacity. Thus, for a given level of performance, a shared bus architecture will require more memory than a shared memory system, which increases cost.
- *Some means is required to arbitrate for the shared bus.* A shared bus appears very much like an internal, high-speed, shared-media LAN. As such, each port must contend for use of the bus. Once access is granted, the port uses the bus to transfer a frame from its local memory (input queue) to the local memory (output queue) of the target destination port.
- *Multiple input queues may be required.* Depending on the worst-case bus latency, there may be a need for a prioritized arbitration mechanism

and/or multiple input queues at different priority levels. This effect is much more prevalent in a crosspoint matrix fabric, and is discussed in detail in Section 15.3.3.5.

The product literature for many early modular internetworking devices prominently displayed and touted their backplane capacity. This was usually a clear sign that the system used a shared bus architecture; the capacity of the shared backplane bus guided the potential user as to the number and data rates of the interfaces that could be configured in the system while sustaining non-blocking operation.[21]

A shared bus architecture does not scale well; it is generally not possible to increase either the data rate or the bus width without redesigning all of the switch port interfaces (in particular, any ASIC devices designed to connect to, and arbitrate for, the shared bus). Most modern switches use either a shared memory or a crosspoint matrix fabric; rarely is there much call for a shared bus anymore. As memories have gotten cheaper, faster, more sophisticated, and/or embedded, the small (if any) improvement possible from a shared bus is usually not enough of a change to provide sufficient benefit.

15.3.3 Crosspoint Matrix

As depicted in Figure 15.14, a crosspoint matrix switch fabric creates a transient connection between an input and an output port for the duration of a frame (or subset of a frame) exchange. There is effectively a matrix of electronic switches available to create a connection between every possible input and output port pair. The fabric control logic connects a given input to the appropriate output(s) on a frame-by-frame basis, in a matter of nanoseconds, and then disconnects the ports in preparation for the next frame exchange. A crosspoint matrix fabric is often called a *crossbar;* the terms are synonymous.

Because every input port can be connected to some output port at the same time, the total data transfer capability of the crosspoint matrix can be much larger than that of a shared bus, and actually grows with the number of ports.

15.3.3.1 Multicasting in a Crosspoint Matrix Fabric

Unlike a shared memory or shared bus architecture, a crosspoint matrix provides no natural means to transfer frames from one input port simultaneously to multiple output ports. There are two common approaches to dealing with multicast traffic in a crosspoint matrix:

[21] For example, the first family of products from Wellfleet (later Bay Networks, then Nortel Network) used a standard VMEbus as the shared backplane. Operating with a 10 MHz clock and a 32-bit-wide bus, the system had an aggregate capacity of 320 Mb/s; this was considered quite a high-performance device at the time (late 1980s).

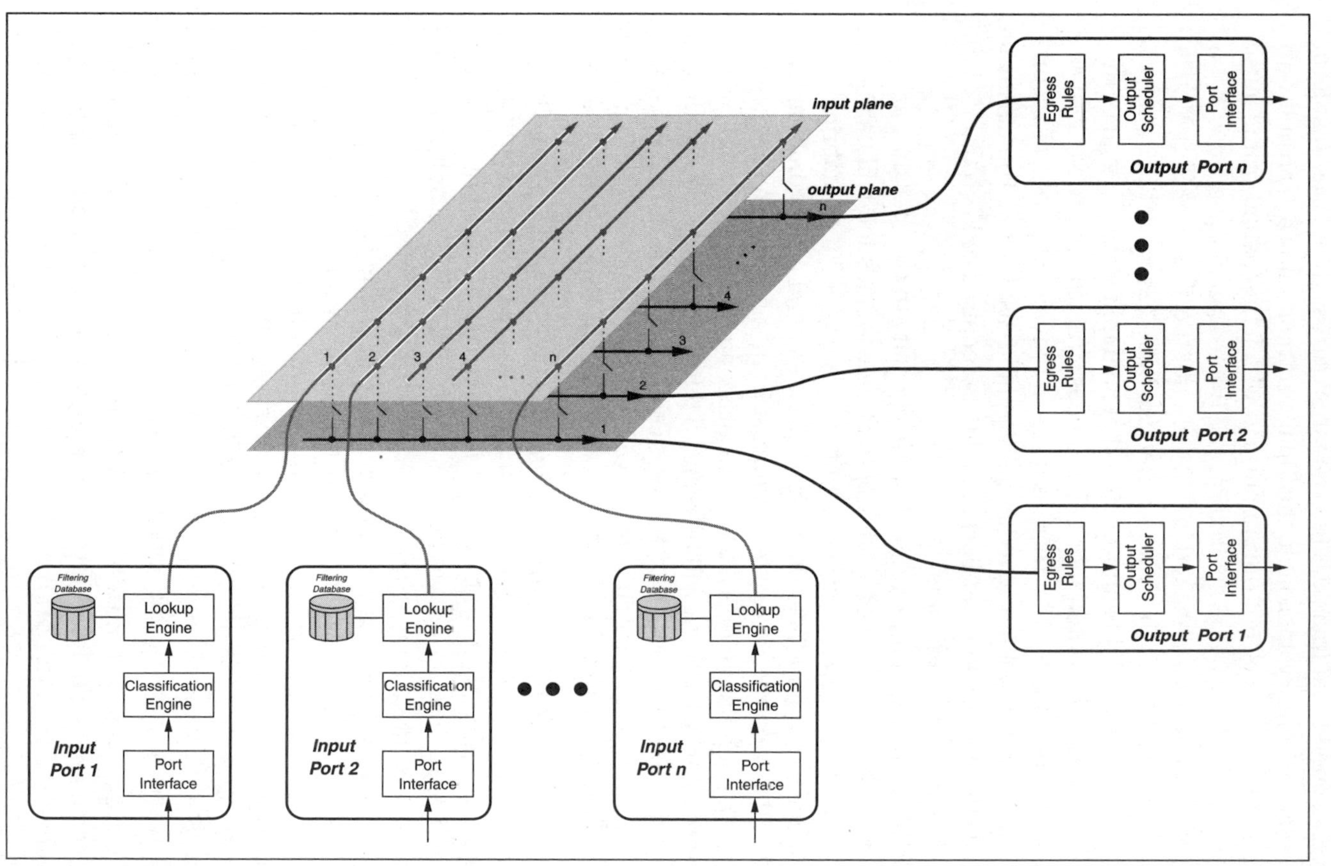

Figure 15.14 Crosspoint matrix fabric.

- *Use multiple unicast transfers.* Simply put, any time a frame needs to be transferred to multiple output ports, the input port can execute a series of individual transfers to each target across the fabric. Just as in the shared memory approach, the input port maintains a Transmit Port Map indicating the set of output ports to which the instant frame must be transferred. As fabric arbitration and frame transfer proceeds, each target output port is checked off the list until the Transmit Port Map is all zeros, after which the frame buffer can be released by the input port.

  The advantage of this approach is that it simplifies the design of the crosspoint matrix switch fabric. If multicast frames are propagated as multiple unicast transfers, there is no need to make any special accommodation within the fabric to handle the multicast traffic. The disadvantage is the increased input port complexity required to keep track of the progress of multicast transfers.

  While it may seem wasteful of fabric capacity to transfer the same frame multiple times, consider that the frame in question will be using bandwidth on all of the target output ports anyway.[22] If the fabric is designed to support the sum of the capacities of all ports combined, it will still be non-blocking when multicast frames are transferred separately to each output port. Any overprovisioning of capacity that was factored into the design will be reduced due to the frame replication caused by multicast traffic. The design can still handle the total capacity, but queuing delay (switch latency) will increase to the extent that multicast traffic comprises a significant portion of the total offered load.

- *Provide a dedicated multicast data path.* Alternatively, a switch can provide one (or more) logical output ports that are used specifically for multicast traffic. The multicast port is effectively a shared bus that is routed to each of the output ports in addition to the unicast line for that port, as depicted in Figure 15.15.

  This approach makes sense when multicast traffic is expected to be a small portion of the total offered load and the switch fabric is blocking in nature or has little excess capacity. By offloading the multicast traffic from the individual port outputs on the switch matrix, we avoid the frame replication discussed earlier and dedicate most of the capacity for unicast traffic, which is assumed to comprise the bulk of the frame load. The disadvantages of this approach are:

  - Each output port must be equipped to receive frames from its dedicated unicast output line from the switch fabric as well as from the shared multicast port output.

[22] Some frames may not actually be transmitted at the output due to the operation of the Egress Filter (see Section 15.4.1), but this is generally a very small fraction of the total traffic and can be ignored.

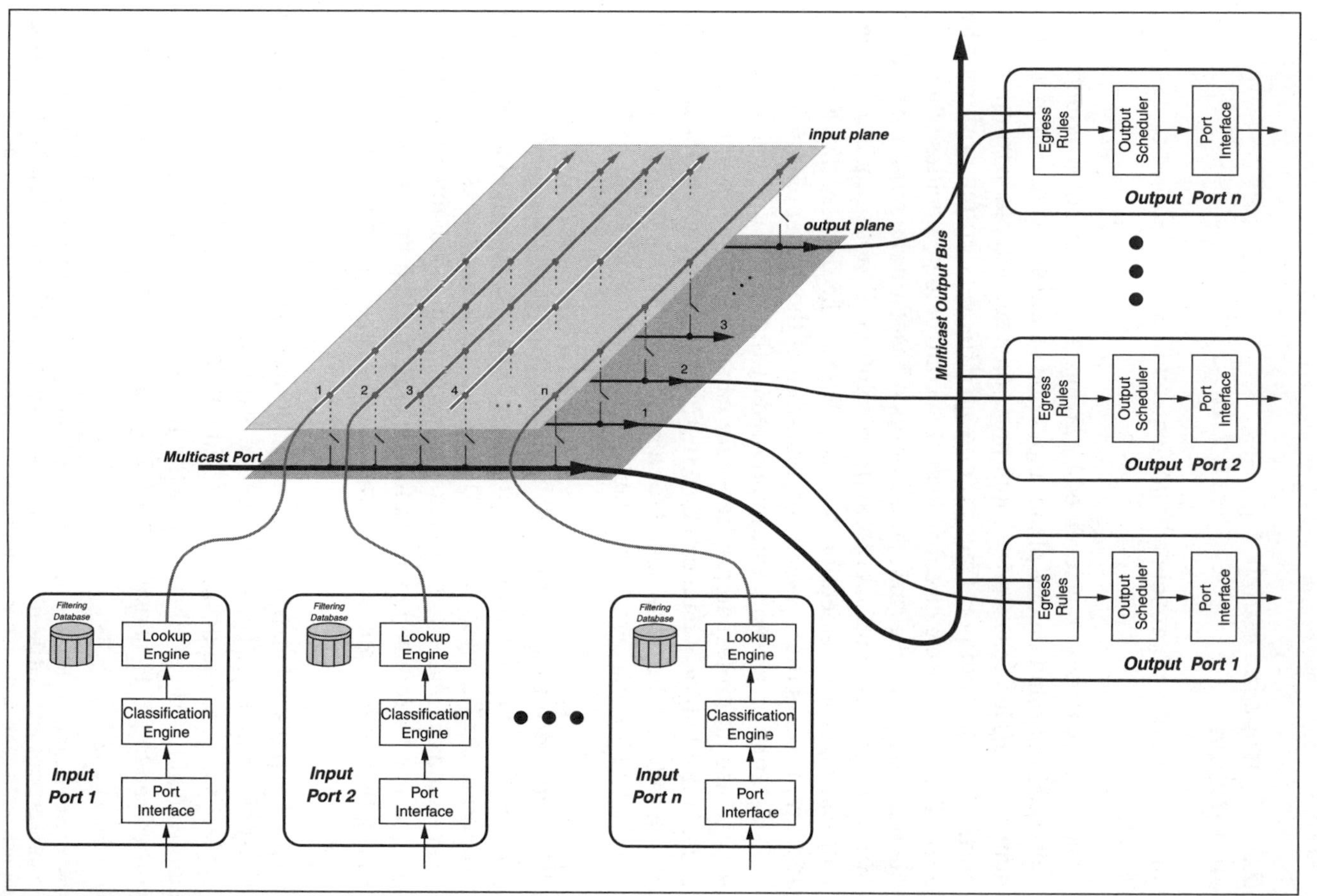

Figure 15.15 Shared multicast port.

- The capacity of the shared multicast bus may be a limiting factor if multicast traffic comprises a significant fraction of the total load.[23]

15.3.3.2 Crosspoint Matrix Implementation

There are two popular approaches to implementation of the crosspoint matrix:

- A *physical matrix* can be created by laying down strips of conductive material in parallel on one plane (input ports) and strips of conductive material at right angles to the input ports on a second plane (output ports).[24] Each input port trace is connected to every output port trace by a transistor switching circuit; the switch control logic decides which of the transistor switches are closed or open based on the requests made by the input port controllers and the resolution of those requests by the fabric arbitrator (see Section 15.3.3.5). That is, the depiction in Figure 15.14 represents the physical configuration of the crosspoint matrix.

  Depending on the data rate supported by the fabric, it is often necessary to use multiple material traces for each port (both input and output). Multiple bits of data can then be transferred at each clock tick, which reduces the clock speed for a given rate of data transfer at the expense of increasing the pin count for the switch ports on the fabric chip.

- A *logical matrix* can be created by defining the signals for each output port as a logic function derived from the signals at the input ports, under control of the fabric arbitrator. That is, a crosspoint matrix can be built from standard digital logic blocks. As with the physical matrix, clock speeds can be reduced by defining each input and output in terms of multiple parallel signals at the expense of increasing the pin count at the fabric interface.

In general, a physical matrix can be smaller and less complex, resulting in a lower-cost switch fabric. The disadvantage is that the integrated circuitry must typically be custom-designed and laid out; it is not generally possible to build a physical matrix in silicon using the conventional IC design tools used for synthesized logic. The advantage of a logical matrix is that because it uses

[23] At least one switch fabric IC offers the capability to make a tradeoff between the amount of shared multicast capacity and the number of unicast ports that can be used. That is, the system designer can assign any of the fabric's output ports for multicast use; the shared multicast bus aggregates the selected number of multicast ports into a single logical channel. Those ports not assigned to multicast service can be used as unicast outputs.

[24] Normally, polysilicon is used for the conductive material in an integrated circuit.

synthesizable logic it becomes much more portable across semiconductor manufacturing processes and requires less specialized design skills.

Depending on the clock speed and the width of the port interface to the matrix, a huge switching capacity can be created. For example, a 16-port, 16-bit-wide (16 signals per port) matrix running on a 100 MHz clock has an effective data transfer capability of 25.6 Gb/s. Such a fabric would be suitable for huge numbers of 100 Mb/s ports and/or quite a few Gigabit Ethernet ports.[25]

15.3.3.3 The Head-of-Line Blocking Problem

Crosspoint matrices can provide an extremely port-scalable, high-capacity switch fabric. However, they suffer from a systemic problem known as *head-of-line blocking.* Consider what happens when multiple input ports must contend for the availability of a single output port. Figure 15.16 depicts a situation where a lot of traffic is destined for output port 9; ports 1, 2, and 3 each have frames queued and waiting for port 9 to become available. Assuming that the switch arbitration algorithm is fair, those frames will be transferred to port 9 in an orderly manner. The switch capacity will be evenly distributed among all of the input ports that have traffic destined for the single target output port.

The problem is with port 4. Port 4 has frames queued and waiting to be transferred to a variety of output ports. However, the first frame in the queue is destined for output port 9, which we know to be experiencing short-term congestion. Since only one input port at a time is able to transfer frames to output port 9, each input port with a frame queued for port 9 must wait its turn. Assuming fair, round-robin scheduling, port 4 may have to wait for ports 1, 2, and 3 to transfer their respective frames to port 9 before it gets to unload the frame at the head of its queue. In the meantime, there are frames waiting in port 4's input queue behind the frame destined for port 9. These frames are targeted at uncongested ports; that is, the target output ports (ports 6, 1, and 3 in Figure 15.16) are idle and awaiting traffic. However, port 4 cannot proceed to transfer those frames because the frame at the head of the line is blocking progress.

Note that this situation is not a result of any flaw in port 9; there is a transient overload condition where the traffic targeted at port 9 temporarily exceeds that output link's capacity. The switch is (properly) resolving that short-term congestion by spreading the offered load over time. During that spreading time, frames must wait in queues within the switch. Ideally, we would like the frames to wait in the output queue for port 9, but we need to transfer frames across the switch

[25] An ASIC implementation of such a crosspoint matrix would require ($16 \times 16 \times 2 =$) 512 pins just for the input and output port connections. Additional pins would be needed for switch control, power, and so on.

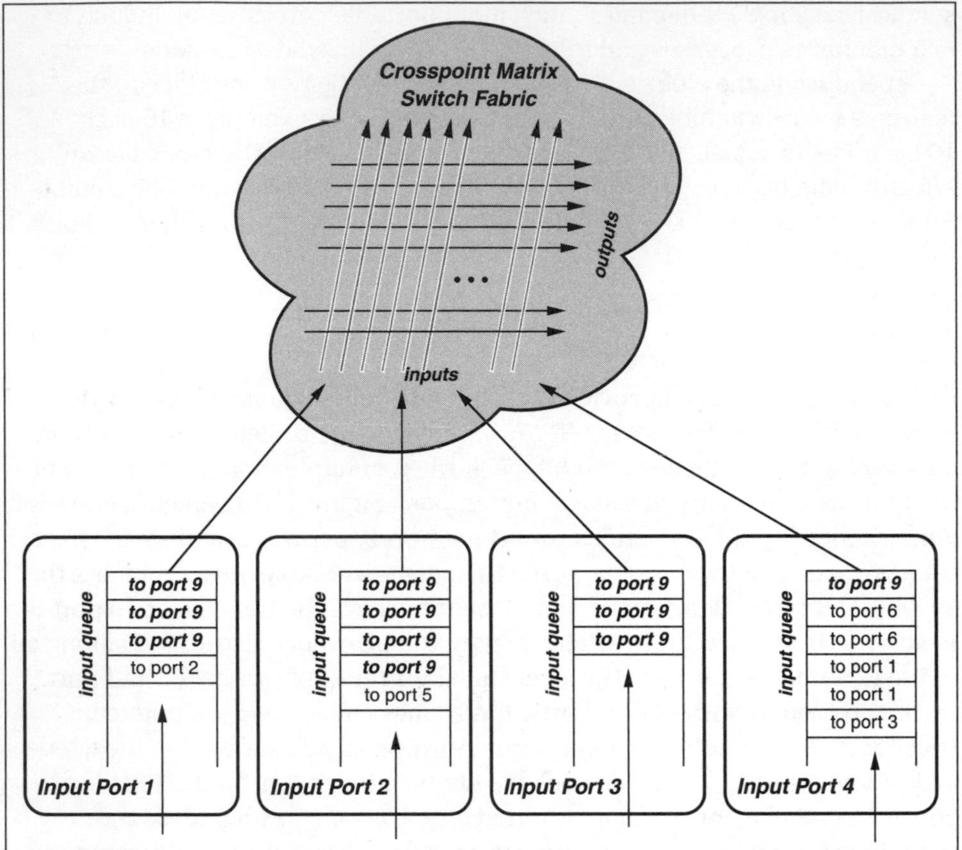

Figure 15.16 The head-of-line blocking problem.

fabric to achieve that state. To the extent that the switch fabric capacity is also experiencing transient congestion due to the many-to-one traffic pattern, some of the frames are still in the input queues waiting to cross the fabric. It is this condition that leads to the blocking problem.

Head-of-line blocking reduces the aggregate throughput of the switch as a function of traffic patterns. If some ports regularly experience short-term congestion (e.g., ports connected to servers that are often the target for heavy offered load), throughput can be reduced on other ports that are completely uncongested. This is an undesirable situation; there is no good reason to reduce the throughput between ports 4 and 6 just because ports 1, 2, and 3 are sending a lot of traffic to port 9.

15.3.3.4 Solving the Head-of-Line Blocking Problem

A number of solutions to the head-of-line blocking problem have been implemented in practical switches, including:

- Queue lookahead
- Priority queues
- Per-output-port input queues

Each one differs in complexity of implementation and effectiveness in eliminating the blocking effect.

15.3.3.4.1 Queue Lookahead

One of the simplest approaches is to implement a lookahead mechanism on the input queue. Each input port arbitrates for the target output port as determined by the frame at the head of its queue. When multiple input ports contend for the same output port (e.g., port 9 in Figure 15.16), one of the input ports will be granted access and the others will be temporarily blocked. When this occurs, the blocked input port can look ahead to the next frame in its input queue to see if the target output port needed by that second frame is available. If it is, the port can transfer that second frame rather than the one at the head of the line. Once transferred, the input port can once again arbitrate for the frame at the head of the queue and, if necessary, repeat the lookahead algorithm if the congested output port is still unavailable.

The hardware required for a simple one-stage queue lookahead is not especially complex and does not significantly increase the cost of the queue management logic. Of course, the mechanism is effective only if there is a single frame blocking the head of the line. If both the first and second frames in the queue are destined for congested output ports, then all of the other frames in the queue are still blocked (e.g., input port 1 in Figure 15.16). However, the probability that two frames are both head-of-line blockers is lower than the probability that only one frame is causing trouble.[26]

Queue lookahead is most effective when the fabric arbitration mechanism provides a means to make a *standing request*, that is, to request an output port and have the switch provide notification when it is available without further action on the part of the input port. That way, the frame at the head-of-the-line will always be assured of delivery, regardless of the time distribution of the traffic destined for the congested output port. The input port can continue to process lookahead frames until the fabric arbitrator tells it that that (congested) output port has become available, ending the head-of-line block.

15.3.3.4.2 Priority Queues

An alternative approach to solving the head-of-line blocking problem is to equip each input port with multiple queues representing different priority levels, as depicted in Figure 15.17.

[26] The probability can be reduced further by incorporating a two-level lookahead, although this increases the hardware complexity. At some point (typically one or two levels), lookahead schemes provide diminishing returns, and it becomes more practical to implement one of the multiple-input-queue mechanisms discussed in Sections 15.3.3.4.2 and 15.3.3.4.3.

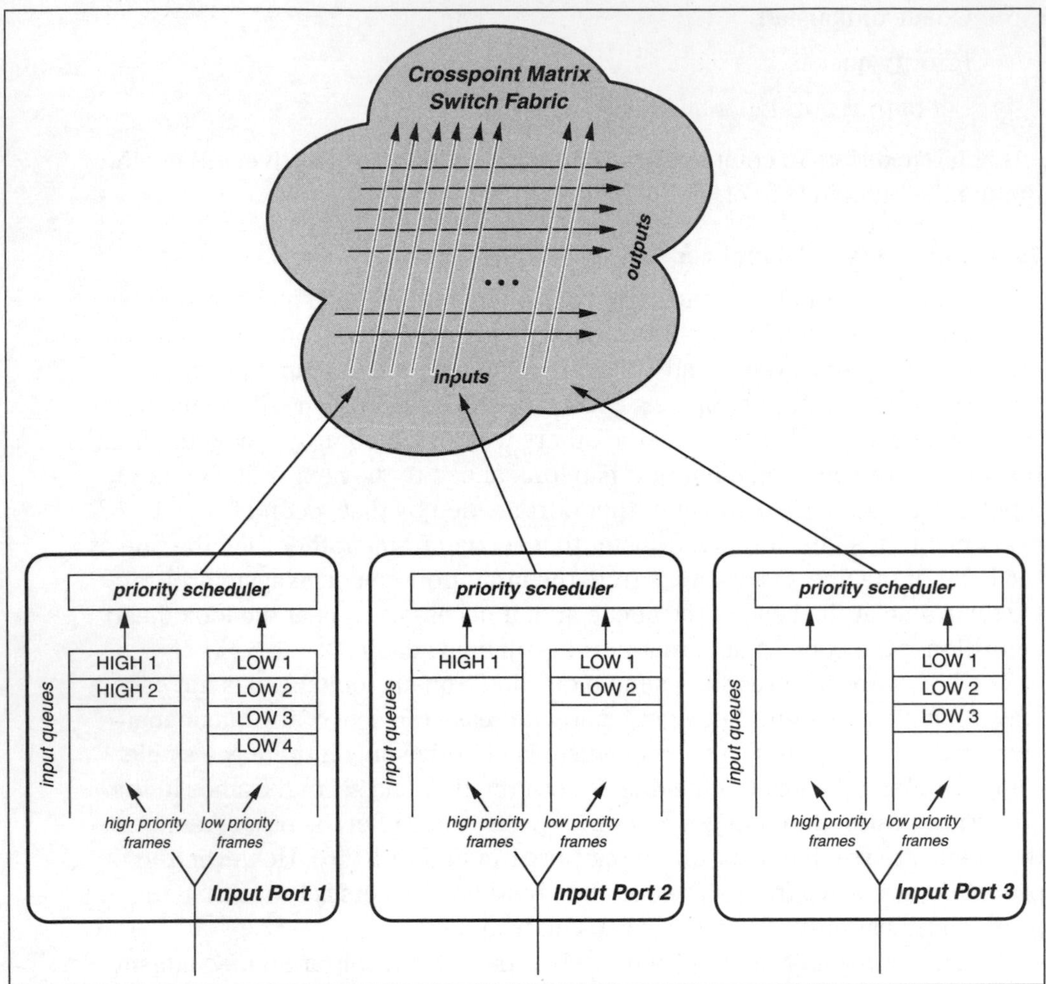

Figure 15.17 Priority input queues.

Frames are placed into one of the input queues based upon the priority as determined by the Classification Engine (and recorded in the internal switch header). The input port nominally schedules frames for fabric arbitration in priority order; that is, frames in the high-priority queue(s) receive preferential treatment relative to frames in the lower-priority queue(s).[27] Frames will be

[27] In theory, any of the mechanisms discussed could be used for output queue scheduling (e.g., weighted fair queuing; see Chapter 13). In practice, strict priority is generally adequate and implies simpler queue management logic. A strict priority policy will starve lower-priority queues only when the sustained, steady-state, high-priority offered load exceeds the capacity of the switch fabric or its output ports. In a LAN switch environment, this is presumed not to be the case; sustained overload indicates a configuration problem (i.e., inadequate capacity) that cannot be resolved by complex priority mechanisms.

processed from lower-priority queues when all higher-priority queues are either empty or currently experiencing head-of-line blocking.

Thus, head-of-line blocking may still occur, but at least a low-priority frame will never block one of higher priority. In addition, queue lookahead can be implemented in addition to priority queuing, further reducing the probability of blocking (especially for the higher-priority queues).

A few points should be noted regarding the implementation of priority input queues:

- Priority queues can be implemented on any input port without regard to whether this mechanism is being used on other input ports. That is, the fact that an input port has multiple queues and is selecting frames for fabric arbitration according to priority classification is invisible to the switch fabric or to other ports on the switch. Thus, to the extent that it is known in advance on which ports head-of-line blocking is anticipated, the additional cost can be incurred only when needed.
- Queue priority can be effectively combined with arbitration priority (see Section 15.3.3.6). If the switch fabric itself supports arbitration at multiple priority levels, the input queues can be mapped to the fabric arbitration priorities.
- The number of priority levels or queues provided does not have to be the same as either the number of priorities resolved by the Classification Engine or the number of Classes of Service provided at the output ports. The purpose of prioritization at the input queue is to avoid having high-priority traffic head-of-line-blocked by lower-priority traffic. Regardless of input queue priority, all frames will still end up in an output queue and be scheduled according to their (end-to-end) user priority. Just as user priority is mapped to the available Classes of Service in the output queues, user priority is mapped to the available number of input queues and/or switch arbitration priority levels.

15.3.3.4.3 Per-Output-Port Input Queues

One complete solution to the head-of-line blocking problem is to provide an input queue for each possible output port, as depicted in Figure 15.18.

At the point where the Receive data path is ready to transfer a frame across the fabric, it must of course know the target output port. Rather than placing all of the frames waiting to be transferred into a single input queue (or a set of prioritized queues), a port can maintain a separate input queue for each possible output port. A scheduler selects frames from the non-empty queues in a fair (e.g., round-robin) manner. If the target output port is available, the input port transfers the first frame in that queue across the fabric. If the target output port is busy, the input port moves on to the next non-empty queue. This mechanism completely eliminates head-of-line blocking, since the unavailabil-

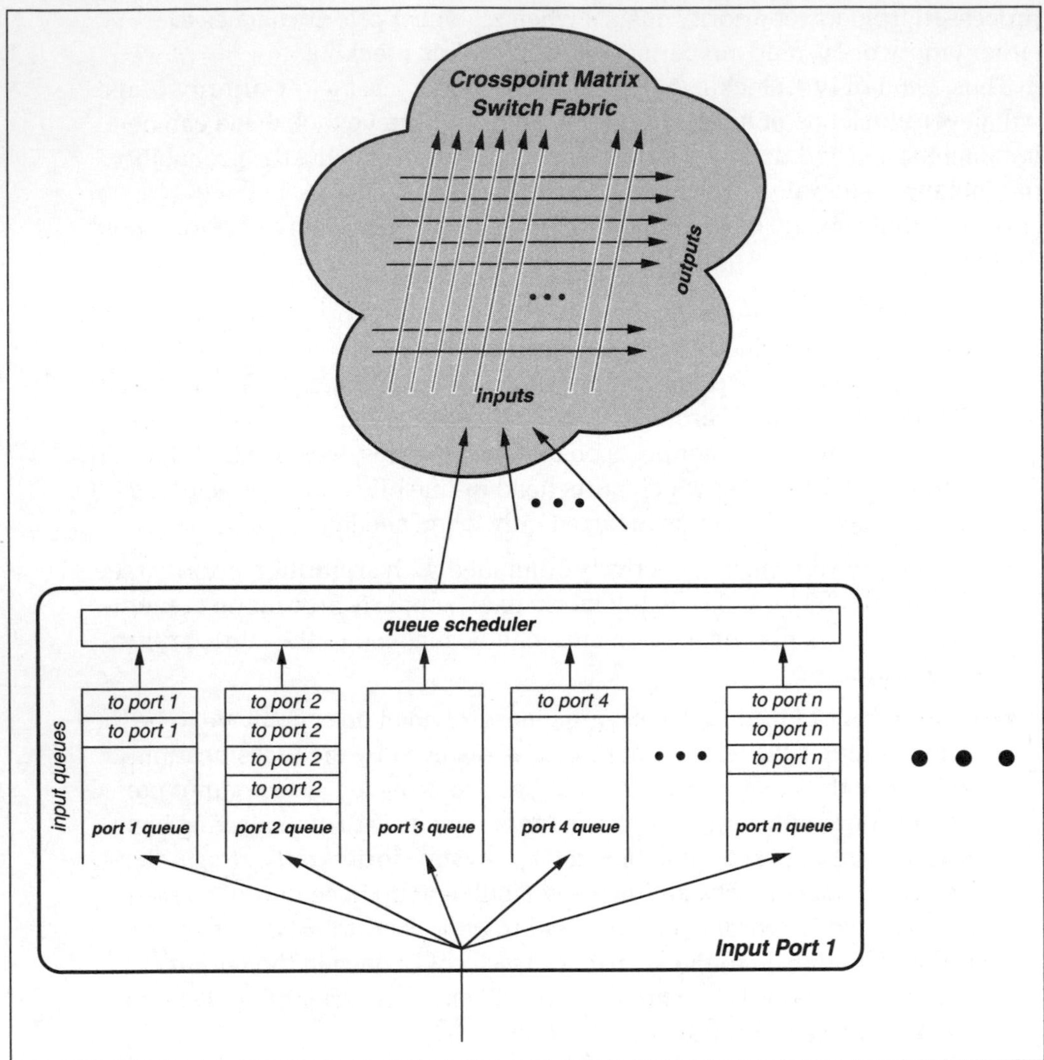

Figure 15.18 Per-output-port input queues.

ity of a given output port will never prevent traffic from moving to those ports that *are* available; the condition never occurs where a frame destined for an available port is waiting behind a frame that cannot currently be transferred.

As in the case of the queue lookahead scheme (see Section 15.3.3.4.1), per-output-port queuing works best if the fabric arbitration mechanism provides a means to make a standing request, that is, to have the switch provide notification when a previously-requested output port becomes available. The input port can continue to process frames for uncongested ports until the fabric arbitrator tells it that that (previously congested) output port is now available for use.

It is also possible to combine per-output-port queues with priority queues.

Each output port can be served by multiple queues at different priority levels. On a per-port basis, high-priority frames will be given precedence over lower-priority frames, as discussed in Section 15.3.3.4.2.

The price for this ultimate solution is not so much an increase in the total amount of input queue memory required—it is the same number of frames being queued either way—but in the complexity of the queue memory data structures and of the hardware used to manage and schedule those queues. The cost and complexity of a per-output-port queuing system can get quite high in a switch with a large number of ports. As always, we are riding the curve of semiconductor technology; as ICs become more dense and logic becomes less expensive, complexity of per-port queue mechanisms becomes ever more practical.

15.3.3.5 Arbitrating for the Fabric Connection

In a shared memory fabric, each port attempting to write into or read from the shared memory must by necessity arbitrate for the right to use the memory data path.[28] However, once access is obtained, any input port can store data destined for any output port, and an output port can read data written by any input port. Similarly, the input ports on a switch must arbitrate for the right to post data onto a shared bus fabric, but the data transfer itself can be to any output port (or to multiple output ports simultaneously). Neither a shared memory nor a shared bus fabric embodies the concept of arbitrating for the right to send or receive data between a particular pair of switch ports.

A crosspoint matrix is different. Transient data paths are created between specific input and output ports as needed for data transfer. When an input port wishes to transfer a frame across a crosspoint matrix fabric, it must request access from itself to a specific target output port. In contrast, an input port in a shared memory or shared bus architecture only needs to request the use of the common fabric.

As depicted in Figure 15.19, crosspoint matrices must provide a mechanism for:

- Each input port to submit requests for a path to a selected output port
- Arbitrating among multiple simultaneous requests for the same output port
- Granting requests as a result of the arbitration
- Enabling the fabric control logic to create the desired path at the appropriate time

[28] This arbitration is unrelated to the switching application; any shared memory requires a mechanism to allocate access among its multiple potential users.

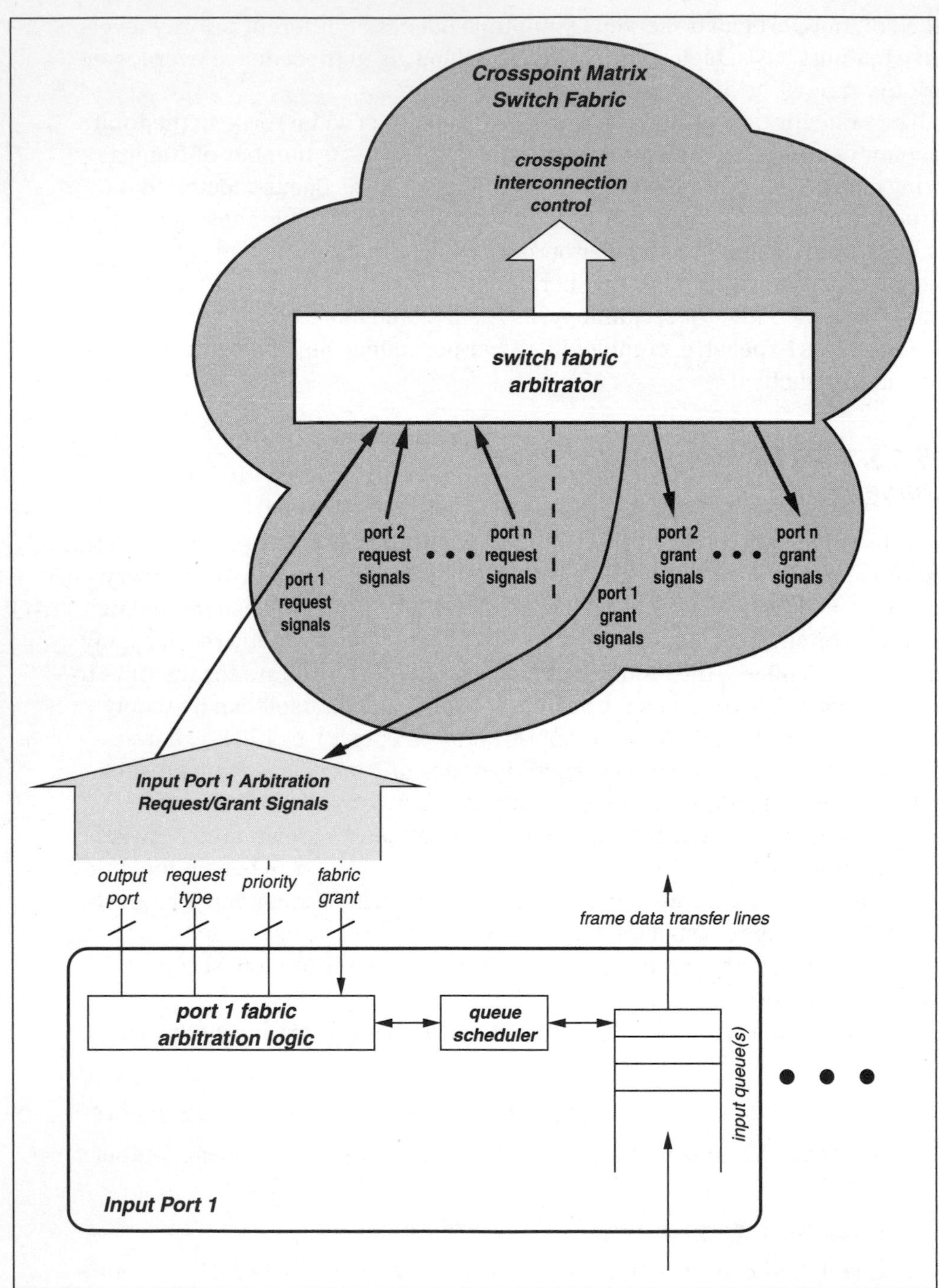

Figure 15.19 Crosspoint matrix arbitration.

15.3.3.5.1 Arbitration Request Types

Under conditions of heavy offered load, it is important that the arbitration scheme operate both efficiently and in a fair and controlled manner. While the details of the arbitration logic tend to be highly product- and implementation-dependent, most crosspoint matrix arbitrators support one or more of the following types of fabric requests from the input ports:

Immediate request An input port can request access to a particular output port for immediate use. If the target port is available, the arbitrator responds by issuing a grant to the requesting input port. If not, the grant is denied, and no further action is taken by the arbitrator. The input port is free to make further requests for the same or different output ports at a later time.

An immediate request might be appropriate for the first request made for a frame at the head of a queue equipped with lookahead capability (see Section 15.3.3.4.1). If the request is granted, the input port can transfer the frame and proceed to the next frame in the queue. If the request is denied, the input port can make a standing request for the same output port (see below) followed by an immediate request for the next frame in the queue (lookahead).

Synchronous request A second form of request asks for an output port and waits until the grant is issued. In this mode, the request-and-grant is a synchronous, atomic operation; no additional requests can be made by the input port until the outstanding request is granted (or times out due to some abnormal condition).

Synchronous requests are appropriate for simple, single-input-queue systems that incorporate neither priority nor lookahead features. There is no need to provide additional port logic complexity if the design cannot take advantage of it.[29]

Standing request Some crosspoint arbitrators provide a means for an input port to request that it be notified when a desired output port becomes available. The arbitrator maintains an internal list of standing requests individually for each output port. When an output port becomes available, the fabric arbitrator decides which input port is to be granted access (based on the scheduling algorithm, priority level, etc.) and notifies the lucky winner that its request can be granted. The input port can then make an immediate or synchronous request, knowing that it will be successful.

Standing requests are appropriate for more complex systems that support lookahead, priority, and/or per-output-port queuing. Any time an

[29] Time spent waiting for a grant against a synchronous request is exactly that time during which the input port is head-of-line blocked.

immediate request is denied, the input port can issue a standing request and move on to process a frame destined for a different output port. The input port will be notified when its standing request is fulfilled and can take appropriate action at that time.

The capability to support standing requests imposes greater complexity on the logic both in the input ports and in the fabric arbitrator, but can provide significant improvements in switch fabric utilization and performance.

15.3.3.5.2 In-Band versus Out-of-Band Arbitration

The implementation of a high-speed, high-port-density crosspoint matrix is often limited by the sheer number of pins required to move signals into and out of the fabric chip(s). To achieve data rates of 1000 Mb/s or higher, we often have to resort to 8- or 16-bit-wide interface paths; as the port density of the switching fabric increases, the number of pins on a switch chip can multiply into the hundreds or thousands.

In addition to the pins needed to move data through the fabric, we need a way to issue arbitration requests and grants between the input ports and the switch chip. Two approaches are commonly used to achieve this end:

- On switch fabrics that are not severely pin-limited (e.g., those that have relatively low port density or that only support lower data rates, such that a 1- or 2-bit-wide data path can be used), we can simply add additional pins for the arbitration control. Each input port makes its requests on signal pins dedicated to the arbitration function; the switch can issue output port grants on similarly dedicated lines.[30]
- When pins are at a premium, we generally opt to make arbitration requests through the same data path used for frame transfers across the fabric. That is, output port requests are structured as "frames" being sent to the arbitrator within the fabric chip. Similarly, grant commands can be issued by the fabric arbitrator and sent to the respective ports through the fabric data output paths. In exchange for the reduction in pin count, we have:
  - *Increased the complexity of both the port and the fabric arbitration logic.* Information passing across the fabric interface must be parsed to separate arbitration requests and grants from data frame transfers.[31]

[30] In some switch designs, the grant signals are common to all ports. This reduces the number of pins required, but requires that the signaling on the output port grant lines be fast enough to accommodate the sum of the input port request rates with minimal delay.

[31] Usually, some special codes or flag bits in the frame headers are used to uniquely identify arbitration requests. There is no need to parse or assign 48-bit addresses in the arbitrator.

- *Reduced the available bandwidth by using some of the data interface capacity for arbitration exchanges.* In practice, a switch designed for in-band arbitration signaling must include extra capacity to account for this effect.

15.3.3.6 Priority Levels in the Switch Fabric

Now, to make things *really* complicated, we can provide multiple priority levels for the switch arbitration. Under this scheme, an input port makes requests not only for a particular output port and request type but at a specified priority level. The arbitrator uses the request priority level as an input to the algorithm used to resolve contention for an output port. Higher-priority requests will be granted ahead of lower-priority requests for the same port. Note that the number of priority levels provided by an arbitrator is completely independent of any other priority mechanisms in the switch (e.g., classification priorities or output queue Classes of Service). The purpose of prioritization here is to schedule the switch fabric in the manner that moves the most important traffic to the output ports in the most expeditious manner.[32]

15.3.4 Input versus Output Queues

Regardless of the design of the fabric, any switch works best when the frames get to the output queue(s) as soon as possible. If there are frames in an output queue and the output port is available, those frames can be sent immediately. If the output port is available, but frames are still waiting on the input side of the switch fabric, the output port is unnecessarily idled; we can't send frames that are still sitting in an input queue. Thus, if frames have to wait, it is better to wait in an output queue than in an input queue; this maximizes channel utilization at the output.[33]

15.3.4.1 Input Queues and Shared Memory Switch Fabrics

Note that with a shared memory architecture there really isn't any input queue with respect to the switch fabric. Frames are stored in memory in one of two states:

[32] Typical fabrics provide two, four, or eight levels of priority.

[33] This is a practical application of the "hurry up and wait" syndrome. We want to speed frames through the Receive data path processing and across the switch fabric, even if they will have to sit in an output queue waiting for transmission.

- *The frame is awaiting processing by the Lookup and/or Classification Engine.* At this point in the process, we do not yet know the output port(s) to which we need to transfer the frame. The memory is being used for temporary storage within the Receive data path; there is no issue of head-of-line blocking on such frames, since they are not yet queued for transfer across the switch fabric.
- *The frame has been inserted into the appropriate output queue(s) and is awaiting transmission.* Once the Lookup Engine has completed its task, it knows the output port(s) to which it wants to transfer the frame. This transfer is effected by linking the appropriate buffer pointer into the output queue for the target port(s). As this can be an atomic operation performed by the Lookup Engine, we never have frames awaiting transfer across the fabric for which we know the target output port. While there may be buffers within the Receive data path to provide time for frame processing, a shared memory architecture needs no input queue to the fabric itself.

15.3.4.2 Input Queues, Output Queues, and Flow Control

Recall from Chapter 8 that the PAUSE flow control mechanism allows a device to request that its full duplex partner stop sending frames for a period of time. Typically, this action would be taken because the instant device (e.g., a switch port) sees that there will be imminent buffer overflow if frames continue to arrive.

Once frames are transferred to an output port within a switch, it becomes rather difficult to use the PAUSE mechanism to prevent buffer overflow. Frames on output queues have typically arrived from a multitude of different input ports. When the output queue begins to grow, how does the switch know on which input port to assert flow control? Without a crystal ball (or an amazing traffic-anticipation heuristic, which amounts to the same thing), it is impossible to predict the port on which future frames will arrive that will cause the troubled output queue to overflow.

PAUSE flow control is effective only with an architecture that maintains input queues to the switch fabric. If an input queue is in danger of overflow, we know a priori that any overrun will be caused by frames arriving from the input port feeding that queue. Thus, we can apply high-water marks on the input queue and assert PAUSE flow control as needed.

Even with an input-queued system, flow control becomes problematic if link aggregation is being used. Since neither the fabric arbitration mechanism nor the aggregator's frame collector will typically know the algorithm being used by the link partner to distribute frames across the multiple links, it is not generally possible to determine which physical link within the aggregation will receive the frames that ultimately cause queue overflow. Unless we are willing to throttle an entire aggregation as a result of a single, traffic-intensive conversation, flow control can only be used to prevent overflow of the individual physical link queues within the frame collector, not the aggregated input queue to the switch fabric. IEEE 802.3x flow control was designed specifically to prevent buffer overflow under transient overload conditions in memory-constrained, input-queued switches. As a result of:

- Rapidly decreasing memory costs
- The emphasis on rapid transfer of frames from input ports to output queues in modern switch designs
- The widespread use of link aggregation

PAUSE flow control has becomes less useful and effective than originally intended. While it is often provided as a product feature in commercial switches, most users disable the function.

15.4 Switch Data Transmit Path Functions

Ultimately, the switch fabric delivers a stream of frames to each output port. These frames may have entered the switch from a single input or from a multitude of input ports. In any case, we need to perform some additional checks and processing before sending them onto the physical link. Figure 15.20 depicts the logical blocks present in the output port (transmit) data path. The sections that follow look at the operations performed within each of these blocks.

15.4.1 Output Filters

For each frame targeted at a given output port, we need to perform two VLAN-related qualification tests before actually queuing it for transmission. As discussed in Chapter 12, the Egress Filter determines whether the output port is in the member set for the VLAN to which the frame belongs. A frame should never be sent on a port that is not in the member set for its associated VLAN. Under most conditions, frames will never be forwarded through the switch fabric to output ports not in the VLAN member set. However, it is possible that, due to inconsistent static entries in the Filtering Database or the operation of Shared VLAN Learning, frames will appear at the output that should not be sent on that port. The Egress Filter detects and prevents this condition.

For each frame that should properly be transmitted on the output port, the Egress Rules function determines whether it must be sent tagged or untagged. This decision is made on a per-frame basis, as a function of the VLAN to which

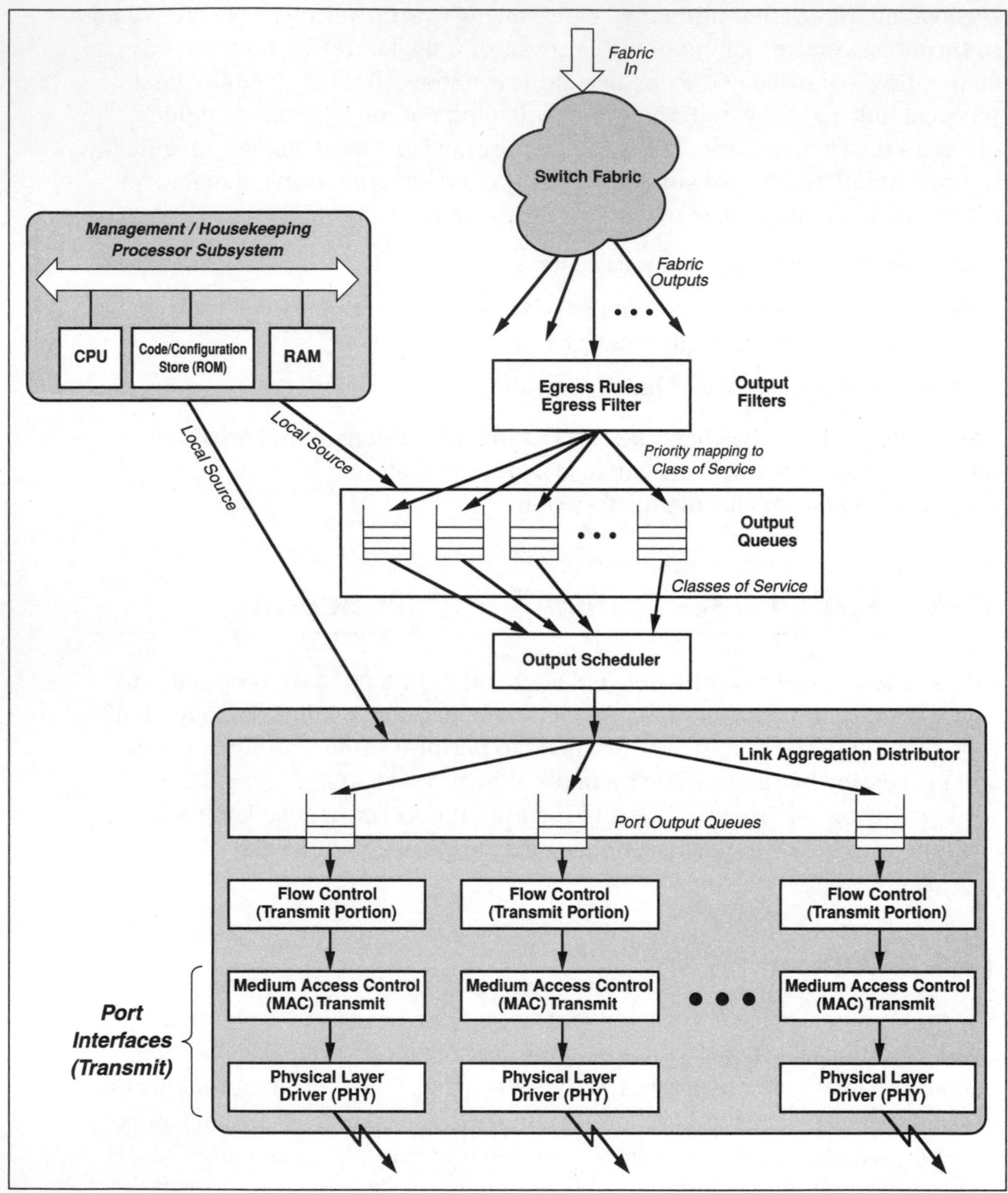

Figure 15.20 Switch output data flow (transmit path).

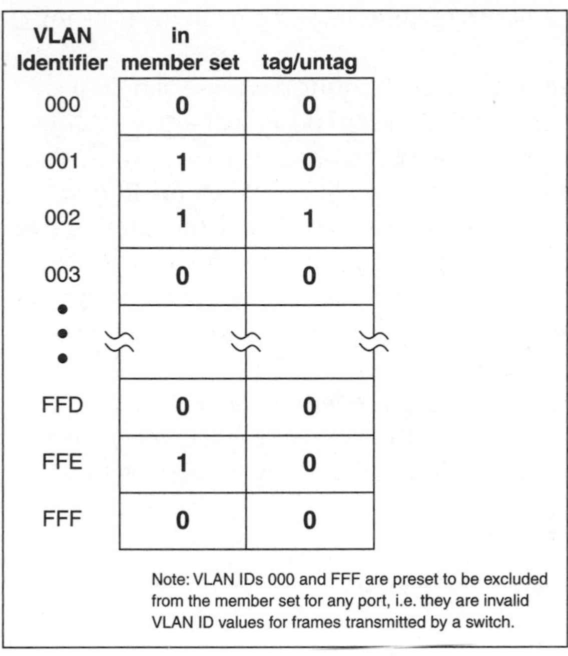

Figure 15.21 Output filter table. VLAN IDs 000 and FFF are preset to be excluded from the member set for any port; that is, they are invalid VLAN ID values for frames transmitted by a switch.

this frame belongs. For each VLAN for which this output port is in the member set, frames will be sent either all tagged or all untagged under administrative control. The setting of the Egress Rule is based on whether any tag-unaware devices must receive frames for this VLAN on the link to which this output port connects.

The Egress Rules and the Egress Filter can be applied simultaneously through the use of a simple output filter table (depicted in Figure 15.21). For each of the 4,096 possible values of the VLAN Identifier, 1-bit indicates whether the port is in the member set (Egress Filter), and 1 indicates whether frames should be sent tagged or untagged (Egress Rules).[34] Note that no complex lookup mechanism is needed; the VLAN identifier in the internal switch header can be used as a pointer directly into the output filter table. In addition, the output filter table requires only 1 Kbyte of memory.

Once the tagging decision is made, all of the information needed to create the tag (if necessary) is already present in the internal switch header. The VLAN identifier, priority, and other information were all determined by the Classification Engine when the frame was received; at this point in the

[34] For a VLAN for which the port is not in the member set, the setting of the tag/untag bit is irrelevant.

process we are only deciding whether to include those fields in the transmitted frame.[35]

In the steady-state, the configuration of the filtering database should prevent a switch from attempting to forward frames to ports that are not in the forwarding state according to the operation of the Spanning Tree Protocol. However, there may be transient or boundary conditions when the filtering database has not yet converged to a new, stable state; that is, the filtering database cannot always be depended on to implement spanning tree port states. The Egress Filter can prevent unwanted transmission of data frames onto ports that are in inappropriate states; if a port is defined as not being in the member set of any VLAN, all frames forwarded through the switch fabric will be discarded at the output. The housekeeping processor can still submit BPDUs for transmission on ports that are in the *listening* or *learning* states by inserting them directly into the output queue following the Egress Filter (see the following text).

15.4.2 Output Queues and Priority Handling

Frames passing all of the qualification tests from the output filters are then placed into one of the output queues on that port. It is in the output queues that the various Classes of Service (CoS) offered by the switch are implemented; there will generally be one queue for each CoS. The internal switch header contains each frame's priority as determined by the Classification Engine; this priority is mapped to a CoS (and hence, an output queue) as discussed in Chapter 13.

The number of output queues is typically in the range of one to eight. This is an implementation tradeoff; more output queues provide greater granularity in the CoS offered at the expense of a more complex memory data structure, and possibly a greater total memory requirement.

Frames are dequeued and submitted for transmission according to the priority policy implemented in the output queue scheduler. Scheduling policies may include strict priority, weighted fair queuing, and so on (see Chapter 13). Regardless of the policy, the end result is a single stream of frames delivered for transmission on the output port in the desired priority order.[36]

The housekeeping processor should be able to locally source frames at any

[35] Another way to look at this process is to consider every frame as being tagged by the switch upon receipt. The tag used is either one contained explicitly in the received frame or one generated implicitly by the Classification Engine. The Egress Rules decision then becomes whether to strip the tag or to leave it intact.

[36] As discussed in Chapter 2, some commercial switches are capable of implementing proprietary transmission policies, for example limiting broadcast or multicast traffic to a specified maximum number of frames per unit time. Such policies are easily implemented in the output scheduler.

point in the output process flow. That is, frames may be inserted into one of the priority queues, directly into the single, prioritized output stream, or even into the individual physical link output queues following the Link Aggregation Distributor (see Section 15.4.3). The point at which frames are locally sourced is a function of the application submitting the frames:

- Higher-layer application traffic (SNMP, HTTP, Telnet, etc.) may be submitted into one of the normal output queues at a priority level commensurate with the application.
- Spanning tree BPDUs may be inserted directly into the output stream from the priority scheduler, effectively stepping to the head of the queue (see Chapter 5).
- Link Aggregation Control Protocol (LACP) messages may be inserted into the individual physical link queues of an aggregated link as necessary (see Section 15.1.1 and Chapter 9).

It can generally be assumed that if the housekeeping processor is locally sourcing frames, they do not need to be qualified by the output filter.[37]

15.4.3 Link Aggregation Distributor

If the output port comprises an aggregation of multiple physical ports, we need to take the stream of frames coming from the output scheduler and assign each one to a specific physical interface. The decision is made according to the distribution algorithm implemented within the Aggregator (see Chapter 9). The Distributor determines the conversation to which each frame belongs (based on a set of conversation mapping rules) and assigns it to one of the available physical interfaces.

The Distributor may also need to independently source frames onto the underlying physical ports on its own behalf; for example, it may generate Marker messages when transferring conversations from one physical port to another in the aggregation.

15.4.4 Transmit Flow Control

Under normal conditions, the Transmit Flow Control module transparently passes frames submitted by the Distributor (or output scheduler) to the Transmit MAC. It neither modifies nor interferes with frame transmissions unless the Receive Flow Control module has detected, parsed, and decoded a PAUSE frame containing a non-zero value for the pause_time parameter (see Chapter 8 and Section 15.2.2). In that case, the Transmit Flow Control module essen-

[37] If you can't trust your own internal management processor, who *can* you trust?

tially halts the interface; it simply does not allow frames to be submitted to the MAC until the pause timer expires (or is cleared by receiving a PAUSE frame with a 0 value for pause_time).

The method used to halt frame flow is implementation-dependent. Typically, some internal mechanism (e.g., a DMA engine or memory controller) will simply prevent additional frame buffer pointers from being linked into the MAC controller's transmit queue.

If the switch needs to assert flow control to its partner, it can always insert a PAUSE frame into the transmit stream, regardless of whether data frame forwarding has been halted or not. The signal to assert flow control might come from the housekeeping processor, or possibly from a queue buffer manager on the receive side of the interface (e.g., the Link Aggregation Collector or the switch fabric input queues).

15.4.5 Hey, Kids! What Time Is It?[38]

There is one final qualification test to perform before we can finally send the frame. At the input port, we timestamped each frame upon arrival. We now need to compare that timestamp with the current time to see if the frame has overstayed its welcome.

As discussed in Chapter 2, a bridge must place an upper bound on the transit delay experienced by a frame between receipt and retransmission through an output port.[39] Unless this upper bound can be guaranteed by design, the timestamp mechanism ensures that frames are discarded rather than forwarded with excess delay.

15.4.6 Port Interfaces (Transmit)

We have been examining, qualifying, modifying, and manipulating the frames so much that it's almost a shame to have them leave the switch forever through the output port. Oh, I forgot—that's the reason the switch exists in the first place! The Transmit Port Interface implements the MAC and PHY functions appropriate to the technology and medium being used on this particular port.

On a shared (half duplex) channel, the Transmit MAC performs the necessary channel arbitration functions for the LAN technology in use (CSMA/CD, Token Passing, etc.). On a full duplex link, there is no need to contend for channel use with any other station; the MAC can transmit frames whenever they are available to be sent. The Physical interface (PHY) converts the data

[38] Send me an e-mail if you know the answer to this question.

[39] IEEE 802.1D/Q-compliance requires that this limit be not more than 4 seconds, with a default value of 1 second [IEEE98a, IEEE98d].

stream emanating from the MAC into electrical or optical signals appropriate for the medium in use.

In a typical end station application, the Transmit MAC generates the proper FCS for all outgoing frames. In a switch, two possibilities exist:

- *The forwarded frame is not identical (bit-for-bit) to the frame as it was received.* The switch may have modified the contents of the frame between reception and transmission as the result of inserting, modifying, or stripping of a VLAN tag or due to frame format conversions between dissimilar LAN technologies on the input and output ports. If the forwarded frame is not exactly identical to the received frame, a new FCS must be computed before transmission. Typically, this function will be performed in hardware by the Transmit MAC entity.[40]
- *The forwarded frame is identical to the frame as it was received.* If every bit in the forwarded frame is exactly the same as in the received frame, then the original FCS is still valid. Rather than calculate the FCS in the Transmit MAC, the switch should simply forward the frame with the received FCS. This implies that the Transmit MAC entity must be able to enable or disable FCS generation on a frame-by-frame basis. The switch port can determine whether frame modifications have been made by inspecting the flag bits in the internal switch header.

Ladies and gentlemen, the frame has left the switch. It is gone, but not forgotten; a hint of its transitory encounter will live on forever in the network management frame counters.

[40] Methods for preserving FCS integrity when a recalculation is needed are discussed in Chapter 3, *Bridging between Technologies.*

APPENDIX

Protocol Parsing

This appendix provides a decision tree that allows a device to determine from an incoming frame which protocol is in use, regardless of the encapsulation method used. This is particularly useful as part of a classification engine for implementing protocol-based VLANs, as discussed in Chapter 11, *Virtual LANs: Applications and Concepts*. The decision tree is presented with respect to Ethernet networks only, because:

- Ethernet-based switches are by far the most common.
- Only Ethernet supports a native Type field. It is primarily because frames may be encapsulated in native Type format or LLC/SNAP formats that the protocol parsing task becomes complex. A Token Ring or FDDI device needs to implement only the subset of the decision tree presented here that deals with LLC and SNAP encapsulation.

The decision tree supports parsing of IP, IPX, DECnet, Local Area Transport (LAT), NetBIOS, and AppleTalk. Where appropriate, related protocols within each family (e.g., ARP along with IP, DEC MOP with DECnet) have been included.

Frame Format

A received frame is assumed to be in the format displayed in Figure A.1.

All lengths shown are in bytes. The LLC fields shown are present only if the Type/Length field indicates Length (i.e., ≤ 0x05DC). The SNAP fields are present only if the LLC DSAP and SSAP fields indicate SNAP encapsulation (i.e., 0xAA). If the frame is VLAN-tagged, the tag is inserted between the source address and the Type/Length field; the decision tree operates on the fields shown, now shifted in position by the length of the VLAN tag.

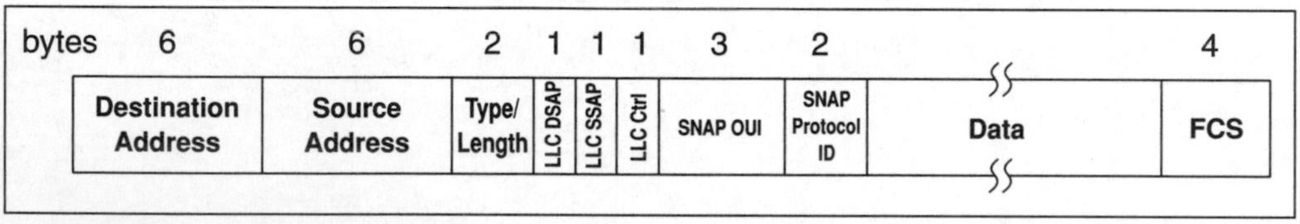

Figure A.1 Format of received frame.

Decision Flow

Upon receiving a frame, use the flow chart in Figure A.2 and Tables A.1 and A.2 to decode the protocol type.

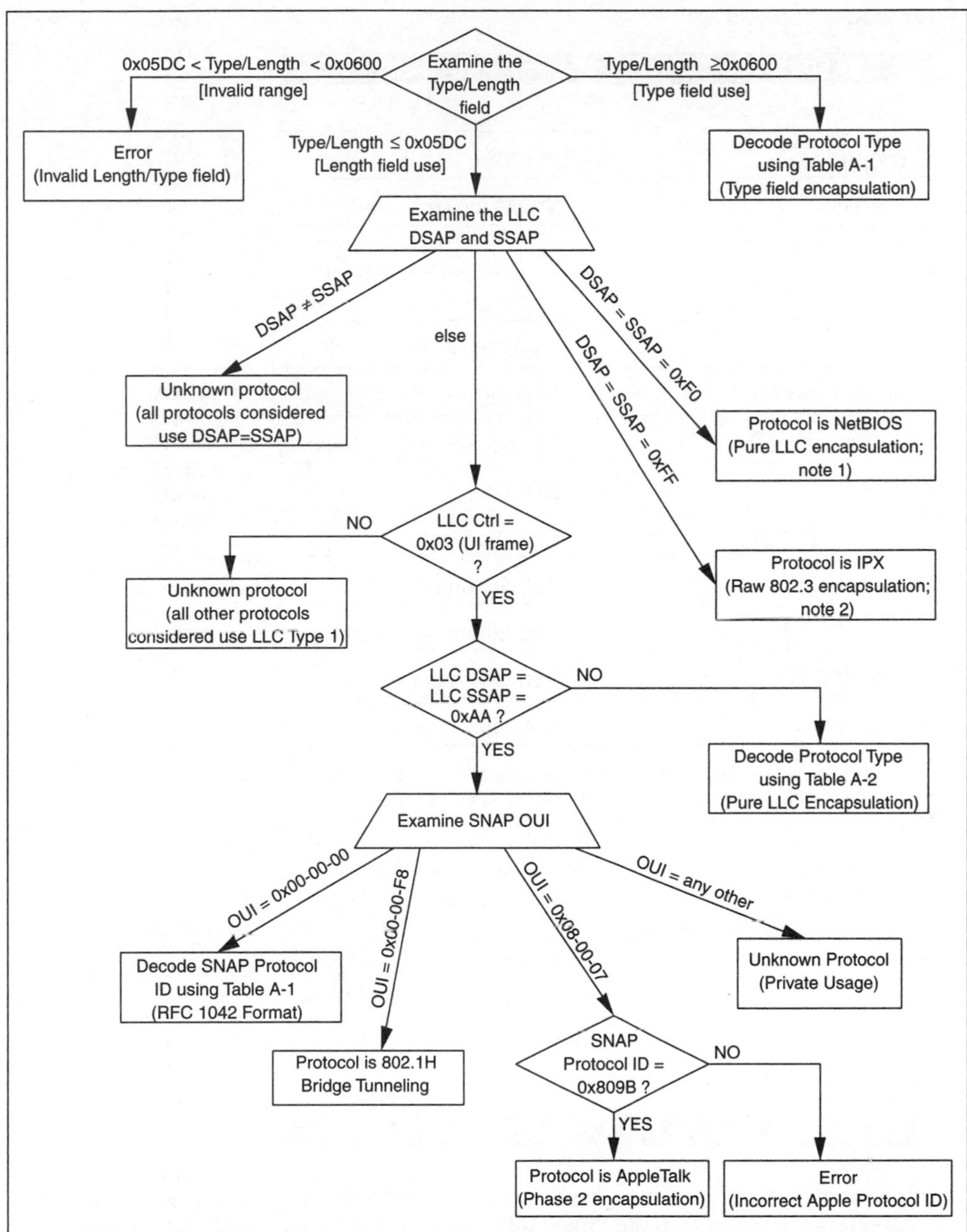

Figure A.2 Protocol decision tree flowchart.[1] NetBIOS is the only protocol considered that uses LLC Type 2 (connection-oriented LLC), so the parsing of NetBIOS is shown before the check of the LLC Control field.[2] No known protocol uses 0xFFFF for its LLC DSAP and SSAP. This value implies IPX using raw 802.3 encapsulation, since the first field in the IPX header is the header checksum. IPX always disables header checksumming and indicates this by using 0xFFFF as the checksum value.

Table A.1 Protocol IDs

VALUE	PROTOCOL
0x0800	IP
0x0806	IP-ARP
0x8035	IP-RARP (rarely used)
0x8137	IPX
0x809B	AppleTalk[1]
0x80F3	AppleTalk ARP[2]
0x6001, 0x6002	DEC MOP
0x6003	DECnet Routing Protocol
0x6004	DEC LAT
0x6005, 0x6006	DEC Diagnostics
0x8038	DEC Spanning Tree
0x803D	DEC Ethernet Encryption
0x803F	DEC LAN Monitor
Others	Not applicable

[1] AppleTalk Phase 1 uses Type field encapsulation, with 0x809B as the Type value. AppleTalk Phase 2 uses SNAP encapsulation, with SNAP OUI = 0x08-00-07.

[2] AppleTalk ARP Phase 1 uses Type field encapsulation, with 0x80F3 as the Type value. In Phase 2, AppleTalk ARP uses SNAP encapsulation, with SNAP OUI = 0x00-00-00.

Table A.2 LLC SAPs

VALUE	PROTOCOL
0x06	IP[1]
0x42	802.1D spanning tree
0xE0	IPX/SPX (so-called 802.2 encapsulation)
Others	Not applicable

[1] While this format is theoretically permissible, commercial IP devices do not use Pure LLC encapsulation with the 0x06 SAP. Stations use either Type field encapsulation (on Ethernet LANs) or RFC 1042 (SNAP, with 00-00-00 OUI) encapsulation (on non-Ethernet LANs).

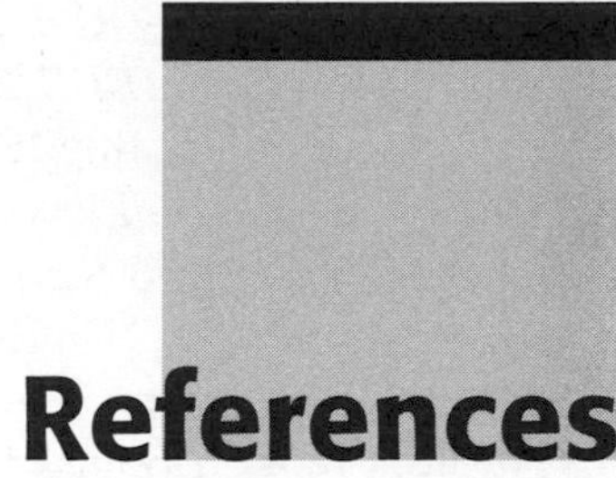

References

[ABBO80] Abbott, Edwin A., *Flatland: A Romance of Many Dimensions*, ©1984 Turtleback Editions (originally published 1880).

[ADAM79] Adams, Douglas, *The Hitchhiker's Guide to the Galaxy*, Harmony Books, 1979.

[AMD96] Kalkunte, Mohan, and Kadambi, Jayant, "Performance Simulations of 1 Gb/s Networks," presented to IEEE 802.3z Task Force, May 1996.

[ANSI79] ANSI Standard X3.66, *Advanced Data Communication Control Procedures (ADCCP)*, 1979.

[ANSI95] ANSI Standard X3.263, *FDDI Twisted Pair–Physical Medium Dependent (TP-PMD)*, revision 2.2, March 1995.

[APPL90] Sidhu, Gursharan S., Andrews, Richard F., and Oppenheimer, Alan B., *Inside AppleTalk™*, 2d ed., ©1990 Addison-Wesley.

[BAXT95] Baxter, Michael A., and Sayre, Dr. Edward P., "Closing the High Speed Signal Integrity Design Loop—The Design, Simulation and Characterization of a QuickRing™ Backplane System," Proceedings of the 1995 High-Performance System Design Conference.

[CARL98] Carlo, James T., et al., *Understanding Token Ring Protocols and Standards*, ©1998 Artech House.

[CHES91] Chesson, G., "The Evolution of XTP," *Proceedings of the Third International Conference on High Speed Networking*, North-Holland, Amsterdam, 1991.

[CHOU85] Choudhury, G. L., and Rappaport, S. S., "Priority Access Schemes Using CSMA-CD," *IEEE Transactions on Communications*, vol. COM-33, no. 7, pp. 620–626, July 1985.

[CIAM98] Ciampa, R., *Flexible Intelligent Routing Engine (FIRE): The Third-Generation Layer 3 Switching Architecture from 3Com*, 3Com Corp., 1998.

[COHE80] Cohen, D., "On Holy Wars and a Plea for Peace," *IEEE Computer Magazine*, no. 14, pp. 48–54, 1981.

[COME95] Comer, Douglas E., *Internetworking with TCP/IP*, vol. 1: *Principles, Protocols, and Architecture*, ©1995 Prentice Hall.

[COME98] Comer, Douglas E., and Stevens, David L., *Internetworking with TCP/IP*, vol. 2: *Design, Implementation, and Internals*, ©1998 Prentice Hall.

[DALA81] Dalal, Y. K., and Printis, R. S., "48-Bit Absolute Internet and Ethernet Host Numbers," Proceedings of the Seventh Data Communications Symposium, 1981.

[DEC82] Digital Equipment Corporation, "DECnet DIGITAL Network Architecture (Phase IV) General Description," May 1982.

[DIX80] Digital Equipment Corp., Intel Corp., and Xerox Corp., "The Ethernet: A Local Area Network—Data Link Layer and Physical Layer Specifications," version 1.0, September 1980.

[DIX82] Digital Equipment Corp., Intel Corp., and Xerox Corp., "The Ethernet: A Local Area Network—Data Link Layer and Physical Layer Specifications," version 2.0, November 1982.

[FLOY93] Floyd, S., and Jacobson, V., "Random Early Detection Gateways for Congestion Avoidance," *IEEE/ACM Transactions on Networking*, August 1993.

[HAMM75] Hammond, J. L., Brown, J. E., and Liu, S. S., "Development of a Transmission Error Model and an Error Control Model," Technical Report RADC-TR-75-138, Rome Air Development Center, 1975.

[HEIM83] Heimel, C., *Sex Tips for Girls*, Simon & Schuster, 1983.

[IBM82] International Business Machines Corp., "A Building Planning Guide for Communication Wiring," September 1982.

[IBM87] International Business Machines Corp., "Token-Ring Network Architecture Reference," 2d ed., IBM document SC30-3374-02, August 1987.

[IBM94] International Business Machines Corp., "IBM 8229 Manual," 1st ed., IBM document GA27-4025-00, March 1994.

[IEEE90a] ISO/IEC Standard 10038, *Media Access Control (MAC) Bridges* [ISO publication of IEEE Standard 802.1D], 1990.

[IEEE90b] IEEE Standard 802, *Overview and Architecture*, 1990.

[IEEE90c] ISO/IEC Standard 8802-4, *Token-passing bus access method and physical layer specifications* [ISO publication of IEEE Standard 802.4], 1990.

[IEEE93a] ISO/IEC Standard 10038, *Media Access Control (MAC) Bridges* [ISO publication of IEEE Standard 802.1D], 1993 revision.

[IEEE93b] IEEE 802.1F, *Common Definitions and Procedures for IEEE 802 Management Information*, 1993 (reaffirmed 1998).

[IEEE94] ISO/IEC 15802-4, *System load protocol* [ISO publication of IEEE Standard 802.1E], 1994.

[IEEE95a] IEEE 802.1H, *Recommended Practice for Media Access Control (MAC) Bridging of Ethernet V2.0 in IEEE 802 Local Area Networks*, 1995.

[IEEE95b] IEEE Standard 802.3u, *Media Access Control (MAC) Parameters, Physical Layer, Medium Attachment Units, and Repeater for 100 Mb/s Operation, Type 100BASE-T*, 1995.

[IEEE95c] ISO/IEC Standard 15802-2, *LAN/MAN management* [ISO publication of IEEE 802.1B], 1995.

[IEEE97] IEEE Standard 802.3x, *Specification for 802.3 Full Duplex Operation*, 1997 (now published as part of [IEEE98e]).

[IEEE98a] ISO/IEC Standard 15802-3, *Media Access Control (MAC) Bridges* [ISO publication of IEEE Standard 802.1D], 1998 edition.

[IEEE98b] ISO/IEC Standard 8802-2, *Logical Link Control* [ISO publication of IEEE Standard 802.2], 1998.

[IEEE98c] ISO/IEC Standard 15802-5, *Remote MAC Bridging* [ISO publication of IEEE Standard 802.1G], 1998.

[IEEE98d] IEEE Standard 802.1Q, *Virtual Bridged Local Area Networks*, 1998.

[IEEE98e] ISO/IEC Standard 8802-3, *Carrier sense multiple access with collision detection (CSMA/CD) access method and physical layer specifications* [ISO publication of IEEE Standard 802.3], 1998.

[IEEE98f] ISO/IEC Standard 8802-5, *Token Ring access method and Physical layer specifications, Amendment 1: Dedicated Token Ring operation and fibre optic media* [ISO publication of IEEE Standard 802.5r and 802.5j], 1998.

[IEEE98g] IEEE Standard 802.3ac, *Carrier sense multiple access with collision detection (CSMA/CD) access method and Physical layer specifications, Frame Extensions for Virtual Bridged Local Area Network (VLAN) Tagging on 802.3 Networks*, November 1998.

[IEEE98h] ISO/IEC Standard 8802-5, *Token Ring access method and physical layer specifications* [ISO publication of IEEE Standard 802.5], 1998.

[IEEE99a] Draft Standard P802.1r, *Supplement to Media Access Control (MAC) Bridges: GARP Proprietary Attribute Registration Protocol (GPRP)*, draft 1.0, January 1999.

[IEEE99b] Draft Standard P802.3ad, *Supplement to Carrier Sense Multiple Access with Collision Detection (CSMA/CD) Access Method and Physical Layer Specifications: Link Aggregation*, draft 3.0, November 1999.

[IEEE00] IEEE Standard 802, *Overview and Architecture*, 2000.

[ISO84] ISO/IEC Standard 8073, *Information Technology—Open System Interconnection—Connection Oriented Transport Protocol Specification*, 1984.

[ISO87] ISO Standard 8473, *Information Processing Systems—Data Communications—Protocol for providing the connectionless-mode network service*, 1987.

[ISO89a] ISO/IEC Standard 9314-2, *Information Processing Systems—Fibre Distributed Data Interface—Part 2: FDDI Token Ring Media Access Control (MAC)*, 1989.

[ISO89b] ISO/IEC Standard 9314-2, *Information Processing Systems—Fibre Distributed Data Interface—Part 1: FDDI Token Ring Physical Layer Protocol (PHY)*, 1989.

[ISO89c] ISO/IEC Standard 9596, *Information Technology—Open Systems Interconnection—Common Management Information Protocol Specification (CMIP)*, 1989.

[ISO90] ISO/IEC Standard 9314-3, *Information Processing Systems—Fibre Distributed Data Interface—Part 3: FDDI Token Ring Physical Layer Medium Dependent (PMD)*, 1990.

[ISO91] ISO/IEC 10039, *Information Technology—Open Systems Interconnection—Local Area Networks—Medium Access Control (MAC) Service Definition*, 1991.

[ISO93] ISO/IEC 4335, *Information technology—Telecommunications and information exchange between systems—High-level data link control (HDLC) procedures—Elements of procedures*, 1993.

[ISO94] ISO/IEC Standard 7498-1, *Information Technology—Open System Interconnection—Basic Reference Model: The Basic Model*, 1994.

[ISO95] ISO/IEC 15802-1, *Information technology—Telecommunications and information exchange between systems—Local and metropolitan area networks—Common specifications—Part 1: Medium Access Control (MAC) service definition*, 1995.

[KLEIN75] Kleinrock, L., and Tobagi, F., "Random Access Techniques for Data Transmission over Packet-Switched Radio Channels," Proceedings of the National Computer Conference, 1975.

[KNUT98] Knuth, Donald E., *The Art of Computer Programming: Sorting and Searching*, vol. 3, ©1998 Addison-Wesley.

[LELA94] Leland, W., Taqqu, M., Willinger, W., and Wilson, D., "On the Self-Similar Nature of Ethernet Traffic," *IEEE/ACM Transactions on Networking*, February 1994.

[MALA90] Malamud, Carl, *Analyzing Novell Networks*, ©1990 Van Nostrand Reinhold.

[MALA93a] Malamud, Carl, *Exploring the Internet: A Technical Travelogue*, ©1993 Prentice Hall.

[METC76] Metcalfe, R. M., and Boggs, D. R., "Ethernet: Distributed Packet Switching for Local Computer Networks," *Communications of the ACM*, vol. 19, no. 7, July 1976.

[PACE96] Wang, Peter, "Class-of-Service (CoS) Implementation for PACE," 3Com Technology Brief, version 0.96b, May 1996.

[PACE98] 3Com Corporation, "PACE™ Technology: The Realization of Multimedia-Enabled Ethernet," Document 500676-001, October 1998. Available at www.3com.com/technology/tech_net/white_papers/500676.html.

[PERK98] Perkins, D., *RMON: Remote Monitoring of SNMP-Managed LANs*, ©1998 Prentice Hall.

[PERL92] Perlman, Radia, *Interconnections: Bridges and Routers*, ©1992 Addison-Wesley.

[PETER72] Peterson, W. W., and Weldon, T. J., *Error Correcting Codes*, 2nd ed., MIT Press, 1972.

[RFC791] Postel, J., "Internet Protocol," September 1981.

[RFC792] Postel, J., "Internet Control Message Protocol," September 1981.

[RFC826] Plummer, D. C., "Ethernet Address Resolution Protocol: Or converting network protocol addresses to 48 bit Ethernet address for transmission on Ethernet hardware," November 1982.

[RFC1028] Davin, J., Case, J. D., Fedor, M., and Schoffstall, M. L., "Simple Gateway Monitoring Protocol," November 1987.

[RFC1042] Postel, J., and Reynolds, J., "A Standard for the Transmission of IP Datagrams over IEEE 802 Networks," February 1988.

[RFC1094] Sun Microsystems, "NFS—Network File System Protocol specification," March 1989.

[RFC1123] Braden, R. T., "Requirements for Internet hosts—application and support," October 1989.

[RFC1157] Case, J. D., Fedor, M., Schoffstall, M. L., and Davin, C. "Simple Network Management Protocol (SNMP)," May 1990.

[RFC1191] Mogul, J. C., and Deering, S. E., "Path MTU discovery," November 1990.

[RFC1213] McCloghrie, K., and Rose, M. T., "Management Information Base for Network Management of TCP/IP-based Internets: MIB-II," March 1991.

[RFC1390] Katz, D., "Transmission of IP and ARP over FDDI Networks," January 1993.

[RFC1493] Decker, E., Langille, P., Rijsinghani, A., and McCloghrie, K., "Definitions of Managed Objects for Bridges," July 1993.

[RFC1504] Oppenheimer, Alan, "Appletalk Update-Based Routing Protocol: Enhanced Appletalk Routing," August 1993.

[RFC1512] Case, J., and Rijsinghani, A., "FDDI Management Information Base," September 1993.

[RFC1513] Waldbusser, S., "Token Ring Extensions to the Remote Network Monitoring MIB," September 1993.

[RFC1525] Decker, E., McCloghrie, K., Langille, P., and Rijsinghani, A., "Definitions of Managed Objects for Source Routing Bridges," September 1993.

[RFC1531] Droms, R., "Dynamic Host Configuration Protocol," October 1993.

[RFC1661] Simpson, W., "The Point-to-Point Protocol (PPP)," July 1994.

[RFC1748] McCloghrie, K., and Decker, E., "IEEE 802.5 MIB using SMIv2," December 1994.

[RFC1749] McCloghrie, K., Baker, F., and Decker, E., "IEEE 802.5 Station Source Routing MIB using SMIv2," December 1994.

[RFC1757] Waldbusser, S. "Remote Network Monitoring Management Information Base," February 1995.

[RFC2074] Bierman, A., and Iddon, R., "Remote Network Monitoring MIB Protocol Identifiers," January 1997.

[RFC2178] Moy, J., "OSPF Version 2," July 1997.

[RFC2205] Braden, R., et al., "Resource ReSerVation Protocol (RSVP)—Version 1 Functional Specification," September 1997.

[RFC2233] McCloghrie, K., and Kastenholz, F., "The Interfaces Group MIB using SMIv2," November 1997.

[RFC2325] Slavitch, M., "Definitions of Managed Objects for DRQ-Type Heated Beverage Devices using SMIv2," April 1998.

[RFC2328] Moy, J., "OSPF Version 2," April 1998.

[RFC2544] Bradner, S., and McQuaid, J., "Benchmarking Methodology for Network Interconnect Devices," March 1999.

[RFC2613] Waterman, R., Lahaye, B., Romascanu, D., and Waldbusser, S., "Remote Network Monitoring MIB Extensions for Switched Networks Version 1.0," June 1999.

[RFC2665] Flick, J., and Johnson, J., "Definitions of Managed Objects for the Ethernet-like Interface Types," August 1999.

[RFC2674] Bell, E., Smith, A., Langille, P., Rijsinghani, A., and McCloghrie, K., "Definitions of Managed Objects for Bridges with Traffic Classes, Multicast Filtering and Virtual LAN Extensions," August 1999.

[ROSE94] Rose, M., and McCloghrie, K., *How to Manage Your Network Using SNMP: The Networking Management Practicum*, ©1994 Prentice Hall.

[ROSE96] Rose, Marshall T., *The Simple Book—An Introduction to Networking Management*, 2nd ed., ©1996 Prentice Hall.

[SEIF83] Seifert, Rich, "Introduction to Ethernet," presentation at Digital Equipment Corporation User's Society (DECUS), Spring 1983.

[SEIF89] Seifert, Rich, *Choosing Between Bridges and Routers*, ©1989 Infonetics Research Institute (2nd ed. ©1990, 3rd ed. ©1991).

[SEIF90] Seifert, Rich, "Have Remote Bridge Vendors Made a Big Blunder?" *Data Communications*, April 1990.

[SEIF91] Seifert, Rich, "Ethernet: 10 Years After," *BYTE*, January 1991.

[SEIF93] Seifert, Rich, *The Design and Planning of Enterprise-Wide AppleTalk Internetworks*, ©1993 Apple Computer.

[SEIF96] Seifert, Rich, *The Use of Backpressure for Congestion Control in Half Duplex CSMA/CD LANs*, ©1996 Networks and Communications Consulting. Available by anonymous ftp at ftp://ftp.netcom.com/pub/se/seifert/TechRept15.pdf.

[SEIF98] Seifert, Rich, *Gigabit Ethernet: Technology and Applications for High-Speed LANs*, ©1998 Addison-Wesley.

[SHAH93] Shah, Amit, and Ramakrishnan, G., *FDDI: A High Speed Network*, Prentice Hall, 1993.

[SPUR97] Spurgeon, Charles, *Practical Networking with Ethernet*, ©1997 International Thomson Computer Press.

[STEV94] Stevens, W. Richard, *TCP/IP Illustrated*, vol. 1: *The Protocols*, ©1994 Addison-Wesley.

[TANEN88] Tanenbaum, Andrew S., *Computer Networks*, ©1988 Prentice Hall.

[TERP94] Terplan, K., and Huntington-Lee, J., *Applications for Distributed Systems and Network Management*, ©1994 John Wiley & Sons.

[WEIN98] Weinstein, Eric, *CRC Concise Encyclopedia of Mathematics*, CRC Press, 1998. See also www.treasure-troves.com/math/BirthdayProblem.html.

[WEIS98] Weiss, Mark A., *Data Structures and Algorithm Analysis in C*, ©1998 Addison-Wesley.

[WIRB98] Wirbel, Loring, "Allayer's Architecture Allows Easy Scaling," *EE Times*, April 1998.

[WONG87] Wong, A. W., Vernon, A. J., and Field, J. A., "Evaluation of Path-Finding Algorithm for Interconnected Local Area Networks," *IEEE Journal on Selected Areas of Communications*, vol. SAC-5, December 1987.

[WYCK95] Wyckoff, John, et al, *NetWare Link Services Protocol: Advanced Theory of Operation*, Novell, November 1995.

Glossary

This glossary provides a compilation of the technical terms, acronyms, and abbreviations used throughout the book. This list is not intended to be a comprehensive network glossary. In particular, the definitions and expansions provided reflect the use of these terms only within this book; that is, other definitions for the same terms may be appropriate in different contexts.

Terms

1BASE5 A baseband Ethernet system operating at 1 Mb/s over one pair of UTP cable. See also *StarLAN*.

10BASE-F A generic designation for a family of 10 Mb/s baseband Ethernet systems operating over optical fiber.

10BASE-FB A baseband Ethernet system operating at 10 Mb/s over two multimode optical fibers using a synchronous active hub.

10BASE-FL A baseband Ethernet system operating at 10 Mb/s over two multimode optical fibers using an optional asynchronous active hub.

10BASE-FP A baseband Ethernet system operating at 10 Mb/s over two multimode optical fibers using a passive hub.

10BASE-T A baseband Ethernet system operating at 10 Mb/s over two pairs of Category 3 (or better) UTP cable.

10BASE2 A baseband Ethernet system operating at 10 Mb/s over thin coaxial cable. Also known as *Cheapernet.*

10BASE5 A baseband Ethernet system operating at 10 Mb/s over thick coaxial cable.

10BROAD36 A broadband Ethernet system operating at 10 Mb/s over three channels (in each direction) of a private CATV system.

100BASE-FX A baseband Ethernet system operating at 100 Mb/s over two multimode optical fibers.

100BASE-T A generic designation for a family of 100 Mb/s baseband Ethernet systems operating over both twisted pair and optical fiber cable.

100BASE-T2 A baseband Ethernet system operating at 100 Mb/s over two pairs of Category 3 (or better) UTP cable.

100BASE-T4 A baseband Ethernet system operating at 100 Mb/s over four pairs of Category 3 (or better) UTP cable.

100BASE-TX A baseband Ethernet system operating at 100 Mb/s over two pairs of STP or Category 5 UTP cable.

100BASE-X A generic designation for 100BASE-T systems that use 4B/5B encoding (100BASE-TX, 100BASE-FX).

100VG-AnyLAN A designation for a LAN system using the Demand Priority access method, as standardized by IEEE 802.12.

1000BASE-CX A baseband Ethernet system operating at 1000 Mb/s over two pairs of 150 STP cable.

1000BASE-LX A baseband Ethernet system operating at 1000 Mb/s over two multimode or singlemode optical fibers using longwave laser optics.

1000BASE-SX A baseband Ethernet system operating at 1000 Mb/s over two multimode optical fibers using shortwave laser optics.

1000BASE-T A baseband Ethernet system operating at 1000 Mb/s over four pairs of Category 5 UTP cable.

1000BASE-X A generic designation for 1000 Mb/s Ethernet systems that use 8B/10B encoding (1000BASE-CX, 1000BASE-LX, 1000BASE-SX).

Acceptable frame filter A qualification function implemented in an input port of a VLAN-aware switch. The acceptable frame filter may be set either to Admit All or Admit All Tagged.

Access domain The set of stations among which MAC arbitration can occur. Stations on the same shared LAN are in the same access domain; stations in separate access domains do not contend for use of a common communications channel.

Access priority The priority used to determine access privileges on a shared LAN segment relative to other stations that have frames queued. Access priority only carries local significance on a LAN. See also *User priority.*

Active monitor A device in a Token Ring LAN that is responsible for handling many boundary conditions and housekeeping functions, including generation of a common clock, elastic buffering, and removal of circulating high-priority tokens.

Actor In Link Aggregation, the device on a point-to-point link at the end in question. See also *Partner.*

Address A unique identifier of a station or network interface.

Aggregated link A set of two or more physical links that appear to higher-layer entities as if they were a single higher-capacity link.

Aggregator The entity that performs the operations required to make multiple physical links function as an aggregated link.

Aging process Within the Spanning Tree Protocol, the process that removes dynamic entries from the filtering database when the stations with which those entries are associated have been inactive for a specified time (the aging time).

Aging time Within the Spanning Tree Protocol, the time after which a dynamic filtering database entry will be removed if its associated station has been continuously inactive.

AppleTalk A protocol suite developed by Apple Computer, used in Macintosh computers and other compatible devices.

Application A process or program running on a station or stations in the network.

Application flow A stream of frames or packets among communicating processes within a set of end stations.

Application-based VLAN A catenet where the association of a frame to a VLAN is determined by application-specific information in the frame.

Application layer The highest layer of the seven-layer OSI model, responsible for generic application services and program interfaces to user applications.

ARP cache A data structure that provides the current mapping of 32-bit IP addresses to 48-bit MAC addresses.

Auto-Negotiation A technique used in Ethernet systems that operate over point-to-point links, where the device at each end of the link can learn the capabilities of the device at the other end and automatically configure itself to the highest common set of capabilities (e.g., data rate, duplexity, and/or flow control).

Backbone A network used primarily to interconnect other networks.

Backoff The mechanism used in the Ethernet MAC (CSMA/CD) to reschedule a transmission in the event of a collision.

Backpressure A technique used to stop a station from sending frames by using the half duplex MAC mechanisms afforded by the underlying LAN (e.g., Carrier Sense or collision detection).

Bandwidth The data-carrying capacity of a device or communications channel. Usually expressed in bits per second.

Best-effort service A service provided by an architectural layer entity where frames or packets are delivered with high probability but with no absolute guarantee.

Big Endian (1) A method of ordering bits within a byte such that they are transmitted from the most significant bit first to the least significant bit last. (2) A method of ordering bytes within a multi-byte field such that they are transmitted from the most significant byte first to the least significant byte last. See also *Little Endian.*

Bit An atomic unit of data representing either a 0 or a 1.

Bit stuffing A technique that provides a unique frame delimiter pattern yet maintains payload data transparency by inserting an extra 0 bit after every occurrence of five 1 bits in the payload data stream.

Bit time The length of time required to transmit 1 bit of information; equal to the reciprocal of the data rate.

Blocking In connectionless networks, a characteristic of a switch, switch fabric, or network interface implying that it is not capable of handling traffic at the maximum frame and/or data arrival rate without having to discard traffic (in the worst-case) due to a lack of internal resources.

Blocking state A stable state in the Spanning Tree Protocol in which a bridge port will receive BPDUs but will neither receive nor transmit data frames.

Bottleneck A point in a data communications path or computer processing flow that limits overall throughput or performance.

Bounded system A device with a fixed predetermined configuration (e.g., number of ports, port technologies, and data rates).

Bridge An internetworking device that relays frames among its ports based upon Data Link layer information (e.g., MAC addresses and/or VLAN identifiers). Also known as a *switch* or a *Layer 2 switch.*

Bridged LAN Synonymous with *catenet.*

Bridge Identifier In the Spanning Tree Protocol, a catenation of a Bridge Priority value and the bridge's MAC address. The bridge with the numerically-lowest Bridge Identifier value will become the Root Bridge in the spanning tree.

Bridge Number A locally-assigned, ring-unique number identifying each bridge in a source routed catenet.

Bridge port A network interface on a bridge.

Bridge Priority An administratively-controlled value that is catenated with the bridge's MAC address to create a Bridge Identifier.

Bridge transit delay The delay between the receipt of a frame on one port and the forwarding of that frame onto another port of a bridge.

Broadcast address A well-known multicast address signifying the set of all stations.

Brouter A device combining the functions of a bridge and a router. See also *Swouter.*

Browser An application program providing a graphical user interface to Internet or intranet services.

Buffer A block of memory used to temporarily store data while it is being processed.

Burst mode A modification to the flow control algorithm originally used in the NetWare (IPX) protocol suite. In burst mode, a station may continue to transmit information even if there are multiple outstanding packets awaiting acknowledgment.

Byte An 8-bit unit of data.

Call-back unit A device that calls a user at a pre-programmed telephone number when a connection is requested to prevent unauthorized access from unknown locations.

Campus switch A switch used within a campus backbone. Campus switches are generally high-performance devices that aggregate traffic streams from multiple buildings and departments within a site.

Canonical format Synonymous with *Little-Endian* format.

Carrier Sense In Ethernet, the act of determining whether the shared communications channel is currently in use by another station.

Catenet A collection of networks (typically LANs) interconnected at the Data Link layer using bridges. Also known as a *bridged LAN.*

Chassis switch A switch implemented in a modular fashion, with a base chassis and a set of plug-in blades chosen for a particular application environment.

Cheapernet A slang term for thin-wire coaxial Ethernet (10BASE2).

Classification Engine The module within a switch that is responsible for examining incoming frames and classifying them as to VLAN association, priority, and so on.

Client (1) Application software (typically resident in an end-user workstation) designed to operate through cooperation and communication with a companion server application (typically resident in a dedicated multitasking computer system). (2) An architectural entity using the services of a lower-layer service provider (e.g., a Transport entity may be a client of a Network layer service provider).
See also *server.*

Coaxial cable A communications medium built as a pair of concentric cylindrical conductors. Used in 10BASE5 and 10BASE2 Ethernet systems.

Collapsed backbone A method of interconnecting networks by using a switch or router as a central relay device.

Collector The module within a Link Aggregator responsible for gathering frames received from multiple, underlying physical links. See also *Distributor.*

Collision A simultaneous transmission attempt by two or more stations on a shared Ethernet LAN.

Collision detection The act of detecting a collision.

Collision domain The set of stations among which a collision can occur. Stations on the same shared LAN are in the same collision domain; stations in separate collision domains do not contend for use of a common communications channel.

Collision fragment The portion of an Ethernet frame that results from a collision. On a properly configured and operating LAN, collision fragments are always shorter than the minimum length of a valid frame.

Communications channel The medium and Physical layer devices that convey signals among communicating stations.

Communications medium The physical medium used to propagate signals across a communications channel (e.g., optical fiber, coaxial cable, twisted pair cable).

Configuration Message In the Spanning Tree Protocol, a BPDU that carries the information needed to compute and maintain the spanning tree.

Congestion The state where the offered network load approaches or exceeds the locally-available resources designed to handle that load (e.g., link capacity or memory buffers).

Connectionless A communications model in which stations can exchange data without first establishing a connection. In connectionless communications, each frame or packet is handled independently of all others.

Connection-oriented A communications model in which stations establish a connection before proceeding with data exchange and in which the data constitutes a flow that persists over time.

Consultant A person who borrows your watch, then charges you for the time of day. See also *Guru*.

Conversation As used in Link Aggregation, a set of traffic among which ordering must be maintained.

Copy port Synonymous with *Mirror Port*.

Core switch A VLAN-aware switch that connects exclusively to other VLAN-aware devices. See also *Edge switch*.

Crossbar A common name for a crosspoint matrix switch fabric.

Crosspoint matrix A switch fabric designed to provide simultaneous transient connections between any input port and any available output port.

Cut-through A mode of switch operation where frames can be forwarded before they are fully received.

Datagram (1) A frame or packet transferred using connectionless communications. (2) A frame or packet sent using best-effort service. (3) An IP packet.

Data Link layer The second layer of the seven-layer OSI model, responsible for frame delivery across a single link.

D-compliant A bridge or switch that complies with IEEE 802.1D.

Decapsulation The process of removing protocol headers and trailers to extract higher-layer protocol information carried in the data payload. See also *Encapsulation.*

Decoder The entity within the Physical layer responsible for converting signals received from a communications channel into binary data. See also *Encoder.*

Dedicated bandwidth A configuration in which the communications channel attached to a network interface is dedicated for use by a single station and does not have to be shared. See also *Microsegmentation* and *Shared bandwidth.*

Dedicated media A configuration in which the physical communications medium used to connect a station to either a hub or another station constitutes a point-to-point link between the devices.

Default De-reason that de-network is down.

Default port A switch port configured to be the target destination port for traffic received on other ports and for which the lookup process fails.

Default priority The priority assigned to a received frame when none of the administratively-configured policy rules apply to it.

Deferral The mechanism by which a half-duplex Ethernet station withholds its own transmissions when another station is currently using the shared communications channel.

Departmental switch Synonymous with *workgroup switch.*

Designated Bridge In the Spanning Tree Protocol, the bridge responsible for forwarding traffic from the direction of the Root Bridge onto a given link.

Designated Port In the Spanning Tree Protocol, a port through which a Designated Bridge forwards traffic onto a given link in the direction away from the Root Bridge.

Desktop switch A switch used to connect directly to end user devices. A desktop switch usually provides an uplink port for connection to a backbone or workgroup switch.

Device driver The software used to provide an abstraction of the hardware details of a network or peripheral device interface. Device drivers allow higher-layer entities to use the capabilities of a device without having to know or deal with the specific implementation of the underlying hardware.

Disabled state A stable state in the Spanning Tree Protocol state machine in which a bridge port will not receive or transmit any frames (including BPDUs).

Disinterested link A communications link that carries traffic between a sender and a receiver, neither of which is directly connected to that link.

Distributed backbone A shared-bandwidth network used to interconnect other networks, where the backbone communications medium (rather than a central relay device) is used to attach to the lower level networks. See also *Collapsed backbone.*

Distribution function The algorithm used by a Distributor to assign conversations to particular physical links within an aggregation.

Distributor The module within a Link Aggregator responsible for assigning frames submitted by higher-layer clients to the individual underlying physical links. See also *Collector.*

E1 A T-carrier technology commonly used in Europe, capable of multiplexing 32 DS-0 (64 Kb/s) channels for a total data-carrying capacity of 2.048 Mb/s.

Edge switch A switch located at the boundary between a VLAN-unaware domain and a VLAN-aware domain of a catenet. Edge switches must be capable of determining VLAN membership by inspecting implicitly tagged frames and applying a set of VLAN association rules. See also *Core switch.*

Egress Filter A qualification function implemented in an output port of a VLAN-aware switch. The Egress Filter will discard a frame if it belongs to a VLAN for which the output port is not in the member set or if the Egress Rule entity has determined that the frame is to be sent untagged and the value of the CFI and/or NCFI bits in the VLAN tag is such that the frame may contain embedded MAC addresses in the wrong bit order for this type of LAN, but the switch does not have the capability to find the embedded addresses and change their bit order to make the application work properly.

Egress Rule The rule used to determine whether a frame is transmitted in tagged or untagged format on the output port of a switch. If a frame belonging to a given VLAN is sent tagged, every device that is a member of that VLAN and directly connected to that port must be tag-aware.

Encapsulating bridge A bridge that encapsulates LAN frames for transmission across a backbone.

Encapsulation The process of taking data provided by a higher-layer entity as the payload for a lower-layer entity and applying a header and trailer as appropriate for the protocol in question. See also *Decapsulation.*

Encoder The entity within the Physical layer responsible for converting binary data into signals appropriate for transmission across the communications channel. See also *Decoder.*

End-of-Frame Delimiter A symbol or set of symbols used to indicate the end of the Data Link (or MAC) encapsulation. See also *Start-of-Frame Delimiter.*

End-of-Stream Delimiter A symbol or set of symbols used to indicate the end of the Physical layer encapsulation. See also *Start-of-Stream Delimiter.*

End station A device that runs end user applications and that is the source and sink of frames on a network.

Enterprise network The set of Local, Metropolitan, and/or Wide Area Networks and internetworking devices comprising the communications infrastructure for a geographically-distributed organization.

Enterprise switch A switch used within an enterprise backbone. Enterprise switches are generally high-performance devices operating at the Network layer that aggregate traffic streams from sites within an enterprise.

Error control A procedure used to recover from detected errors, for example Positive Acknowledgment and Retransmission.

Error detection A procedure used to detect whether received information contains errors. See also *Frame Check Sequence.*

Error rate The ratio of bits (or frames) received in error to the total number of bits (or frames) received.

Ethernet The popular name for a family of LAN technologies standardized by IEEE 802.3.

Explorer frame In source routing, a frame used either to perform route discovery or to propagate multicast traffic. There are two types of explorer frames: Spanning Tree Explorers and All Routes Explorers.

Fast EtherChannel A proprietary method of Link Aggregation developed by Cisco Systems.

Fast Ethernet An Ethernet system operating at 100 Mb/s.

Fast path The code thread that is traversed most often and that is usually highly optimized for performance.

Filtering The process of inspecting frames received on an input port of a switch and deciding whether to discard or forward them.

Filtering database A data structure within a bridge that provides the mapping from Destination Address to bridge port (in a D-compliant bridge), or from the combination of Destination Address and VLAN to bridge port (in a Q-compliant bridge).

Flooding The action of forwarding a frame onto all ports of a switch except the port on which it arrived. Normally used for frames with multicast or unknown unicast Destination Addresses.

Flow control A mechanism that prevents a sender of traffic from sending faster than the receiver is capable of receiving.

Forwarding The process of taking a frame received on an input port of a switch and transmitting it on one or more output ports.

Forwarding Delay A parameter of the Spanning Tree Protocol that defines the delay (temporal hysteresis) imposed between transitions from the *listening* to the *learning* state and from the *learning* to the *forwarding* state.

Forwarding state A stable state in the Spanning Tree Protocol state machine in which a bridge port will transmit frames received from other ports as determined by the bridge forwarding algorithm.

Fragmentation A technique whereby a packet is subdivided into smaller packets so that they can be sent through a network with a smaller Maximum Transmission Unit. See also *Reassembly.*

Frame The Data Link layer encapsulation of transmitted or received information.

Frame Check Sequence A block check code used to detect errors in a frame. Most LANs use a CRC-32 polynomial as their FCS.

Framing The process or method of delimiting the beginning and end of a frame.

Full duplex A mode of communication whereby a device can simultaneously transmit and receive data across a communications channel. See also *Half-duplex*.

Functional group addressing A technique used for multicasting in Token Ring LANs in which specific bits within a 48 bit MAC Destination Address are associated with predefined functional entities. A frame so addressed will be received by all devices that have implemented the functions corresponding to the bits set within the address.

Gateway (1) A device capable of relaying user application information among networks employing different architectures and/or protocol suites. (2) An internetworking device operating at the Transport layer or above. (3) An old term for an IP router. (4) A marketing name for anything that connects anything to anything else.

Gigabit Ethernet An Ethernet system operating at 1000 Mb/s.

Globally-administered address A device or interface identifier whose uniqueness is ensured through the use of an assigned Organizationally-Unique Identifier, typically by the manufacturer of the device or interface. See also *Locally-administered address*.

Group address Synonymous with *multicast address*.

Guru Great Understanding, Relatively Useless. See also *Consultant*.

Half duplex A mode of communication in which a device can either transmit or receive data across a communications channel, but not both simultaneously. See also *Full duplex*.

Hardware address Synonymous with *unicast address*.

Hash function An algorithm that distributes items evenly into one of a number of possible buckets in a hash table.

Header A protocol-specific field or fields that precede the encapsulated higher-layer data payload (e.g., the MAC addresses in a Data Link frame). See also *Trailer*.

Head-of-line blocking A condition in which a switch is prevented from processing further queue entries because of a lack of resources to service the first entry in the queue.

Hello time In the Spanning Tree Protocol, the interval between Configuration Messages as generated by the Root Bridge.

High-water mark An indicator that the number of entries or bytes in a queue has risen above a predetermined level. See also *Low-water mark*.

Hop count A measure of the number of routers through which a packet has passed.

Host In an IP network, a synonym for *end station*.

Housekeeping processor An embedded computer used to support various utility, diagnostic, and initialization functions within a device.

Hub (1) A central interconnection device as used in a star-wired topology. See also *Repeater* and *Switching hub*. (2) A repeater.

Implicit tag A method of mapping an untagged frame to its associated VLAN by inspection of the frame's contents.

Individual port A switch port that cannot form an aggregated link with any other port.

Ingress Filter A qualification function implemented in an input port of a VLAN-aware switch. The Ingress Filter can be configured to discard any received frame associated with a VLAN for which that port is not in the member set.

Ingress Rule A rule used to classify a frame as to its VLAN association. Synonymous with *VLAN association rule*.

Interframe gap The spacing between time-sequential frames.

Intermediate station Synonymous with *internetworking device*.

Internet A well-known set of networks interconnected by routers using the Internet Protocol. Home of the World Wide Web, USENET, and many other facilities.

internet See *internetwork*.

Internet Protocol The internetwork protocol used in the Internet, specified in [RFC791]. Abbreviated *IP*.

internetwork A set of networks interconnected at the Network layer by routers.

internetworking device A device used to relay frames or packets among a set of networks (e.g., a bridge or router).

internetwork protocol The protocol used to move frames from originating source stations to their ultimate target destinations (through routers, if necessary) across an internetwork. IP, IPX, and DDP are all examples of internetwork protocols.

Invariant A characteristic of an architectural layer entity that does not change with implementation; that is, higher layer entities can depend on the invariant behaviors of their lower-layer service providers.

isoEthernet A variant of Ethernet developed by National Semiconductor Corp. (and standardized in IEEE 802.9a) that provides an isochronous communication channel in addition to a 10 Mb/s Ethernet LAN.

Jabber control A method used to prevent a device from transmitting continuously and thereby disrupting a shared communications channel.

Jam In Ethernet, the process of sending an additional 32 data bits following the detection of a collision to ensure that all parties to the collision properly recognize the event as such.

Jumbo frame A frame longer than the maximum frame length allowed by a standard. Specifically used to describe the dubious practice of sending 9-Kbyte frames on Ethernet LANs.

Key The means used to identify a set of aggregatable links from the perspective of the system comprising those links. All links that are assigned the same key are aggregatable; any links with different keys are not aggregatable.

LAN segmentation The practice of dividing a single LAN into a set of multiple LANs interconnected by bridges.

LAN switch A switch that interconnects Local Area Networks.

Layer entity An architectural abstraction of the module that implements the functions defined at a given layer of the protocol stack.

Layer 2 switch Synonymous with *bridge.*

Layer 3 switch Synonymous with *router.*

Layer 4 switch A router that can make routing policy decisions based on Transport layer information (e.g., TCP port identifiers) encapsulated within packets.

Leaky VLAN A VLAN that may, under certain boundary conditions, carry frames that do not belong to that VLAN. Leaky VLANs typically result from devices that improperly implement the VLAN association and/or forwarding rules either to reduce cost or as a result of sloppy design practices.

Learning process The process whereby a bridge builds its filtering database by gleaning address-to-port mappings from received frames.

Learning state A transition state in the Spanning Tree Protocol state machine where a bridge port is learning address-to-port mappings to build its filtering database before entering the forwarding state.

Length Encapsulation The Ethernet frame format where the Length/Type field contains the length of the encapsulated data rather than a protocol type identifier. Length Encapsulated frames typically use LLC to multiplex among multiple higher-layer protocol clients. See also *Type Encapsulation.*

Lifetime control A method used to place an upper bound on the time that a packet may be present in an internetwork. Lifetime control prevents packets from being circulated endlessly in a routing loop.

Line driver An electronic or optical device used to convey line signals onto a physical communications medium. See also *Line receiver.*

Line receiver An electronic or optical device used to extract line signals from a physical communications medium. See also *Line driver.*

Link Aggregation The process of combining multiple physical links into a single logical link for use by higher-layer link clients. Link Aggregation can increase both the capacity and availability of a communications channel.

Link-constrained protocol A protocol designed to operate only over a single link, with no intervening internetworking devices (e.g., the Spanning Tree and Link Aggregation Control Protocols). Frames from link-constrained protocols must never be forwarded by a bridge or router.

Link cost A metric assigned to a link, used to compute the spanning tree. Normally the link cost is inversely proportional to the data-carrying capacity of the link.

Listening state A transition state in the Spanning Tree Protocol state machine in which a bridge port is listening for BPDUs transmitted by other bridge ports to determine whether it should proceed to the learning state.

Little Endian (1) A method of ordering bits within a byte such that they are sent from the least significant bit first to the most significant bit last. (2) SA method of ordering bytes within a multi-byte field such that they are sent from the least significant byte first to the most significant byte last. Also known as *canonical format.* See also *Big Endian.*

Load balancing The practice of allocating traffic across multiple devices, interfaces, or communications links to evenly distribute offered load and obtain maximum benefit from the available resources.

Local Area Network A network with a relatively small geographical extent. Typically, Local Area Networks operate at high data rates, exhibit low error rates, and are owned and used by a single organization.

Locally-administered address A device or interface identifier whose uniqueness is established by a network administrator rather than by the manufacturer of the device or interface. See also *Globally-administered address.*

LocalTalk An Apple Computer-proprietary LAN technology employing CSMA/CA access control at a data rate of 230 kb/s. LocalTalk is implemented in all Apple Macintosh computers and most Apple-compatible devices.

Logical address Synonymous with *multicast address.*

Lookup Engine The entity in the receive (input) path of a switch port responsible for determining the appropriate output port(s) to which a given frame should be transferred.

Lookup process The process and/or algorithms implemented by a Lookup Engine.

Low-water mark An indicator that the number of entries or bytes in a queue has dropped below a pre-determined level. See also *High-water mark.*

MAC address A bit string that uniquely identifies one or more devices or interfaces as the source or destination of transmitted frames. IEEE 802 MAC addresses are 48 bits in length and may be either unicast (source or destination) or multicast (destination only).

MAC address–based VLAN A catenet where the association of a frame to a VLAN is determined by the source MAC address in the frame.

MAC algorithm The set of procedures used by the stations on a LAN to arbitrate for access to the shared communications channel (e.g., CSMA/CD, Token Passing).

Managed object An atomic element of an SNMP MIB with a precisely defined syntax and meaning, representing a characteristic of a managed device.

Marker Generator The entity within a Link Aggregation Distributor that generates Marker messages as needed for conversation transfer among the physical links in the aggregation.

Marker message A message used to delimit the end of the frame data stream for a given set of conversations on a physical link within an aggregation.

Marker Protocol A mechanism used to accelerate the transfer of a conversation from one physical link to another within an aggregation.

Marker Responder The entity within a Link Aggregation Collector that responds to Marker messages inserted in a frame stream.

Marker Response The response to a Marker message, indicating that the Marker message was received by the Link Aggregation Collector in the partner device.

Media Access Control The entity or algorithm used to arbitrate for access to a shared communications channel.

Microsegmentation A network configuration model in which each individual station connects to a dedicated port on a switch. See also *Dedicated bandwidth.*

Mirror Port A switch port configured to reflect the traffic appearing on another one of the switch's ports. Also known as a *copy port.* See also *Monitored Port.*

Modem A device used to convert digital data to or from analog signals for transmission across an analog communications channel.

Monitored Port A port on a switch whose traffic is replicated to a Mirror Port for the purpose of external traffic monitoring. See also *Mirror Port.*

MTU Discovery A process whereby a station can determine the largest frame or packet that can be transferred across a catenet or internetwork without requiring fragmentation.

Multicast address A method of identifying a set of one or more stations as the destination for transmitted data. Also known as a *logical address* or *group address.*

Multicast pruning A technique whereby traffic is propagated only on those links necessary to deliver it to the devices listening to a particular multicast address. See also *Source Pruning.*

Multimedia The application that justifies whatever the heck you are trying to sell.

Multimode fiber An optical fiber that allows signals to propagate in multiple transmission modes simultaneously, ultimately limiting both its bandwidth and maximum extent. Typically manufactured in 50 μm or 62.5 μm diameters. See also *Singlemode fiber.*

Multiplex The process of combining multiple signals or traffic streams into a single signal or stream. Multiplexed signals are separated upon receipt by a demultiplexer.

Multiport NIC A single device that comprises multiple instantiations of a network interface.

NetWare A network operating system and related software components developed by Novell.

Network A set of devices and communication links that allow computers to intercommunicate.

Network administrator (1) A person responsible for managing the day-to-day operations of a network. (2) The person blamed for all computing problems, whether they are related to the network or not.

Network architecture A model of the operation and behavior of devices attached to a network, typically as a series of layered protocol entities.

Network interface A subsystem that provides the means for a computer or internetworking device to attach to a communications link.

Network layer The third layer of the seven-layer OSI model, responsible for routing packets across an internetwork.

Network management The process of configuring, monitoring, controlling, and administering network operation.

Network management agent An entity (typically a combination of software and hardware) within a device that is responsible for gathering network management information and reporting it to a network management station as appropriate.

Network management station A device that communicates with network management agents throughout a network. Typically it comprises a workstation operated by a network administrator, equipped with network management other relevant applications software. Also known as a *network manager*.

Nibble A 4-bit unit of data (half of a byte).

Non-blocking In connectionless networks, a characteristic of a switch, switch fabric, or network interface implying that it is capable of handling traffic at the maximum frame and data arrival rates without ever having to discard traffic due to a lack of internal resources.

One-armed router A router (typically connected to a VLAN-aware switch) that forwards traffic among multiple logical networks through a single physical interface.

Operating system The software responsible for managing the underlying hardware in a computer. Generally provides an abstraction of the hardware platform to ease software development and the user interface.

Optical fiber A communications medium capable of carrying and directing light signals. Normally extruded or drawn from transparent glass or plastic material.

Overprovisioning A technique of providing more capacity (e.g., switching or communications link capacity) than is actually needed for a given application, usually with the intent of reducing delay and/or simplifying the overall system design.

Packet The Network layer encapsulation of transmitted or received information.

Partner The device at the other end of a point-to-point link (e.g., Link Aggregation partner). See also *Actor.*

Path cost The sum of the link costs between a given bridge port and the Root Bridge, used to compute the spanning tree.

pause_time The parameter of an Ethernet flow control message that indicates the length of time for which a device should cease data transmission.

Physical address Synonymous with *unicast address.*

Physical layer The lowest layer of the seven-layer OSI model, responsible for transmission and reception of signals across the communications medium.

ping A utility program used to test for network connectivity by using the Echo Request and Echo Response mechanisms of ICMP.

Port A network interface on a bridge, switch, or station.

Port-based VLAN A catenet where the association of a frame to a VLAN is determined by the switch port on which the frame arrived.

Port Identifier A value assigned to a port that uniquely identifies it within a switch. Port Identifiers are used by both the Spanning Tree and Link Aggregation Control Protocols.

Port mirroring A process whereby one switch port (the *Mirror Port*) is configured to reflect the traffic appearing on another one of the switch's ports (the *Monitored Port*).

Port number A locally-assigned, bridge-unique number identifying each port on the bridge.

Port Priority An administratively-controlled value that is catenated with a Port number to create a Port Identifier.

Preamble A frame field used to allow a receiver to properly synchronize its clock before decoding incoming data.

Presentation layer The sixth layer of the seven-layer OSI model, responsible for converting information between a local format and a common network format.

Priority The principle whereby preferential treatment is given to certain network devices, applications, or traffic over others.

Priority regeneration A technique used in a VLAN-aware switch to map locally-significant, natively-signaled user priority levels into globally significant values.

Priority tag A tag adhering to the syntax of IEEE 802.1Q, but used solely to indicate frame priority as opposed to a VLAN association. From a VLAN perspective, a priority-tagged frame is considered to be untagged. See also *Tagged frame* and *Untagged frame.*

Promiscuous mode A mode of operation of a network interface in which it receives (or attempts to receive) all traffic regardless of Destination Address.

Protocol A set of behavioral algorithms, message formats, and message semantics used to support communications between entities across a network.

Protocol analyzer A network management tool that is used to parse and decode frames for the purpose of monitoring and/or isolating faults in a network.

Protocol-based VLAN A catenet in which the association of a frame with a VLAN is determined by the Network layer protocol encapsulated by the frame.

Protocol stack A set of layered protocol entities that implement a given network architecture. Also known as a *protocol suite*.

Pseudo-CAM A subsystem, typically comprising a conventional RAM and a Lookup Engine, that emulates the operation of a content-addressable memory.

Q-compliant A bridge or switch that complies with IEEE 802.1Q.

Queue lookahead A technique used to avoid head-of-line blocking by processing entries beyond the first one in a queue.

Reassembly The process of reconstructing a packet from its fragments. See also *Fragmentation*.

Relay entity The architectural abstraction within an internetworking device (e.g., a bridge or router) that transfers data among the ports of the device.

Remote bridge A bridge that has at least one port connected to a WAN link to allow a catenet to span geographically dispersed LANs.

Repeater A device used to interconnect LAN segments at the Physical layer (e.g., a 10BASE-T hub). See also *Hub*.

Ring Number A locally-assigned, catenet-unique value identifying each ring in a source routed catenet.

RMON probe A device capable of passively monitoring network traffic, gathering statistics related to that traffic, and reporting it to a network management station using SNMP.

Root Bridge In the Spanning Tree Protocol, the bridge in the catenet with the numerically-lowest value for its Bridge Identifier, which is responsible for initiating regular Configuration Messages.

Root Port In the Spanning Tree Protocol, the port through which a Designated Bridge forwards traffic in the direction of the Root Bridge.

Route Descriptor A catenation of a Ring Number and a Bridge Number within the routing information field of a source routed frame.

Route Discovery The process of determining the available route(s) between a pair of stations in a source routed catenet.

Router An intermediate station operating as a Network layer relay device.

Route Request A frame sent to initiate the Route Discovery process.

Route Response A frame sent by the target of Route Discovery in response to a Route Request.

Route Selected frame A frame sent to indicate which of the available routes has been selected by the Route Discovery process.

Routing The process of relaying packets between networks.

Server (1) Application software (typically resident in an dedicated, multitasking computer system) designed to operate through cooperation and

communication with a companion client application (typically resident in an end user workstation). (2) An architectural entity providing services to a higher-layer client.
See also *Client.*

Service interface The means by which a client application or protocol uses the services provided by an underlying architectural layer.

Service provider An architectural entity providing services to a client (e.g., the Network layer may be a service provider to a Transport client).

Session layer The fifth layer of the seven-layer OSI model, responsible for process-to-process communication.

Shared bandwidth A characteristic of a communications channel in which the available capacity is shared among all of the attached stations. See also *Dedicated bandwidth.*

Shared bus A type of switch fabric that uses a common communications channel (e.g., a backplane) as the mechanism for frame exchange among the switch ports.

Shared media A physical communications medium that supports the connection of multiple devices, each of which may transmit and/or receive information across the common communications channel. Shared media systems require some method for the attached stations to arbitrate for the use of the common channel. See also *Dedicated media* and *MAC algorithm.*

Shared memory A type of switch fabric that uses a common memory pool as the mechanism for frame exchange among the switch ports.

Singlemode fiber An optical fiber that allows signals to propagate in only one transmission mode. The reduced distortion relative to multimode fiber allows singlemode fiber to support higher data rates and longer distances. Typically manufactured in diameters of 5 to 10 μm. See also *Multimode fiber.*

Sink The ultimate destination of a frame or packet on a network. A sink absorbs and removes the frame or packet from the network, as opposed to relaying or forwarding it to another link. See also *Source.*

Sliding window A technique used to provide flow and/or error control whereby the sender is allowed to transmit only that information within a specified window of frames or bytes. The window is shifted (slid) upon receipt of proper data acknowledgments from the receiver.

slotTime A parameter of the Ethernet MAC algorithm that defines (1) the maximum round-trip delay of the LAN, (2) the minimum length of transmitted frames, (3) the maximum length of a collision fragment, and (4) the quantum of retransmission for calculating backoff times.

Slow Protocol A class of protocols designed such that they never emit more than a specified maximum number of frames-per-second. This characteristic enables their implementation in low-performance microprocessors. Examples include LACP and the Marker Protocol used in Link Aggregation.

Sniffer A trade name for a popular protocol analyzer product from Network Associates (formerly Network General Corporation). See also *Protocol analyzer.*

Source The original sender of a frame or packet on a network. A source generates new frames that may be forwarded by internetworking devices, and which are absorbed by the ultimate destination. See also *Sink.*

Source pruning A technique used within Multicast Pruning in which the source of a multicast stream is turned off if it is known that there are no stations currently listening to the stream. See also *Multicast Pruning.*

Source routing A method of bridging where the path through the catenet is determined by the communicating end stations rather than the bridges, and frames carry explicit routing information. Used exclusively in Token Ring and some FDDI LANs.

Source Routing Bridge A bridge used in a source routed catenet.

Spanning forest A set of multiple spanning trees in a single catenet. Traffic for any given VLAN propagates over a single spanning tree in the forest.

Spanning tree A loop-free topology used to ensure that frames are neither replicated nor resequenced when bridged among stations in a catenet.

Spanning Tree Protocol A protocol used by bridges to determine, establish, and maintain a loop-free topology that includes every reachable link in a catenet. Standardized by IEEE 802.1D.

Stackable switch A switch equipped with a means of connection to other similar switches such that the set of interconnected switches can be configured and managed as if it were a single switch.

Standards Committee An excuse to travel to interesting places at nice times of the year to drink beer and discuss arcane technical issues with 400 geeks.

Standing request A method of switch fabric arbitration where an input port requests the use of a specified output port and is notified at a later time (by the fabric arbitrator) when that request can be granted.

StarLAN A commercial product name for products implementing 1BASE5 Ethernet technology. See also *1BASE5.*

Start-of-Frame Delimiter A symbol or set of symbols used to indicate the beginning of the Data Link (or MAC) encapsulation. See also *End-of-Frame Delimiter.*

Start-of-Stream Delimiter A symbol or set of symbols used to indicate the beginning of the Physical layer encapsulation. See also *End-of-Stream Delimiter.*

Station An addressable device capable of communicating on a network. See also *End station* and *Intermediate station.*

Store-and-forward A mode of switch operation where frames are completely received before they are forwarded onto any of the output ports of the device. See also *Cut-through.*

Stream The Physical layer encapsulation of transmitted or received information.

Strict priority A method of priority scheduling where higher priority traffic is always processed before lower priority traffic. See also *Weighted fair queuing.*

Structured wiring A systematic method of providing a communications infrastructure within a building or campus. Structured wiring systems provide standardized cabling characteristics and wiring conveniences, which allows organizations to use the same infrastructure for multiple communications technologies and eases the administrative burden of equipment and personnel moves, additions, and changes.

Subnet-based VLAN A catenet where the association of a frame to a VLAN is determined by the network portion of the IP Source Address contained within the frame.

Subnet mask A 32 bit field that, when logically ANDed with an IP address, produces the network portion of that address. The bits of a subnet mask are set to 1 for those bits that correspond to the network portion of the associated IP address and to 0 otherwise.

Switch Synonymous with *internetworking device.*

Switched LAN A LAN characterized by the use of a switching hub rather than a repeater hub as the central device.

Switch fabric The mechanism used to transfer frames from the input ports of a switch to its output ports.

Switching hub A switch used as a central interconnection device in a star-wired topology.

Switch mirroring A process whereby one switch port is configured to reflect the traffic appearing on all other ports of the switch.

Swouter A device that combines the functions of a switch and a router. See also *Brouter.*

Symbol An encoded bit or group of bits. A symbol is the atomic unit of data at the Physical layer of the OSI model.

Synchronous bandwidth A feature available in some FDDI LANs in which a portion of the network capacity can be reserved for use by one or more specially-equipped stations.

Synchronous request A method of switch fabric arbitration in which an input port requests the use of a specified output port and waits until that request is granted.

T1 A T-carrier technology capable of multiplexing 24 DS-0 (64 kb/s) channels, for a total data-carrying capacity of 1.536 Mb/s.

Tag-aware domain A region of a virtual bridged network in which all devices are tag-aware.

Tag-awareness A property of a device that supports and can use VLAN tags.

Tagged frame A frame that includes a VLAN tag.

Task Force A subcommittee within an IEEE 802 Working Group that is responsible for the development of a particular standard or standards.

T-carrier A family of telecommunications technologies supporting the digital signaling hierarchy at data rates in multiples of 64 kb/s (e.g., T1, T3).

Throughput A measure of the rate of data transfer between communicating stations, typically in bits-per-second.

Time to Live A field within an IP packet used for lifetime control. Routers decrement the Time to Live field; packets can be discarded if the value ever reaches 0.

Token A mechanism used to administer access control among stations on a Token Bus or Token Ring LAN. Under normal conditions, only the station in possession of the token may transmit frames.

Token Bus A LAN whose MAC algorithm uses token passing among stations on a logical bus topology (e.g., IEEE 802.4, ARCnet).

Token domain The access domain of a LAN using a token passing MAC (e.g., Token Bus or Token Ring). See also *Access domain.*

Token-passing A method of arbitrating access to a shared LAN where control is passed among the attached stations through the use of a token.

Token reservation A mechanism that allows stations to arbitrate for the future use of a token at a given priority level.

Token Ring A LAN whose MAC algorithm uses token passing among stations on a logical ring topology (e.g., IEEE 802.5).

Topology The physical or logical layout of a network.

Topology change An event that evokes recomputation of the spanning tree in a catenet.

Trailer A protocol-specific field or fields that follow the encapsulated higher-layer data payload (e.g., the FCS in a Data Link frame). See also *Header.*

Translational bridge A transparent bridge that interconnects LANs that use different frame formats (e.g., an Ethernet-to-FDDI bridge). A translational bridge must map the salient fields between the dissimilar frame formats used on its ports.

Transparent bridging A method of bridging in which the path through the catenet is determined by the bridges themselves and stations can communicate without any knowledge of the presence or action of those bridges. Standardized by IEEE 802.1D and IEEE 802.1Q.

Transport layer The fourth layer of the seven-layer OSI model, which typically provides reliable end-to-end message delivery across the underlying potentially unreliable network.

Trap An unsolicited message sent from a network management agent to a network management station, usually to signal a significant event.

Trunk A common name for an aggregated link.

Tunnel A device used to encapsulate one protocol within another, often at the same layer of their respective architectures. Used to transport information among devices using one form of communication (called the *native protocol*) across an infrastructure that only supports a different form (called the *foreign protocol*) without translating between the semantics of the two protocols. Examples include transportation of AppleTalk packets across an IP internetwork. See also *Encapsulating bridge.*

Twisted pair A communications medium consisting of two helically-intertwined copper conductors.

Type Encapsulation The Ethernet frame format in which the Length/Type field identifies the protocol type of the encapsulated data rather than its length. See also *Length Encapsulation.*

Unicast address A method of identifying a single station as the source or destination of data. Also known as a *physical address* or *hardware address.*

Unmanaged switch A switch that does not support any remote network management capability.

Untagged frame A frame that does not include a VLAN tag. See also *Priority tag.*

Uplink port A switch port designed to connect to a backbone switch or network. An uplink port often supports a higher data rate than the attachment ports of the switch.

User priority The priority associated with the application submitting a frame. User priority is carried end-to-end across a catenet. See also *Access priority.*

Virtual bridged network A catenet that comprises one or more VLAN-aware devices, allowing the definition, creation, and maintenance of virtual LANs.

Virtual LAN A subset of the stations, applications, and/or links within a catenet, as defined by their logical relationship rather than their physical connectivity.

VLAN association rule An algorithm used to map a frame to the VLAN to which it belongs.

VLAN-awareness A property of a device that supports and can use VLAN capabilities within a catenet.

VLAN tag A field inserted into a frame that provides an explicit indication of the VLAN association for that frame.

VMEbus An industry-standard computer and internetworking backplane technology developed by Motorola. Believe it or not, VME is not an abbreviation for anything.

Weighted fair queuing A method of priority scheduling that provides preferential treatment for higher priority traffic while preventing total starvation of lower priority traffic under sustained overload conditions. See also *Strict priority*.

Wide Area Network A network with far-reaching geographical extent. Typically, the links comprising Wide Area Networks are owned by, and leased from, common carriers, which imposes a recurring cost as a function of distance and/or data rate.

Wire speed The maximum frame and data arrival rate possible on a given network interface. Wire speed on a 100 Mb/s Ethernet implies rates of 100 million bits-per-second and 148,809.5 frames-per-second.

Wiring closet A room used to house and interconnect network and/or telecommunications equipment. Hubs, switches, and routers are typically installed in wiring closets.

Workgroup switch A switch used within a single department or workgroup. A workgroup switch typically aggregates traffic from desktop switches and provides an uplink to backbone networks and/or workgroup servers.

Working Group A subcommittee within IEEE 802 that is responsible for the development of standards relating to a particular technology.

Zone A set of logically-related devices within an AppleTalk internetwork. Devices in the same zone can communicate as a single workgroup regardless of whether they are on the same or different networks. An AppleTalk zone constitutes a Network layer VLAN.

Acronyms and Abbreviations

AARP	AppleTalk Address Resolution Protocol
AC	Access Control
ADSP	AppleTalk Data Stream Protocol
AFP	AppleTalk Filing Protocol
ANSI	American National Standards Institute
API	Application Program Interface
ARB	All Routes Broadcast
ARCnet	Attached Resource Computer network
ARE	All Routes Explorer
ASCII	American Standard Code for Information Interchange
ASIC	Application-Specific Integrated Circuit
ASN.1	Abstract Syntax Notation 1
ASP	AppleTalk Session Protocol
ATM	Asynchronous Transfer Mode
ATP	AppleTalk Transaction Protocol
AURP	AppleTalk Update-based Routing Protocol

BER	Bit error rate
BGP	Border Gateway Protocol
BOOTP	Bootstrap Protocol
BPDU	Bridge Protocol Data Unit
CAM	Content-addressable memory
CATV	Community Antenna Television
CCITT	International Consultative Committee for Telephone and Telegraph
CDDI	Copper Distributed Data Interface
CFI	Canonical Format Indicator
CLNP	Connectionless Network Protocol
CMIP	Common Management Interface Protocol
CMT	Connection Management
CoS	Class of Service
CPU	Central Processing Unit
CRC	Cyclic Redundancy Check
CSMA/CA	Carrier Sense, Multiple Access with Collision Avoidance
CSMA/CD	Carrier Sense, Multiple Access with Collision Detection
DA	Destination Address
DDP	Datagram Delivery Protocol
DDR	Double-Data Rate
DEC	Digital Equipment Corporation
DECnet	Digital Equipment Corporation Network Architecture
DEUNA	Digital Ethernet UNIBUS Network Adapter
DHCP	Dynamic Host Configuration Protocol
DIX	Digital–Intel–Xerox
DMA	Direct Memory Access
DOS	Disk Operation System
DQDB	Distributed Queue Dual Bus
DRAM	Dynamic Random Access Memory
DRP	DECnet Routing Protocol
DSAP	Destination Service Access Point
DTMF	Dual-Tone Multi-Function
DTR	Data Terminal Ready; Dedicated Token Ring
E-RIF	Embedded Routing Information Field
ECC	Error-Correcting Code
ECL	Emitter-Coupled Logic
ED	End Delimiter
EEPROM	Electrically-Erasable Programmable Read-Only Memory
EIA	Electronic Industries Association
EMI	Electromagnetic Interference
FC	Frame Control
FCS	Frame Check Sequence

FDDI	Fiber Distributed Data Interface
FIFO	First in first out
FIRE	Flexible Intelligent Routing Engine
FLR	Frame loss rate
FOIRL	Fiber-Optic Inter-Repeater Link
FPGA	Field-Programmable Gate Array
FS	Frame Status
FTP	File Transfer Protocol
GARP	Generic Attribute Registration Protocol
Gb/s	Gigabits-per-second
GMRP	GARP Multicast Registration Protocol
GVRP	GARP VLAN Registration Protocol
HDLC	High-Level Data Link Control
HILI	High-Level Interface
HTTP	Hypertext Transfer Protocol
IBM	International Business Machines
IC	Integrated Circuit
ICMP	Internet Control Message Protocol
IEEE	Institute of Electrical and Electronics Engineers
IETF	Internet Engineering Task Force
IFG	Interframe Gap
IP	Internet Protocol
IPX	Internetwork Packet eXchange
ISDN	Integrated Services Digital Network
ISO	Internal Organization for Standardization
ISP	Internet Service Provider
ITU	International Telecommunications Union
IVL	Independent VLAN Learning
kb/s	Kilobits-per-second
LACP	Link Aggregation Control Protocol
LAN	Local Area Network
LAT	Local Area Transport
LAVc	Local Area VAXcluster
LF	Largest Frame
LFSR	Linear Feedback Shift Register
LLC	Logical Link Control
LRU	Least-recently used
LSAP	Link Service Access Point
LSB	Least significant bit; least significant byte
LVDS	Low-Voltage Differential Signaling
MAC	Media Access Control
MAC_PDU	Media Access Control Protocol Data Unit
MAN	Metropolitan Area Network

MAP	Manufacturing Automation Protocol
Mb/s	Megabits-per-second
MIB	Management Information Base
MIS	Management Information System
MLT-3	Multi-Level Threshold (3); Mario, Luca, and Tazio
MOP	Maintenance-Oriented Protocol
ms	Milliseconds
MSB	Most significant bit; most significant byte
MTU	Maximum Transmission Unit
NBP	Name Binding Protocol
NCFI	Non-canonical Format Indicator
NCP	NetWare Core Protocol
NetBEUI	NetBIOS Extended User Interface
NetBIOS	Network Basic Input/Output System
NFS	Network File System
NIC	Network interface card; network interface controller
NOS	Network Operating System
ns	Nanoseconds
opcode	Operation code
OSI	Open Systems Interconnect
OSPF	Open Shortest-Path-First
OUI	Organizationally-Unique Identifier
PAgP	Port Aggregation Protocol
PAN	Personal Area Network
PAR	Positive Acknowledgment and Retransmission; Project Authorization Request
PATRICIA	Practical Algorithm To Retrieve Information Coded In Alphanumeric
PC	Personal computer
PCI	Peripheral Component Interconnect
PDU	Protocol Data Unit
PHY	Physical Layer Interface
Pid	Protocol Identifier
PL_PDU	Physical Layer Protocol Data Unit
POP	Point of Presence; Post Office Protocol
PPP	Point-to-Point Protocol
ps	Picoseconds
PVID	Port VLAN Identifier
QoS	Quality of Service
RAM	Random Access Memory
RARP	Reverse Address Resolution Protocol
RDRAM	Rambus Dynamic Random Access Memory
RED	Random Early Discard; Random Early Detect

RFC	Request for Comments
RII	Routing Information Indicator
RIP	Routing Information Protocol
RISC	Reduced Instruction-Set Computer
RMON	Remote MONitor
ROM	Read-Only Memory
RSVP	Resource reSerVation Protocol
RT	Routing Type
RTMP	Routing Table Maintenance Protocol
SA	Source Address
SAP	Service Access Point; Service Advertisement Protocol
SD	Start Delimiter
SDU	Service Data Unit
SFD	Start-of-Frame Delimiter
SGMP	Simple Gateway Management Protocol
SGRAM	Synchronous Graphic Random Access Memory
SMDS	Switched Multimegabit Data Service
SMT	Station Management
SMTP	Simple Mail Transport Protocol
SNA	Systems Network Architecture
SNAP	Sub-Network Access Protocol
SNMP	Simple Network Management Protocol
SNMPv2	Simple Network Management Protocol version 2
SNMPv3	Simple Network Management Protocol version 3
SONET	Synchronous Optical Network
SPX	Sequenced Packet eXchange
SR-TB	Source Routing-to-Transparent Bridge
SRAM	Static Random Access Memory
SRB	Source Routing Bridge
SRF	Specifically-Routed Frame; Source Routed Frame
SRT	Source Route/Transparent Bridge
SSAP	Source Service Access Point
SSE	Silicon Switching Engine
SSRAM	Synchronous Static Random Access Memory
STE	Spanning Tree Explorer
STP	Spanning Tree Protocol
SVL	Shared VLAN Learning
TAG	Technical Action Group
TB	Transparent Bridge
TC	Topology Change
TCI	Tag Control Information
TCP	Transmission Control Protocol
Telnet	Network Teletype

TIA	Telecommunications Industries Association
TLV	Type-Length-Value
TP-4	Transport Protocol Class 4
TP-PMD	Twisted Pair Physical Medium Dependent Sublayer
TPZ	Timber Preservation Zone; Timber Production Zone
TREN	Token Ring Encapsulation
TTL	Time to Live
TXI	Transmit Immediate
UDP	User Datagram Protocol
UI	User Interface
UTP	Unshielded twisted pair
VAX	Virtual Address eXtensions
VLAN	Virtual Local Area Network
VMS	Virtual Memory System
VPID	VLAN Protocol Identifier
VPN	Virtual Private Network
WAN	Wide Area Network
WDM	Wavelength-Division Multiplexer
WFQ	Weighted Fair Queuing
WG	Working Group
XLII	eXtended LAN Interface Interconnect
XNS	Xerox Network System
XTP	eXpress Transport Protocol
ZIP	Zone Information Protocol
μs	Microseconds

Index